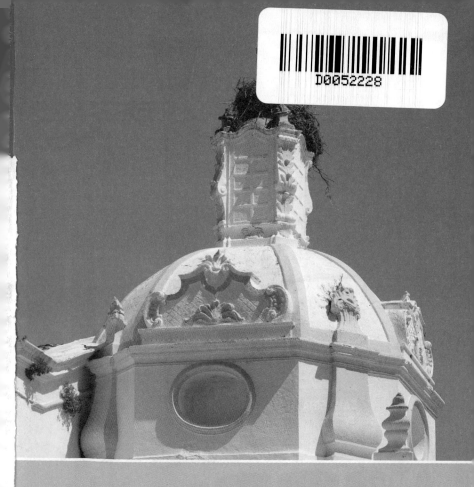

THE ROUGH GUIDE TO

Portugal

written and researched by

Jules Brown, Mark Ellingham, John Fisher and
Matthew Hancock

Contents

Introduction to
Portugal

Once a powerful seafaring kingdom that dominated the merchant routes to Africa, South America and the Orient, Portugal today is a friendly, low-key place with a laidback vibe and a fantastic coastline, much of it fringed by golden sands and endless dunes. Its rolling interior is perfect for exploring on foot, by kayak, by bike or even on horseback – though a large part of the country's charm comes from languorous days on the beach, dining on fabulously fresh seafood and kicking back with a beer to watch the sunset over the Atlantic. The legacy of Portugal's former wealth and power can be seen in its historic cities – yet the capital, Lisbon, superbly sited on the Tejo river estuary, is as popular today for its lively clubbing scene as for its grand Manueline monuments and medieval alleyways. Porto meanwhile, the country's second city and a UNESCO World Heritage Site, is the best place to sample some of the many varieties of Portugal's other notable contribution to the world, port wine.

Portugal's borders have changed little since it became an independent country in the twelfth century. **Mountains** make up the bulk of the frontier with Spain, with the large **rivers** of the Minho in the north and the Guadiana in the south adding to this natural divide. Early Portuguese monarchs fortified the border with a series of **walled towns**, many sited on dramatic hilltops, and these make the border areas some of the most fascinating to visit.

Beaches and high mountains aside, the rest of Portugal is a diverse and verdant country of deep valleys and rolling hills dotted with stone-built villages. For generations, families have eked out a living from the steeply terraced **vineyards** of the mountainous north, and from the **cork oak plantations** roamed by wild boar that dominate the vast agricultural plains of the south.

ABOVE CARVOEIRO BEACH

Portugal's prestige and economy have never regained the heights they attained during the **golden ages** of the fifteenth to eighteenth centuries. The country spent most of the twentieth century in deep poverty under the dictatorial rule of Prime Minister Dr Salazar, and while joining the European Union had great initial benefits – funding new roads and communications – Portugal has struggled badly in the recent years of economic crisis. Yet although it remains one of the EU's weakest economies, Portugal is a remarkably unified country – there are no minorities agitating for independence, while rivalry between the north and south consists of little more than gentle mockery. Indeed Portugal is generally a very tolerant nation, and has integrated a substantial population from its **former colonies** in Africa, Asia and Brazil with relative ease. Contemporary Portuguese tastes are influenced by the flavours, sounds and styles of Brazil, Angola and Mozambique in particular.

It's a **Catholic** country – there are ancient churches in every community – and while support for the institutions of the Church may have waned, a belief in **traditional values** remains. The Portuguese have embraced contemporary life without ever quite getting rid of the more appealing aspects of previous centuries. Fully wired town centres have wi-fi hotspots and cell-phone shops by the score, but they also have a butcher, a baker and (quite literally) a candle-stick maker. Children will be both seen and heard at any time of the day or night, as the family remains at the centre of most things.

When times were hard at home, the Portuguese traditionally emigrated to pastures new, but their homeland's blend of tolerance and tradition, its bucolic scenery and year-round sunshine, persuade most emigrants to return at some stage – and it is this same allure that makes the country so appealing to visitors. Prepare to be charmed.

Where to go

The south-facing coast of the **Algarve** is the country's tourist epicentre and justifiably so – it is here that you'll find the archetypal picturesque Portuguese cove beaches, fringed by rock stacks and gentle cliffs, and it doesn't take much to escape the high-rise resorts and golf courses. If it is **beaches** you are after, however, you have almost the entire west coast of the country to choose from. There are expansive stretches of sand not only on the

PORTUGUESE AZULEJOS

Brightly-coloured decorative tiles have been used throughout Portugal since the birth of the nation, making up everything from immense religious scenes covering entire walls of churches to simple geometric patterns on the back of park benches. It was the Moors who introduced the craft in the eighth century – the word derives from the Arabic *al-zulecha*, meaning "small stone". Less studied than stained glass, less famous than frescoes, many *azulejos* are handcrafted works of art, though even mass-produced factory items add flamboyance to otherwise dull buildings. You'll find them all over the country – on churches, houses, cafés and shops, even motorway bridges and metro stations. The **Museu Nacional do Azulejo** in Lisbon (see p.68) is dedicated to them, or you can marvel at the ingenuity and adaptability of the art while catching the train at **Pinhão station** (see p.295), spending the night in the **Palácio do Buçaco** (see p.197) or visiting the church of **São Lourenço** in the Algarve (see p.456).

Algarve's western coast, but also in the southern Alentejo, on the coast around Lisbon and north to Figueira da Foz, and along the **Minho coast** north to the Spanish border.

Many of these beaches extend as far as the eye can see, and are rarely busy even in high summer, but as they face the full power of the Atlantic, they can be dangerous for swimming. It's no big surprise then that many attract serious surfers instead, with **Peniche**, **Figueira da Foz** and **Nazaré** all major surf destinations.

The south of the country is dominated by the enormous **Alentejo** region, whose wide-open spaces, country estates, olive plantations and vineyards invite long drives and leisurely exploration. Here you'll find a Mediterranean-type climate, sun-drenched, whitewashed villages bedecked with flowers and, in early summer, every spire and treetop capped by a stork's nest. Closer to Lisbon is the flat hinterland of the **Ribatejo**, breeding ground for Portugal's finest horses and for the bulls that still fight in bullrings around the country. Beyond, lies the historic heartland of **Estremadura**, whose closely grouped towns feature some of Portugal's most famous monuments.

OPPOSITE PORTO RIVERSIDE

The north of Portugal feels immediately different, and far less Mediterranean in look and temperament – the rolling hills are green and lush, and the coastline cooler, even in summer. Terraced vineyards cling to the steep slopes of the **Douro River**, its valley shadowed by one of Europe's most memorable train rides. Further north still lie the remote towns and villages of **Trás-os-Montes**, while to the west **Peneda-Gerês** is Portugal's only national park, a surprisingly verdant landscape of wooded mountains and gushing streams.

Standout city is, of course, **Lisbon**, with its dazzling hilltop and riverside location and alluring mix of old-world charm and modern flair. It's not too much of a stretch to describe it as one of Europe's must-see capitals, though the charms – and wines – of **Porto**, wedged into the Douro river valley, also make an excellent case for a long weekend city break. Other Portuguese towns and cities might not have the same profile, but they are both historical and beautiful – like **Guimarães**, the country's first capital, the religious centre of **Braga**, the handsome university town of **Coimbra**, and **Évora**, another university town with Roman antecedents.

Beyond these attractions, how long have you got? Because in just about every town and village there's a surprise to be discovered. Likeable **Tomar** is home to the impressive headquarters of the Knights Templar, while **Aveiro** is an unexpected treat, set on a series of canals lined with colourful houses. There are sumptuous **monasteries and abbeys** at Batalha, Mafra and Alcobaça and extraordinary **fortified towns** at Almeida, Elvas and Bragança; while in **Fatima**, Portugal boasts one of the world's most revered Catholic shrines.

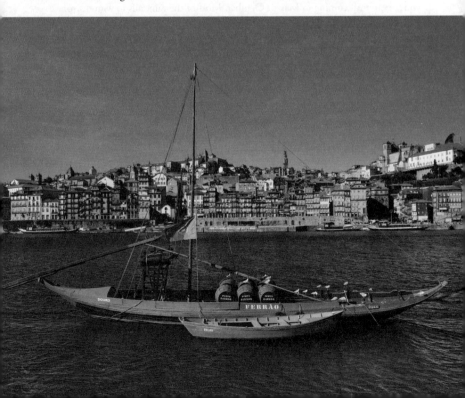

FOOD FROM AFAR

Portugal's former status as an important trading nation has had a huge influence on world cuisine. The **tempura** method of deep-frying was introduced to the Japanese by sixteenth-century Portuguese traders and missionaries, while the fiery curry-house mainstay **vindaloo** derives from a **vinho** (wine) and **alho** (garlic) sauce popular in Portuguese Goa. Indeed, the use of **chillis** in the East only began when the Portuguese started to import them from Mexico. **Bacalhau** (dried salt cod) started life as a way of preserving fish on board the Portuguese voyages of exploration; another, less exotic, export is marmalade (although the local **marmelada** is actually made from quince). Meanwhile, dishes from Portugal's former colonies crop up time and time again in Portuguese restaurants. Keep an eye out for *mufete* (beans with palm oil and fish) and chicken *piri-piri* (chicken with chilli sauce), which originated in **Angola** and **Mozambique**, *caril de camarão* (shrimp curry) and *chamuças* (samosas) from **Asia**, and **Brazilian** meals such as *feijoada* (pork and bean stew), *picanha* (sliced rump steak) and *rodizio* (barbecue meat buffet).

When to go

A weather map of endless suns sums up the situation across the whole of Portugal in **summer**, certainly between June and September, when usually the only daytime variation across the country is a degree or two further up or down the scale from 30ºC. In July and especially August (the Portuguese holiday month), the coastal resorts are at their busiest and prices reach their peak. It's also too hot to do much exploring – if you want to do any serious hiking, or even just walk around the cities, towns and archeological sites, you're better off coming in May or October. Most of the rain falls in **winter**, from November to March, though you can just as easily experience bone-dry winter months and downpours in May and June. The crisp, sharp sunshine makes winter an appealing time to visit central Portugal, while in the south, especially on the coast, it is mild all year round. In the north, on the other hand, it's pretty cold, especially inland where snow is common along the mountainous border areas.

Perhaps the best times of year to visit are in **spring** (ie, from February) – when dazzling flowers carpet hillsides and the almond blossom lights up the countryside – and early **autumn** (October), when the weather is warm but not too hot and the summer crowds have thinned out. The sea, too, is warm in autumn, though the official swimming season only lasts from the beginning of June to mid-September; outside these months – no matter how lovely the weather – outdoor pools and river beach facilities close.

AVERAGE DAILY TEMPERATURES AND MONTHLY RAINFALL

	Jan	Mar	May	Jul	Sep	Nov
LISBON						
Max/min (ºC)	14/8	18/10	22/13	27/17	25/16	17/12
Rainfall (mm)	111	109	44	3	33	93
PORTO (COSTA VERDE)						
Max/min (ºC)	13/5	15/7	19/10	25/15	24/14	17/8
Rainfall (mm)	159	147	87	20	51	148
FARO (ALGARVE)						
Max/min (ºC)	15/9	18/11	22/14	28/20	26/19	19/13
Rainfall (mm)	70	72	21	1	17	65

Author picks

Our authors have visited every corner of
Portugal to bring you some unique travel
experiences. Here are some of their own
personal favourites.

Stay in a castle Be a king or queen for the night
at the lovely, tranquil *Forte de São João da Barra*
(p.452), overlooking the Reserva Natural Ria
Formosa, or the *Pousada Dom Afonso II* (p.422) –
a historic castle, which has had a stylish,
contemporary makeover.

Great walks Fantastic walking trails abound
including the epic Rota Vicentina through the
unspoilt southwest of the country (p.425) and
some terrific mountain paths in the north's
Parque Nacional da Peneda-Gerês (p.339).

Classic journeys The drive or train ride along
the Douro (p.298) is our favourite – from Porto to
the Spanish border, with lashings of local wine
along the way.

Party time Let your hair down (and look out for
the plastic hammers) at Porto's riotous Festa de
São João (p.277).

Coastal beauty spots The tiny Algarve village
of Benagil (p.465) marks the start of a clifftop
path that leads past an awesome sea cave,
while the pretty resort of Vila Nova de Milfontes
(p.426) faces a tranquil estuary on the wild
Alentejo coast.

Delightful towns Favourites include the ancient
hilltop settlements of Marvão (p.403) and
Monsaraz (p.409), both with sublime views over
the Alto Alentejo, though beautiful Belmonte
(p.245) runs a close second.

Magnificent markets Foodies will find the local
fish and seafood at Olhão market unbeatable
(p.441), while Estremoz market (p.395) sells some
of the best Alentejan crafts and local produce,
and Barcelos in the Minho (p.319) is the country's
most traditional market.

> Our author recommendations don't end
> here. We've flagged up our favourite places
> – a perfectly sited hotel, an atmospheric
> café, a special restaurant – throughout the
> Guide, highlighted with the ★ symbol.

FROM TOP CAVE, BENAGIL; ESTREMOZ MARKET; FESTA DE SÃO
JOÃO

things not to miss

It's not possible to see everything that Portugal has to offer in one trip – and we don't suggest you try. What follows, in no particular order, is a selection of the country's highlights, including fascinating architecture, outstanding natural wonders, amazing beaches, one stupendous market and a peerless custard tart. Each entry has a page reference to take you straight into the Guide, where you can find out more. Coloured numbers refer to chapters in the Guide section.

1 ALGARVE BEACHES
Page 486
The region has some of Europe's finest beaches and there are few more impressive than Praia da Bordeira.

2 MONSARAZ
Page 409
Many of the medieval houses in the fortified hilltop village of Monsaraz have been converted into atmospheric guesthouses.

3 CANAL TRIP, AVEIRO
Page 206
Float through the canals and lagoons of fascinating Aveiro on a brightly coloured boat.

7

8

9 BATALHA
Page 157

The "Battle Abbey" is one of the greatest achievements of Portuguese architecture.

10 KAYAKING ON THE MONDEGO RIVER
Page 196

Even novice kayakers will be enchanted by this gentle float down a verdant valley.

11 ALFAMA, LISBON
Page 65

A village in the heart of the capital, with streets so narrow and precipitous that few cars can enter.

12 SINTRA
Page 111

The hilltop retreat near Lisbon is one of the most scenic in the country, surrounded by opulent palaces and country estates.

13 PARQUE NACIONAL DA PENEDA-GERÊS
Page 339

The country's only national park offers alluring trails past gushing streams and alpine scenery.

14 PASTÉIS DE BELÉM
Page 95

These delicious flaky custard tartlets have been made and served warm with cinnamon and icing sugar sprinkled over them for more than a century at the *Antiga Confeitaria de Belém*.

9

10

21

22

21 SURFING
Page 139

Peniche offers consistently good surfing in a country that is blessed with rolling Atlantic waves.

22 FEIRA DE BARCELOS
Page 319

The country's liveliest and most colourful market shows that rural traditions are alive and well.

23 SERRA DA ESTRELA
Page 235

The highest mountains in Portugal conceal windswept uplands, remote villages and challenging hiking trails.

24 PORTO'S RIVERFRONT
Page 266

The historic riverside *bairro* of Ribeira is now a UNESCO World Heritage Site.

23

Itineraries

Whether you've got a few days, a week or longer, here are three itineraries to give you a taste of Portugal's varied attractions. Our Grand Tour takes in the country's unmissable historic towns and natural attractions, while the wine route will guide you around remote rural gems. We also recommend the best beaches in a country famed for its fabulous sands.

GRAND TOUR OF PORTUGAL

Portugal is a small country so you can easily see the best of it quickly. The Grand Tour takes in the must-see destinations.

❶ **Lagos** The Algarve's most historic town, from where the great navigators departed in the Age of Discoveries. See p.474

❷ **Évora** A superbly preserved Alentejan town containing Portugal's finest Roman temple. See p.384

❸ **Elvas** Explore the walls – with their far-reaching views – that encircle this fortified border town. See p.404

❹ **Lisbon** One of Europe's most fascinating capitals is a captivating mix of ancient and contemporary – and beautifully located, overlooking the Tejo river estuary. See p.56

❺ **Coimbra** A former Portuguese capital, the ancient university town also has the superb Roman site of Conímbriga on its doorstep. See p.178

❻ **Serra da Estrela** The country's highest mountains – with its only ski resort – make a great destination for a night in the hills. See p.235

❼ **Porto** A unique city, famed for its wines, football team and amazing riverside cityscape. See p.256

❽ **Parque Nacional da Peneda-Gerês** This wild, rugged mountain region, hugging the border with Spain, is ideal for a walking holiday – or for a panoramic drive. See p.339

WINE ROUTES

Portugal produces terrific wines and its vineyards tend to nestle in bucolic countryside – views and booze, our favourite combination.

❶ **Quinta Miradouro** Cliff Richard's wine estate in the Algarve is a good introduction to Portuguese wines – with the chance of spotting the great man himself. See p.460

❷ **Alentejo wine route** Some of the best Portuguese wines are produced in this beautiful inland region, with top producers located near the historic towns of Beja, Évora and Estremoz. See p.392

❸ **Rota do Vino do Dão** Check out the classic reds produced along the Dão valley. See p.200

❹ **Port wine lodges** No visit to Porto is complete without a tour of the port wine lodges in Vila Nova da Gaia, many overlooking the Douro River. See p.270

❺ **Peso da Régua** The classic port-wine estates can be visited from this town on the Douro, which is also home to the headquarters of the Rota do Vinho do Porto and the Douro Wine Institute's exhibition centre. See p.289

ABOVE VINEYARDS, PESO DA RÉGUA; PRAIA DA MARINHA, ALGARVE

❻ Pinhão The main centre for quality ports with a classic backdrop of Douro wine terraces. **See p.295**

❼ Melgaço Portugal's northernmost outpost is the centre for the country's famed *vinho verde*. The Solar do Alvarinho offers tastings and tours of local estates. **See p.332**

LIFE'S A BEACH

Most people come to Portugal for its beaches and there are hundreds to choose from – here's a tour of the best.

❶ Foz do Minho, Minho Portugal's northernmost beach is a hidden gem, a sandy bank facing Spain across the Rio Minho river estuary. **See p.326**

❷ Nazaré, Estremadura This former fishing village has a great town beach – and is also where the world's largest-ever wave was surfed. **See p.149**

❸ Caparica A favourite for surfers and day-trippers from Lisbon. **See p.120**

❹ Galapos, Parque Natural da Arrábida This beautifully positioned bay has calm waters in one of Portugal's loveliest natural parks. **See p.124**

❺ Comporta, Alentejo Deserted sands stretch as far as the eye can see at this remote part of the northern Alentejo. **See p.422**

❻ Porto Covo, Alentejo The Portuguese love this unspoilt coast, studded with idyllic sandy coves. **See p.424**

❼ Praia do Amado, Algarve A wild and wonderful stretch of sand with its own surf school in a remote corner of the Algarve. **See p.486**

❽ Praia da Marinha, Algarve A classic cliff-backed cove beach, perfect for families. **See p.465**

ELEVADOR DE SANTA JUSTA, LISBON

Basics

Getting there

There are regular direct flights to Lisbon, Faro and Porto from all over Europe and some US cities, though travellers from outside Europe may find it cheaper to fly via London and arrange onward travel from there. If you want to see some of France or Spain en route, or are taking a vehicle, there are overland combinations of ferry, rail and road to consider, though these nearly always work out pricier than flying. Package holidays and tours can be good value, whether it's an Algarve beach holiday or escorted walking tour – and travel agents and specialist tour operators can also provide car rental, hotel bookings and other useful services.

Air, train and ferry fares are at their highest in school holidays and summer (basically Easter to September), and around Christmas/New Year and Easter week. The cheapest flights from the UK and Ireland are usually with the budget airlines, though watch out for the airport taxes, which can cost more than the flight itself, while luggage allowances and allocated seating are also charged as extra. Major scheduled airlines are usually (though not always) more expensive, while specialist flight, discount or online agents can sometimes offer special student and youth fares plus a range of other travel-related services.

Flights from the UK and Ireland

Flying to Faro, Lisbon or Porto takes two to three hours from airports around the UK and Ireland, and usually the cheapest flights are with **budget airlines** such as easyJet (Ⓦ easyjet.com), Jet2 (Ⓦ jet2.com), Ryanair (Ⓦ ryanair.com), Aer Lingus (Ⓦ aerlingus .com), Monarch Airlines (Ⓦ flights.monarch.co.uk), thomsonfly (Ⓦ flights.thomson.co.uk) or flybe (Ⓦ flybe.com). Between them they fly direct from around twenty regional British airports, plus Belfast and Dublin, and although Faro on the Algarve is the most common destination you should be able to find a route that suits you. Not all routes are daily or

year-round: some Algarve flights are summer-only, and other Lisbon or Porto routes have a reduced winter service. **Fares** vary wildly and, depending on promotions, can be as low as £20 or €25 each way, though you'll have to travel off-peak and book a long time ahead to get this sort of deal. Around £100 total for a return flight is more common, but if you're tied to school holidays or book late you're likely to pay nearer £150–200 return.

The main scheduled airlines flying to Portugal are the **national carriers** TAP (Ⓦ flytap.com) and British Airways (Ⓦ ba.com): TAP flies regular services from London to Lisbon and Porto, while BA serves Lisbon and Faro. You'll also be able to arrange add-on sections to London from regional UK airports. They are not necessarily more expensive than the budget airlines, and flight times may be more convenient – that said, you're unlikely to get a rock-bottom deal and the fully flexible fares offered can run into the hundreds.

Flights from the US and Canada

The only direct nonstop services **from the United States** are from New York (Newark) to Lisbon with United Airlines (Ⓦ united.com) or TAP (Ⓦ flytap .com), with fares starting at US$1000 return. Flight time is around seven hours. From all other cities you'll need a connecting flight, either via New York or via a European airport with airlines such as BA (Ⓦ ba.com), Lufthansa (Ⓦ lufthansa.com) or Air France (Ⓦ airfrance.com) – in which case you can add four or five hours to your total travel time, depending on the connection. TAP can also arrange onward flights from Lisbon to Porto or Faro.

From Canada to Portugal, most airlines route through New York or Europe, though SATA (Ⓦ sata .pt) sometimes has direct flights from Toronto to Lisbon or Porto (about 11 hours).

Flights from Australia, New Zealand and South Africa

There are no direct flights to Portugal **from Australia or New Zealand**, but many airlines offer through-tickets with their partners via their European or Asian hubs. Flights via Asia are generally the cheaper option, but fares don't vary as much between airlines as you might think, and in the end you'll be basing your choice on things like flight timings, routes and possible stopoffs. If you're seeing Portugal as part of a wider European trip, you might want to aim first for the UK, since there's a wide choice of cheap flights to Portugal once there. Or consider a Round-the-World fare, with most basic options able to offer Lisbon as a standard stopover. **From South Africa**, TAP (Ⓦflytap.com) and South Africa Airways (Ⓦflysaa .com) fly to Lisbon with a change of plane in Maputo, or you can fly with one of the major European airlines via their home hub.

Trains

Getting from London to Lisbon by train involves taking the **Eurostar** (Ⓔeurostar.com) from London St Pancras to Paris, then Paris to Irun on the Spanish border by high-speed train (TGV) and finally the overnight Sud-Express "train-hotel", which gets you into Lisbon at about 7.30am. It's an enjoyable route, well worth considering, though the cheapest **fares** start at around £200 return (with couchette accommodation on the overnight train) – and the connections are such that you will probably have to spend a night in Paris. For Porto you change at Coimbra, while there are also direct connections from Lisbon to the Algarve. The alternative route to Portugal is **via Madrid** – this takes two nights (overnight trains from Paris to Madrid and then Madrid to Lisbon), but gives you a day in Madrid en route. The overnight trains have seats (not really recommended) as well as couchettes and cabins complete with showers, plus restaurant, buffet bar and lounge. Our "Overland from Spain" section has more on the various routes.

The best first stop is the excellent Ⓦseat61.com, which provides full route, ticket, timetable and contact information. You can book the whole journey **online** with Rail Europe (Ⓦraileurope.co.uk) or call a specialist **rail agent** such as the Spanish Rail Service (☎0203 137 4464, Ⓦspanish-rail.co.uk) or European Rail (☎020 7619 1083, Ⓦeuropeanrail .com). If you live outside the UK, you can book Eurostar and overnight train tickets through Ⓦraileurope.com. These contacts can also provide information about **rail passes** (principally InterRail and Eurail), which have to be bought before leaving home – our "Getting around" section (see p.28) has more details.

Overland from Spain

It's easy to travel by **train** from Spain to Portugal, and there are some rewarding stops en route. Rail passes are valid, though you'll be liable for supplements on many trains.

From Madrid (Chamartin station), the overnight Lusitania Trenhotel takes ten hours and thirty minutes to Lisbon (change at Entroncamento in Portugal for Coimbra and Porto). Prices start at €60 one way, €97 return, for a second-class seat, or €85 one way, €135 return, for the cheapest berth (four-bed cabin); there are also singles, doubles and *gran classe* cabins available. Tickets can be bought in Madrid at Chamartin, through the Spanish (Ⓦrenfe.es) or Portuguese (Ⓦcp.pt) railway companies' websites, or from one of the rail agents mentioned in "Trains", above.

From the northeast, the overnight Sud-Express from the French border at **Hendaye/Irun** to Lisbon (around 13hr) passes through San Sebastian and Salamanca, entering Portugal at Vilar Formoso in Beira Alta and then calling at Portugal's highest town, Guarda; change at Coimbra for Porto. Tickets start at €70 one way, €110 return (€94/150 for the cheapest six-bed berth), and again can be bought online or from agents.

From northwestern Spain, two trains a day connect **Vigo** in Galicia to Porto (around 3hr), passing the border at Tuy/Valença on the River Minho, then following the river and coast down via Vila Praia de Âncora, Viana do Castelo and Barcelos.

From **Granada, Córdoba and Seville** in southern Spain you are well placed to get a bus to the border at Ayamonte/Vila Real de Santo António, for onward transport by bus or train along the Algarve coast.

There are numerous other border **road crossings**, but if you're in a rental car check first whether you're covered to take the vehicle between countries. The major routes from Madrid or Salamanca make for an easy motorway drive to Portugal's biggest cities, but there are some excellent minor routes into the country as well – like those from Zamora to Bragança or Miranda do Douro, or from Cáceres to Castelo Branco.

Driving from the UK

Driving the 2000km or so from the UK to Portugal, using the standard cross-Channel services or Eurotunnel (Ⓦeurotunnel.com) through the Channel Tunnel, takes two full days. It's not a cheap option (factoring in the cross-Channel trip, fuel, tolls, overnight stops and meals), but it is a good way of seeing France and Spain on the way.

The best way of cutting down the driving time is to catch the ferry to northern Spain, though this still leaves a six- to eight-hour drive before you reach Portugal. Brittany Ferries (Ⓦbrittany -ferries.co.uk) sails to **Santander** from Plymouth (1 weekly; 20hr) and Portsmouth (2 weekly; 24hr) and to **Bilbao** from Portsmouth (2 weekly; 24hr). A car-and-2-passengers **fare** starts at £324 one-way from Plymouth to Santander, £335 from Portsmouth to Santander, and £355 to Bilbao, though in summer and school holidays return fares can rocket. In winter the website often features special deals (it's cheaper for foot passengers, though everyone has to book some form of seating or cabin accommodation).

Package holidays, tours and city breaks

Standard **package holidays** concentrate on hotels and self-catering apartments and villas in the Algarve's main beach resorts, and bargains can be found online or at any UK high-street travel agent for as little as £125 per person for a seven-night flight-and-accommodation package off season. There are often really good deals for families, though obviously the more bells and whistles you want (beachfront accommodation, pool, kids' clubs etc), the more you pay, while prices are always significantly higher during school holidays.

Other **specialist tour operators** offer a wide range of fly-drive holidays based around accommodation in historic manor houses and *pousadas*, while some feature activities such as birdwatching, horseriding, hiking, biking and wine tours. Prices vary wildly depending on the standard of accommodation, and whether the tours are fully inclusive or not (with guides and meals etc). Most tour operators should also be able to tailor-make a holiday, and arrange flights, accommodation, insurance and car rental.

City breaks are mainly to Lisbon, though you'll also find Porto and even short breaks to the Algarve offered. UK prices start at around £200 for a three-day (2-night) break, including return flights and B&B in a modest hotel. Adding extra nights or upgrading your hotel is usually possible too. The bigger US operators, such as American Express and Delta Vacations, can also organize short city breaks to Lisbon on a flight-and-hotel basis.

SPECIALIST TOUR OPERATORS

Martin Randall Travel UK ☎ 020 8742 3355, Ⓦ martinrandall .com. Leading cultural tour specialist, offering small-group,

expert-led trips either along the Douro by train and boat or to the historic centre of the country. Departures a couple of times a year, from around £1700.

BIRDWATCHING, BOTANICAL AND ADVENTURE

09°West, Portugal ☎ 211 991 086, Ⓦ 09west.com. Lisbon-based company offering a range of hiking, birdwatching, surfing and photography tours throughout the country.

Formosmar, Portugal ☎ 289 817 466, Ⓦ formosmar.com. Kayaking, bike tours, walking tours and birdwatching, around the Ria Formosa in the Algarve.

Limosa Holidays UK ☎ 01692 580623, Ⓦ limosaholidays.co.uk. Birdwatching in the Alentejo and Algarve. There's some walking involved, and the holidays (from around £1700 for a week) include flights, meals and transport.

Nature Trails Portugal ☎ 926 543 289, Ⓦ caminhosdanatureza .pt. Guided and self-guided hikes and cycle trips, mostly in the south of the country.

Naturetrek UK ☎ 01962 733051, Ⓦ naturetrek.co.uk. Offers 7- or 8-day spring and autumn botanical and birdwatching trips in the southern Alentejo and the Algarve (around £1300), including gentle walking.

FOOD AND DRINK

Arblaster & Clarke UK ☎ 01730 263111, Ⓦ winetours.co.uk. Sophisticated wine-tour specialist offering Douro vineyard walks, port-harvest trips, and escorted Portugal tours – from around £1700 for a week's all-inclusive guided wine tour.

HORSERIDING

Equitour UK ☎ 0800 043 7942, US ☎ 1 800 656 6163; Ⓦ equitour.com. Horseriding holidays in the Alentejo – a week for around £1000 (not including flights), with accommodation at a private country resort.

WALKING AND CYCLING

Easy Rider Tours US ☎ 1 800 488 8332, Ⓦ easyridertours.com. Guided cycling and sightseeing tours in various Portuguese regions, from a leisurely Sintra tour to a nine-day mountain-to-coast trip, with prices ranging from $3000–4000.

Portugal Walks UK ☎ 0965 753 033 or Portugal ☎ 965 753 033, Ⓦ portugalwalks.com, Ⓦ pedalinportugal.com. A good range of group and individual guided and self-guided walking and cycling holidays in the Algarve, Alentejo, Lisbon coast and north Portugal. Typically, a four-night self-guided walk starts at around €300, a week's guided group walking from around €600, or cycling for around €1300 (all excluding flights).

Ramblers Worldwide Holidays UK ☎ 01707 331133, Ⓦ ramblersholidays.co.uk. Long-established walking-holiday operator with guided walking trips along the Douro and Minho rivers, as well as the Algarve and the northern national and natural parks. From around £665 per week.

Getting around

Portugal is not a large country and you can get almost everywhere easily and efficiently by train or bus. Regional trains are often cheaper and some lines very scenic, but it's almost always quicker to go by bus – especially on shorter or less obvious routes. You'll obviously have a great deal more flexibility if you drive, and you'll be able to visit more out-of-the-way places in a short trip.

By train

Comboios de Portugal (**CP**; enquiries on ☎808 208 208, Ⓦcp.pt) operates all trains. For the most part it's an efficient network with modern rolling stock, while there are some highly picturesque lines in the north that are among the country's best

PORTUGAL: TRAINS

attractions, notably the Douro line from Porto to Pocinho. Be aware that rural train stations can sometimes be a fair way from the town or village they serve – Portalegre station and town are 12km apart, for example. **Timetables** (*horários*) for all lines are available from stations and on the CP website, which has a good English-language version.

Most **train services** are designated Regionais (R) or Interregionais (IR), covering the country from Faro in the south to Valença do Minho in the north. Intercidades (IC) are faster and more expensive services, connecting Lisbon to the main regional centres; while the modern, high-speed Alfa Pendulares (AP) trains run from Lisbon to Faro, and from Lisbon to Braga via Santarém, Coimbra, Aveiro and Porto. Urban services (*urbanos*) in Lisbon (to Cascais, Sintra, Setúbal and Vila Franca de Xira) and Porto (to Aveiro, Braga and Guimarães) provide a useful commuter link to local towns, while both cities also have an underground metro system.

Tickets, fares and rail passes

Most visitors simply buy a **ticket** every time they travel; first-class is *primeira classe* or *conforto*, second-class is *segunda classe* or *turística*. Always turn up at the station with time to spare since long queues often form at the ticket office. However, at unstaffed regional stations you can just pay the ticket inspector on board, while major stations have credit-card ticket machines for long-distance IC or AP tickets (on the day of travel or up to thirty days in advance); and you can also buy IC and AP tickets on the CP website.

Fares are extremely good value. A typical regional journey, across the Algarve from Faro to Vila Real de Santo António for example, only costs around €5.50; the Lisbon-to-Porto route costs around €25 second-class/€36 first-class by Intercidade, or around €31/43 on the fastest Alfa Pendular service. It's cheapest on all services if you avoid travelling on Friday afternoons, Sunday afternoons, Monday mornings, national holidays and the day preceding a national holiday. There are fifty-percent **discounts** for children under 12 (under-4s go free), and thirty percent for over-65s (ID required; ask for a *bilhete terceira idade*) and Euro 26 card-holders – but discounts aren't given on AP trains, nor on some weekend IC trains. **Seat reservations** are obligatory on IC and AP trains, though they are included in the ticket price.

The major pan-European **rail passes** (InterRail and Eurail) are only worth considering if you're visiting the country as part of a wider European tour. However, both schemes also have single-country Portugal passes, which might prove better value. The **InterRail Portugal Pass** (raileurope.co.uk) is only available to European residents and allows three, four, six or eight days' train travel within one month, with under-26, second- and first-class versions available. For anyone else, **Eurail** (eurail .com) also has Portugal passes, typically offering three, four or six days' travel within a month, again in various classes. You can check current prices on the websites, but bear in mind that it often works out cheaper to buy individual tickets as you need them, and it's certainly more convenient to be able to choose buses on some routes. All these passes also have to be bought before you leave home, and you'll still be liable for supplements and seat reservations on long-distance and high-speed trains.

By bus

Buses connect almost all of the country's towns and villages, with services operated by a wide array of private companies. It can be a little confusing at times: at some bus stations you may find two or more companies running services to the same towns; conversely, buses going to the same destination may leave from different terminals. However, there is a national network of **express buses**, with Rede Expressos (rede-expressos.pt) offering a daily service to destinations across the country – you can book tickets online or buy them at bus stations and ticket desks (often in cafés by the bus stop/station). Buying tickets in advance is a wise idea, but even in summer in tourist areas the day before is usually fine. **Fares** are good value: the Lisbon–Porto express route and Faro–Lisbon both cost around €20. Under-4s travel free, under-12s half-price, and there are discounts for under-26s and senior citizens over 65 with relevant identification.

Local and rural bus services go virtually everywhere you're likely to want to go, with the notable exception of some of the natural parks, like the Serra da Estrela, Serra de Malcata and Montesinho. However, services are often restricted to one or two departures a day, or geared towards school and market times – meaning early-morning weekday departures, sometimes only during term times. Many local services are reduced – or nonexistent – at weekends.

The local **bus station** – Rodoviária or Camionagem – is usually the best place to check services and routes. Most companies have timetables posted in the ticket-office window and copies to give away, though outside the Algarve

DISTANCE CHART (KMS)

	Aveiro	Beja	Braga	Bragança	Castelo Branco	Coimbra	Évora	Faro	Guarda
Aveiro	–	380	120	320	216	64	306	499	180
Beja	380	–	500	560	254	333	78	152	360
Braga	120	500	–	230	330	170	425	620	260
Bragança	320	560	230	–	310	314	484	697	203
Castelo Branco	216	254	330	310	–	160	175	390	106
Coimbra	64	333	170	314	160	–	255	455	169
Évora	306	78	425	484	175	255	–	215	282
Faro	499	152	620	697	390	455	215	–	495
Guarda	180	360	260	203	106	169	282	495	–
Leiria	121	265	238	380	170	67	190	390	236
Lisbon	242	193	361	510	250	196	150	300	365
Portalegre	310	181	410	390	80	240	104	317	188
Porto	68	50	53	255	277	118	370	575	220
Santarém	185	195	310	450	169	138	118	300	281
Setúbal	290	139	417	560	270	246	108	250	372
Valença do Minho	194	580	91	323	407	250	502	702	348
Viana do Castelo	140	524	49	280	355	194	448	648	295
Vila Real	185	512	107	138	264	207	440	661	160

it's rare to find anyone who speaks English. Turismos often have bus timetables too, though you can't always count on them being up to date.

By car

A massive EU-funded construction programme has improved roads right across the country – particularly in previously remote areas such as Trás-os-Montes and Beira Alta – and what appears to be a minor route on a map can turn out to be a beautifully engineered highway. But there are still plenty of winding, poorly maintained rural roads – and you can expect to encounter highway repairs, farm vehicles, roaming animals and locals laden with wood or produce on almost any countryside journey. Other than on city approaches and during rush hour, **traffic** is generally light, though as car ownership has increased dramatically in recent years so too has congestion. It's worth noting, too,

---

PORTUGAL'S TOP FIVE DRIVES

1. From Entre-os-Rios, the **N222** heads high above the south bank of the Douro, before hugging the water as far as pretty Pinhão. See p.289
2. Drive across the highest mountains in Portugal, from Seia to Covilhã on the **N339**. See p.242
3. The trans-Trás-os-Montes **N103** snakes around northern Portugal's wildest terrain, skirting the Parque Natural de Montesinho. See p.375
4. The vertiginous **N379-1** crosses the Serra de Arrábida mountains high above the Baia de Setúbal, providing stunning coastal views. See p.124
5. The **N265** from Serpa to Mértola is a bucolic back-route through the Alentejo's stunning Parque Natural do Vale do Guardiana. See p.420

Leiria	Lisbon	Portalegre	Porto	Santarém	Setúbal	Valença do Minho	Viana do Castelo	Vila Real
121	242	310	68	185	290	194	140	185
265	193	181	50	195	139	580	524	512
238	361	410	53	310	417	91	49	107
380	510	390	255	450	560	323	280	138
170	250	80	277	169	270	407	355	264
67	196	240	118	138	246	250	194	207
190	150	104	370	118	108	502	448	440
390	300	317	575	300	250	702	648	661
236	365	188	220	281	372	348	295	160
–	128	170	185	70	180	314	261	271
128	–	228	314	79	50	443	390	403
170	228	–	360	145	192	484	434	344
185	314	360	–	254	362	123	71	117
70	79	145	254	–	121	384	331	340
180	50	192	362	121	–	492	440	450
314	443	484	123	384	492	–	53	198
261	390	434	71	331	440	53	–	155
271	403	344	117	340	450	198	155	–

that Portugal's accident statistics are some of the worst per capita in the EU, and drink-driving is not uncommon, despite the strict laws and advertising campaigns.

Most **main roads** are prefixed EN – Estrada Nacional – or just N, with the faster regional highways denoted as IP (Itinerário Principal) or IC (Itinerário Complementar). On the whole, they are two-lane roads, with passing lanes on hills, though stretches near some towns and cities are dual carriageway.

You can pay by credit card at most petrol stations for **fuel** (gasolina) – unleaded is sem chumbo, diesel gasóleo.

Motorways and tolls

The **motorway** (auto-estrada) network (prefixed with "A") comprises four- or six-lane toll roads (signposted "Portagem") that link the Algarve with Lisbon, Porto, the main inland towns and the north. Most of the motorways have **toll gates** – take a ticket when you join the motorway, then hand it in at the next toll gate or when you leave, and you'll be told what to pay. Don't drive through the lane marked "Via Verde" (an automatic debit-payment lane), but use any lane with a green light above it – you pay in cash, or with Visa or MasterCard.

However, some formerly toll-free motorways now use **number plate-recognition** cameras to charge. If you have your own car, there are three somewhat complex ways to pay: full details are on ⓦ portugaltolls.pt. For those renting a car, you need to pay for road usage at a post office – just tell the post office your car registration number and they will tell you what you owe. However, you can currently only pay two to five days after you have used the road, which is not much good if you are using the motorway to the airport for a flight home. In theory, you could be chased for the bill, but it is unlikely.

The tolls are considered expensive by the Portuguese, who tend to use the older routes where possible; driving up the A1 from Lisbon to Porto, for example, costs around €22, while Lisbon to Faro costs around €25. However, it's always much quicker by motorway and, with some sections virtually deserted, they are a pleasure to drive.

ADDRESSES

Addresses in Portugal are written as: Rua Garrett 32-2º, which means Garrett Street no. 32, 2nd floor; "esq" or "E" (for *esquerda*) after a floor number refers to a flat or office on the left-hand side, "dir" or "D" (for *direita*) is right, *esquina* means corner or junction, and R/C stands for *rés-do-chão* (ground floor). You will often see the following abbreviations used in addresses: Av (for Avenida, avenue) and Trav (Travessa, alley).

Rules of the road

Traffic drives on the right: **speed limits** are 50kph in towns and villages (often enforced by tripped "Velocidade Controlade" traffic lights), 90kph on normal roads, and 120kph on motorways and interregional highways. Unless there's a sign to the contrary at road junctions (and there rarely is), vehicles coming from the right have **right of way** – it can be horribly confusing, but most drivers use common sense to interpret whose turn it is. Other **road signage** is also poor, particularly at round-abouts, city exits and highway access roads, where signs simply dry up for no reason; often, too, there's little or no warning of turnings at slip-roads and junctions; or destinations may be signposted in one direction and not the other.

Driving licences from most countries are accepted, so there's no need to get an international one before you leave. Many **car insurance** policies cover taking your car to Portugal; check with your own insurer. However, you're advised to take out extra cover for motoring assistance in case your car breaks down: try motoring organizations like the RAC (Ⓦ rac.co.uk) or the AA (Ⓦ theaa.co.uk). Alternatively, you can get 24-hour assistance from the Automóvel Clube de Portugal (Ⓦ acp.pt), which has reciprocal arrangements with foreign automobile clubs.

If you're **stopped by the police** in Portugal, they'll want to see your personal ID or passport, driving licence, and papers for the car (including ownership papers if it's your own car). By law, you should also have a red warning triangle and a fluorescent yellow jacket in the car (provided in rental cars). It pays to be patient and courteous since the police can – and do – levy on-the-spot fines for speeding, parking and other offences. Pleading ignorance won't get you anywhere.

Parking

Many towns and beach resorts are now flooded with traffic, especially in summer, so you may find problems finding a central parking space. Some cities, such as Coimbra, have park-and-ride schemes, while in Porto there are huge car parks at suburban metro stations. When **parking in cities**, do as the locals do and use the empty spaces pointed out to you. A tip of €0.50 to the man doing the pointing will pay them for "looking after" your car. **On-street parking** is usually metered, even in the smallest towns. The price varies, but averages €0.50 an hour, though it's generally free from 8pm until 8am the next morning on weekdays, on Saturday afternoons and all day Sunday. **Garage parking** is always more expensive – up to €10 a day – but where it's available it is the most secure option.

Car and motorbike rental

Car rental is relatively inexpensive and usually cheapest of all arranged in advance through one of the large multinational chains. Check their websites for special offers. Otherwise, rental agencies (including local firms) are found in all the major towns and at the airports in Lisbon, Porto and Faro. Local rates start at €150 a week with unlimited mileage, theft cover and collision damage waivers. Minimum age for rental is 21, though up to and including the age of 24 you'll have to pay a supplement.

Collision **insurance** is vital, since without it you'll be liable for costs should the vehicle be damaged – and this includes even minor scratches, easily acquired down unmade tracks or in crowded car parks. Ensure that all visible damage on a car you're picking up is duly marked on the rental sheet. It's definitely worth considering paying the extra charge to reduce the "excess" payment levied for any damage, but these waiver charges (by the day) soon add up. However, you can avoid all **excess charges** in the event of damage by taking out an annual insurance policy with Ⓦ Insurance 4carhire.com, which also covers windscreen and tyre damage.

You can also rent mopeds, scooters and low-powered (80cc) **motorbikes** in many resorts, with costs starting at around €30 a day. You need to be at least 18 (and over 23 for bikes over 125cc) and to have held a full licence for at least a year. Rental should include helmet and locks along with third-party insurance. Helmet use is obligatory.

CAR RENTAL COMPANIES

Auto Jardim Ⓦ auto-jardim.com
Avis Ⓦ avis.com
Budget Ⓦ budget.com

Europcar Ⓦ europcar.com

Hertz Ⓦ hertz.com

Taxis

Travelling by taxi in Portugal is relatively cheap by European standards, and meters are used in towns and cities – an average journey across Lisbon or Porto costs around €8–13. Additional charges are made for carrying luggage, travelling at weekends or between 10pm and 6am (twenty percent more), and for calling a cab by phone – these charges are all posted inside the cab. You may have to rely on taxis more than you expect, since bus and railway stations are often some way removed from town centres, while in rural areas there may be no other way to reach your next destination. Outside town limits, the journey is usually charged by the kilometre – the driver should be able to quote you a figure for the trip.

By bike

Cycling is increasingly popular in Portugal, both as a sport and a way to get from A to B, despite the hilly terrain of the interior. In addition, dedicated cycle paths are beginning to appear in major cities, such as Lisbon and Porto, as are long-distance cycle paths along former railways lines, such as the Ecopista do Dão near Coimbra and the Ecopista da Linha do Tâmega near Amarante. Specialist outlets, plus hotels, campsites and youth hostels, rent bikes from €10–20 a day: we give details in the guide.

Portugal's woeful road-accident statistics mean that defensive riding is essential – reflective and fluorescent clothing (or sashes) at night is recommended. In general, it's best to assume that drivers will not obey road signs or regulations – just be prepared. Minor country roads have far less traffic to contend with, but locals know them such backwards and so speeding – even around blind corners – is the norm. For more information on cycling abroad, contact the UK's national cycling organization, the **CTC** (Ⓦ ctc.org.uk), though you'll have to join to access their tours and notes on cycling in Portugal.

Collapsible bikes can be taken for free on regional and interregional trains (ie, the slow ones), so long as they're dismantled and stowed in a bag or other cover. Otherwise, bikes can be taken on the Lisbon and Porto urban lines and regional trains from Coimbra – there's usually a small charge during the week, free at weekends. The CP website (Ⓦ cp.pt) has the latest details.

Accommodation

Accommodation in Portugal is pretty good value, certainly compared with other western European countries. In almost any town you can find a basic guesthouse or small hotel offering a simple double or twin room for as little as €40, though you'll pay more in Algarve resorts in summer, in the mountains in the winter, or year-round in Lisbon. Moving upmarket, you're often spoilt for choice by some wonderful manor houses and a network of comfortable hotels known as pousadas, many in historic buildings or sited in places of natural beauty. Even in high season you shouldn't have much problem finding a bed in most regions, though the best places in Lisbon and the Algarve are often booked up days ahead, so advance reservations here are advised.

In hotels, a *quarto duplo* has two single beds, and a *quarto casal* has a large double bed for a couple. A single room – *quarto solteiro* or *individual* – costs around three quarters of the price of a double. Ask to see the room before you take it, and don't be afraid to ask if there's a cheaper one available (rooms without private bathrooms often cost considerably less). In higher-grade hotels, you'll often get a better rate by booking online or simply by asking, especially out of season or at the end of the day.

Lastly, a word of warning: between November and April, night-time temperatures throughout Alentejo, the mountain Beiras and Trás-os-Montes can plummet to below freezing, and even along the coast temperatures of under 5ºC are common. However, few B&Bs or guesthouses have any form

---

ACCOMMODATION PRICES

All establishments listed in this book have a price quoted. It represents the rate for the **cheapest available double/twin room in high season** (ie, Christmas/ New Year, Easter, July and August, and other local holidays), which means that at other times you'll often be able to stay for a lower price than that suggested. Breakfast is included, unless otherwise stated. For youth hostels we give the euro price for a dorm bed instead, and for campsites we give the price of a pitch plus the price per extra adult, if relevant.

ACCOMMODATION ALTERNATIVES

Useful websites that can provide alternatives to standard hotel and hostel accommodation in Portugal.

Airbnb ⓦ airbnb.com
CouchSurfing ⓦ couchsurfing.org
Vacation Rentals by Owner ⓦ vrbo.com

of heating other than the odd plug-in radiator, so check out the facilities before taking a room. Similarly, in the height of summer check for a fan or air conditioning, as nights can be very warm.

Guesthouses and private rooms

A simple **guesthouse** is known as an *alojamento local* – these come with or without en-suite facilities and don't always provide breakfast, but are usually perfectly comfortable and often in characterful old townhouses. In seaside resorts and smaller villages, you can also often rent a **room** in a private house, known as a **dormida** or **quarto** – just look around for signs in windows, or check with the local turismo. Room quality and facilities vary greatly; some are little more than a bed in a converted attic, others come with modern bathrooms and air conditioning. Always ask where the room is before you agree to take it – you could end up far from the town centre or beach. Breakfast is not usually included.

Rates for *alojamentos locais* and *quartos* average around €40–50 a night, though in the Algarve in high season expect to pay up to twice as much.

Hotels

Hotels are all classified with one to five stars, and can vary from old buildings with plenty of character, sometimes with owners to match, to top-notch, stylish, luxury resorts. A one-star hotel (which may still be known by its former name as a *pensão* or *resedencial*) – usually costs around €40 and may not have en-suite bathrooms or indeed much else other than the bed, a heavy (and almost never used) wardrobe, and perhaps a chair or table. More upmarket places will have modern en-suite rooms, plus TVs, heaters and air conditioning. Breakfast is usually included, but don't expect much more than coffee, bread and preserves, and possibly some sliced ham and cheese.

At two- and three-star hotels, en-suite doubles cost up to €80; many three-star places these days have air-conditioned rooms with cable/satellite TV, and even swimming pools, so they can be pretty good value. For rooms with all mod cons in four- and five-star hotels, you'll pay anything from €100 to €200, while the very fanciest places – boutique hotels in the Algarve or luxury hotels in Lisbon, for example – attract an international clientele and can pretty much charge what they like. Some cosier places of four- or five-star quality, often in a converted historic building or manor house in a rural location, are known as **estalagems**, or inns. All hotels and inns serve breakfast, usually (though not always) included in the price. In one- and two-star hotels it tends to be continental-style; more substantial buffet breakfasts are provided at three-star places and up.

Pousadas

Pousadas de Portugal (ⓦ pousadas.pt) is a chain of over forty hotels that have either been converted from historic properties such as old monasteries or castles, or purpose-built in dramatic countryside settings. Formerly government-run, they are now efficiently managed by the Portuguese hotel chain Pestana, and can be found all over the country, especially in the Alentejo and the north. The

UNUSUAL PLACES TO STAY

Convento de São Francisco, Mértola. Spend the night in a former monk's cell. See p.421
Casa do Abrigo, Ilha da Berlenga. Bed down at the old fort on an island nature reserve. See p.141
A Lagosta Perdida, Montesinho. A haven for hikers at the boutique-style "Lost Lobster". See p.374
Navio Gil Eannes, Viana do Castelo. Budget dorms on an old hospital ship. See p.326
Paço de Calheiros, Ponte de Lima. Stay at the country retreat of a count. See p.336
Quinta do Rio Alcaide, Porto de Mós. Relax in the spring-fed pool at this converted paper mill. See p.161
Quinta Nova, Pinhão. Chic rooms and amazing views at a gorgeous Douro wine estate. See p.297
Santos, Guarda. The cosy rooms here nestle inside the city walls. See p.227
Vila Galé Albacora, Tavira. Stay in style in a former tuna-fishing village. See p.449

PICK OF THE POUSADAS

Alcácer do Sal, Alentejo. Dramatic views from a fabulous castle. See p.422
Beja, Alentejo. A tranquil retreat in a former convent. See p.418
Estoi, Algarve. A palatial blend of contemporary style and old-fashioned elegance. See p.440
Évora, Alentejo. Sumptuous comforts in southern Portugal's most charming town. See p.391
Flor da Rosa, Alentejo. How many old convents have a snooker room in the cloister? See p.398
Óbidos, Estremadura. A superb, intimate castle conversion. See p.143
Porto. A magnificent Baroque riverside palace in Portugal's second city. See p.275
Tavira, Algarve. Designer-style ancient convent. See p.449
Viseu, Beira Alta. A dramatic conversion of a former hospital. See p.223

converted historic buildings are particularly fine, making full use of the old cloisters and chapels, etc, and some have been well modernized by Portugal's top architects. Others are more like small country houses, with an old-fashioned elegance and charm, while facilities and service throughout are equivalent to those in four- and five-star hotels. Most also have a swimming pool, lovely gardens and a good restaurant.

Prices vary considerably depending on the season, day (more expensive on Fri & Sat nights) and location, but start at around €100–120 per night, rising to €170–200 for the finest properties. That said, a whole host of promotions (through the website) offer rooms from around €90, and there are good deals most of the year for anyone over 55. Another popular approach is to book a self-drive holiday based around the *pousadas*, with seven nights' accommodation plus car starting at around €700.

You can book the *pousadas* through their website, or through the official agents Keytel in the UK (Ⓦ keytel.co.uk) or Petrabax in the US (Ⓦ petrabax.com).

Rural tourism: country and manor houses

An increasingly popular alternative is to stay in a privately owned **country or manor house**. Promoted under the banner of Turismo no Espaço Rural (TER), most are reasonably priced and are subdivided into the following categories: "HR" or Hotéis Rurais (traditional, country hotels); "TH" or Turismo de Habitação (old manor houses and palaces); "CC" or Casas no Campo (simpler country houses); and "AG" or Agro-Turismo (farmhouses, often on working farms or wine estates).

You can book many of these properties via **CENTER** (Central Nacional de Turismo no Espaço Rural ☎ 258 931 750, Ⓦ center.pt), a non-profit-making organization which aims to help residents maintain their properties and traditional ways of life – without their support, many houses would either be sold, developed or abandoned. Alternatively, check the websites of the organizations it represents (namely Ⓦ solaresdeportugal.pt, Ⓦ aldeiasdeportugal.pt and Ⓦ casasnocampo.net).

Properties range from simple farmhouses offering a couple of rooms on a bed-and-breakfast basis, to country manors complete with period furnishings. *Quintas* or *herdades* are farm estate houses, and you can even stay in palaces (*palácios*), owned by Portuguese aristocrats who have allowed their ancient seats to become part of the scheme.

There are hundreds of properties available, all of which have been inspected and approved by the government tourist office. **Rates** start at around €60 a night, though the grandest places might charge up to €120 for a double/twin room, or a little more for self-contained apartments or cottages within the grounds (sleeping up to six). Large breakfasts are invariably included, while many will provide dinners made from local ingredients, sometimes accompanied by wine and other produce made on the estate. Others offer activities like fishing, rambling, horseriding and wine tasting.

Villas and apartments

Virtually every area of the country has some sort of self-catering **villa** or **apartment** available for rent, from basic one-room studios to five- or six-bedroom houses complete with grounds and pool. Most UK and European tour operators can find you a suitable place (usually but not exclusively in the Algarve), though in summer the best places are booked up months in advance. The minimum rental period is usually a week, and the best deals are often packages, including flights and car rental, with endless tour companies such as First Choice (Ⓦ firstchoice.co.uk) and Thomson (Ⓦ thomson.co.uk), or Minho specialists such as Portuguese Affair (Ⓦ portugueseaffair.com), and

Western Algarve experts Star Villas (W starvilla.com). While the Algarve has a year-round international trade, and prices to match, other **Portuguese resorts** (such as Peniche, Figueira da Foz or Viana do Castelo) are pretty quiet outside Easter, July and August and will have plenty of locally available accommodation.

Youth hostels

There are around fifty **youth hostels** (*pousadas de juventude*) in Portugal, under the umbrella of the youth organization Movijovem and affiliated to the Hostelling International network (W hihostels.com). You'll need a valid membership card, available from your home-based youth-hostel association, or you can join on your first night at any hostel. There are full details of each hostel on the W pousadas juventude.pt website (also in English), and you can book directly with the hostels, or online or call central reservations on ☏ 707 203 030.

Some hostels are a bit on the basic side, and others are geared towards schools and groups, but they are all in convenient locations for sightseeing or outdoor activities. As well as dorm beds, you can often get larger family rooms or apartments, and even en-suite double rooms. Some of the newer ones – at Parque das Nações (Lisbon), Lousã, Idanha-a-Nova and Guimarães, for example – have been very well designed, while many others have wi-fi, cafés, bars and bike rental as standard. At Alcoutim and Portimão (Algarve) there are swimming pools; stylish Aljezur/Arrifana (Algarve) has a great cliff-top position; while other particularly good hostel locations include Vilarinho das Furnas (in Peneda-Gerês National Park), Areia Branca (on the beach, close to Peniche), and Lagos and Leiria (good buildings in historic towns).

Prices vary according to season, location and facilities, but dorm beds in most cost between €12 and €18 per person (high season is basically July, August, Easter, Christmas and other public holidays); we have given prices for individual hostels throughout the guide.

There's also a growing network of **independent and boutique hostels**, particularly in surf resorts in the Algarve, Alentejo and Estremadura coast, and also increasingly in Lisbon and Porto. Prices are similar to those at the *pousadas de juventude*, though the vibe tends to be more backpacker- than family-oriented, and some of the new boutique city hostels (such as the *Rivoli Cinema Hostel* in Porto and *Lisbon Lounge* or *Travellers House* in Lisbon) are very classy indeed.

Camping

There are hundreds of campsites, though many are huge, town-sized affairs by or near the beach that also have space for campervans/RVs, caravans and permanent bungalows and apartments. Needless to say, these get very crowded with Portuguese families in summer, though there are also plenty of smaller rural sites offering a quieter experience. The **Roteiro Campista** has details of over 200 campsites on its website (W roteiro-campista.pt; also in English) and booklet, which is widely available in bookshops in Portugal.

Charges are usually per person and per caravan or tent, with showers and parking extra; even so, it's rare that you'll pay more than €8 per person, although those operated by **Orbitur** (W orbitur .com) – usually with bungalows on site as well – are more expensive. The cheapest place to camp is usually the **municipal campsite** in each town, though these vary in quality and can be very crowded – they are not always recommended.

A few sites require an **international camping card** which gives discounts at member sites and serves as useful identification: many campsites will take it instead of your passport, and it covers you for third-party insurance when camping. The card is available from most home motoring or cycling organizations and camping and caravan clubs, or check W campingcardinternational.com.

Camping outside campsites is legal, though there are restrictions – for example, you can't camp on tourist beaches or in natural parks (other than in designated camping areas). With a little sensitivity you can pitch a tent for a short period almost anywhere else in the countryside, but it's always best to ask locally first – the potential fire risk is taken very seriously in Portugal.

Food and drink

Portuguese food doesn't have the same high profile as other European cuisines, with menus usually relying on a traditional repertoire of grilled fish and meat, hearty stews and casseroles, and the ubiquitous salted cod (bacalhau), nearly all served with the same trio of accompaniments – rice, potatoes and salad. There are, of course, blindingly good exceptions to the norm in every town – crispy suckling pig from the local grill house, sardines straight from the boat and slapped on the

barbecue, a slow-cooked ragout of wild boar in a country tavern – and these are the kind of simple, earthy dishes that Portugal excels in. Most restaurants are also extremely good value, while Portuguese wine (and not just the famous port) enjoys a growing worldwide reputation – if you're not yet familiar with them, you'll soon come to relish a refreshing glass of vinho verde on a hot day, or a gutsy Alentejo red with your bife.

There's far more choice, style and invention in Lisbon, Porto, the Algarve and in wine regions such as the Douro, where international dishes are widely available and some enterprising chefs are adding a contemporary twist to traditional Portuguese cuisine. But out in the regions, and particularly in rural areas, simple, traditional menus still dominate. It's surprising, since the Portuguese originally introduced many spices and ingredients to a global market, but other than the odd Chinese or Indian restaurant, pizza place or Brazilian grill house most towns tend to feature resolutely local restaurants. Fast-food joints are widespread, though they are found more often in shopping malls than town centres. We have included a detailed **menu reader** in the Language section (see p.512).

Breakfast, snacks and sandwiches

At **breakfast**, any café, *pastelaria* (pastry shop) or *confeitaria* (confectioners) can provide a croissant or brioche, some toast (*uma torrada*; a doorstep with butter), a simple sandwich (a *tosta mista* is grilled ham and cheese) or some sort of cake or pastry. A *padaria* is a bakery, and any place advertising *pão quente* (hot bread) will also usually have a café attached.

Classic Portuguese **snacks** include *folhadas* (meat- or cheese-stuffed pasties), *croquetes* (deep-fried meat patties), *pastéis* or *bolinhos de bacalhau* (salt-cod fishcakes), *iscas de bacalhau* (battered cod fishcakes with egg), *chamuças* (samosas), *bifanas* (a grilled or fried pork sandwich), and *prego no pão* (steak sandwich).

If you see a sign saying **petiscos**, you can sample Portugal's version of tapas. The range, however, is rarely extensive, and apart from olives, *tremoços* (pickled lupin seeds), a small round of cheese or some small fried fish these dishes tend towards the challenging – stewed snails or octopus salad, for example, or the unspeakable, ubiquitous *orelhas de porco* (crunchy pig's ears).

Restaurants

The quickest way to get trampled to death is to come between the Portuguese and their lunch.
A Small Death in Lisbon, Robert Wilson

Portuguese **restaurants** (*restaurantes*) run the gamut, from rustic village eatery to designer hot spot, while meals are also served in a **tasca** (a tavern) and, less commonly these days, a **casa de pasto** (a cheap local dining room). A **cervejaria** is literally a "beer house", usually more informal than a restaurant and typically serving up steaks and seafood. A **marisqueira** is also a seafood place, while a **churrasqueira** specializes in char-grilled meat.

At lunch, most places offer a **prato do dia** (dish of the day), which is often cheaper than choosing from the menu. Many places also offer a more formal **ementa turística** – not a "tourist menu" as such, but a three-course set meal of the day, which may include soup, a drink or dessert: the lot can cost as little as €7–12. Prices, in any case, are rarely off-putting, and for €15–30 a head you could eat

---

VEGETARIAN PORTUGAL

Portuguese cuisine is tough on strict **vegetarians** and you'll be eating a lot of omelettes, chips, salads and pizzas. Nearly everywhere does a basic vegetable soup, though beware of the **caldo verde** – a kale, onion and potato broth – which usually comes with *chouriço* in. Portuguese fruit is a particular joy, especially in the Algarve, Estremadura and Beira Baixa, and any market should turn up some excellent local produce. You may even find officially certified *biológico* – **organic** – produce, though it has yet to make much of an impact on mainstream food-buying habits.

In Lisbon, Porto and some parts of the Algarve, there is a reasonable selection of **vegetarian restaurants**, even macrobiotic ones, together with Chinese, Italian and Indian establishments where you should be able to eat well. Also, most towns have **health-food shops** (or supermarkets with health-food sections) where you can find cereal bars, gluten-free biscuits, dried fruit and the like.

well in most restaurants in Portugal, provided you don't choose lobster or quaff the vintage port.

The default size for servings is huge. Indeed, you can usually have a substantial meal by ordering a cheaper **meia dose** (half-portion), or **uma dose** (a portion) between two. Meals are often listed in two sizes on the menu and it's perfectly acceptable to choose a smaller portion. **Lunch** is usually served noon to 3pm; **dinner** from 7.30pm onwards; don't count on being able to eat much after 10pm outside cities and tourist resorts.

Once seated in a Portuguese restaurant, you will be bought a plate of **appetizers**, which may just be bread and portions of butter and sardine spread, but sometimes includes cheese, *chouriço*, prawns or other titbits. None of it is free and you will be charged for everything that you eat – if you don't want it, just say *não quero isto* ("I don't want this"), and make sure you check the bill afterwards. Beware, too, the near-ubiquitous serenade of the traditional Portuguese **television**, even in upmarket or otherwise romantic or fancy restaurants. A request to turn it down or, heaven forbid, off is likely to be met with bemusement.

Portuguese cuisine

Most Portuguese are convinced that theirs is the finest cuisine in the world. You may beg to differ – though you're in for a long argument if you voice a contrary opinion – but, at its best, Portuguese food marries locally sourced ingredients (especially fish, seafood, pork and game) with a straightforward preparation that lets the flavours shine through. There is regional variation, though not as much as you'd think – in fact, many ostensibly regional dishes turn up on menus across the country. In most day-to-day restaurants fancy sauces and fresh vegetables are rare, and the predominant dressing for grills and roasts is olive oil, garlic and lemon, though coriander, cumin and paprika are commonly used in cooking.

Fish and seafood

In any resort or river port you can get fabulous **seafood**, from prawns to barnacles, while **fish** on offer usually includes bream (*dourada*), sea bass (*robalo*), hake (*pescada*), *carapau* (mackerel), salmon (*salmão*, often farmed) and trout (*truta*). The most typical Portuguese fish dish is **bacalhau** (dried, salted cod), which is virtually the national dish with reputedly 365 different ways of preparing it – served with a boiled egg and black olives, made into a pie, char-grilled or cooked in a traditional

copper *cataplana*, the list is endless. The best for first-timers to try are *bacalhau á bras* (fried with egg, onions and potatoes) and *bacalhau com natas* (baked in cream).

Grilled **sardines** provide one of the country's most appetizing smells, and you should definitely try a fish or seafood **cataplana**, named after the wok-like lidded copper vessel in which it's cooked. Also typical of the seaside is **arroz de marisco**, mixed seafood in a soupy rice; *massa de peixe/marisco* is a similar dish but with noodles – *cataplanas*, *arroz* and *massa* dishes are usually served for a minimum of two people. Other specialities include a **caldeirada de peixe**, basically a fish stew, and **açorda** (a bread stew traditionally made from stale bread mixed with herbs, garlic, eggs and whatever farmers found to hand), often served with prawns. *Migas* and *xarém* are regional variations of *açorda*.

Meat and game

Grilled **beef, chicken and pork** are the mainstays of most menus – pork is especially loved in Portugal, whether it's steaks, chops, ribs, belly or leg. Particularly sought-after is the *porco negra*, from the black Alentejan pigs, fed on acorns to give them a sweet flavour. **Presunto** is Portugal's equivalent of Parma ham – a smoked leg of pork preserved in sea salt and cured for months or years. The grill or **barbecue** (*no churrasco*) sees a lot of action, and grilled chicken (almost a second national dish) is usually enlivened by the addition of piri-piri (chilli) sauce. Also ubiquitous are *porco à alentejana* (pork cooked with clams), which originated, as its name suggests, in the Alentejo, and *rojões* (chunks of roast pork, served with black pudding) from the north (mainly Minho and Douro). **Leitão** (spit-roast suckling pig) is at the centre of many a communal feast, particularly in the Beiras; **cabrito** (roast kid) is ubiquitous in mountain areas; while another festive Beiras speciality is **chanfana** (goat stew). Duck (*pato*) is usually served shredded and mixed with rice (*arroz de pato*); rabbit is served in rural areas (*a caçadora*, hunter's style, as a stew), and things like wild boar (*javali*), partridge (*perdiz*) or quail (*cordoniz*) are often on menus too.

The Portuguese have long believed that if you eat an animal, you may as well eat all of it, and offal is common. **Alheiras** are sausages made from bread and chicken, with their roots in the Inquisition, when Jews copied the Catholic passion for sausages while avoiding pork – the best come from Mirandela in Trás-os-Montes, and are served grilled or steamed. You might need to steel yourself for a couple of special dishes: Porto's **tripas** (tripe) dishes incorporate beans and spices but the heart of the dish is still recognizably chopped stomach-lining; while **cozido à portuguesa** is a boiled "meat" stew in which you shouldn't be surprised to turn up lumps of fat, cartilage or even a pig's ear. Other traditional dishes use pig's or chicken's blood as a base – the words to look for are *sarrabulho* and *cabidela*.

Cheese

There's a huge range of **regional Portuguese cheese**, a sizeable quantity of which is still handmade (the label D.O.P. guarantees that it was made in its traditional area). A *queijo de cabra* or *cabreiro* is goats' cheese, sheep is *ovelha*, cow is *vaca*, cured is *curado*. *Queijo fresco* and *requeijão* are unpressed curds of sheep's milk, similar to cottage cheese.

Particularly recommended local cheeses to look out for are **Queijo da Serra (or Queijo Serrano)** from the Serra da Estrela, which has an almost liquid texture – the traditional method is to cut out a hole on top and scoop up the contents by spoon – and **Azeitão**, a sheep's milk cheese from near Lisbon, which crumbles slightly when you cut it and has a pleasantly astringent taste.

Vegetables and salad

Accompanying nearly every dish will be **potatoes**, either fried or roast in the case of most meat dishes or boiled if you've ordered fish. The distinction is less marked in tourist resorts on the Algarve and elsewhere, but trying to get chips to come with your grilled trout or salmon in a rural town simply invites incomprehension – fish comes with boiled potatoes and that's that. Most dishes are also served with a helping of rice and salad. Other **vegetables** occasionally make an appearance, like carrots, cabbage or broccoli, usually boiled to within an inch of their lives – a more interesting choice is *grelos* (turnip tops), often turned into a purée, while winter and early spring is the time for chestnuts (*castanhas*), which appear in soups and stuffings. **Salad** is the more common accompaniment to every meal; a *salada mista* is a simple mixed salad of lettuce, tomatoes and onions.

Desserts, cakes, pastries and fruit

In most restaurants, the **dessert** menu rarely goes further than fruit salad, ice cream or things like chocolate mousse and rice pudding. Anything described as a *doce de casa* (house dessert) is invariably a heart-stopping wedge of sugar, cream and egg (our favourite Portuguese recipe begins "Take sixty egg yolks…").

In cake shops, cafés and tea rooms you can seriously indulge yourself in pastries (*pastéis*), buns (*bolinhos*), rolls (*tortas*), tarts (*tartes*) and cakes (*bolos*). There are hundreds of local specialities, starting with the classic Lisbon **pastéis de nata** (custard tarts) and then continuing in glorious profusion by way of *queijadas de Sintra* (Sintra "cheesecakes", not that they contain any cheese), *palha de ovos* (egg pastries) from Abrantes, *bolo de anjo* ("angel cake"), *mil folhas* (millefeuille pastries), *bolinhos* made with beans (*feijão*), carrot (*cenoura*) or pumpkin (*chila*), *bolos de arroz* (rice-flour muffins) and *suspiros* ("sighs" – meringues). From Averiro, there are incredibly sweet egg-based **ovos moles** wrapped in wafers, while anything labelled **doces conventuais** ("convent desserts") owes its origins to the gastronomic inspiration of nuns past.

Seasonal **fruit** ranges from spring cherries and strawberries to summer melons, peaches and apricots. The grapes arrive in late summer and autumn, as do most pears, apples, plums and figs, while winter is the time for citrus fruits, pomegranates, and immensely sweet *dióspiros* (persimmon or date-plums). Available year-round are bananas from Madeira, and sweet and aromatic pineapples from the Azores.

Wine

Portugal's **wine regions** – notably Alentejo, Bairrada, Dão, Estremadura, Ribatejo and the Douro – have acquired a strong reputation in recent years. Most wines are made in small cooperatives with local grape varieties, many peculiar to Portugal (including some wonderfully named varieties of grape such as Dog strangler and Bastardo).

Portuguese wine lists (ask for the *lista de vinhos*) don't just distinguish between *tinto* (red), *branco* (white) and *rosé*, but between *verde* ("green", meaning young, acidic and slightly sparkling) and *maduro* ("mature", meaning the wines you're probably accustomed to). You'll find a decent selection from around the country in even the most basic of restaurants, and often in half-bottles, too.

Some of the best-known *maduros* are from the **Douro** region: the reds tend to be expensive, though a good, crisp, reasonably priced white is Planalto. Red wines from the **Dão** region (a roughly triangular area between Coimbra, Viseu and Guarda, around the River Dão) taste a little like burgundy, and they're available throughout the country. Quinta de Cabriz from Carregal do Sal (near Viseu) is an excellent mid-range Dão red. The **Alentejo** is another area with a growing reputation – wines from Reguengos de Monsaraz have the strength and full body typical of that region, notably the Monte Velho reds and Esporão Reserva whites from the Herdade de Esporão vineyard. Among other smaller regions offering interesting wines are Colares near Sintra (rich reds), Bucelas in the Estremadura (crisp, dry whites) and Alenquer from Ribatejo (refreshing whites).

The light, slightly sparkling **vinhos verdes** – "green wines", in age not colour – are produced in quantity in the Minho. They're drunk young as most don't improve with age, but are great with meals, especially shellfish. There are red and rosé *vinhos verdes*, though the whites are the most successful. Casal Garcia and Gato are the two labels you see everywhere; far better are Ponte de Lima and Ponte da Barca. For real quality, try the fuller-strength Alvarinho from Monção and Melgaço, along the River Minho.

Portuguese **rosé wines** are known abroad mainly through the spectacularly successful export of Mateus Rosé. This is too sweet and aerated for most tastes, but other rosés are definitely worth sampling.

Portugal also produces a range of sparkling **wines**, known as *espumantes naturais*. The best of these come from the Bairrada region, north of Coimbra, though Raposeira wines – a little further north from near Lamego – are more commonly available.

Fortified wine, spirits and beer

Port (*vinho do Porto*), the famous fortified wine or *vinho generoso* ("generous wine"), is produced from grapes grown in the vineyards of the Douro valley and mostly stored in huge wine-lodges at Vila Nova de Gaia, facing Porto across the Rio Douro. You can visit these for tours and free tastings; we give full details in the Guide.

Madeira (*vinho da Madeira*), from the island of the same name, comes in four main varieties: Sercial (a light, dry aperitif), Malvasia (very sweet, heavy dessert wine), Vermelho (a sweeter version of Sercial) and Boal or Malmsey (drier versions of Malvasia). Also worth trying are the sweet white **moscatel** dessert wines from Setúbal, which – like port and Madeira – also come as yearly vintages.

Domestic **brandy** (the best is *maciera*) and **gin** are fairly unsophisticated and frighteningly cheap. Be warned that the typical Portuguese measure of spirits involves the waiter or bartender pouring from the bottle until you beg them to stop. Order by name if you'd like an international brand that you've heard of.

Local firewaters – generically known as **aguardente** – include *bagaço* (made from distilled grape husks), *aguardente de figo* (from figs), *ginginha* (from cherries), *brandymel* (a honey brandy) and the very strange *Licor Beirão* (a kind of cognac with herbs). In the Algarve, the best-known firewaters are *brandy mel*, made from the strawberry tree and which tastes a bit like schnapps, and *amêndoa amarga*, made from almonds.

Portugal's main **beer** (*cerveja*) brands, found nationwide, are Sagres and Super Bock, and you'll also see Cristal and Cintra, not that there's much to distinguish any of them. The standard beer in Portugal is a typical European-style lager (around five percent strength), but the main brands also offer a *preta* (black) beer – a kind of slightly fizzy lager-stout – as well as wheat, fruit-flavoured and non-alcoholic versions, none particularly successful. From the tap, order *um imperial* (or *um fino* in the north) if you want a regular glass, and *uma caneca* for half a litre. For bottled beer, ask for a mini (20cl) or a *garrafa* (33cl).

Coffee, tea and soft drinks

The Portuguese take their **coffee** very seriously, and you can order it a variety of ways. A simple coffee (*uma bica* or *um café*) is small, black and strong, like an espresso; *um carioca* is also small and black, but weaker; *uma chinesa* is large, black and strong. Ordering *um garoto* in Lisbon and the south, or *um pingo* in the north will get you an espresso-sized coffee with milk; while *um galão* is large and milky but weak, like a latte, and is often served in a glass. If you prefer your coffee reasonably strong and not too milky, ask for *um meia de leite*.

Tea (*chá*) is usually served black; *com leite* is with milk, and to be sure of getting tea with a slice of lemon (as opposed to a lemon-tea drink) ask for *um chá preto com limão*. Herbal teas are known as *infusões*, the most common being camomile (*camomila*), mint (*menta*) and lemon verbena (*lúcia-lima*).

Fresh orange juice (*sumo de laranja*) – rather surprisingly for an orange-producing country – can be awkward to find; adding the word *natural* or *fresca* should get you the real thing. If there is a juicer available, ask for it *da maquina* to get it freshly squeezed. **Mineral water** (*água mineral*) – of which the best-known national brands are Vimeiro, Pisões, Pedras Salgadas and Vidago – comes either still (*sem gás*) or carbonated (*com gás*).

The media

Foreign-language newspapers (including the European editions of British papers, plus the International Herald Tribune, Le Monde and the like) can be bought in the major towns, cities and resorts, usually the same day in Lisbon and much of the Algarve or a day late elsewhere. For an English-language view of what's happening in Portugal, the weekly Portugal News (W theportugalnews.com) is widely available, while The Resident (W algarveresident.com) is aimed at expats, principally in the Algarve.

Newspapers and magazines

The most respected Portuguese daily **newspapers** are the Lisbon-based *Diário de Notícias* (W dn.pt) and *Público* (W publico.pt) and Porto's *Jornal de Notícias* (W jn.pt). While the traditional *Diário de Notícias* is associated by many with the former Salazar regime, *Jornal de Notícias* is more liberal in outlook, and stylish *Público* has the youngest, most sophisticated feel, good for politics and the arts. All have useful daily listings information (with good Friday supplements). The best-selling tabloid is the right-wing *Correio da Manhã* (W cmjornal.xl.pt), while business daily *Jornal de Negócios* (W negocios.pt) keeps you up to date with economic issues, and the weekly *Expresso* (W expresso.sapo.pt) has lots of meaty articles on politics, economics and culture. For fans of Portuguese **sport** (mainly football), *A Bola* (W abola.pt), *O Jogo* (W ojogo.pt) and *Record* (W record.xl.pt) cover the daily ins and outs of teams and players. Popular current-affairs **magazines** include the long-standing *Visão*, while for coverage of the C-list celeb and reality TV scene you need a copy of *Caras* (ie, Faces), a bit like a Portuguese *Hello!*

Television and radio

There are four domestic **channels** – the state-run RTP1 and 2, and the private channels SIC and TVI. The best is 2, which is a mix of films from all over the world, National Geographic-style documentaries and daily coverage of the arts. The other three channels are heavy on game shows, variety shows, reality TV, and imported or adapted American and British series. Films are nearly always shown in their original language (ie, subtitled rather than dubbed), while you also get a full diet of *telenovelas* (soaps). Some of the most popular soaps are actually Brazilian (saucy historical romps a speciality), though home-produced imitations such as the teen-soap *Morangos com Açúcar* (Strawberries with Sugar) also achieve high ratings.

Most Portuguese households and businesses get their TV via **cable or satellite** subscription. Even in small two- and three-star hotels you'll often get a couple of foreign-language channels (BBC World, CNN, Eurosport, MTV), while four- and five-star places usually offer an endless range of foreign-language channels plus pay-for movie channels.

Portugal has a plethora of national and local **radio stations**. Antena 1 mixes golden oldies and Portuguese music with news on the hour. Antena 2 has classical music, while Antena 3 has the best contemporary sounds and new Portuguese music. Rádio Comercial is the best of the independent stations, playing Bryan Adams and the like during the day but better at night. Radio Renascença is a mainstream station of a religious persuasion; the associated RFM has a younger target audience but its playlist hasn't changed in years. With a short-wave radio you'll be able to tune into the **BBC World Service** (W bbc.co.uk/worldservice).

Festivals

Almost every village in Portugal has its own festival (festa) or traditional pilgrimage (romaria), usually to celebrate the local saint's day or the regional harvest. Some are little more than an excuse for the villagers to hold a low-key procession and picnic or barbecue and dance, while others have become serious celebrations lasting several days and attracting tourists from all over the world.

The great weekly **feiras**, like that at Barcelos in the Minho, were originally simply markets, but nowadays are a combination of agricultural show, folk festival, amusement park and, admittedly, tourist bazaar. Most towns also put on concerts, dances, processions and events throughout the year (especially between June and September), while an increasing number of **music festivals** are held in Portugal, from jazz to electro.

Only the major highlights are picked out in the **festival calendar** below. Other local festivals and events are covered in the guide (the Lisbon and Porto chapters both have full listings of festivals in those regions), or check with local turismos and have a look at the websites of the various town halls (Câmara

Municipal: usually ⓦ cm-nameoftown.pt), which always carry news about forthcoming festivities.

Among major **national events**, Easter week and the Santos Populares festivities – associated with St Anthony (June 12/13), St John (June 23/24) and St Peter (June 28/29) – stand out. All are celebrated throughout the country with religious processions. Easter is most magnificent in Braga, where it is full of ceremonial pomp, while the saints' festivals tend to be more joyous affairs. In Lisbon, during the saint's day *festa* for Santo António, the Alfama becomes one giant street party. In Porto, where St John's Eve is the highlight of a week of celebration, everyone dances through the streets all night, hitting each other over the head with leeks or plastic hammers.

JANUARY

6 Epiphany (Dia de Reis) The traditional crown-shaped cake *bolo rei* (king's cake) with a lucky charm and a bean inside is eaten; if you get the bean in your slice you have to buy the cake next year.

FEBRUARY

Carnaval Many areas now have Rio-like carnival parades, with Lisbon and the Algarve towns being good destinations. But **Carnaval** has much older traditions steeped in springtime fertility rites, and for a glimpse of what it was like before thongs and spangles, check out the masked merry-making of the **Entrudo dos Comprades** (p.293), near Lamego.

MARCH/APRIL

Easter Holy week (Semana Santa) religious processions in most places, most majestically in Braga, and at São Brás de Alportel in the Algarve (the **Festa das Tochas**). The **Festa da Mãe Soberana** in Loulé (Algarve) is one of the country's largest Easter festivals. Another good location is Tomar, where the floral crosses of the procession are ceremoniously destroyed afterwards.

MAY

Early May Queima das Fitas The "burning of the ribbons", celebrating the end of the academic year, reaches its drunken apogee in Coimbra and other university towns.
3 Festa das Cruzes The "Festival of the Crosses" is the biggest annual event in Barcelos (Minho).
13 Fátima (Peregrinação de Fátima) Portugal's most famous pilgrimage commemorates the Apparitions of the Virgin Mary; also in October (see p.161).
End of May (or early June) Corpus Christi Vaca das Cordas is a "running of the bull" ceremony in Ponte de Lima with roots in classical mythology.

JUNE

First weekend Festa de São Gonçalo Prominent saint's day celebrations in Amarante.
First week Rock in Rio-Lisboa Europe's largest rock festival (an offshoot of the enormous Rock in Rio fest) is held in even numbered years.

First two weeks Feira Nacional da Agricultura Held at Santarém, for ten days from the first Friday, with dancing, bullfighting and an agricultural fair.
Second & fourth weeks Santos Populares (Popular Saints) Celebrations in honour of Santo António (St Anthony, June 12–13), São João (St John, 23–24) and Pedro (St Peter, 28–29) throughout the country.
Arraial Pride Lisbon's increasingly popular gay pride event changes exact date and venue annually but usually takes place towards the end of the month in venues such as Terreiro do Paço and Belém.

JULY

Throughout the month Sintra Music Festival Performances by international orchestras, musicians and dance groups in parks, gardens and palaces in and around Sintra, Estoril and Cascais. An offshoot of the festival is the "Noites de Bailado" – ballet, dance and opera in Sintra's Centro Cultural Olga Cadaval.
First week Festa dos Tabuleiros Tomar's biggest and most spectacular procession takes place every four years, with the next two being in 2015 and 2019; (see p.167).
First two weeks Festa do Colete Encarnado Held in Vila Franca de Xira, with Pamplona-style running of bulls through the streets.

AUGUST

Second week Festival Sudoeste Much-heralded four-day rock, indie and electro music festival at Zambujeira do Mar, Alentejo coast (see p.429).
First weekend Festas Gualterianas The major festival in Guimarães has been held since the fifteenth century.
First weekend Festa do Nossa Senhora da Boa Viagem Seafaring is celebrated at Peniche with religious processions by boat and on land.
Third weekend Romaria da Nossa Senhora da Agonía Viana do Castelo's major annual religious celebration, plus carnival and fair (see p.322).

SEPTEMBER

First week Romaria de Nossa Senhora dos Remédios The annual pilgrimage in Lamego comes to a head at the end of the first week, though events start in the last week of August (see p.292).
First week Festa Avante! The Portuguese Communist Party's big annual bash sees three days of live music, events, rallies and speeches.
Second & third weekends Feiras Novas The "New Fairs" – a traditional festival and market – held in Ponte de Lima.
Third or fourth week Festa de São Mateus A week's worth of celebrations in Elvas (Alentejo), including a huge religious procession plus the usual fairs and fireworks.

OCTOBER

First two weeks Feira de Outubro More bull-running and bullfighting in Vila Franca de Xira.
13 Fátima The second great pilgrimage of the year at Fátima.

NOVEMBER

First two weeks Feira Nacional do Cavalo The National Horse Fair, held in Golegã (see p.170).

11 São Martinho Celebrations in honour of St Martin, with roots in pre-Christian harvest festivals coincides with the first tastings of the year's wine, roast chestnuts and Água Pé – a weak wine made from watered-down dregs. At its most traditional in northern Trás-os-Montes, Beira Baixa (particularly Alcains), Golegã, and Penafiel east of Porto.

DECEMBER

24 Christmas (Natal) The main Christmas celebration is midnight Mass on December 24, followed by a traditional meal of *bacalhau*, turkey or – bizarrely in Trás-os-Montes – octopus.
31 New Year's Eve (Noite de Ano Novo) Individual towns organize their own events, usually with fireworks at midnight, and the New Year is welcomed by the banging of old pots and pans.

Sports and outdoor activities

Internationally famed for its beaches, golf courses and tennis centres, Portugal also has an ideal climate for a variety of other outdoor pursuits including surfing, windsurfing, walking and adventure sports. Spectators can enjoy top-class football throughout the country, or seek out Portugal's own brand of bullfighting.

Adventure activities

The **outdoor activity** scene is rapidly expanding, with many regions now offering paragliding, abseiling, rap jumping, rafting, canyoning, caving, mountain biking and 4WD expeditions. There's most scope in the mountain areas – notably the Serra da Estrela and Peneda-Gerês parks – and on the major rivers (Douro, Mondego and Zêzere), but many of the smaller natural parks and reserves also have local adventure outfits. It's always worth contacting operators in advance, since activities are sometimes only for groups and are always heavily subscribed at weekends and during summer holidays. Prices vary considerably, but you can expect to pay from €50 for a day's guided mountain walking, or €50–80 for whitewater rafting or canyoning.

Swimming

Portugal is on the Atlantic, which tends to be cooler than the Mediterranean in summer, but warmer in the winter. The **Algarve** has the country's most popular sandy beaches, many of them sheltered in coves – the sea is warmest on the eastern Algarve, and remains swimmable year-round if you're hardy. The western coast has some stupendous stretches of beach, but they face the full brunt of the ocean, so you need to beware the heavy undertow and don't swim if you see a red or yellow flag. The EU blue flag indicates that the water is clean enough to swim in – Portugal has an impressive 275 – and that the beach has lifeguards. For a full rundown of the country's blue flag beaches, see W blueflag.org.

An unsung glory of central and northern Portugal is its **river beaches** – you'll see signs (*praia fluvial*) everywhere directing you to quiet bends in the local river or to weirs or dramatic gorges. Often, the local municipality erects a summer bar (usually open June to September), and there are usually picnic and barbecue areas, and public toilets. Many towns also have a summer outdoor **swimming pool** (*piscina*), also only open from June to September. At indoor municipal pools (open all year) you may have to show your passport, and you'll have to wear a swimming cap.

Bullfighting

Although a traditional Portuguese sport, **bullfighting** (*tourada*) is nowhere near as popular as it used to be – though you can still watch it, if you really want. Afficionados claim that it is less cruel than in Spain as the bulls are not killed in public, though critics say that it is more cruel as the bull is injured and taunted in the ring, then killed later anyway. Whatever your views, the sport is still legal in Portugal and there are regular fights during the **bullfighting season** (April to October) at bullrings around the country, including Lisbon and Albufeira.

Ribatejo, east of Lisbon, is where many of the bulls (and horses) are bred, and local festivals around here involve bullfights and bull-running through the streets, such as at Vila Franca de Xira and Santarém.

Football

Football is Portugal's favourite sport bar none and it is no surprise to the natives that one of the world's greatest players (Cristiano Ronaldo) and top managers (José Mourinho) hail from the country. The national team came closest to glory in the 2004 European Championships, held in Portugal – they were beaten in the final by surprise winners Greece, though the real legacy was the construction of several excellent stadiums, including the Estádio do Dragão in Porto and Benfica's Estádio da Luz.

The leading clubs, inevitably, hail from the country's big cities, Porto and Lisbon. Over the last two decades **FC Porto** has swept up every title available, including the national league on many occasions (the win of 1999 made it a unique five times in a row), the European UEFA Cup/Europa League in 2003 and 2011 (when they went the entire league season undefeated under manager Villas-Boas), and – its crowning glory – the European Champions League title in 2004. Lisbon-based **Benfica** experienced a similar golden age in the 1960s, when Mozambique-born striker Eusébio was at his masterful height. The other big team is **Sporting**, also from Lisbon. Just about every Portuguese citizen supports one of these three teams and, in the provinces, usually one of the lesser, local outfits as well. Of these, Sporting Braga (who reached an all-Portuguese Europa League final in 2011) is the most consistent.

Ticket prices for a clash between two big names average €30–80, depending on the seat, while tickets for other games cost about half that. The Liga Portuguesa (W lpfp.pt) season runs from the end of August to mid-May, most matches being played on Saturdays and Sundays. Live televised matches are regular fixtures in bars and restaurants, usually on Friday or Sunday evenings, often other days too.

TEAMS AND TOWNS

Some of Portugal's tourist spots are also home to top league football teams with regular visits from the likes of Porto, Sporting and Benfica – though if you look at the fixtures list you may be totally unaware where the match is being played. This is because team names don't always match the names of the town they represent. Taking off the ending of –ense or –enses (which roughly means from the town of) will often help. Here is a list of some top football towns followed by their very different club names:

Barcelos Gil Vicente (W gilvicentefc.pt)
Belém (Lisbon) Belenenses (W osbelenenses.com)
Coimbra Académica (W academica-oaf.pt)
Figueira da Foz Naval (W naval1demaio.net)
Funchal (Madeira) Marítimo (W csmaritimo.pt)
Olhão Olhanense (W scolhanense.com)
Vila do Conde Rio Ave (W rioave-fc.pt)

Golf

Portugal is a year-round **golf** destination, though exclusivity is often the key word. Some of the country's finest hotels and villa complexes have golf courses attached, or have connections with a golf club, and the best deals are usually on special golf-holiday packages. Otherwise, green fees on 18-hole courses start at around €40, though multi-play packages and discounts are nearly always available. The Greater Lisbon area and the Algarve have the bulk of the courses: for more information consult a specialist tour operator or check out the websites W portugalgolf.pt and W algarvegolf.net.

Tennis

Many larger Algarve hotels also have year-round **tennis courts**. If you want to improve your game, the best intensive coaching is at the Vale do Lobo Tennis Academy (packages organized by Light Blue Travel; W lightbluetravel.co.uk) or the Praia da Luz Ocean Club near Lagos (Jonathan Markson Tennis; W marksontennis.com).

Horseriding

Horseriding stables around the country offer one-hour or full-day rides, often on Lusitano thoroughbred horses. The main areas for tourist rides are Estoril and Sintra, the Algarve and the Alentejo, while the province of Ribatejo lies at the heart of

---

WATCHING THE FOOTBALL

If you're going to the game, or watching on TV, you need to know the basics if you want to join in. Arriving after kick-off, ask *resultado?* (what's the score?) and settle down in time to watch the *guarda-redes* (goalkeeper) make a complete *frango* (cock-up) of a save. The *meio-campo* (midfield) looks decidedly dodgy and your *ponte de lance* (centre forward) keeps getting caught *fora-de-jogo* (offside) – that's when he's not being clattered from behind. That's a *falta!* (foul!) and a *grande penalidade!* (penalty!), surely? If he scores, the TV commentators will invariably celebrate Brazilian-style – *golo!* (try goooooaaaaalllll!) – before referring to the *festa nas bancadas* (party on the terraces) that's now under way. If, on the other hand, you're losing, heaven forbid your team resorts to punting it aimlessly up the field, route-one style – sad to say, the long-ball game is known disparagingly as *o jogo Inglês* (the English game).

Portugal's equestrian traditions. Prices start from around €25 for an hour's trek, rising to around €100–120 for a full day, which usually includes a picnic lunch. For details of *centros hípicos* (riding schools) in a particular area, contact the local tourist office.

Skiing

The only **skiing** is in the Serra da Estrela (usually possible from December to February, sometimes March), though you wouldn't specifically travel to Portugal for it. The slopes lie just below the *serra*'s highest point, Torre, with access easiest from Covilhã via Penhas da Saude. The four lifts, ski school, and ski and snowboard rental are operated by Turistrela at the Estância Vodafone (W skiserradaestrela.com); a day's gear rental starts at €25, one-hour lessons from €30, and you can also book reasonably-priced ski packages. The year-round artificial run at Ski Parque, near Manteigas, is another option, and this also doubles as an outdoor activity and adventure centre.

Surfing and windsurfing

Surfing in Portugal is renowned throughout Europe, though the currents and the raw power of the swell here require a high level of expertise. Indeed in January 2013, American surfer Garrett McNamara rode what is thought to be the largest wave ever (30 metres high) off the coast of Nazaré in Estremadura. Supertubos on the south side of Peniche (Estremadura) is the original surf destination in Portugal – it's one of the few breaks to work in northerly winds – while Ericeira and, of course, Nazaré on the Estremadura coast, both attract highly talented local surfers and travelling pros. There are international competitions held at all these places, as well as at Espinho south of Porto (popular with bodyboarders) and Figueira da Foz near Coimbra, while the more protected west coast of the Algarve, around Sagres, is excellent for beginners and experienced surfers alike.

The biggest **windsurfing** destinations are Guincho and Praia Grande, north of Lisbon, and round Sines on the Alentejo coast. We've highlighted rental outfits and surf camps in nearly all these places, while good websites include W wannasurf.com and W beachcam.pt (in Portuguese) for breaks, photos, reports, surf-savvy weather and wave height forecasts, and W surfing portugal.com, home to the Federação Portuguesa de Surf, which organizes competitions.

Kayaking

Some adventure outfits can organize river **kayaking**, with the Rio Mondego offering an excellent gentle introduction that starts from near Penacova (p.196), and is basically a relaxing half-day float downriver towards Coimbra. In addition, sea-kayaking is increasing in popularity, particularly along the more sheltered southern Algarve coast. Many Algarve resorts now hire out kayaks, if you want to go independently, or offer guided kayak trips that explore the local coves and beaches.

Diving

Scuba diving for beginners is best off Praia do Carvoeiro near Lagoa in the Algarve, where Tivoli Diving (W tivoli-diving.com) and Divers Cove (W diverscove.de) offer standard dives with equipment rental for around €45, plus night and wreck dives for experienced divers, and full four-day PADI-accredited Open Water courses from €450. On the west coast, conditions can be more trying, with a strong undertow, though there are more sheltered waters between Lisbon and Cascais.

Walking

Portugal only has one **national park** – the Parque Nacional Peneda-Gerês, in the Minho – but there are over thirty other **protected areas**, designated as *parques naturais* (natural parks), *reservas naturais* (natural reserves) or other specifications. You'll find them all listed and profiled on the website of the government's Instituto da Conservação da Natureza (W icn.pt – some information in English available). All the main parks, and many of the minor ones, are covered in the guide and between them account for some of Portugal's most dramatic landscapes – from the high-mountain scenery of the Serra da Estrela to the limestone caves of the Serras de Aire e Candeeiros, or the island hideaway of the Ilha Berlenga to the lagoons, dunes and marshes of the Ria Formosa.

Throughout the guide we've recommended **walks and hiking trails** wherever possible. All the parks have information centres, and most promote trails and tours within their area. Marked walking routes are becoming more popular, but signage and trail maintenance are extremely patchy. English is rarely spoken, even at major information centres, making it difficult to find out about the status of routes, while there is a real paucity of proper walking maps: we recommend the best ones in our "Maps" section (see p.51).

Shopping

Though most large towns in Portugal have at least one out-of-town shopping centre, in the majority of places people still do much of their purchasing in traditional shops and markets. Old town centres look like they haven't changed much for thirty years or more, with a butcher, a baker and a candlestick-maker on every corner, not to mention a florist, a grocer and a hardware store.

We've pointed out regional handicrafts, specialist shops and markets throughout the guide, but there's a general rundown below of things you'll see and might want to buy. Some of the town accounts also have their own dedicated shopping sections. Specialist craft and souvenir shops might be able to arrange shipping home for you; otherwise, go to the local post office, where all kinds of insured, registered and signed-for services are available (see ⓦ ctt.pt, which has an English-language version).

Prices are fixed in shops everywhere, though you might be able to negotiate small discounts when buying large souvenirs (or buying in bulk). Open-air markets are a bit more flexible, though don't try haggling for food, drink, clothes or anything that has obviously got a price attached to it – for everything else you can try asking for the best price, and you may get a discount.

Markets

A town's **mercado municipal** (municipal market) is the place to buy meat, fish, fruit, veg and bread. In larger towns they are open daily (not Sunday), usually from 7 or 8am until lunchtime; smaller towns might have a market just once or twice a week. Often, a town's regular market is supplemented by a larger weekly affair, sometimes at a different site in the open air, where you'll also be able to buy clothes, shoes, ceramics, baskets, furniture, flowers, toys, tools and a million-and-one other things you never knew you needed. In the case of the great **weekly markets** at Barcelos (Minho; Thurs), Viana do Castelo (Minho; Fri), Ponte da Barca/Arcos de Valdevez (Minho; Wed), Carcavelos (Lisbon; Thurs), Estremoz (Alentejo; Sat) and Loulé (Algarve; Sat), or the monthly markets at Évora (Alentejo; second Tues) and Santarém (Ribatejo; second/fourth Sun), these constitute a major reason to visit in the first place. The best **flea market** in the country is Lisbon's Feira da Ladra (Tues & Sat), just the place to buy a candelabra or a set of dusty postcards.

Minimarkets, supermarkets and malls

In small villages and towns the **minimercado** (minimarket) is as convenient as convenience-shopping gets, which isn't very if you want a store bigger than someone's front room. **Supermercados** tend to lie on the outskirts of towns – Intermarché, Pingo Doce, Jumbo, Continente and Mini-Preço are the main supermarket names, selling pretty much everything you would expect (though choices can be more limited in out-of-the-way locations), while the pile-'em-high German-owned Lidl is increasingly prevalent. In Lisbon, Porto, Coimbra and the Algarve, the **mall** is king. Geared up for whole days out, these giant shopping centres have hundreds of stores, plus cafés, fast-food restaurants, cinemas and kids' entertainment.

Ceramics

Highest-profile souvenirs are probably **ceramics** of all kinds, from traditional *azulejo* tiles to elaborate figurines, cookware to sculpture. The virtual symbol of Portuguese tourism, the ceramic Barcelos cockerel (see p.320), perches on every

---

THE CHINESE SHOP

There's scarcely a town in Portugal that doesn't have a **Loja Chinês**, a Chinese-run emporium selling everything under the sun. In many ways, they fulfil the same function as a "pound" or "dollar" shop, selling basic household items really cheaply – if you need two-dozen toilet rolls, a set of tupperware, fifty wine glasses or a washing-up bowl, this is where you come. But they are also good for dirt-cheap toys and electronics – all made in the Far East, guaranteed to break after a couple of hours – and for all those things you never knew you needed, like a Portuguese flag, a *Star Wars* light sabre or an alarm clock shaped like a man on a toilet.

tat-shop shelf. You can buy rustic, brown kitchen **earthen-ware** in every market and supermarket for just a few euros, but interesting regional variations include Barcelos' own brown-and-yellow pottery ware, black earthenware (from Tondela) and the almost Aztec-style patterns typical of Santa Comba Dão in the Viseu region. Porches is the centre for the Algarve's pottery and ceramics, while Caldas da Rainha in Estremadura is probably the best-known ceramics town – caricatured rustic **figurines** and floral- and animal-inspired plates and bowls have been produced here since the nineteenth century. Estremoz in the Alentejo has an even older heritage, and is also known for its elaborate figurines and its flower- and leaf-festooned pottery.

Carpets, rugs, blankets, tapestries, linen and lace

Hand-stitched **Arraiolos carpets** (from the town of the same name in Alentejo) have a worldwide reputation, and they cost a fortune, but there's nothing to stop you looking. **Tapestries** from Portalegre (Alentejo) have been known since the seventeenth century, and the *colchas* or **embroidered bedspreads** of Castelo Branco (Beira Baixa) for just as long – again, the high prices and lengthy ordering times mean these are unlikely spur-of-the-moment purchases for most visitors. Hand-woven woollen **rugs and blankets** are a more realistic buy, with particularly fine examples from Reguengos de Monsaraz (Alentejo) – you can hang them on a wall. Rustic woolly blankets (and fleece-lined slippers) are also a feature of the mountain villages of the Serra da Estrela – Sabugeiro has hundreds of them displayed in its souvenir shop windows. For embroidered **linen and lace** it's Vila do Conde (north of Porto) that is the best-known centre, though many other fishing towns – such as Peniche and Nazaré in Estremadura – also have a strong bobbin-lace tradition. The biggest and best pieces command high prices, but there's plenty of reasonably priced work available too.

Food and drink

Port wine is the most popular buy, with cheap run-of-the-mill stuff available in supermarkets or gathering dust above the salt cod in old-fashioned grocery stores. For specific names and vintages you need to have done your homework since a recent vintage (not yet ready to drink) starts at around €30, with the serious stuff commanding prices of €100 and upwards. Visiting a lodge in Porto or along the Douro is by far the best way to immerse yourself in the subject. Don't miss a drink in the *solares* in Porto or Lisbon either, where you can sample individual glasses from hundreds of different varieties.

Virtually every region in Portugal produces **table wine**, often remarkably good. Regional wine routes (past vineyards and estates open to the public) are well signposted, particularly in the Douro, Alentejo, Ribatejo and Dão valley.

Taking food home is more problematic, depending on your country's importation laws, but no one is going to object to a bottle of **olive oil** – the best are now sold like wines, from single estates, particularly in the Douro, where production is an adjunct to the wine business. Other suggestions include a jar of mountain **honey** from the Serra da Estrela, or packs of mountain **herbs and teas**, particularly from the Serra do Gerês. Portuguese **cheeses and hams** are excellent, though to take them home you may have to get them vacuum-packed (you can buy them like that at Lisbon airport).

Clothes, shoes and accessories

Portugal's textiles industry has traditionally been one of the most important in Europe, and though this has suffered badly from cheap rivals from the Far East, you can still pick up brand-name seconds from many of Portugal's weekly markets. For quality **designer clothes**, however, you have to head to the upmarket malls or larger city centres, particularly Lisbon's Avenida da Liberdade (for international names) or the Bairro Alto (for local cutting-edge styles). Fátima Lopes and Maria Azevedo are current style icons, while Ana Salazar is a more established leading name. Some of the larger shopping centres also have designer boutiques; indeed the giant Freeport mall at Alcochete (W freeport.pt) is Europe's largest designer discount outlet. Leather goods have a fair reputation in Portugal, particularly **bags and shoes** (and belts and briefcases) – most big towns and shopping centres will have a decent selection, though a common complaint is that Portuguese shoe shops don't always stock the larger or wider sizes you might require. **Gold and silver** filigree work is notable – there are some fine shops in Lisbon and Porto – and you'll be able to pick up cheap, hippy-style jewellery at beaches along the Algarve, especially Albufeira.

Travelling with children

As Portuguese society largely revolves around family life, the country is very child-friendly and families will find it one of the easiest places for a holiday. The two main worries for parents in Portugal are cars – which are usually fast moving – and the strong sun. Keep young children covered up between 11am and 3pm, make them wear a hat, and always apply a high-factor sunscreen. Be aware, too, that many castles and monuments are unrailed and may have very steep drops, while sea bathing – especially on the west coast – can be hazardous, with dangerous undertows. Cobbled town centres and stepped alleys are also difficult for anyone with a toddler and a pushchair.

Most **hotels and pensions** can provide an extra bed or a cot (*um berço*) if notified in advance. There is usually no charge for babies and small children who share their parents' room, while discounts of up to fifty percent on accommodation for older children are not uncommon. Babysitting and child supervision are available at most four- and five-star places, though you'll have to pay.

Children are welcome in all **cafés and restaurants** at any time of the day. Indeed, waiters often go out of their way to spend a few minutes entertaining restless children; tots may even find themselves being carried off for a quick tour of the kitchens while parents finish their meals in peace. Highchairs (*cadeirinha de bebé*) are normally the clip-on-table variety. Specific child menus are rare, though restaurants will nearly all serve half-portions (*meia dose*) as a matter of course – these are still too much for most children to finish, but the Portuguese often simply order a *dose* or two between the family. Note, however, that restaurants rarely open much before 7.30pm (so British children may need to adjust to eating later than they are used to) and local children are often still up at midnight.

Specific changing facilities in restaurants, cafés and public toilets are largely nonexistent, and when you do find them – such as in larger shopping centres – they are usually in women's toilets only.

Fresh milk (*leite pasteurizado*) for **babies** is sold in larger supermarkets; mornings are best as it tends to sell out by mid-afternoon – *gordo* is full-fat, *meio-gordo* half-fat and *magro* skimmed milk. Mini-mercados, smaller shops and cafés generally only stock UHT, which is what most Portuguese kids drink. Nappies/diapers (*fraldas*) are widely available in supermarkets and pharmacies, as are formula milk, babies' bottles and jars of baby food – though don't expect the full range of (or indeed any) organic or salt-free choices you might be used to at home.

Most **museums, sights and attractions** don't usually charge for small children, while under-12s get in for half-price. On public transport, under-5s go free while 5- to 11-year-olds travel half-price on trains but pay full fare on metros and buses.

Travel essentials

Costs

Portugal remains one of the EU's least expensive destinations, and simple meals and drinks, accommodation and public transport are all still pretty good value. Lisbon, Porto and the Algarve are inevitably the most expensive places to visit, but even here you'll get a better deal on most things than in many other European countries.

As far as a **daily budget** goes, if you always share a room in the cheapest hotels, use public transport and stick to inexpensive restaurants you could have a reasonable time on somewhere between €70 and €80 a day. Stay and eat in fancier places in the main cities and you're looking at more like €120 a day, though if you're holidaying in five-star beach resorts or city boutique hotels this figure won't even cover your room. There's more information about specific prices in the "Accommodation", "Getting around" and "Food and drink" sections.

Most museums, galleries and attractions are fairly inexpensive (and some are free on one day of the week), but even so it pays to take along any **student/youth discount cards** you may be entitled to, such as the Euro 26 card (**W** euro26.org; also available in Portugal at post offices, youth hostels, and at branches of the Caixa Geral de Depósitos bank – ask for a *Cartão Jovem*). Any **entrance fees** noted in this guide are for the full adult price; children usually get a discount. **Senior travellers** in Portugal are also entitled to discounts at most museums (it's always worth showing your senior citizen's card or ID), as well as on trains and at the country's *pousadas*.

Crime and personal safety

By European standards, Portugal is a remarkably crime-free country – people really do still leave their cars and house doors unlocked in the country. However, there's the usual **petty theft** in the cities and larger tourist resorts, particularly in the form of pickpockets on public transport and in bus and train stations. Best advice is not to carry too much cash or too many valuables, and leave your passport in the hotel safe where possible. Drivers should never leave anything visible in the car (preferably, don't leave anything in the car at all). Violence directed at tourists is rare – if you are threatened, hand over your valuables and run. In an **emergency**, dial ☎112 for the police or an ambulance.

There are two main police forces: the metropolitan **Polícia de Segurança Pública** (PSP) and the more rural **Guarda Nacional Repúblicana** (GNR), both of which can handle incidents involving tourists. Most police officers in the Algarve speak some English, but elsewhere it's less usual, so confusion can easily arise. To this end, showing deference is wise: the Portuguese still hold respect dear, and the more respect you show a figure in authority, the quicker you'll be on your way.

Portugal is rarely a dangerous place for **women travellers** and you only need to be particularly wary in parts of Lisbon at night (around Cais do Sodré, at the top end of Avenida da Liberdade, on the metro and on the Cais do Sodré–Cascais train line), in the darker alleys near the river in Porto, and in streets immediately around train stations in the larger towns (traditionally red-light districts). If you are on your own or feel uncomfortable anywhere, you should be able to get around at night by taxi. On the whole, though, the country is formal to the point of prudishness.

Electricity

Mains voltage is 220V, which works fine with equipment intended for 240V. Plugs are the European two round pin variety; adaptors are sold at airports, supermarkets and hardware stores.

Entry requirements

EU citizens need only a valid passport or identity card to enter Portugal, and can stay indefinitely. Citizens of Canada, the US, Australia and New Zealand do not need a visa for stays of up to ninety days. Most other nationals (including South Africans) will have to apply for a visa from a Portuguese embassy or consulate before departure. Entry conditions can change, however, so it's advisable to check the current situation before leaving home.

If necessary, an extension to your stay can be arranged once you're in the country. Extensions are issued by the nearest District Police headquarters or the Foreigners' Registration Service – **Serviço de Estrangeiros e Fronteiras** (☒sef.pt) – which has offices in most major tourist centres. You should apply at least a week before your time runs out and be prepared to prove that you can support yourself without working. Extended-stay and work visas are also available from Portuguese embassies or consulates in your own country.

For most EU citizens, their passport or ID is sufficient to allow them to stay indefinitely as employees, self-employed or students. However, you will need to register with various agencies if you are **staying in Portugal**, to access health care etc, and will require a *numero de contribuinte* (social security number) to do just about anything else, from opening a bank account to settling an electricity bill.

Gay and lesbian travellers

Though traditionally a conservative society, Portugal has become increasingly tolerant of homosexuality, at least in the cities and in the Algarve. In more rural areas, however, old prejudices are ingrained and coming out is still a problem for many. As there is no mention of homosexuality in law, gays have the same rights as heterosexuals by default and the legal age of consent is 16. The best contact is the **Associação ILGA Portugal** (☒ilga-portugal.pt; English information available), which operates the Centro LGBT (Rua de São Lázaro 88, Lisbon; ☎218 873 918; Wed–Sat 6–11pm), an information centre and helpline, which organizes the country's annual Pride festival. The biggest scene is in Lisbon, which has a number of gay bars and clubs.

Health

The **European Health Insurance Card** (☒ehic.org.uk) gives EU citizens access to Portuguese state public-health services under reciprocal agreements – show it and your passport at a health centre or hospital for treatment. While this will provide free or reduced-cost medical care in the event of minor injuries and emergencies, it won't cover every eventuality – and it only applies to EU citizens in possession of the card – so travel insurance is also essential.

Tap water is generally safe to drink, although most Portuguese prefer bottled water (it's very inexpensive in supermarkets). Otherwise, just use common sense: wash and peel fruit and vegetables, and avoid eating snacks that appear to have been sitting in display cabinets for too long. **Mosquitoes** can be a menace in the summer, but mosquito-repellent lotion and coils are widely sold in super-markets and pharmacies. Use a high-factor **sun block** as the sun is extremely powerful.

For minor complaints go to a **farmácia** (pharmacy); most have a green neon cross outside. There's one in virtually every village and English is often spoken. Pharmacists are highly trained and can dispense drugs that would be prescription-only in Britain or North America. Opening hours are usually Monday to Friday 9am to 1pm and 3 to 7pm, Saturday 9am to 1pm. Local papers carry information about 24-hour or night-time pharmacies (*farmácias de serviço*) and the details are also posted on every pharmacy door.

In an **emergency** dial ☎112. Treatment is at the local **Centro da Saúde** (Health Centre) or **hospital**, and somebody usually speaks at least some English. Contact details of other English-speaking doctors can be obtained from British or American consular offices or, with luck, from the local tourist office or a major hotel. Basic treatment is free for EU citizens with the EHIC card, though you'll have to pay for X-rays, lab tests and the like; otherwise you'll be charged for everything and will have to claim it back from your insurance, so get receipts.

Insurance

You should take out a comprehensive travel **insurance policy** before travelling to Portugal, to cover against loss, theft and illness or injury. A typical policy will provide cover for the loss of baggage, tickets and – up to a certain limit – cash or cheques, as well as cancellation or curtailment of your journey. Most policies exclude so-called dangerous sports unless an extra premium is paid:

in Portugal this can mean most watersports and scuba diving are excluded, though probably not things like hiking or bike tours.

If you need to make a claim, you should keep receipts for medicines and medical treatment, and in the event you have anything stolen, you must obtain an official **statement from the police** (a *formulário de participação de roubo*).

Internet

The government has invested a lot in commu-nications technology and Portugal is surprisingly switched-on and wireless for a place of its size. Internet cafés can be found in most towns and resorts, charging from around €2 per hour (often free for wi-fi). You can also get online at larger post offices (access by credit card or by buying a prepaid net card), while free **municipal internet** places (called Espaços Internet; locations on ⓦ espacos internet.pt) are widespread, even in very small towns. You can generally also find a PC to use in libraries, youth centres, hostels and many hotels. **Wireless** access is available in bars, shopping malls, town squares and other public "hot spots", though sometimes you need to sign up and pay for an hour's or day's use. If you take your own laptop make sure you've got insurance cover and all the relevant adaptors for recharging.

Laundry

Small guesthouses don't really like you doing your laundry in your room – to avoid an incident, it might be better to ask first if there's somewhere you can wash your clothes. Hotels generally have a laundry service, but it's usually pretty expensive. It's far better to take your clothes to the local *lavandaria*, where you can get them washed, dried and even ironed at a very reasonable cost – you may have to come back the next day to pick them up.

Mail

Post offices (*correios*; ❶ctt.pt) are normally open Monday to Friday 8.30 or 9am to 5.30 or 6pm, the smaller ones closing for lunch. Larger branches sometimes open on Saturday mornings, while the main Lisbon and Porto offices have longer hours. There's an office-finder on the website which gives exact hours and contact details for every post office in Portugal. However, it's often quicker to buy **stamps** (*selos*) from coin-operated vending machines in streets or inside the offices, or from newsagents. Letters or cards should take three or four days to arrive at destinations in Europe, and seven to ten days elsewhere. *Correio azul* is the equivalent of airmail or first-class, and theoretically (but not always in practice) takes two or three days to Europe, five elsewhere.

Maps

The best available **country map** is Michelin's *Portugal* (1:400,000) and there are also three regional Michelin maps (north, centre and south) at 1:300,000, while Michelin's *Lisboa Planta Roteiro* is the nearest to an *A–Z* of the city. A good bookshop or travel store in your own country should be able to provide any of these maps, or buy online from specialist stores such as ❶stanfords.co.uk or ❶randmcnally.com. Tourist offices and car rental outlets in Portugal can also usually provide you with a reasonable **road map**, while other maps and more detailed regional plans can be bought at motorway service stations and town and city bookshops.

For **walking and hiking**, the only serious choices are the 1:25,000 topographic sheets (the so-called "Série M888") produced by the Instituto Geográfico do Exército (❶igeoe.pt). These cover the entire country, though some haven't been updated for years. Even so, they are the best you'll get, and you can order them online from the Institute, or buy them at various bookshops in Portugal; outlets are listed on the website.

Money

Portugal's currency is the **euro** (€), and notes are issued in denominations of 5, 10, 20, 50, 100, 200 and 500 euros, and coins in denominations of 1, 2, 5, 10, 20 and 50 cents and 1 and 2 euros. Up-to-the-minute currency **exchange rates** are displayed at ❶xe.com.

You'll find a **bank** (*banco*) or savings bank/building society (*caixa*) in all but the smallest towns:

standard opening hours are Monday to Friday 8.30am to 3pm. In Lisbon and larger Algarve resorts, some banks also open in the evening, while others have automatic currency exchange machines. **Exchange bureaux** (*câmbios*), which you'll find in Lisbon, Porto and the Algarve, tend to have longer working hours, closing on weekdays at around 6pm, and also opening on Saturdays.

By far the easiest way to get money is to use your bank debit card to withdraw cash from an **ATM** (known as a Multibanco), found in even the smallest towns, as well as on arrival at the airports. You can usually withdraw up to €300 a day and instructions are available in English. Make sure you have a PIN that's designed to work overseas, and take a note of your bank's emergency contact number in case the machine swallows your card. Most European **debit cards** can also be used directly in shops, petrol stations etc, to pay for purchases.

All major **credit cards** are accepted in hotels, restaurants and shops, and for tours, tickets and transport, though don't count on being able to use them in many small hotels, family businesses and rural areas.

Opening hours and public holidays

Opening hours for shops, cafés, restaurants, museums and tourist offices in Portugal tend to be a fluid concept, especially outside the main towns and resorts. Many open late or close early (or don't open at all) if the weather's bad or if not many people are around. We give the official opening hours in the Guide.

PUBLIC HOLIDAYS

January 1 New Year's Day (Dia Um de Janeiro)
Shrove Tuesday February/March Carnival (Carnaval)
Good Friday March/April (Sexta Feira Santa)
April 25 Liberty Day, commemorating the 1974 Revolution (Vinte Cinco de Abril)
May 1 Labour Day (Dia do Trabalhador)
June 10 Portugal Day (Dia de Portugal)
August 15 Feast of the Assumption (Festa da Assunção)
December 8 Immaculate Conception (Imaculada Conceiçaõ)
December 25 Christmas Day (Natal)

Shops and businesses generally open from 9/9.30am until 12.30/1pm and 2.30/3pm until 6/7pm. Most also open all day Saturday from 9am to 7pm, especially in towns and cities. Larger **shopping centres and malls** stay open seven days a week, often until midnight. **Restaurants** tend to close one day a week, often Sunday or Monday.

Opening hours for **museums, churches and monuments** vary enormously, but almost all close on Mondays (or Wednesdays for palaces), as well as on Christmas Day, New Year's Day, Good Friday and other public holidays. Some opening hours are **seasonal**, and usually in Portugal "summer" means from Easter until September and "winter" from October until Easter.

On national **public holidays** (see box, p.51) transport services are much reduced. Most museums and galleries also close for the day, though other tourist facilities – restaurants, souvenir shops and the like – tend to stay open. There are also endless **local festivals**, saints' days and holidays when entire villages, towns, cities and regions grind to a halt: for example, June 13 in Lisbon and June 24 in Porto. In 2013, four out of Portugal's fourteen public holidays were suspended for five years in response to the economic crisis. The controversial measure aims to boost economic activity, but it remains to be seen whether the holidays will be reinstated in the future.

Phones

All Portuguese **phone numbers** have nine digits. Landlines start with a 2, mobiles with a 9. Numbers starting with 800 are free; 808 are local-rate calls. To **call Portugal from abroad**, dial your country's international access number + 351 (country code) + nine-digit number. You can search for national phone numbers and addresses for free online at ⓦpai.pt or ⓦ1820.pt.

The cheapest way of making a call from a public telephone is with a **telephone card** (*carta telefónico*), available from post offices, newsagents, supermarkets and kiosks. The national operator is **Portugal Telecom** (ⓦptcom.pt), which issues its own cards for national and international use (various types and denominations, from €5), though cards are also issued by several competitors. Avoid making any calls from hotel phones, which always have very high charges. **Calling home from Portugal**, dial ❶00 (Portugal's international access code) + your country code + city/area code minus initial zero + number.

Portugal has one of the highest densities of **mobile phone** (*telemóvel*) ownership in the world. Most European mobile phones will work in Portugal, but

even though prices are coming down it's expensive to use your own mobile extensively while abroad. You could always simply buy a local **SIM card** for your mobile, though this depends on the model and service provider – Vodafone has shops all over Portugal, for example, including at Lisbon airport.

Smoking

In common with most EU countries, **smoking** is prohibited in all public spaces in Portugal. The ban was introduced in 2008 by the then Prime Minister José Sócrates, who was promptly spotted lighting up on a plane to Venezuela. While not all laws are closely followed by the Portuguese, this one is generally observed – though, of course, smokers can indulge at restaurants and cafés, if they sit at the outside tables.

Taxes

Value Added Tax (known as **IVA**) varies depending on the goods or services purchased, but can be as high as 23 percent – it's almost always included in the advertised price, though. Non-EU residents can **claim back the sales tax** on purchases that come to over €61.35. You need to ask the shop for a declaration and then present this to customs at the airport before you fly home: details on ⓦglobal-blue.com.

Time

Portugal is in the same time zone as the UK, following GMT in winter. Clocks go forward an hour at the end of March and back an hour at the end of October. If you're coming from Spain, turn your watch back one hour.

Tipping

There is no hard and fast rule for **tipping**, which is not really a Portuguese custom. In a café, restaurant or for taxis, it's customary to round up the bill to the nearest euro or, for big amounts, the nearest note – so leave €25 for a bill of €23.50, for example. You shouldn't feel obliged to leave any tip at all for other services – though needless to say, any you do leave will be gratefully received.

Toilets

Public toilets are neither numerous nor obvious, though a number of cities have installed coin-operated automated toilets. You can generally use the toilets in cafés, though (in theory) you'll have to order something first and sometimes ask for the key. The "facilities" in some places may leave you dazed, though on the whole there's been a significant upgrade in recent years – whoever has the contract for installing automatic light and flush facilities in Portugal is on a roll. A sign reading *Lavábos, Casa de banho* or WC will head you in the right direction, then it's *homens* or *cavalheiros* for men and *senhoras* or *mulheres* for women.

Tourist information

The Portuguese national tourist board, **Turismo de Portugal** (Ⓦ visitportugal.com), is a good source of information when planning your trip, while in Portugal itself you'll find a tourist office in most of the larger towns. **Regional offices** offer a broadbrush approach to the region they represent, and some also have useful websites.

On the ground, local or municipal **turismos** can at least supply a town map or accommodation information, though the service available varies wildly from place to place. English is only routinely spoken in offices in the larger towns and resorts, and, while some offices are extremely helpful and professional, others treat your visit almost as an intrusion. Often, the best you'll get is a fistful of brochures and directions to the bus station/museum/ferry office where you'll have to ask all over again.

USEFUL TOURIST WEBSITES

Ⓦ **visitportugal.com** (all Portugal)

Ⓦ **visitlisboa.com** (Lisbon area)

Ⓦ **turismodocentro.pt** (Coimbra and central Portugal)

Ⓦ **visitportoandnorth.com** (Porto and the north)

Ⓦ **visitalgarve.com** (Algarve)

Ⓦ **rt-planiciedourada.pt** (Alentejo)

Ⓦ **ipmuseus.pt** (the Museums Institute website)

Travellers with disabilities

Portugal is slowly coming to terms with the needs of travellers with disabilities, though you should not expect much in the way of special facilities.

However, people are generally ready to help and will go out of their way to make your visit as straightforward as possible.

Lisbon, Porto and Faro **airports** have ramps, lifts and adapted toilets. You'll also find **ramped access** to some museums and public buildings, while adapted WCs can be found at some train stations and major shopping centres. It's worth bearing in mind that many guesthouses and budget hotels are located on the first floor or higher and don't have lifts. However, most four- and five-star hotels have lifts, ramps and specially adapted bedrooms and bathrooms, while many manor houses and farmhouses have guest rooms on the ground floor.

At **train stations**, wheelchair access is usually possible as far as the platform, but getting from the platform on to the train can be difficult. Parts of Lisbon's **metro** system are also problematic, though Porto's newer system is generally more accessible. Self-drive vehicles with automatic gearsticks are available from the larger car-rental companies, and there are reserved disabled parking spaces across the country (though they are not always respected).

Portugal's old **town centres** – specifically their steps and cobblestone alleys – pose their own problems. However, a number of attractive medieval towns and villages have been rehabilitated as part of central Portugal's Aldeias Históricas scheme, which has also meant the construction of some smooth wheelchair-accessible pathways alongside the cobbles.

Some **organizations** at home may be able to advise you further about travel to Portugal, such as the UK-based Holiday Care (Ⓦ holidaycare.org.uk), or Access Travel (Ⓦ access-travel.co.uk), a small **tour operator** offering Algarve accommodation suitable for the disabled. In Portugal, **Accessible Portugal** (Ⓦ accessibleportugal.com) is a specialist in wheelchair and disabled holidays and offers city breaks, tours, accommodation and transfers. The government organization that promotes awareness of the disabled is the **Instituto Nacional Para a Reabilitação** (Ⓦ inr.pt), which has a useful website, though it is only in Portuguese.

Lisbon and around

CASTELO DE SÃO JORGE

1

Lisbon and around

Mainland Europe's westernmost capital, Lisbon is a fascinating and inspiring place to spend a few days, thanks to its wonderful waterfront location, balmy climate and quirky range of attractions that combine a place-that-time-forgot feel with a modern vibrancy that few European cities can match. For much of the twentieth century, Lisbon had little contact with the outside world and, even today, the city retains one foot firmly in the early 1900s. Its hills and cobbled alleys are still served by ancient trams and funiculars that rattle along streets where old-fashioned shops and cafés far outnumber the multinationals. Lisbon's revolution of 1974 and later entry into the EU, however, allowed the city's other foot to stride into the twenty-first century, with a range of excellent modern museums and adventurous architectural projects. Immigrants from Brazil and Portugal's former colonies in Africa add an exotic appeal to the city's culture, and Lisbon is now home to some of Europe's hottest Latin American and African bands and clubs, sitting cheek by jowl with the city's traditional fado bars and restaurants.

A short way inland from Lisbon, the UNESCO heritage site of Sintra enjoys a cool mountainside location, which made it a favoured summer destination for Portugal's royals – their ornate and extravagant palaces make for a fascinating day-trip. It is also just a short hop from Lisbon to some fantastic Atlantic beaches: locals favour the southern coast, with miles of sands along the Costa da Caparica or the small cove beaches between the historic port of Setúbal and the resort of Sesimbra. Easiest to reach, however, are the town beaches of bustling Estoril and the former fishing village of Cascais, both easily accessible by train.

Lisbon

Strung out over a series of hills facing the glistening waters of the broad estuary of the Tejo, **LISBON** is one of Europe's most handsome cities. Although its modern suburbs are ungainly, the historic centre is relatively compact and easy to explore in just a day or two. The oldest part of the city, the warren of streets that make up the Alfama, sits below the spectacularly sited Moorish Castelo de São Jorge, its ruined walls facing another hill, the Bairro Alto or upper town, famed for its bars, restaurants and vibrant nightlife. The valley between these hills makes up the Baixa, or lower town. This neat

ANTIGA CONFEITARIA DE BELÉM

Highlights

❶ Alfama Getting lost in the winding, narrow streets and alleys of Lisbon's oldest quarter is half the fun. **See p.65**

❷ Castelo de São Jorge Despite its bloody past, the castle makes a tranquil haven from the busy city, with its pretty gardens, strutting peacocks and dazzling rooftop views. **See p.68**

❸ Bairro Alto Lisbon's "upper town" is *the* place for a lively night out, with its huge selection of vibrant bars, clubs and restaurants. **See p.71**

❹ Mosteiro dos Jerónimos The magnificent Manueline monastery houses the tomb of Vasco da Gama. **See p.79**

❺ Museu Gulbenkian Lalique's fantastic Art Nouveau jewellery, Flemish masters and Impressionist paintings are all included in this awe-inspiring collection of priceless art and antiquities. **See p.84**

❻ Antiga Confeitaria de Belém Don't miss a melt-in-the-mouth, tasty, flaky, warm custard tart, best eaten in the tiled surroundings of Belém's most traditional café. **See p.95**

❼ Palácio Nacional, Sintra A splendid royal retreat in the beautiful, wooded summer residence of kings. **See p.111**

HIGHLIGHTS ARE MARKED ON THE MAPS ON P.58 AND PP.60–61

1

grid of grand eighteenth-century buildings was erected on the rubble of the earthquake which flattened much of the city in 1755, a planned commercial district rebuilt around the historic squares of Praça do Comércio, on the riverfront, and the broad Rossio. From here, the palm-lined Avenida da Liberdade is the main artery inland, rising to the green slopes of the city's central Parque Eduardo VII. Key attractions beyond the historic centre include the fantastic art collection of the Museu Gulbenkian, just north of the park; the Museu de Arte Antiga west of the centre; and the modern art of the Berardo Collection, 6km to the west in Belém, the suburb from which Portugal's great navigators set sail: the sublime Mosteiro dos Jerónimos monastery is one of several monuments built here to celebrate their achievements. Finally, 5km to the east lies the Parque das Nações, the futuristic site of Lisbon's Expo 98, whose main attraction is one of Europe's largest oceanariums.

Brief history

Named Allis Ubbo (calm harbour) by the **Phoenicians**, the administrative capital of Lusitania was renamed Olisipo by the **Romans** when they settled in the western half of Iberia in 210 BC. During the early 700s, **Moors** from North Africa began to exploit

LISBON & AROUND

ATLANTIC OCEAN

N

HIGHLIGHTS

4 Mosteiro dos Jerónimos

6 Antiga Confeitaria de Belém

7 Palácio Nacional, Sintra

0   10
kilometres

trading links from the city they called Lishbuna to their territories to the south, and the city flourished. The Moors set up the Alcáçova – a Muslim palace – on the site of today's castle and settled around some hot springs (alhama, today's Alfama). In 1147, Catholics from the north under Afonso Henriques laid siege to Lisbon's castle with a band of ruthless **European crusaders** and, after seventeen weeks of resistance, the Moors finally gave in – they were either killed or forced to live as "New Christians" in the quarter still known as Mouraria. In 1150, with Afonso Henriques now Portugal's first monarch, the Sé (cathedral) was established on the site of the main mosque, and in 1255 Lisbon became the capital of a **Christian** country.

The discoveries

By the fifteenth century, Lisbon was the capital of an expansionist country whose navigational expertise had set up trading routes round half the world. **Vasco da Gama** sailed from Belém to open up a sea route to India in 1498, and within sixty years Lisbon controlled ports from Brazil in the west to Macau in the east. Lisbon became one of the wealthiest cities in Europe, able to fund lavish buildings such as the Torre de Belém, the Mosteiro dos Jerónimos and the palace at Terreiro do Paço. By the early eighteenth century, further funds flooded in from newly discovered gold in Brazil, but this second "golden age" came to a sudden halt with the **Great Earthquake of 1755** (see box, p.74). Under the **Marquês de Pombal**, a new city was rapidly rebuilt in a grid pattern (today's Baixa district), but Lisbon never recovered its economic clout. The city briefly flourished in the mid-nineteenth century when the Botanical Gardens were considered the best in Europe. A public works programme laid out the Avenida da Liberdade and a series of funicular street lifts were built to serve its hills.

The Salazar era

Political turmoil in the early 1900s saw the end of the Portuguese monarchy and ushered in the reign of **Dr António de Oliveira Salazar**, who ruled Portugal with an iron fist from 1928–68. An economist, Salazar's policies generated sufficient wealth to fund a wartime Expo in Belém in 1940, the Cristo Rei statue overlooking the Tagus and the impressive Ponte 25 de Abril suspension bridge (originally named the Ponte Salazar). But most of the population failed to prosper under his rule, and by the **1974 revolution** which ushered in democracy, most of Lisbon was stuck in a time warp with little or no economic development.

The modern city

Entry into the EU and a series of events – including **Expo 98** and hosting the **European Championships in 2004** – saw money and development pour into the city, bequeathing new rail and metro lines and Europe's longest bridge, Ponte Vasco da Gama. The historic *bairros* (districts) and riverfront have also been given makeovers. If some of the renovation has somewhat diminished the erstwhile lost-in-time feel of the city, it has also injected a wave of optimism that has made Lisbon one of Europe's most exciting capitals.

The Baixa

The tall, imposing buildings that make up the **BAIXA** (Lower Town, pronounced bye-sha) house some of Lisbon's most interesting shops and cafés. Many of the streets are pedestrianized and, by day, they thrum with business folk and street entertainers. When the offices close, however, the whole area is strangely quiet. Facing the river, these streets felt the full force of the 1755 earthquake that destroyed much of the capital. The king's minister, the Marquês de Pombal, swiftly redesigned the sector with the grid pattern that is evident today, framed by a triangle of broad squares, **Praça do Comércio** to the south, with **Praça da Figueira** and **Rossio** to the north. Within this triangle, three main streets are dissected by nine smaller streets, many of which took

1

GREATER LISBON

■ ACCOMMODATION
Alegria	9
As Janelas Verdes	13
Avenida Park	3
Britania	6
Dom Carlos Parque	4
Dom Sancho I	7
Heritage Liberdade	10
Inspira Santa Marta	5
Lisboa Plaza	8
Pousada de Juventude de Lisboa	1
Sheraton Lisboa	2
Suíço Atlântico	11
York House	12

● RESTAURANTS
Casanova	11
Bela Ipanema	7
Eleven	4
Frango da Guia	1
Marisqueira Santa Marta	6
Picanha	9
Ribadouro	8
Túnel de Santos	10

◆ CAFÉS
Deli Deluxe	12
A Linha d'Água	3
Botequim do Rei	5
Versalles	2

HIGHLIGHTS
1. Alfama
2. Castelo de São Jorge
3. Bairro Alto
5. Museu Gulbenkian

BARS AND CLUBS
Kremlin 2
Lux 1

FADO
O Senhor Vinho 3

SHOPS
Amoreiras 2
El Corte Inglés 1

1

their names from the crafts and businesses carried out there, like **Rua da Prata** (Silversmiths' Street) and **Rua dos Sapateiros** (Cobblers' Street). Today, banks and chain stores disturb these divisions somewhat, though plenty of traditional stores remain; the central section of **Rua da Conceição**, for example, is still lined with shops selling beads and sequins. Pombal also wanted the grid's churches to blend in with his harmonious design, so much so that they are almost invisible – walk along **Rua de São Julião** and the facade of the church of Oliveira is barely distinguishable from the offices alongside it, though its tiled interior is delightful.

Rossio

Praça Dom Pedro IV (popularly known as **Rossio**) has been the city's main square since medieval times and it remains the hub of commercial Lisbon. Its central space sparkles with Baroque fountains and polished, mosaic-cobbled pavements. During the nineteenth century, Rossio's plethora of cafés attracted Lisbon's painters and writers, though many of the artists' haunts were converted to banks in the 1970s. Nevertheless, the outdoor seats of the square's remaining cafés are perennially popular meeting-points. On the northwestern side of the square, there's a horseshoe-shaped entrance to **Rossio station**, a mock-Manueline complex with the train platforms an escalator ride above the street-level entrances. Opposite, the square's grandest building is the **Teatro Nacional de Dona Maria II**, built in the 1840s. Here, prior to the earthquake, stood the Inquisitional Palace, in front of which public hangings, autos-da-fé (ritual burnings of heretics) and bullfights used to take place.

Rua das Portas de Santo Antão

One of Lisbon's first streets to be pedestrianized, **Rua das Portas de Santo Antão** is also its liveliest. Running north from the Teatro Nacional de Dona Maria II, the cobbled street is lined with seafood restaurants and theatres and is packed with a healthy mix of tourists and locals. Most of its restaurants have tables outside which are great for people watching – though this is one of the only streets in town where waiters will try and lure you into their premises if they have tables to fill. The *portas* in the name refer to the town gates through which the street once passed, and though the gates have long gone, it still exudes a sense of history. At no.96, the domed **Coliseu dos Recreios** opened as a circus in 1890 and is now one of the city's main concert venues. Look out, too, for some famous watering holes, including *Solmar* at no.108, one of the city's best-known *cervejarias* little changed from the 1950s and *Ginginha Sem Rival* at no.7, a titchy bar serving the potent *ginginha* cherry liqueur.

Casa do Alentejo

Rua das Portas de Santo Antão 58 · Daily 10am–10pm · Free · ☎ 213 469 231 · Ⓜ Rossio or Restauradores

A restaurant, café-bar and cultural centre, the **Casa do Alentejo** is a sumptuously decorated pseudo-Moorish palace, little changed for decades. Originally a seventeenth-century mansion and later a casino, it has been a centre dedicated to culture from the Alentejo district since the 1930s. You can just wander in and look around the beautifully tiled interior – some of the decorative tiles are from the original mansion – but most visitors head upstairs to the dining room or the café-bar, with its neighbouring ballroom, an amazing, slightly rundown room hung with chandeliers.

Praça da Figueira

Once the site of Lisbon's main market, the **Praça da Figueira** has been one of Lisbon's main squares since the 1940s, though the recent addition of an underground car park has detracted somewhat from its former grandeur. Slightly quieter than the neighbouring Rossio, its cafés offer appealing views of the green slopes of the Castelo de São Jorge above.

THE BAIXA & CHIADO

ACCOMMODATION

Borges	7
Chiado	8
Florescente	1
Gerês	3
Lisboa Tejo	5
Insulana	6
Lisbon Lounge Hostel	9
Metrópole	4
Travellers House	10
VIP Executive Suites Eden	2

CAFÉS

A Brasileira	11
Benard	12
Confeitaria Nacional	7
Leitaria Académica	10
Martinho da Arcada	14
Nicola	6
Suíça	5
Vertigo	9

RESTAURANTS

A Berlenga	4
Bom Jardim/Rei dos Frangos	1
Casa do Alentejo	2
Floresta Santana	10
João do Grão	8
Tão	13

BAR AND CLUB

A Ginginha	1

—25— Tram

0 _____ 100
metres

SHOPS

Ana Salazar	2
Armazéns do Chiado	4
FNAC	3
Livraria Bertrand	5
Manuel Tavares	1
Napoleão	7
Santos Ofícios	6
Storytailors	8

Barreiro & River Cruises ▼

1

Elevador de Santa Justa
Rua de Santa Justa • Daily: June–Sept 7am–11pm; Oct–May 7am–10pm • €5 return • Ⓜ Baixa-Chiado

Built in 1902 by a disciple of Gustav Eiffel, Raul Mésnier, the impressive and eccentric-looking **Elevador de Santa Justa** street lift creaks its way up 32 metres above the Baixa. The exit at the top comes out next to the Bairro Alto's Convento do Carmo, but you can stop first for a drink at the *elevador's* own pricey rooftop café, which has great views over the city and the elaborate metal framework of the lift itself.

Núcleo Arqueológico
Rua dos Correeiros 9 • Book in advance for guided tours on Thurs at 5pm & Sat hourly 10am–noon & 3–5pm; tour 30–45min • Free • ☎ 211 131 004 • Ⓜ Baixa-Chiado

One of Lisbon's smallest but most fascinating museums, the **Núcleo Arqueológico**, lies beneath the Baixa's streets. During the construction of the BCP bank in the 1990s, excavations revealed the remains of Roman fish-preserving tanks, a fifth-century Christian burial place and Moorish ceramics, which can all be seen in this tiny museum. Most of the exhibits are viewed through glass floors or from cramped walkways beneath the modern bank.

Rua Augusta and Arco da Rua Augusta
The mosaic-paved **Rua Augusta** is the Baixa grid's main pedestrianized thoroughfare, filled with shops, cafés, market stalls and buskers. It ends in a huge arch, the **Arco da Rua Augusta**, adorned with statues of historical figures, including the Marquês de Pombal and Vasco da Gama. Acting as a gateway to the city, the arch was built to celebrate Lisbon's reconstruction after the earthquake, although it wasn't completed until 1873.

Museu Design Moda
Rua Augusta 24 • Tues–Thurs & Sun 10am–8pm, Fri & Sat 10am–10pm • Free • Ⓦ mude.pt • Ⓜ Baixa-Chiado or Terreiro de Paço

Inside a grand former bank, the **Museu Design Moda** houses an impressive collection of design and fashion classics from the 1930s to today, amassed by former stockbroker and media mogul Francisco Capelo. The museum's ever-changing exhibits include design classics by Charles and Ray Eames and Phillipe Starck, as well as Capelo's fashion collection – haute couture from the 1950s, 1960s street fashion and designer brands of the 1990s, with examples from the likes of Paco Rabanne, Pierre Cardin and Alexander McQueen.

Praça do Comércio
Originally built on the site of a royal palace, the arcaded **Praça do Comércio** is Lisbon's main riverfront square, and it was here that Dom Carlos I was assassinated in 1908 during the country's attempts to become a republic. One of Portugal's monarchs is still honoured here, however: the statue at the centre of the square is Dom José, who was king when the city was redeveloped following the 1755 earthquake.

Praça do Comércio's **riverfront** provides a natural focus for the area. In the hour or two before sunset, people linger in the golden light to watch the orange ferries ply between the **Estação Fluvial** and Barreiro on the opposite side of the Tejo. The secluded **Patio da Galé**, tucked into the western arcades, hosts frequent events. The square is also a major **transport interchange** – the starting point for tram and bus tours of the city, as well as home to the city's main tourist office. It is also the place in Lisbon you are most likely to be offered a dodgy watch or "hasheesh".

Lisbon Story Centre
Praço do Comércio • Daily 10am–8pm • €7 • ☎ 211 941 099, Ⓦ visitlisboa.com • Ⓜ Terreiro de Paço

The eastern arcades of Praça do Comércio were renovated in 2012 to become Ala Nascente, a hub of somehat touristy cafés and shops, the highlight of which is the **Lisbon Story Centre**. This gives a potted, visual account of the history of the city – good for a rainy day, though somewhat pricey for what you get. There are six zones, each dedicated to a phase in Lisbon's history, from ancient myths to the present via the Discoveries. The zones consist of multimedia displays, models, paintings, photos, narrations and filmed re-enactments of key moments – the highlight is a somewhat gory 4D film depicting the 1755 earthquake, and a "virtual" scale model of the modern city.

The Alfama

The Alfama is Lisbon's oldest and most atmospheric quarter, a labyrinthine maze of narrow streets, steps and alleys wrapped round the steep lower slopes of the **Moorish castle**. Walking round the area is a must for any Lisbon visit. It's the street life that's the interest here, much of it continuing in the same way as it has for centuries,

ALFAMA & CASTELO

● SHOPS	
A Arte da Terra	2
Casa do Fado e da Guitarra Portuguesa	1

■ BARS AND CLUBS	
Costa do Castelo	2
Portas do Sol	4

■ FADO AND MUSIC CLUBS	
A Baiuca	5
A Parreirinha de Alfama	3
Chafarica	1
Clube do Fado	6
Onda Jazz	7

● CAFÉS	
Miradouro de Santa Luzia	5
Pois Café	8

● RESTAURANTS	
Arco do Castelo	2
Barracão de Alfama	6
Casanova	4
Cruzes Credo	9
Lautasco	3
Malmequer-Bemmequer	7
Rêsto do Chapitô	1

■ ACCOMMODATION	
Ninho das Águias	1
Solar do Castelo	2
Solar dos Mouros	3

1

with children playing in the roads and alleys, and families cooking fish on tiny grills outside their houses. Appropriately in an area which is home to many **fado clubs**, there is also a museum dedicated to the Portuguese music, while around the Alfama are further distractions in the form of the city's **cathedral**, two historic churches containing national pantheons, a fantastic **market**, and museums dedicated to a Roman theatre, decorative arts and – further east – Portuguese tiles.

The Sé

Largo da Sé • Daily 10am–7pm • Free • **Treasury** Mon–Sat 10am–5pm • €2.50 • **Cloister** Mon–Sat 10am–7pm, Sun 2–7pm • €2.50 • ☎ 218 876 628 • Tram #28

Lisbon's squat, military-looking cathedral – **the Sé** – is Romanesque in style, with a surprisingly plain and sombre interior. This is because many of its original embellishments were destroyed by the 1755 earthquake, though restoration work in the 1930s saw the reconstruction of the huge and impressive rose window. The cathedral was founded in 1150 on the site of Moorish Lishbuna's main mosque, shortly after the city was taken from the Moors under the direction of the Englishman Gilbert of Hastings, who became Lisbon's first bishop.

Most things of value were placed in the **Treasury**, including the remains of St Vincent, which, according to legend, arrived in Lisbon in a boat guided by ravens – the birds are still a symbol for the city today. Of more interest, however, is the thirteenth-century **cloister**, which is currently being excavated, to reveal the remains of a sixth-century Roman house and Moorish public buildings.

Casa dos Bicos

Rua dos Bacalhoeiros • Mon–Fri 10am–6pm, Sat 10am–2pm • €3 • ☎ 218 810 900, Ⓦ josesaramago.org • Ⓜ Terreiro de Paço or tram #25

The **Casa dos Bicos** means the "House of Points", which aptly describes its curious walls, studded with pyramid-shaped stones. It was built in 1523 for the son of the Viceroy of India, though only the facade of the original building survived the earthquake. It is now owned by the Saramargo organization and hosts regular recitals and exhibitions dedicated to the Nobel Prize for Literature-winning Portuguese author José Saramago, who died in 2010.

Casa do Fado e da Guitarra Portuguesa

Largo do Chafariz de Dentro 1 • Tues–Sun 10am–6pm • €5 • ☎ 218 823 470, Ⓦ museudofado.pt

Set in the renovated Recinto da Praia, a former water cistern and bathhouse, the **Casa do Fado e da Guitarra Portuguesa** is an engaging museum outlining the history of fado and Portuguese guitar by way of wax models, paintings, sounds and descriptions of the leading characters and styles of this very Portuguese music. It's an excellent introduction to fado and worth seeing before you visit a fado house. There's also a good shop for fado CDs and a small café.

ALFAMA WALKS AND VIEWPOINTS

The easiest place to start a wander around the Alfama is along the road below the Sé, which becomes Rua de São João de Praça. Follow this as it twists its way down to the Alfama's lower square, **Largo do Chirariz de Dentro**, home to many of the city's best fado bars and clubs. From here, head uphill and you'll probably get lost in the maze of alleys that wend up past the church of São Miguel to emerge by the **Largo das Portas do Sol**, a viewpoint with a tremendous outlook – a solitary palm rising from the stepped streets against the dome of Santa Engrácia and the Tejo beyond. Just round the corner, in front of the Igreja da Santa Luzia, the **Miradouro da Santa Luzia** has perhaps the city's best views across the Alfama and the river.

1

Museu do Teatro Romano

Entrance on Patio de Aljube • Tues–Sun 10am–1pm & 2–6pm • Free • ☎ 218 820 320, ⓦ museu-teatroroman.pt • Tram #28

You can see the sparse ruins of the **Teatro Romano** (57 AD), set behind a grille just off to the left at the junction of ruas São Mamede and Saudade. The finds excavated from the site can be visited at the small adjacent **Museu do Teatro Romano**, which has multimedia explanations of the theatre's history.

Museu de Artes Decorativas Portuguesas

Largo das Portas do Sol 2 • Mon–Sat 10am–5pm • €4 • ☎ 218 814 600, ⓦ fress.pt • Tram #28

Inside a seventeenth-century mansion, the lovely **Museu de Artes Decorativas Portuguesas** displays what was once the private collection of banker Ricardo do Espírito Santo Silva, who offered it to the nation in 1953. Here, you can see some of the best examples of seventeenth- and eighteenth-century applied arts in the country. Highlights include a stunning sixteenth-century tapestry depicting a parade of giraffes, beautiful carpets from Arraiolos in the Alentejo, and oriental quilts that were all the rage in the seventeenth century. The museum also has a courtyard café.

São Vicente de Fora

Largo de São Vicente • Tues–Sun 10am–6pm • Church free; Monastery €4 • Tram #28 or bus #34 from Santa Apolónia station and ⓜ Martim Moniz

The church of **São Vicente de Fora** takes its name from its original position *fora* (outside) the city walls. Built on the site where Crusaders perished while fighting the Moors, it remains one of Lisbon's most interesting churches. Begun in 1582 under the Italian architect Felipe Terzi, it was finally inaugurated in 1629 only to be partially destroyed by the earthquake of 1755. It was then restored and in 1855, the former monastic refectory became the official burial site for the kings and queens of the House of Bragança. You can see the tombs here of pretty much all the Portuguese monarchs from João IV to Manuel II, the last Portuguese king, who died in exile in England in 1932. Look out too for the tomb of Catherine of Bragança, the widow of England's Charles II. Upstairs rooms trace the history of La Fontaine's fables illustrated on 38 tile panels, but save some energy to climb to the roof for spectacular views out over the city. There's also a lovely café by the entrance.

Feira da Ladra

Tues & Sat 9am–3pm • Tram #28 or bus #34 from Santa Apolónia station and ⓜ Martim Moniz

Lisbon's twice-weekly **Feira da Ladra** ("thieves market") sprawls colourfully around the elongated square of Campo de Santa Clara below the impressive dome of the Santa Engrácia church. Goods on sale include unwanted bric-a-brac and old junk, but you'll also find cheap clothes, CDs, crafts, books, prints, antiques of varying quality and the odd novelty (such as night-vision goggles or souvenirs from Portugal's former colonies). Best of all, though, are the people who run the stalls, a motley collection of Lisbon's most interesting characters.

Santa Engrácia

Campo de Santa Clara • Tues–Sun: May–Oct 10am–6pm; Nov–April 10am–5pm • €3 • Tram #28 or bus #34 from Santa Apolónia station and ⓜ Martim Moniz

The white dome of **Santa Engrácia** makes it one of the most recognizable buildings on the city skyline. Begun in 1682, it was not completed until 1966, leading to the expression "a job like Santa Engrácia", one that is never finished. Since 1916, the church has been the **Panteão Nacional**, housing the tombs of eminent Portuguese figures, including former presidents, the writer Almeida Garrett and Amália Rodrigues, Portugal's most famous fado singer. You can go up to the terrace for dazzling views across the river and city below.

LISBON'S AZULEJOS

Lisbon has some of Portugal's best *azulejos* – brightly coloured, decorative ceramic tiles – and you can see a variety of styles decorating houses, shops, monuments and even metro stations. The craft of decorative tile-making was brought over by the Moors in the eighth century. Originally, the tiles were painted using thin ridges of clay to prevent the lead-based colours from running into each other, and the early Portuguese tiles were produced using the same techniques: the early sixteenth-century **geometric tiles** in the Palácio Nacional in Sintra (see p.111) are a fine example. Portuguese *azulejos* developed their own style around the mid-sixteenth century when a new Italian method – introduced to Iberia by Francisco Niculoso – enabled images to be painted directly onto the clay thanks to a tin oxide coating which prevented running.

At first, **religious imagery** was the favoured form – such as those in the Bairro Alto's Igreja de São Roque (see p.71) – but during the seventeenth century decadent and colourful images became popular. The wealthy Portuguese began to commission large *azulejo* panels displaying battles, hunting scenes and fantastic images influenced by Vasco da Gama's voyages to the East, while huge panels were also commissioned for churches – these often covered an entire wall and became known as *tapetes* (carpets) because of their resemblance to rugs. By the late seventeenth century, blue and white tiles influenced by **Dutch tile-makers** were popular with Portugal's aristocracy, and their favoured images were flowers and fruit. The early eighteenth century saw highly-trained artists producing elaborately decorated, multicoloured **ceramic mosaics**, often with Rococo themes.

After the Great Earthquake, more prosaic tiled facades, often with **Neoclassical designs**, were considered good insulation devices, as well as protecting buildings from rain and fire. By the mid-nineteenth century, *azulejos* were being mass-produced to decorate shops and factories, while the end of the century saw the reappearance of figurative designs, typified by the work in the *Cervejaria da Trindade* (see p.97), a vaulted beer-hall in the Bairro Alto. By the 1900s, Portugal had become the world's leading producer of decorative tiles, with **Art Deco** designs taking hold in the 1920s. Lisbon's metro stations boast some of the best of the more modern tiles, with work by artists such as Eduardo Nehry, whose tiles light up Campo Grande, and António da Coata, whose Alice-in-Wonderland-inspired white rabbit can be seen at Cais do Sodré station.

Museu Nacional do Azulejo

Rua da Madre de Deus, about 1.5km east of Santa Apolónia station • Tues–Sun 10am–6pm • €5; free on Sun before 2pm • ☎ 218 103 340, �🌐 mnazulejo.imc-ip.pt • Bus #794 from Praça do Comércio or Santa Apolónia

One of the most appealing of Lisbon's small museums, the **Museu Nacional do Azulejo** traces the development of tile-making from Moorish days to the present via its hugely impressive collection of *azulejos* covering the main styles of tile from the fifteenth century to the present day. The museum is housed within the church and cloisters of Madre de Deus, a former convent dating from 1509. The church has a Baroque interior, installed after the earthquake of 1755, and retains some striking eighteenth-century tiles depicting scenes from the life of Santo António. Most of the museum is set around the church cloisters, which house many more delights, including Portugal's longest *azulejo* – a 36-metre tiled panorama of pre-earthquake Lisbon, completed in around 1738 – and some fascinating examples of the large *azulejo* panels known as *tapetes* (carpets). There's also a lovely garden **café**.

Castelo de São Jorge

Castelo Daily: March–Oct 9am–9pm; Nov–Feb 9am–6pm • **Câmara Escura** Daily 10am–5pm every 30min weather permitting • €7.50 • ☎ 218 800 620, 🌐 castelodesaojorge.pt • Tram #28 from Rua da Conceição in the Baixa; bus #37 from Praça da Figueira, or tram #12 from Martim Moniz to the Santa Cruz area just east of the castle

Superbly sited on a hilltop with the city and river laid out below, the **Castelo de São Jorge** is rightly Lisbon's most popular attraction. Part of its appeal lies in the fact that

1

much of it is little more than a shell whose restored walls enclose grassy areas where peacocks shelter and cats doze beneath trees. There was probably a castle here in the Iron Age and by the time the city was under Moorish rule, the building was sufficiently robust to repel the invading Christians for several months until Lisbon finally fell to Afonso Henriques in 1147. Initially, Portugal's monarchs lived in the castle, but they moved out when Manuel I built a new palace down by the river. After that, the castle served as a barracks, prison and children's home until the late twentieth century when it was substantially renovated to become the tourist attraction you see today.

The castle **museum** is in the old Alcáçova (the former palace where the kings lived), with a small multimedia exhibition that details the history of the city together with archeological finds. Inside the Tower of Ulysses, a **Câmara Escura** periscope focuses on sights round the city with English commentary – though the views are almost as good from the neighbouring towers.

Santa Cruz and Mouraria

Take time to explore the areas immediately around the castle. Turn left from the castle exit and you are in the tiny **Santa Cruz** quarter, a village in its own right with a school, church and bathhouse. To the north and west of the castle is **Mouraria**, named because this was where the Moors were forced to live when expelled from the castle – today, it's an atmospheric area with some good local cafés.

Cais do Sodré and Bica

Down on the waterfront, **Cais do Sodré** (pronounced *kaiysh doo sodray*) is a colourful, but slightly down-at-heel suburb enlivened by some good restaurants, clubs and bars. Many of its **waterfront warehouses** have been converted into upmarket cafés and restaurants and by day, in particular, a stroll along its atmospheric riverfront is very enjoyable. Cais do Sodré is also the main departure point for **ferries** over the Tejo – a ride over to the little port of Cacilhas (see p.119) is recommended – while the eponymous station is the terminus for the **rail line** out to Cascais.

Mercado da Ribeira

Av 24 de Julho • Tues–Sat 5am–2pm; flower section open til 7pm • Ⓦ espacoribeira.pt • Ⓜ Cais do Sodré

The **Mercado da Ribeira** is Lisbon's main and most historic market. The first market here was built on the site of an old fort at the end of the nineteenth century, though the current structure only dates from 1930. The main market downstairs sells an impressive array of spices, fruit and vegetables, with a separate, aromatic flower section.

Elevador da Bica

Entrance on Rua de São Paulo • Mon–Sat 7am–9pm, Sun 9am–9pm • €3.60 return • Ⓜ Cais do Sodré

With its entrance tucked into an arch on Rua de São Paulo, the **Elevador da Bica** is one of the city's most atmospheric funicular railways. Built in 1892 and originally powered by water counterweights – though now operated electrically – the *elevador* leads up towards the Bairro Alto, via a steep residential street. Take time to explore the surrounding steep side-streets of the Bica neighbourhood, too, a warren of tightly-knit houses, little shops and fine local restaurants.

Miradouro de Santa Catarina

Just off Rua M. Saldanha, Bica district • **kiosk** Daily 10am–dusk, weather permitting • Tram #28

Set on the cusp of a hill, high above the river, the railed **Miradouro de Santa Catarina** has spectacular views over the city and river. Here, in the shadow of the statue of the Adamastor – a mythical beast from Luís de Camões's *Lusiads* – a collection of guitar-strumming New Age hippies often gathers around an appealing **drinks kiosk** (daily 10am–dusk, weather permitting), which has a few outdoor tables.

Chiado

1

On the west side of the Baixa, the area known as **Chiado** – the *nom de plume* of the poet António Ribeiro and pronounced *she-ah-doo* – was Lisbon's original upmarket shopping area. Many of its former stores were destroyed by a fire in 1988, although the original *belle époque* atmosphere has since been superbly re-created under the direction of eminent Portuguese architect Álvaro Siza Vieira.

Chiado remains a smart shopping district, famed for its cafés especially along Rua Garrett. Of these, **A Brasileira**, Rua Garrett 120, is the most famous, once frequented by Lisbon's literary set and now usually mobbed by tourists.

Museu do Chiado

Rua Serpa Pinto 4 • Tues–Sun 10am–6pm • €4, free on Sun until 2pm • ☎ 213 432 148, ⓦ museudochiado-ipmuseus.pt • Ⓜ Baixa-Chiado

The stylish **Museu do Chiado** incorporates the former Museum of Contemporary Art, whose original home was damaged during the Chiado fire. The new museum was constructed around a nineteenth-century biscuit factory, hence the presence of the old ovens. Its three floors display the work of some of Portugal's most influential artists since the nineteenth century, including some wonderful decorative panels by José de Almada Negreiros, recovered from the San Carlos cinema. Highlights include the beautiful sculpture *A Viúva* (The Widow) by António Teixeira Lopes and some evocative scenes of the Lisbon area by Carlos Botelho and José Malhoa. It also hosts some excellent temporary exhibitions: check the website for details.

Bairro Alto

High above the central city, to the west of the Baixa, the **Bairro Alto** – meaning upper town – has a sleepy, residential feel during the day, its maze of narrow streets enlivened by a few bohemian boutiques. At night, however, it comes to life as many of the city's best bars, restaurants and fado clubs open for business. Many of the Bairro Alto's most interesting thoroughfares lie west of Rua da Misericórdia, a confusing grid of streets, whose buildings are often liberally defaced with graffiti. Traffic is restricted to residents only, and though dodgy characters offering hash still lurk on the corners round the market building on Rua da Atalaia, it's essentially safe at any time if you keep valuables out of sight.

Igreja de São Roque

Largo de Trindade Coelho • **Church** Mon 2–6pm, Tues, Wed, Fri–Sun 9am–6pm • Free • **Museu de São Roque** Tues–Wed & Fri–Sun 10am–6pm, Thurs 2–9pm • €2.50, free on Sun from 10am–2pm

Built by Jesuits in the sixteenth century, the **Igreja de São Roque** has a bland Renaissance facade that gives no hint of its interior riches. Inside, impressive *azulejos* and marble decorate the side chapels, while the **Capela de São João Baptista** is thought

---

TRANSPORT TO THE BAIRRO ALTO

To reach the Bairro Alto, you can simply climb the steep Calçada de Glória, but it's more fun to approach via one of the quirky funiculars, which were originally powered by water displacement, and then by steam, until electricity was introduced. Most conveniently, the **Elevador da Glória** (Mon–Fri 7am–midnight, Sat 8.30am–2am, Sun 9am–midnight; €3.60 return), built in 1885, trundles up from the Praça dos Restauradores, dropping you at the top of the hill on Rua de São Pedro de Alcântara: the adjacent gardens here provide a superb view across the city to the castle. The **Elevador da Bica** (see p.70) drops you on Rua Loreto at the foot of the Bairro Alto, while the **Elevador de Santa Justa** (see p.64), brings you out beside the Convento do Carmo.

1

THE GREAT EARTHQUAKE

Anyone who witnessed the shocking images of Japan's tsunami in 2011 will have some idea of the disaster which befell Lisbon on November 1, 1755. A quake of around 8.7 on the Richter scale – the largest earthquake ever to hit Europe – struck at 9.30am when many people were attending Mass for All Souls' Day. Survivors fled to the open spaces of the riverfront, many to be engulfed by a giant tsunami that followed some forty minutes later. Fires then burned for up to five days and tens of thousands of people lost their lives. The event put a halt to Portuguese colonial expansion, but also led to the development of the study of seismology.

to be one of the most expensive and lavish chapels of its era. Dom João V commissioned the papal architect to design and build the chapel in Rome, with no expense spared. It was shipped to Lisbon in 1749, but its intricate array of ivory inlays, gold, lapis lazuli and mosaics of John the Baptist took some four years to reassemble and the result is truly remarkable. The most valuable treasures of the church are kept in the adjacent **Museu de São Roque**, which also displays sixteenth- to eighteenth-century paintings and a fairly uninspiring collection of church relics.

Convento and Museu Arqueológico do Carmo

Largo do Carmo • Mon–Sat: June–Sept 10am–7pm; Oct–May 10am–6pm • €4 • ☎ 213 478 629, ⓦ museuarqueologicodocarmo.pt

The pretty, enclosed Largo do Carmo holds the entrance to the **Convento do Carmo**, whose beautiful Gothic arches rise majestically above the ruins. Built between 1389 and 1423, and once the city's grandest church, it was badly damaged by the 1755 earthquake. In the nineteenth century its shell was used as a chemical factory but today it houses the splendidly capricious **Museu Arqueológico do Carmo**, home to many of the treasures from Portugal's monasteries which had been dissolved after the 1834 Liberal revolution. The nave is open to the elements, with columns, tombs and statuary scattered in all corners. Inside, on either side of what was the main altar, are the main exhibits, centring on a series of tombs. Largest is the beautifully carved, two-metre-high stone tomb of Ferdinand I; nearby, that of Gonçalo de Sousa, chancellor to Henry the Navigator, is topped by a statue of Gonçalo himself, holding a book to signify his learning. Other noteworthy pieces include sixteenth-century Hispano-Arabic *azulejos*, an Egyptian sarcophagus (793–619 BC), whose inhabitant's feet are just visible beneath the lid, and, even more alarmingly, two pre-Columbian mummies which lie in glass cases, alongside the preserved heads of a couple of indigenous Peruvians.

Praça do Príncipe Real

North of the tight Bairro Alto grid, the streets open out around the leafy **Praça do Príncipe Real**, one of the city's loveliest squares. Laid out in 1860 and surrounded by the ornate homes of former aristocrats – now largely turned into offices – the square is the focal point of Lisbon's gay scene, though by day it is largely populated by children in the play park and locals playing cards under the trees.

Museu da Água Príncipe Real

Praça do Príncipe Real • Mon–Sat 10am–6pm; tours Wed & Sat at 11am & 3pm, Fri 1pm • €2.50 • Bus #758 or #778 from Chiado

Praça do Príncipe Real's central pond and fountain are built above a covered reservoir that houses the **Museu da Água Príncipe Real**. Steps lead down inside the eerie nineteenth-century reservoir, where you can admire brick and vaulted ceilings, part of a network of underground water supplies that link up with the Aqueduto das Águas Livres (see p.75). Tours – not for claustrophobics – take you along one of these, a humid 410-metre tunnel that exits at the viewpoint of Miradouro de São Pedro.

Museus de Politécnica

Rua Escola Politécnica 56 • Tues–Fri 10am–5pm, Sat & Sun 11am–6pm; closed Aug • €5 per museum, or a combined ticket costs €6, including entry to Jardim Botânico • ⓦ mnhn.ul.pt • Bus #758 or #778 from Chiado

The Museus de Politécnica feature two minor museums within Lisbon Polytechnic: the **Museu de História Natural** exhibits a rather sad collection of stuffed animals tracing the evolution of Iberian animal life, while the more appealing **Museu da Ciência** includes an imaginative interactive section among its otherwise pedestrian geological displays. Look out for the temporary exhibits, which can be more rewarding.

Jardim Botânico

Rua Escola Politécnica 58 • April–Oct Mon–Fri 9am–8pm, Sat & Sun 10am–8pm; Nov–March closes at 6pm • €2, or a combined ticket costs €6, including entry to the Museus de Politécnica; Butterfly house €1 • Bus #758 or #778 from Chiado

Beyond the museums, the entrance to the enchanting **Jardim Botânico** is almost completely invisible from the surrounding streets. Portuguese explorers introduced many plant species to Europe, and these gardens, laid out between 1858 and 1878, form an oasis of twenty thousand exotic plants from around the world. There's also a **butterfly house**, called the Lugartagis, which is a greenhouse for breeding butterflies.

Avenida da Liberdade and around

The grand, palm-lined **Avenida da Liberdade** is a 1.3-kilometre-long avenue climbing from the upper fringes of the Baixa to Lisbon's main park, Parque Eduardo VII. Laid out in the late nineteenth century and modelled on the Champs-Élysées, the broad avenue and its little kiosks form the focal point of various events during the year, including a parade on June 12–13 for St Anthony. It was once was the exclusive address for some of Lisbon's most respected figures, such as António Medeiros, whose rich **art collections** are on display in his former home. On the western side of the avenue it's a short walk to the historic **Praça das Amoreiras**, the finishing point of the massive **Aqueduto das Águas**.

Elevador da Lavra

Largo da Anunciada • Mon–Sat 7am–9pm, Sun 9am–9pm • €3.60 return • ⓜ Restauradores or Avenida

Dating back to 1882, the **Elevador do Lavra** is a historic street lift that rises from the northern end of Rua das Portas de Santo Antão up one of the city's back-breaking hills, to drop you in a little-visited suburb. It is the *elevador* least used by tourists but, like the other more famous lifts to the Bairro Alto, this one is great fun to ride. Once you've trundled up the hill, it's a short walk to the little **Jardim do Torel**, a park with great views back over the Baixa.

Casa-Museu Medeiros e Almeida

Rua Rosa Araújo 41 • Mon–Fri 1–5.30pm, Sat 10am–5.30pm • €5, free on Sat 10am–1pm • ⓦ casa-museumedeirosealmeida.pt • ⓜ Avenida

The **Casa-Museu Medeiros e Almeida**, set in the former home of art collector and industrialist António Medeiros e Almeida (1895–1986), gives you a real taste of the opulence of this district of Lisbon in the nineteenth century. Parts of the house have been kept as they were when he lived there, while other rooms display his priceless collection of works, including 2000-year-old Chinese porcelain, an important collection of sixteenth- to nineteenth-century watches, and dazzling English and Portuguese silverware. There are sumptuous eighteenth-century tiles (*azulejos*) in the Sala de Lago, a room also filled with bubbling decorative fountains.

Mãe d'Água and the Aqueduto das Águas Livres

Praça das Amoreiras • **Mãe d'Água** Mon–Sat 10am–6pm • €2.50 • ☎ 218 135 522 • ⓜ Rato

The delightful **Praça das Amoreiras** is one of Lisbon's nicest squares, dominated on its west side by the arches of the **Aqueduto das Águas Livres**. Stretching some 60km into

1

the hills above Lisbon, this enormous aqueduct was built in 1748 to pipe fresh water into the city for the first time. On the south side of the square, the **Mãe d'Água** water cistern marks the end of the line for the aqueduct, its reservoir contained within a cathedral-like stone building with Gothic lion heads. The water cistern now hosts occasional exhibitions and has great views from its roof. You can walk over the 60-metre-high central section of the aqueduct itself, which takes about fifteen or twenty minutes: the entrance is around 1km north of Praça das Amoreiras, at Calçada da Quintiha 6 in Campolide (bus #718 from Amoreiras; March–Oct Mon–Sat 10am–6pm; €2.50).

São Bento

São Bento, downhill and west from the Bairro Alto, was home to Lisbon's first black community – originally slaves from Portugal's early maritime explorations. However, the area today is best known for the Neoclassical parliament building, the **Palácio de São Bento** (or Palácio da Assembléia), originally a Benedictine monastery before the abolition of religious orders in 1834. Since the Portugese government still sits here, it can only be visited by prior arrangement (☎213 919 000), though you get a good view of its steep white steps from tram #28, which rattles right by.

Casa Museu Amália Rodrigues

Rua de São Bento 193 • Tues–Sun 10am–1pm & 2–6pm • €5 • ☎ 213 971 896, ⓦ amaliarodrigues.pt • Bus #706 from Praça do Comércio

The **Casa Museu Amália Rodrigues** is inside the house where Portugal's most famous fado singer lived from the 1950s until her death in 1999. The house has been preserved as it was when she lived there, with artefacts tracing the life and times of the daughter of an Alfama orange-seller who became an internationally famous singer. Revered in her lifetime, her death resulted in three days of national mourning, and her record covers, film posters and everyday belongings are lovingly displayed here.

West Lisbon

West of the Bairro Alto sits the leafy district of **Estrela**, best known for its gardens and enormous **basílica**. To the south lies opulent Lapa, Lisbon's diplomatic quarter, where sumptuous mansions and grand embassy buildings peer out majestically towards the Tejo; it's also home to the superb **Museu Nacional de Arte Antiga**, Portugal's national gallery. Down below, on the riverfront, the regenerated district of **Santos** is known as "the design district", with some of the city's coolest new shops and bars.

Basílica and Jardim da Estrela

Basílica Daily 7.30.am–1pm & 3–8pm • Free • Tram #28 from Praça Luís de Camões in Chiado, or #25 from Praça do Comércio

With its landmark white dome being visible from much of the city, the impressive **Basílica da Estrela** was commissioned by Queen Maria I (whose tomb lies inside), and completed in 1790. Opposite it, is the **Jardim da Estrela**, a luxuriantly leafy park with a pond-side café, a well-equipped children's playground and even a library kiosk for those who fancy absorbing a spot of Portuguese literature under the palms.

Museu Nacional de Arte Antiga

Rua das Janelas Verdes 95 • Tues 2–6pm, Wed–Sun 10am–6pm • €5, free Sun 10am–2pm • ☎ 213 912 800, ⓦ mnaa.imc-ip.pt • Bus #760 from Praça do Comércio, or a short walk from tram #25

Portugal's national gallery, the **Museu Nacional de Arte Antiga** is home to the largest collection of Portuguese fifteenth- and sixteenth-century paintings in the country, as well as European art from the fourteenth century to the present day, and a rich display of applied art showing the influence of Portugal's colonial explorations. All of this is beautifully displayed in a seventeenth-century palace, once owned by the Marquês de Pombal. The palace was built over the remains of the Saint Albert monastery,

1

most of which was razed in the 1755 earthquake, although its beautiful chapel can still be seen today. The attractive garden and café (hours as for museum; free entry) are worth a visit in their own right.

The collection

The museum helpfully highlights its top ten works of art to guide you round the extensive collection. Principal highlight is **Nuno Gonçalves**'s *Altarpiece for Saint Vincent* (1467–70) showing Lisbon's patron saint being admired by people from all walks of life, their faces looking remarkably modern. Equally impressive is **Hieronymus Bosch**'s stunningly gruesome *Temptation of St Anthony* in room 57 – unusually, there's also an image on the back, showing the arrest of Christ. Elsewhere, seek out the altar panel depicting the *Resurrection* by Raphael; Francisco de Zurbarán's *The Twelve Apostles*; a small statue of a nymph by Auguste Rodin and works by Albrecht Dürer, Cranach, Fragonard and **Josefa de Óbidos**, considered one of Portugal's greatest female painters.

The **Oriental art collection** includes inlaid furniture from Goa, Turkish and Syrian *azulejos*, Quing Dynasty porcelain and a series of late sixteenth-century Japanese *namban* screens (room 14), showing the Portuguese landing at Nagasaki. The Japanese saw the Portuguese traders as southern barbarians (*namban*) with large noses – hence their Pinocchio-like features.

Santos

Southeast of the Museu Nacional de Arte Antiga, **Santos** was formerly a run-down riverside area of factories and warehouses, where people only ventured after dark for its well-known nightclubs. Its squares and streets are not particularly alluring, but over the years, artists and designers have moved into the inexpensive and expansive warehouse spaces and it's now become the city's trendy art district, where many of the country's top designers showcase their products, especially around **Largo de Santos**. Hip bars and restaurants have followed in their wake, though much of the district remains fairly run-down – and the area around the Museu da Marioneta (see below) retains an earthy, villagey feel to its cobbled backstreets.

Museu da Marioneta

Rua Esperança 146 • Tues–Sun 10am–1pm & 2–5.30pm • €5, free on Sun 10am–1pm • ☎ 213 942 810 • Tram #25, then a short walk

Contemporary and historical puppets from around the world are displayed in the well-organized **Museu da Marioneta** (puppet museum), housed in a former eighteenth-century convent. Highlights include shadow puppets from Turkey and Indonesia, string marionettes, Punch and Judy-style puppets, and faintly disturbing, almost life-sized contemporary figures by Portuguese puppeteer Helena Vaz. There are also video displays and projections, while the final room shows Wallace and Gromit-style plasticine figures and how they are manipulated for films.

Alcântara and the docks

Loomed over by the enormous Ponte 25 de Abril suspension bridge, Lisbon's docks at **Alcântara** have a decidedly industrial hue, with a tangle of railway lines, flyovers and cranes dominating the skyline. Nevertheless, the area is well known for its nightlife, mainly thanks to its dockside warehouse conversions that shelter cafés, restaurants and clubs. It's also home to two good museums tracing Portugal's trading links with the Orient.

Museu do Oriente

Avenida Brasilia • Tues–Thurs, Sat & Sun 10am–6pm, Fri 10am–10pm • €5, free on Fri 6–10pm • ☎ 213 585 200, ⓦ museudooriente.pt • Tram #15 or #18, or train to Alcântara Mar

Housed in an enormous 1930s *Estado Novo* building, the **Museu do Oriente** traces the cultural links that Portugal has built up with the Orient. Highlights of its extensive

1

collection include valuable nineteenth-century Chinese porcelain, an amazing array of seventeenth-century Chinese snuff boxes and, from the same century, Japanese armour and entire carved pillars from Goa. The top floor is given over to displays on the Gods of Asia, featuring a bright collection of religious costumes and shrines used in Bali and Vietnam, together with Taoist altars, statues of Buddha, some fine Japanese Shinto masks and Indonesian shadow puppets. Vivid images of Hindu gods Shiva, Ganesh the elephant god and Kali the demon are counterbalanced by some lovely Thai amulets. There is also a decent top-floor restaurant.

Doca de Santo Amaro

Tram #15 or train to Alcântara Mar

The intimate **Doca de Santo Amaro** nestles right beneath the humming traffic and rattling trains crossing Ponte 25 de Abril. This small, almost completely enclosed marina is filled with bobbing sailing boats and lined with tastefully converted warehouses. Its international cafés and restaurants are more pricey than usual for Lisbon, but the constant comings and goings on the Tejo provide plenty of free entertainment. Leaving Doca de Santo Amaro at its western side, you can pick up a pleasant riverside path that leads all the way to Belém, twenty minutes' walk away.

Ponte 25 de Abril

Resembling the Golden Gate Bridge in San Francisco, the hugely impressive **Ponte 25 de Abril** was opened in 1966 as a vital link between Lisbon and the southern banks of the Tejo. Around 2.3km in length, the bridge rises to 70m above the river, though its main pillars are nearly 200m tall. It was originally named Ponte de Salazar after the dictator who ruled Portugal from 1932 to 1968, but took its present name to mark the date of the revolution that overthrew Salazar's regime in 1974. You'll pass over it if you take a bus or train south of the Tejo.

Museu do Centro Científico e Cultural de Macau

Rua da Junqueira 30 • Tues–Sun 10am–6pm • €3, free Sun 10am–2pm • ⓦ cccm.pt • Tram #18

The **Museu do Centro Científico e Cultural de Macau** is dedicated to Portugal's trading links with the Orient and its former colony of Macau, which was handed back to Chinese rule in 1999. There are model boats and audio displays detailing early journeys, and exhibits of Chinese art from the sixteenth to the nineteenth centuries, including an impressive array of opium pipes and ivory boxes.

Belém and Ajuda

Tram #15 (signed Algés) from Praça da Figueira via Praça do Comércio (20min) or Oeiras train from Cais do Sodré

With its maritime history, attractive riverside location and slew of good museums, **Belém** (pronounced *Ber-layng*) is rightly one of Lisbon's most popular suburbs. It was from here that Vasco da Gama set off for India in 1497, and the vast **Mosteiro dos Jerónimos** was built here to honour his safe return. Along with the monastery and the landmark **Torre de Belém**, the suburb boasts a group of small museums, most of them set up under the Salazar regime during the Expo in 1940 – though the best of the lot, the **Berrardo Collection**, is a more recent addition. Just to the north of Belém is **Ajuda**, famed for its palace and ancient botanical gardens. When planning your trip, bear in mind that quite a few of the sights at Belém are closed on Mondays, and many are free on Sunday mornings.

Mosteiro dos Jerónimos

Praça do Império • Daily: May–Sept 10am–6.30pm; Oct–April 10am–5pm; restricted access to church on Sat mornings and during Mass • Free; cloisters €7, free on Sun 10am–2pm; combined ticket with Torre de Belém €10, plus Palácio da Ajuda €13 • ☎ 213 620 034, ⓦ mosteirojeronimos.pt • Tram #15

If there's one building that symbolizes the golden age of the Portuguese discoveries, it's the **Mosteiros dos Jerónimos**, which dominates the north side of the Praça do Império. Now a UNESCO World Heritage Site, the monastery and its adjacent church were built to fulfil a promise that Portugal's king, Dom Manuel, made should Vasco da Gama return safely from his inaugural voyage to India in 1498. The fact that the spices he returned with were more than enough to fund the building was, perhaps, a happy coincidence. Construction duly began in 1502 under the architect Diogo de Boitaca, who had made his name on the Igreja de Jesus in Setúbal, considered to be the first ever Manueline building.

Appropriately, **Vasco da Gama's tomb** now lies just inside the fantastically embellished entrance to the church. Crowned by an elaborate medley of statues, including Henry the Navigator, the 32-metre-high entrance was designed by the Spaniard João de Castilho, who took over the building of the church in 1517; the portal now forms the obligatory backdrop to weekend wedding photos. The church's interior is even more dazzling, displaying the maritime influences typical of Manueline architecture: the pillars are carved to resemble giant palms fanning out into a ceiling resembling

---

TRANSPORT AROUND BELÉM

A 45-minute circular Yellowbus hop-on, hop-off **minibus tour** (9.30am–5pm: May–Oct daily every 30min; Nov–April Mon–Fri hourly, Sat & Sun every 30min; €10) departs from in front of the Mosteiro dos Jerónimos, heading up to the palace at Ajuda then back via the Torre de Belém.

a delicate jungle canopy. The church also contains the **tomb of Luís de Camões** (1527–1570), Portugal's greatest poet and recorder of the discoveries, alongside the tombs of former presidents and dignataries.

Equally impressive is the adjacent monastery, gathered round sumptuously vaulted **cloisters** with nautical symbols carved into the honey-coloured limestone. You can still see the twelve niches where navigators stopped for confession before their voyages of exploration, until the Hieronymite monks were forced out during the dissolution of 1833. In 2007, the monastery was again influential in blessing future trade: the Treaty of Lisbon was signed here to cement the format of the European Union.

Museu de Arqueologia

Praça do Império • Tues–Sun 10am–6pm • €5, free Sun 10am–2pm • ⓦ mnarqueologia-ipmuseus.pt • Tram #15

The **Museu de Arqueologia** is housed in a neo-Manueline extension to the monastery, added in 1850. It has a small section on Egyptian antiquities, but concentrates on relatively dull Portuguese archeological finds, though there are a few fine Roman mosaics that were discovered in the Algarve, and its temporary exhibits can be rewarding.

Museu da Marinha

Praça do Império • Tues–Sun: May–Sept 10am–6pm; Oct–April 10am–5pm • €5 • ⓦ museumarinha.pt • Tram #15

With its entrance opposite the Centro Cultural de Belém, the enormous **Museu da Marinha** is large enough to display real vessels – among them fishing boats and sumptuous state barges, a couple of seaplanes and even some fire engines. Fascinating for kids and anyone interested in maritime history, it also houses various models of historical ships and some artefacts from Portugal's former colonies.

Torre de Belém

Tues–Sun: May–Sept 10am–6.30pm; Oct–April 10am–5.30pm • €5, free on Sun 10am–2pm; combined ticket with Mosteiro dos Jerónimos €10, plus Palácio da Ajuda €13 • ☎ 213 620 034, ⓦ torrebelem.pt

Reached via a narrow walkway and jutting into the river, the impressive **Torre de Belém** (Tower of Belém) has become an iconic symbol of Lisbon. It typifies the Manueline style that was prominent during the reign of Manuel, its windows and stairways embellished with arches and decorative symbols representing Portugal's explorations into the New World. Built as a fortress to defend the mouth of the River Tejo, it took five years to complete, though when it opened in 1520 it would have been near the centre of the river – the earthquake of 1755 shifted the river's course. Today, visitors are free to explore the tower's various levels, which include a terrace facing the river from where artillery would have been fired. You can then climb a very steep spiral staircase up four levels – each with a slightly different framed view of the river – to a top terrace where you get a blowy panorama of Belém. You can also duck into the dungeons, a low-ceilinged room used to store gunpowder and lock up prisoners.

Museu de Arte Popular

Avenida de Brasília • Wed–Sun 10am–1pm & 2–6pm • €2, free on Sun 10am–1pm • ☎ 213 011 282, ⓦ map.imc-ip.pt • Tram #15

In a space which feels slightly too large for its exhibits, the charming **Museu de Arte Popular** chronicles Portugal's folk art, from beautiful wood and cork toys to ceramics, rugs and fascinating traditional costumes, including amazing cloaks from the Trás-os-Montes region. Black-and-white photos and old films of folk costumes and dances complete the appeal.

Padrão dos Descobrimentos

Avenida da Brasília • Daily: May–Sept 9am–7pm; Oct–April 10am–6pm • €3 • ⓦ padraodosdescobrimentos.egeac.pt • Tram #15

You can't miss the **Padrão dos Descobrimentos** (Monument to the Discoveries), an angular concrete monument in the shape of a caravel. It was built in 1960 to

BELÉM & AJUDA

RESTAURANTS AND CAFÉS
Antiga Confeitaria
de Belém 1
Floresta Belém 2
Quadrante 3

—18— Tram

0   250
metres

Rio Tejo

commemorate the 500th anniversary of the death of Henry the Navigator, whose statue stands at the front of the monument, alongside other Portuguese legends. Inside is a temporary exhibition space, though you'll probably just head up in the lift to the top of the momument for some fine views of the river, and to look down on the giant marble mosaic map of the world that has been set into the pavement below.

Centro Cultural de Belém
Praça do Império • Ⓦ ccb.pt • Tram #15

Built to host Lisbon's Presidency of the European Union in 1992, the stylishy pink marble **Centro Cultural de Belém** is one of the city's main cultural centres and is home to the wonderful **Berardo Collection**, as well as putting on regular cultural exhibitions and concerts, plus live entertainment at the weekend. For the best views of its surroundings, drop into the café, whose garden esplanade overlooks the river and the Monument to the Discoveries.

Berardo Collection
Daily 10am–7pm • Free • ☎ 213 612 878, Ⓦ museuberardo.com • Tram #15

With its entrance via the first floor of the Centro Cultural de Belém, the **Berardo Collection** is a unique collection of modern art amassed by wealthy Madeiran Joe Berardo. Some of the most celebrated artists of the current and last centuries are displayed, though note that the collection is so large that not all of it can be shown at once, and two floors are given over to temporary exhibits. The best parts of the permanent collection (some of which should be on display) include Eric Fischl's giant panels of sunbathers; Andy Warhol's distinctive *Judy Garland*; and Chris Ofili's *Adoration of Captain Shit*, made with elephant dung. Portugal's Paula Rego is well represented, with works such as *The Past and Present* and *The Barn*, while Francis Bacon, David Hockney, Picasso, Miró, Man Ray, Max Ernst and Mark Rothko usually feature, along with various video artists.

Jardim do Ultramar and the Presidência da República
Jardim Entrance on Calçada do Galvão • Daily: May–Sept 10am–6pm; Oct–April 10am–5pm • €2 • **President's Palace** Entrance on Praça Afonso de Albuquerque • Tours Sat 11am–4pm, Sun 2.30–4pm • €5 • Ⓦ museu.presidencia.pt • Tram #15

The leafy **Jardim do Ultramar** is a green oasis with hothouses, ponds and towering palms, a lovely place for a shady walk. In the southeastern corner of the garden lies the Portuguese President's official residence, the pink **Presidência da República**, which is open for guided visits at weekends, when the public can look round its lavish state rooms.

Museu dos Coches
Praça Afonso de Albuquerque • Tues–Sun 10am–6pm • €5, free on Sun 10am–2pm • Ⓦ museudoscoches.pt • Tram #15

Recently rehoused in a modern building, the **Museu dos Coches** (Coach Museum) was opened in 1905 on the initiative of the queen, Dona Amélia, and contains one of the largest collections of carriages and saddlery in the world. The sumptuously decorated and ornate coaches date from the sixteenth to nineteenth centuries, including a very rare coach designed for King Felipe I (Spain's King Philip II). The collection also includes sedan chairs and children's buggies.

Museu da Electricidade
Avenida de Brasília • Tues–Sun 10am–6pm • Free except for temporary exhibits • ☎ 213 028 190 • Tram #15

Down by the riverside, the extraordinary redbrick **Museu da Electricidade** is an early twentieth-century electricity generating station with cathedral-like windows. The museum's highlights include its enormous original generators, steam turbines and winches – all looking like something out of a science-fiction film. It also makes a fascinating backdrop for regular temporary exhibitions.

FESTA DE SANTO ANTÓNIO, ALFAMA (P.65) >

Palácio Nacional da Ajuda

Largo da Ajuda • **Palácio** Mon, Tues & Thurs–Sun 10am–5.30pm • €5, free on Sun 10am–2pm; combined ticket with Torre de Belém €10, plus Mosteiro dos Jerónimos €13 • **Jardim Botânico d'Ajuda** Daily: May–Sept 9am–8pm; Oct–April 9am–7pm • €2 • Tram #18 from Praça do Comércio, or bus #729 from central Belém or Calçada da Ajuda

The massive nineteenth-century **Palácio Nacional da Ajuda** sits on a hillside above Belém. The Portuguese royal family ordered its construction in 1802, but it was incomplete when they were forced to flee to Brazil during the invasion of Napoleon's troops in 1807. Despite this, Dom João moved into the palace when he returned to Portugal in 1821. Most of what you see today was commissioned by João's granddaughter Dona Maria II and Dom Ferdinand, and gives an eye-popping insight into the opulent life the royals lived: the queen could warm her feet on a polar-bearskin rug when she got out of bed; there's an enormous throne and ballroom, while the banqueting hall, full of crystal chandeliers, is highly impressive. Opposite the palace, the attractive **Jardim Botânico d'Ajuda** is one of the city's oldest botanical gardens – a fine example of formal Portuguese gardening boasting some great views over Belém.

North Lisbon

On a steep slope to the north of the centre, **Parque Eduardo VII** is the city's main park, whose views and tropical greenhouses make for a pleasant escape from the bustle of the city. Northwest of the park, the **Fundação Calouste Gulbenkian** is Portugal's premier cultural centre, combining one of Europe's richest art collections at the Museu Gulbenkian with Portuguese contemporary art at the Centro de Arte Moderna. Beyond are further attractions at Campo Pequeno's **Praça de Touros** (bullring) and the **Jardim Zoológico**, the city's zoo, which lies around 2km north west of the Gulbenkian.

Parque Eduardo VII

Estufa fria Daily: April–Sept 9am–6pm; Oct–March 9am–5pm • **Estufa Quente** closes 30min earlier • €3.10 • Ⓜ Parque or Marquês de Pombal

The sloping **Parque Eduardo VII**, with its formally laid out lawns and shrubs, was named in honour of the British King Edward VII when he visited the city in 1903. Its main attraction is the **Estufas** (hothouses), one *quente* (hot) planthouse and one *fria* (cool), filled with tropical plants, pools, palms and cacti. Beyond the hothouses, the top of the park has a viewing platform with commanding views over the city: you can walk over the grassy hillock beyond (with its olive trees, lake and café) to the Gulbenkian museum (see below).

Fundação Calouste Gulbenkian

Avenida de Berna • Ⓦ gulbenkian.pt • Ⓜ Praça de Espanha or São Sebastião

The **Fundação Calouste Gulbenkian** is Portugal's foremost cultural organization, the legacy of oil magnate Calouste Gulbenkian (see box opposite). The centrepiece to his foundation is this purpose-built arts complex, built in the late 1960s within neatly landscaped grounds. It hosts concerts, performances and temporary exhibitions (check the website for details), though most people come to see the **Museu Gulbenkian**, where the magnate's amazing art collection includes priceless artworks from around the world, dating from ancient Egyptian times to the late twentieth century. Across the gardens, the **Centro de Arte Moderna** has more contemporary art, mostly from Portugal but also featuring international names.

Museu Gulbenkian

Tues–Sun 10am–5.45pm • €4, combined ticket with Museu de Arte Moderna €7, free on Sun • Ⓦ museu.gulbenkian.pt

The biggest joy about the **Museu Gulbenkian** is the chance it offers to compare and contrast pieces of art from so many places in the world and from so many different

CALOUSTE GULBENKIAN

Calouste Sarkis Gulbenkian was the Roman Abramovich of his era, making his millions from oil but investing in the world's best art rather than footballers. Born of wealthy Armenian parents in Istanbul in 1869, he followed his father into the oil industry and became oil consultant to the Ottoman court. In 1911 he set up the Oil Petroleum Company, raking in 5 percent of the company's vast profits, most of which he invested in England where he chose to live. During World War II, his Turkish background made him unwelcome in Britain, so Gulbenkian moved to Portugal, which offered him tax-free status and a secure home. By his death in 1955, he had accumulated one of the best private art collections in the world. His dying wish was that all his collection should be displayed in one place, and this was granted in 1969 – a century after his birth – with the opening of the Museu Calouste Gulbenkian. The museum continues to buy works of art with his funds to this day, much of it for the Centro de Arte Moderna, which was opened in 1984.

periods of history. The diverse collection ranges from ancient Egytian sculptures to twentieth-century Lalique jewellery, via works by heavyweights such as Manet, Monet, Renoir, Turner and Rembrandt.

You start off in the small **Egyptian room** displaying art from the Old Empire (c.2700 BC) up to the Roman era, followed by the **Greco-Roman room** which features amazingly preserved glassware, jewellery and coins. Then move to the **Eastern Islamic arts** section with its Turkish tiles, mosque lamps, sumptuously illustrated manuscripts and fine carpets, while art from the **Far East** includes Chinese porcelain and stunning fourteenth-century lacquerwork from Japan.

The highlight, however, is the **painting collection** – a kind of romp through some of the best art from the European schools, including Flemish masters from the fifteenth century, Rubens' graphic *The Love of the Centaurs* (1635) and eighteenth-century works by Fragonard, Guardi and Gainsborough – in particular the stunning *Portrait of Mrs Lowndes-Stone*. The big names of nineteenth- to twentieth-century France (Degas, Millet) are all represented, as are Sargent and Turner: don't miss his vivid *Wreck of a Transport Ship* (1810).

Leave time, too, to explore the **Sèvres porcelain**, Louis XV and Louis XVI furniture and assorted Italian tapestries and textiles. The final room features the amazing **Art Nouveau jewellery** of René Lalique (1860–1945); the highlight is the fantastical *Peitoral-libélula* (Dragonfly breastpiece) brooch, half-woman, half-dragonfly, decorated with enamel work, gold, diamonds and moonstones.

Centro de Arte Moderna José Azeredo Perdigão

Entrance also on Rua Dr Nicolau de Bettencourt • Tues–Sun 10am–5.45pm • €4, combined ticket with Museu de Arte Moderna €7, free on Sun • ⓦ cam.gulbenkian.pt

The **Centro de Arte Moderna** can be reached by walking across the gardens from the Museu Calouste Gulbenkian, via an impressive array of sculptures (including a Henry Moore). Inside, the collection embraces Pop Art, installations and sculpture – some witty, some baffling, but all thought-provoking. Twentieth-century Portuguese artists feature strongly: look out for the Lisbon scenes by **Carlos Botelho** (1899–1982), and **Paula Rego**'s portraits: her *Mãe* is outstanding (see box, p.109). Other big names in Portugal are **Almada Negreiros** (1873–1970), whose self-portrait is set in the café *A Brasileira* and the Futurist colours of **Amadeu de Sousa Cardoso** (1887–1918). Powerful photos by **Fernando Lemos** also feature, as do pieces from major international artists such as David Hockney and Antony Gormley, though these are sometimes lent to other museums.

Next to the museum, there's a perennially popular self-service restaurant, particularly good for vegetarians.

1 Praça de Touros

Campo Pequeno • Ⓦ campopequeno.com • Ⓜ Campo Pequeno

Built in 1892, the **Praça de Touros do Campo Pequeno** is an impressive Moorish-style bullring seating nine thousand spectators, and Portuguese bullfighting takes place weekly from Easter to September. Surrounded by a ring of lively cafés and restaurants, the bullring also hosts visiting circuses, concerts and occasional events, while beneath it is an underground shopping and cinema complex. Check the website for events and to buy tickets.

Jardim Zoológico

Praça Marechal Humberto Delgado • Daily: March–Sept 10am–8pm; Oct–Feb 10am–6pm • **Reptile house and cable car** Daily 11am until 30min before closing time • **Amusement park** Daily 11am until 60min before closing time • €18, under-12s €12.50 • Ⓦ zoolisboa.pt • Ⓜ Jardim Zoológico

Opened in 1884, the **Jardim Zoológico** has been greatly improved over recent years and now makes for an enjoyable day out, especially if you have children. There's a small cable car, which offers a fine aerial view of many of the enclosures, a reptile house, a boating lake and various animal "shows" – sea lions, macaws and the like – as further diversions. Just by the entrance, the **Animax** amusement park has further rides to rid parents of a few euros.

Parque das Nações

The former Expo 98 site, **Parque das Nações** – the Park of Nations – lies on the northeastern fringes of the city, and remains a huge attraction for Lisboetas who come here en masse at weekends – it's also a popular riverfront residential area. The main highlight is the **Oceanário** (Oceanarium), though there are plenty of other attractions, from water gardens to a cable car, as well as bars, shops and restaurants, many overlooking Olivais docks and the 17-kilometre-long Vasco da Gama bridge. The park is also home to a couple of venues that host major international bands and sporting events: the **Pavilhão Atlântico** (Atlantic Pavilion) is Portugal's largest indoor arena; while the elegant **Pavilhão de Portugal** (Portugal Pavilion), with its distinctive, sagging concrete roof, is a multipurpose arena designed by Álvaro Siza Vieira, Portugal's best-known architect.

Oceanário de Lisboa

Esplanada Dom Carlos I • Daily: May–Sept 10am–8pm; Oct–April 10am–7pm • €13, under-12s €9 • Ⓦ oceanario.pt

Designed by Peter Chermayeff and resembling a set from a James Bond film, the **Oceanário de Lisboa** is one of Europe's best and largest oceanariums, containing around eight thousand fish and marine animals. Its main feature is the enormous central tank, the size of four Olympic-sized swimming pools, which you can look into from different levels to get close-up views of the sharks and rays. Perhaps even more impressive are the re-creations of various ocean ecosystems, such as the Antarctic tank containing frolicking penguins, and the Pacific tank, where otters bob about and play in the rock pools. These

---

TRANSPORT AROUND THE PARQUE

Both the metro and bus #28 from Praça do Comércio leave you in the **Estação do Oriente**, an impressive glass-and-concrete bus and train interchange designed by Spanish architect Santiago Calatrava. From the station, head through the Vasco da Gama shopping centre to the main **Posto de Informação** (daily 10am–8pm; Oct–April until 7pm; ☏ 218 919 333, Ⓦ portaldasnacoes.pt), which has details of current events.

A **road train** (hourly: May–Sept daily 10am–7.30pm; Oct–April Sat & Sun 10am–6pm; €4) trundles anticlockwise round the whole park, starting and finishing in front of the Pavilhão Atlântico. From here, you can also **rent bikes** (from around €5 an hour), a good way to get round the flat, traffic-free lanes. It is not too taxing, however, to walk to the principal attractions, or you can take the scenic cable car (see p.88).

PARQUE DAS NAÇÕES

RUA JOÃO PINTO RIBEIRO · AVENIDA DA · PRAÇA DO VENTUROSO · BOA ESPERANÇA · ROTUNDA DOS VICE-REIS · AVENIDA DA BOA ESPERANÇA

Parque do Tejo

Torre Vasco da Gama

ESTRADA DE MOÇAMBIQUE

R. MANUEL DR. DR. RUI GOMES DE OLIVEIRA

RUA MANUEL

RUA CONSELHEIRO LOPO VEZ

PASSEIO DO CANTÁRICO

AVENIDA DOM JOÃO II

AVENIDA DO ATLÂNTICO

RUA DO MAR A CHINA

RUA DO POLO NORTE

ALAMEDA DOS OCEANOS

RUA DO ROJADOR

RUA DO ROJADOR

RUA DA PIMENTA

Garcia de Orta Gardens

Teleférico

Feira Internacional de Lisboa (FIL)

Pavilhão Atlântico

Bus Station

VIA RECÍPROCA

Oriente (M)

Estação do Oriente

AVENIDA DO ÍNDICO

Centro Vasco da Gama

Bike Hire

ⓘ

Nautical Centre

AVENIDA DE BERLIM

AVENIDA DO PACÍFICO

Rhizone ⊙

River Gate

Council of Ministers

Pavilhão de Portugal

RUA DO CARIBE

PASSEIO DO BÁLTICO

AVENIDA DOM JOÃO II

RUA DA CENTIEIRA

ALAMEDA DOS OCEANOS

CAIS PORTUGUÊS

Olivais Dock

Rio Tejo

Casino

RUA DO MAR DO NORTE

N

Oceanário

RUA DO POLO SUL

AVENIDA DE PÁDUA

ESPLANDA DOM CARLOS I

Pavilhão do Conhecimento Ciência Viva

Oceanário Ticket Office

PASSEIO DE NEPTUNO

PRAÇA PRÍNCIPE PERFEITO

Jardins da Água

PASSEIO DE ULISSES

Teatro Camões

RUA PEDRO E INÊS

0 ——— 100
metres

■ **BARS AND CLUBS**
Azul Profundo   **3**
Havana   **1**
República da Cerveja   **2**

● **RESTAURANTS**
D'Bacalhau   **1**
Senhor Peixe   **2**

■ **ACCOMMODATION**
Pousada da Juventude
  Parque das Nações   **1**

1

areas are separated from the main tank by invisible acrylic sheets, which give the impression that all the marine creatures are swimming together in the same space. On the darkened lower level, smaller tanks contain shoals of brightly coloured tropical fish and other warm-water creatures. Find a window free of the school parties and the whole experience becomes the closest you'll get to deep-sea diving without getting wet.

Pavilhão do Conhecimento Ciência Viva

Alameda dos Oceanos · Tues–Fri 10am–6pm, Sat & Sun 11am–7pm, last entry 1hr before closing · €7, under-17s €4 · ⓦ pavconhecimento.pt

The **Pavilhão do Conhecimento Ciência Viva** (Knowledge Pavilion for Live Science) hosts excellent temporary exhibitions on subjects such as 3D animation and the latest computer technology, and is usually bustling with school parties. The permanent interactive exhibits – such as creating a vortex in water, a film of detergent the size of a baby's blanket or immobilizing shadows – are particularly good and there's also a cybercafé offering free internet access.

The cable car

Mid-June to mid-Sept Mon–Fri 11am–8pm, Sat & Sun 10am–8pm; mid-Sept–mid-June daily 10am–7pm; €4 one way, €6 return

The ski-lift-style **cable car** rises up to 20m as it shuttles you across Olivais docks, with commanding views en route. The south end starts near the **Jardim da Água** (Water Garden), crisscrossed by ponds linked by stepping stones, with enough fountains, water gadgets and pumps to keep kids occupied for hours. The northern end drops you just beyond the **Jardim Garcia de Orta**, a leafy waterside garden displaying plant species from Portugal's former colonies. The garden is overlooked by the **Torre Vasco da Gama**, Lisbon's tallest structure at 145m, which was once part of an oil refinery and now houses a five-star hotel.

ARRIVAL AND DEPARTURE	**LISBON**

BY AIR

The airport (☏ 218 413 700, ⓦ ana.pt) lies around 9km north of the city centre and has a tourist office (daily 7am–midnight; ☏ 218 450 660), ATMs, 24-hour exchange bureau and car rental agencies.

GETTING TO/FROM THE CENTRE

By taxi The easiest way into the city centre is by taxi and, depending on traffic conditions, a journey to Rossio should take around 20 minutes and cost around €15, plus €2.50 extra for baggage: note that fares are slightly higher between 10pm and 6am, at weekends and on public holidays. The tourist office at the airport sells taxi vouchers, priced according to the zone or destination you are travelling to. The vouchers allow you to jump the airport taxi queue, but otherwise cost more than a metered ride.

By metro Aeroporto station is at the far end of the red Oriente metro line. To get to the city centre (around 25 minutes €1.40) you'll need to change trains at either Alameda or Saldanha.

By bus Aerobus #1 (ⓦ yellowbustours.com; every 20–30min from 7am–11pm; €3.55, tickets valid all day on city buses) departs from outside the terminal and runs to Praça do Marquês de Pombal, Praça dos Restauradores, Rossio, Praça do Comércio and Cais do Sodré train station. Aerobus #2 runs to Sete Rios (for the bus station) and to the financial centre. The cheaper local bus #44 (every

10–15min from 6am–midnight; €1.75) leaves from outside the terminal to Praça dos Restauradores and Cais do Sodré station, though this is less convenient if you have a lot of luggage.

BY BUS

Sete Rios The main bus station is opposite the zoo at Sete Rios (ⓦ Jardim Zoológico on the Gaivota line), 2.5km north of Rossio, and has an information office that can help with all bus arrival and departure details (☏ 707 223 344, ⓦ rede-expressos.pt). You can usually buy tickets if you turn up half an hour or so in advance, though for the summer express services to the Algarve and Alentejo coast it's best to book a seat (through any travel agent) a day in advance. Destinations Albufeira (6–8 daily; 3hr 10min); Coimbra (at least hourly; 2hr 20min); Faro (5–6 daily; 3hr 45min); Porto (hourly; 3hr 30min).

BY CAR

Parking If you are driving, head straight for an official car park: central locations include the underground ones at Restauradores; Parque Eduardo VII; Parking Berna on Rua Marquês de Sá da Bandeira near the Gulbenkian; and the Amoreiras complex on Avenida Engenheiro Duarte Pacheco. Expect to pay around €2 an hour or €12 per day. Wherever you park, do not leave valuables inside: the break-in rate is extremely high.

BY TRAIN
INTERNATIONAL AND LONG-DISTANCE TRAINS

Estação Santa Apolónia All international and most long-distance trains arrive at Estação Santa Apolónia (fares and timetable info on ☎808 208 208, ⓦcp.pt), which is on the Gaivota metro line; you can take any bus heading west from outside the station to Praça do Comércio (a 15min walk). At the station there's a helpful information office (Tues–Sat 7.30am–1pm; ☎218 821 606) and an exchange bureau. Most trains also call at Oriente station at Parque das Nações, which is on the red Oriente metro line and more convenient for the airport and for the north or east of Lisbon. There are bus links to towns north and south of the Tejo from here.

Destinations Coimbra (hourly; 2hr–2hr 50min); Faro (2–3 daily; 3hr 20min); Madrid (1 daily; 9hr 30min); Porto (hourly; 2hr 50min–3hr 20min).

LOCAL TRAINS

Estação do Rossio Local trains – from Sintra or Queluz via Sete Rios, by the main bus station – emerge right in the heart of the city at Estação do Rossio (☎213 433 747), a mock-Manueline complex with the train platforms an escalator ride above street-level entrance.

Cais do Sodré Services from Cascais and Estoril arrive at the other local station, Cais do Sodré (☎213 424 780), on the Caravela metro line – you can either walk the 500m east along the waterfront to Praça do Comércio or take any of the buses heading in that direction.

GETTING AROUND

Most places of interest are within easy walking distance of each other, though it's fun to use Lisbon's public transport system at some stage. As well as the tram, bus, *elevador* (funicular), ferry or metro, taxis are widely used and are among the cheapest in Europe. Although Lisbon ranks as one of the safer European cities, it does have its share of pickpockets, so take special care of your belongings when using the metro and buses.

Lisbon metro map

1

BUYING TICKETS

Buses, trams and *elevadores* in the city are operated by Carris (☎ 213 613 000, ⊛ carris.pt), while the metro is run by a separate company (☎ 213 558 457, ⊛ metrolisboa.pt). You can just buy a single ticket (*bilhete simples*, €1.80 for buses, €2.85 for trams, or €1.40 for the metro: €3.60 return for *elevadores*) each time you ride, but it's much better value to buy one of the available travel passes.

Passes A day-pass (*bilhete 24 horas rede* €6) allows unlimited travel on buses, trams, *elevadores* and the metro until midnight of that day – the first time you buy one, you'll also need to pay for a Viva Viagem card (€0.50), which you can recharge each day or load up with credits for up to €15, after which €1.25 is deducted for each journey by bus or metro. Cards and passes are available at main metro stations.

BY TRAM, ELEVADOR AND BUS

Most trams, buses and *elevadores* run every ten to fifteen minutes throughout the day, from around 6.30am to midnight: stops are indicated by a sign marked *paragem*, which carries route details.

Trams (*eléctricos*) These run on five routes, trundling round the city's oldest and steepest streets, and are worth taking for the sheer fun of it. The most famous route is #28, which runs from Martim Moniz to Prazeres: try and get on at either terminal as the most interesting stretch – from São Vicente to the Estrela gardens via the Alfama and the Baixa – has become so popular that standing-room-only is the norm.

Buses (*autocarros*) These run just about everywhere in the Lisbon area, filling in the gaps to reach the more outlying attractions. Clubbers can take advantage of the *Madrugada* ("Dawn Service") night buses, which operate 12.30–5am. Most night services run to and from Cais do Sodré station, including the useful #201 to the docks via Santos.

Elevadores The three funicular railways and one street lift – each known as an *elevador* – offer quick access up to Lisbon's highest hills and the Bairro Alto (see box, p.71).

BY CAR

Apart from Saturday afternoons and Sundays, when the city is quiet, driving round Lisbon is best avoided, though it can be useful to hire a car to visit outlying sights, such as Sintra.

Parking is very difficult in central Lisbon, so it's best to head for one of the central underground car parks (see p.88). Pay-and-display spots on the street get snapped up quickly and some of the local unemployed get by on tips for guiding drivers into empty spots.

BY TAXI

Fares Lisbon's cream taxis are inexpensive, as long as your destination is within the city limits; there's a minimum charge of €3.25 and an average ride across town will cost around €8–13. Fares are twenty percent higher from 10pm to 6am, at weekends and on public holidays. All taxis have meters, which should be switched on, and tips are not expected.

Taxi ranks Outside the rush hour taxis can be hailed quite easily in the street, or alternatively head for a taxi rank, found outside the stations, at Rossio, at the southern end of Avenida da Liberdade, and at Estação Fluvial – you can expect to queue during morning and evening rush hours. At night, your best bet is to ask a restaurant or bar to call a cab for you, or phone yourself (€1 extra): try Rádio Taxis ☎ 218 119 000; Autocoope ☎ 217 996 460; or Teletáxi ☎ 218 111 100.

BY METRO AND LOCAL TRAIN

Metro The most central of Lisbon's metro (Metropolitano) stations are those at Restauradores, Rossio and Baixa-Chiado. Although it's unlikely that you'll need to stray from the central zone, the metro is the quickest way to reach outlying sights, including the airport, the Gulbenkian museum, the zoo, bus station and the Oceanarium. The metro runs daily from 6.30am to 1am.

Local trains The local train line from Cais do Sodré station runs west along the coast to Belém (€1.55), or to Estoril and Cascais (€2.45 to either). Other local trains depart from the central Rossio station to Queluz (€1.55) and Sintra (€2.45 one way).

BY FERRY

Ferries (⊛ transtejo.pt) cross the Rio Tejo at various points, offering terrific views of Lisbon. The most useful and picturesque route is from Cais do Sodré to Cacilhas (every 15min; daily 5.40am–2.30am; €1.20). Another attractive route runs from Belém to Porto Brandão and Trafaria (every 30min–1hr; Mon–Sat 6.30am–11.30pm, Sun 7.30am–11.30pm; €1.15), from where you can catch buses to Caparica.

TRAM ROUTES

#12 runs from Praça da Figueira to Largo Martim Moniz via the Alfama.
#15 A modern "supertram" from Praça da Figueira to Algés via Belém; buy tickets in advance or take exact change for automatic ticket machines.
#18 from Rua da Alfândega via Praça do Comércio and Cais do Sodré to the Palácio da Ajuda.
#25 from Rua da Alfândega to Campo Ourique via Praça do Comércio, Cais do Sodré, Lapa and Estrela.
#28 from Largo Martim Moniz to Prazeres, via the Alfama, Baixa, Chiado, São Bento and Estrela.

THE CARTÃO LISBOA

If you're planning some serious sightseeing, consider buying a **Cartão Lisboa** (Lisbon Card; €18.50 for one day, €31.50 for two, or €39 for three), which entitles you to unlimited rides on the city's buses, trams, metro and *elevadores* plus entry to around 25 museums, including the Gulbenkian and Museu de Arte Antigua, as well as discounts of around 25 to 50 percent at other sights and attractions. It's available from all the main tourist offices, including the one in the airport.

INFORMATION

Lisbon Welcome Centre The main Lisbon tourist office, the Lisbon Welcome Centre, is down by the riverfront in Praça do Comércio (daily 9am–8pm; ☎ 210 312 810, ⓦ visitlisboa.com) and can supply accommodation lists, bus timetables and maps.

Y Lisboa The Y Lisboa tourist office on Rua Jardim do Regedor 50 (daily 10am–8pm; ☎ 213 472 134), to the east of Praça dos Restauradores, has information aimed at young and student travellers.

Portuguese tourist board On the western side of Praça dos Restauradores in the Palácio da Foz, the main Portuguese tourist board (daily 9am–8pm; ☎ 213 463 314, ⓦ visitportugal.com) is useful for information on destinations outside Lisbon.

"Ask Me" In summer, smaller "Ask Me" kiosks are dotted round town near the main tourist sights, such as on Rua Augusta, Baixa, and opposite Belém's Mosteiro dos Jerónimos.

TOURS

Bus tours Yellow buses (☎ 213 582 334, ⓦ yellowbustours.com) operates two circular hop-on, hop-off open-top bus trips: the two-hour Circuito Tejo (May–Oct every 30min from 9.15am–6.45pm; Nov–April every 45min from 9.45am–5.45pm; €15) visits Lisbon's main sites, with clearly marked stops across the city; while the Olisipo tour (every 45min: May–Oct from 10am–7pm; Nov–April from 10am–5pm; €15; 1hr 45min) runs from Praça do Comércio to Parque das Nações via the Alfama and Campo Pequeno.

River cruises Two-and-a-half-hour cruises up the Rio Tejo depart from Praça do Comércio's Estação Fluvial (April–Nov daily at 3pm; €20; ☎ 808 203050, ⓦ transtejo.pt). The price includes a drink and a bilingual commentary, with stops at Parque das Nações and Belém (tide permitting).

Tram tours Eléctrico das Colinas (Hills Tour; July–Sept every 20min from 10am–7pm; Oct–June every 30min

9.45am–6.15pm; €18; ☎ 213 613 010, ⓦ yellowbustours.com) takes passengers on an eighty-minute ride in an antique tram from Praça do Comércio, around Alfama, Chiado and São Bento.

Walks Highly recommended, themed two-hour guided walks are offered by Lisbon Walker (☎ 218 861 840, ⓦ lisbonwalker.com; €15). Departing daily from Praça do Comércio at 10am and 2.30pm, they give expert insight into the quirkier aspects of the city's sights including legends, secret histories and spies.

Wine tours For an excellent introduction to local wines, Vitis-route (☎ 912 002 847, ⓦ vitis-route.com) will pick you up from your hotel and take you to two or three vineyards in the Lisbon area for tastings. As well as the expert knowledge of vintner João, the price (around €150 per person) includes drinks, two meals and a visit to local villages.

ACCOMMODATION

Lisbon has no shortage of sumptuous places to stay, including historic buildings and palaces. It also has a reputation for some excellent independent hostels. Between June and September, rooms can be harder to find without an **advance reservation** and prices are at their highest – though August can be less expensive as many people head for the beach. Many of Lisbon's top **hotels** are lined up along and around the Avenida da Liberdade, while the Baixa and the Chiado also have a fair selection of more upmarket places which could not be more central. The most atmospheric part of town is around the Alfama and the castle, while the Bairro Alto is ideal for nightlife, but can be noisy after dark.

BAIXA AND CHIADO

Borges Rua Garrett 108 ☎ 213 461 951, ⓦ lisbonhotelborges.com; ⓜ Baixa-Chiado; map p.63. This is a traditional three-star hotel in a great position for Chiado's shops and cafés. Double or triple rooms are plain and small but good value, though the place often fills with tour groups. **€90**

⭐ **Chiado** Rua Nova do Almada 114 ☎ 213 256 100, ⓦ hoteldochiado.com; ⓜ Baixa-Chiado; map p.63. Stylish hotel designed by Álvaro Siza Vieira – the architect responsible for the Chiado redevelopment – with Eastern-inspired interior decor. The cheapest rooms lack much of a view, but the best ones have terraces with stunning castle vistas, a view you get from the bar terrace too. Rooms are

1

not huge but are plush and contemporary. Limited parking available. **€125**

Florescente Rua das Portas de Santo Antão 99 ☎213 426 609, ⓦ residencialflorescente.com; ⓜ Restauradores; map p.63. One of this pedestrianized street's best-value options, where many of the rooms are spick-and-span and come with TV, a/c and small bathroom. However, others are windowless and less appealing, and be prepared for street noise. Internet access on request. **€65**

Gerês Calçada da Garcia 6 ☎218 810 497, ⓦ pensao geres.com; ⓜ Rossio; map p.63. The beautifully tiled entrance hall sets the tone in one of the city's more atmospheric central guesthouses, located on a steep side-street just off the Rossio. The variously sized rooms are simply furnished and all have TVs and showers. There's also internet access on request. No breakfast. **€55**

Insulana Rua da Assunção 52 ☎213 427 625, ⓦ insulana.net; ⓜ Baixa-Chiado; map p.63. On the top floor of an old Baixa building, above a series of shops, this decent guesthouse has smart en-suite rooms with satellite TV. The bar overlooks a quiet pedestrianized street. **€65**

Lisboa Tejo Rua dos Condes de Monsanto 2 ☎218 866 182, ⓦ evidenciatejohotel-lisbon.com; ⓜ Rossio; map p.63. This historic Baixa townhouse has been given a superb makeover, and now combines bare brickwork with cutting-edge design. Wood-floored rooms aren't huge but come with modems and minibars, and downstairs is a boutiquey, Gaudí-inspired bar. **€135**

Metrópole Rossio 30 ☎213 219 030, ⓦ almeidahotels .com; ⓜ Rossio; map p.63. Centrally located early-twentieth century hotel, with most of the comfortable rooms (as well as the airy lounge bar) offering superb views over Rossio and the castle. However, you pay for the location and the square can be pretty noisy at night. **€185**

VIP Executive Suites Eden Praça dos Restauradores 24 ☎213 216 600, ⓦ viphotels.com; ⓜ Restauradores; map p.63. Compact studios and apartments sleeping up to four people, in the impressively converted Eden Theatre. Get a ninth-floor apartment with a balcony and you'll have the best views and be just below the rooftop pool and breakfast bar. All studios come with dishwashers, microwaves and satellite TV. Disabled access. Studios **€100**

ALFAMA AND CASTELO

Ninho das Águias Costa do Castelo 74 ☎218 854 070; map p.65. Beautifully sited, simple guesthouse with a view-laden terrace garden on the street looping around

the castle – this is one of the most popular budget options in Lisbon, so book well in advance. Climb up the staircase and past the birdcages to the rooms, which are bright but spartan, though avoid the dingy basement room. Those with a private bath cost €5 more. No breakfast. **€50**

Solar do Castelo Rua das Cozinhas 2 ☎218 870 909, ⓦ heritage.pt; map p.65. Boutique hotel in a historic eighteenth-century mansion abutting the castle walls on the site of the former palace kitchens. Just fourteen bright, modern rooms cluster round a tranquil Moorish courtyard, where breakfast is served in summer. **€200**

Solar dos Mouros Rua do Milagre de Santo António 6 ☎218 854 940, ⓦ solardosmouros.com; map p.65. A tall, beautifully renovated townhouse done out in a contemporary style with its own bar. Each of the twelve rooms offers superb views of the river or castle and comes with DVD player and a/c. There's plenty of modern art to enjoy if you tire of the view. Breakfast extra. **€130**

BAIRRO ALTO AND AROUND

Belver Príncipe Real Rua da Alegria 53 ☎213 407 350, ⓦ belverhotels.com; map pp.72–73. This small four-star sits on a quiet street just below the Bairro Alto. Just eighteen rooms, each with modern decor and some with balconies – the best ones boast superb city views. If your budget can stretch, go for the top-floor suite with stunning vistas (€140). **€80**

Casa de São Mamede Rua da Escola Politécnica 159 ☎213 963 166, ⓦ casadesaomamede.pt; map pp.72–73. On a busy road, this superb seventeenth-century townhouse comes with period fittings, a bright breakfast room and even a grand stained-glass window. The rooms are rather ordinary but all have TV and a/c. Ask about special deals for families, too. **€90**

Globo Rua do Teixeira 37 ☎213 462 279, ⓦ blueangel hotel.com; map pp.72–73. Located in an attractive town-house with a bar/TV room. The budget rooms are simple but clean and reasonably large (though those at the top are a little cramped and some have no windows). The best rooms have showers and views. No breakfast. **€40**

Londres Rua Dom Pedro V 53 ☎213 462 203, ⓦ pensaolondres.com.pt; map pp.72–73. This wonder-ful old building has soaring ceilings and a wide range of pleasant rooms with satellite TV, spread across four floors; the best ones have their own showers (**€70**), while rooms 402, 409 or 411 have fine city views. Also has rooms sleeping three or four. **€40**

OUR FIVE FAVOURITE PLACES TO STAY

Best views: *Ninho das Águias* (see p.92)   **Retro chic**: *Heritage Liberdade* (see p.93)

Boutique: *Chiado* (see p.91)   **Eco-friendly**: *Inspira Santa Marta* (see p.93)

Budget: *The Independente* (see p.93)

LX Boutique Rua do Alecrim 12 ☎ 213 474 394, ⓦ lxboutiquehotel.pt; ⓜ Cais do Sodré; map pp.72–73. A tasteful makeover of an old townhouse has made *LX Boutique* into a popular small hotel with its own chic restaurant. The floors are all named after Portuguese poets and fado singers, and the rooms are stylish and individual, with shutters and tasteful lighting – try and get one with river views rather than looking over the unsalubrious Rua Nova do Carvalho. **€100**

★ **The Independente** Rua de São Pedro de Alcântara 81 ☎ 213 461 381, ⓦ theindependente.pt; map pp.72–73. Part hostel and part boutique hotel, this fantastic old building was once the Socialist Party HQ and Swiss Embassy and has far-reaching views over Lisbon. The lower floors house dorms (sleeping 6–12), each with towering ceiling, while up the light internal stairwell there are quirky double rooms in the roof spaces, the best with balconies offering river views. There's a downstairs bar and patio and the place offers a range of activities, from bar crawls and guided walks to cycle hire. Dorm beds **€12**; doubles **€50**

AVENIDA DA LIBERDADE AND AROUND

Alegria Praça Alegria 12 ☎ 213 220 670, ⓦ alegrianet .com; ⓜ Avenida; map pp.60–61. A friendly, simple place in a great position, on a leafy square (and next to a police station). The spacious, brightly coloured rooms all have TV, but expect some street noise. No breakfast. **€78**

Britania Rua Rodrigues Sampaio 17 ☎ 213 155 016, ⓦ heritage.pt; ⓜ Avenida; map pp.60–61. Designed in the 1940s by influential architect Cassiano Branco, this is an Art Deco gem with huge airy rooms, each with traditional cork flooring and marble-clad bathroom. The hotel interior, with library and bar, has been declared of national architectural importance – and the service is friendly and pleasant too. **€175**

Dom Carlos Parque Av Duque de Loulé 121 ☎ 213 512 590, ⓦ domcarloshoteis.com; ⓜ Marquês de Pombal; map pp.60–61. This is a decent three-star option in a good position near the park, with fair-sized rooms, all with bath, cable TV and minibar. There's also a downstairs bar with plasma TVs. Garage parking. **€116**

Dom Sancho I Av da Liberdade 202 ☎ 213 513 160, ⓦ hoteldomsancholisbon.com; ⓜ Avenida; map pp.60–61. One of the few inexpensive options right on the Avenida, set in a grand old mansion with high ceilings and decorative cornices. The large en-suite rooms come with satellite TV and a/c – though the front rooms are noisy. **€65**

Heritage Liberdade Av da Liberdade 28 ☎ 213 404 040, ⓦ heritage.pt; ⓜ Restauradores; map pp.60–61. In a superb mansion, this hotel blends traditional and contemporary style. Though the dining area/bar is small (and the gym/plunge pool even smaller), the rooms more than compensate: they are spruce with tiled bathrooms, retro taps and great cityscapes from top-floor rooms. **€190**

Inspira Santa Marta Rua de Santa Marta 48 ☎ 210 440 900, ⓦ inspirasantamartahotel.com; ⓜ Avenida; map pp.60–61. The facade of a traditional townhouse hides a modern boutique hotel which boasts impressive green credentials, including low-energy lighting and recycled or local products. Sheng fui-designed rooms are compact but comfy with glass-wall showers and – unusually for Lisbon – coffee-making facilities and free minibars. There are also spa facilities, a games room, stylish restaurant and bar. **€125**

★ **Lisboa Plaza** Trav Salitre 7 ☎ 213 218 218, ⓦ heritage.pt; ⓜ Avenida; map pp.60–61. Part of the small, local, highly recommended Heritage chain, whose hotels are all in beautifully renovated historic buildings – this is a tasteful, understated former family home with marble bathrooms, bar and a fashionable rooftop terrace, a short walk from the main Avenida. Friendly staff and good for families. Limited disabled access. **€135**

Suíço Atlântico Rua da Glória 9 ☎ 213 461 713, ⓦ turim hoteis.com; ⓜ Restauradores; map pp.60–61. During World War II this was known to be the spies' favourite hangout – now it's a popular budget hotel in a good location. Rooms are fairly standard, though some come with balconies looking down on to seedy Rua da Glória. The bar and bright breakfast room are the highlights. **€65**

LAPA

As Janelas Verdes Rua das Janelas Verdes 47 ☎ 213 968 143, ⓦ heritage.pt; bus #727, #760 or tram #25 from Praça do Comércio; map pp.60–61. This discreet eighteenth-century townhouse is just metres from the Museu Nacional de Arte Antiga. It has well-proportioned rooms with marble-clad bathrooms, period furnishings, and a delightful walled garden with a small fountain where breakfast is served in summer. The top-floor library and terrace have stunning river views. **€180**

York House Rua das Janelas Verdes 32 ☎ 213 962 435, ⓦ yorkhouselisboa.com; bus #727, #760 or tram #25 from Praça do Comércio; map pp.60–61. Located in a sixteenth-century Carmelite convent (and hidden from the main street by high walls), the rooms here are chic and minimalist. The best are grouped around a beautiful interior courtyard, where drinks and meals are served in summer, and there's a highly rated restaurant. **€150**

NORTH LISBON

Avenida Park Av Sidónio Pais 6 ☎ 213 532 181, ⓦ avenidapark.com; ⓜ Parque; map pp.60–61. A slightly old-fashioned hotel, but with good-sized rooms – beg for one with a view over the park for no extra price – on a quiet street. **€100**

Sheraton Lisboa Rua Latino Coelho 1 ☎ 213 120 000, ⓦ sheratonlisboa.com; ⓜ Picoas; map pp.60–61. The 1970s high-rise is something of an icon in this part of

1

Lisbon and is now a mecca for those seeking five-star spa facilities. Its dated exterior hides some very modern attractions including a heated outdoor pool, swanky rooms and a spectacular top-floor bar and restaurant – dubbed Lisbon's eighth hill, it commands the best views of the city you'll find outside a plane. **€120**

HOSTELS

Lisbon Lounge Hostel Rua de São Nicolau 13-4° ☎218 885 312, ⓦ lisbonloungehostel.com; ⓜ Rossio; map p.63. Understandably popular independent hostel in a great old Baixa townhouse full of stripped floorboards and comfy sofas. There's an airy lounge, communal kitchen and laundry service. Dorms sleep four, six or eight, and there are some twin-bed rooms too. Dorm beds **€25**; twins **€32**

Oasis Hostel Rua Santa Catarina 24 ☎213 478 044, ⓦ oasislisboa.com; ⓜ Baixa-Chiado or tram #28; map pp.72–73. In a lovely old townhouse with its own patio garden – complete with palm tree – this welcoming hostel is a stone's throw from the fashionable Miradouro Santa Catarina. Dorm beds **€14**; doubles **€32**

Pousada da Juventude Parque das Nações Rua de Moscavide 47–101, Parque das Nações ☎218 920 890, ⓦ microsites.juventude.gov.pt/portal/en; ⓜ Oriente; map p.87. Five minutes' walk northeast of Parque das Nações, towards the bridge, this well-equipped modern youth hostel has eighteen four-bed dorms and ten double

rooms. There's also a pool table and disabled access. Dorm beds **€17**; doubles **€45**

Pousada da Juventude de Lisboa Rua Andrade Corvo 46 ☎213 532 696, ⓦ microsites.juventude.gov.pt/portal /en; ⓜ Picoas; map pp.60–61. This is the main city hostel, set in a rambling old building, with a small bar (6pm–midnight) and canteen. Thirty rooms sleeping four or six (with shared bathrooms), or doubles with private shower rooms. There's also a TV room on the top floor, and breakfast is included in the price. Disabled access. Dorm beds **€17**; doubles **€45**

Travellers House Rua Augusta 89 ☎210 115 922, ⓦ travellershouse.com; ⓜ Baixa-Chiado; map p.63. Right on Lisbon's main pedestrianized street, this award-winning independent hostel has a wonderful high-ceilinged lounge, bean bags and DVD room. Dorm beds **€28**; doubles **€70**

CAMPSITE

Lisboa Camping Estrada da Circunvalação, Parque Florestal de Monsanto ☎217 628 200, ⓦ lisboa camping.com; bus #714 from Praça da Figueira via Belém. The main city campsite – with disabled facilities, restaurants, a swimming pool and shops – is 6km west of the city centre, in the expansive hilltop Parque de Monsanto. The entrance is on the park's west side. Though the campsite is secure, take care in the park after dark. Open all year. Pitch **€32**

EATING

Lisbon has some of the best-value cafés and restaurants of any European city, serving large portions of good Portuguese food at sensible prices. A **set menu** (*ementa turística*) at lunch or dinner will get you a three-course meal for around €15, though you can eat for even less than this by sticking to the ample main dishes and choosing the daily specials. **Seafood** is widely available – there's an entire central street, Rua das Portas de Santo Antão that specializes in it. Options for **vegetarians** are somewhat limited, though *Tão* (see p.96) and *Terra* (see p.97) are worth seeking out. Indian and Chinese restaurants also offer good vegetarian options, as do some of the museum cafés, such as at the Centro de Arte Moderna at the Gulbenkian.

CAFÉS

Lisbon's cafés are its pride and joy, ranging from atmospheric turn-of-the-twentieth-century artists' haunts to Art Deco wonders. The cafés listed below are good for breakfast, coffee and cakes or just a beer during the afternoon.

BAIXA AND CHIADO

A Brasileira Rua Garrett 120 ☎213 469 547; ⓜ Baixa-Chiado; map p.63. Opened in 1905 and marked by a bronze of Fernando Pessoa outside, this is the most famous of Rua Garrett's old-style coffee houses – its outside tables are usually packed. Livens up at night with a more youthful clientele swigging beer outside until 2am, though the attractive interior is its real appeal. Daily 8am–2am.

Benard Rua Garrett 104 ☎211 373 133; ⓜ Baixa-Chiado; map p.63. Often overlooked because of its

proximity to the better-known *A Brasileira*, this old-style café has an equally ornate interior and an outdoor terrace on Chiado's most fashionable street. It also serves superb cakes, ice cream and coffees. Mon–Sat 8am–midnight.

Confeitaria Nacional Praça da Figueira 18 ☎213 424 470; ⓜ Rossio; map p.63. Opened in 1829 and little changed since, with a stand-up counter selling pastries and sweets below a mirrored ceiling. There's a small side room for sit-down coffees and snacks and a few outdoor tables. Daily 9am–8pm; Oct–April closed Sun.

Leitaria Académica Largo do Carmo 1–3; ⓜ Baixa-Chiado; ☎213 469 092; map p.63. Take a table in one of the city's nicest, quietest squares, outside the ruined Carmo church. Good for drinks, it also does light lunches. Mon–Sat 7am–midnight, Sun 7am–8pm.

Martinho da Arcada Praça do Comércio 3 ☎218 879 259; ⓜTerreiro do Paço; map p.63. Beautiful café-restaurant beneath the arches, little changed from the beginning of the twentieth century when it was frequented by the writer Fernando Pessoa. The restaurant is somewhat formal, but you can always just call in for a coffee and *pastel de nata* in the attached stand-up café, or have less formal lunches at the outdoor tables. Mon–Sat 7am–11pm.

Nicola Rossio 24 ☎213 460 579; ⓜRossio; map p.63. A former haunt of Lisbon's literary figures, dating back to the seventeenth century, this grand old place is a good stop for breakfast. Outdoor seats are always at a premium and it has occasional live fado. Mon–Sat 9am–10pm, Sun 10am–7pm.

Suíça Rossio 96 ☎213 214 090; ⓜRossio; map p.63. Famous for its cakes and pastries; you'll have a hard job getting an outdoor table here, though there's plenty of room inside – the café stretches across to Praça da Figueira, where the best tables are. Daily 7am–9pm.

Vertigo Trav do Carmo 4 ☎213 433 112; ⓜBaixa-Chiado; map p.63. An arty crowd frequents this bare-brick walled café with an ornate glass ceiling. Occasional art exhibits and a good range of cakes and snacks. Mon–Sat 11am–11pm, Sun 10.30am–6.30pm.

ALFAMA, CASTELO AND THE EASTERN RIVERFRONT

Deli Deluxe Av Infante Dom Henrique, Armazem B, Loja 8; ⓜSanta Apolónia; map pp.60–61. A modern deli with delectable cheeses, cured meats and preserves, though the riverside café at the back is even more appealing. Grab a seat outdoors and enjoy the range of goodies from croissants to speciality teas, yoghurts, bagels, salads and cocktails. Tues–Fri noon–midnight, Sat 10am–midnight.

Miradouro de Santa Luzia Miradouro de Santa Luzia ☎218 863 968; map p.65. This hilltop suntrap sits just below the viewpoint of the same name. Drinks and meals are slightly pricey but you pay for the views, which are fabulous. Daily 9am–11pm

★ **Pois Café** Rua São João da Praça 93–95 ☎218 862 497; map p.65. With its big comfy sofas and laidback ambience, walking into this Austrian-run café feels like eating in someone's large front room. A friendly, young crowd, light meals and home-made snacks, including a great *Apfelstrudel*. Tues–Sun 11am–8pm.

BAIRRO ALTO AND CAIS DO SODRÉ

Esplanada Praça do Príncipe Real ☎962 311 669; map pp.72–73. Glass pavilion in the square with outdoor seats beneath the shady trees. Great for lunch, as it does a good range of salads, quiches and vast wholemeal sandwiches from around €5. Daily 9am–11pm.

BELÉM

Antiga Confeitaria de Belém Rua de Belém 84–92 ☎213 637 423; map p.81. No visit to Belém is complete without a coffee and hot *pastel de nata* (custard-cream tart) liberally sprinkled with *canela* (cinnamon) in this cavernous, tiled pastry shop and café, which has been serving them up since 1837. Daily 8am–midnight; Oct–May closes at 11pm.

NORTH LISBON

A Linha d'Água Jardim Amália Rodrigues, Parque Eduardo VII ☎213 814 327; ⓜSão Sebastião; map pp.60–61. Facing a small lake, this glass-fronted café is at the northern end of the park. It's a tranquil spot to sip a coffee or beer, and serves good-value buffet lunches. Daily 10am–8pm.

Botequim do Rei Alameda Cardeal Cerejeira, Parque Eduardo VII ☎213 160 891; ⓜParque; map pp.60–61. The food here is fairly average, but the outdoor seating, in the park right by a small lake, is particularly appealing, making this a lovely spot for a drink or snack. Tues–Sun 10am–10pm.

★ **Versailles** Av da República 15A ☎213 546 340; ⓜSaldanha; map pp.60–61. One of Lisbon's most traditional cafés full of bustling waiters circling the starched tablecloths. It's busiest at around 4pm, when Lisbon's best-dressed elderly dames gather for a chat beneath the chandeliers. Daily 7.30am–10pm.

RESTAURANTS

There are hundreds of restaurants in central Lisbon, many of which serve no-nonsense local food, or inexpensive foreign dishes from the former colonies. Note that on Saturday nights you should reserve a table for the more popular places, such as those in the Bairro Alto and Alfama. Restaurants in the Baixa are good for lunch as most have inexpensive set menus aimed at local workers, while Chiado is the upmarket shopping district with some good places to eat on its fringes, and Cais do Sodré, by the river, is generally cheap and cheerful. For more upmarket

---

OUR FIVE FAVOURITE RESTAURANTS

Best views: *Rêsto do Chapitô* (see p.96)
Budget: *Bom Jardim/Rei dos Frangos* (see p.96)
Modern Portuguese: *Cantinho do Avillez* (see p.96)

Quirky: *Bota Alta* (see p.97)
Traditional: *Varina da Madragoa* (see p.98)

1

international food, try the *docas* at Alcântara with its a range of fashionable restaurants, most facing the river, or the riverfront Passeio das Tágides out at Parque das Nações, with its long line of moderately priced bars and restaurants specializing in international cuisine.

BAIXA

A Berlenga Rua Barros Queirós 29 ☎ 213 422 703; ⓜ Rossio; map p.63. Atmospheric *cervejaria* with live crabs and seafood displayed in its window. Take a seat for a plate of prawns at the bar, or sit down at the main restaurant for good-value fish, meat and seafood. Mains range from €8–12. Daily noon–midnight.

Bom Jardim/Rei dos Frangos Trav de Santo Antão 11–18 ☎ 213 424 389; ⓜ Restauradores; map p.63. The "King of Chickens" has branches on two sides of an alleyway connecting Restauradores with Rua das Portas de Santo Antão. There are plenty of tables outdoors, too. A tasty spit-roasted half-chicken with chips is yours for around €6, though it also serves other meat and fish dishes for around €9. Daily noon–11.30pm.

Casa do Alentejo Rua das Portas de Santo Antão 58 ☎ 213 469 231; ⓜ Restauradores; map p.63. A centre dedicated to Alentejan culture with its own restaurant, "Alentejo House" has an ornate interior dining room where you can enjoy sound Alentejan dishes such as *carne de porco à alentejana* (grilled pork and clams) from around €11. Daily noon–3pm & 7–10.30pm.

Floresta Santana Calçada Santana 18 ☎ 963 945 338; ⓜ Rossio; map p.63. A short (uphill) walk from the bustle of the Baixa but a world away in terms of atmosphere: very much a local with excellent-value meals served in a friendly, family-run place. The fish and meat is fresh and generous and desserts are home-made and huge. Two courses with wine should come to under €10. Daily 10am–11pm.

João do Grão Rua dos Correeiros 222–228 ☎ 213 424 757; ⓜ Rossio; map p.63. One of the best in a row of somewhat touristy restaurants on this pedestrianized street, where appealing outdoor tables tempt you to sit down and sample the reasonably priced Portuguese salads, fish and rice dishes. The marble- and *azulejo*-clad interior is just as attractive. Daily noon–3.30pm & 6–11pm.

Tão Rua dos Douradores 10 ☎ 218 850 046; ⓜ Baixa-Chiado; map p.63. For a healthy lunch, head to this fashionable, very good value, Eastern-inspired organic restaurant, with set meals from around €7. Tasty vegetarian sushi, risottos, grilled aubergines and salads, along with the occasional fish dish. Mon–Fri noon–3pm & 6.30–11pm.

ALFAMA, CASTELO AND THE EASTERN RIVERFRONT

Arco do Castelo Rua do Chão da Feira 25 ☎ 218 876 598; map p.65. This cheerful Goan restaurant specializes in dishes from Portugal's former Indian colony, including a tempting shrimp curry, Indian sausage and spicy seafood. Despite being right opposite the entrance to the castle, it is good value with mains from around €9. Mon–Sat noon–midnight.

Barracão de Alfama Rua de São Pedro 16 ☎ 218 866 359; map p.65. An unpretentious tiled *tasca* popular with locals, and with non-touristy prices: you can have a full meal here for under €15. Portions are generous with fine fish and grills. There are a few outdoor tables at the back in summer. Daily 11am–midnight.

Casanova Loja 7 Armazém B, Cais da Pedra à Bica do Sapato ☎ 218 877 532; ⓜ Santa Apolónia; map p.65. The bustling *Casanova* offers pizza, pasta and crostini accompanied by fine views from its outside terrace. It's phenomenally popular and you can't book, so turn up early. Around €18 for a full meal. Daily 12.30pm–1.30am.

Cruzes Credo Rua Cruzes da Sé 29 ☎ 218 822 296; map p.65. This fashionable little café-restaurant has a jazzy ambience and serves tasty *petiscos* snacks and some less usual (for these parts) dishes such as bruschetta, hummus and burgers (€5–7). It's also a tranquil spot for a drink. Daily 10am–2am.

Lautasco Beco do Azinhal 7 ☎ 218 860 173; map p.65. There are tables in a pretty courtyard with fairy lights, making this a particularly romantic spot for a night out. The food can be less impressive than the setting, but the *cataplana* for two is recommended and works out less expensive than other mains (from €12). Reservations advised. Mon–Sat 10am–3pm & 7–10.30pm; closed one month in winter.

Malmequer-Bemmequer Rua de São Miguel 23–25 ☎ 218 876 535; map p.65. Cheerily decorated and moderately priced place, overseen by a friendly owner. You can have charcoal-grilled meat and fish from around €8 (try the *salmão no carvão*, or grilled salmon). Wed–Sun 12.30–3.30pm & 7.30–10.30pm, Tues 7.30–10.30pm.

★ **Rêsto do Chapitô** Costa do Castelo 7 ☎ 218 867 734; map p.65. Multipurpose venue incorporating a theatre, circus school, restaurant and jazz bar. The restaurant is in an upstairs dining room, reached via a spiral staircase, and serves a range of imaginative mains such as black pork with ginger and mushroom risotto from €16. The outdoor esplanade commands terrific views over Alfama. Daily noon–6pm & 7.30pm–midnight.

CHIADO AND CAIS DO SODRÉ

★ **Cantinho do Avillez** Rua dos Duques de Bragança 7 ☎ 211 992 369, ⓦ cantinhodoavillez.pt; ⓜ Baixa-Chiado; map pp.72–73. In a bright, white space, with tram #28 rattling by its door, this laidback but classy canteen is the place to sample cuisine from Lisbon's top chef, José Avillez, but at affordable prices. Delectable main courses from €15–18 include the likes of scallops with sweet potatoes, mushrooms and aparagus, or tuna with ginger. Mon–Sat 12.30–3pm & 7.30pm–midnight.

1

Casa Liege Rua da Bica Duarte Belo 72–74 ☎ 213 422 794; ⓜ Baixa-Chiado; map pp.72–73. Small and bustling *tasca* at the top of the Elevador da Bica, packed at lunchtimes thanks to its filling and inexpensive dishes such as grilled chicken, sausages and fine *pastéis de bacalhau*. Good house wine, too. Mon–Sat 11am–11pm.

Pharmacia Rua Marechal Saldanha 1 ☎ 213 462 146; map pp.72–73. Part of the Pharmaceutical Society and Museum, this traditional building with a terrace on lawns facing the Tejo is a terrific spot for a quirky café-restaurant decked out with retro pharmacy fittings. The speciality here is tapas (from around €7). It also does fine steaks, or just pop in for a drink. Tues–Sun 1pm–1am.

Porto de Abrigo Rua dos Remolares 16–18 ☎ 213 460 873; ⓜ Cais do Sodré; map pp.72–73. This longestablished and atmospheric restaurant near the main market has a little stained-glass window and serves goodvalue dishes from around €9, such as octopus, salmon and *açorda de camarão* (shrimps with garlicky bread sauce). Mon–Sat 11am–11pm.

BAIRRO ALTO, PRÍNCIPE REAL AND AROUND

1˚ de Maio Rua da Atalaia 8 ☎ 213 426 840; ⓜ Baixa-Chiado; map pp.72–73. This buzzing *adega* offers simply cooked, grilled fish and meats with boiled veg and potatoes. You can watch the chef cook through a hatch at the back, adding to the theatrics. Good daily specials, with mains from around €10. Arrive early to bag a table. Daily noon–3pm & 7–11pm.

Bistro 100 Maneiras Largo da Trindade 9 ☎ 210 990 475; ⓜ Baixa-Chiado; map pp.72–73. In a fine Art Nouveau building, this is the latest offering from Sarajevoborn chef Ljubmar Stanisic, whose restaurant and canteen serve a fascinating mixture of classy mains (suckling pig, fresh fish; around €25) and upmarket comfort foods such as salmon sausages and deluxe hamburgers (€17). Mon–Sat 11am–11pm.

★ **Bota Alta** Trav da Queimada 37 ☎ 213 427 959; map pp.72–73. An attractive old tavern with quirky, bootthemed decor (its name means "high boot") that attracts queues for its large portions of traditional Portuguese food (mains from around €10). It's always packed and the tables sit cheek by jowl; try to get there before 8pm. Mon–Fri noon–2.30pm & 7–10.30pm, Sat 7–10pm.

Cervejaria da Trindade Rua Nova da Trindade 20 ☎ 213 423 506; map pp.72–73. Huge and famous vaulted beer hall-restaurant – the city's oldest, dating from 1836 – with some of Lisbon's loveliest *azulejos* on the walls and a pretty patio garden. It specializes in shellfish, though other dishes are also good (from €10 or so), as is the beer. Daily 10am–midnight.

Comida de Santo Calçada Engenheiro Miguel Pais 39 ☎ 213 963 339; map pp.72–73. Popular, pricey but fun Brazilian restaurant serving classic dishes such as *feijoada*

(a bean stew), and a fantastic *ensopadinho de peixe* (fish in coconut); also good vegetarian options, with mains €15–18. Daily 12.30–3.30pm & 7.30pm–1am; June–Sept closed Mon.

Pap Açorda Rua da Atalaia 57–59 ☎ 213 464 811; map pp.72–73. This renowned restaurant attracts Lisbon's fashionable elite to its chandelier-hung dining room converted from an old bakery. *Açorda* – the house speciality – is a sort of bread and shellfish stew, but there are excellent regional dishes, too, such as mixed fish with aleoli. Mains from €17. Reservations recommended. Tues–Sat 12.30–2pm & 8–11.30pm.

Terra Rua da Palmeira 15 ☎ 707 108 108; map pp.72–73. Attractive vegetarian and vegan restaurant with a lovely patio garden and good-value salads and pasta dishes available as an all-you-can-eat buffet (around €16). Also serves fine Italian ice creams. Tues–Sun 1.20–3.30pm & 7.30–midnight.

AVENIDA DA LIBERDADE AND AROUND

Bela Ipanema Av da Liberdade 169 ☎ 213 572 316; ⓜ Avenida; map pp.60–61. Bustling café/bar/restaurant by the São Jorge cinema. The bar attracts a steady stream of locals with its pastries, light lunches, beers and coffees; the small dining area serves good-value food (two courses with wine around €15), with outdoor tables facing the avenue. Mon–Sat 7am–midnight.

Marisqueira Santa Marta Travessa do Enviato de Inglaterra 1 117 ☎ 213 525 638; ⓜ Avenida; map pp.60–61. Slightly touristy but spacious restaurant specializing in seafood: there's a tank with bubbling crabs in one corner. Service is attentive and reasonably priced meals (mains from around €12) end with a complimentary glass of port.

★ **Ribadouro** Av da Liberdade 155 ☎ 213 549 411; ⓜ Avenida; map pp.60–61. The Avenida's best *cervejaria*, serving a decent range of grilled meat and fresh shellfish (but no fish) from around €15. If you don't fancy a full meal, order a beer with a plate of prawns at the bar. Very popular, so turn up early or book a table. Daily noon–1am.

SÃO BENTO, LAPA AND SANTOS

Picanha Rua das Janelas Verdes 96, Lapa ☎ 213 975 401; map pp.60–61. Just up from the Museu de Arte Antiga, with an intimate, ornately tiled interior, this specializes in *picanha* (thin slices of beef) accompanied by black-eyed beans, salad and potatoes. Great if this appeals to you (as that's all they do), and for a fixed price of around €15 you can eat as much of the stuff as you want. Mon–Fri 12.45–3pm & 7.45–11.30pm, Sat & Sun 7.45–11.30pm.

Túnel de Santos Largo de Santos 1 ☎ 912 151 850; map pp.60–61. Lively, modern café-restaurant with outdoor seating facing the square. Inside, a cosy brick-vaulted interior space attracts a young crowd for inexpensive grills, snacks and salads (around €8 and up). Mon–Sat 8am–10pm.

1

Varina da Madragoa Rua das Madres 34 **☎**213 965 533; map pp.72–73. Once the haunt of Nobel Prize for Literature winner José Saramago, and it's easy to see why he liked it: a lovely, traditional restaurant with grape-embellished *azulejos* on the walls and a menu featuring superb Portuguese dishes such as *bacalhau*, trout and steaks; around €25 for a full meal. Tues–Fri 12.30–3.30pm & 7–11.30pm, Sat 7.30–11.30pm.

ALCÂNTARA AND THE DOCKS

Alcântara Café Rua Maria Luísa Holstein 15, Alcântara **☎**213 621 226; map p.78. Elite designer bar-restaurant blending industrial and modern architecture. One of the city's trendiest in decor and clientele, but expect to pay over €30 a head for a meal. Daily 8pm–3am.

Café na Fábrica LX Factory, Rua Rodrigues Faria 103 Edf E **☎**967 382 848; map p.78. Set in a small but cosy wooden shed-like warehouse, this arty space is very popular for lunch, with wraps, quiches, baguettes and salads from around €6.50. There are also a few outdoor tables. Mon–Fri 9.30am–7pm, Sat & Sun noon–8pm.

Espalha Brasas Armazém 12, Doca de Santo Amaro **☎**213 962 059; map p.78. Superb grilled meats, tiger prawns and fish kebabs can be enjoyed at the riverside tables of this fashionable dockside restaurant which has a bright upstairs room with great views over the river. Daily specials from around €14. Mon–Sat noon–4am.

Malaca Too LX Factory, Rua Rodrigues Faria 103 Edf G **☎**213 477 082; map p.78. This fantastic space has tables wedged between giant old printing presses – a surprising backdrop for fresh, oriental cuisine ranging from wonton soups and green curries to fresh fish, from around €14. Daily noon–midnight.

BELÉM

Floresta Belém Praça Afonso de Albuquerque 1 **☎**213 636 307; map p.81. One of the best-value places along this stretch, attracting a largely Portuguese clientele, especially for weekend lunches. Great salads, grills and fresh fish from around €8 inside or on a sunny outdoor terrace. Tues–Sat noon–4pm & 6.30pm–midnight, Sun noon–4pm.

Quadrante Centro Cultural de Belém **☎**213 612 400; map p.81. Good-value self-service food (salads,

sandwiches and rice dishes) is available from two separate counters inside the Centro Cultural de Belém. The inside is no great shakes, but head out to the roof-garden terrace for exhilarating views over Belém and the river. Daily 10am–10pm; Oct–April Sat & Sun closes at 9pm.

NORTH LISBON

Eleven Rua Marquês da Fronteira **☎**213 862 211, **ⓦ**restauranteleven.com; **ⓜ**Marquês de Pombal; map pp.60–61. At the top of Parque Eduardo VII, this Michelin-starred restaurant hits the heights both literally and metaphorically. The interior is both intimate and bright with wonderful city views. Quality here is expensive but not outrageous, with set menus from around €75 or a tasting menu at around €90. Dishes feature black pork with chestnut gnocchi or pumpkin risotto with scallops, and there's a fine wine list. Mon–Sat 12.30–3pm & 7.30–11pm.

Frango da Guia Campo Pequeno **☎**217 961 031; **ⓜ**Campo Pequeno; map pp.60–61. This restaurant takes its inspiration from the Algarve village of Guia, which is famed for its spit-roast chicken. One of several restaurants in a lovely space within the bullring's outer walls, with outdoor seating, it's recommended for its good-value chicken (around €6) though it also serves tasty steaks and other grills (around €8–9). Daily noon–11.30pm.

PARQUE DAS NAÇÕES

D'Bacalhau Rua do Pimenta 43–45 **☎**218 941 297; **ⓜ**Oriente; map p.87. If you want to sample some of the alleged 365 recipes for *bacalhau* – salted cod – this is a good place to come, as it serves quite a range of them, from €9: *bacalhau com natas* (with a creamy sauce) is always tasty. It also serves other dishes, including a selection of fresh fish from €12. Mon–Sat noon–11.30pm, Sun noon–3pm.

Senhor Peixe Rua da Pimenta 35–37 **☎**218 955 892; **ⓜ**Oriente; map p.87. "Mr Fish" is widely thought to serve up some of the best fresh seafood in Lisbon – check the counter for the day's catch or choose a lobster from the bubbling tank. Most dishes – from around €15 – are grilled in the open kitchen. Tues–Sat noon–3am & 7.30–11pm, Sun noon–3pm.

DRINKING AND NIGHTLIFE

Lisbon's **nightlife** is legendary, though don't expect to see any action much before midnight. There are some great bars where you can get a drink at any time of the day, but clubs – which may not open much before 11pm – generally operate on a "minimum consumption" policy: you buy a ticket at the door which you can get stamped each time you buy a drink at the bar. Designed to stop people dancing all night without buying a drink, which many Portuguese would happily do, the price varies hugely: perhaps €10 if it's a quiet night, more likely around €20–30; keep hold of your ticket to prove you have "consumed" enough (otherwise you pay on exit). The traditional centre of Lisbon's nightlife is the **Bairro Alto**, an intriguing blend of student bars, designer clubs, fado houses and restaurants. The slightly seedy Cais do Sodré district can best be described as up and coming, while neighbouring **Santos** is rapidly gaining a trendy reputation, with some established names. Bars and clubs in **Alcântara and the docks** tend to attract a slightly older, wealthier crowd to those in the centre.

BAIXA

A Ginginha Largo de São Domingos 8; Ⓜ Rossio; map p.63. Everyone should try *ginginha* – Portuguese cherry brandy – once. There's just about room in this microscopic joint to walk in, down a glassful and stagger outside to see the city in a new light. Daily 9am–10.30pm.

ALFAMA AND CASTELO

Costa do Castelo Calçada do Marquês de Tancos 1B Ⓣ 218 884 636; map p.65. Terrace-café/bar/restaurant with a long list of cocktails and mid-priced pasta and fish dishes. There's occasional live music and poetry readings at weekends. Mon–Sat noon–midnight.

Portas do Sol Largo Portas do Sol Ⓣ 218 851 299; map p.65. With its entrance hidden below street level, this hip spot is an obligatory venue for anyone into sunsets. It's a chic indoor space, though most people head for the comfy sofas and outside seats on the giant terrace with grandstand views over the Alfama. Pricey drinks, coffees and cocktails, but worth it. Mon–Thurs 10am–midnight, Fri & Sat 1am–2am.

SANTA APOLÓNIA

Lux Armazéns A, Cais da Pedra a Santa Apolónia Ⓣ 218 820 890, Ⓦ luxfragil.com; Ⓜ Santa Apolónia; map pp.60–61. This three-storey converted meat warehouse has become one of Europe's most fashionable places to be seen, attracting the likes of Prince and Cameron Diaz. Part-owned by actor John Malkovich, it was the first place to set up in the docks opposite Santa Apolónia station. There's a rooftop terrace with amazing views, a middle floor with various bars, comfy chairs and sofas, amazing projection screens, and music from pop to jazz and dance, while the downstairs dancefloor descends into frenzy at times. The club is also increasingly on the circuit for touring bands. Tues–Sun midnight–6am.

BAIRRO ALTO

Alface Hall Rua do Norte 96 Ⓣ 213 433 293; map pp.72–73. This quirky café-bar is in a former print works. Now part of a hostel and filled with retro chairs and artefacts, its high ceilings and comfy sofas make it an ideal place to hang out for live music, usually jazz on Wed–Sun from 10pm. Daily 5pm–2am.

Ártis Rua do Diário de Notícias 95 Ⓣ 213 424 795; map pp.72–73. *Ártis* is a fashionable little tapas bar where you can sample a range of local wines with tasty snacks such as pork with coriander and garlic and local cheeses. Tues–Fri 6pm–2am, Sat & Sun 6pm–3am.

Cinco Lounge Rua Ruben A Leitão 179 Ⓣ 213 424 033; map pp.72–73. Run by an affable Brit, this New York-style bar has become legendary for its cocktails, with over a hundred to choose from the classics to totally wacky concoctions. A great place to chill out. Daily 9pm–2am.

Clube da Esquina Rua da Barroca 30 Ⓣ 213 427 149; map pp.72–73. A buzzy little corner bar with ancient radios on the wall and DJs spinning discs on a good, old-fashioned turntable. Great for people-watching and always lively. Daily 9.30pm–2am.

Decadente Bar Rua de São Pedro de Alcântara 81 Ⓣ 213 461 281; map pp.72–73. Attached to a boutique hostel, this small, fashionable bar attracts a youthful, laidback crowd. It's best on Thursday and Saturday evenings when there is often live music, usually Latin or jazz. Daily 6pm–2am.

★ **Enoteca** Rua da Mãe de Água Ⓣ 213 422 079; map pp.72–73. Tucked into steps downhill from Praça do Príncipe Real, this extraordinary wine bar can be hard to find. It is set in the bowels of a nineteenth-century bathhouse and now serves upmarket wines and other drinks, along with *petiscos* (snacks). Tues–Sun 6pm–2am.

Frágil Rua da Atalaia 126 Ⓣ 213 469 578, Ⓦ fragil.com. pt; map pp.72–73. An icon of cool for years before the owner opened *Lux*, this club is partly gay and wholly pretentious – it's best after 1am. Ring the bell and look your best to get past the style police. Thurs–Sat 11pm–4am.

Maria Caxuxa Rua da Barroca 6–12 Ⓣ 965 039 094; Ⓜ Baixa-Chiado; map pp.72–73. This arty lounge-bar has plenty of space for big sofas and eclectic decor – including record players and aged machinery – though these get lost in the crowds when the DJ pumps up the volume as the evening progresses. Daily 5pm–2am.

★ **Pavilhão Chinês** Rua Dom Pedro V 89 Ⓣ 213 424 729; map pp.72–73. Once a nineteenth-century tea- and coffee-merchant's shop, this is now a bar set in a series of comfortable rooms. Most are completely lined with mirrored cabinets containing some 4000 artefacts from around the world, including a cabinet of model trams. There is waiter service and the usual drinks are supplemented by a long list of exotic cocktails. Mon–Sat 6pm–2am, Sun 9pm–2am.

Portas Largas Rua da Atalaia 105 Ⓣ 218 466 379; map pp.72–73. Atmospheric, black-and-white-tiled *adega* with cheapish drinks, music from fado to pop, and a varied, partly gay crowd, which spills out onto the street on warm evenings. Often a starting point for clubbers moving on to *Frágil*. Daily 6pm–2am.

Solar do Vinho do Porto Rua de São Pedro de Alcântara 45 Ⓣ 213 475 707, Ⓦ www.ivdp.pt; map pp.72–73. Opened in 1944, the Port Wine Institute's Lisbon base lures in visitors with over 300 types of port, starting at around €3 a glass and rising to over €25 for a glass of vintage J.W. Burmester. Drinks and snacks such as cheese and hams are served at low tables in the comfortable eighteenth-century former Palácio Ludovice, and though the waiters are notoriously snooty, it's still a good place to kick off an evening. Mon–Fri 11am–midnight, Sat 2pm–midnight.

1

OUR FIVE FAVOURITE BARS

Best views: *Portas do Sol* (see p.99)
Best cocktails: *Cinco Lounge* (see p.99)
Best wines: *Enoteca* (see p.99)

Classic Lisbon: *Portas Largas* (see p.99)
Quirky: *Pavilhão Chinês* (see p.99)

CAIS DO SODRÉ AND SANTOS

Café Tati Rua da Ribeira Nova 36 ☎213 461 279; Ⓜ Cais do Sodré; map pp.72–73. This is one of the new breed of arty café-bars opening in the down-at-heel area around the market. With stripped walls and old furniture, it has tatty chic decor and a very appealing range of snacks, teas, cakes and wines. Popular for Sunday brunch, it's also lively on Wednesday and Sunday evenings for live jazz. Tues–Sun 11am–1am.

Kremlin Escadinhas da Praia 5 ☎216 957 101, Ⓦ grupo-k.pt; map pp.60–61. The tough door policy, based on its reputation as one of the city's most fashionable nightspots, has put off many old-hand clubbers, but this is still the place to go for all-night dancing. Tues–Sat midnight–10am.

Le Chat Jardim 9 de Abril ☎966 537 387; map p.78. A modern, glass-sided café-bar adjacent to the Museu Nacional de Arte Antiga, *Le Chat* has a terrific terrace which gazes over the docks and Ponte 25 de Abril. Great at any time of the day, it's a particularly fine spot for a cocktail or sundowner. Sun–Wed noon–midnight, Thurs–Sat noon–3am.

Pensão Amor Rua do Alecrim 19 ☎213 143 399; Ⓜ Cais do Sodré; map pp.72–73. The "Pension of Love" is a striking former "house of ill-repute" which has retained its eighteenth-century burlesque fixtures and fittings for its current incarnation as a trendy bar/club. Risqué photos, frescoes and mirrors line the walls of a series of ornate rooms, where you can buy cocktails and drinks, browse books in a small bookstore or enjoy occasional live concerts. Mon–Wed noon–2am, Thurs & Fri noon–4am, Sat 6pm–4am.

Sol e Pesca Rua Nova do Carvalho 44 ☎213 467 203; Ⓜ Cais do Sodré; map pp.72–73. Once a shop selling fishing equipment, this hip bar is located on an up-and-coming street better known for its strip joints. The fishing equipment is now part of the decor, and you can still purchase tinned fish to enjoy with bread and wine. Mon–Sat noon–11pm.

AVENIDA DA LIBERDADE

Ritz Clube Rua da Glória 57 ☎212 241 604; Ⓜ Avenida; map pp.72–73. One of Lisbon's most famous and atmospheric clubs, recently reopened after a facelift. Founded as a cabaret club in 1908, the place retains most of its original fittings, a fantastic backdrop for a varied cultural programme (live music, DJ sets, cinema and performing arts), with a separate bar and restaurant area where you can chill out. Sun–Wed 9pm–4am, Thurs–Sat 9pm–6am.

ALCÂNTARA AND THE DOCKS

Doca de Santo Armazém CP, Doca de Santo Amaro ☎213 963 535; map p.78. Though it's slightly set back from the river, this large, palm-fringed club, bar and restaurant has a great cocktail bar on the esplanade. Mon–Thurs 12.30pm–1am, Fri–Sun 12.30pm–4am.

Op Art Doca de Santo Amaro ☎213 956 797, Ⓦ opartcafe.com; map p.78. Located in splendid isolation on the fringes of the Tejo, this small glass pavilion morphs from a simple restaurant serving moderately priced grills into an evening bar. In summer, you can sprawl on dockside beanbags and gaze over the river. After 1am, the mood changes again with vibrant dance sounds. Tues–Fri & Sun 3pm–2am, Sat 3pm–6am.

PARQUE DAS NAÇÕES

Azul Profundo Doca da Olivais; Ⓜ Oriente; map p.87. Sunny esplanade bar overlooking the glittering docks. Offers a good range of well-priced snacks, fruit juices and wicked *caipirinha* cocktails. Daily 10am–2am; Oct–April closes at 10pm.

Havana Rua da Pimenta 115–117; Ⓜ Oriente; map p.87. Lively Cuban bar with an airy interior and outdoor seating. The pulsating Latin sounds ramp up a notch after 11pm when it turns into more of a club. Daily noon–2am; Oct–April Sat & Sun only.

República da Cerveja Passeio das Tágides 2–26 ☎218 922 590; Ⓜ Oriente; map p.87. In a great position close to the water's edge and facing the Vasco da Gama bridge, this modern bar-restaurant specializes in some fine international beers, though sticking to the local Superbock will save a few euros. Steaks and burgers are also on offer, and there's live music Thurs to Sat. Daily 12.30pm–1am; Oct–Feb closes at midnight.

GAY AND LESBIAN BARS AND CLUBS

Gay and lesbian nightlife focuses on the Bairro Alto and Praça do Príncipe Real, where a generally laidback group of clubs and bars attracts people of all ages. In "Directory" (see p.106) there's further information on the gay and lesbian scene in Lisbon.

Finalmente Rua da Palmeira 38, Príncipe Real ☎213 479 923; map pp.72–73. A first-class disco with lashings of kitsch. Weekend drag shows (at 2am) feature skimpily dressed young *senhoritas* camping it up to high-tech sounds. Daily 11am–6am.

Sétimo Céu Trav de Espera 54, Bairro Alto ☎213 466 471; map pp.72–73. Popular with gays and lesbians, this is an obligatory stop for beers and *caipirinhas* served by the Brazilian owner. The great atmosphere spills out onto the street. Mon–Sat 10pm–2am.

Trumps Rua da Imprensa Nacional 104B ☎963 160 602, ⓦtrumps.pt; map pp.72–73. Popular gay disco-club with a reasonably relaxed door policy, which sees a good lesbian turnout, though a bit cruisy midweek. Fri & Sat 11.45pm–6am.

LIVE MUSIC AND PERFORMING ARTS

No visit to Lisbon is complete without listening to **fado** – the city's most traditional music – but there's plenty else on offer if this doesn't appeal to you. The many emigrants from Portugal's former colonies have cemented the popularity of **music from Africa** (especially Cabo Verde, Guinea Bissau, Angola and Mozambique) and, of course, Brazil. The Portuguese love their **pop and rock** and big names frequently perform at the venues listed on p.102. The city also has one of Europe's oldest **jazz clubs** and a loyal jazz following. To find out what's on, the best **listings** are in *Agenda Cultural*, a free monthly magazine produced by the town hall, which details current **theatre and opera** shows as well as live music (in Portuguese). An online version is available on ⓦagendalx.pt. You can usually buy tickets on the night, or, for bigger events, from music store FNAC (Rua do Nova do Almada 104–110, Chiado) or online at ⓦticketline.pt.

FADO

Lisbon is the best place in the country to hear fado, a traditional soulful type of music which has its roots in the clubs of the Bairro Alto and Alfama. Most clubs are small and serve food, and though you don't have to eat, they usually charge a minimum fee (rarely below €15), which

you are expected to spend on food or drink, or you pay on exit. Some of the touristy places can be extremely tacky; we've highlighted below the more authentic experiences.

A Baiuca Rua de São Miguel 20 ☎218 867 284; map p.65. Nightly fado *vadio* (using amateur performers) can be heard in this great little tiled *tasca* which serves decent

---

LISBON'S EVENTS CALENDAR

Carnival February/March: Brazilian-style carnival parades and costumes, mainly at Parque das Nações.

Lisbon half-marathon March: The half-marathon traces a route across Ponte Vasco da Gama, finishing in Parque das Nações (ⓦmaratonaclubeportugal.com).

Peixe em Lisboa March/April: Fish festival held in Pátio da Galé, with masterclasses by top chefs (ⓦpeixeemblisboa.com).

Rock in Rio May: A five-day biannual mega rock festival held in even years, in Parque Bela Vista to the north of the centre (ⓦrockinrio-lisboa.sapo.pt).

Santos Populares June: Street-partying to celebrate the saints' days – António (June 13), João (June 24) and Pedro (June 29). Celebrations for each begin on the evening before the actual day. Santo António is Lisbon's main event.

Arraial Pride June: Gay Pride event, in various venues (ⓦarraialpride.ilga -portugal.pt).

Handicrafts Fair June/July: A state-run handicrafts fair, with live folk music, is held in Estoril on the Avenida de Portugal, near the Casino. A similar event occurs during the same period at FIL (ⓦfil.pt), at the Parque das Nações.

Sintra Music Festival June/July:

Performances by international orchestras, musicians and dance groups in parks, gardens and palaces in and around Sintra (ⓦestorilportugal.com/events).

Super Bock Super Rock July: Rock festival featuring local and international bands in various venues (ⓦsuperbock.pt).

Jazz em Augusto August: Jazz festival at the Gulbenkian's open-air amphitheatre (ⓦmusica.gulbenkian.pt), with a similar event in Cascais.

Festival dos Oceanos August: Ocean-themed festival featuring concerts, environmental awareness events and fireworks at various riverside venues (ⓦfestivaldosoceanos.com).

São Martinho November 11: Saint's day celebrated by the traditional tasting of the year's wine which is drunk with hot chestnuts, in memory of St Martinho, who shared his cape with a poor man.

Natal December: The build-up to Christmas begins in early December with Europe's tallest Christmas tree filling the centre of Praça da Comércio. Distinctive hooped *bolo-rei* (dried-fruit "king cake") appear in shops and *pastelarias*.

New Year's Eve December 31: There are usually fireworks in Praça do Comércio, at Cascais and the Parque das Nações.

fresh fish and grills from €15. Very atmospheric. Thurs–Mon 7.30–11pm.

A Parreirinha de Alfama Beco do Espírito Santo 1 ☎218 868 209; map p.65. Just off Largo do Chafariz de Dentro, this is one of Lisbon's best fado venues, owned by famous fado singer Argentina Santos, and often attracting leading stars and an enthusiastic local clientele. Reservations are advised when the big names appear. The minimum charge is around €15, but expect to spend about €40 with food. Daily 8pm–3am.

A Severa Rua das Gáveas 51–61, Bairro Alto ☎213 428 314, ⊛asevera.com; map pp.72–73. A city institution, named after a nineteenth-century Gypsy singer Maria Severa. Big fado names and big prices. Minimum consumption around €20. Mon, Tues & Thurs–Sun 8pm–3am.

Clube do Fado Rua de São João da Praça 94, Alfama ☎218 852 704, ⊛clube-de-fado.com; map p.65. Intimate place with stone pillars and an old well; frequented by a mainly local clientele. Attracts small-time performers, up-and-coming talent and the occasional big names. Minimum charge around €20. Daily 8pm–2am.

O Senhor Vinho Rua do Meio à Lapa 18, Lapa ☎213 972 681, ⊛srvinho.com; map pp.60–61. For a truly authentic fado experience, seek out this famous club in upmarket Lapa. It features some of the best singers in Portugal, hence the high prices (at least €50 all in). Reservations are advised. Mon–Sat 7.30pm–2am.

Tasca do Chico Rua do Diário de Notícias 39, Bairro Alto ☎213 431 040; map pp.72–73. Atmospheric little bar (a fine spot for a drink) which morphs into a very popular fado bar on Mondays and Wednesdays, when crowds pack in to hear the moving songs from 8pm. Daily 7pm–2am.

AFRICAN AND BRAZILIAN

B. Leza Largo Conde-Barão 50, Santos ☎213 963 735; map pp.72–73. Live African music on most nights in this wonderful sixteenth-century building, with a dancefloor, Cape Verdean food and table service. Tues–Sun 8pm–6am.

Chafarica Calçada de São Vicente 81, Alfama ☎218 867 449; map p.65. Tiny, pricey but huge fun Brazilian bar with tropical decor and live music from 11pm at weekends. Mon–Sat 10pm–4am.

JAZZ

Hot Clube de Portugal Praça de Alegria 48, off Av da Liberdade ☎213 619 740, ⊛hcp.pt; ⓜAvenida; map pp.72–73. Dating from 1948 – making it one of Europe's oldest jazz clubs – the *Hot Clube* hosts top names in the jazz world, along with local performers. Tues–Sat 10pm–2am.

Onda Jazz Arco de Jesus 7, Alfama ☎218 873 064, ⊛ondajazz.com; map p.65. One of Lisbon's best jazz clubs, where you can also eat, with regular top acts along

with local musicians. Wednesday-night jamming sessions, with live shows nightly from 10.30pm. Tues–Sat 8pm–2am.

CLASSICAL MUSIC, OPERA AND THEATRE

For details of ballet performances, check the website of the renowned Lisbon-based Companhia Nacional de Bailado (⊛cnb.pt).

Casino Alameda dos Oceanos, Parque das Nações ☎218 929 000, ⊛casinolisboa.pt; ⓜOriente; map p.87. This state-of-the-art casino (Sun–Thurs 3pm–3am, Fri & Sat 4pm–4am) offers the usual gambling fodder, but the stunning space – with its glass-cylinder entrance hall – also hosts top shows from Broadway and London as well as major concerts in the performance hall, which has a retractable roof.

Centro Cultural de Belém Praça do Império, Belém ☎213 612 400, ⊛ccb.pt; map p.81. This modern cultural centre has both a large and small auditorium hosting a range of music and dance, from jazz to classical.

Fundação Calouste Gulbenkian Av de Berna ☎217 823 000, ⊛gulbenkian.pt; ⓜSão Sebastião; map pp.60–61. There are three concert halls (including an outdoor amphitheatre) at the Gulbenkian, with performances ranging from jazz to chamber to classical, with prestigious guest soloists.

Lisbon Players Rua da Estrela 10, Lapa ☎213 961 946, ⊛lisbonplayers.com.pt; map pp.60–61. Check out performances by this amateur but highly rated English-speaking theatrical group consisting largely of expat actors.

Teatro Nacional de Dona Maria Rossio, Baixa ☎213 250 827, ⊛teatro-dmaria.pt; ⓜRestauradores; map p.63. Puts on regular performances of Portuguese and foreign plays.

Teatro Nacional de São Carlos Rua Serpa Pinto 9, Chiado ☎213 253 000, ⊛tnsc.pt; ⓜBaixa-Chiado; map p.63. The opera season runs from September to June, and there's a regular classical music programme inside this lovely building.

Ze dos Bois Rua da Barroca 59, Bairro Alto ☎213 430 205, ⊛zedebois.org; map pp.72–73. Rambling art venue in a former eighteenth-century palace that hosts various installations, art-house films and exhibitions along with occasional concerts. Usually Wed–Sun 11pm–2am.

LARGE VENUES

Coliseu dos Recreios Rua das Portas de Santo Antão 96, Baixa ☎213 240 580, ⊛coliseulisboa.com; ⓜRestauradores; map p.63. Main indoor city-centre rock, pop and classical venue set in a lovely domed building, originally opened in 1890 as a circus.

Pavilhão Atlântico Parque das Nações ☎218 918 440, ⊛pavilhaoatlantico.pt; ⓜOriente; map p.87. Big-name stars play at Portugal's largest indoor venue, which holds up to 20,000 spectators.

CLOCKWISE FROM TOP MUSEU GULBENKIAN (P.84); CERVEJARIA DA TRINDADE (P.97); VIEW OVER THE ALFAMA (P.65) >

1

CINEMA

Virtually all cinemas show **films with the original soundtrack** (usually American or English) and Portuguese subtitles. Ticket prices are low, usually around €8 (cheaper at matinées and on Monday): you can find listings on ⓦagendalx.pt. There are multi-screen complexes at Amoreiras, Edifício Monumental (ⓜSaldanha), El Corte Inglês (ⓜSão Sebastião), Vasco da Gama in Parque das Nações (ⓜOriente) and Colombo Shopping Centre (ⓜColégio Militar-Luz). As well as the following art-house venues (see below), Lisbon hosts a couple of **film festivals**: the Indie Lisboa **film festival in April/May**, showcases independent cinema from around the world (ⓦindielisboa.com), while the ten-day Festroia takes place in Setúbal in June (ⓦfestroia.pt).

Instituto da Cinemateca Portuguesa Rua Barata Salgueiro 39 ☎213 596 200, ⓦcinemateca.pt; ⓜAvenida; map pp.60–61. The national film theatre, with twice-daily shows ranging from contemporary Portuguese films to anything from Truffaut to Valentino. It

also has its own small cinema museum.

São Jorge Av da Liberdade 175 ☎213 103 400, ⓦcinema saojorge.pt; ⓜAvenida; map pp.60–61. Lisbon's most central cinema shows a mixture of mainstream and art-house movies: it also hosts the odd temporary exhibition and fair.

SPORTS

Football is the biggest game in Lisbon, and it's usually easy to get match tickets (see below), while summer-season **bullfights** at the Praça de Touros do Campo Pequeno, just off Avenida da República, are the other main spectacle (see p.86). Otherwise, you're going to need to travel out of the capital for sports, either for **golf**, on the upmarket courses around Estoril and Cascais (consult ⓦportugalgolfe.com), or **watersports**, namely surfing at Caparica and windsurfing at Guincho.

FOOTBALL

Daily soccer tabloid *Bola* has fixtures, match reports and news, as does the website ⓦlpfp.pt. To buy advance tickets for big games – which cost between €10 and €40 – go to the kiosks (not the turnstiles) at the grounds, or check the club websites.

Benfica Estádio da Luz, Avenida Gen. Norton Matos ☎217 210 500, ⓦslbenfica.pt; ⓜColégio Militar-Luz. Though less successful than Porto in recent years, Lisbon's most famous football team are still national and international giants. Their awesome stadium was completely rebuilt in preparation for the 2004 European Championships;

it was here that Portugal lost in the final to Greece in front of 65,000 disbelieving spectators.

Sporting Club de Portugal (Sporting Lisbon) Estádio José Alvalade, Rua Professor da Fonseca ☎217 516 000, ⓦsporting.pt; ⓜCampo Grande. Benfica's traditional city rivals play at the nearby stadium, also purpose-built for Euro 2004 and featuring state-of-the-art design, with a capacity of 54,000.

Belenenses Estádio do Restelo, Avenida do Restelo, Belém ☎213 010 461, ⓦosbelenenses.pt. Lisbon's third team play in a beautifully located stadium in Belém, though they last won the title back in 1946.

SHOPS AND MARKETS

Lisbon has a fantastic array of **independent shops**, many unchanged for centuries, some extremely cutting edge. There are also some impressive contemporary **shopping malls**, many of which incorporate supermarkets on the ground floor, as well as the more traditional markets, such as the Alfama's Feira da Ladra **flea market**. The Bairro Alto and Chiado are the main centres for alternative **designer clothes** and crafts, while international designer names cluster along Avenida da Liberdade. **Antique shops** tend to be concentrated along Rua do Alecrim in Chiado, Rua Dom Pedro V in the Bairro Alto, and along Rua de São Bento, between Rato and São Bento. Traditional **shopping hours** are Monday to Friday 9.30am to 7 or 8pm (some shops close for an hour at lunch), Saturday 9am to 1pm. However, many of the Bairro Alto shops are open afternoons and evenings only, usually 2 to 9pm or so.

ANTIQUES, ARTS AND CRAFTS

A Arte da Terra Rua de Augusto Rosa 40 ☎212 745 975; map p.65. Within historic stables opposite the Sé – some of the handicrafts are displayed in the stone horse troughs – this is a beautiful space selling a range of local arts and crafts, from jewellery and cork products to postcards, preserves and souvenirs. Mon–Sat 11am–8pm, Sun 11am–6pm.

A Vida Portuguesa Rua Anchieta 11, Chiado;

ⓜBaixa-Chiado; map pp.72–73. Somewhat sparse and expensive but evocative collection of retro toys, crafts and ceramics, beautifully displayed and packaged in a former grocer's shop. Mon–Sat 10am–8pm.

Cork and Co. Rua das Salgadeiras 10, Bairro Alto ☎216 090 231; ⓜBaixa-Chiado; map pp.72–73. Portugal supplies around 50 percent of the world's cork, and this shop displays the versatility of the product with a range of tasteful cork goods, from cork bags and bracelets to cork umbrellas. Mon–Wed noon–10pm, Thurs–Sat noon–midnight.

Fábrica Sant'anna Rua do Alecrim 95, Chiado; ⓜ Baixa-Chiado; map pp.72–73. If you're interested in Portuguese tiles – *azulejos* – check out this factory shop, founded in 1741, which sells copies of traditional designs and a great range of pots and ceramics. Mon–Fri 9.30am–7pm, Sat 10am–2pm.

Santos Ofícios Rua da Madalena 87, near the Sé; ⓜ Terreiro do Paço; map p.63. Small shop stuffed with a somewhat touristy collection of regional crafts including some attractive ceramics, rugs, embroidery, baskets and toys. Mon–Sat 10am–8pm.

Solar Albuquerque Rua Dom Pedro V, 66–72 Bairro Alto ☎ 213 465 522; map pp.72–73. A huge treasure-trove of antique tiles, plates and ceramics dating back to the sixteenth century – great for a browse. Daily 10am–7pm; July & Aug closed Sat & Sun.

BOOKS AND MUSIC

Casa do Fado e da Guitarra Portuguesa Largo do Chafariz de Dentro 1, Alfama; map p.65. The shop attached to this museum (see p.66) sells an excellent selection of fado CDs, and the staff give expert advice. Tues–Sat 10am–6pm.

FNAC Armazéns do Chiado, Rua do Carmo 2, Chiado ⓜ Baixa-Chiado; map p.63. A good range of English-language books, along with an extensive music department and decent selection of computer equipment. Also has a desk selling tickets to major events. Daily 10am–10pm.

Livraria Bertrand Rua Garrett 73, Chiado; ⓜ Baixa-Chiado; map p.63. Portugal's oldest general bookshop opened in 1773, and was once the meeting place of the literary set. Today it sells a good range of novels in English, plus foreign magazines. Mon–Thurs 9am–8pm, Fri & Sat 9am–10pm, Sun 2–10pm.

CLOTHES AND ACCESSORIES

Ana Salazar Rua do Carmo 87, Chiado; ⓜ Baixa-Chiado; map p.63. The main Lisbon outlet of one of the country's best-known designers, with adventurous styles mostly aimed at women. Mon–Sat 10am–7pm.

Espaço Fátima Lopes Rua da Atalaia 36, Bairro Alto; map pp.72–73. Flagship store for Lisbon's biggest names in fashion; bold, colourful and confident clothes to reflect the mood of Portugal's wannabes. Mon–Fri 10am–1.30pm & 2.30–8pm, Sat 11.30am–2.30pm & 3.30–8.30pm.

Fabric Infinit Rua Dom Pedro V 74, Bairro Alto; map pp.72–73. Upmarket store selling one-off and unique designer jewellery, shoes and home products; should you tire of browsing there's an attractive café, selling organic produce, complete with Zen-garden patio at the back. Tues–Sat 11am–7pm.

Storytailors Calçada do Ferragial 8, Chiado; ⓜ Baixa-Chiado; map p.63. Set in a suitably stylish bare-brick eighteenth-century former warehouse, the shop interior is as magical as its designer clothes inspired by fairy tales. Its haute couture range has been snapped up by the likes of Madonna, Janet Jackson and Lily Allen. Tues–Sat noon–8pm.

MARKETS

Feira da Ladra Campo de Santa Clara; map pp.60–61. Lisbon's main Tuesday- and Saturday-morning flea market (see p.67).

Mercado da Carcavelos Carcavelos, on the train line to Cascais. Wonderful rambling Thursday-morning market opposite the train station, for clothes and ceramics.

Mercado da Ribeira Av 24 de Julho, Cais do Sodré; ⓜ Cais do Sodré; map pp.72–73. One of Lisbon's most atmospheric covered markets, selling a great selection of fruit, veg and flowers.

SHOPPING CENTRES AND SUPERMARKETS

Amoreiras Entrance on Av Engenheiro Duarte Pacheco 103, ⓦ amoreiras.com; ⓜ Rato; map pp.60–61. This postmodern shopping centre was one of the first in Lisbon, with some 250 shops, cinemas, restaurants and a hotel. Daily 10am–11pm.

Armazéns do Chiado Rua do Carmo 2, Chiado ⓦ armazensdochiado.com; ⓜ Baixa-Chiado; map p.63. A well-designed shopping centre spread over six floors. The top floor has a series of cafés and restaurants, most offering great views over town. Daily 10am–10pm.

Centro Colombo Av Colégio Militar-Luz ⓦ colombo.pt; ⓜ Colégio Militar-Luz. Iberia's largest shopping complex boasts some four hundred national and international stores, restaurants, cinemas and children's play areas. Daily 9am–midnight.

Centro Vasco da Gama Av Dom João II, Parque das Nações ⓦ centrovascodagama.pt; ⓜ Oriente; map p.87. Three floors of national and international stores beneath a glass roof permanently washed by running water. Also restaurants, children's areas and disabled access. Daily 9am–midnight.

El Corte Inglês Av António Augusto de Aguiar ⓦ elcorteingles.pt; ⓜ São Sebastião; map pp.60–61. Giant Spanish department store spread over nine floors, selling everything from gourmet foods, clothes and sports goods to CDs, books and toys. Mon–Sat 10am–10pm.

WINE AND FOOD

Manuel Tavares Rua da Betesga 1A, Baixa; ⓜ Rossio; map p.63. This small, century-old shop sells a great selection of chocolate and national cheeses, plus a basement stuffed with vintage wines and ports. Mon–Sat 9.30am–7.30pm.

1

Napoleão Rua dos Fanqueiros 70, Baixa, junction with Rua da Conceição ⓦ napoleao.co.pt; ⓜ Terreiro do Paço; map p.63. Great range of port and wine, with knowledgeable, English-speaking staff. Mon–Sat 9.30am–8pm.

DIRECTORY

Embassies and consulates Australia, Av da Liberdade 200–2°, ⓜ Avenida (☎ 213 101 500); Canada, Av da Liberdade 198–200, ⓜ Avenida (☎ 213 164 600); Ireland, Rua da Imprensa à Estrela 1–4°, tram #28 to Estrela (☎ 213 929 440); South Africa, Av Luís Bivar 10, ⓜ Picoas (☎ 213 192 200); UK, Rua de São Bernardo 33, ⓜ Rato (☎ 213 924 000); US, Av das Forças Armadas, ⓜ Jardim Zoológico (☎ 217 273 300).

Gay and lesbian The Centro Comunitário Gay e Lésbico de Lisboa at Rua de São Lázaro 88 (☎ 218 873 918; Wed–Sat 6pm–11pm; ⓜ Martim Moniz) is Lisbon's main gay and lesbian community centre, with its own café. The centre organizes events and is happy to give details of gay-friendly venues. It is run by ILGA whose comprehensive website (ⓦ ilga-portugal.pt) is in English and Portuguese.

Hospital The privately run British Hospital, Rua Tomás da Fonseca (☎ 217 213 400 100, ⓦ bhlxxi.galileisaude.pt), has English-speaking staff and doctors on call from 8.30am to 9pm. There are various other public hospitals around the city.

Left luggage There are 24hr lockers at the airport (in level 1 of car park 1), the main train stations and bus station (around €8 a day depending on size of bag).

Lost property For anything lost on public transport, call ☎ 218 535 403. Major losses should be reported to the police station (see below).

Police The tourist police station is in the Foz Cultura building in Palácio Foz, Restauradores ☎ 213 421 634 (daily 24hr). You need a report from here in order to make a claim on your travel insurance.

Post office The main post office is at Praça dos Restauradores 58 (☎ 213 238 700; Mon–Fri 8am–8pm, Sat & Sun 9am–6pm), from where you can send airmail and *correio azul* (express mail – the fastest service). There's a 24hr post office at the airport. Stamps (*selos*) are sold at post offices and anywhere that has the sign "Correio de Portugal – Selos" displayed.

Around Lisbon

The most popular excursions from the city are to the beach resorts west along the coast from Belém, which can be reached by train from Cais do Sodré (see p.90). There are fine beaches at places such as **Oeiras**, though you only really reach the ocean proper at **Estoril** and **Cascais**. For large, wild stretches of sand, head north to **Guincho**, or cross the Tejo by ferry to reach the **Costa da Caparica**, a thirty-kilometre stretch of beach to the south of the capital. Further south still, there are good, clean beaches at **Sesimbra** and in the **Parque Natural da Arrábida**, a superb unspoilt craggy reserve, while the large town of **Setúbal** is noted for its Igreja de Jesus, Portugal's oldest Manueline building. Heading inland also pays dividends, with sights such as the elegant **Palácio de Queluz**, while the beautiful town of **Sintra**, a UNESCO World Heritage site in the hills above Lisbon, is a must.

The Estoril coast

Stretching for over 30km west of Lisbon, **the Estoril coast** makes for an easily accessible and enjoyable trip from the city – the train line that hugs this dramatic coast is worth the trip alone. Much of the coast is backed by a seafront promenade, along which you can walk or cycle, and the lively resorts of **Estoril** and **Cascais** in particular make pleasant alternatives to staying in Lisbon.

GETTING AROUND   **THE ESTORIL COAST**

By train The Linha de Cascais train runs along the Estoril coast stopping at Belém (though fast trains do not stop here), then the beaches of Oeiras, Carcavelos and stations beyond to Estoril and Cascais at the end of the line. It leaves Cais do Sodré station every twenty minutes (Mon–Thurs & Sun 5.30am–1.30am, Fri & Sat 5.30am–2.30am; €2.45).

By road The attractive N6 coastal highway (Avenida Marginal) passes through most of the centres along the seafront; the faster A5 motorway (Auto-Estrada da Oeste) is an inexpensive toll road that runs further inland from Lisbon to Estoril – drive west past Amoreiras and follow the signs.

1

Oeiras

The first suburb of any size after Belém is **OEIRAS** (pronounced *oo-air-esh*), where the Rio Tejo officially turns into the sea. The riverside walkways and the beach here have recently been cleaned up, though most people still swim in the ocean pool alongside the sands. The only reason to stop here is to see the **Palácio do Marquês de Pombal**, at Largo Marquês de Pombal, the erstwhile home of the rebuilder of Lisbon. Now an adult education centre, the grand house can be visited by appointment only (☎ 214 465 300, ⓦ egeac.pt), although the attractive gardens are open daily (9am–9pm, until 6pm from Oct–April; free).

Carcavelos

The next town along the line, **CARCAVELOS** has the most extensive sandy beach on this part of the coast and is popular with surfers and windsurfers. To reach the beach, it's a ten-minute walk from the station along the broad Avenida Jorge V. Try to visit Carcavelos on Thursday morning, when the town hosts a huge **market**; turn right out of the station and follow the signs.

Estoril

With its fine beach, casino and surviving grandiose villas dotted among the modern apartments, you can see why **ESTORIL** (pronounced *é-stril*) was the favoured haunt of exiled royalty during the earlier half of the last century. These days it's a lively resort, its centre consisting of the palm-lined **Parque do Estoril**, surrounded by bars and restaurants and the enormous **casino**. The **Feira Internacional Artesanato** – handicrafts and folk music festival – is held here in July.

The casino

Tues–Sat 3pm–3am • Free • Semiformal attire required • ☎ 214 667 700, ⓦ casino-estoril.pt

During World War II, **Estoril Casino** was a popular hangout for exiled royalty and spies, including James Bond author Ian Fleming who was based here to keep an eye on double agents. He used his experience at the casino as inspiration for his first Bond novel, *Casino Royale*.

Praia de Tamariz

The resort's fine sandy beach, **Praia de Tamariz**, is backed by cafés, restaurants and a **seafront promenade** that stretches northwest to Cascais, 2km away. A stroll between the two towns is recommended, drifting from beach to bar; the walk takes around twenty minutes. From July to mid-September, a free firework display is held above the beach every Saturday night at midnight.

ARRIVAL AND INFORMATION   ESTORIL

By train The train station is on Estoril's through-road; take the underpass from the station to reach the beach on one side and the town the other.

Information Estoril's turismo is across the main road from the station, at the bottom of the park (daily: June–Sept 9am–8pm; Oct–May 10am–1pm & 2–6pm; ☎ 214 663 813, ⓦ estoril-portugal.com), and can provide advice on private rooms and details of the area's various golf clubs.

ACCOMMODATION AND EATING

Deck Bar Arcadas do Parque 21 ☎ 214 680 366. Facing the park, just back from the turismo, this great little restaurant and café has outdoor tables. A good spot for a drink or snack, it also serves a range of dishes from omelettes and pasta to *bacalhau* and seafood; main courses €8–10. Tues–Sat 8am–2am.

Jonas Bar Passeio Marítimo, Monte Estoril ☎ 214 676 946. On the seafront promenade, around five minutes north of Estoril towards Cascais, this is a laidback beach café-bar facing the waves. As well as cocktails and fresh juices, it also serves light lunches and snacks. Daily 8am–2am; Oct–April closes at 8pm.

Smart Rua Maestro Laçerda 6, by Rua José Viana 63 ☎ 214 682 164, ⓦ hotel-smart.net. The best budget choice for accommodation, with pleasant rooms and its own pool and bar in a building originally built as an architect's summer house. Free wi-fi and parking. €75

1

Cascais

At the end of the train line, **CASCAIS** (*cash-kaysh*) is a handsome resort of grand mansions and former fishermen's houses wrapped round a bay dotted with **sandy beaches**. There's a flash marina and a fort (now a hotel) that guards the harbour, as well as a cluster of appealing museums, including the wonderful **Casa das Histórias**, dedicated to the artist Paula Rego. While the beaches can get pretty mobbed in summer, it has a young vibe and **lively nightlife**.

The mosaic-paved and partly pedestrianized streets of Cascais **old town** have almost as much allure as its beaches. Just off the main drag, it is worth seeking out the bustle of the local **fish market** (Mon–Fri after the day's tide), while for a wander away from the crowds, stroll up beyond Largo 5° de Outubro into the pretty network of houses on the west side of town, in the streets north of the graceful **Igreja da Assunção**.

1

Museu do Mar

Rua Júlio Pereiro de Melo • Tues–Sun 10am–5pm • Free • ☎ 214 815 906

The modern and engaging **Museu do Mar** relates the town's relationship with the sea, via a fascinating collection of model boats, fossils and stuffed fish. There are also stories about and finds from various local shipwrecks, that children, in particular, will enjoy.

Casa das Histórias

Av da República 300 • Daily 10am–6pm • Free • ⓦ casadashistoriaspaularego.com

You can't miss the distinctive ochre towers of the modernist **Casa das Histórias** – a museum which, unusually, is dedicated to a living artist, Paula Rego, who was made a Dame by the British Queen in 2010. The museum, designed by famous architect Eduardo Souto de Moura, features around 120 of Rego's disturbing but beautiful collages, pastels and engravings, as well as those by her late husband Victor Willing.

Museu Biblioteca Conde Castro Guimarães

Av Rei Humberto II de Itália • Tues–Fri 10am–5pm, Sat & Sun 10am–1pm & 2–5pm • Free • ⓦ cm-cascais.pt

On the seafront side of the leafy expanses of the Parque Municipal da Gandarinha, with its mini-zoo and small lake, stands the **Museu Biblioteca Conde Castro Guimarães** within the former grand mansion of the counts of Guimarães. It is now a house museum, and you are free to wander round the opulent rooms filled with period furniture, paintings and the antiques that the family bequeathed to the nation. Its most valuable exhibit is some rare, illuminated sixteenth-century manuscripts.

Palácio da Cidadela

Passeio D. Maria Pia • Open for exhibits only • Free • ☎ 213 614 660

Cascais' **Palácio da Cidadela** was built in the seventeenth century to help defend the mouth of the Tagus, but by 1870, it had become a summer home for the royal family – a role it continued for Portugal's presidents after the birth of the republic in 1910. Completely renovated in 2004, the fortress now houses a hotel and a cultural space that is open to the public for various temporary exhibitions. Just below the fortress is the entrance to the **Marina de Cascais**, an enclave of expensive yachts serviced by restaurants, bars and boutiques.

PAULA REGO

Paula Rego (born 1935) shot to international prominence in 1990 when she was appointed Artist in Residence at London's National Gallery, and she is now considered one of the world's leading figurative painters. In 2011, she was listed as one of the top 100 most influential living women in *The Guardian* newspaper. Although she has spent most of her life in England – she married English artist Vic Willing – her formative years were spent in Salazar's Lisbon, where she was born. She had a sheltered childhood within the confines of a wealthy family home and she still feels bitter about the way her mother became a "casualty" of a society which encouraged wealthy women to be idle, leaving work to their servants. Her women are portrayed as typical of the servants of her childhood: stocky and solid. Other adults are usually viewed with the unsentimental eye of a child, and she paints hairy, bony, yet powerful female figures. Power and dominance are major themes of her work; she revives the military outfits of postwar Portugal for her men and dresses many of her women like dolls in national costume. Several of her pictures convey sexual opposition, the result of a background dominated by the regimes of the Roman Catholic Church and a military dictatorship. Her images are rarely beautiful, but are undoubtedly amusing, disturbing and powerful.

1

Santa Marta Lighthouse
Rua do Farol • Tues–Fri 10am–5pm, Sat & Sun 10am–1pm & 2–6pm • Free

The distinctive blue-and-white-striped **Santa Marta Lighthouse** now doubles as a small museum that traces the building's history from a fort in the eighteenth century to the development of optical devices. Don't miss the fine terrace café.

Praia do Guincho

Regular buses from Cascais bus station run the 6km west to **Praia do Guincho**, an enormous sandy beach which curves round a large bay. Often the waves are too big to swim here (take great care of dangerous undertows), though it's a superb place for surfing and windsurfing if you know what you're doing – legs of the World Windsurfing Championships are often held here in August.

ARRIVAL AND INFORMATION   CASCAIS

By train The train station is on Largo da Estação, a couple of minutes' walk from the centre of town.
By bus The bus station is opposite the train station, beneath Cascais Village Shopping, with regular buses to Cabo da Roca (approx hourly; 40min), Guincho (every 1–2 hours; 20 min) and Sintra (approx hourly; 1hr).

Information Cascais turismo is set in an old mansion on Rua Visconde da Luz (June–Sept Mon–Sat 9am–7pm, Sun 10am–6pm; Oct–May daily 10am–1pm & 2–6pm; ☎ 214 868 204), where the staff will usually phone around on your behalf for private rooms.

ACCOMMODATION

Baía Av Combatentes da Grande Guerra ☎ 214 831 033, ⓦ hotelbaia.com. Modern seafront hotel overlooking the harbour, with a great rooftop pool and bar and a highly regarded restaurant. It has over a hundred rooms, all with a/c and satellite TV, and many with a sea view (book ahead in summer for these). **€130**

★ **Farol Design Hotel** Av Rei Humberto II de Italia 7 ☎ 214 823 490, ⓦ farol.com.pt. Right on the seafront, this is one of the area's most fashionable hideaways, neatly combining traditional and contemporary architecture. A new designer wing has been added onto a sixteenth-century villa, and the decor combines wood and marble with modern steel and glass. The best rooms have sea views and terraces. There's also a restaurant, fantastic fairy-lit outside bar and seapool facing a fine rocky foreshore. **€260**

Pergola House Av Valbom 13, Cascais ☎ 214 840 040, ⓦ pergolahouse.com. Sumptuous century-old mansion bang in the centre of town with its own garden, stucco ceilings and wonderfully ornate, tiled dining room. Each room has a distinct character, and some have their own balconies. **€130**

★ **Solar Dom Carlos** Rua Latina Coelho 8 ☎ 214 828

115, ⓦ solardomcarlos.com. The best-value place in town, set in a sixteenth-century mansion on a quiet backstreet in the pretty western side of Cascais. Dom Carlos once stayed here, hence the royal chapel, which still survives. The tiled interior stays cool in summer, there's a garden and car parking, while the attractive rooms come with satellite TV and fridge. Parking. **€70**

Vila Bicuda Rua dos Faisões, Cascais ☎ 214 8960 200, ⓦ vilabicuda.com. A very well run, upmarket villa complex set in its own landscaped grounds with two large swimming pools. Excellent for families, the modern villas are well equipped and the complex has its own great café, shop and (pricey) Italian restaurant. But you'll need a car – it's around 3km from central Cascais towards Guincho. **€130**

CAMPSITE

Orbitur Guincho Lugar da Areia, EN247, Guincho ☎ 214 870 450, ⓦ orbitur.pt. Attractive campsite set among pine trees close to Guincho beach, which is served by bus from Cascais. The site, with its own tennis courts, minimarket and café, also has bungalows and caravans for rent. Orbitur members get a ten-percent discount. Pitch **€21**

EATING AND DRINKING

RESTAURANTS AND CAFÉS

Esplanada Santa Marta Av Rei Humberto II de Italia ☎ 214 837 779. This is one of the best places to enjoy charcoal-grilled fish (around €8) served on a tiny terrace overlooking the sea and a little beach. Tues–Sat 10am–10pm.

Jardim dos Frangos Av Combatentes da Grande Guerra 68 ☎ 214 861 717. Permanently buzzing with

people and sizzling with the speciality grilled chicken (around €7), which is devoured by the plate-load at indoor and outdoor tables. Daily 10am–midnight.

Music Bar Largo da Praia da Rainha 121 ☎ 214 820 848. Decent pasta, grills and fish (from €12) can be had in this restaurant with superb views from its interior or at tables on the patio above the beach. Daily 10am–10pm; Oct–May closed on Mon.

O Pescador Rua das Flores 10 ☏ 214 832 054. The best of a row of restaurants near the fish market, this offers superior fish meals and good service. A meal will set you back a good €25, but main courses such as tuna cooked in garlic are sublime. Mon–Sat noon–3.30pm & 6.30–11pm.

O Solar do Bitoque Rua Regimento 19 de Infantaria, Loja 11 ☏ 918 580 343. *Bitoques* are thin steaks, and this lively local with outdoor seating specializes in various types as well as inexpensive burgers, salads and fresh fish; most mains under €6. Mon–Sat 10am–midnight.

Santini Av Valbom 28F ☏ 214 833 709. Opened by an Italian immigrant just after the Second World War, *Santini*'s ice creams are legendary in these parts. Fresh, natural ingredients produce delicious fruity flavours such as mango, strawberry, lemon and passion fruit or "classics" such as chocolate, pistachio, almond and caramel. Daily 11am–midnight.

BARS

Bar Salamandra Praia da Duquesa ☏ 214 820 287. Just up from the station towards Estoril, with a great view of the seafront, this buzzing bar has something for everyone, from bar games to live TV sports and frequent live music (jazz and rock). Also serves snacks. Daily noon–2am.

Chequers Largo Luís de Camões 7 ☏ 214 830 926. Lively English-style pub with sports TV and so-so food; the big draw is the outdoor tables on the attractive square. Daily: May–Sept 8am–2am; Oct–April 8am–8pm.

Sintra

The attractive, verdant town of **SINTRA** warrants at least a day of anyone's itinerary, though two or three days would allow you to make the most of its fabulous surroundings. The cooler air of the hilltop town made it the preferred summer retreat for Portugal's royalty; over the years it has also attracted the rich and famous, and inspired countless writers, including Lord Byron (who begins his epic poem *Childe Harold* in "Cintra's glorious Eden") and Gothic-novel writer William Beckford. It was awarded UNESCO World Heritage status in 1995 because "the cultural landscape of the Serra and the town of Sintra represents a pioneering approach to Romantic landscaping that had an outstanding influence on developments elsewhere in Europe".

The town's historic centre spreads across the slopes of several steep hills. Dominating the centre of **Sintra-Vila** are the tapering chimneys of the **Palácio Nacional**, surrounded by an array of tall houses painted in pale pink, ochre or mellow yellow, many with ornate turrets and decorative balconies peering out to the plains of Lisbon far below. All this is highly scenic – though summer crowds can swamp its narrow central streets, and once you've seen the sights, you're best off heading to the surrounding attractions up in the hills. Easiest to reach are the **Castelo dos Mouros** and the extraordinary **Palácio da Pena** – both visible on the wooded heights above town – or the lush gardens of **Monserrate**, though you'll need a car to see the **Convento dos Capuchos**.

Sintra's annual **festa** in honour of St Peter is held on June 28 and 29, while in July and August the **Sintra Music Festival** puts on classical performances in a number of the town's buildings, including the Palácio Nacional. The end of July also sees the **Feira Grande** in São Pedro, with crafts, antiques and cheeses on sale.

Palácio Nacional

Largo da Rainha Dona Amélia • Mon, Tues & Thurs–Sun 10am–6.30pm; Oct–May closes at 5.30pm • €9, free on Sun 10am–2pm • ⓦ pnsintra.imc.pt

Best seen early or late in the day to avoid the crowds, the sumptuous and wonderfully atmospheric **Palácio Nacional** largely dates from the reign of Dom João I (1385–1433), making it the oldest surviving palace in Portugal, though sadly, after the fall of the monarchy in 1910, most of the surrounding walls and medieval houses were destroyed. Embellished by a series of monarchs – notably Manuel I (1495–1521) – the palace displays a range of architectural styles from Moorish tiles to Manueline decorations and Gothic battlements.

On the lower floor of the palace, you'll pass through the beautiful **Sala dos Cisnes** (Hall of Swans), a reception room named after the painted swans on its ceiling, and the **Sala das Pegas** (Hall of Magpies). The story goes that Dom João I had the room

1

SINTRA-VILA

Summer tramway

Palácio Nacional

Centro Cultural O. Cadaval

Market

ESTEFÂNIA

PR. DA REPÚBLICA

Museu do Brinquedo

Câmara Municipal

Buses

Train Station

SEE INSET

SINTRA-VILA

PR. DA REPÚBLICA

VOLTA DO DUQUE

Parque da Liberdade

Quinta da Regaleira

Santa Maria

SÃO PEDRO DE SINTRA

São Pedro

Castelo dos Mouros

Chalet Condessa d'Edla

SANTA EUFÉMIA

Palácio da Pena

Ticket Office

N

SINTRA

0   100
metres

Cruz Alta

Colares & Praia das Maças   Ericeira & Mafra

Monserrate (4km) & Cabo da Roca

Convento dos Capuchos

Convento dos Capuchos

Portela de Sintra & Bus Station

Algueirão

Lisbon, Cascais & Queluz

ACCOMMODATION	
Casa do Valle	3
Chalet Relogio	5
Nova Sintra	2
Piela's	1
Sintra Jardim	4

RESTAURANTS, CAFÉS AND BARS	
Adega das Caves	1
Cantinho de São Pedro	6
Casa da Piriquita	2
Fonte da Pipa	4
Páteo do Garrett	5
Tulhas	3

STRANGE HAPPENINGS IN SINTRA

Sintra has been a centre for **cult worship** for centuries: the early Celts named it Mountain of the Moon after one of their gods and the hills are scattered with laylines and mysterious tombs. Locals say batteries drain in the area faster than elsewhere and light bulbs seem to pop with monotonous regularity. Some claim this is because of the angle of iron in the rocks, others that it is all part of the **mystical powers** that lurk in Sintra's hills and valleys. There are certainly plenty of **geographical and meteorological quirks**. In the woods around Capuchos, house-sized boulders litter the landscape as if thrown by giants, while a white cloud – affectionately known as the queen's fart – regularly hovers over Sintra's palaces even on the clearest summer day. Exterior walls seem to merge with the landscape as they are quickly smothered in a thick layer of ferns, lichens and moss. And its castles, palaces, mansions and follies shelter tales of Masonic rites, insanity and eccentricity that are as fantastical as the buildings themselves.

---

decorated with as many magpies as there were women at court, implying that they were all magpie-like gossips after he was allegedly caught canoodling with one of the servants.

Best of the upper floor is the gallery above the palace chapel. Beyond here, a succession of state rooms leads to the **Sala das Brasões**, a dazzling domed hall embellished with 72 coats of arms representing Portuguese nobility. Finally, don't miss the **kitchens**, whose roofs taper into the 33-metre-high chimneys which are the palace's distinguishing features.

Museu do Brinquedo

Rua Visconde de Monserrate 29 • Tues–Sun 10am–6pm • €4, children €2 • ⓦ museu-do-brinquedo.pt

Housed in a former fire station, the impressive **Museu do Brinquedo** houses what was once a fascinating private toy collection. The huge array of toys over three floors is somewhat confusingly labelled, but look out for the 3000-year-old stone Egyptian toys, as well as Hornby trains from the 1930s and some of the first-ever toy cars, produced in Germany in the early 1900s. Perhaps the most interesting section is that on early Portuguese toys, containing papier-mâché cars, tin-plate animals, wooden trams and trains, as well as a selection of 1930s beach toys, including beautifully painted buckets.

Quinta da Regaleira

Daily: April–Sept 10am–8pm; Oct & Feb–March 10am–6.30pm; Nov–Jan 10am–5.30pm • 90min tours every 30min–1hr; reservations essential • €10; unguided visits €6 • ☏ 219 106 650, ⓦ regaleira.pt

Just a five-minute walk out of town on the Seteais–Monserrate road, **Quinta da Regaleira** is one of Sintra's most elaborate estates, laid out at the turn of the twentieth century, and declared a UNESCO World Heritage Site in 1995. The estate was designed by Italian architect and theatrical set designer Luigi Manini for wealthy landowner António Augusto Carvalho Monteiro. The Italian's sense of the dramatic is obvious: the principal building, the mock-Manueline **Palaçio dos Milhões**, sprouts turrets and towers, though the interior is sparse apart from some more elaborate Rococo wooden ceilings and impressive Art Nouveau tiles. The surrounding **gardens** are more impressive and shelter fountains, terraces, lakes and grottoes. The most memorable feature is the Initiation Well, inspired by the initiation practices of the Knights Templar and Freemasons. Entering via a Harry Potter-style revolving stone door, you can walk down a moss-covered spiral stairway to the foot of the well and through a tunnel, which eventually resurfaces at the edge of a lake.

Monserrate

Estrada da Monserrate • Daily: April–Sept 9.30am–8pm; Oct–March 10am–6pm • €7 • optional guided tours of the palace daily at 10am & 3pm, €5 extra • ⓦ www.parquesdesintra.pt • Bus #435 from Sintra station via Sintra-Vila, about every 30min; €2

About an hour's walk beyond the Quinta da Regaleira, the fabulous gardens and palace of **Monserrate** is most associated with William Beckford, a wealthy MP and author of

1

the Gothic novel *Vathek*. He rented the estate from 1793 to 1799, after he was forced to leave Britain when caught in a compromising position with a 16-year-old boy. He set about improving the place, by landscaping a waterfall and re-creating elements of his estate at Fonthill in Wiltshire.

Half a century later, a second immensely rich Englishman, Sir Francis Cook, bought the estate, with scarcely less ambitious plans. Cook imported the head gardener from Kew to lay out succulents and water plants, tropical ferns and palms, and just about every known conifer. For a time Monserrate boasted the only lawn in Iberia and it remains one of Europe's most richly stocked gardens, with over a thousand different species of subtropical trees and plants.

From the entrance, paths lead steeply down through tree ferns and lush undergrowth to a ruined chapel, half-engulfed by a giant banyan tree. From here, lawns take you up to Cook's main legacy, the construction of a great **palace** inspired by Brighton Pavilion, with its mix of Moorish and Italian decoration – the dome is modelled on the Duomo in Florence. The interior has largely been restored after years of neglect and you can now admire the amazingly intricate plasterwork which covers almost every wall and ceiling. Don't miss the billiard room, with superb views over the coast. The park also has a decent café.

Castelo dos Mouros

Daily: April to mid-Oct 9.30am–8pm; mid-Oct to March 10am–6pm • €7 • ⓦ www.parquesdesintra.pt • Bus #434 from Sintra station or Sintra-Vila; €5

From Sintra, it's a pleasant, if steep, walk up to the spectacular ruined ramparts of the **Castelo dos Mouros**, the "Castle of the Moors" (30–40min): start at the Calçada dos Clérigos, near the church of Santa Maria, where a stone pathway leads all the way up to the lower slopes, where you can see a Moorish grain silo and a ruined twelfth-century church. To enter the castle itself, you'll need to buy a ticket from the road exit. Built in the ninth century, the castle was taken from the Moors in 1147 by Afonso Henriques, Portugal's first monarch: the ruins of a Moorish mosque remain. The castle walls were allowed to fall into disrepair over subsequent centuries, though they were restored in the mid-nineteenth century under the orders of Ferdinand II. The castle is partly built into two craggy pinnacles, and views from up here are dazzling both inland and across to the Atlantic. Recent excavations have revealed the ruins of Muslim houses, thirty Medieval Christian graves and ceramic vases dating back to the fifth century BC.

Palácio da Pena

Estrada da Pena • Daily: April–Sept 9.45am–7pm; Oct–March 10am–6pm • Palace, gardens & Chalet Condessa d'Edla €13.50; gardens only €7; Chalet Condessa d'Edla & gardens €9 • ⓦ www.parquesdesintra.pt • Bus #434 from Sintra station or Sintra-Vila to the ticket office, every 20min; €5

From the ticket office, it's a short ride on a shuttle bus (€3 return) or a twenty-minute walk up through the gardens – a stretch of rambling woodland with a scattering of lakes and follies – to the fantastical **Palácio da Pena** itself. Resembling something out of a Shrek film, with its ornate medley of domes, statues and towers, the palace was built in the late 1840s by the German Baron von Eschwege on the site of a former monastery – whose chapel remains inside the palace today. Queen Maria II's husband, Ferdinand of Saxe-Coburg-Gotha, requested some of the embellishments, which embrace various architectural styles from Moorish to Manueline. The palace was subsequently used as a summer retreat for the royals, and Queen Amélie, mother of the last King of Portugal, stayed the night here before the royals were driven into exile at the birth of the Republic in 1910.

The inside of the palace is also highly impressive, packed with furniture, paintings and imposing statues – the ballroom and royal dining room are particularly lavish. You can also look round the mock-alpine Chalet Condessa d'Edla in the grounds, built by Ferdinand in the 1860s as a retreat for his second wife.

Convento dos Capuchos

9km southwest of Sintra on the EN247-3 • Daily: April to mid-Oct 9.30am–8pm; mid-Oct to March 10am–6pm • €6 • ☎ 219 237 300, ⓦ www.parquedesintra.pt

Built in 1560, the **Convento dos Capuchos** is known as the "cork convent" because of its cork doors and cell-like rooms, cut from rock and also lined with cork. This natural insulation gave the resident monks a modicum of comfort in otherwise incredibly basic conditions. It's hard not to be moved by the simplicity of the place, which was occupied for almost three hundred years before finally being abandoned in 1834 by its seven remaining monks. You can enter some of the **penitents' cells** by crawling through 70cm-high doors; here, and on every other ceiling, doorframe and lintel, panels of cork are attached, which were taken from the surrounding woods. Elsewhere, you'll come across a washroom, kitchen, refectory, tiny chapels, even a bread oven set apart from the main complex.

1

ARRIVAL AND DEPARTURE   SINTRA

By train Sintra station is on Avenida Dr Miguel Bombarda, a ten- to fifteen-minute walk from Sintra-Vila, the historic centre of the town, with trains from Lisbon's Rossio and Sete Rios stations every twenty minutes (45min; €2.45 one way).

By bus Buses from Cascais (approx hourly; 1hr), stop outside Sintra train station.

INFORMATION AND PASSES

Information Sintra turismo (daily: June–Sept 9am–8pm; Oct–May 9.30am–1.30pm & 2.30–6pm; ☎ 219 231 157, ⓦ www.cm-sintra.pt) lies just off the central Praça da República. There's also a small turismo desk at Sintra station (daily 9am–7pm).

Cultural Landscape of Sintra Pass If you are planning to visit most of Sintra's attractions, it may be worthwhile buying an all-inclusive pass (€32), which is valid for 30 days and covers entry to the Palácio Nacional, Monserrate, the Castelo dos Mouros, the Palácio da Pena and the Convento dos Capuchos.

GETTING AROUND

Local buses Local buses depart across the street from the train station, with services to and from Cabo da Roca (every 1–2 hr; 40min), and the Sintra beaches. Hop-on, hop-off bus #434 takes a circular route from Sintra station and Sintra-Vila to the Pena Palace and the Castelo dos Mouros via São Pedro (every 20min; €5), while bus #435 goes from Sintra station and Sintra-Vila to Quinta da Regaleira and Monserrate gardens (approx every 30min; €2).

Bus pass If you want to visit several sights in the area, including the coast, consider a Day-rover (Turístico Diário) ticket, which allows travel on all the local buses run by Scotturb (ⓦ scotturb.com; €10).

Tram There is also a summer tram that runs from Sintra to the coast via Colares, but services are erratic, so check with the Sintra tourist board first.

ACCOMMODATION

Casa do Valle Rua da Paderna 2 ☎ 219 244 699, ⓦ casadovalle.com. Though steeply downhill from the historic centre, this charming guesthouse still commands unbeatable views across the wooded slopes of Sintra. There are various rooms, from top-floor doubles with the best views, to ground-floor rooms with their own terraces. All the rooms access a beautiful garden with its own pool. Good for families, with interconnecting rooms. €90

Chalet Relogio Estrada da Pena 22, Sintra-Vila ☎ 219 241 550, ⓦ chaletrelogio.com. Nineteenth-century architect Luigi Mannini, who worked on the Quinta Regaleira (see p.113), designed this wonderful mansion with a distinctive clock tower. Individual rooms are simply furnished but enormous, with big windows and high ceilings, and there's a rambling garden too. It's a long walk into town but bus #434 passes outside. €65

Nova Sintra Largo Afonso d'Albuquerque 25, Estefânia ☎ 219 230 220, ⓦ novasintra.com. This hotel is in a big mansion above a decent restaurant, which has a raised café-terrace overlooking the busy street. Modern rooms, all with cable TV, bath and shiny marble floors. €80

Piela's Av Desiderio Cambournac 1–3, Estefânia ☎ 219 241 691, ⓦ comcafepielas.com. Popular budget accommodation in a swish, renovated townhouse on a busy road above a cybercafé. The welcoming English-speaking proprietor offers rooms of varying sizes, each with TV. Triples also available. No breakfast. €65

★ **Sintra Jardim** Trav dos Alvares, São Pedro ☎ 219 230 738, ⓦ residencialsintra.blogspot.com. The best mid-range option in the area, this rambling old building has soaring ceilings, wooden floors and oodles of character. There's a substantial garden with a swimming pool and the giant rooms can easily accommodate extra beds – so it's great for families. You'll need to book ahead in summer; in winter there's a log fire in the communal lounge. €80

EATING AND DRINKING

There's a great **market** – with antiques and crafts, as well as food – in São Pedro's main square on the second and last Sunday of every month. Good restaurants are thin on the ground; the best concentration is at São Pedro, a twenty-minute walk from town. Local specialities include *queijadas da Sintra* – sweet cheese pastry-cakes.

Adega das Caves Rua de Pendoa 2, Sintra-Vila ☎ 219 239 848. Bustling café-bar beneath *Café Paris*, attracting a predominantly youthful local clientele; good-value salads and baguettes as well as inexpensive grills from around €9. Daily 9am–2am.

Cantinho de São Pedro Praça D. Fernando II 18, São Pedro de Sintra ☎ 219 230 267. Large, stone-walled restaurant overlooking an attractive courtyard just off São Pedro's main square. Slightly formal service but excellent food at reasonable prices. Try the daily specials, which are

1

usually good value. On cool evenings, a log fire keeps things cosy. Daily noon–3pm & 7.30–10pm.

Casa da Piriquita Rua das Padarias 1, Sintra-Vila ☏219 230 626. On the uphill alley off the main square, this tearoom and bakery is always busy with locals queueing to buy *queijadas da Sintra* and the similarly sticky *travesseiros*. Its more modern sister branch, up the hill at no. 18 (closed Tues), has a big outdoor terrace. Thurs–Tues 9am–midnight.

Fonte da Pipa Rua Fonte da Pipa 11–13, Sintra-Vila ☏219 234 437. This laidback bar with low lighting is one of the few bars in this part of town, and sits next to the lovely fountain (*fonte*) the street is named after. Daily 9pm–2am.

★ **Páteo do Garrett** Rua Maria Eugénia Reis F. Navarro 7, Sintra-Vila ☏219 243 380. Bar-restaurant with a dark interior, though the lovely, sunny patio has great views over the village. It serves standard Portuguese meals, or just pop in for a drink. Mains such as monkfish rice from around €12. May–Dec Thurs–Tues 11am–11pm; Jan–April closes at 2pm.

Tulhas Rua Gil Vicente 4, Sintra-Vila ☏219 232 378. Imaginative cooking in a fine building, converted from old grain silos. The giant mixed grills at €24 for two people will keep carnivores more than happy, while the weekend specials (around €9) are usually excellent. Thurs–Tues noon–3.30pm & 7–10pm.

The Sintra coast

West of Sintra the road winds around through the hills to **PRAIA GRANDE**, the best beach on this section of coast, certainly for surfers. In August the World Bodyboarding Championships are held here, along with games such as volleyball and beach rugby. Plenty of inexpensive cafés and restaurants spread along the beachside road. Just north of Praia Grande is the larger resort of **PRAIA DAS MAÇÃS**, a lively little holiday village with plenty of bars and restaurants sprawled round a broad expanse of sand – a good place to spend a day or two. Sintra's **historic tramway** offers the most picturesque, if rather slow, route to the coast: opened in 1904, the tram trundles along from the northeast part of Sintra to the coast at Praia das Maçãs via Colares.

The most visited part of this coast, however, is **CABO DA ROCA**, 14km southwest of Praia Grande and officially the most westerly point in mainland Europe – the tourist office in the souvenir shop and café here sells a certificate to prove it. It's an enjoyable trip to get here, though the cape itself offers little more than a lighthouse below which Atlantic breakers slam the cliffs.

ARRIVAL AND INFORMATION

THE SINTRA COAST

By bus Bus #441 runs from Sintra train station to Praia Grande and Praia das Maçãs (every 1–2hr; around 30min). Bus #403 runs approx hourly to Cabo da Roca from both Sintra (40min) and Cascais train stations (40min).

By tram The tram runs from the start of the N247, just north of Avenida Heliodora Salgado in Sintra-Estefânia to Praia das Maçãs (50min; €2). Its current schedule is

April–Sept Fri–Sun 5 daily, but check the local timings with the Sintra tourist board as service interruptions seem to be the norm.

Information The Cabo da Roca turismo is in the souvenir shop on the headland (daily 9am–8pm; Oct–May closes at 7pm; ☏219 280 891, ⊛www.cm-sintra.pt).

ACCOMODATION AND EATING

Arribas Av A. Coelho 28, Praia Grande ☏219 289 050, ⊛hotelarribas.pt. This modern three-star hotel dominates the seafront at the north end of the sands. The rooms, however, are enormous and the hotel boasts sea pools, a restaurant and café-terrace with great sea views. €120

O Loureiro Rua Pedro A. Cabral 6, Praia das Maçãs ☏219 292 442. Overlooking the beach, *O Loureiro* is strong on seafood, with the fresh fish and grilled squid dishes being reliably tasty. Mains around €9. Fri–Wed

11am–3pm & 7–11pm.

São Saturnino Azóia ☏219 289 686, ⊛saosat.com. Reached down a steep track – look for the sign on the left on the way to Azóia/Cabo da Roca – this former convent dates from the twelfth century and sits in a valley where time seems to stand still. The six rooms, three suites and self-catering apartment all come with wooden beams and low ceilings. There's a small outdoor pool and lots of terraces with stunning views. €180

Palácio de Queluz

Largo do Palácio, Queluz Belas • Mon & Wed–Sun 9am–5pm; May–Sept gardens open til 6pm • €9, free on Sun 10am–2pm; gardens only €3 • Portuguese Horsemanship display May–July, Sept & Oct Wed at 11am • ⓦ www.parquesdesintra.pt • Take the Sintra line train from Rossio to Queluz-Belas station (every 20min; 20min, €1.85): turn left out of the station and walk down the main road for fifteen minutes, following signs through the town until you reach a vast cobbled square, Largo do Palácio

Around 13km northwest of Lisbon city centre and 16km southeast of Sintra, the **Palácio de Queluz** is one of Portugal's most sumptuous palaces. Commissioned in 1747 by Dom Pedro, brother of King José I, its striking Rococo exterior and formal gardens were clearly influenced by the Palace of Versailles. It was built as a summer residence for the royals, but ended up being the permanent home of the Dona Maria I, aka Maria the Mad. She married her uncle Dom Pedro, and became queen after José I's death in 1777, but after the death of her husband in 1786, Maria suffered severe mental problems and is said to have alarmed visitors who could hear her screaming from her palace bedroom. The palace was occupied and pillaged by French forces during the Napoleonic wars, when the Portuguese royal family fled to Brazil, though plenty of priceless works of art survived. These can still be seen today, supplemented by further artworks that were installed on the royal family's return to the palace in 1821. Today the palace is preserved as a museum, though it is still pressed into service now and again to accommodate state guests and dignitaries, as well as hosting events for the Sintra music festival.

The palace and gardens

Visitors first enter the **Throne Room**, lined with mirrors surmounted by paintings and golden flourishes. Beyond is the more restrained **Music Chamber** with its portrait of Queen Maria above the French grand piano. Smaller quarters include bed and sitting rooms, a tiny oratory swathed with red velvet, and a **Sculpture Room**, whose only exhibit is an earthenware bust of Maria. Another wing comprises an elegant suite of public rooms – smoking, coffee and dining rooms – all intimate in scale and tastefully decorated. The **Ambassador's Chamber**, where diplomats and foreign ministers were received during the nineteenth century, echoes the Throne Room in style, with one side lined with porcelain chinoiserie. In the end, though, perhaps the most pleasing room is the simple **Dressing Room** with its geometric inlaid wooden floor and spider's-web ceiling of radial gilt bands.

Outside, the formal **gardens** consist of low box hedges and weatherworn statues spreading out from the protection of the palace wings, while small pools and fountains, steps and terracing form a harmonious background to the building.

South of the Rio Tejo

The south bank of the river Tejo was linked to Lisbon only by ferry until 1966, when the "Salazar Bridge" was built. Renamed the **Ponte 25 de Abril** after the 1974 Revolution, this huge suspension bridge opened up the south bank to the encroaching city. **Cacilhas** is the port you'll arrive at if you come by ferry, while **Caparica** is the main resort along the superb Costa da Caparica, which stretches for some 20km to the south.

Cacilhas

Ferry from Cais do Sodré daily 5.40am–2.30am; every 15min; €1.20; ⓦ transtejo.pt

The most enjoyable way to approach the southern bank of the Rio Tejo is to take the ferry from Lisbon's Cais do Sodré to **CACILHAS**. The blustery ride grants wonderful views of the city, as well as of the Ponte 25 de Abril, though it's the line of **seafood restaurants** along the riverfront that attracts most Lisboetas to make the crossing. The moderately priced riverside *Cervejaria Farol* is a good bet, though if you head towards the bridge along the Cais do Ginjal you'll find plenty of others with great Lisbon outlooks.

1

Elevador Panorâmico da Boca do Vento
Daily 8am–midnight • €2 return

Just along the waterfront from the Cacilhas ferry terminal is the foot of the **Elevador Panorâmico da Boca do Vento**, a sleek, modern elevator which whisks you up the cliff face to the old part of Almada. From the top there are fantastic views over the river and city, while the surrounding streets are highly atmospheric.

Cristo Rei
Av Cristo Rei 61 • Daily 9.30am–6.30pm • €5 • ⓦ cristorei.pt • Bus #101 from Cacilhas

On a steep cliff above Almada, facing Lisbon across the Tejo, stands the Rio-like **Cristo Rei** (Christ the King) statue, built in 1959 as part of a church. A lift shuttles you up the interior of the statue to a viewing platform, 80m above the ground, with dramatic vistas over the Ponte 25 de Abril, the river and the city.

Caparica
Allegedly named after the discovery of a cloak (*capa*) full of golden coins, the beach resort of **CAPARICA**, at the northern end of the Costa da Caparica, is Lisbon's main seaside resort. It's high-rise, tacky and packed at weekends in summer, but don't let that put you off – the family atmosphere, restaurants and beachside cafés full of tanned surfers make it a thoroughly enjoyable day out. From the main **Praça da Liberdade** (home to the market, supermarkets and banks), the pedestrianized **Rua dos Pescadores** – lined with cafés, restaurants and inexpensive guesthouses – heads down to the seafront. The **beach** itself stretches north towards Lisbon and south away into the distance. The water is of good quality, though beware the dangerous undertow.

A **mini-railway** (May–Sept daily every 30min from 9am–7pm; €6.50 return, or €4.50 for first nine stops; ⓦ transportesalmada.ageneal.pt) runs along the 8km or so of dunes to Fonte da Telha – if you're after solitude, just take the train to the last stop and walk. There are nineteen mini-train stops, most with a beach-café or two, and each with its own particular atmosphere: the earlier stops tend to be family-oriented, later ones are on the whole more fashionable, while stop 18–19 is something of a gay hangout.

ARRIVAL AND INFORMATION | CAPARICA

By bus From Cacilhas take the Via Rapida bus (approx every 30min, daily 7am–9pm; 30min). Alternatively, buses leave from Areeiro in Lisbon (every 30–60min, daily 7am–12.45am; 40min–1hr). In summer, buses stop at the bus park in town near the beginning of the sands. In winter, they use the station in Praça Padre Manuel Bernades, in which case it is best to get off at the first stop in Caparica, on the edge of the leafy Praça da Liberdade, five minutes back from the beach.

Information The turismo is near the beach at Frente Urbana de Praias (Mon–Fri 9.30am–1pm & 2–5.30pm, Sat 9.30am–1pm; ☎ 212 900 071, ⓦ www.cm-almada.pt).

ACCOMMODATION

Orbitur Av Afonso de Albuquerque ☎ 212 901 366, ⓦ orbitur.pt. Caparica's most central campsite is well-equipped, complete with a café and minimarket, though it gets pretty packed in August. Pitch **€21**

Real Caparica Hotel Rua Mestre Manuel 18 ☎ 212 918 870, ⓦ realcaparicahotel.com. Close to the beach and the centre, this small hotel is one of the best-value central options, with some of the en-suite rooms having sea-facing balconies. **€70**

EATING AND DRINKING

O Barbas Rua Praia 13 ☎ 212 900 163. This is the best of the dozens of fish and seafood restaurants in a row of modern wood-framed buildings on the promenade. It serves up affordable paella, *cataplana* and fresh fish (around €9). Mon, Tues & Thurs–Sun noon–2am.

Tarquinio Bar Muralha da Praia ☎ 212 900 053. At the back of the beach near the centre of town, this is a popular surfers' hangout with great cocktails, snacks, and beanbags to lounge on. Tues, Wed & Sun 10am & 2am, Fri & Sat 9am–2am.

Setúbal and Palmela

1

Some 50km south of Lisbon, **SETÚBAL** is a bustling and fairly industrial port, though its historic, pedestrianized centre is both lively and highly attractive, set round a series of squares and narrow alleys filled with decent shops and restaurants. It's a pleasant place to spend some time – take a dolphin trip or look round the remarkable Igreja de Jesus – while its ferry link over the wide Sado estuary gives easy access to miles of long sandy beaches.

Igreja de Jesus

Largo de Jesus • Tues–Sun 9am–noon & 2–5pm, closed public hols • Free

Stranded in a somewhat bleak stretch of town, the **Igreja de Jesus** is one of the most important churches in Portugal. It was founded in 1490, and was a pioneer of the Manueline style that was developed by its architect Diogo de Boitaca (see box, p.166). Its most striking feature is its twisted columns, resembling ropes and made using the local stone from Arrábida. The beautiful *azulejo* tiles were seventeenth-century additions.

Casa da Baía

Av Luísa Todi 468 • Mon–Wed & Sun 9am–10pm, Thurs–Sat 9am–midnight • Free • ☎ 265 545 010, ⓦ mun-setubal.pt

Housed in an eighteenth-century former convent, which later became an orphanage, **Casa da Baía** is still partly run by former orphans. It now houses the city's tourist office as well as a cultural centre and exhibition space, with its own wine shop, restaurant and café in the internal courtyard.

1

Casa do Corpo Santo

Rua Corpo Santo 7 • Oct–April Tues–Fri 9am–12.30pm & 2–5.30pm, Sat 3–7pm; Sept–May Tues–Fri 9am–12.30pm & 2–5.30pm, Sat 2–6pm • ☎ 265 534 222 • €1.20

Take a peek inside the small but beautiful **Casa do Corpo Santo**, built in 1714 as a nobleman's palace and later used as a fishermen's fraternity. It's now a small museum celebrating the fisherman's craft. The upper floor has a painted ceiling, Baroque chapel and walls decked in superb *azulejos* showing scenes of São Pedro, patron saint of fishermen.

Castelo São Felipe

The **Castelo São Felipe**, signposted off the western end of Avenida Luísa Todi, is half an hour's walk from town. Built on the orders of Spanish king Felipe II in 1590, it's a grand structure, harbouring an *azulejo*-lined chapel and protected by sheer walls of overpowering height. Legend has it that a series of secret tunnels connects the castle with the coast, but any proof was lost in the Great Earthquake of 1755. Part of the castle is now a *pousada* (see p.123) but the ramparts and bar are open to nonguests and there are superb views over the mouth of the Sado estuary.

Tróia

Across the Sado estuary from Setúbal loom the high-rise apartments of **Tróia**, a surprisingly glitzy resort complete with marina and golf course, which looks like it's been beamed in from the Algarve. It sits at the tip of a large sand-spit which is fringed on the Atlantic side by a superb, sandy **beach** – if you have your own transport, however, you're best off heading further south to the quieter sands at Comporta (see p.422).

Tróia Ruinas Romanas

1km northeast of the Tróia passenger ferry terminal, and just northwest of the car ferry terminal • June–Aug Tues–Sat 10am–1pm & 3–6.30pm; Sept–May Sat 10am–1pm & 3–5.30pm • €5 • ☎ 265 499 400

The **Ruinas Romanas** are an impressive site that was once the Roman town of Cetobriga. It grew up from the first century AD as a fish-salting centre, before being

---

JOSÉ MOURINHO: THE SPECIAL ONE

Setúbal's most famous son, **José Mourinho**, is one of Europe's most successful and controversial football managers. Born in Setúbal on January 26, 1963, Mourinho grew up supporting Vitória Setúbal where his father was goalkeeper. He began his managerial career coaching their junior team after a modest playing career, which included a spell at Sesimbrense of Sesimbra, up the coast. His big break, however, was being former England manager Bobby Robson's translator at Barcelona. He exploited what he learnt from the English manager to turn round the fortunes of the previously useless União Leiria, which alerted Porto to his managerial talents. Under Mourinho, Porto swiftly landed the Portuguese league, Portuguese Cup and UEFA Cup (all in 2003), and they were crowned European Champions in 2004. His fame was cemented when he moved to Chelsea later that year and promptly won back-to-back league titles (they had not won a league title previously for half a century). Calling himself "the special one", Mourinho was booted out by the London club in 2007 when it was felt he was getting bigger than the club itself, but after a year off – mostly spent back in Setúbal – his career blossomed further, when he moved to Inter Milan. Here, he not only won back-to-back Italian league titles, but also picked up the European Champions League in 2010. His phenomenal success continued when he moved to Real Madrid, where he won the Spanish league title in 2011, and he was subsequently lured back to London in 2013 for a second stint with Chelsea. Nevertheless, his off-the-field persona always attracts controversy. He stirred up the Italian media with the same aplomb as he did in the UK and made himself unpopular in some quarters of Spain after poking the Barcelona coach in the eye.

Despite his wealth and international profile, Mourinho remains loyal to his Portuguese roots. He married his childhood sweetheart (they have two children) and continues to visit his family in Setúbal. Not surprisingly, he has become a Portuguese national hero.

abandoned in the sixth century, probably after an earthquake and tsunami. You can still see the stone tanks where the fish were preserved before being exported to Rome.

Palmela

The small town of **PALMELA**, 10km north of Setúbal, has an impressive medieval **castle**, whose stunning views look out over the coast and the Parque Natural da Arrábida. It is also the centre of a wine-producing area, hence the town's major annual event, the **Festa das Vindimas**. Held in September, it celebrates the first of the year's wine harvest, with processions, fireworks, grape-treading and running of the bulls.

ARRIVAL AND GETTING AROUND   SETÚBAL AND PALMELA

By bus Setúbal and the surrounding area are served by TST buses (ⓦtsulddotejo.pt), which arrive at and depart from the bus station on Av. 5 de Outubro, a five-minute walk from the pedestrianized centre.

Destinations Cacilhas (hourly; 50min–1hr); Lisbon's Praça de Espanha (every 30min; 1hr); Palmela (Mon–Fri approx hourly; 20min).

By car The fast A2 from Ponte 25 de Abril whisks you to Setúbal from Lisbon in around forty minutes; it's about the same from Lisbon airport via Ponte Vasco da Gama. You can usually park along the eastern edges of the main Avenida Luísa Todi.

By light railway Setúbal and Palmela are both on the Fertagus light railway line (ⓦfertagus.pt) from Lisbon's Entrecampos and Sete-Rios stations (hourly; 50min to

Palmela; 1hr to Setúbal).

By train Conventional trains run from Lisbon's Entre-campos station to Setúbal (approx every hour; 1hr 10min; timetable on ☎707 127 127, ⓦcp.pt) which drop you at Praça do Brasil, north of the town centre; local trains use the more central Praça Quebedo station at the eastern end of Avenida 5 de Outubro.

By ferry Car ferries depart daily from Setúbal across the Sado estuary to Tróia (approx every 35min; 6.45am–10.30pm; from Tróia 7.20am–11pm; €3.25 per person, cars from €12.50; ☎265 235 101, ⓦwww.atlanticferries.pt); expect long queues in summer. There's also an hourly passenger catamaran (approx hourly; 6.20am–1am; from Tróia 6.45am–1.30am; €3.25 per person).

INFORMATION AND ACTIVITIES

Information Setúbal's turismo is in the Casa da Baía (see p.121), Avenida Luísa Todi 468 (Mon–Wed & Sun 9am–10pm, Thurs–Sat 9am–midnight; ☎265 545 010, ⓦmun-setubal.pt).

Dolphin-watching tour Vertigem Azul, Rua Praia da Saúde 11D, near the harbour (☎265 238 000, ⓦvertigemazul.com), runs wonderful three-hour dolphin-watching trips to see a

resident pod of bottle-nosed dolphins, either in the Sado estuary or along the coast (daily weather permitting at 9.30am & 2.30pm, minimum eight people required; €30 per person).

Jeep safari Mil Andanças, Avenida Luísa Todi 121 (☎265 532 979, ⓦmil-andancas.pt) runs day-long jeep safaris to local wine estates (€40 per person; price includes wine tasting and lunch).

ACCOMMODATION

SETÚBAL

Bocage Rua de São Cristovão 14 ☎265 543 080, ⓦhoteisbocage.com. This is the town's best budget option, right in the heart of the pedestrianized old town. The rooms are attractive and well-maintained with private bathrooms, a/c and TVs. **€50**

Hotel do Sado Rua Irene Lisboa 1–3 ☎265 542 800, ⓦhoteldosado.com. Perched on a hilltop above a residential part of town, this renovated mansion has a modern extension with plush rooms, the best sharing the great views from the terrace and restaurant. **€150**

Pousada de Juventude de Setúbal Largo José Afonso ☎265 573 545, ⓦmicrosites.juventude.gov.pt/portal /en. Futuristic, modern hostel right in the middle of one of Setúbal's main squares, close to the docks. It has six four-bed rooms and 12 doubles with or without bath. Dorm beds **€12**; doubles **€27**

Pousada São Filipe Castelo São Filipe ☎265 550 070, ⓦpousadas.pt. The top spot around Setúbal in all ways, with rooms built within the chunky walls of the castle. Front rooms command superb views over the estuary, though avoid those housed in – and still resembling – the former cells. The restaurant (open to nonguests) serves upmarket Portuguese and international cuisine (mains around €20), or you can just enjoy the views with a drink on the terrace. Parking. **€180**

PALMELA

Pousada de Palmela Castelo de Palmela, Palmela ☎212 351 226, ⓦpousadas.pt. Once the headquarters for the Order of Santiago, the convent in the castle has been restored and extended into a fabulous *pousada*, incorporating the original cloisters within the design and boasting panoramic views from all points. There's also a quality in-house restaurant. **€150**

1

EATING AND DRINKING

Good-value fish and seafood **restaurants** abound at the waterside Doca dos Pescadores. There are also plenty of places to eat around the atmospheric **Mercado Municipal** (Mon–Sat 7am–2pm); in summer, the market area is considerably expanded with clothes and touristy bric-a-brac. Nightlife in Setúbal revolves around the outdoor café-bars along Avenida Luísa Todi and the grid of streets north of the Doca dos Pescadores.

A Champanheria Av Luísa Todi 414 ☎ 265 220 996. Classy oyster and champagne bar-restaurant whose owner is a champion of the Slow Food Movement – there are two menu options: four starters and a meat or fish main from €30–40, or eight starters and a main for €43–54. Tues–Sat 12.30–3pm & 7–11pm, Sun 12.30–4pm.

Adega dos Frades Rua M. Afonso Pala 19 ☎ 265 231 425. On a quiet pedestrianized backstreet, this simple old-town bar/restaurant serves bargain lunchtime grills for under €8, with plenty of locals (and a TV) for company. Mon–Fri noon–3pm (until 8pm for drinks and snacks).

Novo 10 Av Luísa Todi 422–426 ☎ 265 525 212. Local hero José Mourinho (see box, p.122) is said to favour this *marisqueira* with a big outdoor terrace facing the avenue, and it is easy to see why – great fish and seafood with moderate prices (mains around €12). Mon, Tues & Thurs–Sun noon–midnight.

Tasca da Fatinha Rua da Saúde 56 ☎ 265 232 800. Good waterside restaurant right on the fisherman's dock, dishing up piles of fresh fish (around €8–9) straight from the outside grill. Daily noon–midnight.

Parque Natural da Arrábida

The craggy, scrub- and wood-covered slopes of the Serra da Arrábida rise to around 500 metres above a dramatic coastline dotted with cove beaches. It's stunningly beautiful, though surprisingly little known to tourists: home to wildcats, badgers, polecats, buzzards and Bonelli's eagles, the region has had protected status since 1976 and makes up the **Parque Natural da Arrábida.** Walking guides are available from the park's main office in Setúbal (see p.125), though to get the most of the park you'll need a car – indeed, the spectacular N379-1 ranks as one of the most dramatic drives in Portugal. Note, however, that from July to August, a one-way system is in place on the narrow coastal road through the park, which operates westwards-only from 8am to 7pm (though the inland N10 and N379-1 roads operate both ways).

Convento da Arrábida

Wed & Sun only • Reservations esseential on ☎ 212 197 620, ⓦ foriente.pt • €5

Accessible on the N379-1, the highly picturesque, stacked white buildings of the **Convento da Arrábida** were built by Franciscan monks in 1542. Abandoned in the late nineteenth century, the buildings were restored in the 1950s and are now owned by the Fundação Orient, who use the spaces for seminars and conferences. Tours take in the original monastery building, gardens, shrines and the lodgings for pilgrims – with stunning ocean views from most of the site.

Portinho da Arrábida and Galapos

The most attractive destination on the coast, around 4km south of the convent down the winding N10, is the tiny harbour village of **PORTINHO DA ARRÁBIDA**, where a cluster of waterside restaurants and former fisherman's houses face the clear waters of the Bay of Setúbal – walk round the bay to the east to reach the coast's best beach, **Galapos**, which you can also reach from the coast road to Setúbal. Portinho's harbour is guarded by a tiny seventeenth-century fort, now housing the **Museu Oceanográfico** (Tues–Fri 10am–4pm, Sat 3–6pm, closed Sat in August; ☎ 212 189 791; €2.10) which displays marine animals from the region both live – in a small aquarium – and stuffed.

Praia da Figueirinha and the coast road

The six to seven kilometres of snaking coast road from Portinho da Arrábida towards Setúbal are dotted with various superb cove beaches – look for parking signs or the huddle of cars above them. **Praia da Figueirinha** is the largest and most accessible beach,

1

a lovely stretch of sand, though the waters here – as elsewhere on this coast – tend to be colder than on the western beaches facing the main Atlantic.

José Maria da Fonseca wine vaults and museum
Rua José Augusto Coelho, Vila Nogueira de Azeitão • Daily 10am–noon & 2.30–5.30pm • €3 • ☎ 212 198 940, ⓦ jmf.pt

The highlight of the otherwise unexceptional village of Vila Nogueira de Azeitão (just outside the park boundary) is the **José Maria da Fonseca wine vaults and museum**. The company has been producing quality wines in this region since the nineteenth century, including the local Setúbal Moscatel. The tour of the vaults, which lasts 45 minutes, makes an interesting diversion, and includes a free tasting.

GETTING AROUND

By bus Getting round by public transport is tricky. In July and August buses from Setúbal run along the coast as far as Praia da Figueirinha roughly every 30min (daily 9am–7pm). The rest of the year, you can only skirt round the park on buses from Setúbal to Sesimbra via Vila Nogueira de

PARQUE NATURAL DA ARRÁBIDA

Azeitão (Mon–Fri 11 daily, Sat & Sun 4 daily) that take the main road, well back from the coast. Vila Nogueira de Azeitão is also served by buses from Lisbon to Setúbal (approx every 30min; 50min).

INFORMATION AND ACTIVITIES

Information The Parque Natural da Arrábida information office is in Setúbal on Rua Claudio Lagrange (Mon–Fri 9am–12.30pm & 2–5.30pm; ☎ 265 541 157), and can provide information on walking in Arrábida.
Diving and boat trips Certified divers can rent equipment from the Centro de Mergulho diving school, Pontinha

da Arrábida Casa 5 (☎ 9212 183 656, ⓦ portinhodivers .com), or you can take diving lessons; the waters here are some of the clearest on the entire Portuguese coast. In summer, the company also offers boat trips along the coast.

ACCOMMODATION

Casa d'Adôa Pontinha da Arrábida Casa 3 ☎ 936 011 143, ⓦ casadaadoa.com. This lovely house right on the seafront has fresh rooms and a sunny patio garden. It has a variety of rooms, but all come with minibar, a/c and satellite TV, and two have kitchenettes, including a larger family room (€150). Breakfast €7. **€60**

Picheleiros Vale de Picheleiros S. Caetano ☎ 212 181 322, ⓦ clubecampismobarreiro.pt. This well-equipped campsite, just outside Azeitão (a short drive from the park and the coast), comes complete with minimarket, café and children's playground. Pitch **€9**

EATING

★ **O Galeão** Portinho da Arrábida ☎ 212 180 533. The best of the restaurants facing the water, with a terrace resting on stilts so you can guiltily peer down

at the relatives of what's probably on your plate: sea-fresh fish and seafood, from €10–14. Mon & Wed–Sun 11am–11pm; Oct–May from 6pm.

Sesimbra and around

The main resort on the Bay of Setúbal, **SESIMBRA** is largely a day-trip destination for Lisbon residents who come here for the long sandy strip of beach facing relatively still waters. Apartment buildings mushroom across the low, bare hills beyond the narrow streets of the attractive old centre, whose endless rows of café-restaurants are all filled to the gills in summer. The crowds, however, are largely Portuguese and out of season it's an atmospheric place, with elderly fishermen gathering in groups on the seafront promenade to chat. It also makes a good base to explore the coast to the west, including the wild **Cabo Espichel** and the southern stretches of the **Costa da Caparica**.

Fortaleza de Santiago
Sesimbra was an important port during the Portuguese Discoveries, when Dom Manuel lived here for a while. The town's fort, **Fortaleza de Santiago**, was built in the seventeenth century as part of the country's coastal defences, but in the eighteenth

1

century it became a seaside retreat for the Portuguese monarchs. Today, it is undergoing renovation to create a Museum of the Sea.

Porto de Abrigo

It's a pleasant walk from the centre of Sesimbra along the seafront Avenida dos Náufragos to Sesimbra's fishing port, **Porto de Abrigo**, with its brightly coloured boats. Various **boat trips** operate out of the port in summer; get the latest timetables from the tourist office.

Castelo de Sesimbra

Daily 7am–8pm; Oct–May closes at 7pm • Free

High above Sesimbra, the imposing Moorish **Castelo** is a short drive or a stiff half-hour climb from the centre. Dating from the tenth century, it was substantially renovated in the 1930s: within the walls are a pretty eighteenth-century church, Nossa Senhora do Castelo, a café, exhibition space and a cemetery. Climb round the battlements, which give amazing panoramas over the surrounding countryside and coastline.

Cabo Espichel and Nossa Senhora do Cabo

Eleven kilometres west from Sesimbra lies **Cabo Espichel**, a dramatic cape facing the full force of the Atlantic. Here you'll find the eighteenth-century church of Nossa Senhora do Cabo, lined on two sides by arcaded lodgings for pilgrims, with a weatherworn chapel perched above the rocks beyond. The whole place has an end-of-the-world air – and it seems appropriate that dinosaur footprints have been discovered on the nearby Praia dos Lagosteiros.

Costa da Caparica

It's an easy drive from Sesimbra to the southern beaches of the **Costa da Caparica**, a surprisingly verdant and undeveloped stretch of coast. A few kilometres to the north of Cabo Espichel is the little village of **Aldeia do Meco**, from where a path cuts down to the superb beach of **Praia do Meco**, though take care of the huge breakers here. The calmest strip of beach is by the **Lagoa de Albufeira**, a little further south, where you'll find a sheltered lagoon, popular with sea birds and fine to swim in.

ARRIVAL AND INFORMATION

SESIMBRA AND AROUND

By bus Sesimbra's bus station is halfway up Avenida da Liberdade, a five-minute walk from the seafront.
Destinations Aldeia do Meco (Mon–Sat 3–4 daily, Sun 1 daily; 30min); Cabo Espichel (1 daily at 2.50pm, return 3.30pm; 20min); Lagoa de Albufeira (1–2 daily; 40min); Lisbon's Praça de Espanha (hourly; 1hr); and Setúbal (hourly; 30min).
By ferry and bus Coming from Lisbon in summer, it's usually much quicker to take the ferry across to Cacilhas

and pick up the hourly bus there (around 45min), as the main bridge road is often jammed with traffic.
By car In season and at weekends, parking in central Sesimbra is a nightmare – head for the signed free car park near the football stadium.
Information Sesimbra's turismo is on Largo da Marinha 26, just back from the seafront Avenida dos Náufragos (daily 9.30am–1pm & 2–5.30pm; ☎212 288 540, ⓦ cm-sesimbra.pt).

ACCOMMODATION

Hotel do Mar Rua Gen. Humberto Delgado 10 ☎212 288 300, ⓦhoteldomar.pt. Enormous, slightly impersonal three-star spreading uphill above Sesimbra's western beach. The older parts are showing their age, but most rooms command superb sea views, as does the top-floor restaurant. There's also a garden with pool. Parking. **€160**
Náutico Av dos Combatantes 19 ☎212 233 233, ⓦresidencialnautico.com. Steeply uphill above the western end of the beach (and the *Hotel do Mar*), this is

Sesimbra's best affordable option: a comfortable modern place with spacious rooms, some with great sea views (balcony rooms are €15 extra). **€75**
Sana Park Av 25 de Abril 11, Sesimbra ☎212 289 000, ⓦsanahotels.com. An excellent upmarket choice, this boutiquey hotel has glass lifts, sauna and pool, restaurant and groovy rooftop bar (open to nonguests). The plush rooms are all en suite, though you'll pay a fair bit more for a sea view. **€130**

1

CAMPSITES

Campimeco Praia das Bicas, Aldeia do Meco ☎ 212 683 393, ⌨ roteiro-campista.pt. About 2km northwest of Aldeia do Meco, just off Praia das Bicas, a fabulous stretch of sand, this large campsite comes complete with tennis courts, restaurant, pool and minimarket. Pitch €7

Forte do Cavalo Porto de Abrigo, Sesimbra ☎ 212 288 508, ⌨ roteiro-campista.pt. This is a well-located campsite just past the fishing port, a short walk from central Sesimbra and the beach; there's a fine café as well as a minimarket and games room. Pitch €8

EATING AND DRINKING

Sesimbra's local delicacy is *salmonete* (red mullet), which in these parts feeds off a certain seaweed that makes it extra flavoursome. At night, families crowd the line of restaurants east of the fort, along Avenida 25 de Abril, and round the little Largo dos Bombaldes, with its warren of cobbled alleyways and inexpensive restaurants spilling uphill. West of the fort along the seafront is where most of the music **bars and cafés** are found.

SESIMBRA

A Sesimbrense Rua Jorge Nunes 19 ☎ 212 230 148. Friendly family-run local just back from Largo dos Bombaldes (keep going past *Toni Bar*), serving no-nonsense soups, sardines, salads and grills from €7–10, with a few outdoor seats in summer. Mon & Wed–Sun noon–10pm.

Bolina Rua Prof. Fernandes Marquês 4 ☎ 212 288 093. Sesimbra's biggest and best club is just off the western seafront, but doesn't start to get lively until after midnight. Tues–Sun 11am–7am; Oct–May weekends only.

Pedra Alta Largo dos Bombaldes 13 ☎ 212 231 791. For a quality fish or shellfish meal, this is hard to beat, and though it's in a prime position with outdoor seats on the square, prices are not outrageous (around €25 a head). Dishes include the fabulous fish baked in salt and lobster stews. Tues–Sun noon–11.30pm.

Por do Sol Av dos Náufragos 23-1° ☎ 212 232 251. For a change from the usual Portuguese fare, the "Sunset" serves a range of good-value pizza, pasta and salad (around €6–7) in an upstairs dining room with superb views across the beach. Daily 12.30–3pm & 7.30–11pm.

X-up Avenida dos Naufragos 13 ☎ 212 234 193. This sophisticated cocktail bar is right on the seafront: it's a great place for a drink, with regular party nights and guest DJs. Daily 10am–4am.

LAGOA DE ALBUFEIRA

O Lagoeiro Estrada Lagoa de Albufeira, Lagoa de Albufeira ☎ 212 681 929. Just back from the beach overlooking the lagoon, *O Lagoeiro* is the perfect spot for grills, drinks or snacks – the speciality is *caldeirada* (a tasty fish stew). Around €15 a head. Tues–Sun noon–11pm.

Estremadura and Ribatejo

ILHA DA BERLENGA

Estremadura and Ribatejo

Head north out of Lisbon and the sights soon stack up in the historic provinces of Estremadura and Ribatejo. The monastery at Alcobaça, the extraordinary abbey at Batalha and the headquarters of the Knights Templar in Tomar – some of the most famous buildings in Portugal – are all easily accessible, even by public transport, and offer a fascinating glimpse into the country's tangled past. Other attractions are equally high profile, from the walled medieval town of Óbidos to the tremendous castle at Leiria, while the obscenely ornate palace-monastery of Mafra always intrigues. Heads are also turned by the shrine at Fátima, the country's (and, indeed, one of the world's) most important pilgrimage sites.

Along the Estremaduran coast, the main resorts are the holiday fleshpots of **Nazaré** and **Ericeira**, though there are several smaller, perhaps more charming resorts – notably **São Martinho do Porto** – and plenty of less crowded beaches too, while ferries sail from **Peniche** to the remote offshore bird sanctuary of the **Ilha da Berlenga**. Inland, getting off the beaten track means delving into the spectacular underground caverns around **Porto de Mós** and viewing the amazing nearby sauropod tracks, all of which lie within the **Parque Natural das Serras de Aire e Candeeiros**.

Contrasting with the fertile agricultural land and market gardens of Estremadura is the flatter plain of the Ribatejo – the traditional bull-breeding territory that runs alongside the banks of the **Rio Tejo**. The river valley itself boasts some of Portugal's richest **vineyards**, while it's **Santarém**, the Ribatejo capital, which has the province's longest history.

Ericeira

Perched on a rocky ledge 30m above a series of fine sandy beaches, **ERICEIRA** offers one of the few natural harbours between Cascais and Peniche. During the nineteenth century boats left from here to trade with countries as far away as Scotland and Brazil. Later, it provided a welcome escape route for Portugal's last monarch, Dom Manuel II – "The Unfortunate" – who hightailed it to the harbour at Ericeira on October 5, 1910, fleeing into exile as Portugal finally jettisoned its monarchy.

Although it's now much more built-up on the outskirts, and a busy resort in peak season when people flock here from Lisbon, Ericeira remains a laidback place of narrow lanes and whitewashed houses picked out in cobalt blue. It's also renowned for excellent seafood – the town name is said to derive from the words *ouriços do mar* (sea urchin).

ÓBIDOS

Highlights

❶ Iberian Wolf Recovery Centre While away an afternoon with the wolves in the woods near Mafra. **See p.135**

❷ Ilha da Berlenga Take the boat from Peniche to a rocky, windswept island bird-sanctuary. **See p.140**

❸ Óbidos After the coach tours have left, enjoy the atmospheric streets of this walled medieval town. **See p.141**

❹ Nazaré For seaside frolics, you can't beat the biggest, brashest resort on the Estremaduran coast. **See p.147**

❺ Alcobaça The twelfth-century monastery at Alcobaça is one of Europe's most impressive Cistercian monuments. **See p.150**

❻ Grutas de Mira de Aire Visit the most spectacular underground caves in the country. **See p.159**

❼ Pegadas dos Dinossáurios Don't miss the tracks of Portugal's dinosaurs – as clear today as when they were made 175 million years ago. **See p.160**

❽ Tomar The stunning Convento de Cristo is the undisputed highlight, but Tomar itself is a gem of a town. **See p.164**

HIGHLIGHTS ARE MARKED ON THE MAP ON P.132

Around Praça da República

Virtually the whole of the town centre is pedestrianized, with the pretty **Praça da República** at its hub, ringed with cafés and *pastelarias*; there's a daily market nearby. Below town, the working fishermen's port of **Porto de Pesca** is overlooked by the whitewashed chapel of Santo António (patron saint of Portuguese fishermen), and there's a beach by the port, though it's a bit scrappy and often crowded.

ESTREMADURA & RIBATEJO

ATLANTIC OCEAN

N

Coimbra
Penela
Pedrógão
Praia da Vieira
Pombal
Rio Zêzere
Castelo Branco
Praia Velha
Marinha Grande
Leiria
São Pedro de Moel
Água de Madeiros
Pedra do Ouro
Batalha
Ourém
Castelo Branco
Nazaré ④
São Jorge
Porto de Mós ⑥ Fátima
⑧ Tomar
Barragem do Castelo do Bode
⑤
Grutas de Mira de Aire
Alvados
S. António ⑦ Pegadas dos Dinossáurios
São Martinho do Porto
Alcobaça
Minde
Constância
Foz do Arelho
PARQUE NATURAL SERRAS DE AIRE E CANDEEIROS
Entroncamento
Castelo de Almourol
Abrantes
Ilha da Berlenga
② Baleal
Caldas da Rainha
Lagoa de Óbidos
Golegã
Peniche
③ Óbidos
Salinas Naturais de Rio Maior
Rio Maior
Chamusca
Atouguia da Baleia
Areia Branca
Lourinhã
Santarém
Alpiarça
Ponte de Sor
Porto Novo
Santa Cruz
Cartaxo
Almeirim
Torres Vedras
Alenquer
São Lourenço
Arruda dos Vinhos
Azambuja
Salvaterra de Magos
Coruche
① Iberian Wolf Recovery Centre
Ericeira
Sobreiro
Vila Franca de Xira
Foz de Lizandro
Mafra
RESERVA NATURAL DO ESTUÁRIO DO TEJO
Sintra
Queluz
Alcochete
LISBON
Montijo
Vendas Novas
Cascais
Barreiro
Setúbal
ATLANTIC OCEAN
The Algarve

HIGHLIGHTS

① Iberian Wolf Recovery Centre
② Ilha da Berlenga
③ Óbidos
④ Nazaré
⑤ Alcobaça
⑥ Grutas de Mira de Aire
⑦ Pegadas dos Dinossáurios
⑧ Tomar

0   20
kilometres

The beaches

The main street, Rua Dr Eduardo Burnay, leads from Praça da República towards the town's principal beach, **Praia do Sul**, while north of the port is **Praia do Norte**, with **Praia do São Sebastião** a fifteen-minute walk beyond, past the next headland.

You can also take a bus from Praça dos Navegantes to reach less-developed beaches further out: at **Foz de Lizandro** (2km south), the river guarantees safe bathing whatever the state of the sea, while the World Surfing Championships have been held at **Praia da Ribeira d'Ilhas** (3km north). Indeed, the Ericeira coast is famous as the heartland of Portuguese surfing, and was named a World Surfing Reserve in 2011 (currently, one of only four in the world).

2

ARRIVAL AND DEPARTURE   ERICEIRA

By bus The bus station is up on the main N247 highway, but passengers are dropped at the top of Rua Prudêncio Franco da Trindade, which leads down in a couple of minutes to the main square. There are useful services to Lisbon (7 daily; 1hr 20min), Mafra (hourly; 20min) and Sintra (hourly; 45min).

By car Ericeira is a quick (45min) drive from Lisbon on the A21 motorway via Mafra. There's limited access to the old town by car, and parking is easiest near the market (free) or in the underground Parque Navegantes at Praça dos Navegantes (expensive).

INFORMATION AND ACTIVITIES

Information Turismo, Rua Dr Eduardo Burnay 46 (daily 10am–6pm, mid-July to Aug until 10pm; ☎ 261 863 122).
Surfing For World Surfing Reserve information see ⓦ worldsurfingreserves.org. There are surf shops in town,

and surf schools and camps at São Sebastião, Ribeira d'Ilhas and Foz do Lizandro beaches, including Na Onda (ⓦ ericeirasurf.com).

ACCOMMODATION

Hotels and guesthouses are generally good value, though anywhere in the main part of town can be guaranteed to be noisy in high season. The ones listed below are open all year round (not all are), and prices are generally a good bit lower outside July and August.

Fortunato Rua Dr Eduardo Burnay 7 ☎ 261 862 829, ⓦ pensaofortunato.com. A range of simple en-suite rooms, some with a terrace (for which you'll pay €5 extra): the best are the west-facing ones at the top with good views of Praia do Sul. Breakfast is included but only June–Sept. Garage parking available. **€55**

Vila Galé Largo dos Navegantes 1 ☎ 261 869 900, ⓦ www.vilagale.pt. A ritzy modern four-star hotel on the seafront. The 200 spacious rooms feature dark woods and tasteful fabrics, and some also have a sea view and wide terrace. There's an outdoor pool, indoor health club, an alfresco bar-restaurant and manicured gardens. Parking available. **€120**

★**Vilazul** Calçada da Baleia 10 ☎ 261 860 000, ⓦ hotelvilazul.com. Cheery two-star hotel with blue-shuttered windows: the spacious rooms have cane chairs, a/c and plenty of closet space. There's a third-floor bar and terrace which offers rooftop and partial sea views, while breakfast is served in the downstairs restaurant. **€63**

★**Vinnus** Rua Prudêncio Franco da Trindade 19 ☎ 261 866 933, ⓦ residencialvinnus.com. Close to the market and main square (with parking opposite), this is the best budget option. Some of the en-suite rooms have small balconies, and others have a kitchenette. No credit cards or breakfast. **€45**

EATING AND DRINKING

Ericeira has a glut of good restaurants, thanks to holiday-makers from Lisbon who demand a decent dinner. Local seafood specialities are the coastal shellfish or *arroz* (rice), *massada* (pasta) and *feijoada* (beans) *de mariscos* – rich, soupy servings of seafood made for sharing. You'll pay more if you eat with a sea view – the better-value restaurants tend to be in the town centre. The bars around the modern Praça dos Navegantes, near Praia do Sul, attract a young crowd, especially at weekends, but most of the "in" places (for which, read surfer-friendly) are out of town.

Adega Típica Rua Alves Crespo 3 ☎ 261 862 149. Traditional, rustic *adega* with a good-value menu of fish, grilled meats and pasta. Locals as well as tourists like it,

which means it's pretty reliable. Mains from €10. Daily 11am–11pm.

ACCOMMODATION
Fortunato	3
Vila Galé	4
Vilazul	2
Vinnus	1

RESTAURANTS
Adega Tipica	4
O Gafanhoto	3
Mar à Vista	1
Tik Tak	2
Tik Tak Tapas	5

★ **Mar à Vista** Largo das Ribas ☎261 862 928. A wonderful place above the Praia dos Pescadores, with three basic nooks to dine in and the freshest shellfish in Ericeira. It's a great place for *cataplanas*, *arroz* dishes, or crab and lobster, though expect to pay around €30 a head. Thurs–Mon noon–10pm.

★ **O Gafanhoto** Rua da Conceição ☎261 861 514. There are few frills in this friendly backstreet joint, but you get a decent choice of char-grilled meat and freshly caught fish at budget prices (from around €9). Wed–Mon noon–4pm & 7–11pm.

Tik Tak Rua 5 de Outubro 7 ☎261 863 246. A fashionable place with outdoor tables on a cobbled street, serving great meat kebabs and Brazilian grills (try the *picanha*) as well as fish (dishes mostly €10–16). Its sister bar-restaurant *Tik Tak Tapas* (Rua do Ericeira 15; closed Thurs) is a good spot for a drink and tapas. Mon–Fri 7–11pm, Sat & Sun noon–3pm & 7–11pm.

Mafra and around

The small town of **MAFRA** is synonymous with the vast monastery-palace, the **Mosteiro Palácio Nacional de Mafra**, built by the recklessly extravagant king Dom João V. It's only 12km from Ericeira, so makes an easy half-day trip from the coast, or you can see it en route from Lisbon or Sintra. Drivers will also be able to call in at the nearby **Tapada de Mafra** park and at the craft village at **Sobreiro**, on the road between Mafra and Ericeira.

Mosteiro Palácio Nacional de Mafra

Terreiro Dom João V • Mon & Wed–Sun 10am–5.30pm, last entry 4.30pm; guided tours take 60–75min • €6, under-14s free, and free on
Sun 10am–2pm • ☎ 261 817 550, ⓦ ipmuseus.pt

Construction of the **Mosteiro Palácio Nacional de Mafra** started in 1717, and it was
originally planned to be a modest Franciscan monastery, built to honour the birth of
the king's first child. But Dom João V's reign coincided with Portuguese holdings in
Brazil producing vast mineral wealth, and this bonanza changed everything. The simple
monastery became a lavish palace, with hundreds of monks in residence to care for
the royal souls. The resulting building was a magnificent, over-the-top Baroque
statement of intent, completed in just thirteen years by the gruelling labour of
thousands (of whom hundreds died). The oft-quoted figures tell a tale of grandiose
excess – a 200-metre-long facade, 1200 rooms, over 5000 doorways and windows,
156 staircases, and two soaring bell towers over the basilica containing 92 bells.

There's little humanity or empathy at work in the seemingly endless royal apartments,
and it's hard to imagine a life lived in these cavernous chambers. All the rooms are
re-creations from when João VI fled to Brazil in 1808 in the face of the French advance
and took all the furniture and valuables with him. However, there is at least one
original piece – the bed in which the last Portuguese monarch, Manuel II, slept the
night before he went into exile in England. Some of the rooms are simply shocking,
like the **Sala dos Troféus**, where the furniture, including the chandeliers, is made from
antlers and upholstered in deerskin. The undoubted highlight is the stupendously
decorated **library**, with its 90-metre-long tiled floor. Forty thousand books are still in
place here, kept free of insect infestation by a colony of tiny bats that lives in the eaves.

Tapada Nacional de Mafra

Portão de Codeçal, Mafra • Daily 9.30am–5.30pm • Walking trails €5; train €8 • Reservations advised Mon–Fri ☎ 261 817 050, Sat & Sun
and hols ☎ 261 814 240, ⓦ tapadademafra.pt

Six kilometres north of Mafra on the Gradil road is the **Tapada de Mafra**, once the
palace's extensive hunting grounds. The park is still entirely walled, and there are
wild boar and deer within, though it's now set up for public visits with walking and
mountain-bike trails. Access to the trails is limited to certain hours in the morning
and afternoon, and it'll take two or three hours to get round. There are also falconry

---

WATCH OUT, WOLVES ABOUT

In a hidden forest valley just 20km north of Lisbon, the **Iberian Wolf Recovery Centre** houses
a dozen or so wolves in natural enclosures. There are only around three hundred wolves left in
the wild in Portugal, mostly in the northern mountains, with another two thousand in Spain.
Those living at the centre were brought here after being rescued from illegal captivity or were
transferred from other zoos – they won't be released again into the wild.

The centre is run by the not-for-profit organization **Grupo Lobo** (ⓦ lobo.fc.ul.pt), which
campaigns for wolf preservation and public education, and offers **guided visits** to see the
wolves (Sat, Sun and public holidays: May–Sept at 4.30pm & 6pm, Oct–April at 3pm & 4.30pm;
€5, under-18s €3; ☎ 261 785 037 or ☎ 917 532 312; English spoken); you have to book in
advance, but the day before is usually fine. You'll get to walk around the enclosures and see
some of the wolves up close, and you can then buy as many postcards, T-shirts, key-rings
and wolf-adoption packs as you can manage to boost the centre's funds. They also have
a volunteer programme.

To get there, follow the brown signs for the "Centro de Recuperação do Lobo Ibérico", which
is 7km from Malveira, off the N8 Torres Vedras road; look for the turn at the Picão/Carapiteira
junction and then it's 2km up a minor road, eventually a track (but fine for cars), which leads to
the reception centre.

displays and children's and family activities, while at weekends and public holidays, you can tour the park on a road train.

Aldeia Típica

Sobreiro, 5km northwest of Mafra on N116 • Daily 10am–6pm • ☎ 261 815 420

En route to Ericeira, at the small village of **Sobreiro**, you'll find the **Aldeia Típica** craft village, which was established by artist José Franco. It's particularly geared up for families, who enjoy looking round the traditional workshops, water mills and craft outlets, all displaying tools, furniture and artefacts collected over many years. The *adega* here is a good place to stop for lunch, serving local wine, bread and moderately priced meals.

ARRIVAL AND INFORMATION   MAFRA

By bus Mafrense buses run hourly from Lisbon Campo Grande (1hr 15min) or from Sintra station (30min), stopping near the monastery/palace. There are also hourly buses from Ericeira (20min). A vast car park outside the palace soaks up the day-trip trade.

Information The turismo is in the palace, to the right of the basilica (Mon & Wed–Fri 10am–5pm, Sat & Sun 10am–1pm & 2–5pm; ☎ 261 817 170, ⓦ cm-mafra.pt).

Torres Vedras and around

TORRES VEDRAS is a pleasant if fairly nondescript town, though for a short period during the Peninsular War against the French it was at the forefront of a desperate European struggle. With Lisbon judged to be under threat, the Duke of Wellington ordered the secret construction of the Linhas de Torres, the so-called "Lines of Torres Vedras". Within a year in 1810, Wellington's troops, plus gangs of militias and conscripted locals, built an extraordinary network of almost 150 forts and impregnable defensive positions. The British–Portuguese forces then carried out a scorched-earth policy in front of the Lines and sheltered behind them, thwarting the under-supplied French army, which was subsequently forced to retreat to Spain. Wellington's seemingly desperate tactic was a military triumph – though the cost to the local population was severe.

There's little evidence of this drama on display in the modern town, bar some surviving fortress ruins nearby. Still, there's a pleasant kernel of cobbled lanes in the centre, at its best around the central Praça 25 de Abril, where an obelisk commemorates the battles. Otherwise, the **castelo** is the only notable sight and, after a drink at one of the cafés on the square it's probably time to move on – Lourinhã or the local beaches to the northwest make a better overnight stop, while Alenquer and the Ribatejo wine country are just a thirty-kilometre drive to the east.

Castelo

Tues–Sun 10am–1pm & 2–6pm • Free

Above the old town of Torres Vedras sits the **Castelo**, which was once a popular royal residence. It was here, in 1414, that Dom João I confirmed the decision to take the Moroccan outpost of Ceuta – the first overseas venture leading towards the future Portuguese maritime empire. The castle was reduced to rubble by the earthquake of 1755, but the battlements have been restored and in spring the slopes are carpeted with red poppies.

Praia de Santa Cruz and around

Thirteen kilometres northwest of Torres Vedras, the resort of **Praia de Santa Cruz** marks the start of a string of local beaches that runs all the way north to Peniche. Santa Cruz itself is eminently missable, its wide beaches backed by a contagious rash of apartments and villas, and boasting a campsite the size of an independent country. Far better to push on the 5km north to the duned sands of **Porto Novo** (follow signs initially for Lourinhã), which has restricted its development to a strip of four simple guesthouses with restaurants, just above the sandy bay at the mouth of the Rio Maceira.

Areia Branca

If you're looking for an overnight beach stop somewhere near Torres Vedras, **Areia Branca** ("White Sand") is the most enticing option. Little more than a fishing village thirty years ago, it's now been fully developed but it remains a congenial place of low-rise apartments filling a shallow bowl above a sandy beach, with a promenade of café-bars where surfers hang out. To stretch your legs and soak up the views, follow the walk signposted 3km up the coastal road to the seventeenth-century Forte de Paimogo.

ARRIVAL AND DEPARTURE   AREIA BRANCA

By bus Regular daily buses run to Areia Branca from Peniche (6 daily; 30min) and from Torres Vedras, via Lourinhã (8 daily; 40min).

By car It's a direct 21km drive from Torres Vedras to Areia Branca. There's parking near the beach.

ACCOMMODATION AND EATING

Casal dos Patos Alameda Ver o Mar 1 ☎ 261 413 768, ⓦ casaldospatos.online.pt. This German-owned property is a hilltop villa with great views, sited on the road directly above the beach. There are four double rooms (closed Nov–Feb) – though not all have the views – and a cottage (available by the night, open all year) that sleeps up to four. €70, cottage €80

Pousada da Juventude Praia de Areia Branca ☎ 261 422 127, ⓦ microsites.juventude.gov.pt/portal/en. For once, budget travellers have the edge in town, as there's a good youth hostel right on the sands, where you can wake to the sound of crashing waves. Dorm beds €15, doubles €45

Residencial Dom Lourenço Av António José do Vale ☎ 261 422 809, ⓦ domlourenco.com. On the road out of town, this straightforward seaside hotel has fine if functional rooms and apartments, and a decent restaurant below (mains €9–12). Doubles €50, apartments €70

Lourinhã

Just inland, 3km from the beach at Areia Branca, the small market town of **LOURINHÃ** touts itself as "Capital dos Dinossáuros", on account of the many Jurassic-era fossils retrieved from the local coastline, now on display at the local museum. Once you've seen this, visited the **market** (mornings only, closed Sun & Mon) – there's also an outdoor market on the first Monday of every month – and climbed up to the church viewpoint, you've basically exhausted Lourinhã's attractions.

Museu da Lourinhã

Rua João Luís de Moura 95 • Daily 10am–12.30pm & 2.30–5.30pm, until 6.30pm June–Aug; closed Mon May–Sept • €4 • ☎ 261 414 003, ⓦ museulourinha.org

The excellent **Museu da Lourinhã**, right in the centre of town, is definitely worth a visit. It has a separate dinosaur pavilion containing, among other things, dinosaur egg nests and the oldest dinosaur embryos in the world. These are pretty amazing, and tend to overshadow the rest of the museum, but the rooms devoted to local trades and crafts are fascinating too.

INFORMATION   LOURINHÃ

Turismo Largo António Granjo, by the main square (Mon–Fri 9am–12.30pm & 2–5.30pm; ☎ 261 410 127, ⓦ cm-lourinha.pt). Pick up leaflets for a couple of local

waymarked walks, including the 7km trail out to the beach at Areia Branca.

ACCOMMODATION AND EATING

There's a simple **hotel** in town, and the turismo also has details of a couple of local *turismo rural* options. A few fairly basic **restaurants** line up around the central square and along the pedestrianized street beyond the museum. The town is known for its *aguardente Lourinhã*, Portugal's only demarcated brandy, so expect to be offered a nip at the end of a meal.

Peniche

In the fishing town of **PENICHE**, determined touts hawk rooms and a glut of harbourside seafood restaurants vie for tourists. But although the balance of life is changing here, Peniche has yet to be seduced entirely from its roots. Gangs of fishermen still repair nets at the harbourside, while the first weekend in August sees the boisterous festival of **Nossa Senhora da Boa Viagem**, during which there's a blessing of the fleet, plus fireworks, bands and dancing in the street.

The town was an island up until the fifteenth century, when the surrounding area silted up and now a narrow isthmus, with gently sloping beaches either side, connects it to the mainland. Unsightly development stretches along the coast, but inside the walled town there is a small grid of narrow streets dominated by a fortress, as well as a busy harbour and marina. Boats from here run out to the Ilha da Berlenga (see p.140), while there's an enjoyable regional **market** held on the last Thursday of the month.

Fortaleza de Peniche

Campo da República • Tues–Fri 9am–12.30pm & 2–5.30pm, Sat & Sun 10.30am–12.30pm & 2–5.30pm • €1.55, under-16s free • ☎ 262 780 116

The sixteenth-century **Fortaleza** was a much-feared jail during the years of Portugal's dictatorship, and later housed refugees from the former colonies. Despite a fresh coat of paint here and there, it's still a formidable place of bare yards and high walls; the bleak *parlatório* (prisoners' receiving room) houses a small exhibition commemorating those imprisoned here. Further within the fort is the municipal museum, while on the top floor you can see the old cells and solitary-confinement pens.

Along the coast

Beyond the fortress, to the west, it's 2.5km to the tip of **Cabo Carvoeiro**, a rugged peninsula topped by a lighthouse, where the waves smash against the weathered rock pillars. South of town (along the Caldas da Rainha–Lisbon road) and east towards Baleal/Ferrel, you'll find the duned **surf beaches**, with periodic beach bars, boardwalks and surf-camps. **Baleal** itself, 5km northeast of Peniche, is an islet-village joined to the mainland by a narrow causeway, with fine sand beaches either side, and bar-restaurants overlooking the sands at both ends.

2

Atouguia da Baleia

The other local excursion is the five-kilometre drive east along the N114 (Caldas da Rainha–Lisbon road) to the village of **Atouguia da Baleia** – *baleia* means "whale". These magnificent creatures were hunted off the shores here when Atouguia was a thriving port. The parish church of São Leonardo is full of small treasures, such as a curious fourteenth-century stone relief of the Nativity and a calcified whalebone propped up in the corner.

ARRIVAL AND DEPARTURE   PENICHE

By bus The bus station lies outside the town walls – it's a 10min walk into the centre, across the Ponte Velha to the main Rua Alexandre Herculano.
Destinations Areia Branca (6 daily; 30min); Baleal (July & Aug hourly; Sept–June Mon–Fri 6 daily; 15min); Caldas da Rainha (3–7 daily; 45min); Lisbon (9 daily; 1hr 45min); Óbidos (3–7 daily; 30min); São Martinho do Porto (3 daily;

1hr); Torres Vedras (8 daily; 50min).
By car There's pay parking all over town, including by the gardens outside the turismo and on the harbour front, and there's free parking up by the fortress. At Baleal, there's a large car park on the mainland side of the causeway.
By boat The harbour, for boats to Berlenga (see p.141), is close to the fortress.

INFORMATION AND ACTIVITIES

Information Turismo, Rua Alexandre Herculano (daily: July & Aug 9am–8pm; Sept–June 9am–1pm & 2–5pm; ☎ 262 789 571, ⓦ cm-peniche.pt).
Boat trips Sea-charter companies based at the harbour offer fishing trips and cruises, either around the local coastline (from €15) or out to Berlenga.

Watersports Peniche is a big watersports centre, particularly for surfing, but also for diving. Dive operators include Haliotis (ⓦ haliotis.pt), based in the *Hotel Praia Norte*, 1km north of Peniche centre – one-day dive trips in the gin-clear waters off Ilha Berlenga cost around €75, though cheaper coastal dives are also available.

ACCOMMODATION

In July and August accommodation can be tricky to find without an advance reservation, though the turismo can help find private rooms. The official **town-centre** choices are exclusively small guesthouses, with the two larger resort-style three-star hotels both a short way out of town by the Baleal roundabout. There's also more **beachfront accommodation** to the south of town at Consolação beach. All prices ebb and flow with the season – in high summer rooms go for €70, though at any other time of the year you're more likely to pay around €40.

Casa das Marés Praia do Baleal, 5km northeast of Peniche ☎ 262 769 200/255/371, ⓦ casadasmares1.com,

ⓦ casadasmares2.com and ⓦ casadasmares.com. At the far end of Baleal village (over the causeway), by the chapel,

---

SURFING AT PENICHE

Peniche has some of the best and most consistent surfing in the country. The turismo hands out a free **surf-guide** to the local beaches, including Supertubos and the other local breaks. You can rent gear from Rip Curl, Rua Alexandre Herculano (☎ 262 787 206), or from any of the local **surf-camps**, including Baleal Surfcamp (ⓦ balealsurfcamp.com), PH Surf School (ⓦ penichehostel.com) and Peniche Surf Camp in Baleal (ⓦ penichesurfcamp.com). Group lessons cost from €35 (individual sessions from €80), while each camp also has accommodation (hostel-style or apartments and private rooms). One-week inclusive courses for beginners cost around €500 in July and August, cheaper outside high season.

this is actually three conjoined houses, each offering B&B, with views either of the sweeping sands or back across to Peniche. Breakfast is served on the terrace overlooking the small fishermen's beach where the boats are winched ashore. There's parking at the front. **€90**

Casa do Castelo Atouguia da Baleia, 5km east of Peniche on N114 ☎ 262 750 647, ⓦ casacastelo.com. Across the road from Atouguia church, this elegant family home is set in lovely tree-shaded gardens – there's a swimming pool too. It's a typically charming, traditional Portuguese country house, and makes an elegant alternative base for the seaside. **€90**

★ **Maciel** Rua José Estêvão 38 ☎ 262 784 685,

ⓦ residencial-maciel.com. The best budget option in town is classier than its neighbours, with a highly polished interior of wooden floors, rugs, plants and coordinated decor. **€60**

★ **Peniche Hostel Backpackers** Rua Arquitecto Paulino Montêz 6, 1st floor ☎ 969 008 689, ⓦ peniche hostel.com. A friendly surfers' and backpackers' place in a renovated house just inside the town walls, across from the turismo. It's kind of boutiquey, with two small, four-bed mixed dorms and three double rooms available, plus a kitchen and lounge. They can arrange lessons at their own surf school, and you can also rent boards and bikes. Dorm beds **€20**, doubles **€50**

EATING AND DRINKING

A dozen or so **restaurants** along Avenida do Mar all offer grilled fish at reasonable prices (mains from around €10), plus pricier *arroz* and shellfish dishes. To check out the daily catch, visit the **Mercado Municipal** (off Rua Arquitecto Paulino Montêz; closed Mon), full of voluble fishwives sipping a *bica* as they exchange news. Your best bet for a drink and a view of the world going by is one of the handful of harbourside **bars** on Avenida do Mar, while Baleal beach has a few bars popular with the surf crowd.

★ **A Sardinha** Rua Vasco da Gama 81 ☎ 262 781 820, ⓦ restauranteasardinha.com. The best of the backstreet options is a good-value, family-run place serving the full range of fish and seafood, from sardines to lobster, with dishes starting from around €9. You can sit outside on the narrow street in summer. Daily 11.30am–4pm & 6.30–10.30pm.

Estelas Rua Arquitecto Paulino Montêz ☎ 262 782 435. Acclaimed as the best restaurant in town, serving super-fresh fish and seafood in a breezy contemporary dining room. Most mains are from €15–20, and it's the place to try classics like *cataplana de marisco* or a large grilled *robalo* (seabass). Mon, Tues & Thurs–Sun noon–4pm & 7pm–midnight.

Hó Amaral Rua Dr Francisco Seia 7 ☎ 262 782 095. A bit more refined than the harbourside restaurants, and a bit pricier (mains €10–15), but it makes for a cosy dinner. Swordfish comes grilled with stewed onions (*cebolada*), while the house specials are *frigideira* (a mix of prawns, clams, squid and cuttlefish) or *arroz de tamboril* (monkfish rice). Mon–Wed & Fri–Sun noon–3pm & 7–11pm.

Onda Azul Largo da Ribeira 38 ☎ 262 787 224. The "Blue Wave" has harbour views from its outdoor terrace, so it's a popular lunch choice. There's the usual grilled-fish menu in three languages, though daily specials are always worth a look, such as roast octopus with potatoes in olive oil. Mon–Wed & Fri–Sun noon–3pm & 7–11pm.

Ilha da Berlenga

The craggy, ocean-ravaged **Ilha da Berlenga** lies 10km offshore from Peniche – it's usually visible from Cabo Carvoeiro. Taking up just two-and-a-half square kilometres, the island is uninhabited except for a few fishermen, because the island has been declared a **natural reserve**, home to thousands upon thousands of sea birds, including gulls, puffins and cormorants. The birds are entirely dominant – visitors, you get the feeling, are just about tolerated as long as they don't venture into the ubiquitous perching and roosting areas.

At the main landing dock, with its small fleet of fishing boats, there's a tiny sandy beach that's a mere golden notch in the cliffs. This gets ridiculously busy in summer, though you're unlikely to come to Berlenga just for the beach. The water is lovely however, and fantastic for snorkelling. The only buildings on the island are a few huts and concrete houses above the harbour, a lighthouse on the heights and – across one shoulder of the island, reached by the only track – the highly romantic seventeenth-century **Forte de São João Baptista**, on a rocky islet the other side of a stone bridge. Striding out across the island seems like an attractive idea, but be warned – there's no shade, and the ever-present screeching, swooping birds make a restful picnic unlikely.

2

ARRIVAL AND DEPARTURE

By ferry The ferry from Peniche is operated by Viamar (€20 return, under-12s €10; ☎ 262 785 646, ⓦ viamar-berlenga .com) and takes around 45 minutes – longer if the sea is rough (it can be a very bouncy ride). Departures are from Peniche harbour below the fort and run mid-May to mid-September, with up to three ferries a day in July and August (9.30am, 11.30am & 5.30pm; return at 10.30am, 4.30pm & 6.30pm), and one daily at other times (10am; return at 4.30pm). There's a limit of 300 tickets sold each day (ticket office open 8.30am–noon & 3–5.30pm). In July and August, get there in good time for a ticket; outside these months it's not usually a problem.

Boat trips Other companies with offices on Peniche harbour front, including Turpesca (☎ 262 789 960 or ☎ 963 073 818) and Julius (☎ 262 782 698 or ☎ 917 601 114, ⓦ julius-berlenga.com.pt), operate boat trips to Berlenga all year round except December. Departures depend on the weather and season, but in summer there are several daily excursions, usually departing in the morning and including a stop on the island and a visit to the caves along the coastline. Ticket prices are pegged to those of Viamar ferry, so you shouldn't pay more than €20 for the trip.

ACCOMMODATION AND EATING

Facilities on the island are limited, though it's remote and interesting enough a destination to attract a fair number of tourists. There's a campsite, a hostel, one hotel and a small minimarket (only open in summer when everything else is). There's also a bar and restaurant at the hotel, but as everything is shipped in, prices are high. Advance reservations are essential everywhere – don't turn up expecting to stay without one.

Área de Campismo de Berlenga ☎ 262 789 571, ⓔ campismo.berlenga@cm-peniche.pt. Reservations for the small island campsite need to be made through Peniche turismo. It's not exactly a luxury spot, more a rocky ledge in a fantastic location, and you'll need to be pretty self-sufficient unless you plan on eating in the hotel. It's only open from 1 July to 15 September. Pitch €10.30

★ **Casa do Abrigo** Forte de São João Baptista ☎ 912 631 426 (Mon–Fri after 7pm), ⓔ berlenga reservasforte@gmail.com. This rudimentary refuge housed in the fort can't be beaten for location, if not sybaritic comfort. There are simple private bed spaces for 1 or 2 people (*cubatas*) and dorms (sleeping up to six). It's a cold-water shower, generator-off-at-midnight kind

of place – bring your own cooking utensils (there is a kitchen), sleeping stuff and towels. Only open 15 May to 15 September; it's a bit cheaper outside July and August and if you stay more than two nights. Dorm beds €20; *cubata* bed spaces €22

Residencial Mar e Sol ☎ 262 750 331, ⓦ restaurantemaresol.com. There are just six rooms at the only hotel, above the harbour. It's seriously overpriced on a Saturday night in August (€130), but is down to €50 at the start and end of the season. Meals in the restaurant are based around the fish landed at the harbour below, which is pretty good for food miles (dishes start at around €14). Restaurant open noon–4pm & 8–10pm. Closed Nov to mid-April. €80

Óbidos

ÓBIDOS is thoroughly charming – a very small town, completely enclosed by medieval walls – and although much was rebuilt after the 1755 earthquake, it retains a captivating feel with its cobbled alleys and whitewashed houses. To the Portuguese it's known as the "Wedding City", after a custom whereby the ancient kings gave the village to their queens as a wedding present. Perhaps more curiously still, five hundred years ago the sea reached the foot of the ridge on which Óbidos stands and boats were once moored below its walls. As the sea later retreated, it left a fertile green plain and the distant Lagoa de Óbidos, with the town now marooned inland.

Naturally enough, such an attractive, history-laden place attracts visitors by the coach-load, while the land below the walls shows ever-increasing development. However, it's really just the main street that gets overly congested, and you only need to climb the side alleys or the perimeter walls to escape the throngs. Óbidos also hosts an annual **summer festival** from July to September, which includes a ten-day medieval fair, plus opera at the castle, and other concerts and events (details from the turismo).

2

Rua Direita

The main entrance to town is through the **Porta da Vila**, housing a tiled oratory, beneath which someone is usually displaying handmade lace. Beyond stretches the main street, **Rua Direita**, a run of restored houses, gift and craft shops, galleries and cafés. Ginjinha d'Óbidos, the local cherry liqueur, is much in evidence, along with the ubiquitous ceramics and embroidery.

Rua Direita climbs eventually to Dom Dinis's massively towered **castle**, whose keep now houses a rather splendid *pousada*. There's also access at various points to the **town walls** – at times, a hair-raising walkway with no handrail – from where you can enjoy the views over the surrounding plain.

Museu Municipal

Praça de Santa Maria, off Rua Direita • Tues–Sun 10am–1pm & 2–6pm • €1.50 • ☎ 262 955 557

The handsome central square, overlooked by pillory and portico, is flanked on one side by the former town hall, now the **Museu Municipal**, notable principally for its work by **Josefa de Óbidos** (1630–1684), one of the most renowned of all Portuguese painters. Although she was born in Seville, Josefa lived here in Óbidos in a convent for most of her life. First known for her etchings and miniature paintings, she later moved on to wonderfully detailed, full-scale religious works of art. Her portrait of powerful priest Faustino das Neves is the museum's highlight (though it's not always on display).

Igreja de Santa Maria

Praça de Santa Maria • Daily: April–Sept 9.30am–12.30pm & 2.30–7pm; Oct–March 9.30am–12.30pm & 2.30–5pm • Free

At the back of the main square, the **Igreja de Santa Maria** has a homely interior lined with blue seventeenth-century *azulejos* and an altarpiece attributed to Josefa de Óbidos. The church was the venue of the wedding of the 10-year-old king, Afonso V, who married his 8-year-old cousin, Isabel, in 1444.

ARRIVAL AND INFORMATION   ÓBIDOS

By bus Buses stop outside the Porta da Vila, by the turismo, with regular services to Caldas da Rainha (every 30min–1hr; 15min), Nazaré (7 daily; 1hr) and Peniche (3–7 daily; 30min). **By car** It's an easy drive to Óbidos from Caldas da Rainha (6km to the north) or Peniche (24km west), while from Lisbon it's around an hour's drive up the A8 motorway. There's a large car park by the turismo, immediately outside the Porta da Vila; or there's free parking over the road in the wasteground lot by the aqueduct.

By train There's a minor train station at Óbidos (services from Caldas da Rainha, São Martinho and Leiria), but it's a fair walk from the walls, below the town.

Information Turismo, outside the Porta da Vila (May–Sept daily 9.30am–7.30pm; Oct–April Mon–Fri 9.30am–6pm, Sat & Sun 9.30am–12.30pm & 1.30–5.30pm; ☎ 262 959 231, �🌐 cm-obidos.pt).

ACCOMMODATION

Accommodation generally scores high on charm, especially in the old townhouses or country manors that play on Óbidos' genteel image. Most is mid-range or above – budget travellers should hunt out private rooms advertised in the windows of houses along Rua Direita, where you should be able to get something for €50 or €60.

★ **Casa das Senhoras Rainhas** Rua Padre Nunes Tavares 6 ☎ 262 955 360, �🌐 senhorasrainhas.com. The only serious rival to the *pousada* is this exceptional boutique-style hotel at the bottom of the old town, by the walls. Rooms are charming rather than cutting-edge, with smart marble bathrooms and a soothing colour scheme – some have a private terrace – and there's a lovely courtyard. The restaurant (closed Tues, & Wed lunch) meanwhile offers a fine-dining experience – say seafood gazpacho and pork loin with a *moscatel* glaze – for around €50 a head. **€120**

★ **Casa de São Tiago** Largo de São Tiago 1 ☎ 262 959 587, ⟨⟩ casas-sthiago.com. Beautifully restored family house, dripping with vines and climbing flowers, just below the castle on Rua Direita. It's peaceful and friendly, and the rooms have wrought-iron bedsteads, tiles and rugs, and views either over the lemon trees or to the castle walls. Breakfast is served in the walled courtyard. **€80**

Casa d'Óbidos Quinta de São José, 1km south of town, near Senhor da Pedra church ☎262 950 924, ⓦcasa dobidos.com. Classy nineteenth-century manor house in lovely gardens, with a swimming pool and tennis court. There are half a dozen rooms in the house, and four rustic cottages in the grounds. Minimum two-night stay. €90

Estalagem do Convento Rua Dr João de Ornelas ☎262 959 216, ⓦestalagemdoconvento.com. A minor convent just outside the walls (lower gate) has been converted into an atmospheric hotel of squeaky tiled floors, granite arches, oak beams and stone staircases. The traditionally furnished rooms overlook an internal garden, courtyards or the countryside, and you can park right outside. €90

★ **Louro** Rua da Antiga Estrada Real, Casal da Canastra ☎262 955 100, ⓦhotelouro.com. A modern, refurbished inn, around 500m from the walls – walk away from Porta da Vila, past the car parks. The en-suite rooms offer a comfortable night at a good price (and outside July–Oct rates drop to €50–60). The rear rooms have valley and town-wall views, parking is easy, and there's a mani-cured garden and outdoor pool. €70

Pousada do Castelo ☎210 407 630, ⓦpousadas.pt. One of the country's finest *pousadas*, sited within the castle and approached through an intimate courtyard overlooked by carved windows. There are only 17 rooms, 8 of them in a new wing, all done in a lavish Portuguese country style, and making good use of the original stone walls and other features. The top room is the duplex suite in one of the castle towers, complete with canopied bed fit for a king. Guests tend to eat in the restaurant (mains around €25), where there's a classy take on traditional country food. For parking, follow the *pousada* signs. €200

Rainha Santa Isabel Rua Direita ☎262 959 323, ⓦobidoshotel.com. The carefully preserved facade hides an up-to-date twenty-room hotel with lounge and bar. There's a period feel inside – wooden floors and beams, blue-tiled bathrooms, dried flowers and leather armchairs – while the rooms vary in size and outlook, though the best have rooftop views. €80

EATING AND DRINKING

Restaurants are geared towards day-trippers, so prices are high and multi-language menus ubiquitous. To eat with the locals you need to head 1km out of town (on the Caldas da Rainha road, 15min walk) to the cobbled square by the unfinished rotunda church of Senhor da Pedra, where there's a handful of moderately priced restaurants serving grills, fish and rice dishes.

RESTAURANTS

Adega do Ramada Trav Josefa d'Óbidos, off Rua Direita ☎262 959 462. Cosy little grill house with summer esplanade seating in the alley. Steaks, lamb chops, pork, sea bass and salmon (€12–14) are all prepared on the outdoor charcoal grill. Tues–Sun noon–3pm & 7–10pm; Oct–April closed Sun 7–10pm.

O Pretensioso Largo do Postigo 2 ☎262 950 021. The dishes are a little different at this old house set inside the lower walls, such as a *bacalhau papillote* with an almond-and-*broa* crust or duck with a honey and port-wine sauce (mains €13–18). If the weather's kind you can also eat in the charming garden, shaded by an orange tree. Tues–Sun noon–3pm & 7–11pm.

★ **Vila Infanta** Largo do Santuário do Senhor da Pedra, 1km south, Caldas da Rainha road ☎262 959 757. The best-value meals are just out of town at this friendly, family-run grill restaurant, where you can eat a full meal for around €15, which is the price of a main course at many places in Óbidos. Mon, Tues & Thurs–Sun noon–3pm & 6.30–10pm.

BARS

Ibn Errik Rex Rua Direita 100 ☎262 959 193. A garrulous owner presides over this townhouse bar, which has been in business for half a century. Bottles hang from every available space, and there's a carafe of the local *ginjinha* on every table. Mon & Wed–Sun 11am–2am.

Lagar da Mouraria Trav da Mouraria, near Santa Maria church ☎919 937 601. Idiosyncratic bar fashioned from an old wine press – there are seats in the stone chambers and an enormous, gnarled wooden beam bisecting the room. They do tapas-style snacks and food too. Daily 11am–2am.

Caldas da Rainha

CALDAS DA RAINHA means "Queen's Spa", and was named for Dona Leonor, wife of Dom João II. She was sufficiently taken by the therapeutic powers of the bubbling waters here that she founded a hospital in 1484, around which the town gradually grew up to service the growing popularity of the **spa**. Its heyday was probably in the nineteenth century, although Caldas today shows little of its regal past: once through the drab modern outskirts, however, there's a pleasant centre focused on the modern spa buildings and the spreading municipal park beyond, which contains two diverting museums. Caldas is also not a bad place for souvenir hunting: its **embroidery** has a national reputation, though it's best known as a **ceramics** centre. There's a lively outdoor fruit, vegetable and flower **market** every morning in the central Praça da República – Monday sees the addition of clothes, shoes and household goods.

Hospital Termal Rainha Dona Leonor

The lanes running downhill from the central Praça da República lead to Largo da Rainha Dona Leonor and the buildings of the royal spa complex, notably the **Hospital Termal** (founded the year after the queen's first visit, in 1485) and the **Balneário Novo** (New Baths) built in 1855. Around the back of the spa, the hospital church **Nossa Senhora do Pópulo** (built 1500) is covered in blue-and-yellow *azulejo* tiles and has an impressive Manueline belfry. Inside the sacristy, there's a *Virgin and Child* by Josefa de Óbidos.

Museu de José Malhoa

Parque Dom Carlos I • Tues–Sun 10am–12.30pm & 2–5pm • €3, free Sun morning, and under-14s free • ☎ 262 831 984, ⓦ mjm.imc-ip.pt

Pretty much everything of interest in Caldas lies in, or just outside, the **Parque Dom Carlos I**, an extensive landscaped park around a small lake and a garden café. The main attraction here is the **Museu de José Malhoa**, largely dedicated to the works of the Caldas-born painter **José Malhoa** (1855–1933), Portugal's leading nineteenth-century exponent of naturalism, a master of costume, genre scenes and country life. There are also works by many of Malhoa's contemporaries on display, particularly those of the so-called "Grupo do Leão", a collection of artists, writers and intellectuals (named after a Lisbon beer-hall), of which Malhoa was a prominent member. In the basement, don't miss the ceramics by **Rafael Bordallo Pinheiro** (1846–1905), notably his masterpiece, the life-sized models representing the Passion.

It's Pinheiro who is most closely associated with the famous Caldas da Rainha pottery. His naturalist tableware (cabbage-leaf bowls, butterfly plates and the like) is still hugely popular, while in the enduring caricature of "Zé Povinho" – a bearded peasant in black hat, with no respect for authority – Pinheiro created a true Portuguese archetype.

Faianças Artisticas Fabrica Bordallo Pinheiro

Rua Rafael Bordallo Pinheiro 53 • **Factory shop** Mon–Sat 10am–7pm, Sun 2–7pm • **Casa-Museu San Rafael** Tues–Fri 9am–1pm only • Free • ☎ 262 880 568, ⓦ bordallopinheiro.pt

The ceramics factory founded by Rafael Bordallo Pinheiro in 1884, the **Faianças Artisticas Fabrica Bordallo Pinheiro**, lies on the street that bears his name, which runs around the back of the municipal park. The factory shop ("Loja") is filled with colourful glazed earthenware, from typical figurines to contemporary dinner services; the adjacent **Casa-Museu San Rafael** displays a selection of remarkable historical pieces by Pinheiro and his craftsmen.

Museu da Cerâmica

Rua Illídio Amado, just up the road from the Pinheiro factory • Tues–Sun 10am–12.30pm & 2–5pm • €2, free on Sun 10am–12.30pm • ☎ 262 840 280

The other place to pursue the subject of Caldas' ceramics is the **Museu da Cerâmica**. It's set in a delightful rustic stone villa, and contains more of Pinheiro's original work as well as providing an overview of the whole history of Caldas pottery. There are some extraordinary naturalistic pieces here – lobster-garlanded dishes, griffins entwined with snakes, fish-head jars, cabbage-leaf bowls – all protected from harm by staff who follow you around the creaking floors at a not-so-discreet distance.

CLOCKWISE FROM TOP FÁTIMA (P.161); CONVENTO DE CRISTO, TOMAR (P.165); IBERIAN WOLF SANCTUARY (P.135) >

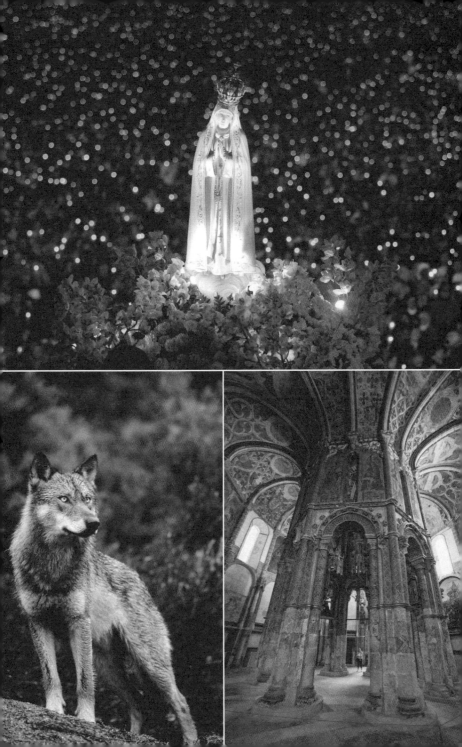

ARRIVAL AND DEPARTURE

By bus The bus station (Terminal Rodoviário) is at Rua Coronel Soeiro Brito 35, around a 5min walk from Praça da República.

Destinations Foz do Arelho (3–8 daily, though hourly on Sat & Sun in July & Aug; 20min); Leiria (2–4 daily; 1hr 20min); Lisbon (hourly; express service 1hr 10min, otherwise 1hr 30min); Nazaré (3–10 daily; 45min); and Óbidos (every 30min–1hr; 15min).

By car Caldas is 6km north of Óbidos. There's pay parking in Praça 25 de Abril and along Rua de Camões in front of the park, though if you continue around the park heading out of town, the street parking becomes free.

By train The train station is on the west side of the town; it's a 5min walk from there to the turismo, down Avenida 1 de Maio. Heading north from Caldas da Rainha, the trains stay inland until São Martinho do Porto, 13km south of Nazaré – for Foz do Arelho, you need to take the bus instead.

Destinations Leiria (6 daily; 1hr); Lisbon (up to 11 daily; 1hr 15min–2hr); and São Martinho do Porto (6 daily; 10–15min).

CALDAS DA RAINHA

INFORMATION

Turismo Praça 25 de Abril (Mon–Fri 9am–7pm, Sat & Sun 10am–1pm & 3–7pm; ☏ 262 839 700, ⓦ www.cm-caldas -rainha.pt), at the side of the modern town hall. From here, Praça da República is a five-minute walk away: walk down Rua Engenheiro Duarte Pacheo from the turismo, turn right on Rua Heróis da Grande Guerre, then left down pedestrianized Rua Almirante Cândido dos Reis.

ACCOMMODATION

Casa dos Plátanos Rua Rafael Bordallo Pinheiro 24 ☏ 262 841 810. The in-town manor-house option is this restored eighteenth-century property set in a quiet corner behind the spa and park. No credit cards. Closed Nov–Jan. €70
Central Largo Dr José Barbosa 22 ☏ 262 831 914, ⓦ residencialcentral.com. Located in a quiet, restored square between the market (Praça da República) and the spa (Largo da Rainha Dona Leonor), the rooms here have laminate floors and updated bathrooms, and some have French windows you can throw open onto the square. No breakfast. €40
Dom Carlos Rua de Camões 39A ☏ 262 832 551, ⓦ domcarlosportugal.com. Traditional old hotel, opposite the park. It's a bit musty, and furnishings and decor have seen better days, but it's a useful standby if you just want a bed for the night. No credit cards. €40

EATING AND DRINKING

Sabores d'Italia Praça 5 de Outubro 40 ☏ 262 845 600, ⓦ saboresditalia.com. It's rare to get proper Italian food in Portugal and, while you'll pay for the experience here, it's worth it. They serve homemade pasta and daily fish and meat specials (€14–21), plus pizzas too (€8–14). Tues–Sun 12.30–2.30pm & 7–10pm.

Tijuca Rua de Camões 89 ☏ 262 824 255. The best budget choice, a simple basement restaurant opposite the park, with a traditional menu and most dishes costing €6–9. The chicken casserole (*frango na púcara*) is good, served in an earthenware pot. Mon–Sat noon–3pm & 7–10pm; closed Wed in summer.

Foz do Arelho

The small village of **FOZ DO ARELHO**, 8km west of Caldas da Rainha, sits 1km back from a beautiful, sheltered lagoon beach, which is overlooked by a couple of cafés. The road continues a further 500m or so to another tremendous beach where river meets ocean, and here there's a promenade of fancier bars and restaurants. It's not really overdeveloped – this is more a holiday-home place than a resort – and outside July and August you'll have the wide, white sands to yourself. On the lagoon itself, the **Lagoa de Óbidos**, fishermen stand in the shallow waters next to their boats, attending to their nets.

ARRIVAL AND DEPARTURE

By bus There are direct buses out to Foz from Caldas da Rainha several times a day, a twenty-minute ride.
By car With a car you can drive northwest from Caldas along the N360, which takes you past the tranquil Lagoa de Óbidos, and then out along the coast via Foz do Arelho on a breezy clifftop route – a much better option than taking the busy N8 or the motorway.

ACCOMMODATION

Penedo Furado ☎ 262 979 610, ⦿ hotelpenedofurado .com. This is the best of two small hotels, signposted to the right up a side street as you pass through the village. It's a homely place with spacious rooms and distant lagoon views – prices shoot up in August, but are better value the rest of the year. **€60**

Quinta da Foz ☎ 262 979 369, ⦿ quinta-dafoz.com.

The other good option is *Quinta da Foz*, right in the village (off the square), a sixteenth-century manor house with five pretty rooms to let and two separate small apartments. Expect echoing quarters, vintage tiles and antique beds – the rooms include breakfast but the apartments don't. Doubles **€120**; apartments **€85**

EATING AND DRINKING

The presence of some rather fashionable bars in Foz village and dotted around the lagoon tells you what kind of place this is in summer, when the city crowds descend from Lisbon. Much of the action is out at the ocean beach where a line of bars and seafood restaurants vies for your attention. They're all a bit showy, a bit pricey and often a bit disappointing.

O Central Rua Almeida Grandela 81 ☎ 262 978 523. Best place to eat in the village is this bar and restaurant on the main through-road. A welcoming family dishes up

bumper-sized platters of grilled meat and fish, *cozido* and *bacalhau*, and you'll spend €8–10 at lunch, perhaps twice that at dinner. Daily 11am–11pm.

São Martinho do Porto

Lying 10km north of Foz, **SÃO MARTINHO DO PORTO** is the main resort between Peniche and Nazaré. However, it's low-key and largely low-rise and, compared with Peniche and Nazaré, is an easy-going place favoured by families. The reason for São Martinho's popularity is its beach, a glorious sweep of sand that curls around the bay and shelves gently into the sea, making its waters wonderfully warm. There's also a good northern beach on the open Atlantic coastline beyond the bay, pounded by surf. You can spend another happy day tramping the boardwalks and dune paths around the bay, or climbing the ochre cliffs above the quayside to the lighthouse. There's also an older part of São Martinho to explore, up the steep hill behind the more modern bay-side streets – the easiest way up is to take the **ascensor** (daily: June–Sept 10am–midnight; Oct–May 10am–9pm; free), from inside the turismo building, which whisks you to an upper square with sweeping town and bay views.

ARRIVAL, DEPARTURE AND INFORMATION

By bus and train The train station (services from Caldas da Rainha and Leiria) is on Largo 28 de Maio, while buses stop a bit closer in on Rua Conde de Avelar, with both terminals only a short walk from the seafront.

Information The turismo is in the heart of the town, two blocks from the bay promenade, on Rua Vasco da Gama (May–Sept Tues–Sun 10am–1pm & 3–7pm; Oct–April Tues–Sun 10am–1pm & 2–6pm; ☎ 262 989 110).

ACCOMMODATION AND EATING

★ **Atlântica** Rua Miguel Bombarda 6 ☎ 262 980 163, ⦿ residencial-atlantica.com. The best budget option, a jaunty blue-and-white guesthouse that's just two blocks from the seafront. The downstairs restaurant, the *Carvalho* (meals around €15–20), is as good as any of the eating places in the centre, and has a summer terrace. **€50**

Palace do Capitão Rua Capitão Jaime Pinto 6 ☎ 262 985 150, ⦿ palacecapitao.com. The finest accommodation in

town is a beautifully restored mansion overlooking the central promenade. The inlaid parquet floors and hand-painted wallpaper set the tone for what is an elegant house with comfortable rooms – though not all have sea views. Out of season doubles can cost as little as €60–80. They have an elegant *Casa de Chá* too, which makes a rather nice place for afternoon tea and cakes. **€100**

Nazaré

Some websites and holiday brochures claim **NAZARÉ** as one of Portugal's most picturesque seaside resorts, and if you come out of season you might just about agree.

But in summer, the crowds are far too heavy for the place to cope with and the enduring characteristics are lines of souvenir stalls and identikit fish restaurants with a touch of hard-edged hustle. While elderly local women still don traditional headscarves and embroidered aprons, their trays of fish have been replaced by cheap souvenirs and signs advertising rooms – and the colourful sardine boats that used to be hauled up along the beach at night now dock at an out-of-town harbour. However, as long as you don't expect a cosy village, and are steeled for peak-season crowds, Nazaré is highly enjoyable, with all the restaurants, facilities and knockabout cheer of a busy resort. It's not just summer either that rocks: New Year's Eve on Nazaré beach is one of the biggest parties in Portugal, while the annual Carnaval parades are rumbustious all-night affairs.

NAZARÉ

ACCOMMODATION
Mar Bravo	2
Miramar Hotel & Spa	4
Praia	6
Quinta do Campo	5
Ribamar	3
Vila Conde Fidalgo	1

RESTAURANTS AND BARS
A Tasquinha	3
Casa O Santo	1
O Casalinho	2

The beach

The long sweep of the seafront promenade is backed by a tight warren of narrow alleys and streets filled with houses advertising rooms and simple restaurants, with the occasional small square letting in the light. The main **beach** is a large expanse of clean sand, packed with bathers and multicoloured sunshades in summer, while further beaches stretch north beyond the headland. The water might look inviting on calm, hot days, but it's worth bearing in mind that swimming off these exposed Atlantic beaches can be dangerous – always heed warning signs and swim only where directed to do so. It's no coincidence that Nazaré has a worldwide reputation among **surfers** seeking serious waves – in 2013, Hawaiian surfer Garrett McNamara broke the world record for the largest wave ever surfed, a 30-metre-high monster off the coast at Nazaré.

Sítio

Ascensor da Nazaré (funicular), lower station at Largo do Elevador · Daily 7am–midnight, until 2am in Aug · €2.20 return

The original settlement here was built at **Sítio**, 110m up the rock face above the north end of the town, to avoid pirate raids. Legend tells of a twelfth-century knight, Dom Fuas Roupinho, who, while out hunting, was led up the cliff by a deer. The deer dived into the void and Dom Fuas was saved from following by the timely vision of Nossa Senhora da Nazaré, in whose name a church was subsequently built. You can reach Sítio and the church by taking the funicular from town, which rumbles up to a *miradouro* at the top.

The main church square is ringed by souvenir shops and patrolled by formidable *varinhas* (fishwives) touting huge mounds of dried fruit and nuts. The views down to the town and beach are sensational, while following the waymarked **footpath** signs from the square takes you out to the *farol* (lighthouse). It's the first section of a thirteen-kilometre circular trail that connects the town to Sítio (via funicular) by way of beach and pine forest.

ARRIVAL AND INFORMATION

NAZARÉ

By bus The bus station is on Avenida Vieira Guimarães, just a minute or two from the seafront.

Destinations Alcobaça (up to 9 daily; 20min); Caldas da Rainha (3–10 daily; 45min); Leiria (10 daily; 1hr 10min); Lisbon (6 daily; 2hr); Óbidos (3 daily; 1hr); and São Martinho do Porto (3 daily; 20min).

By car A one-way system filters traffic away from the narrow streets and up and down the flanking thoroughfares. There's pay parking in a large car park behind the market, or free spaces along the seafront starting after the cultural centre and library (heading towards port and marina).

By train The nearest train station is 6km inland, at Valado, on the Alcobaça road, though connecting buses do run regularly into town. It's easiest, however, to come by bus.

Information Nazaré's turismo, is at the Centro Cultural de Nazaré, on Av da República, which runs the length of the beach, and is where you'll find most of the town's hotels and restaurants (July & Aug daily 9am–9pm; April–June & Sept 9.30am–12.30pm & 2.30–6.30pm; Oct–March daily 9.30am–1pm & 2.30–6pm; ☎ 262 561 194, ⓦ cm-nazare.pt).

ACCOMMODATION

Nazaré is awash with **private rooms** and you'll be approached by touts throughout town – expect to pay up to €60 in high season, though much less for most of the year. In August a local bus runs on a circuit from town out to the two nearby **campsites** and back (*Orbitur* ⓦ orbitur.pt, and *Vale Paraíso* ⓦ valeparaiso.com), but there's no transport there the rest of the year.

★ **Mar Bravo** Praça Sousa Oliveira 71 ☎ 262 569 160, ⓦ marbravo.com. The most upmarket seafront choice has smallish rooms but all have an ocean view and are handsomely styled with good marble bathrooms. There's an equally refined fish and seafood restaurant downstairs, some say the best in town, where you can eat really well for €30 or so. **€80**

Miramar Hotel & Spa Rua Abel da Silva, Pederneira ☎ 262 550 000, ⓦ miramarnazarehotels.com. Contemporary four-star hotel sited on the eastern heights above Nazaré – it's a steep 1km above town and beach, in the old village of Pederneira, and you'll really need a car. Views are sensational – from rooms, pool, terrace, restaurant and breakfast balcony – while there are also some one- and

2

two-bed apartments surrounding a small courtyard, across from the hotel. Rates are pretty good – as low as €60 a night in winter. **€90**

★ **Praia** Av Vieria Guimarães 39 ☎ 262 569 200, ⓦ hotelpraia.com. Designer four-star hotel that's actually a couple of hundred metres from the beach (despite the name) but otherwise fully lives up to expectations. The rooms have blond-wood furniture, smart bathrooms and big balconies with sea or hill views; there's a year-round rooftop pool (covered in winter) and a terrific terrace with sweeping views. Rates as low as €70 out of season. **€120**

Quinta do Campo Valado dos Frades, 6km east of Nazaré ☎ 262 577 135, ⓦ aquintadocampo.com. A rather grand estate whose eight double rooms are traditional but elegant, with heavy wood furniture and immaculate white linen. There are also extensive grounds that contain a pool and tennis courts. **€80**

Ribamar Rua Gomes Freire 9 ☎ 262 551 58. Rooms (above a restaurant) are small, with frilly fabrics and tiny bathrooms tiled with *azulejos*. Some have the original wooden flooring and plaster cornicing, while others overlook the beach, though you'll pay a bit more for a sea view. **€50**

★ **Vila Conde Fidalgo** Av da Independência Nacional 21 ☎ 262 552 361, ⓦ condefidalgo.planetaclix.pt. The best budget choice is set back up the hill from the sea (10min walk), with parking outside. It's a secluded complex of simple rooms and apartments, separated by plant-filled patios and ceramic-tiled walkways. Furnishings are basic but adequate, with a fridge and TV in each room, and kitchenettes in the apartments (which can sleep four). No breakfast and no credit cards. Doubles **€50**; apartments **€70**

EATING AND DRINKING

The main concentrations of **restaurants**, **cafés** and **bars** are along the seafront Avenida da República, in the squares and alleys behind, and near the lower funicular station. Menus are broadly similar – plenty of grilled fish – and prices at most don't vary by more than a euro or two.

★ **A Tasquinha** Rua Adrião Batalha 54 ☎ 262 551 945. Just far enough off the seafront to be a locals' choice, this is the hands-down winner for very reasonably priced tavern-style food. It's a wooden bench and check-tablecloth joint, and you may have to queue, but it's worth it for the tasty meat and fish grills or special dishes like *atum cebolada* (tuna with onions), with most options costing €8–11. Tues–Sun noon–3pm & 7–11pm.

Casa O Santo Trav do Elevador 11 ☎ 262 085 128. This cosiest of *adegas* is the nearest thing to a pub in town,

good for a thimbleful of local wine or a beer and some fresh clams or prawns. Daily noon–midnight.

O Casalinho Praça Sousa Oliveira 7 ☎ 262 551 328. Alfresco dining in the square, or in the contemporary dining room. Service is with a smile, and you can expect good sea bass, squid kebabs, sardines, grilled bream and the like for around €10 – it's not really the place to go if you don't want fish. Mon, Tues & Thurs–Sun noon–3pm & 7–11pm.

Alcobaça

The vast Cistercian monastery at **ALCOBAÇA** was founded in 1153 by the first king of Portugal, Dom Afonso Henrique, to celebrate his decisive victory over the Moors at Santarém six years earlier. Building started soon after and – with royal patronage assured – by the end of the thirteenth century it was the wealthiest and most powerful monastery in the country. Nearly a thousand monks and lay-brothers lived here running a veritable business empire based on market-gardening, farming, fishing, forestry and trading. Notorious tales of the lavish lifestyle at Alcobaça were a staple of the writings of early travellers, who found the monastic excesses shocking and titillating in equal measure. The dissolution of the Portuguese monasteries in 1834 put an end to all this, but the buildings still stand as an extraordinary monument to another age.

ALCOBAÇA FESTIVALS

The middle of November every year sees the **Mostra de Doces Conventuais**, a weekend of feasting on conventual sweets and pastries and fruit liqueurs from convents, monasteries and cake shops in Portugal, Spain and France. During the **Cister Música** (ⓦ cistermusica.com) festival in May or June you can catch concerts in the abbey and elsewhere.

A visit to the monastery can comfortably occupy a couple of hours. Alcobaça itself is a small and fairly unremarkable town, though the Rio Baça winds attractively through the few remaining old-town streets. The ruined hilltop castle provides the best overall view of the monastery, while down below in town there's a large market building (the market is held on Monday) and attractive public gardens.

Mosteiro de Alcobaça

Daily: April–Sept 9am–7pm; Oct–March 9am–5pm; last entry 30min before closing • Monastery €6, under-14s free & free on Sun before 2pm; entry to church free; joint ticket with Batalha and Tomar's Convento do Cristo €15 • ☎ 262 505 120, ⓦ mosteiroalcobaca.pt

For centuries a centre of study, contemplation and religious doctrine, the **Mosteiro de Alcobaça** still possesses an overwhelming power that's also at least partly related to its historic and architectural significance. Founded in the very early years of the Portuguese kingdom, its overall construction took centuries, with major expansions and additions mirroring each notable era of Portuguese imperial might. In particular, Alcobaça stands as the first great early-Gothic building in Portugal – both abbey church and medieval cloister are the largest of their types in the country, while the church is also the burial place of Dom Pedro and Dona Inês de Castro, whose story echoes down through the ages as one of enduring love. The monastery has had multiple uses since Portugal's religious orders were dissolved in 1834 – from prison and barracks to school and nursing home – and today it's effectively a museum, owned and run by the state.

Sala dos Reis

The ticket desk for the monastery is immediately inside the church, on the left, by the entrance to the **Sala dos Reis** (Hall of Kings). The monarchs in question are those who ruled Portugal for its first six hundred years, from founder Afonso Henrique to Dom José I, who died in 1777 and under whom the final additions and alterations were made to the monastery. Their statues are all on display, along with vivid eighteenth-century *azulejos* that tell the story of the founding of the monastery.

Claustro do Silencio

From the Sala dos Reis you enter the heart of the monastery, the **Claustro do Silencio** (Cloister of Silence), off which are located the wider monastic quarters. It was built in the reign of Dom Dinis (probably finished in around 1311) and is a beautiful space – indeed, it's one of the largest cloisters in Europe. In the sixteenth century a Manueline upper

---

DOM PEDRO AND DONA INÊS DE CASTRO

The two extraordinary, carved, fourteenth-century tombs in the abbey church at Alcobaça shine a light on a doomed medieval romance. **Prince Pedro** (1320–1367), son of Afonso IV and heir to the Portuguese throne, was married to Constance of Castile, but fell in love with her maid, **Inês de Castro** (1320–1355), who was from a noble Galician (ie Spanish) family. The two continued an affair, despite the disapproval of the king, who feared a creeping Spanish influence in the Portuguese court. Following Constance's death in 1345, Afonso IV banished Inês and forbade her marriage to Pedro, but the pair wed in secret in Bragança in the far north of the country. With Inês's brothers and other Spanish nobles favoured by Pedro, and Afonso in danger of losing control of his court, the king moved to more radical measures, and ordered his daughter-in-law's murder. She was killed in Coimbra in 1355, sparking a revolt by Pedro against his own father. Afonso died two years later, and when Pedro succeeded to the throne in 1357 he assuaged his grief with the commissioning of two elaborate tombs, which he placed foot to foot in the abbey church – allegedly, so that they could see each other when they rose again. Inês' corpse was transferred here from **Coimbra** and ceremonially reinterred – not before, according to gory legend, Pedro placed her rotting body on the throne and insisted the court honour his lost queen by kissing her hand.

storey was added by notable architect João de Castilho, giving the medieval Gothic cloister a renewed grace and elegance. There's also a beautiful hexagonal *lavabo* with Renaissance fountain, which was where the monks washed before entering the refectory.

Refectory and kitchen

The monks took their meals in the **refectory**, but the celebrated feasting at Alcobaça came with an attached duty – as they ate, the Scriptures were read to the assembled brothers from the elegant stone pulpit. The medieval **kitchen** was lost to renovations in the seventeenth century. By the time awed travellers were enjoying monastic hospitality a century later, the food was prepared in the vast, arcaded "new" eighteenth-century kitchen, whose scale still retains the power to impress. An enormous central chimney rests on wrought-iron legs, with water brought into the building via a hydraulic canal system – the size of the water-basin set into the floor gives you an idea of just how much pot-boiling and pan-scrubbing went on here.

ARRIVAL AND INFORMATION   ALCOBAÇA

By bus From the market and the nearby bus station it's a five-minute signposted walk to the monastery, crossing the river en route.

Destinations Batalha (8 daily; 30min); Leiria (4 daily; 45min); Lisbon (3 daily; 2hr); and Nazaré (up to 9 daily; 20min).

By car There's free parking in the large car park off the avenue above the monastery, and plenty more near the market and gardens. The town centre has improved immeasurably since through-traffic was diverted away from the monastery, opening up the facing square, Praça 25 de Abril.

Information The turismo, Praça 25 de Abril (daily: May–Sept 10am–1pm & 3–7pm; Oct–April 10am–1pm & 2–6pm; ☎262 582 377, ⍟cm-alcobaca.pt), is on the square, opposite the monastery, and can supply wholly unnecessary maps of the town.

ACCOMMODATION AND EATING

Alcobaça has a limited but relatively inexpensive choice of **accommodation**, mostly near Praça 25 de Abril, where a ring of cafés and restaurants has grandstand views. **Restaurants** are predictably touristy, with little to choose between them – for cheap meals, locals favour the restaurant at the *Corações Unidos*.

António Padeiro Rua Dom Maur Cocheril 27 ☎262 582 295. Just up the alley from the main square, this long-standing restaurant is a refined spot for a meal. The food's traditional, like everywhere in town, but it's the best place for something like *cabrito*, *cozido* or grilled fish, with lunch dishes from around €8, otherwise mains at €11–15. Daily noon–3.30pm & 7–10.30pm.

Challet Fonte Nova Rua da Fonte Nova 8 ☎262 598 300, ⍟challetfontenova.pt. A boutique hotel in an aristocratic nineteenth-century villa, furnished with antiques but tempered with an interior-designer's eye. They have an associated spa as well, with the house secreted on a backstreet off Rua Frei Estevão Martins, to the side of the turismo. Parking. **€120**

Dona Inês de Castro Rua Costa Veiga 44 ☎262 582 012, ⍟hotel-inesdecastro.com. Modern three-star hotel, a five-minute walk from town (follow the Lisbon–Évora signs at the roundabout) and looking out across fields to the back of the monastery. **€60**

Corações Unidos Rua Frei António Brandão 39 ☎262 582 142, ⍟coracoesunidos.pt. Large rooms in a dated guesthouse, just off the square, some with side views to the monastery. The old-fashioned restaurant downstairs is a reliable place for an inexpensive meal (the *ementa turística* is €12) – *frango na púcara*, a tasty chicken casserole, is the house speciality, with *cozido* served on a Sunday. Restaurant open noon–3pm & 7–11pm. **€40**

Leiria

The old royal castle at **LEIRIA** peers out over a charming town that comes as something of a surprise for many visitors. Surrounded by modern suburbs and a swirling one-way system, it holds no great sights save the castle itself, but the pretty old streets and squares in the centre are worth a wander. As a student town Leiria has enough good restaurants and bars to make the evenings go with a swing, while it's also handily poised for the fine beaches of the Pinhal de Leiria to the west.

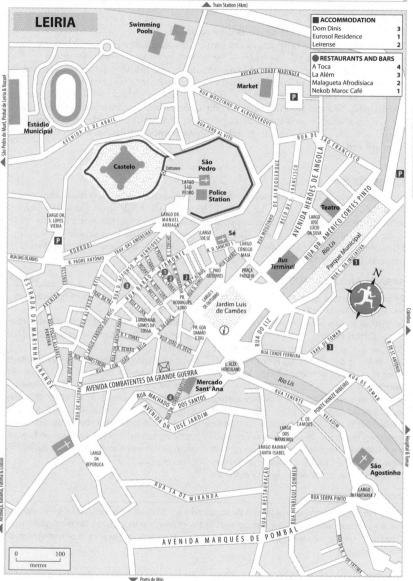

Praça Rodrigues Lobo

The old town spreads out around the arcaded **Praça Rodrigues Lobo**, named for the statue of the local poet (1580–1622) who became one of Portugal's most famous early writers. In fact, Leiria's literary connections go back even further than this – in 1480, the town had one of Portugal's first printing presses, which was run by Jews who printed in Hebrew. An antiques and crafts fair is held in the square on the second Saturday of each month.

Castelo de Leiria

Rua do Castelo • April–Sept Tues–Sun 10am–6pm; Oct–March Tues–Sun 9am–5pm • €2.25

Leiria's **Castelo** was an early site in the battle for control of what was to become the kingdom of Portugal. Taken from the Moors by Afonso Henriques in the twelfth century, it became a royal favourite and in the fourteenth century was the main residence of Dom Dinis. It's been much altered since (the battlements are modern reconstructions), though it's still an impressive sight, crowning the crags above town. You can see the former royal palace within the castle walls, while inside the keep is a small museum containing displays of armour and archeological finds. There's also the shell of the old church of **Nossa Senhora da Penha**, which dates from around 1400.

Largo da Sé

Outside the walls, on the edge of the old town, stands the sixteenth-century cathedral, or **Sé**, which was built during the reign of Dom João III. Look across the square here to the impressively tiled pharmacy opposite – once the meeting place of a literary circle surrounding novelist **Eça de Queirós**, who lived in Leiria for a year in 1870–71. His novel, *The Sin of Father Amaro* (1876), draws heavily on his experiences in this provincial cathedral city.

ARRIVAL AND INFORMATION   LEIRIA

By bus It's easiest to arrive by bus, as the bus terminal is right in town on Avenida Heróis de Angola.

Destinations Alcobaça (4 daily; 45min); Batalha (5 daily; 15min); Coimbra (10 daily; 50min); Fátima (Mon–Sat 7 daily, Sun 2; 35min–1hr); Lisbon (9 daily; 1hr 10min); Porto de Mós (3 daily; 35min); São Pedro de Moel (July & Aug up to 10 daily, Sept–June 2–3 daily; 30min); and Tomar (4 daily; 1hr).

By car Leiria is about 35km northeast of both Alcobaça and Nazaré, and 70km (under an hour's drive) south of Coimbra. Driving into Leiria, if you follow the signs for "centro", you end up in a one-way system of some devilment. Although metered street parking and pay car parks are widely advertised, parking in the centre can be pricey. Far better to avoid the one-way system and park in the free car parks on the outskirts (near the market and river), which isn't too long a walk into town.

By train The train station is 4km north of town – either wait for a connecting bus into the centre, or take a taxi (around €6).

Destinations Caldas da Rainha (6 daily; 1hr); Figueira da Foz (6 daily; 45min–1hr 20min); Lisbon (4 daily; 2hr–3hr 20min); and São Martinho do Porto (6 daily; 35–50min).

Information The turismo is on Jardim Luís de Camões (daily 10am–1pm & 3–6pm; ☎244 814 770, ⓦcm-leira .pt), a 5min walk across from the bus station. In the square outside the turismo, there's an Adam-and-Eve fountain: though it's of no artistic merit – let's just say that Adam is pleased to see you.

ACCOMMODATION

The very cheapest accommodation is found in the narrow old-town streets off Praça Rodrigues Lobo – though note that none of these places has parking, and you won't be able to drive to them to unload. The town's youth hostel closed in 2013, and it was unclear at the time of writing if it would reopen (latest news on ⓦmicrosites.juventude .gov.pt/portal/en).

Dom Dinis Trav de Tomar 2 ☎244 815 342, ⓦhotel ddinis.pt. Across the bridge from the turismo, and up a steep side-street – it's signposted and there's adjacent parking. It doesn't look much from the outside, but the rooms are bright and double-glazed against street noise. €45

Eurosol Residence Rua Comissão da Iniciativa 13 ☎244 860 460, ⓦeurosol.pt. Leiria's central four-star choice provides stylish, modern apartments (studios, or one- and two-bedroom), plus gym, sauna, pool and underground parking – it's signposted from the ring road.

The adjacent sister hotels, the *Eurosol Leiria* and *Jardim*, are further out of the centre, but have similar facilities and prices plus fine city views. Web rates are often real bargains. €90

★ **Leiriense** Rua Afonso de Albuquerque 6 ☎244 823 054, ⓦhotelleiriense.com. A firm favourite for some years, offering cool, quiet rooms with parquet floors and handsome wooden furniture. There are a fair few single and twin rooms, so it's useful for solo travellers. The location is ideal, and it's good value for money. €40

EATING AND DRINKING

There are some good **restaurants** in the old town, with a particular cluster on Rua Correia Mateus, while some more contemporary places can be found around the Jardim Luís de Camões. Pretty Praça Rodrigues Lobo has the most popular **cafés** in town, while the **bar scene** is concentrated on Largo Cândido dos Reis and Rua Barão de Viamonte – you'll find all kinds of places tucked away in the alleys off here, from student dives to quite sophisticated lounge bars.

RESTAURANTS

★ **A Toca** Rua Dr Correia Mateus ☎ 244 832 221. Come here for large portions of traditional, well-cooked food – the *bife a vaca* arrives sizzling in an earthenware dish and the *lulas grelhado* is excellent. It's the best restaurant on the street, with meals for around €15. Mon–Fri & Sun noon–3pm & 7–10.30pm.

Lá Além Rua Maria da Fonte 6 ☎ 937 377 770. An Alentejan bar-restaurant with terrace, tucked up a side alley. It's a cheapish place (mains from around €7) to try *migas*, grilled lamb, steaks and other specialities from Portugal's south. Mon & Wed–Sun noon–2am, Tues 7pm–2am.

Malagueta Afrodisíaca Rua Gago Coutinho 17 ☎ 244 831 607. Contemporary style that comes as something of a shock in old-town Leiria, and a fun menu to boot – though whether every dish is aphrodisiacal, you'll have to wait until you've eaten to find out. Expect plenty of fragrant curries – fish and prawn – but also a good chicken *fajita*, Brazilian *vatapá* (fish in palm oil), and a rare vegetarian selection. Dishes mostly €8–12. Mon–Fri 12.30–11pm, Sat & Sun 7pm–midnight.

BAR

Nekob Maroc Café Rua Gago Coutinho 23 ☎ 244 892 082, ⓦ nekob.com. Right in the heart of the old town, this fashionable Moroccan bar is a popular choice for a night out. Daily 8pm–3am.

Pinhal de Leiria and its beaches

One of the finest stretches of coastline in the country flanks the **Pinhal de Leiria**, a sprawling pine forest west of Leiria and stretching north of São Pedro de Moel. It's what passes for an ancient forest in Portugal – the pines were first planted by farmers in the fourteenth century as a protective measure against encroaching sand dunes. Later, the trees were an essential resource when it came to fitting out ships during the Portuguese "Discoveries". There are **bike lanes** and tracks throughout the forest, while beyond the dunes lie vast white-sand beaches soaking up the thundering breakers from the Atlantic. By public transport, the only realistic target is the small resort of São Pedro de Moel, though bikers and drivers will be able to find better, more isolated spots. Expect any of the **beaches** near São Pedro to be packed in July and August – the straight, fast, coastal road north and south has been upgraded to cope with heavy summer traffic. Come any other time and you'll have the sands to yourself.

São Pedro de Moel

SÃO PEDRO DE MOEL, 22km west of Leiria, is a largely laidback resort where old buildings have been renovated and new ones erected with an eye for tradition. Although it's now firmly a holiday place, it still resembles in part the fishing village it once was, with many houses boasting wooden balconies, louvred windows and climbing roses. A restored cobbled square sits back from a small central beach, while just to the north, 1km past the lighthouse, **Praia Velha** provides a fantastic sweep of sand. You can walk here – follow signs for "praias" from the roundabout – though the equally fine southern beaches of **Paredes** and **Pedra do Ouro** are a short drive away.

A bike lane runs through the trees all the way from São Pedro to the more developed resort of **Praia da Vieira**, 10km north (or a 15min drive), with a long line of beachfront cafés and deckchairs staked out under bamboo parasols.

ARRIVAL AND DEPARTURE   SÃO PEDRO DE MOEL

By bus Buses from Leiria to São Pedro sometimes involve a change at Marinha Grande, the congested small town halfway between Leiria and the coast (2–3 daily, more in summer; 30min).

2

ACCOMMODATION

Even in high season you should be able to find accommodation, since most local visitors come for the day or stay in holiday homes here. Still, making an advance reservation in August isn't a bad idea. Several places advertise "*quartos*" on the road down from the roundabout towards the clifftop; bear left near the church and you'll soon find the square and beach at the bottom of town.

★ **Água de Madeiros** Água de Madeiros, 3km south of São Pedro de Moel ☎ 244 599 324, ⓦ aguade madeiros.com. Sitting in a valley cleft, near often deserted sands (out of season, at least). There are twelve simple but cosy rooms, some of which have sea views, plus a bar, pool and terrace. The beach is just 100m away. **€75**

Mar & Sol Av da Liberdade 1 ☎ 244 590 000, ⓦ hotel maresol.com. São Pedro's main hotel sits on the cliffs above the sea. It's a three-star that's had a face-lift, so the rooms are now in cool, contemporary colours (they've all got a balcony but sea views cost €15–30 more), and the swish restaurant has big picture windows overlooking the beach. **€70**

Miramar Rua dos Serviços Florestais ☎ 244 599 141. The largest of several guesthouses with unexciting rooms, just down from the roundabout. It's a family-friendly place – some rooms have bunk-beds, and there's a restaurant downstairs – but despite the balconies it can be a bit dark and poky. You might want to ask to see a couple of rooms first. **€60**

Parque Orbitur Rua Volta do Sete ☎ 244 599 168, ⓦ orbitur.pt. The closest campsite to town is also the best, in the trees and just 600m from the beach. The site has a pool with slides, plus bar and restaurant, as well as rooms, chalets and bungalows for rent. Pitch **€18.40** plus **€5.40** per adult; doubles **€44**

EATING AND DRINKING

Brisamar Rua Dr Nicolau Bettencourt 23 ☎ 244 599 520, ⓦ brisamar.com.pt. Regarded as the best in town, and augmenting its Portuguese menu with things such as Greek salad, pasta or tuna steak (mains from around €12). But you have to sit inside and there's no sense of being at the seaside. It's a block over from the *Miramar*. Daily 12.30–3pm & 7.30–10pm; Oct–June, closed Mon.

Estrela do Mar Av Marginal ☎ 244 599 245, ⓦ quinta dafalca.com. Hard to beat for location, tucked into the cliffs above the main beach and with a lot of outdoor seating. You should just be able to get a drink outside meal times and soak up the views. Otherwise, the fish choice depends on what's been caught that day, and mains cost from around €10. Daily noon–11pm; closed Thurs in winter.

★ **O Pai dos Frangos** Praia Velha ☎ 244 599 158. Unmissable beach restaurant, which prepares sensational mixed kebabs (pork and bacon-wrapped prawns), plus grilled chicken, seafood rice and fresh fish (most dishes €8–12). There's no better place for lunch – on the small outdoor terrace, or at tables by the huge picture windows. Tues–Sun 11am–11pm; shorter hours in winter.

Batalha

Eleven kilometres south of Leiria stands the Mosteiro de Santa Maria da Vitória, widely known as the **Mosteiro da Batalha** (Battle Abbey). Built to commemorate a great national victory – the defeat of Castilian forces at the decisive Battle of Aljubarrota in 1385 – the abbey in turn became a great national monument. Successive monarchs lavished funds upon its construction, and over two centuries Batalha became one of Portugal's most celebrated buildings – a hybrid Gothic and Manueline masterpiece that's both royal pantheon and an expression of national pride.

Most visitors see the abbey and leave – to be honest, there isn't anything attractive about the village itself, though it's peaceful once the tour buses have left. To complete the trip – and learn more about the history behind the founding of the abbey – it's also worth driving out to **São Jorge**, 4km south of present-day Batalha and site of the actual battle in question, where there's a useful interpretation centre.

Brief history

The dynasty of Burgundian kings lasted over 250 years, until 1383 and the death of Fernando I. Even during the good times, in the early years of the Portuguese kingdom, Castilian Spanish nobles and kings had an eye for making trouble – the death of a Portuguese king seemed like too good an opportunity to miss, especially since

Fernando's widow Leonor, now ruling as regent, subsequently married her only daughter Beatriz to Juan I of Castile. With an illegitimate heir of Fernando's also contesting the throne – one João, Grand Master of the noble Portuguese house of Aviz – the stage was set for a showdown, which duly came at the **Battle of Aljubarrota** (August 14, 1385). Although the sheer force of numbers and power all seemed to be on the side of Castile, they had not bargained on a canny promise that João made to the Virgin Mary – he vowed that if the Portuguese won, she would get a brand-new abbey and eternal gratitude. João's army prevailed in a battle that sealed the independence of Portugal, the first stones of the "Battle Abbey" were laid the following year in 1386, and Grand Master João became Dom João I (initial king of the Aviz dynasty which subsequently ruled until 1581).

Mosteiro da Batalha

Largo Infante Dom Henriques, Batalha • Daily: April–Sept 9am–6.30pm; Oct–March 9am–5.30pm; last admission 30min before closing • Main church free; Cloisters and Capelas Imperfeitas €6, free on Sun before 2pm; joint ticket with Alcobaça and Tomar's Convento do Cristo €15 • ☎ 244 765 497, ⓦ mosteirobatalha.pt

The abbey at Batalha took more than a century to build, though the overall ornate French-Gothic structure owes its style and substance to the work of the first two long-serving architects, Afonso Domingues and the Catalan architect known as Master Huguet. English influences are explained by the Portuguese Crown's alliance with England since 1373 – Dom João I later married Philippa of Lancaster, the daughter of John of Gaunt – and it's possible to see the hand of medieval English architects in the abbey's nave and chapterhouse. With a wealthier, more confident age came a richer design, and in the late fifteenth and early sixteenth centuries Batalha's architects worked in a masterful Manueline style, transforming the abbey into a dazzling statement of Portuguese pride. Batalha has been in the hands of the state since the dissolution of the monasteries in 1834 and is, in essence, a museum.

Capela do Fundador

It's the **Capela do Fundador** (Founder's Chapel) that lies at the heart of Batalha's raison d'être. The abbey might have had its origins in thanks for divine help in battle, but Dom João I put it to work to bolster his authority and that of the House of Aviz by ordering the construction of a royal pantheon (completed by the architect Huguet around 1433). João and his English wife Philippa were its first occupants – their joint tomb is a suitably regal affair, and their statues, rather cutely, hold hands, to symbolize the enduring relationship between Portugal and England. Four royal princes also have tombs in the chapel, all of them sons of João and Philippa and three of them very definitely eclipsed by the fourth and most famous – **Prince Henry the Navigator**, the man who drove the first wave of Portuguese explorations south to Africa.

Claustro Real and Sala do Capítulo

The first departure from the overall Gothic tenor of the abbey can be seen in the **Claustro Real**, or Royal Cloister. Diogo de Boitaca – royal architect to Dom Manuel I – arrived at the abbey in 1509 with a commission to spend some of the kingdom's increasing wealth, and added intricate carved decorations to the cloister, typical of the daring Manueline style. The columns supporting the arches and stone screens are an ornate, entwined tangle of spirals, branches, leaves, flowers and shells.

Opening off one side of the cloister is the abbey's chapterhouse, the **Sala do Capítulo**, the nerve-centre of the early abbey, where the monks congregated to discuss important matters. It's the undoubted masterpiece of the architect Huguet, with a daring star-vaulted ceiling, 19 metres across, that has no visible support. Legend has it that only condemned prisoners were allowed to work on its construction because the vault was considered so unsafe, and that Huguet had to sleep beneath his completed ceiling on the first night to prove his doubters wrong. However, it did stay up – and has done for centuries – and the chapterhouse now commemorates Portugal's "unknown soldiers", with ceremonial sentries watching over a tomb containing the remains of two unidentified combatants from World War I.

Capelas Imperfeitas

Behind the apse of the main church are the so-called **Capelas Imperfeitas** (Unfinished Chapels) – you have to leave the main complex to see them and walk around the back. They were commissioned by Dom Duarte, crowned king in 1433 on the death of his father João I, and were intended as Gothic funereal chapels, but work stopped with the early death of the king in 1437 and that of his architect Huguet a year later. There matters may have rested, but for the later intervention of Dom Manuel and his millions, and more importantly his masterful architects, notably Mateus Fernandes who worked here from 1490 onwards. The towering, fifteen-metre-high portal was transformed into an extraordinary Manueline latticework, while inside the octagonal space virtually every inch bristles and froths – tree branches, ropes, angels, molluscs, linked chains, vegetation, keyhole arches and many other conceits in delicate stone. The seven interior funereal chapels were eventually completed – two contain the tombs of Dom Duarte and his wife Leonor, placed here much later – but the upper storey is still unfinished, giving the chapels their name.

São Jorge: the battle site

The Battle of Aljubarrota was fought on a plain 10km northeast of Aljubarrota itself, at the small hamlet of **São Jorge**, 4km south of Batalha. When the fighting was over a small chapel was built and remains at the entrance to the village today. The battle lasted only one hour, but it was a hot day and the commander of the victorious Portuguese forces, Nuno Álvares Pereira, complained loudly of thirst; a jug of fresh water is still placed daily in the porch of the chapel in his memory. Legend has it that Aljubarrota itself was defended by its baker, Brites de Almeida, who fended off the Castilian army with her baking spoon. This fearsome weapon dispensed with seven soldiers, whom Brites promptly baked in her oven.

Centro de Interpretaçao da Batalha de Aljubarrota

Av Dom Nuno Álvares Pereira, São Jorge • May–Sept Tues–Sun 10am–7pm; Oct–April Tues–Sun 10am–5.30pm • €7, under-17s €3.50 • ☎ 244 480 060, ⓦ fundacao-aljubarrota.pt • The centre and battle site are signposted on the IC2/N1, a short drive from Batalha. A tourist-train service runs from outside the abbey on Sat & Sun (departures every 30min, while centre is open; €2 each way)

A short path leads from the chapel to the impressive **Centro de Interpretaçao da Batalha de Aljubarrota**, which tackles the battle itself, the contemporary political intrigue and much more besides. It takes a hands-on multimedia approach, so not only do you visit the battlefield but then see a video re-enactment of the day's combat; there's also plenty for children to do, and a café on site.

ARRIVAL AND DEPARTURE   BATALHA

By car The large abbey car park is the most convenient place to leave your car, though there's plenty of overspill parking in the village beyond.

By bus Buses stop on the cobbled square-cum-car park,

Largo 14 de Agosto de 1385, at the top end of which the abbey is visible, on the right, standing alone surrounded by a bare plaza. There are regular services to and from Fátima (4 daily; 25min), Leiria (5 daily; 15min) and Lisbon (5 daily; 2hr).

ACCOMMODATION AND EATING

There are some budget rooms in town, and a decent hotel or two in the vicinity, though Batalha doesn't really warrant an overnight stop (Alcobaça or Leiria are nicer places to stay). The **cafés** that flank the abbey plaza are the best places to soak up the views, though none of the **restaurants** stands out – all offer standard menus at moderate prices.

Casa do Outeiro Largo Carvalho do Outeiro 4 ☎ 244 765 806, ⓦ casadoouteiro.com. Signposted 100m up a side road, this small boutique hotel with swimming pool has fifteen bright rooms, all with terrace (though only some have the abbey view). It's very contemporary – white walls, wooden floors, stylish furniture and plenty of light – while the owner Odete is responsible for much of the artwork and the preserves and cakes served at breakfast. **€65**

Restaurante Vitória Largo da Misericórdia ☎ 244 765 678. The *churrasqueira* here, beneath the guesthouse of the same name, is where the locals come for grilled chicken and pork, straight from the grill at bargain prices. There's a shaded terrace for diners. It's just up from the bus stop (or, from the main road, behind Totta bank) – if it's busy then *Casa das Febras*, across the way, offers more good-value dining. Daily noon–3pm & 7–10pm.

2

Porto de Mós and around

Eight kilometres south of Batalha lies the small riverside town of **Porto de Mós**, with its distinctive castle. Further south and east extends the **Parque Natural das Serras de Aire e Candeeiros**, a mix of rugged limestone hills, crags and upland farmland divided by ancient stone walls. There are walking trails in both the Aire and Candeeiros ranges, but the *parque natural* is better known for its fabulous **underground caves**, which all lie in a rough triangle between Porto de Mós and Fátima, on the west side of the A1 motorway. Meanwhile, across the motorway on the east side of the Serra de Aire, Portugal has its own Jurassic Park where you can walk with dinosaurs at the **Pegadas dos Dinossáurios**.

Castelo de Porto de Mós

Porto de Mós • May–Sept Tues–Sun 10am–12.30pm & 2–6pm; Oct–May Tues–Sun 10am–12.30pm & 2–5.30pm • Free • ☎ 244 499 637, ⓦ municipio-portodemos.pt

High above town, nestled in the folds of the hills, the grandiose **Castelo de Porto de Mós** was built in the thirteenth century. It was given to Nuno Álvares Pereira in 1385 by the grateful Dom João I, in recognition of the general's victory at the Battle of Aljubarrota – significantly, the Portuguese army had rested here on the eve of the battle – and was later turned into a fortified palace. Severely damaged in the earthquake of 1755, the castle has been renovated piecemeal since, and now boasts rather too pristine electric-green tiled towers.

The caves

There are three sets of caves open to the public in the natural park (and a fourth, Moeda, off the N356 road between Batalha and Fátima), but unless you are a real fan, a visit to one will probably suffice. As it happens, the largest and most spectacular, at Mira de Aira, is the only one directly accessible by bus.

Grutas de Mira de Aire

Mira de Aire, 13km southeast of Porto de Mós • Daily: April & May 9.30am–6pm; June & Sept 9.30am–7pm; July & Aug 9.30am–7.30pm; Oct–March 9.30am–5.30pm • €6.20, under-11s €3.60, under-5s free; combined entry with Parque Aquático €10.35, under-11s €6.60 • ☎ 244 440 322, ⓦ grutasmiradaire.com

It's a fabulous thirteen-kilometre drive out into the hills along the N243 from Porto de Mós to the **Grutas de Mira de Aire**, Portugal's largest show caves. There's parking right outside, or it's a signposted one-kilometre walk from the town bus stop. The 45-minute guided tour ends up at a natural lake filled with fountains 110m below the surface, taking in a galaxy of stalactites, stalagmites and oddly shaped rock formations with curious names – "Octopus Gallery", the "Organ", the "Conch" – en route. To exit, you take the lift up and emerge beside the **Parque Aquático** water park (summer only), which is a great place to cool off – there are half-day and full-day tickets available for this, and you can visit independently of the caves. Outside on the road, several cafés and restaurants cater for the crowds.

Grutas de Alvados and Santo António

July & Aug daily 10am–6.30pm; Sept–June Tues–Sun 10am– 5pm • Each site €5.80, under-11s €3.60, or combined ticket (Visita Conjunta) €9, under-11s €6 • ⓦ grutasalvados.com, ⓦ grutassantoantonio.com

The **Grutas de Alvados** contain a variety of natural halls and underground lakes, though it's the **Grutas Santo António** that are the bigger draw – the latter has the most impressive stalagmites and stalactites of any of the local caves. The turn-off for these caves is signposted from the N243 before you reach Mira de Aire – you could jump off the Mira de Aire bus, but it's then a three-kilometre walk to Alvados and then another 1km to Santo António.

Pegadas dos Dinossáurios

Estrada de Fátima, Bairro • Tues–Sun 10am–12.30pm & 2–6pm; mid-March to mid-Sept Sat & Sun open until 8pm • €2 • ☎ 249 530 160, ⓦ www.pegadasdedinossaurios.org • The site is just outside the village of Bairro, off the N360 – you'll pick up the signs at Boleiros if you head towards Fátima (via Minde) after seeing the caves

In a quarry around 10km south of Fátima, paleontologists made an extraordinary discovery in 1994 – namely the oldest and longest set of preserved sauropod tracks found anywhere in the world. The tracks date back 175 million years, and were made as the large herbivores plodded through a shallow lagoon, later preserved as limestone. They are now on display *in situ* at the excellent **Monumental Natural das Pegadas dos Dinossáurios**, where a gravel walkway circles the site on high before dropping down to the quarry floor. You can clearly see the footprints (*pegadas*) – hundreds of them, exceptionally well preserved – and follow their route across the stone. By the spacing, paleontologists reckon that some of the sauropods were up to 30m long. There's an explanatory film (in Portuguese) shown at the ticket office, though it's hard to resist the temptation to make straight for the tracks.

ARRIVAL AND INFORMATION   PORTO DE MÓS

By bus The bus station (services from Leiria via Batalha, and from Alcobaça) is a short walk from the riverside gardens. There are two or three useful weekday bus services from Porto de Mós to Mira de Aire with Rodoviária do Tejo (ⓦrodotejo.pt), currently departing at 9.35am (during school terms), 12.05pm and 2.30pm; it's a thirty-minute journey. A return service leaves Mira de Aire at

around 1.30pm and 6.30pm, though other regional services may also pass through Mira de Aire and Porto de Mós.

Information Turismo, Jardim Público (May–Sept Tues– Sun 10am–1pm & 3–7pm; Oct–April Tues–Sun 10am–1pm & 2–6pm; ☎ 244 402 318, ⓦ www.municipio-portodemos .pt).

PASS THE SALT

Of all the things uncovered in the Aire e Candeeiros natural park over the years (stalactites, Roman cobblestones, dinosaur footprints), the oddest is surely salt – mined here since ancient times. It's still produced near the town of Rio Maior, at the foot of the Serra dos Candeeiros, where a wide bed of concrete-lined **salt pans** (*marinhas do sal*) exploits the bed of rock salt under the local mountains. Workers at the cooperatively owned **Salinas Naturais de Rio Maior** pump salty water from a well and then subject it to various concentration and evaporation techniques in the tanks and pans on view. It's a process that has been going on, in some shape or form, since the twelfth century. There's most activity between June and September, but you can see something at most times of the year since many of the old wooden salt sheds have been turned into craft stores, salt shops and rustic taverns, and there are even a couple of restaurants where you'll get a good grill-lunch with the salt workers. The sheds themselves are curious works, with weathered boards, gnarled olive-wood posts and ancient wooden locks. The salt pans lie 3km north of Rio Maior (off the IC2/N1), but signposting is patchy. Coming into the town centre, follow scant signs for "Marinhas do Sal" and "Salinas" (on the Alcobertas road); you're there when you see the Wild West-style wooden buildings overlooking the salt-beds.

ACCOMMODATION

Casa dos Matos Rua Dom Fuas Rupinho, Alvados ☎ 244 440 393, ⓦ casadosmatos.com. An attractive, contemporary country home on the way to the Alvados caves, with plenty of exposed stone and coordinated fabrics, plus an outdoor pool and pretty terrace. The breakfasts are good, using locally sourced produce. **€90**

Quinta do Rio Alcaide Rio Alcaide ☎ 966 164 342, ⓦ rioalcaide.com. Nearest to town, 1km out of Porto de Mós, the serene *quinta* is a converted paper mill with guest rooms (including in the windmill), as well as self-catering studios and larger apartments. There's also an attractive swimming pool in the grounds. **€60**

Fátima

The simple farming village of **FÁTIMA** changed forever on May 13, 1917, when – according to the witnesses themselves – the Virgin Mary announced herself to three young children. It was the first of six apparitions that transfixed first Portugal and then the Catholic world, which now regards Fátima as a fixture on its pilgrimage calendar, second only to Lourdes in France. As Fátima's celebrity has increased exponentially, so has its size and importance. Farming village no more, Fátima has a basilica that attracts millions – not to mention hotels, pilgrims' hostels, cafés and restaurants, as well as souvenir shops that each year explore new levels of tackiness.

Quite what you make of it all depends largely on your beliefs – it is, after all, a place built entirely on faith. To see it through the eyes of believers you really need to come during the major **annual pilgrimages** (May 12–13 and October 12–13), when hundreds of thousands of people gather here from throughout the country. Most walk and for a few weeks before the dates each year, it's common to see pilgrims in reflective jackets, marching along Portugal's highways in the blazing heat, with some completing the final part of their journey shuffling penitently down the esplanade on their knees. The death of the last surviving child witness, Lúcia, in 2005, was marked as a national event – amid blanket media coverage she was buried in the basilica in February 2006, and it's no exaggeration to say that the entire country came to a halt to watch.

Santuário de Fátima

Information office, next to Capelinha das Aparições, May–Oct Mon–Sat 9am–6.30pm, Sun 9am–6pm; Nov–April Mon–Sat 9am–6pm, Sun 9am–5.30pm • ☎ 249 539 600, ⓦ santuario-fatima.pt

At the heart of the entire sanctuary is the simple **Capelinha das Aparições** (Chapel of the Apparitions), built on the spot where the Virgin supposedly appeared. This was the first building constructed here, and still marks the end of pilgrimage for millions of visitors each year, though it's now entirely overwhelmed by the other buildings that have sprung up over the intervening years. The mighty **Basílica de Nossa Senhora do Rosário de Fátima** was begun in 1928 and consecrated in 1953 – inside are the tombs of Lúcia, Jacinta and Francisco. In front is the gargantuan esplanade – capable of holding a million worshippers – over which Gregorian chanting wafts from flanking speakers. At the top of the esplanade stands another epic church, the circular **Basílica de Santíssima Trindade** (Holy Trinity Basilica), a dramatic contemporary space that can hold nine thousand pilgrims.

There are regular daily Masses held in both the chapel and main basilica – times are posted (some are in English) – and a torchlit procession at dusk, the largest of which is on the twelfth day of each month.

For all but the most devout, a tour around the rest of the widely advertised "attractions" in town is largely an exploration of the grotesque and the kitsch, from the Wax Museum ("29 scenes!, 112 figures!") to the Museum of Apparitions 1917 ("Be present during the Vision of Hell!"). Every shop window, meanwhile, displays an endlessly inventive array of *artigos religiosos*. You can get an awful lot of tacky souvenirs for just a few euros – Apparition snowflakes, Virgin Mary keyrings, bottled Fátima water, Sister Lúcia desk ornaments – or spend hundreds on a gilded statue of a martyred saint.

2

MIRACLES, SECRETS AND PILGRIMAGES

The three Fátima children – Lúcia, Jacinta and Francisco – were looking after sheep when the **Virgin Mary** descended from Heaven. Celestial lights flashed as she introduced herself and then requested that the children return five more times – each time on the thirteenth of the month – until October, at which time all would be revealed. The children reported their vision and, slowly, over the months, enthusiastic crowds grew at the appointed times – not put off in the slightest by the fact that the Virgin remained stubbornly invisible to anyone other than the three children.

The October gathering was the largest by far, with thousands in collective thrall to an event that became known as the **Miracle of the Sun** – a technicolour burst of light and fire, accompanied by wondrous healings. Of the three children, it was Lúcia only who was chosen to receive – and keep – the famed three **Secrets of Fátima**, directly from the Virgin. She revealed two in the 1940s – unsurprisingly apocalyptic visions and vague prophecies about world war – and wrote the third down in a sealed envelope entrusted to the Pope. After decades of speculation, the third secret was revealed in May 2000, another typically vague prediction that apparently predicted the attempt on Pope John Paul II's life in 1981.

Lúcia's fellow witnesses both died in the European flu epidemic of 1919–20, while **Lúcia** herself later retreated to the Convent of Santa Teresa near Coimbra. Cocooned from the outside world as a Carmelite nun, she was known by all in Portugal as Irmã (Sister) Lúcia. The elderly bespectacled nun made an unlikely pin-up, but her image is as ubiquitous in Fátima as that of the Virgin herself, set poignantly against the fading, black-and-white childhood photographs of Jacinta and Francisco, cast forever in a supporting role by their early deaths.

ARRIVAL AND INFORMATION   FÁTIMA

By bus Fátima's bus station is on Av Dom José Alves Correia da Silva, which is the main through-avenue between the rotundas – turn right along the avenue and walk for 500m to reach the turismo. It has regular connections from Batalha (4 daily; 25min), Leiria (Mon–Sat 7 daily, Sun 2 daily; 35min–1hr) and Tomar (2–4 daily; 45min).

By car With Batalha 18km northwest, Leiria 25km northwest and Tomar 35km east, Fátima and the basilica lie just off the A1 motorway, flanked by two large traffic circles (*rotundas*) – Rotunda Norte, nearest the bus station, is the one with the statues of the three shepherd children. Vast car parks ring the basilica, and provided you don't coincide with a pilgrimage you'll find street parking in the town as well.

By train Fátima is also on the main Lisbon–Porto train line, but the Estação de Fátima is 25km east of town and there's not always an immediate bus connection.

Information Turismo, Av Dom José Alves Correia da Silva (daily 10am–1pm & 3–6pm, longer all-day hours in summer; ☎ 249 531 139, ⓦ www.rt-leiriafatima.pt).

ACCOMMODATION AND EATING

Outside the major pilgrimages and weekends there's plenty of **accommodation** to go round. The turismo's map of town (also viewable online) lists thirty options alone. During the pilgrimages (when most accommodation is booked up months in advance and prices double) people camp around the Basílica. All this said, it's hard to recommend spending the night in Fátima basilica – nearby Ourém is a better option (see below). It really is a very small place, with nothing to do, and while there is also a glut of **cafés and restaurants**, they are all geared towards tourists and pilgrims and none is particularly inspiring.

Ourém

With its cosy nest of medieval lanes, a clutch of old stone houses and a church or two, the pretty town of **OURÉM** lies 12km to the east of Fátima. From the lower new town, Vila Nova de Ourém, a winding road climbs for 2km up to Ourém castle, crowning a hill above the town. Ourém's heyday was in the fifteenth century, when the fourth count of Ourém, Dom Afonso, built several grand monuments and converted the castle into a palace. The castle was virtually destroyed by Napoleon's forces, but is now largely restored. You can walk around its parapet, walls and towers for a marvellous, sweeping panorama, with the basilica of Fátima visible away to the west.

FROM TOP NAZARÉ (P.147); MOSTEIRO DE ALCOBAÇA (P.151) >

ACCOMMODATION AND EATING OURÉM

Pousada de Ourém Largo João Manso ☎ 249 540 930, ⓦ pousadas.pt. The *pousada* has been fashioned from several fifteenth-century buildings to create a stylish hotel, most of whose rooms have far-reaching views (though only three have balconies). There's a nice terrace-bar and courtyard, while across the street from the reception is a fabulous terrace and outdoor pool with more extensive views. The restaurant offers a contemporary twist on traditional regional dishes. **€120**

Tomar

TOMAR is a charming, small town on the banks of the Rio Nabão – close enough to Lisbon for a day-trip, handsome enough and certainly interesting enough to warrant an overnight stay. Its old quarter is typically attractive, laid out as a grid of cobbled streets centred on a fine square, and there are riverside strolls to enjoy and green woods for picnicking. But standing sentry over town, high on the hill above, is the real reason for a visit – the mighty **Convento do Cristo**, founded (along with the town) in 1160 as the headquarters of the Order of the Knights Templar, scourge of the Moors and defenders of the faith. Castle and town both survived Moorish siege and attack in 1190, after which Tomar prospered in line with the gradual establishment of Portugal as a regional and, later, imperial force.

Convento de Cristo

Estrada do Convento • Daily: June–Sept 9am–6.30pm; Oct–May 9am–5.30pm; last entrance 30min before closing; closed public holidays • €6, under-14s free, free on Sun 9am–2pm; combined ticket with Alcobaça and Batalha €15 • ☎ 249 315 089, ⓦ conventocristo.pt • It's a 15min walk uphill from the town centre; free parking outside

The dramatic **Convento de Cristo** is one of Portugal's most important historical buildings – serving, unusually, as both military nerve-centre and religious foundation. It was built by Gualdim Pais, a knight who had served under Afonso Henriques in battles against the Moors in Portugal. In 1157 he was appointed Grand Master of the **Order of the Knights Templar**, and moved their base from Soure in central Portugal, south to strategically important land overlooking the Rio Nabão at what became Tomar. When the powerful Templar order was later suppressed – it was seen as a challenge both to European rulers and the Papacy – it was simply re-established in Portugal in 1319 as the **Order of Christ**, with the castle at Tomar again its headquarters. The Order was later at the centre of Portugal's emerging maritime empire, and under Prince Henry the Navigator – an illustrious Grand Master indeed – the castle also became both lavish palace and monastic centre.

It's an enormous complex, and though you could whip around the main highlights in an hour, a longer tour could easily take two or three hours. You're given a comprehensive English-language guide and floorplan on entry, and there's a café inside with terrace seating.

Charola, nave and portal

The first structure to be built by Gualdim Pais within the new walls was also the castle's defining structure, the **Charola**, a round temple modelled on the Church of the Holy Sepulchre in Jerusalem. It's an outstanding piece of architecture, sixteen-sided on the outside, octagonal on the inside, and must have made a deeply powerful and symbolic impression on the Order's medieval knights – many of whom, like Gualdim Pais himself, had travelled to the Holy Land. Under Dom Manuel I – Grand Master of the Order of Christ as well as king – the chapel was superbly decorated with the polychromatic statues and rich paintings you see today. Prince Henry had earlier added a **nave** to the round temple, greatly expanding the size of the church; Manuel rebuilt this in the flamboyant style that became synonymous with his name, in particular commissioning master architect João de Castilho to add a superb decorative **portal** that links the Charola to the Manueline church.

The cloisters

There are no fewer than eight cloisters in the Convento do Cristo, most added during the fourteenth and fifteenth centuries as the complex underwent massive expansion, in line with its increasing influence. Not only did Prince Henry build himself palatial quarters within the castle, he also expanded the monastic quarters, adding two lovely tiled cloisters, the **Claustro do Cemitério** and the **Claustro da Lavagem**, the latter used for domestic tasks like the washing of monks' robes. The main cloister received its first remodelling under Dom Manuel I and his court architect João de Castilho, but it was Manuel's successor, João III (1521–57), who transformed this central feature of what was by now a full working monastery. Work on the **Claustro Príncipal** began in 1557 and, under first the Spanish architect Diogo de Torralva and then the Italian Filippo Terzi, by 1591 the Convento do Cristo had a magnificent two-storey arcaded Renaissance cloister that's the equal of anything in the country.

Janela do Capítulo

If there's one place in the entire complex that reveals the wealth and care lavished on the buildings – and thus the high regard in which the Convento do Cristo was held for centuries – it's the **Janela do Capítulo** (Chapter House Window). Added to the west

2

MANUELINE ARCHITECTURE

With the new-found wealth and confidence engendered by the "Discoveries" came a distinctly Portuguese version of Late Gothic architecture. Named after King Manuel I (1495–1521), the **Manueline style** is characterized by a rich and often fantastical use of ornamentation. Doors, windows and arcades are encrusted with elaborately carved stonework, in which the imagery of the sea is freely combined with both symbols of Christianity and of the newly discovered lands.

The style first appeared at the Igreja de Jesus (1494–98), in **Setúbal**. This relatively restrained building is the work of Diogo Boitac, who later supervised the initial construction of the great Jéronimos monastery at **Belém** a few kilometres downstream from Lisbon. Commissioned by the king, this is a far more exuberant structure with an elaborately carved south portal opening onto a nave where the vaulting ribs seem to sprout out of the thin, trunk-like columns like leaves from a palm tree. Belém was the point from which many of the Portuguese navigators set forth, and the new building was largely subsidized by the new, lucrative spice trade.

The Jéronimos monastery is the most unified expression of the new style, but Manuel I also commissioned lavish extensions to existing buildings, such as the Convento do Cristo at **Tomar**, which is arguably the most brilliant and original expression of Manueline decoration. The armillary sphere – a navigational instrument – became the personal emblem of King Manuel, and frequently appears in Manueline decoration. It can be seen at the great abbey at **Batalha**, whose Capelas Imperfeitas (Unfinished Chapels) are also smothered in ornamentation (including snails and artichokes) that seems to defy the material from which it's carved. Not all Manueline architecture was ecclesiastical: there were also palaces, like that of the Dukes of Bragança at **Vila Viçosa**, and castles, like the one at **Évora Monte** where the whole of the exterior is bound by a single stone rope. Most famous of all secular constructions is Lisbon's **Torre de Belém**, a fortress built on an island in the River Tejo which incorporates Moorish-style balconies, battlements in the form of shields, and even a carving of a rhinoceros.

Manueline architecture did not continue much beyond the fourth decade of the sixteenth century. Indeed, so meteoric was the rise and fall of Manueline art within the reign of Dom Manuel that, to some extent, it must have reflected his personal tastes. In the reign of Manuel's successor, King João III, a more austere religious atmosphere prevailed in which the decorative excesses of the Manueline style were replaced by the ordered sobriety of Italian classicism.

facade of the nave between 1510 and 1513, it was given the full Manueline treatment by sculptor Diogo de Arruda, who rolled out every maritime and imperial motif he could muster in one masterful decorative sweep around what is – let's not forget – a mere window (albeit a very large window into a very important church). There are twisted ropes, knots and swirls, coral and vegetation, and crosses and globes in glorious profusion. Access to see the window and the west facade is from the **Claustro de Santa Bárbara**, next to the Claustro Príncipal.

Praça da República

The gridded streets of the old town converge on the central **Praça da República**, where you'll find a statue of Tomar's founding father, Gualdim Pais, and a ring of handsome seventeenth-century buildings including the old town hall. Here, the **Igreja de São João Baptista** (Tues–Sat 10am–5pm, July–Sept until 7pm, Sun 11am–5pm; free) dates from at least a century earlier and presents an interesting melange – octagonal bell-tower, sculpted Manueline doorway and paintings inside by Gregório Lopes (1490–1550), one of the most significant artists to emerge from the so-called "Portuguese School" of the sixteenth century.

Museu Hebraico Abraão Zacuto

Rua Dr Joaquim Jacinto 73 • May–Sept Tues–Sun 10am–1pm & 2–6pm; Oct–April Tues–Sun 10am–1pm & 2–5pm • Free

Tomar's excellently preserved fifteenth-century synagogue, now the **Museu Hebraico Abraão Zacuto**, is named after the Spanish astronomer, Abraham Zacuto, who prepared navigational aids for Vasco da Gama. There's little to see inside save some surviving Hebraic inscriptions, as well as gifts donated by visitors, but the fact that it stands at all is reason enough to visit. Following the expulsion of the Portuguese Jews in 1496, the temple was abandoned and later served as a prison and then private house, before being adopted as a national monument – there are long-standing plans to establish a museum and library on the premises.

Museu dos Fósforos

Convento de São Francisco, Av General Bernado Faria • May–Sept Tues–Sun 10am–1pm & 2–6pm; Oct–April Tues–Sun 10am–1pm & 2–5pm • Free

The old convent of São Francisco, facing Varzea Grande, might tempt you with its **Museu dos Fósforos**, which claims Europe's largest collection of matchboxes. Indeed, it does hold 40,000 or so – although its boast of it being "a singular description of universal history and culture" is pushing it a bit.

Aqueduto Pegões

Out of town, you can get great views of the stunning seventeenth-century **Aqueduto Pegões**, built to supply the convent with water. The best place to see it is 2km from Tomar, signposted (Pegões) off the N113 Leiria road, where a double-storey L-shaped sweep strides across a fertile valley.

ARRIVAL AND INFORMATION   **TOMAR**

The adjacent train and bus stations are on Avenida Combatentes da Grande Guerra, within easy walking distance of the centre. Head directly north across the open space of Varzea Grande and you'll soon hit Avenida Dr Cândido Madureira – the turismo is at its western end.

By bus There are regular services to and from Fátima (2–4 daily; 45min), Leiria (4 daily; 1hr), Lisbon (2–4 daily; 1hr 15min–2hr) and Santarém (2–4 daily; 1hr 5min).

By car Tomar is 130km northeast of Lisbon, and the drive

THE FESTA DOS TABULEIROS

Tomar is renowned throughout the country for its **Festa dos Tabuleiros** (literally, the Festival of the Trays). It can be traced back to Queen Isabel who founded the Brotherhood of the Holy Spirit in the fourteenth century, though some believe it to derive from an ancient fertility rite. Whatever its origins, it's now a largely secular event, held at four-yearly intervals during the first week of July; the next event is in 2015.

The festival starts on the first Sunday with the **Cortejo dos Rapazes** or "Boys' Procession" (for schoolchildren), with the **Cortejo do Mordomo** on the following Friday, when the costumed festival coordinators parade their carriages, carts and cattle (symbols of the sacrificial oxen that were once presented).

The main procession is on the final Sunday. The **Cortejo dos Tabuleiros** consists of several hundred young women wearing white, each escorted by a young man in a white shirt, red tie and black trousers. Each woman carries on her head a tray with thirty loaves threaded on vertical canes, intertwined with leaves and paper flowers, and crowned with a cross or a white dove – the symbol of the Holy Spirit. The resulting headdress weighs 15kg, and is roughly person-height – hence the need for an escort to lift and help balance it. There's music and dancing in the flower-filled streets, traditional games, fireworks at dawn and dusk, and a bullfight the night before the procession.

takes around an hour and twenty minutes. Free parking is available on the vast Varzea Grande, in front of the bus station. Anywhere else near the old town, or across the bridge in the more modern part, is either zealously metered or restricted.

By train There are direct trains to Tomar from Lisbon (approx hourly; 1hr 50min–2hr 40min) and Santarém (approx hourly; 45min–1hr), but not from the north of the country. Coming from Porto or Coimbra, you'll have to change at Entroncamento.

Information Turismo Municipal, Av Dr Cândido Madureira (May–Sept daily 10am–1pm & 3–7pm; Oct–April daily 9.30am–1pm & 2.30–6pm; ☎ 249 329 823, ⊛ cm-tomar .pt).

2 ACCOMMODATION

Camping Redondo Rua do Casal Rei 6, Poço Redondo, 10km northeast of Tomar ☎ 249 376 421, ⊛ camping redondo.com. This pretty, rural campsite, under English–Dutch ownership, also has two stone cottages and four wooden chalets to rent – prices run from €55 to €95 a night. There's also budget accommodation in a two-person caravan (€20–40 per night) or pre-erected six-person tents (€35–45). Pool, café-bar (camp dinners in summer) and breakfast are available, and you're only a few kilometres from the local lake. From Tomar, follow signs for IC3 (Coimbra) and then Junceira, Fonte de Dom João and Poço Redondo. Pitch €3, plus €3.50 per adult, plus €2.50 per car

★ **Cavaleiros de Cristo** Rua Alexandre Herculano 7 ☎ 249 321 203, ⊛ cavaleirosdecristo.pt. Quiet, sober rooms with white walls and terracotta-tiled floors; some also have French windows and partial river views. It's a step-up from most of the other budget places in town but prices remain reasonable, and the people welcoming. €50

★ **Estalagem de Santa Iria** Parque do Mouchão ☎ 249 313 326, ⊛ estalagemsantairia.com. This secluded island retreat has spacious balconies onto the park, whose mature trees screen off the traffic. Rooms

are on the tired side, but it's old-fashioned in the nicest possible way, and the restaurant is pretty good value too (mains from €12) in quietly elegant surroundings. Car access is from the riverside avenue across the narrow bridge. Out of season, you'll get some good deals, with rooms down to €70. €85

Quinta do Valle Asseiceira, Santa Cita, 7km south of Tomar ☎ 249 381 165 or ☎ 966 814 613, ⊛ quinta dovalle.com. Lovely old *quinta*, now divided into self-catering apartments sleeping two to four people. Breakfast is included (served in the apartments) and there's an outdoor pool and rambling gardens. Doubles €85; four people €105

Templários Largo Cândido dos Reis 1 ☎ 249 310 100, ⊛ hoteldostemplarios.com. The smartest hotel in the town centre is a large, modern four-star overlooking the river, with a health spa and rather fine indoor pool, plus easy parking. Balconies overlook the riverside lawns. €80

União Rua Serpa Pinto 94 ☎ 249 323 161. This deservedly popular place (book in advance in summer) has an air of grandeur, especially in the lovely breakfast room and period-piece of a bar. Bathrooms might be on the elderly side, but most rooms are generously sized. No credit cards. €40

EATING, DRINKING AND ENTERTAINMENT

Tomar's best **cafés** are the *Santa Iria*, which has a wide terrace by the old bridge, and the century-old *Paraiso* (closed Tues), on the main pedestrianized street. There are plenty of **restaurants**, all reasonably priced, and a cheap grilled-chicken place at the **market** (market day is Friday 7am–1pm). Tomar has a wide cultural programme, detailed in the monthly *Agenda Cultural*, available from the turismo. Look out for performances by the Fatias de Cá **theatre company** (⊛ fatiasdeca.net), who stage spectacular events – Shakespeare productions, *The Name of the Rose*, sound-and-light shows – in the Convento do Cristo or the Mata dos Sete Montes.

RESTAURANTS

A Bela Vista Trav Fonte Choupo 6, off Rua Marquês Pombal ☎ 249 312 870, ⊛ restaurantebelavista.pai.pt. A rustic place by the river with a delightful covered terrace underneath an old house. It serves traditional Portuguese dishes – roast *cabrito* and *leitão* are house specials – but there are also fish and rice dishes, and you'll eat well for €20 a head. Mon 7–10pm, Wed–Sun noon–3pm & 7–10pm.

Restaurante Jardim Rua Silva Magalhães 39 ☎ 249 312 034. Come here for large portions in a backstreet local favourite – it's nothing fancy, the sort of place

where football will be hogging the limelight on the TV. It's mostly a meat place but there's usually a fish choice or two and a few pasta dishes as well. Mains from €7. Mon, Wed–Fri & Sun 9am–3pm & 6pm–midnight, Sat 6pm–midnight.

★ **Restaurante Tabuleiro** Rua Serpa Pinto 148 ☎ 249 312 771. Semi-smart, family-friendly restaurant serving traditional food (roast pork, *bacalhau*, veal, *arroz de peixe*, steak) in coronary-inducing portions – a *dose* (€14) will easily feed two. Desserts are all homemade, and the owner summons up menu guidance in half a dozen languages. Mon–Sat noon–3pm & 7–10pm.

BAR
Theatro Bar Rua do Teatro ☎ 249 321 000. Tomar's coolest bar is just to the side of the theatre, a stripped-down space for drinks, music and DJ sets. The doors open late and don't close until the small hours. Tues–Sat 10pm–4am, Sun 10pm–2am.

East along the Rio Tejo

Around 20km south of Tomar, the Rio Tejo swings east, past the remarkable castle at **Almourol**, to meet the Rio Zêzere at **Constância**, one of the most attractive towns on the Tejo. There's another historic castle at **Abrantes**, 12km further east, and an even more extraordinary one at Belver, east of Abrantes, on the north bank of the Tejo. The whole route is an enjoyable approach to the towns of the northern Alentejo or the Beira Baixa, and it's covered by train (the Lisbon–Covilhã service), but drivers are going to have the best of it since you're unlikely to want to stop anywhere for long.

2

Castelo de Almourol

Vila Nova da Barquinha, 27km south of Tomar • Ferry departures from Cais Junto ao Castelo, opposite the castle • March–Oct Tues–Sun 10am–1pm & 2.30–7pm; Nov–Feb Tues–Sun 10am–1pm & 2.30–5pm; castle open same hours • Ferry €2 return; castle €2 • ☎ 249 720 358

Castles rarely come cuter than the **Castelo de Almourol**, which clings to a craggy islet in the Rio Tejo. You arrive via a little ferry that departs from a car park opposite the castle itself. Once ashore, you can climb through the trees to the castle, where there's a beautiful rural panorama from the tall central keep. Back above the quayside car park, a bar with a shady terrace serves snacks and sandwiches. At weekends, boats also run to the castle from the river esplanade in the village of Tancos, 2km to the west, which is home to the nearest train station.

Constância

3km east of Almourol • By train, get off at Praia do Ribatejo-Constância, the stop after Almourol

Sited at the confluence of the Tejo and Zêzere rivers, the small town of **CONSTÂNCIA** is worth a quick stop. It's typically attractive in that old-town Portuguese way, with a historic centre of cobbled streets and whitewashed buildings. It's best known, however, for its association with **Luís de Camões**, author of Portugal's great national epic poem, *Os Lusíadas* – the riverside Camões gardens are based on those described in the poem. Constância is at its liveliest during the **Festa dos Barqueiros**, on Easter Monday, with parades and traditional boats on the Tejo.

Abrantes

Overlooking the Rio Tejo, 15km east of Constância, **ABRANTES** has a historic kernel of pretty narrow alleys and squares lined with crumbling houses that lies hidden at the centre of a dreary modern town. It looks its best in spring and summer when flowers on Rua da Barca and in the Jardim da República are in bloom; the views are also impressive. The high point – in all respects – is the town's much-restored **castelo** (Tues–Sun 10.30am–1pm & 1.30–6pm; free), constructed in the early fourteenth century, from where there are more sweeping vistas.

Castelo de Belver

Belver, 35km east of Abrantes • April–Sept Tues–Sun 9.30am–12.30pm & 2–6pm; Oct–March Tues–Sun 10am–12.30pm & 2–5.30pm • €1.30, under-14s free, and free on Sun morning

The **Castelo de Belver** is one of the most famous in the country, with a place in dozens of Portuguese legends. The name comes from *belo ver* (beautiful to see), the supposed exclamation of a medieval princess, waking up to look out from its keep at the river valley below. It dates from the twelfth century, when the Portuguese frontier stood at the Tejo, the Moors having reclaimed most of the territories to the south. Stunningly sited – and virtually impregnable, as failed Moorish attack after failed Moorish attack revealed – the beautifully restored battlemented walls and keep are a dramatic reminder of how hard the early Portuguese nation had to work at keeping its independence.

ARRIVAL AND DEPARTURE   CASTELO DE BELVER

Although technically in the Alentejo, Belver is best approached from Abrantes, by public transport at least. **Buses** stop in the village square, while the **train station** is directly below the village beside the river. If you take the train further towards Castelo Branco, look out for the striking rock gorge at Vila Velha de Ródão, known as the Portas do Ródão (see p.252).

Golegã

GOLEGÃ, on the west bank of the Rio Tejo, midway between Tomar and Santarém, is a pleasant riverside town which calls itself "Capital of the Horse", a claim it backs up with black-horse silhouettes hanging outside virtually every business. It is best known for its **Feira Nacional do Cavalo** (National Horse Fair), held during the first two weeks of November. The fair incorporates celebrations for St Martin's Day on November 11, when there's a running of the bulls and a grand parade of red-waistcoated grooms. Other than during the *feira*, Golegã makes for a brief visit: the sixteenth-century **Igreja Matriz** flanks its main square, a couple of cafés put out tables under the trees, while the old market has been turned into a small shopping complex.

Casa-Estúdio Carlos Relvas

Largo Dom Manuel I · Tues–Sun 9.30am–12.30pm & 2–6pm · Free · ☎ 249 979 120, ⓦ casarelvas.com

Golegã's **Casa-Estúdio Carlos Relvas** was the home of Carlos Relvas – father of José Relvas, who proclaimed the Portuguese Republic in Lisbon in 1910. Relvas Senior had an interest in the newly discovered art of photography, early examples of which are displayed, while the house itself is a whimsical pavilion of wrought iron and glass set in landscaped gardens.

Santarém

Strategically sited **SANTARÉM**, set on a plateau on the banks of the Rio Tejo, already had a long history before Portugal was ever an independent nation. An important Roman trading city was sited here, and from the eighth to the twelfth centuries Shantarin was one of the most important and cultured Moorish cities on the Iberian peninsula. Accordingly, its conquest in 1147 by Afonso Henriques was hugely significant and in later medieval times Santarém became a royal favourite, decorated with grand Gothic

BULLS AND WINE – A SCENIC DRIVE

Golegã is one of the main crossing points to the east bank of the Rio Tejo – a **bull-breeding** and vine-growing territory of rich plains and riverside marshes. The **N118** marks the most attractive route along the river, taking in several small towns and *quintas* en route to Santarém, 45km away. There's nothing much to stop for in Chamusca, Alpiarça or Almeirim – the latter once the site of a royal summer palace – but local **wine producers** line the road at intervals, open for sales to the public; look for signs saying *"vinho do produtor"*.

buildings and hosting regular meetings of the Cortes (Parliament). There's little if nothing left of Roman or Moorish times but, with its two exquisite churches and surviving old-town alleys and squares, modern Santarém remains a pleasant place to visit – not least for the unrivalled view across the plains from the Portas do Sol, the former site of the Moorish citadel and Reconquista castle.

Praça Sá da Bandeira

The market and municipal gardens mark the northern edge of the town, with the spacious **Praça Sá da Bandeira** just beyond. This is named for the Marquês de Sá da Bandeira (1795–1876), Portuguese prime minister in the 1830s and the town's most famous son, whose statue is overlooked by the fussy Baroque facade of the Jesuit **Igreja do Seminário** (1676). The largely pedestrianized old town lies beyond, with Rua Serpa Pinto and Rua Capelo e Ivens threading towards the signposted Portas do Sol, about fifteen minutes' walk away, with the best of the churches conveniently en route.

Igreja de Marvila

Largo de Marvila • Wed–Sun 9am–12.30pm & 2–5.30pm • Free

Although one of the oldest churches in town, the **Igreja de Marvila** – at the end of Rua Serpa Pinto – had a Manueline makeover, which is especially noticeable in the sculpted doorway. Inside are brilliant seventeenth-century *azulejos* covering every centimetre of the nave.

Igreja da Graça

Largo Pedro Álvares Cabral • Igreja da Graça and Casa do Brasil, both Wed–Sun 9.30am–12.30pm & 2–5.30pm • Free

The fifteenth-century **Igreja da Graça**, with its impressive rose window, is Santarém's most architecturally interesting church. Inside, it's the elaborately carved sarcophagus of Pedro de Meneses, the first Governor of Ceuta (died 1347), which draws the eye, though Portuguese people know the church as the burial place of **Pedro Álvares Cabral**, discoverer of Brazil in 1500. A simple tombstone set in the floor near the Meneses sarcophagus marks the spot, with Cabral "the discoverer" honoured more prominently outside the church by a heroic statue – cross in one hand, sword in the other. The Cabral family lived in Santarém, and a house by the church thought to be theirs (though with no real evidence) is now the **Casa do Brasil**, a cultural centre with art and other exhibitions.

Igreja de São João de Alporão

Largo Zeferino Sarmento • Currently closed for refurbishment, but normally Wed–Sun 9.30am–12.30pm & 2–5.30pm • ☎ 243 377 290, ⓦ museu-santarem.org

Opposite the fifteenth-century clock tower of the Torre das Cabaças is the city's archeological and medieval art museum, housed in the twelfth-century church of **São João de Alporão**. Its Romanesque portal gives way to a later Gothic interior, containing the remarkable Gothic tomb of one Duarte de Meneses.

Portas do Sol

End of Av 5 de Outubro • Daily: May–Sept 9am–10pm; Oct–April 9am–6.30pm • Free

The Moors, naturally enough, picked the best vantage point for their fortified town, atop the plateau overlooking the Rio Tejo and beyond. Afonso Henriques too, and all subsequent overlords of Santarém, kept the walls secure, though today's stone battlements have been much restored over the centuries. The castle site is now a municipal garden known as the **Portas do Sol**, the "Gates of the Sun" – a pleasant spot to stroll and sip a coffee in the shade of the trees. A swashbuckling statue of Afonso Henriques commemorates his pivotal capture of the town.

ARRIVAL AND INFORMATION   SANTARÉM

By bus The bus station is close to the old centre, on Avenida do Brasil.

Destinations Abrantes (6 daily; 1hr 25min); Fátima (9 daily; 1hr); Lisbon (12 daily; 1hr 15min); Ourém (1 daily; 1hr 10min);

SANTARÉM'S FESTIVALS AND MARKETS

For two weeks in June (starting the first Friday of the month) Santarém's **Feira Nacional da Agricultura** celebrates all things rural and agricultural, with displays of bullfighting, folk dancing, local arts and crafts, and country traditions. The town also hosts an annual **Festival de Gastronomia** (third and fourth week of October), where you can taste all sorts of regional specialities. In addition, a large **market** sprawls around the bullring on the second and fourth Sunday of every month.

and Tomar (2–6 daily; 1hr).

By car It's 80km, and under an hour's drive, from Lisbon to Santarém. Parking in the old town is impossible, though there are pay-parking spaces (free at weekends) around the market and down Avenida Sá da Bandeira, near the bus station. There's also free parking a little way out by Santa Clara church.

By train The train station is 2km below the town, with buses into the centre leaving every 30min; a taxi will cost €5.

Destinations Castelo Branco (6 daily; 2hr–2hr 35min); Covilhã (5 daily; 3hr 5min–4hr 5min); Lisbon (every 30min–1hr; 1hr–1hr 30min); Tomar (roughly hourly; 45min–1hr); and Vila Franca de Xira (every 30min–1hr; 30–40min).

Information Turismo, Rua Capelo e Ivens 63 (Mon–Fri 10am–2pm & 3–7pm, Sat & Sun 9am–1pm & 2–6pm; ☎ 243 304 437, ⓦ cm-santarem.pt).

ACCOMMODATION

★ **Casa da Alcáçova** Largo da Alcáçova 3 ☎ 243 304 030, ⓦ alcacova.com. The premier choice in town, this aristocratic manor house at the shoulder of the Portas do Sol has jaw-dropping river views. Antiques, original fireplaces and magnificent beds (including some four-posters) furnish the eight rooms – dressing gowns and slippers are supplied. Drinks are served in the elegant lounge, and there's a lovely pool and outdoor eating area. Parking available. **€135**

Muralha Rua Pedro Canavarro 12 ☎ 243 322 399. Simple budget rooms in a family-run place adjacent to a surviving chunk of the city walls. A couple have balconies over the street, but otherwise it's fairly unremarkable. No credit cards. **€40**

Umu Av Bernardo Santareno 38 ☎ 243 377 240, ⓦ www.umu.pt. The *Umu*, formerly the *Alfageme*, has had a recent face-lift and its public areas are modern and smart. The bedrooms are relatively spacious, but there's little character and the only views are of the surrounding residential–retail suburb. Plus you're a stiff 500m walk from the centre. In the end, the main selling point is the easy parking, right outside. **€60**

EATING AND DRINKING

Santarém's choice of restaurants is good, though hardly any are open on Sundays. Rua Dr Jaime Figueiredo, the street behind the market, is the place to look for an inexpensive meal. Among local specialities there's *fataça na telha* (mullet cooked on a hot tile), which has its origins in the fishing village of Caneiras, 5km south of town.

Churrasqueira do Mercado Rua Dr Jaime Figueiredo 24 ☎ 243 326 839. A basic grill house behind the market, one of the few places open on a Sunday night – when you'll be watching football with the locals (you should be supporting Sporting). The grilled chicken is really good – the thermonuclear *piri-piri* sauce is optional. Mon–Wed & Fri–Sun 11am–3pm & 7–11pm.

O Saloio Trav do Montalvo 11, off Rua Capelo e Ivens ☎ 243 327 656. Popular with local families, and boasting a little outdoor patio, this traditional, tiled *casa de pasto* is good value for money – most dishes cost €5–7. Mon–Fri noon–9.30pm, Sat noon–4pm.

Taberna do Quinzena Rua Pedro de Santarém ☎ 243 322 804, ⓦ quinzena.com. One of the oldest eating places in the region, in business for well over a century. Traditional snacks, steaks and meat grills are served in a no-nonsense *tasca* with a serious bullfighting obsession – a full meal costs around €20. Mon–Sat 10am–10pm; closed 2 weeks in Aug.

The Ribatejo wine route

Wine has been produced on the banks of the Tejo for around two thousand years and, while it's long had a reputation for quantity rather than quality, the offerings of some new producers have recently begun to acquire an international profile. Even so, few of the local wine towns south of Santarém stand up to a visit in their own right, but if you're not in a hurry the drive down the N3 towards Vila Franca and Lisbon isn't a bad one. Many **vineyards** offer tours and tastings and they are all signposted from the road. The drive can occupy half a day, with lunch taken in either of the two prettiest towns, **Alenquer** or **Arruda dos Vinhos**, or you can take an organized wine tour of the region from Lisbon, which includes tastings at a couple of vineyards and a long boozy lunch (see p.91).

Museu Rural e do Vinho

Cartaxo, 14km south of Santarém • Tues–Fri 10.30am–12.30pm & 3–5.30pm, Sat & Sun 9.30am–12.30pm & 3–5.30pm • €1 •
☎ 243 701 257, Ⓦ www.cm-cartaxo.pt

At the small town of Cartaxo, the self-declared "Capital do Vinho", the **Museu Rural e do Vinho** is the single best place to investigate the subject – as well as the exhibits, you can taste and buy the local wines here. The museum is housed in the signposted Quinta das Pratas, a municipal park and sports complex on the outskirts of town.

2

Azambuja

AZAMBUJA, 13km to the southwest of Cartaxo, is known for its red wines made from the Periquita grape, though the town itself isn't worth a stop. However, for a true off-the-beaten-track sight, follow the signs from town to the **Vala de Azambuja**, a 26-kilometre-long canal built parallel to the river by the Marquês de Pombal, designed to drain the land when the Rio Tejo was in flood. Three kilometres up a dirt road (fine for cars; signposted "Palácio") stand the forlorn ruins of the **Palácio das Obras Novas**, once used as a staging post for the steamers plying the route from Lisbon to Constância in the nineteenth century.

Alenquer

At Carregado, the N3 meets the N1, and offers a choice of routes further into the rolling hills. Five kilometres north, and perched on a hill above the Alenquer river, **ALENQUER** mainly produces lemony flavoured white wines and has some decent local restaurants in which to sample them. Traffic chokes the main road alongside the river, but it's an enjoyable climb up to the attractive upper town, where you can visit the Manueline cloisters of the church and convent of São Francisco, the oldest Franciscan house in Portugal, built during the lifetime of St Francis of Assisi.

Arruda dos Vinhos

It is in the valleys around **ARRUDA DOS VINHOS**, 13km west of Carregado, that the region's vineyards are at their most attractive. It's a pretty town, too, with an enormous eighteenth-century public fountain and handsome Manueline church, but is top-heavy with restaurants and estate agents, both the consequence of the weekend influx of Lisboans.

EATING AND DRINKING

ARRUDA DOS VINHOS

O Fuso Rua Cândido do Reis 94, Arruda dos Vinhos ☎ 263 975 121. A rustic barn of a restaurant where vast slabs of meat and *bacalhau* are grilled over open fires. It's not particularly cheap (meals from around €25) but it is excellent, and you can drink the fresh, Beaujolais-style Arruda (also known as Arruta) red wines. Daily noon–11pm.

Vila Franca de Xira

The bustling west-bank city of **VILA FRANCA DE XIRA**, 45km downriver from Santarém, makes a rival claim to be the capital of the Ribatejo, but it's a poor second to Santarém and only worth the effort of a visit for aficionados of the Portuguese bullfight. The rearing of bulls and horses dominates the local economy: there's a School of Bullfighting here, and posters everywhere announcing forthcoming fights, while Vila Franca celebrates its obsession in café names and statues.

The two great annual events are the **Festa do Colete Encarnado** ("Red Waistcoat Festival", which refers to the costumes of the mounted horsemen of the plains), held over several days in the first two weeks of July; and the **Feira de Outubro** (October Fair), in the first two weeks of the month. On both occasions there are bullfights, with the animals running through the streets chased by the bold (and drunk) – inevitably, injuries are sustained.

Without a bullfight to detain you, it's hard to linger long in the few restored streets around the town hall; it's nicest down at the riverside gardens by the train station, where there's an old fisherman's *bairro* with a couple of restaurants – in March and April local restaurants in town all celebrate the shad, a Tejo river fish.

2

Coimbra and the Beira Litoral

BIBLIOTECA JOANINA, COIMBRA

Coimbra and the Beira Litoral

The province of Beira Litoral is dominated by the city of Coimbra, which, with Guimarães, Lisbon and Porto, forms the quartet of Portugal's historic capitals. Situated on a hill above the Rio Mondego, it's a wonderfully moody place, full of ancient alleys and lanes, spreading around the country's oldest university. As a base for exploring the region, the city can't be beaten, with Portugal's most extensive Roman site, Conímbriga, 16km to the southwest, the castle at Montemor-o-Velho, 32km west, and the delightful spa town of Luso and ancient forest of Buçaco under an hour's journey to the north.

3

Beira's coastline, from Figueira da Foz north as far as Porto, remains one of the least spoiled in Portugal, backed by rolling dunes and pine forests. There's some development around the pretty lagoon town of **Praia de Mira**, but the only major resort is **Figueira da Foz** and even this remains thoroughly local in character. To the north of the region, **Aveiro** is one of Portugal's most attractive provincial towns and sits on an elaborate network of canals.

Following the delightful **Rio Mondego** upstream from Coimbra, you'll come to see why it has been celebrated so often in Portuguese poetry as the "Rio das Musas" – River of the Muses. A tributary of the Mondego, the **Dão**, is the source of some of the country's finest wines, while there's an equally beautiful route along the **Rio Vouga** up to the pretty little town of **Vouzela**. To the north is the impressive convent at **Arouca**, and the *serras* of Freita and Arada, both peppered with remote hamlets and offering more scenic routes for drivers. To the south lies the **Serra do Caramulo**, where the village of **Caramulo** makes a good base for mountain pursuits. East of Coimbra, as the land slowly rises towards the mountain Beiras region and the Serra da Estrela, the first foothills are encountered in the **Serra da Lousã** and the **Serra do Açor**, rustic regions containing a range of pretty settlements such as riverside **Góis** and the incredibly sited, schist village of **Píodão**.

Coimbra

Hugging the banks of a broad stretch of the Rio Mondego, handsome **COIMBRA** (pronounced queem-bra) is famed for its historic hilltop university, dating from 1290, with its stunning Baroque library. Coimbra was capital of a fledgling Portugal from 1143 to 1255 and, for a relatively small town, retains an impressive number of historical monuments, including ancient convents and two cathedrals. Its old town, curving round the hilltop where the university is located, oozes both history and a vibrancy resulting from the presence of around 20,000 students who ensure the city is well-stocked with good-value cafés, bars and restaurants, some playing the city's jaunty version of fado. Though a worthwhile destination at any time of the year, the best time to visit is May, when students celebrate the end of their studies with a series of

Repúblicas p.186
School's out p.188
Coimbra fado p.189
A hike into the Serra da
  Lousã p.192
Góis motorbike festival p.194
Kayaking the Mondego p.196

Forest fires and the Bombeiros
  Voluntários p.203
Aveiro canal trips p.206
Hikes and cycling round Praia de Mira
  p.210
An estuary walk near Figueira da Foz
  p.212

TRADITIONAL BOATS, AVEIRO

Highlights

❶ Velha Universidade, Coimbra Wind your way up to the splendidly sited university, with its striking Baroque library. **See p.184**

❷ Roman ruins at Conímbriga Mosaics, baths, forum, aqueduct and a mighty defensive wall survive at Portugal's finest Roman site. **See p.191**

❸ Serra do Açor Explore this little-visited mountain range full of unexpected delights – schist villages, river beaches, mountain walks and elegant old bridges. **See p.193**

❹ Kayaking down the Mondego Take a gentle paddle down the meandering and

picturesque Rio Mondego between Penacova and Coimbra. **See p.196**

❺ Mata Nacional do Buçaco Spend the day in the shaded Buçaco forest, and then drop down into the neighbouring spa town of Luso for afternoon tea. **See p.197**

❻ Aveiro Cruise on one of the traditional brightly-painted boats, known as *barcos moliceiros*, through the atmospheric canals of Aveiro. **See p.206**

❼ Figueira da Foz Central Portugal's finest resort, boasting one of Europe's widest beaches, and some great local walks. **See p.211**

HIGHLIGHTS ARE MARKED ON THE MAP ON P.180

festivities – come in August when the students have gone and locals are on holiday, and you'll find the town strangely quiet.

Brief history

There was a settlement here in **Roman** times and the remains of the Roman Crypto-porticus are on display in the town's excellent Museu Machado de Castro. The **Moors** occupied the city from 711, using it as a trading centre for almost three hundred years – today's Arco de Almedina gateway marks the entrance to a former Moorish medina.

HIGHLIGHTS

1. Velha Universidade, Coimbra
2. Roman ruins at Conímbriga
3. Serra do Açor
4. Kayaking down the Mondego
5. Mata Nacional do Buçaco
6. Aveiro
7. Figueira da Foz

COIMBRA & THE BEIRA LITORAL

In 1143, shortly after the **Christian** Reconquest of 1064, Coimbra became the country's **capital** thanks to its position between the Christian north and Moorish south. During this time, the Sé Velha was built, along with the Convento de Santa Cruz. With Portugal expanding south, Lisbon became the capital in 1255, though Coimbra took on the role of cultural capital with the founding of its **university** in 1290, one of the world's first universities. For a time the university, too, moved to Lisbon before returning to be permanently housed in Coimbra's former royal palace in 1537. The Biblioteca Joanina was added in the eighteenth century and the university was further expanded by the New State in the twentieth century. Its students now make up around a sixth of the town's population.

Baixa

Curling from the riverfront round the slopes of the upper town, the Baixa, or lower town, is an atmospheric warren of narrow streets and alleys, housing traditional grocers' shops, tiny restaurants, cafés and the odd fashionable boutique. The main shopping streets, both of which are pedestrianized, are **Rua Ferreira Borges** and its continuation, **Rua Visconde da Luz**. Just off the former, the aptly named **Rua Quebra Costas** (Back-breaker Street) ascends steeply to the upper town through the old city gate, **Arco de Aledina**, and is lined with some of the city's most fashionable boutiques and cafés.

Igreja de Santa Cruz

Praça 8 de Maio • Mon–Sat 9am–noon & 2–5pm, Sun 4–5pm • Church and sacristy free; chapterhouse and cloister €2.50 • ☎ 239 822 841

Facing the pretty little Praça 8 de Maio, the Igreja de Santa Cruz is one of the oldest monastery churches in Coimbra and is the resting place of some of the country's earliest monarchs. Dating from 1131, the *azulejo*-lined interior of the church contains the tombs of Afonso Henrique, proclaimed Portugal's first king in 1143, and Sancho I (1185–1211); it was also where St Anthony of Padua studied in the early thirteenth century. In the sixteenth century, at the height of Portugal's maritime expansions, the church was remodelled by Diogo de Boitaca, the architect behind Lisbon's famous Jerónimos monastery. It was Boitaca who added the ornate Sala do Capítulo (chapterhouse) and the beautiful Cloister of Silence, with its scenes from the Passion of Christ by French artist Nicolas de Chanterene. The over-the-top triumphal arch outside the church was added in the nineteenth century.

Sé Velha

Largo da Sé Velha • Mon–Sat 10am–5.30pm • Cathedral free; cloister €2 • ☎ 239 825 273

Coimbra's first cathedral, the **Sé Velha**, was consecrated in 1184 when Portugal was still battling with Moors to the south, hence its narrow slit windows and imposing fortress-like battlements. The only external embellishment is the faded Renaissance Porta Especiosa ("beautiful door") in the north wall. Inside, the sixteenth-century additions are marginally more ornate, with a gilded wooden altarpiece and attractive *azulejos*, while the Gothic cloisters date from 1218. By 1772, the cathedral was supplanted by the less impressive Sé Nova ("new" cathedral), further up the hill.

Museu Nacional de Machado de Castro

Largo Dr José Rodrigues • Tues–Sun & public hols 10am–6pm; Oct–March closed from 12.30–2pm • €4 • ⓦ www.museumachado castro.pt

Housed in an impressive twelfth-century former bishop's palace, Coimbra's most interesting museum, the **Museu Nacional de Machado de Castro**, has finally emerged from years of extensive renovation. The palace was built on top of Portugal's most

3

■ **ACCOMMODATION**
Astória	5
Botânico	6
Moderna	3
Pousada de Juventude	7
Quinta das Lágrimas	1
Tivoli	4
Vitória	

■ **BARS AND CLUBS**
Galeria Bar	4
Mondego Irish Pub	3
NB Club	2
Tropical	1

● **RESTAURANTS AND CAFÉS**
Adega Paço do Conde	2
A Portuguesa	5
Cantinho do Reis	1
Viela	3
Zé Manel dos Ossos	4

COIMBRA

Académica Stadium & Dolce Vita Shopping ▲   Lousã & Penacova ▲   ▲ Lousã

3

N17, Lousã & Coimbra Shopping ▶

Condeixa, Conimbriga, Lisboa & A1 ▶

Condeixa & Conimbriga ▶

RUA PEDRO

Aqueduto de
São Sebastião

ARCOS DO
JARDIM

Entrance

AVENIDA MARROCOS E SOUSA

RUA COMBATENTES DA GRANDE GUERRA

LADEIRA DO SEMINÁRIO

RUA DO BRASIL

RUA DA ARREGAÇA

AVENIDA DR. JÚLIO HENRIQUES

Jardim
Botanico

Seminário

**Paço
Episcopal**

RUA MANUEL DA SILVA & AIO

SEE 'OLD COIMBRA' MAP FOR DETAIL

**Velha
Universidade**

COIMBRA DE LISBOA

RUA DA ALEGRIA

RUA DO BRASIL

**Coimbra
Parque**

AVENIDA DA LOUSÃ

Parque
Manuel
Braga

Parque Verde do
Mondego

P

FOOTBRIDGE

N

Rio Mondego

EMÍDIO NAVARRO

i

Boat
Trips

P

PONTE DE ST. CLARA

AVENIDA INÊS DE CASTRO

AVENIDA JOÃO DAS REGRAS

**Estádio
Universitário**

ROSSIO DE STA.
CLARA

ESTRADA DA GUARDA INGLESA

**Museu
Militar**

**Convento
Santa Clara-
a-Nova**

**Convento
Santa Clara-
a-Velha**

Portugal
dos
Pequenitos

RUA DAS FERREIRAS

**Visitor
Centre**

RUA ANTÓNIO AUGUSTO GONÇALVES

Quinta
das Lágrimas

ANTIGA ESTRADA NACIONAL

CALÇADA DE SANTA ISABEL

0   100
metres

important Roman building, the extraordinary **Cryptoporticus**, a series of first-century underground galleries which you can visit in the basement today. Named after a local eighteenth-century royal sculptor, the museum highlights Coimbra's cultural importance over the years, with a dazzling array of artefacts such as religious sculptures, jewellery – including a beautiful fourteenth-century necklace – ceramics, furniture, textiles and paintings mostly dating from the fourteenth to the eighteenth centuries. There are also some interesting artefacts from the Orient including eighteenth-century snuff bottles, while the museum's café-restaurant boasts fantastic views across town.

Velha Universidade

Paço das Escolas; ticket office on Praça da Porta Férrea • April–Oct daily 9am–7pm; Nov–March Mon–Fri 9.30am–5.30pm, Sat & Sun 10.30am–4.30pm • €10 for all sights; €7 for university, library and Sala dos Capelos; €5 for library and Capela de São Miguel only • ⓦ uc.pt

The imposing modern structures that make up the main university – mostly built in the 1940s and 50s – give little hint of the riches hidden away behind the white facades of the broad Paço das Escolas square. Accessed via the seventeenth-century Porta Férrea (the "iron gate" that once stood here), the **Velha Universidade** is housed in the former royal palaces. You'll need to buy a ticket to look round it, though you're free to enjoy the city views from the terrace to one side of the square.

Biblioteca Joanina and the Academic Prison

Highlight of the Velha Universidade is the Biblioteca Joanina, a Baroque confection of cleverly-marbled wood, gold leaf, imposing frescoed ceilings and elaborate trompe-l'oeil decorations. The ancient library was installed in 1717 by Dom João V, whose portrait surveys his legacy from the library walls, which are lined with some 250,000 books dating back to the twelfth century. At busy times, you'll be ushered on from the library after a few minutes to the so-called Academic Prison in the basement below. This proved that studying was no laughing matter: the windowless cell was used until 1832 to punish badly behaved students.

Capela de São Miguel and Sala dos Capelos

After leaving the library, glance into the adjacent Capela de São Miguel, a sixteenth-century chapel with a splendid eighteenth-century Baroque organ, then head up the grand double stairway from the central square to the Sala dos Capelos. This series of grand rooms was once part of the royal palace and then became an ornate venue for students to sit their exams, beneath the portraits of former monarchs and university rectors. The rooms are still used to award degree certificates: previous graduates include epic poet Luís de Camões, writer Eça de Queirós and twentieth-century dictator Salazar. Don't miss the narrow balcony outside that gives grand views across the town.

The clock tower

Those with a head for heights can climb the somewhat claustrophobic spiral stairs to the top of the eighteenth-century clock tower for spectacular views over the entire area. The tower is nicknamed *cabra* (the goat), an unaffectionate term lamenting its role in summoning students to lessons.

Museu da Ciência

Largo Marquês de Pombal • Tues–Sun 10am–6pm • €4 • ☎ 239 854 350, ⓦ museudaciencia.com

Partly housed in one of the university's original chemistry laboratories, the excellent **Museu da Ciência** (Science Museum) gathers together a substantial collection of scientific paraphenalia that has been in use at the university since the eighteenth century. The collection includes around 24,000 objects ranging from maps and books to botanical collections from Portugal's former colonies, medical equipment, stuffed animals, preserved insects, fossils and rare gemstones. The museum also has more cutting-edge interactive displays and exhibits dedicated to modern science, including a section on light and matter, looking at how light works and how it affects our universe.

Jardim Botânico

Calçada Martim de Freitas • **Gardens** Daily: April–Sept 9am–8pm; Oct–March 9am–5.30pm • Free • ⓦ uc.pt/jardimbotanico
Sky-Garden Daily March & Oct 10am–5.30pm; April–Sept 10am–8pm; Nov & Feb Sat & Sun 10am–5.30pm weather permitting • €24 • ⓦ sky-garden.biz

Partly hidden beneath the impressive sixteenth-century **Aqueduto de São Sebastião**, Coimbra's **Jardim Botânico** is Portugal's oldest botanical garden, founded in the eighteenth century – its main greenhouse, built in 1856, was one of the country's first structures to use iron. Today the garden is a tranquil retreat from the town's bustle, its paths and steps meandering down into sunken lawns past fountains, lakes, shady palms and enormous banyan trees. Other attractions include dazzling azaleas and an impressive collection of medicinal plants. For the more active, the Sky-Garden tree-top adventure course gives you the chance to clamber through the trees along a series of ladders, zip lines and even a suspended bike.

> ## REPÚBLICAS
>
> The grid of streets that spread around the university buildings is made up of the so-called **Repúblicas**, co-operative buildings first set up in the fourteenth century under Dom Dinis to provide subsidized accommodation for students. Generally rambling houses with tiny rooms, they are ideal for a communal student lifestyle – though have the added bonus of coming with their own cooks – and are little changed from the 1960s and 70s, when they were breeding grounds for dissenters to the Salazar regime. In theory they all have an open-door policy for guests should you wish to look around.

Convento de Santa Clara-a-Velha

Rua das Parreiros • Visitor centre Tues–Sun: May–Sept 10am–7pm; Oct–April 10am–5pm • €5, free on Sun 10am–2pm; English-language audio-guide €1.50 • W santaclaraavelha.drcc.pt

Built by the river on flat grassland, the fourteenth-century Gothic convent of **Santa Clara-a-Velha** was founded in 1330 by Queen Isabel, Coimbra's patron saint and wife of Dom Dinis. Isabel was buried here, along with Inês de Castro (see p.151), though when the convent was abandoned in the seventeenth century because of persistent flooding, Isabel's tomb was moved to the higher Santa Clara-a-Nova in 1677 (see below). Neglected and immersed in silt for over three hundred years, the old convent was then carefully excavated and now forms the centrepiece of a fascinating visitor centre in a modern building across the lawns. Here you can find out about religious life in medieval times before looking round the convent itself. The well-preserved interior includes the remains of the tiny cells, tiled floors and a surprisingly neat communal loo.

Convento de Santa Clara-a-Nova

Alto de Santa Clara • Daily: May–Sept 8.30am–7pm; Oct–April 8.30am–6pm • €1, cloister €2 • ☎ 239 441 674

With the original Convent of Santa Clara prone to annual flooding, it was decided to build a new convent on higher ground, and construction of the **Convento de Santa Clara-a-Nova** ("the new") began in 1649. Its exterior has a military appearance – indeed it was used as a hospital during the Peninsular Wars – but once inside you'll find beautiful cloisters (added in 1733) and an attractive Baroque church, housing the ornate stone tomb of Queen Isabel. The Queen's remains, however, were placed in a silver and crystal urn in 1696, which now sits behind the main altar.

Portugal dos Pequenitos

Rossio de Santa Clara • Daily: Jan, Feb & mid-Oct–Dec 10am–5pm; March–May & mid-Sept–mid-Oct 10am–7pm; June–mid-Sept 9am–8pm • €9, under-13s €5.50, under-3s free • W portugaldospequenitos.pt

No time to visit Portugal's most famous monuments? Then head to this enclosed area of parkland, where **Portugal dos Pequenitos** displays a beguiling collection of scale models of the country's major architectural attractions – though since it was built in the 1940s by local collector Bissaya Barreto, there are no contemporary buildings here. Children in particular love clambering around the models of churches, towers and traditional houses. There are also three small but moderately interesting museums featuring miniature copies of costumes, boats and furniture from the sixteenth century to today.

Quinta das Lágrimas

Rua António Augusto Gonçalves • Gardens open to the public mid-March–mid-Nov Tues–Sun 10am–7pm; mid-Nov–mid-March Thurs–Sun 10am–5pm • €2 • ☎ 239 802 380

The **Quinta das Lágrimas** (Estate of Tears), now a luxury hotel (see p.188), was once an estate hideaway for medieval Portugal's star-crossed lovers Dom Pedro and Inês de

Castro. In the gardens, so legend has it, Inês was brutally murdered on the orders of King Afonso IV – her tears (*lágrimas*) as she died lent the estate its name. Her lover, meanwhile, the crown prince Pedro, rose in open revolt against his own father and later extracted a gory revenge upon the murderers (see box, p.151). As well as being home to some ancient plant species, the gardens also host the July Art Festival, with plays, music and exhibitions (⊛festivaldasartes.com).

ARRIVAL AND DEPARTURE COIMBRA

By bus The main bus station is on Avenida Fernão de Magalhães (a 15-minute walk northwest of the centre), for intercity Rede Expressos buses (☎239 827 081, ⊛rede-expressos.pt), Rodoviária Beira Litoral (☎239 855 270, ⊛rede-expressos.pt) regional services, and Transdev services (☎239 270 812, ⊛transdev.pt) to Figueira da Foz, Aveiro, Condeixa-a-Nova and Conímbriga. For Montemor-o-Velho and Figueira da Foz, the Moisés Correia de Oliveira (☎239 828 263) buses stop on Avenida Fernão Magalhães, just up from Largo do Arnado; while Rodonorte, at Bufete Teresinha, Avenida Emídio Navarro (☎239 825 190, ⊛rodonorte.pt), is for services to the mountain Beiras and the north.

Destinations Arganil (2–3 daily; 1hr 40min); Condeixa for Conímbriga (2 daily; 30min); Covilhã (2–4 daily; 3hr 15min); Figueira da Foz (hourly; 1hr–1hr 15min); Góis (2–3 daily; 1hr 15min); Gouveia (3–4 daily; 2hr); Guarda (2–4 daily; 2hr 5min); Leiria (10–14 daily; 50min); Lisbon (at least hourly; 2hr 20min); Luso via Buçaco (Mon–Sat 2–5 daily; 40min); Montemor-o-Velho (approx hourly; 40min–1hr); Penacova (Mon–Fri up to 16 daily; 45min–1hr); Porto (approx hourly; 1hr 30min); Praia de Mira (1–2 daily; 1hr 15min); Santa Comba Dão (hourly; 1hr 20min); Viseu (approx hourly; 1hr 15min–1hr 25min); Vouzela (1–3 daily; 1hr 50min).

By train There are three train stations – Coimbra A, Coimbra B and Coimbra Parque. All long-distance and express trains call only at Coimbra B, 2km to the north, from where local trains connect to Coimbra A – you don't need another ticket but allow 20 minutes' connection time, or take a taxi (around €3.50). Riverside Coimbra A (often just "Coimbra" on timetables) is right at the heart of the city, on the edge of the Baixa. Coimbra Parque, a short walk southeast of the centre, currently only serves bus replacement services to and from Lousã and Serpins after a planned rail upgrade was suspended. You can check train timetables online at ⊛cp.pt.

Destinations Alfarelos for Montemor-O-Velho (every 30min; 35min); Aveiro (hourly; 40min–1hr); Braga (hourly; 2hr–3hr 50min); Figueira da Foz (hourly; 1hr–1hr 10min); Guarda (6–7 daily; 2hr 30min–3hr); Lisbon (hourly; 2hr–2hr 50min); Luso-Buçaco (3 daily; 30min); Porto (hourly; 1hr 15min–2hr 30min); Santa Comba Dão (3 daily; 40min).

GETTING AROUND

You can walk across central Coimbra in around twenty minutes, though the university is right at the highest part of town – and the stepped streets and alleys take it out of you in the summer heat – so you may want to take one of the local buses or the *elevador* street lift.

By bus The local bus network is run by SMTUC (⊛smtuc .pt) – bus #103 (weekdays only) runs from Coimbra A station via the market up to the university, while the #3 (daily) runs along the same route to Praça da República. In addition, the little electric Linha Azul buses (Mon–Fri, plus Sat mornings in summer) run on a circular route through the otherwise pedestrianized Baixa (lower town).

By elevador The useful *elevador* (Mon–Sat 7.30am–10pm, Sun & hols 10am–10pm), rises from next to the market on Avenida Sá da Bandeira to Rua Padre António Vieira, a short walk from the Sé Nova in the upper town.

By taxi There are taxi ranks outside Coimbra A and B train stations, by the police headquarters near Praça 8 de Maio, and in Praça da República. To call a cab, ring Politaxis ☎239 499 090.

Tickets Integrated tickets for buses and the *elevador* are sold on-board buses (€1.50 per journey), though it's cheaper to pre-buy tickets (3 journeys €2; 11 journeys €6.10; one-day pass €3.20) from kiosks and automatic machines dotted around town or from SMTUC transport shops (Mon–Fri 7am–7pm) – there's one in Praça da República and another by the *elevador* next to the market (also open Sat 8am–1pm).

INFORMATION

Coimbra has two **tourist offices**, both equally useful for city enquiries and staffed with English speakers. Both can provide a good, free street map and the useful *Coimbra Viva* guide and cultural agenda.

Turismo de Coimbra (municipal) Praça da Porta Férrea, inside the Biblioteca Geral (general library) of

Coimbra university ☎239 859 884, ⊛turismodecoimbra .pt. Easter–Oct daily 9am–7pm; Nov–Easter Mon–Fri

3

> ## SCHOOL'S OUT
>
> Coimbra's biggest bash of the year is the **Queima das Fitas** (ⓦqueimadasfitas.org) in May, when the ritual academic "burning of the ribbons" is accompanied by the mother of all parties in a week-long, alcohol-fuelled series of gigs, dances and parties. The coloured ribbons worn by students represent the various faculties, and the week's main parade sees decorated faculty floats followed by black-caped students winding down the hill from the university; every night the focus shifts to the riverside arena where big names in music rock the city until the small hours.

10am–5pm, Sat, Sun & hols 10am–4pm.

Turismo Centro de Portugal (regional) Av Emídio Navarro, by Largo da Portagem, facing the Ponte Santa Clara ☎ 239 488 120, ⓦturismodocentro.pt. Oct–Easter Mon–Fri 9am–6pm; Easter–Sept Mon–Fri 9am–8pm, Sat, Sun & hols 9.30am–1pm & 2.30–6pm.

TOURS AND ACTIVITIES

Tours Hop-on-hop-off, one-hour open-top bus tours are run by Fun(tastic) Coimbra and leave from Largo da Portagem (mid-May to Oct Tues–Sun, departures on the hour 10am–noon & 3–5pm; €10; ⓦyellowbustours .com): the bus ticket includes free access to the city's museums. One-hour cruises on the Rio Mondego are run by Odabarca, departing from beside Parque Dr Manuel Braga (May–Sept Tues–Sun departures on the hour from 3–7pm; Oct–April departures at 3, 4 & 5pm; €6; ☎ 969 830 664, ⓦodabarca.com). Odabarca also runs one-hour city tours by tuk-tuk for €7 (or €10 for cruise and tuk-tuk tour).

Watersports O Pioneiro do Mondego runs downriver kayak trips between the nearby town of Penacova and Coimbra (see p.196), as does Caminhos d'Água, who can also arrange windsurfing on the river in Coimbra (ⓦcaminhosdagua.com; 2hr lesson from €50, equipment rental from €10).

ACCOMMODATION

Astória Av Emídio Navarro 21 ☎ 239 853 020, ⓦalmeidahotels.com; map pp.182–183. You can't miss the landmark dome of this historic three-star hotel with grand Art Deco communal areas. Unfortunately its best days have gone, and though all the rooms are a/c and double-glazed, most are in desperate need of a revamp. Nevertheless front rooms have wonderful river views and there's secure parking 200m away. **€112**

★ **Botânico** Bairro de São José 15 ☎ 239 714 824; map pp.182–183. One of Coimbra's best for the price, this well-run place is up near the botanical gardens and, although right on the main road, the rooms are double-glazed and quiet, with polished wooden floors and rugs. **€50**

★ **Casa Pombal** Rua dos Flores 18 ☎ 239 835 175, ⓦcasapombal.com; map p.184. Coimbra's most charming choice – and the only place to stay in the old town – is this very friendly Dutch-run townhouse near the university. Rooms are small but pretty, with wooden floors, rugs and throws, some peering down over the rooftops to the river – room eight has a great view from the bath! A splendid breakfast is served in the tiled dining room and there's a small patio-garden, plus free internet and wi-fi – it's a real home-from-home. En-suite rooms cost more (€68). **€52**

Moderna Rua Adelino Veiga 49 ☎ 239 825 413, ⓦresidencialmoderna.com.pt; map pp.182–183. The entrance is upstairs, through a shopping gallery, and the tiled reception full of knick-knacks lowers expectations further, but the rooms are perfectly fine – they are simply furnished, with a/c and small en-suite bathrooms, some sleeping three to four. Some rooms have a small terrace overlooking the busy pedestrian street below. Free parking round the corner. No credit cards. **€40**

Pousada de Juventude Rua Henrique Seco 14 ☎ 239 822 955, ⓦmicrosites.juventude.gov.pt/portal /en; map pp.182–183. Above Parque Santa Cruz, and ideally sited for the bars and clubs around Praça da República, this decent, modern hostel has standard four- to six-bed dorms as well as private en-suite twin rooms, plus a patio and kitchen. There's 24hr reception, but check-in is only from 6pm–midnight. Buses #6, #7 and #29 from Coimbra A run to the hostel. Dorm beds **€13**, doubles **€30**

Quebra Luz Escada da Quebra-Costas 18 ☎ 912 278 779, ⓦquebra-luz.com; map p.184. On Coimbra's famously steep approach to the old town, this great little guesthouse has four simple but spacious rooms, the best with balconies looking over the street (others face a courtyard garden). The cheapest rooms share a bathroom, but there are also two en-suite rooms (€65). No breakfast. **€45**

Quinta das Lágrimas Rua António Augusto Gonçalves ☎ 239 802 380, ⓦquintadaslagrimas.pt; map pp.182–183. The city's swankiest address lies across the river, a historic stately house set in acres of beautiful gardens and grounds. It's a classy affair with some regally decorated palace and garden rooms, as well as more contemporary rooms. Staff lurk in each corner to attend to every whim. The Garden Spa has various treatments, plus pool, sauna and Turkish bath, and there are two restaurants – the more formal *Arcadas da Capela* boasts a rare (for Portugal) Michelin star. Website deals offer the best rates. **€215**

Tivoli Rua João Machado 4 ☎ 239 858 300, ⓦ tivoli hotels.com; map pp.182–183. The city's most central four-star hotel doesn't have much of a location (out near

the bus station), though it's less than ten minutes' walk to the historic centre. Rooms are reliable and modern, and there's an indoor pool, gym and garage parking. Families get discounts for interconnecting rooms. **€100**

⭐ **Vitoria** Rua da Sota 9–11 ☎ 239 824 049, ⓦ hotel vitoria.pt; map pp.182–183. The best of the budget options near the station has smart en-suite rooms, most decked out with wooden flooring and furniture. You can also get a good breakfast in the family restaurant downstairs (€3.50 extra). **€45**

EATING

⭐ **Adega Paço do Conde** Rua Paço do Conde 1 ☎ 239 825 605; map pp.182–183. Chicken, meat and fish come straight off the outdoor grill at this locally renowned *churrasqueira*, with a dining room either side of a shady covered terrace. Meals around €12, including salad, wine and coffee. Mon–Sat noon–midnight.

A Portuguesa Parque Verde Mondego, Avenida da Lousã ☎ 239 842 140; map pp.182–183. This modern restaurant is in a lovely position at the edge of the riverside park with outdoor tables facing the water. Prices are a notch higher than other places, but so is the quality and service, with tasty *açorda* dishes, fresh fish (around €12) and a superb *arroz de tamboril* (€36 for 2). Daily noon–10pm.

⭐ **Café Santa Cruz** Praça 8 de Maio ☎ 239 833 617; map p.184. Coimbra's most appealing café, set in part of the sixteenth-century monastery buildings next to the Igreja de Santa Cruz. There are tables in the vaulted stone interior, but on a sunny day it's nicer on the terrace above the square. Great for cakes and pastries. Daily 8am–11pm.

Cantinho do Reis Terreiro da Erva 16 ☎ 239 824 116;

map pp.182–183. The sun-trap terrace is the big attraction here, on the edge of an off-the-beaten-track square. The food attracts a steady stream of regulars – it's best for simple fish and grills, with reliable *bacalhau* dishes and a tasty house steak. Around €15, though lunch is cheaper. Mon–Sat noon–1am.

Viela Rua das Azeiteiras 33 ☎ 239 832 625; map pp.182–183. The street's best bargain – the daily €6 lunch runs from soup to dessert, wine included. There's a longer à la carte menu too, all very reasonably priced, and though it's only a simple pack-em-in place, there are also outdoor tables around the corner in a quiet square. Mon–Sat 8pm–2am.

⭐ **Zé Manel dos Ossos** Beco do Forno 12 ☎ 239 823 790; map pp.182–183. Easy to miss, this atmospheric little joint is behind an inconspicuous door, tucked behind *Hotel Astória*. Little more than a few tables, and walls adorned with messages of praise, the service is brisk and friendly, and the regional food excellent – around €15 for a decent meal, from soup to coffee. If you don't want to queue, arrive at opening time. Mon–Fri noon–3pm & 7.30–10pm, Sat noon–3pm.

DRINKING

⭐ **Galeria Bar Santa Clara** Rua António Augusto Gonçalves 67 ☎ 239 441 657, ⓦ galeriasantaclara.com; map pp.182–183. Relaxed gallery-café-bar with a large terrace overlooking Santa Clara-a-Velha and the river beyond. It's a great place for a coffee or a late drink with exhibitions, music nights and other events. Mon–Fri 2pm–2am, Fri & Sat 2pm–3am.

Mondego Irish Pub Parque Verde do Mondego ☎ 239 837 092; map pp.182–183. Right by the river, so ideal for an afternoon beer or sundowner drinks, this relaxed bar hosts live music Thurs & Fri nights. There's also a kids' playground down on the riverside here, plus pedal-cart rental, so it's good for families. Daily noon–4am.

COIMBRA FADO

Coimbra fado is distinguished from the Lisbon variety by the fact that it uses a slightly different guitar and is sung exclusively by males, usually in the traditional dark cape of the university. Themes are often translations of famous poems, and in general it is slightly more upbeat than the Lisbon variation. It's performed year-round in the city's fado clubs, but you'll find it far more atmospheric if you catch an open-air performance in the old town in summer. The student celebrations in May are a good bet for impromptu fado sessions, and this is also the best time for big-name gigs. Fado ao Centro (see p.190) is a good place to get a taster of the music.

Tropical Praça da República 35, corner of Rua Alexandre Herculano ☎ 239 824 857; map pp.182–183. The pick of the República café-bars, this studenty joint on

two levels heaves at the weekends. The pavement tables get swamped, while the barman roves around with trays of ice-cold Super Bocks. Sun–Fri 8am–2am, Sat 8am–4pm.

CLUBS AND FADO CLUBS

★ **À Capella** Rua do Corpo de Deus, Largo da Vitória ☎ 239 833 985, ⓦ acapella.com.pt; map p.184. If you're going to catch just one fado performance, make it here, in the atmospheric surroundings of this converted medieval chapel with its own bar. There's usually one show a night (€10–15), beginning at 9.30pm. Daily 8.30pm–2.30am.
Fado ao Centro Rua Quebra Costas 7 ☎ 913 236 725, ⓦ fadoaocentro.com; map p.184. This small venue is somewhat touristy but a good place to sample relatively short samples (around an hour) of quality Coimbra fado. Performers explain the meaning of the songs, and the price (€10) includes a short film about fado and a free glass of port. April–Sept Mon–Sat 12.30, 3 & 6pm, Sun at 6pm;

Oct–March daily at 6pm.
NB Club Rua Venâncio Rodrigues 11–17 ☎ 968 771 904, ⓦ noitebiba.pt/coimbra; map pp.182–183. Glitzy club attracting a mixture of students and older locals, with top DJs, themed nights and lots of House (though Fridays are often revival nights). Usually Tues–Sat 11pm–4am, but varies according to events.
★ **Quebra** Rua de Quebra Costas 45–49 ☎ 239 821 661, ⓦ quebra.eu; map p.184. Coimbra's top student music bar hangout, tucked away on the steps leading down from the Sé Velha. There's a tiny terrace for drinks, and live music and DJ sets later in the evening – check the website for details. Mon–Fri noon–4am, Sat 2pm–4am.

SPORTS AND THEATRE

Football Founded by students in 1876, Académica claims to be Portugal's oldest football club. It generally struggles to stay in the top division but its modern stadium, Estádio Cidade de Coimbra (Rua Dom Manuel I ☎ 239 090 341, ⓦ academica-oaf.pt), which seats 30,000, is highly

impressive and also hosts summer concerts.
Theatre The Teatro Académico de Gil Vicente (Praça da República ☎ 239 855 630, ⓦ tagv.info) is Coimbra's cultural hub with a full calendar of theatre, art-house movies and music.

SHOPPING

Coimbra Shopping Avenida Dr Mendes Silva 211–251 ☎ 239 708 758, ⓦ coimbrashopping.pt. This large shopping centre has a hypermarket (open from 8.30am) and a vast array of stores including clothes shops (Mango, Sportzone), toy shops, jewellers and just about everything else. Sun–Thurs 10am–10pm, Fri & Sat 10am–11pm.
Dolce Vita Rua General Humberto Delgado 207–211 ☎ 239 798 090, ⓦ dolcevita.pt. Near the city stadium, this giant shopping centre has a range of local and

international stores including Body Shop, C&A and Massimo Duti, as well as cinemas, cafés and restaurants. Sun–Thurs 10am–11pm, Fri & Sat 10am–midnight.
Mercado Municipal Dom Pedro V Rua Olímpio Nicolau Rui Fernandes ☎ 239 833 385. Close to the post office, this is the biggest market in the region, selling a medley of fresh fruit, veg, fish, flowers, clothes and souvenirs. Mon–Sat 7am–7pm.

DIRECTORY

Hospital Hospital da Universidade de Coimbra, Praceta Prof Mota Pinto ☎ 239 400 400, ⓦ huc.min.saude.pt.
Police Main PSP HQ is at Rua Olímpio Nicolau Rui Fernandes (☎ 239 797 640), across from the post office.
Post office The main post office is on Av Fernão de

Magalhães 223, near Largo do Arnado; other central offices are on Rua Olímpio Nicolau Rui Fernandes, just below the market, and on Praça da República (all Mon–Fri 8.30am–6.30pm, Sat 9am–12.30pm).

Conímbriga

Portugal's most important Roman site, **Conímbriga** is just 16km southwest of Coimbra – an easy day-trip – and around a kilometre south of the pleasant market town of **Condeixa-a-Nova** (signed off the IC3 road to Tomar), where you could easily spend the night. The excavations and remains you can see today are just a fraction of the Roman town that flourished from the last year BC until around 4 AD, and which once spread beneath land now occupied by the little village of **Condeixa-a-Velha**, where the remains of a huge amphitheatre remain hidden.

The site

Daily 10am–7pm • Site and museum €4 • ⓦ conimbriga.pt

As you enter the site you'll find a large car park with ticket office, separate museum and two cafés – handy, as you'll need to allow a good two to three hours to see everything. Once through the gates you'll be faced by the remains of a paved **Roman road** which once ran from Olisipo (Lisbon) to Braccara Augusta (Braga). To the right of this is the impressive first-century **House of the Fountains** – covered to protect it from the elements – whose floors still display beautiful polychrome mosaics. To the left of here are the remains of other wealthy family homes – some with mosaic panels – as well as shops.

Up until the fourth century, the inhabitants lived well and peacefully, but their lives changed dramatically when Swabian attacks became increasingly common. Those who could afford to leave quickly departed for the safety of Rome, while those who remained decided to build the site's most prominent feature, a **vast defensive wall** four metres thick, which could only be entered via giant double gates. The wall virtually cut the town in two: the part of town between the wall and today's ticket office was abandoned, with the rest of the town being protected between the wall and the natural defences of a ravine on the other side.

Today, you can see further **houses** beyond the wall: the biggest boasts around forty rooms and was once owned by a first-century aristocrat, Cantaber – reconstructed pillars show how impressive it was. Little remains of the other main structures, which include shops, an early **Christian basilica**, and a **water cistern** that formed part of a 3km-long aqueduct. You can also visit the partially reconstructed **Forum**, a broad space built around a temple dedicated to Roman gods, that was once the hub of the town.

Museu Monográfico de Conímbriga

The small but excellent **Museu Monográfico de Conímbriga** displays fascinating finds from the excavations, presented thematically. Cabinets detail the minutiae of various trades (glass making, ironmongery, weaving, even house building) and aspects of daily life including coins hoarded because of fear of attack and an array of implements that show the Romans were a vain lot: there are sumptuous, carved hair pins and jewellery you'd admire today. The section on health and hygiene contains scalpels, needles and some quite alarming "probing spoons". On the other side of the museum are displayed the larger spoils – statues of torsos, carved lintels, gargoyles from temples, monochromatic mosaics, remarkably bright mural fragments, and inscribed slabs, pillars and tombstones from the necropolis.

ARRIVAL AND DEPARTURE	**CONÍMBRIGA**
By bus Buses from Coimbra to Conímbriga (around 25min) travel via Condeixa-a-Nova, leaving Coimbra Mon–Fri at	9am, 9.30am, 12.30pm and 3.30pm, returning at 12.55pm, 3.55pm and 4.25pm. Weekend services are greatly reduced.

ACCOMMODATION AND EATING

Other than the two cafés, there are no facilities at the site of Conímbriga and the closest restaurants and accommodation can be found in the nearby town of Condeixa-a-Nova, 1km away, which is a pleasant provincial place to spend the night.

O Cabritino Rua Francisco de Lemos 9, Condeixa-a-Nova ☎239 944 111. Just down the road from the *pousada* (towards the centre of town), this is a handsome fine-dining restaurant with a summer terrace and garden. Goat is the speciality, though you can also find good steaks and fresh fish dishes for around €12–16. Mon & Wed–Sun noon–3pm & 7–10.30pm.

O Regional do Cabrito Praça da República 12 ☎239

944 933. Right on Condeixa-a-Nova's main square, with a few outdoor tables, this simple, friendly place is very good value, with main courses from €6: try dishes such as *bacalhau*, salmon or the local speciality – as perhaps you're beginning to realize from the restaurant names – *cabrito* (roast kid goat), usually slow-roasted and served with roast potatoes and greens. Tues–Sun 11am–11pm.

Pousada de Santa Cristina Rua Francisco Lemos, Condeixa-a-Nova ☎ 239 944 025 ⓦ pousadas.pt. In a relatively modern building – built in 1993 on the site of a fourteenth-century palace – this lacks the wow factor of some of Portugal's *pousadas* but still makes a very pleasant base, with comfy rooms (the bottom ones with a terrace) looking over the hills beyond town and the extensive lawns, which feature a refreshing pool. There's also a good in-house restaurant and bar. **€125**

Serra da Lousã

The rugged hills of the **Serra da Lousã**, only 25km southeast of Coimbra, make another fine day-trip from the city, though you'll really need to stay the night if you plan on doing any serious exploration. The handsome town of **Lousã** is the main base (easily accessible by bus from Coimbra), providing access to a series of **aldeais do xisto**, or mountain schist villages, that were largely depopulated in the 1960s but are now gradually being revived and regenerated in response to the increasing interest in rural tourism.

Lousã

LOUSÃ retains an attractive old kernel within the wider modern town, with the forested green slopes of the *serra* rising behind. A few *casas brasonadas* (heraldic mansions) survive in the older streets, while the grand town hall speaks loudly of more important times. The best days to visit are Tuesdays and especially Saturdays, when the covered **market** is in full swing and stallholders come into town from the outlying villages to hawk their produce, including the local speciality, Licor Beirão. It was a pharmacist from Lousã who originally came up with the secret recipe and this sickly sweet, herb-flavoured cognac-like drink is now drunk all over Portugal. Otherwise, Lousã's only real attraction is its miniature **castle**, though if you're not driving it's a stiff uphill walk to reach it. At the castle, there's a river beach and pool, as well as the good but pricey *Burgo* restaurant,

---

A HIKE INTO THE SERRA DA LOUSÃ

This three-hour, six-kilometre circular hike in the **Serra da Lousã** provides marvellous views and a fascinating glimpse of mountain village life.

From the *Burgo* restaurant near Lousã's castle, walk up the stone steps to the end of the picnic areas, and follow the sign to Casal Novo and Talasnal. The steep rocky path climbs for 1km until it reaches a junction; follow the right-hand fork and after 700m or so you will emerge onto a wider track, which you should follow uphill until it joins a second similar track – turn left and continue the ascent. As the path comes clear of the trees your toil is rewarded by stunning views of the valley below. At the top of this path turn left and continue upwards where you'll meet an unsurfaced road; Talasnal is visible to your left – or you can head right to sleepy **Casal Novo**, which spills down the hillside.

Retrace your steps, ignoring the track you came up and continue in the direction of **Talasnal**, probably the most beautiful of the range's villages with a harmonious mix of ruined and restored cottages amid stunning mountain views. Once you've wound round the side of the mountain you descend to the entrance of the village, whose narrow, higgledy-piggledy passageways are worth a wander.

To exit the village, follow the stream downhill, passing numerous small dwellings in various states of repair to your left and right. Continue downwards on a path mostly marked by dry-stone walls on both sides. When the trail meets a T-junction turn left downhill and cross the river via an old stone bridge. Follow the good, easily navigable path all the way back to the river pools, keeping an eye out for occasional fallen logs blocking the path and the dizzy drop to your right. A well-earned dip in the pools below the castle makes a refreshing end to the walk.

beyond which stepped paths climb up the hillside beyond past a succession of caves, terraces and viewpoints.

Aldeias do xisto

Hard lives in the mountains led to the desertion of many typical upland **aldeias do xisto** (schist villages), some of which are beginning to develop fledgling rural-tourism businesses. Five villages above Lousã (Casal Novo, Talasnal, Cerdeira, Chiqueiro and Candal) form part of central Portugal's Schist Village scheme (ⓦaldeiasdoxisto.pt), which promotes sustainable tourism and other projects – such as establishing waymarked walks and craft shops, and reviving village festivals and customs. The website includes details of local adventure-tour outfits as well as the limited accommodation that is available in the villages. You can drive up yourself – even though not all the roads are surfaced, they are usually fine for normal cars – or follow our circular walk from Lousã castle (see box, p.192) which leads to both Casal Novo and **Talasnal**, the latter with the bonus of the restaurant *Ti'Lena* in a restored schist house (see below).

3

ARRIVAL AND DEPARTURE   LOUSÃ

By bus Buses run approx hourly from Coimbra Parque station to Lousã (1hr 10min). There are also 2–4 daily services (Mon–Fri) between Lousã and Góis (45min) and one daily service (Mon–Fri) to Arganil in the Serra do Açor (1hr 10min).

ACCOMMODATION

Martinho Rua das Forças Armadas, Lousã ☎ 239 991 397. Lousã's cheapest accommodation is at the *Martinho* – to get there, head up the hill from the town hall square and turn left. Set inside a low white building, the rooms are simple but pleasant, and some have balconies. **€50**

Meliá Palácio da Lousã Rua Viscondessa do Espinhal, Lousã ☎ 239 990 800, ⓦsolmelia.com. In the old town, beyond the town hall, this boutique hotel is housed in a seventeenth-century former ducal mansion. The chic rooms come in contemporary style, with the best in the original building, though some are in a modern wing. There's also a bar, a restaurant and a swimming pool. **€75**

EATING AND DRINKING

Burgo Nossa Senhora da Piedade, Lousã ☎ 239 991 162. Near the castle, this old water mill has been transformed into a cosy restaurant specializing in dishes from the Serra da Lousã including chestnut soup, *javali* (wild boar), grilled goat and rabbit with chestnuts. Mains around €12–14. Tues–Sat 12.30–3pm & 7.30–10pm, Sun 12.30–3pm.

Casa Velha Praça Sá Carneiro 14, Lousã ☎ 239 991 555. There's a long menu of Portuguese standards and regional cuisine at this rustic-style restaurant, and portions are vast, so a *dose* (around €9–12) easily feeds two. Dishes include *pataniscas de bacalhau* (cod cakes) and *feijoada de lebre* (hare stew with beans). Thurs–Tues 11am–11pm; closed last two weeks of July.

Ti'Lena Talasnal, Serra da Lousã ☎ 933 832 624. In an ancient stone building, this village restaurant is only open at lunch from Friday to Sunday and it's best to call ahead to let them know you're coming. Although the menu is fairly limited (*cabrito, chanfana, bacalhau*), the food is great: expect to pay around €17 for two courses and drinks. Fri–Sun noon–2pm.

Serra do Açor

East of Lousã stretches the **Serra do Açor**, a mountain range that borders the Serra da Estrela further to the northeast. It's a very attractive region, a mix of bucolic river valleys, pine and eucalyptus forest and the higher traditional schist villages of the mountains proper. **Góis**, 20km northeast of Lousã, is the gateway, prettily set in a river valley, with the small market town of **Arganil** another 13km to the north. Less accessible but worth the effort is the marvellous schist village of **Piódão**, high in the peaks.

GÓIS MOTORBIKE FESTIVAL

Góis is pretty quiet for most of the year, though it perks up in August, no more so than for the huge **motorbike rally** (Concentração de Góis) organized by the Góis Moto Clube (@goismotoclube.net). This attracts up to 40,000 bikers for a good-natured four-day festival of bike shows, radical sports, live bands and DJs – a tent city lines the river just outside town, and the roads are packed with preening speedsters.

Góis and around

GÓIS is beautifully set on the Rio Ceira, crossed by an arched sixteenth-century bridge which leads up to a sloping cobbled square backed by a couple of old-town streets. There's not a lot to occupy you here, but it comes into its own in summer (June to early Sept) when boardwalks are erected and white sand imported to construct a fantastic river beach, with a waterside bar and kayaks to rent. Other favourite local **river beaches** include that at **Várzea Pequena**, 5km west, or you can head into the hills for walks around the Góis schist villages – brown signposts off the Lousã road (N342) lead up to the tiny village of **Aigra Nova**, where there's a **craft shop-café** run by a local not-for-profit agency, Lousitânea, at Rua dos Bois (@235 778 644, @lousitanea.org; daily 10am–6pm) and a good circular waymarked **mountain hike** (10km; 4hr) through three other ancient schist villages in varying stages of restoration.

Arganil

The N342 winds through the trees for 13km from Góis, finally descending to the small town of **ARGANIL**, which has a pedestrianized main street full of traditional shops and a couple of cafés by the square. By far the best day to visit is a Thursday when Arganil's regional weekly **market** takes place on the open-air space above town, from early morning onwards. Part market, part bazaar, it sells everything from a garden spade to a dining-room suite, and it's particularly good for cheap clothes, shoes, local basketware and agricultural hardware and supplies. Inside the market building, there's a simple first-floor *churrasqueira* where everyone goes to eat grilled chicken or *leitão* (suckling pig) for lunch – you'll get the works for just a few euros.

Piódão

From Arganil, it's around an hour's beautiful drive via Coja to **PIÓDÃO**, a traditional schist village set on a steeply terraced mountainside. Despite the slight theme-park atmosphere, its narrow streets are great to explore and the whole village affords superb valley views. There's a small **museum** on Largo Cónego Manuel Fernandes Nogueira (daily: June–Sept 10am–1pm & 2–6pm; Oct–May 9am–1pm & 2–5pm; free), which provides an insight into traditional village life with displays on subjects such as emigration and the economy, as well as daily toil. You can follow a couple of short **walks** from Piódão into the countryside – these are well signposted from the village, or pick up walk leaflets from the information office in the musuem.

ARRIVAL AND DEPARTURE   SERRA DO AÇOR

By bus 2–3 daily Rodoviária da Beira Litoral buses run from Coimbra to Arganil (1hr 40min) via Góis (1hr 15min). There are also 2–4 daily services (Mon–Fri) from Lousã to Góis (45min) and one daily service (Mon–Fri) to Arganil via Góis (1hr 10min).

By car You'll have far more flexibility with your own transport – and a car is essential to visit Piódão or any of the secluded picnic spots and river beaches that make this area so beguiling.

CLOCKWISE FROM TOP FIGUEIRA DA FOZ (P.211); CONÍMBRIGA (P.190); COIMBRA OLD TOWN (P.181) >

INFORMATION

Góis turismo Largo Francisco Inácio Dias Nogueira ☎ 235 770 113 (Mon–Fri 10am–1pm & 2–5.30pm, Sat & Sun 10am–1pm & 2–6pm).

Piódão turismo Inside the museum on Largo Cónego Manuel Fernandes Nogueira (daily: June–Sept 10am–1pm & 2–6pm; Oct–May 9am–1pm & 2–5pm).

ACCOMMODATION AND EATING

Casa das Videiras Carapinhal ☎235 778 073, ⓦ bedandbreakfastcentralportugal.com. For a lovely rural retreat, head to this English-owned B&B, 7km west of Góis on the N2, Vila Nova de Poiares road. There's a summer pool, a pretty patio overlooking the grounds and meals are available. **€50**

Casa Santo António Rua de Santo António, Góis 18 ☎ 235 770 120. Just off the central square in a traditional building, the simple, unsigned *Casa Santo António* has the only official accommodation in Góis. It can be chilly in winter, but at other times it's cosy and welcoming, with its own snooker table in the bar and a generous breakfast. **€40**

Penacova and around

PENACOVA, 22km northeast of Coimbra, is spectacularly sited on a crag high above the **Rio Mondego**. There is little to the place itself – a pint-sized square with a town hall, and a modest cobbled historic quarter along the ridge – but for stunning views of river and valley make a beeline for the terrace of the *Café Turismo*, by the side of the town hall. You can walk the 2km from here down to a great little river beach, **Reconquinho**, where you can swim alongside a seasonal café. Penacova's **market** is on the second Thursday of the month – look out for the highly elaborate toothpicks that are a local speciality, hand-carved from willow.

Mosteiro de Lorvão

Lorvão, 7km southwest of Penacova • Tues–Sat 9am–12.30pm & 2–6pm • Free • ☎ 239 474 430

In a beautiful valley in the wooded hills above Penacova, the **Mosteiro de Lorvão** is an ancient monastic foundation that traces its history back to the sixth century AD, making it one of Europe's oldest monasteries. What you see now dates from the sweeping alterations made in the seventeenth and eighteenth centuries. The monastery today houses a psychiatric hospital and a small museum that contains paintings and what was left of the monastic wealth after the place was looted in the nineteenth century. If you visit on the last Sunday of the month, you'll coincide with the village of Lorvão's open-air **market** – or visit one of the village cafés for a *pastel de Lorvão*, an almond-based sweet traditionally made in the monastery.

ARRIVAL AND INFORMATION   PENACOVA

By bus The bus from Coimbra (Mon–Fri 3 daily; 25min) stops in the main square.

Information Penacova's turismo is opposite the town hall (Mon–Fri 9am–5pm, Sat & Sun 10am–1pm & 2–5pm; ☎ 239 470 300, ⓦ cm-penacova.pt).

KAYAKING THE MONDEGO

The Mondego is one of Portugal's only rivers where you can kayak comfortably all year round, and the 18km, 3–4 hour **kayaking trips** (€20 a head) are a real highlight of any visit to the region. Penacova-based O Pioneiro do Mondego (☎ 239 478 385, ⓦ opioneirodomondego .com), was the first company to offer kayaking tours and can arrange pick-ups or meeting points at various spots along the river between Penacova and Coimbra. Once on the river you'll be guided downstream with a gentle current – and the odd rapids – taking you down pine- and eucalyptus-lined valleys, where black kites fish in summer and grapes dangle over the river in autumn. You end up on a river beach where you can swim before being taken back to your starting point.

ACCOMMODATION AND EATING

A Cota Azenha do Rio ☎ 239 474 841. The best place for Penacova specialities, including lamprey rice, eel fritters and steaks, from around €10. The restaurant has lovely river views, although it's way below town by the bridge on the EN110. Daily noon–10pm.

Avenida Avenida Abel Rodrigues da Costa ☎ 239 477 142, ⓦ pensaoavenida.com. Penacova's best budget choice is the traditional *Avenida*, just down the hill from the main square. It is more than a bit on the elderly side and you pay an extra €10 for your own bathroom, but it does have a good, inexpensive restaurant attached. €25

O Panorâmico Largo Alberto Leitão 7 ☎ 239 477 333. Next to the town hall, *O Panorâmico* has a glorious view down the valley and somewhat upmarket fare such as lamprey and duck rice from around €13–15. Daily 11am–11pm.

The Mata Nacional do Buçaco and Luso

Around 30km northeast of Coimbra, the **Mata Nacional do Buçaco** (National Forest of Buçaco) is a walled, former monastic hilltop retreat, with its own royal palace (now a five-star hotel). These days the forest – partly wild and partly landscaped – is a hugely popular outing for Portuguese day-trippers, who descend in droves at weekends for picnics, but it's large enough to escape the crowds and makes a great day out. It's easily accessible by car or bus, or you could walk the two kilometres (steeply uphill) from **Luso**, a little spa town famed for its mineral waters, which bubble out from the main square.

Buçaco forest

Cars €5; pedestrians free • ⓦ fmb.pt

The real joy of Buçaco is the chance to wander freely around 105 hectares of forest, below towering trees, stumbling across hidden water features, lakes and the occasional dazzling view, such as from the **Portas de Coimbra**. There are few signs, but most paths lead back eventually to the focal point of the park, the ornate palace.

Although the forest had been owned by the Bishop of Coimbra since the eleventh century, it was only settled in 1628 when Carmelite monks were granted permission to create their own "desert" on the wooded hilltop. Here, they constructed a series of chapels and hermitages, in an attempt to re-create the ascetic lifestyle of biblical hermits. The **Convento de Santa Cruz** (see p.198) was erected as their main church, and they also created routes lined with chapels to the "Sacred Mount", planting trees in the process. Today you can follow the **Via Sacra**, lined with chapels, to the heights of **Cruz Alta**, a "high cross" at the top of a hill, which gives dazzling views across the surrounding country: it's around a forty-minute walk here from the palace.

In 1810, the convent was used by the Duke of Wellington as a base for what turned out to be a decisive victory in the Battle of Buçaco, before the religious order was finally disbanded in 1834. The area was then developed into a romantic botanical gardens, when today's water features and beautiful **Vale dos Fetos** (Valley of Ferns) were laid out, and many of the 250 species of tree that you can see today were planted, including giant sequoia, cedar, firs and pines.

Palácio do Buçaco

☎ 231 937 970, ⓦ almeidahotels.com

Construction of the royal **Palácio do Buçaco** in the middle of the forest began in 1888, using a team of architects including Luigi Manini, who built the dramatic Quinta da Regaleira in Sintra; indeed, Buçaco has a lot in common with Sintra in terms of both the landscape and the style of architecture. The impressive palace is mock-Manueline, a riot of carvings and beautiful *azulejo* tiles, topped by a dramatic pinnacled turret. The palace was finally completed in 1907, only for the Republic to be declared three years later. Ever since, it's been a five-star hotel, surrounded by sumptuously landscaped gardens.

Tour coaches stop by in droves and as a result casual visitors are discouraged, though you can use the café or bar after 3pm. At other times, there is a public café opposite.

Convento de Santa Cruz
Daily 10am–1pm & 2–6pm • €2

Within the palace grounds you can visit the small but attractive Carmelite **Convento de Santa Cruz**. As you enter, you'll notice that the door and ceiling of the entrance hall are lined with cork. Look out, too, for the curious little side-chapel centred on an image of the Virgin Mary breastfeeding a baby Jesus, around which worshippers have placed wax models of breasts and pregnant women.

Museu Militar

Just outside the forest near the Portas da Rainha • Tues–Sun 10am–12.30pm & 2–5pm • €2

Buçaco's small **Museu Militar** contains charts, uniforms and relics detailing the events leading up to and during the Battle of Buçaco (1810), when the Duke of Wellington used the heights of the area to successfully withstand an attack by French troops. The French sustained heavy losses, one of Napoleon's first setbacks, giving the Duke time to develop the lines of Torres Vedras further south.

Luso

A spa town for well over a hundred years, **LUSO** – 3km downhill by road from Buçaco – still draws crowds of Portuguese to take its waters, and visitors are welcome to try the various treatments at the **Termas de Luso** (May–Oct; ⓦtermasdoluso.com), which has a certain dated charm. Locals fill bottles and plastic containers with free spa water from the **Fonte São João** spring – Luso water is sold all over the country – next to which is an old-fashioned Art Deco *casa do chá* (tea room), with a terrace overlooking the central gardens and spa buildings. There's also a great little daily fruit-and-veg **market** just down from the tourist office, while a souvenir market (lace, basketware, football shirts and regional cakes) sets its stalls out between the town's roundabouts. After a turn around the small town centre (population 3000) and municipal park with its little lake, head up past the souvenir market stalls to pick up the stepped path to Buçaco.

ARRIVAL AND INFORMATION   **LUSO AND BUÇACO**

By bus All non-express buses from Viseu take a short detour through the forest, stopping at the Palácio do Buçaco, and again by the Portas da Rainha (for the military museum) en route to Luso (Mon–Fri 5 daily, Sat 2 daily; 1hr 45min). Services from Coimbra to Luso run 4 daily (Mon–Fri), and 2 daily on Sat (40min).

By train Three afternoon services leave Coimbra A, and take 30 minutes to Luso–Buçaco station; it's a fifteen-minute walk into town from the station – take the road on the left.

Information Luso turismo is opposite the *Grande Hotel*, near the post office on the main Rua Emídio Navarro (June to mid-Sept Mon–Fri 9am–12.30pm & 2–7pm, Sat & Sun 9.30am–1pm & 2.30–6pm; mid-Sept to May daily 9.30am–12.30pm & 2–5.30pm; ☎231 939 133, ⓦturismo -centro.pt). They give out free fold-out maps of the town and forest.

ACCOMMODATION

★ **Alegre** Rua Emídio Navarro 2, Luso ☎231 930 256, ⓦalegrehotels.com. Just 100m up the road to Buçaco, this impressive building with a grand entrance, once home to a count, is full of nineteenth-century style and polished wood. The best of the high-ceilinged rooms have balconies (€15 extra) and great views, and there's also wi-fi, a small bar and a swimming pool in the pretty garden. The owner is a real expert on local history. Parking. **€60**

Familiar Rua Ernesto Navarro 34, Luso ☎231 939 612. Just up the Buçaco road from town, this is a charming old house with a variety of rooms: a few have small balconies and some sleep up to four people. No credit cards. Parking. **€35**

Grande Hotel de Luso Rua Dr Cid de Oliveira 86, Luso ☎231 937 937, ⓦhoteluso.com. You can't fail to miss the yellow, turreted *Grande Hotel* – a four-star Art Deco-era beauty with tastefully designed rooms, most with balconies. There's a huge Olympic-sized outdoor pool, as well as an indoor pool and hot tub, kids' club and parking. **€100**

★ **Imperial** Rua Emídio Navarro 25, Luso ☎231 937 570, ⓦresidencialimperial.com. Great value, and a good location by the *casa do chá* and *fonte*. It's a modern place with comfortable en-suite rooms complete with sturdy furniture – some rooms sleep four, and there's a good, inexpensive restaurant downstairs (which may be closed at quiet times). **€40**

3

EATING

O Cesteiro Rua Monsenhor Raul Mira, Luso ☎ 231 939 360. A five-minute walk from the town centre (keep going past the turismo), this local favourite serves a typical regional menu, including duck rice, roast goat and a good steak, with mains around €8–12. Mon, Tues and Thurs–Sun noon–3pm & 7–10pm.

Pedra de Sal Rua Dr Francisco Diniz 33, Luso ☎ 231 939 405, ⊕ restaurantepedradesal.com. One of Luso's smarter options, with crisp service and a menu featuring the likes of *porco preto*, steak, or squid-and-prawn kebab for around €12–13. Daily noon–2pm & 7–10pm.

The Dão valley wine route

The route northeast from Coimbra along the IP3 sweeps through the **valley of the Rio Dão**, a name synonymous in Portugal with wine. The Dão is a tributary of the Mondego and flows through the heart of the demarcated region where some of the country's finest red wines are produced. Most of the wine estates lie either side of the river valley to the northeast of **Santa Comba Dão**, and you can spend a happy day pottering through the region's small country towns, following winery signs on the **Rota do Vinho do Dão** to pretty villages like **Santar**. It's a hilly, granite area, cold and rainy in winter, but hot and dry in the sweltering summers, when the wooded slopes are particularly susceptible to ravaging forest fires.

Santa Comba Dão and the Dão valley

The small market town of **SANTA COMBA DÃO**, a little over 50km from Coimbra, marks the start of the Dão wine region. Its only claim to fame is as the home town of António de Oliveira Salazar (1889–1970), the Portuguese dictator and leader of an authoritarian regime that lasted forty years, who was born (and is buried) in the nearby village of Vimeiro. There's not much to the town itself, save a very small historic centre and some grandstand views of the tumbling river and the Aguieira *barragem* (reservoir). However, you can explore the surroundings on the disused Dão-valley rail line from Santa Comba Dão to Viseu, which is now the **Ecopista do Dão**, a 48-kilometre cycle-way and footpath, the longest in the country (⊕ ciclovia.com.pt).

Santar

Around 30km northeast of Santa Comba Dão, near Nelas, **SANTAR** is a very attractive village in the heart of Dão vineyards. Cobbled backstreets lined with handsome stone mansions lead up to the main square, where you'll find the Paço dos Cunhas de Santar (Tues–Sun 10am–10pm; free; ☎ 232 960 140, ⊕ daosul.com), a restored seventeenth-century mansion which now runs wine tastings, wine workshops and cookery courses.

ARRIVAL AND DEPARTURE   SANTA COMBA DÃO AND THE DÃO VALLEY

By bus Buses leave Coimbra approx hourly for Santa Comba Dão (1hr 20min).
By train Around three daily trains leave Coimbra B station

for Santa Comba Dão (40min).
By car In order to reach most of the wine estates, which are well signed on the roads, you will need your own car.

ACCOMMODATION AND EATING

Quinta do Rio Dão Escolha Verde ☎ 232 892 784, ⊕ quintadoriodao.com. The charming Dutch-owned *Quinta do Rio Dão* is an organic estate by the river, 2km from Santa Comba Dão. Accommodation is in B&B rooms in the main house or rustic self-catering cottages in the

grounds, and organic orange juice and home-made estate preserves are served at breakfast. You can splash about on the water in the *quinta*'s kayaks or rowing boat, and it's also near the start of the *ecopista*, with bikes available for guests to rent. **€70**

ACTIVITIES

Wine tours and tastings Details of wineries open to the public for tours and tastings are given on the website ⓦ daosul.com. Some estates are small family concerns and require appointments, while others are very much set up for public visits, like the Paço dos Cunhas de Santar (see opposite) and Quinta de Cabriz (daily 9am–10pm; free; ☎ 232 960 140, ⓦ daosul.com), 3km from Carregal do Sal (off the IC12), which makes some terrific reds and interesting sparkling wines, and has its own restaurant.

Serra do Caramulo

Beyond Santa Comba Dão, the IP3 bears away from the Dão valley and the views are soon of the **Serra do Caramulo**, breaking to the northwest. The eastern turn-off point for the mountains is the small, unassuming town of Tondela, 20km from Santa Comba Dão, from where the minor N230 winds through a succession of tiny villages at the heart of the mountain range, including **Caramulo** itself, a twisting 19km from Tondela. This is the only worthwhile overnight stop, with a fantastic museum, and makes a good hiking base; most of the other *serra* villages are little more than hamlets, surrounded by rhododendrons, brightly coloured azaleas and thick green shrubs growing wild on the hillside. After Caramulo, the N230 descends to **Águeda**, western access point to the mountains, 37km from Caramulo, which is close to the main north–south routes between Coimbra and Aveiro/Porto.

3

Caramulo

Tucked beneath the granite outcrops and wind turbines of the high Beiras *serra*, the straggling village of **CARAMULO** glories in some staggering views. It's a somnolent place, with a belvedere garden and vast, shady chestnut trees at its heart, while several waymarked footpaths radiate from the village through neighbouring hamlets and up to the local peaks. The summit of the loftiest, **Caramulinho** (1075m), is a five-kilometre drive from the village, while at **Cabeço da Neve** (a 4km drive) there's another sweeping viewpoint. The best walk is the circular **Rota dos Caleiros** (8.2km; 3–4hr), which is detailed in a leaflet available from the turismo (see below): it picks its way past the old stone aqueducts (*caleiros*) and granite boulders around Caramulinho, with magnificent views east to the Serra da Estrela and west to the Atlantic Ocean.

Museu do Caramulo

Rua Jean Lurçat 42 • Daily 10am–1pm & 2–6pm; closes at 5pm in winter • €7 • ⓦ museu-caramulo.net

The extraordinary **Museu do Caramulo** was founded by two brothers with a love of "art and automobiles" and displays everything from primitive religious sculpture to souped-up Harley Davidsons. Once you've browsed through the Picasso sketches and sixteenth-century tapestries, it's on to the superb collection of vintage cars and motorcycles, most of which are in working order and given a run-out every September for the **Caramulo Motorfestival** (ⓦ caramulo-motorfestival.com).

ARRIVAL AND INFORMATION

CARAMULO

By car There is no public transport to Caramulo, so you'll need a car to explore.

Information Caramulo turismo (Mon–Fri 9am–1pm & 1.30–5pm, Sat & Sun 10am–12.30pm & 2.30–5.30pm; ☎ 232 861 437) is a little way down the Tondela road from the village roundabout, on the left-hand side – you can pick up walking brochures here.

ACCOMMODATION

Hotel do Caramulo Av Dr Abel Lacerda ☎ 232 860 100, ⓦ hoteldocaramulo.pt. Flagship accommodation is the four-star *Hotel do Caramulo*, with spa and leisure facilities, including indoor and outdoor pools, a decent restaurant and bar, and unbeatable views towards the Serra da Estrela. €114

Vouzela and the Rio Vouga

North of Caramulo, and just beyond the fast Aveiro–Viseu road (IP5), **Vouzela** is an attractive Beira town set on the beautiful **Rio Vouga** and makes a fine destination if you feel like taking in a little of backwater Portugal. Bus services run from Coimbra and Aveiro and, on reaching the Vouga, follow the route of the old train line along the river on the N16. For drivers there are equally bucolic approaches, from Caramulo to the south (N228) or from Viseu and the IP5 to the east, from where the minor N337 makes a particularly memorable approach. Beyond the town lies the spa resort of **São Pedro do Sul**, on the Rio Sul, which flows down from the lovely Serra da Arada that flanks Vouzela to the north.

Vouzela

VOUZELA's old centre is built around a shallow river, crossed by a low **Romanesque bridge**, overhung by willow and bordered by attractive manor houses. Beyond are the riverside gardens, manicured lawns and municipal pool, all towered over by the **viaduct** of the former railway which stretches across a narrow terraced gorge. You can cross both bridge and viaduct on an eight-kilometre circular walk – a board at the top of the gardens by the viaduct shows the route. Within Portugal, the town is best known for its *pasteis de Vouzela* (a very sweet egged-based pastry) and the local *vinho Lafões* (a wine similar to *vinho verde*). A good time to visit is the first Wednesday of the month when there's a morning street **market**.

Museu Municipal

Praça Morais de Carvalho • Tues–Fri 9.30am–1pm & 2–5.30pm, Sat & Sun 2–5pm • Free

From the river, narrow Rua São Frei Gil climbs up past manor houses to a small square where you'll find the **Museu Municipal**, housed in eighteenth-century former law courts. The museum has a fairly uninspiring collection of archeological remains and sacred art, though the room of old toys is more diverting. A third room hosts temporary exhibits.

Termas de São Pedro do Sul

Four kilometres northeast of Vouzela is the thermal resort area of **TERMAS DE SÃO PEDRO DO SUL**, possibly the oldest spa in Portugal, though now offering modern treatments (@termas-spsul.com). It was used by the Romans and Portuguese royalty – Dom Afonso Henriques is said to have bathed his wounded leg here after the battle at Badajoz – and remains among the most attractive in the country. Its position beside the Vouga, with pine trees all around, certainly lends it charm and the resort makes for a pleasant side-trip from Vouzela.

ARRIVAL AND INFORMATION

By bus Vouzela bus station is at Avenida Sidónio Pais. Destinations Aveiro (2–3 daily; 1hr 10min); Coimbra (5 daily; 1hr 50min); Lisbon, via Coimbra (3 daily; 4hr 10min); Porto (1–2 daily; 2hr 30min); São Pedro do Sul (1–2 daily; 15min).

VOUZELA AND THE RIO VOUGA

Information Vouzela turismo, Avenida João de Melo 23 (Mon–Sat 10am–1pm & 2–6pm, Sun 2–6pm; reduced hours in winter; @232 771 515, @cm-vouzela.pt), is in an old market building, which also sells local handicrafts.

ACCOMMODATION

Casa de Fataunços Fataunços @351 916 986 085, @casadefatauncos.com. In the village of Fataunços, roughly halfway between Vouzela and São Pedro do Sul, this beautifully restored eighteenth-century manor house is a fantastic country retreat with its own grounds,

swimming pool and tennis court. The house also arranges painting, theatre and dance courses. **€70**

Casa Museu Rua Ribeiro Cardoso 6, Vouzela @232 771 514, @casamuseu.com. Opposite Vouzela's museum, and with similarly historic touches, the eighteenth-century

FOREST FIRES AND THE BOMBEIROS VOLUNTÁRIOS

Portugal's famed green countryside is ravaged each year by **forest fires**, and the problem has worsened markedly in recent years – it's estimated that ninety percent are caused by human activity, whether it's arson or carelessness with cigarettes, bonfires and barbecues. Matters aren't helped by the country's timber industry, which has replaced native tree species with the highly flammable eucalyptus and pine. Peak fire season is midsummer, but in drought years forest fires break out as early as January and as late as November. You don't need to drive through central and northern Portugal for long before seeing the evidence of past fires – hillsides burned black and torched trees – or the telltale plumes of thick smoke from the latest conflagration. On the worst days, ash falls to the streets in distant towns and cities, and major train lines and motorways are closed.

Extraordinarily, the firefighting service that has the unenviable task of dealing with the problem is almost entirely voluntary. The country's 20,000 or so **Bombeiros Voluntários** make up over ninety percent of Portugal's firefighting forces, with the few (and far better equipped) professional corps (Bombeiros Sapadores) based in the cities or working privately for the country's timber and paper-pulp concerns. You'll see Bombeiros Voluntários vehicles in every region – helping out with ambulance duties too as part of their remit – and the volunteers are usually the first and only firefighters on the scene when a blaze breaks out. Equipment and vehicles are often wholly inadequate; in the past, urgent appeals to the EU have led to specialist aircraft and foreign crews arriving to help.

It is, of course, horribly dangerous work and firefighters lose their lives every year. For this reason – and for their astonishing success rate in saving local homes and properties – the Bombeiros Voluntários have an almost heroic status in Portugal. Rare is the town without a street or avenue named after them, while proud **municipal statues and memorials** to their deeds proliferate.

Casa Museu is an elegantly decorated townhouse with stone walls, antique furnishings and pretty rooms. **€60**
Ferreira Rua Barão da Costeiro 3, Vouzela ☎ 232 771 650. Around 50m down the hill from the Praça da República, *Ferreira* is Vouzela's best budget option, a pleasantly old-fashioned place with simple en-suite rooms in an old townhouse. **€30**

EATING

Forno do Rei Rua Escolar 19, Vouzela ☎ 232 779 129. In a cobbled backstreet behind *Ferreira*, the simple, rustic and very friendly *Forno do Rei* provides good local dishes (meals around €7), which are served on the terrace in summer. Mon–Sat noon–10pm, Sun noon–4pm.
O Meu Menino Avenida Sidónio Pais 6, Vouzela ☎ 232 771 335. Just down from the bus station, this large restaurant serves up reasonably-priced local dishes such as *feijoada*, home-made sausages and rabbit: you can eat well here for under €10. Sun–Fri 11am–11pm.
O Regalinho Rua Teles Loureiro 18, Vouzela ☎ 232 771 220. Vouzela's swankiest option, just off Praça da República, where you can expect to pay €12 a dish for good regional food (roast goat, veal, *bacalhau*). Mon & Wed–Sun noon–2.30pm & 7–9.30pm.

Arouca and the Serra da Freita

A twisting 43-kilometre route from Vouzela heads over the 1000m peaks of the **SERRA DA FREITA** to Arouca, via a beautiful, terraced landscape littered with dolmens, crumbling villages and waterfalls. Vines grow on precipitous slopes, while the roads snake through pine forest and then high across the heather-dotted moorland. A regional map available from Arouca turismo details all the local sights and attractions, as well as several breathtaking hikes, and you could easily spend a day or two touring and walking in the hills. **AROUCA** itself is a handsome little town which – though largely unbothered by tourists – is a real gem. The central square holds a couple of pavement cafés, while in the medieval backstreets there are some beautiful old houses decked with wisteria.

Mosteiro de Santa Maria de Arouca

Largo de Santa Mafalada, Av 25 de Abril • Accompanied visits, sometimes in English, Tues–Sun 9.30am–noon & 2–5pm • €3; under-14s free • ☎ 256 943 321, ⓦ museu-de-arouca.pt.vu

Arouca has always been associated with the vast, medieval **Mosteiro de Santa Maria de Arouca**, whose imposing walls loom over the main road that cuts through town. In the kitchen there are huge fireplaces that give an idea of the number of its former inhabitants, while the Baroque church (which you can see without buying a ticket; enter from the main road) holds richly carved choir stalls and a great organ with 1352 notes, played on rare occasions by one of the country's few experts. The convent peaked in importance when Dona Mafalda, of whose dowry it had formed a part, found her marriage to Dom Henriques I of Castile annulled and retired here to a life of religious contemplation. In the museum upstairs, you can see some of Queen Mafalda's most prized treasures, including an exquisite thirteenth-century silver diptych.

3

Geoparque Arouca

Canelas, 10km northeast of Arouca (N326) • **Visitor centre** Sat 10am–noon & 2.30–5pm, Sun 2.30–5pm; private visits also available Tues–Fri with advance reservations • Admission to centre €2, guided walking tour €8 • ⓦ geoparquearouca.com, ⓦ trilobitesdecanelas.com

Local heart rates increased slightly following the discovery of an extraordinary **fossil site** at Canelas, containing an amazing series of 400-million-year-old trilobites and gastropods. This sits within the wider **Geoparque Arouca** and to see the fossils you need first to go to the park visitor centre, which is on the left-hand side of the N326 before you turn off for Canelas.

ARRIVAL AND INFORMATION   **AROUCA**

By bus There are regional buses from Porto to Arouca (via São João de Madeira), though to make the magnificent journey over the Serra da Freita, you'll need your own car.

Information Arouca turismo is on Rua Alfredo Vaz Pinto, behind the main square, Praça Brandão de Vasconcelas (Mon–Fri 9am–12.30pm & 2–5.30pm, Sat & Sun 9.30am–1pm & 2–5.30pm; ☎ 256 943 575, ⓦ cm-arouca.pt).

ACCOMMODATION AND EATING

NaturVeredas Merujal, 1km south of town ☎ 256 947 723, ⓦ naturveredas.com. A nice pine-forest campsite, with little wooden cabins (sleeping 2–4) and a bunkhouse available, as well as a bar-restaurant on site. Tent pitch €2.50 plus €3.50 per adult; 2-person cabins €25; bunkhouse beds €7.50

São Pedro Av Reinaldo de Noronha ☎ 256 944 580, ⓦ hotelspedro.com. Arouca's best hotel is a three-star place, a five-minute walk up the main road from the square (take the left fork, to Castro Daire, at the top). It has reasonably priced rooms – the nicest have balconies and wonderful views. €60

Tasquinha da Quinta Rua 1 de Maio ☎ 256 944 080. Around the corner from the turismo, the *Tasquinha da Quinta* offers excellent regional dishes for around €10, including the local speciality, *arouquêsa* beef. Daily noon–3pm & 7–10pm.

Aveiro and around

The substantial inland town of **AVEIRO** lies south of Porto on the edge of a system of coastal lagoons which stretch for around 40km both north and south. Until the mid-1500s, it was a vibrant coastal port but its economy was devastated when the river mouth silted up and the hinterland turned to swamp. At the beginning of the nineteenth century, however, canals were dug to open up the town and drain the marshes, creating saltpans, and facilitating the harvesting of seaweed, and the town began to flourish once more. Today, Aveiro's economy depends increasingly on tourists, attracted by its canals and colourful houses, and the nearby **Vista Alegre** factory, famed for its ceramics. The town's closest beaches – at **Barra** and **Costa Nova** – are built up and packed in summer,

AVEIRO

3

■ ACCOMMODATION		● RESTAURANTS AND CAFÉS		■ BARS AND CLUBS	
Aveiro Center	6	Meliá Ria	5	Adamasor	2	O Mercantel	1	Caffé da Praça	1	Mercado Negro	4
Aveiro Palace	3	Moliceiro	4	Alexandre	5	O Telheiro	4	Casa de Chá	5	Tertúlia Toc Aqui	3
Aveiro Rossio Hostel	2	Palmeira	1	Mercado do Peixe	3			Clandestino	2		

but still good fun, while the **São Jacinto nature reserve** provides coastal attractions of a more peaceful kind.

Aveiro

Aveiro has a compact centre of handsome buildings and open squares, though what strikes most are its canals, looped over by footbridges and plied by colourful cruise boats. Aveiro grows upon visitors, rather than being thrust upon them: it lends itself rather easily to a couple of days doing not very much, and with no fixed plans you might well end up staying an extra night or two. In this you're ably supported by an excellent range of restaurants and some lively bars, courtesy of the large student population at the Universidade de Aveiro.

Stand on the bridge over the **Canal Central** and most of central Aveiro is within a couple of minutes' walk. The traditional industries are recalled by imposing statues of local workers on the bridge, notably the *salineira* with her salt tray. Pastel-coloured houses line Rua João Mendonça on the north side, with the old town streets and **Mercado do Peixe** (fish market; Tues–Sat 7am–1pm) just behind. Other arms of the canal branch off at intervals, with tiled houses facing each other across the water.

Aveiro has a preponderance of **Art Nouveau buildings** – the turismo is housed in a particularly fine example – the legacy of returning wealthy emigrants in the early years of the twentieth century. At the top of the pedestrianized Rua Coimbra, Praça da República is flanked by the blue snowflake-design tiled facade of the seventeenth-century **Igreja da Misericórdia** and the **Câmara Municipal**, a century older.

Canal Central, the traffic consists largely of *barcos moliceiros*, the traditional
oon boats with raised prows, colourfully adorned with paintings of flowers
ed women. Once used to transport kelp, they now almost exclusively serve
d a trip on them is something of a must. Numerous companies offer
eparting from either side of the Canal Central in front of the turismo
30 minutes or so, daily 10am–6pm, longer hours in July & Aug; 45min;
around €5). The boat trips usually pass down the main canal to local saltpans and back into
town; if you're lucky, your commentary may be accompanied by the odd singing boatman.

Museu de Aveiro

Avenida Santa Joana Princesa • Tues–Sun 10am–5.30pm • €4, free on Sun and public hols until 2pm • ⓦ imc-ip.pt

Aveiro's one must-see attraction, the wonderful town museum, is inside the fifteenth-
century **Convento de Jesus**. Its finest exhibits all relate to Santa Joana, a daughter of
Afonso V who lived in the convent from 1472 until her death in 1489. Barred from
becoming a nun because of her royal station and her father's opposition, she was later
beatified for her determination to escape from the material world (or perhaps simply
from an unwelcome arranged marriage). Her tomb and chapel are strikingly beautiful,
as is the convent itself, and there's a fine collection of art and sculpture – notably a
series of naïve seventeenth-century paintings depicting the saint's life.

Vista Alegre

Ílhavo • **Museum, chapel and palace** May–Sept Tues–Fri 9am–6pm, Sat & Sun 9am–12.30pm & 2–5pm; Oct–April Tues–Fri
9am–6pm, Sat & Sun 10am–12.30pm & 2–5pm • €2.50 • **Vista Alegre shop and factory shop** Mon–Sat 9.30am–7.30pm •
☎ 234 320 600, ⓦ vistaalegreatlantis.com • Buses (signed Ílhavo) leave approx hourly from outside Aveiro station and take 20 minutes

Portugal's celebrated **Vista Alegre** porcelain works was established in 1824 at Ílhavo,
around 5km west of Aveiro. It soon acquired royal patronage and expanded from a
simple porcelain and glass factory to an estate with its own workers' village, along the
lines of the model villages built by enlightened British entrepreneurs of the period.
Today, there's a **museum**, the founder's **palace**, and a tiled and frescoed seventeenth-
century **chapel** to visit, as well as a Vista Alegre **shop** (porcelain, crystal, silverware) and
factory shop for seconds.

Praia da Barra and Costa Nova

Aveiro's nearest beach lies 9km west, at **Praia da Barra**, a large, developed stretch of sand
overlooked by the Iberian peninsula's tallest lighthouse. There's more of the same at
Costa Nova, 3km south of Barra, though the development here is ameliorated by an
attractive line of candy-striped wooden buildings facing inland over the lagoon.

São Jacinto

The reserve entrance is a ten-minute walk from the boat, out of town along the road to Torreira • To visit, call the visitor centre at least
a day in advance (☎ 234 831 063, ⓦ icnb.pt) as numbers are limited • Entry is only allowed Mon–Wed, Fri & Sat between 9 and 9.30am,
or 2 and 2.30pm

On the north side of the lagoon from Aveiro, and accessible by boat from Forte da
Barra, is the beach and nature reserve of **SÃO JACINTO**, a thriving little port with a
handful of dockside cafés and restaurants. With a military base at one end and a forest
of cranes cluttering the skyline, it's not beautiful, but there is an enormous dune-
fringed **beach** twenty minutes' walk away. Parts of the beach, plus the encroaching pine
forest, have been preserved within the **Reserva Natural das Dunas de São Jacinto**, where

boardwalks and paths are laid out through the marram grass and past willow-shrouded ponds. More than a hundred bird species have been spotted here, including goshawk, teal and wigeon. You can pick up a free map from the visitor centre for a self-guided seven-kilometre walk through the reserve, which takes around two and a half hours.

North of São Jacinto the minor N327 (and summer bus service) runs all the way up the lagoon to the beach at **Torreira**. There's another small resort at **Furadouro**, 26km from São Jacinto, where a long stretch of pine-fringed dunes marks the point at which the distinctive Ria countryside finally comes to an end.

ARRIVAL AND INFORMATION
AVEIRO AND AROUND

By bus Tickets for Rede Expressos (express) services to Lisbon, Coimbra and Porto are available from Loja das Revistas, a newsagent in Praça Humberto Delgado (by the bridge in town on the south side) – you can then catch the bus around the corner on Rua Batalhão de Caçadores (opposite the Forum shopping mall).
Destinations Coimbra (4–5 daily; 45min); Figueira da Foz (3–4 daily; 1hr); Lisbon (3–5 daily; 4hr); Porto (roughly hourly; 2hr 45min); Praia de Mira (1 daily; 1hr); and Vouzela (2–3 daily; 1hr 10min).
By car Parking can be difficult, as metered on-street parking is limited to two hours (though free on Sat

afternoon & Sun) – try Largo do Rossio by the canal or the streets around the train station. The covered car park beneath Praça Marquês de Pombal is best for longer stays.
By train The train station is on Largo da Estação, a fifteen-minute walk from the centre.
Destinations Coimbra (hourly; 40min–1hr); Espinho (hourly; 20–40min); Lisbon (hourly; 2hr 30min–3hr 30min); and Porto (hourly; 30min–1hr 15min).
Information Aveiro turismo is at Rua João Mendonça 8 (June–Sept Mon–Fri 9am–8pm, Sat & Sun 9am–6pm; Oct–May Mon–Fri 9am–6pm, Sat & Sun 9.30am–12.30pm & 1.30–5.30pm; ☎ 234 420 760, ⊛ turismo-centro.pt).

GETTING AROUND

By bus Buses to Praia de Barra and Costa Nova depart from outside Aveiro train station, or on Rua Clube dos Galitos, across the bridge from the turismo, about 150m down the canal on the right (approx hourly; Praia de Barra 15min; Costa Nova 25min). For São Jacinto, catch the bus from the Rua Clube dos Galitos stop to the end of the line at Forte da Barra – not be confused with Praia de Barra (approx hourly; 15min). A connecting boat runs from here across the water to São Jacinto (approx hourly; 5min; €1 single).

By bike Bicycles are available free from the green-trimmed "Loja BUGA" kiosk (daily 10am–7pm), at the back of the Forum Aveiro shopping mall, just across the footbridge (in front of the old market). You need to show ID to get a bike, but can use it for a whole morning or afternoon.
By taxi Available in front of the train station, or at the bottom of Rua Viana do Castelo, near the bridge. To book a taxi, call Central de Táxis on ☎ 234 343 266.

ACCOMMODATION

AVEIRO

★ **Aveiro Center** Rua da Arrochela 6 ☎ 234 380 390, ⊛ hotelaveirocenter.com. This good-value family hotel offers cool doubles, triples and family rooms with shower or bath, overlooking a quiet street or a pretty patio at the back. The staff are courteous, there's on-street parking nearby and a generous buffet breakfast included. **€70**
Aveiro Palace Rua de Viana do Castelo 4 ☎ 234 423 001, ⊛ hotelaveiropalace.com. A grand building in a great position, by the bridge and canal, with four-star comforts – plush rooms, an attractive first-floor bar and wi-fi. Good value. **€90**
★ **Aveiro Rossio Hostel** Largo do Rossio, corner Rua João A. de Aveiro 1 6 ☎ 234 041 538, ⊛ aveirorossio hostel.com. Not just a hostel – though it does have very attractive dorms – but also a very appealing guesthouse, with bright, spacious rooms in a high-ceilinged townhouse. There's also a pleasant communal lounge. Dorm beds **€20**; doubles **€65**

Meliá Ria Cais da Fonte Nova ☎ 234 401 000, ⊛ solmelia.com. A short walk out of the old centre, Aveiro's smartest four-star hotel is a striking glass-and-steel box overlooking the canal and artificial lake. Rooms (some with balconies) are pretty stylish too, and there's a spa and pool, restaurant and garage parking (fee charged). **€80**
Moliceiro Rua Barbosa de Magalhães 15–17, Largo do Rossio ☎ 234 377 400, ⊛ hotelmoliceiro.com. The best upmarket choice, a contemporary four-star – rooms in earth tones with dark-wood furniture and marble bathrooms – where you overlook the canal or rear street. There's a good buffet breakfast, and they go the extra mile too, with a drink on check-in. Limited parking out the front. **€120**
Palmeira Rua da Palmeira 7–11 ☎ 234 422 521, ⊛ residencialpalmeira.net. A bright and cheerful budget choice in the old quarter, between the fish market and the Canal de São Roque. The rooms are varied, but most

have a shower or bath, cable TV, and there's a very helpful owner. €45

THE BEACH
Beach campsites The busy, brash, summer beachside campsites are way out of town, at Praia da Barra

(ⓦcampingbarra.com) and Costa Nova (ⓦcamping costanova.com), both with plenty of facilities and rooms, bungalows and apartments for rent, but not really suitable if you're looking for a quiet few days by the beach. Both campsites charge the same price. Pitch €4, plus €4 per adult.

EATING

Aveiro has some excellent **restaurants** that serve local specialities such as eels and shellfish from the lagoons, usually served fried, with rice (*arroz*), or as a stew (*ensopado*), and accompanied by powerful Bairrada wine. You should also try the celebrated Aveiros *ovos moles*, which are very sweet, candied egg yolks.

Adamasor Travessa do Lavadouro 1 ☎234 347 777. Despite the spacious dining area on two floors of a building facing the fish market, this bare-brick *cervejaria* fills up fast with diners seated at its wooden benches, thanks to the enormous portions of fantastic fresh fish, as well as dishes such as *caril de gambas* (prawn curry), *arroz de marisco* (€30 for two) and a few meat dishes from €12–15. Daily 11am–2am.
Alexandre Cais do Alboi 14 ☎234 425 641. A very popular local *churrasqueira*, with grilled meats – quail to steaks – a speciality, but also offering a good selection of fish and seafood, with mains from €9. Mon–Wed & Fri–Sun noon–10pm.
★ **Mercado do Peixe** Largo da Praça do Peixe ☎234 383 511. In the rafters of the fish market, with crisp decor, attentive service and exceedingly fresh fish and seafood for around €10–17, as well as a range of steaks with

various sauces from €15. There's also a good-value weekday lunch deal, and great views out to the Ria or to the square below from the tiny terrace. Mon–Sat noon–3pm & 7.30–11pm, Sun noon–3pm.
O Mercantel Rua António dos Santos 16 ☎234 428 057. Set up by a former fishmarket worker, as you'd expect this place excels in fresh fish such as John Dory, squid and lobster, with mains from €10–17. The *arroz de marisco* (€45 for two) is excellent. Tues–Sun 11.30am–11.30pm.
★ **O Telheiro** Largo da Praça do Peixe 20–21 ☎234 429 473. At this buzzy *adega*, you can sit at the bar, or at rustic wooden benches and tiled tables. It serves a good range of tapas-style starters (all €4–6), tender beef (try the *bife á caçarola*), *enguias fritas* (fried eels) and a terrific *lulas grelhados* (grilled squid); main courses range from €10–16. Tues–Sun noon–10.30pm.

DRINKING AND NIGHTLIFE

The liveliest **bar area** is immediately around the fish market, where tables are scattered across the cobbles. A ten-minute walk from here, there's another line of late-opening canal-side bars along **Cais de São Roque**, some set in renovated salt storage barns. The town's big annual festival is the **Festa da Ria** (last two weeks of Aug), celebrated with boat races, folk dances, and competitions for the best decorated *barcos moliceiros*. The other major event is the **Festa de São Gonçalinho** (second week of Jan).

Caffè da Praça Rua António Santos Lé 18. Downstairs is a fashionable *tasca* where you can buy drinks and *petiscos* (snacks), while upstairs, you'll find a trendy bar with large windows overlooking the canal. Tasca Mon–Sat 7pm–2am; bar daily 9pm–4am.
Casa de Chá Rua Dr Barbosa Magalhães 9–11 ☎916 842 029. Part of the otherwise modest Art Nouveau Museum, this is a great little tea room and bar (also accessed from Travessa do Rossio) that serves tea, cakes and coffee by day and a mean range of cocktails by night. There's a piano to play and a terrace strewn with beanbags. Tues–Thurs 9.30am–2am, Fri & Sat 9am–3am, Sun 11am–9pm.
Clandestino Rua do Tenente Resende 35 ☎960 000 000. There's no sign, and it's easy to miss this fashionable bar, but you should recognize it by its dark-red exterior and location bang next to the Evangelical church. A DJ plays

jazzy, relaxed tunes. Mon–Sat 10pm–3am.
★ **Mercado Negro** Rua João Mendonça 17–2 ⓦmercadonegro-aveiro.blogspot.com. On the top floor of one of the old buildings that looks down on the central canal, this "cultural collective" retains the building's ornate fixtures but fills the space with simple tables, installation art and students drinking coffee and cocktails. It also regularly hosts films, concerts, theatre and other events. July–Sept Tues–Thurs & Sun 9pm–2am, Fri & Sat 9pm–3am; Oct–June Tues 9pm–2am Wed, Thurs & Sun 5pm–2am, Fri & Sat 5pm–3am.
Tertúlia Toc Aqui Praça do Peixe ☎913 006 553. Fashionable fish-market bar, whose name (which isn't signed – it's the one with the blue facade) means "play here", and on more raucous nights, that's exactly what you can do with the instruments that hang on the back wall. Daily 10pm–2am.

SHOPPING

Forum Aveiro Rua Batalhão de Caçadores 10 ☎234 379 500, ⊛forumaveiro.com. On the south side of the bridge, by the canal, this huge shopping mall should cater to your every shopping need, with a whole panoply of local and international shops (Benetton, Levi's, Mango, Body Shop and the like) as well as a Pingo Doce supermarket, restaurants, cinema screens and even a roof garden. Most shops daily 10am–11pm.

DIRECTORY

Football The local club, Beira Mar (⊛www.beiramar.pt), usually do pretty well in Portugal's top league, though rarely get near to filling their state-of-the-art stadium (capacity 32,800) which was built for the 2004 European Championships.

Hospital Hospital Distrital, Av Dr Artur Ravara ☎234 378 300, ⊛hidpedro.min-saude.pt.
Police Praça Marquês de Pombal ☎234 302 510, ⊛psp.pt.
Post office Praça Marquês de Pombal 23 ☎234 380 840 (Mon–Fri 9am–6pm).

Praia de Mira

3

South of Aveiro, **PRAIA DE MIRA** is the only resort of any size until you reach the full-scale development of Figueira. Though very quiet out of season, for most of the year it's a lively place set on a small lagoon known as **Barrinha**, its cobbled quayside planted with palms. Its one long main street spears past the lagoon towards the sea, where a seemingly endless duned beach stretches to either side. It's ideal for beach-lounging, though the resort also makes an ideal base for local walks or cycling (see box below).

The coastline immediately south of Praia de Mira consists of a virtually deserted thirty-kilometre stretch of stupendous beaches, mostly backed by pine trees, planted to stabilize the low-lying dunes. The sands are only easily accessible at a couple of points – **Praia de Tocha**, with its unusual wooden fisherman's houses, around 12km south of Praia de Mira; and the even quieter **Praia de Quiaios** (pronounced Key-aysh), another 11km south (avoid the extremely rutted forest road to get here). Both are popular summer resorts but dead out of season, and you'll need a car to get to them.

ARRIVAL, INFORMATION AND ACTIVITIES   PRAIA DE MIRA

By bus There are infrequent direct buses from Aveiro (1 daily; 1hr), Figueira da Foz (2 daily; 45min) and Coimbra (1–2 daily; 1hr 15min), but you'll usually have to change in Mira, the inland town 7km to the east.
Information The turismo (daily July & Aug 9.30am–12.30pm & 2–6pm; Sept–June Tues–Sat 9am–1pm & 2–5pm, Sun 2–5.30pm; ☎231 472 566, ⊛cm-mira.pt), on Av da Barra, is a restored *palheiro* (hayloft), built on stilts by the water and once typical of the region – it now doubles as a small museum dedicated to Mira's traditions and trades.
Surfing Surf lessons (around €25) and equipment hire are offered by Secret Surf School (☎968 422 146, ⊛secretsurfschool.com).

ACCOMMODATION AND EATING

A Cozinha Avenida da Barrinha ☎231 471 190. The most appealing of the line of places facing the lagoon is the modern *A Cozinha*, where you can sit outside and eat fresh fish or the likes of octopus rice and *feijoada*; mains from €8. Daily noon–3pm & 7.30–midnight.
Mira Villas Aldeamento Mira Villas, ☎231 470 100,

HIKES AND CYCLING ROUND PRAIA DE MIRA

Praia de Mira is very well set up in terms of local walks and cycle routes. The tourist office has leaflets detailing two great walks: the **Route of the Lakes** is a four-hour route round the Barrinha lagoon inland to the Lagoa de Mira and back, while the **Route of the Mills** is a little longer walk via a series of watermills. Alternatively, you can follow the **Pista Ciclo-pedonal**, a 25km cycle route that heads inland along canals towards Mira then north towards Aveiro. You can hire bikes from Veículógico on the main Avenida Brasil 8 (daily 9am–8pm; €11 a day or around €2.50 an hour; ☎931 446 269, ⊛veiculogico.pt).

ⓦ miravillas.com. The upmarket *Mira Villas* is around 2km from the village, close to the lagoon. Set in an exclusive tourist development, it's a modern four-star with its own pool, bar and restaurant. The rooms have small kitchenettes and some have balconies, but you'll need a car to get here. **€125**

Pousada de Juventude Parque Campismo de Jovens ⓣ 231 472 288, ⓦ microsites.juventude.gov.pt/portal /en. The seasonal youth hostel is signposted from the road by the *Orbitur* campsite – advance bookings are essential, as it's usually busy with groups. Only open June–Aug. Dorm beds €̄12̄; doubles €̄27̄

Senhora da Conceição Avenida Cidade de Coimbra 217 ⓣ 231 471 645, ⓦ hotelsradaconceicao.com. On the main avenue by the lagoon and GALP station, this two-star hotel is a good budget option – ask for one of the rooms at the back, which have lagoon views over the rooftops. **€65**

Figueira da Foz

Facing what the town claims to be Europe's widest beach, **FIGUEIRA DA FOZ** is the largest and most bustling seaside resort on this coast, its fabulous beach attracting a vibrant holiday crowd throughout the summer. It's not immediately attractive – ugly high-rises line up along the seafront – though the tight grid of **central old town** streets around the casino brim with shops and pavement cafés that give this working port its own distinct identity.

Most summer visitors, however, are here for the enormous sandy town **beach** which is 2km long and very wide – it takes a good ten minutes to reach the sea across the sands: waves here can be pretty huge, making it a popular spot for **surfers**, who also frequent the nearby **Praia do Cabadelo**, on the other side of the Rio Mondego. At the southern end of the beach are the remains of an old sea fort, Forte de Santa Catarina, and the **Mercado Municipal** (daily 7am–7pm, closes 4pm from Oct–March), good for fresh produce as well as beachwear, lace, embroidery and other crafts.

Museu Municipal Dr Santos Rocha

Rua Calouste Gulbenkian • June to mid-Sept Tues–Sun 9.30am–5.15pm, Sat & Sun 2–6.45pm; mid-Sept to May Tues–Fri 9.30am–5.15pm, Sat & Sun 2–5.15pm • €2

On the edge of the town park, Parque das Abadias, the **Museu Municipal Dr Santos Rocha** displays an impressive collection of items partly amassed by the renowned local collector and archeologist Dr Santos Rocha. It includes a number of fascinating items from Portugal's former colonies, such as Indo-Portuguese furniture and African instruments, as well as some religious sculptures, ancient coins and an impressive archeological section.

Buarcos

Figueira's seafront road and promenade are lined with apartment buildings and cafés as far as the suburb of **Buarcos** at the northern end, 25 minutes' walk away. This is the nicest part of Figueira, with a row of candy-striped fish restaurants right on the beach and a huddle of pastel-coloured fishermen's houses lurking behind what remains of the old defensive sea wall. It's also home to the tiny **Núcleo Museológico do Mar** at Rua Governador Soares Nogeuria 32 (ⓦ figueiradigital.com; Tues–Fri 9.30am–12.45pm & 2–4.45pm, Sat & Sun 2–6.45pm; closes 5pm from Oct–April; free), which records the area's former seafaring life, and explores how fishing and fishermen have shaped the town with models, photos, pictures and diagrams.

Serra da Boa Viagem and Parque Aventura

Parque Aventura Serra da Boa Viagem • May–Sept daily 10am–9pm • 2hr €10, 3hr €15 • ☎ 916 536 555, ⓦ lusoaventura.com

North of Buarcos and the Cabo Mondego headland, the **Serra da Boa Viagem** is a hilly, wooded reserve with shaded picnic areas and woodland walks, including one detailed on a turismo pamphlet (*Rota da Boa Viagem*). You can test your climbing skills here at the **Parque Aventura**, an aerial forest adventure course with zip wires, rope bridges, clamber nets and treetop obstacles – there's a height and age restriction on some of the routes. From central Figueira, the Serra is a ten-minute drive or an energetic 30-minute cycle; follow the signpost from the coastal road at the end of Buarcos.

AN ESTUARY WALK NEAR FIGUEIRA DA FOZ

Figueira da Foz turismo has details of several waymarked walks in the area, including the four-kilometre **Rota das Salinas**, an interesting estuary route around the saltpans that you glimpse from the bridge on the way into town. The walk begins 7km out of Figueira, at Armazens de Lavas, where you can leave your car by the small Núcleo Museológico do Sal (Wed–Sun 10.30am–12.30pm & 2–6.30pm; mid-Sept to April closes at 4pm and on Wed; €1), which details the history of salt production in these parts. Salt has been produced in the Mondego estuary for almost a thousand years, and around fifty *salinas* still operate between May and September each year. A boardwalk leads out across the saltpans, past weatherbeaten plank huts with salt bags piled outside. The well-signposted circular route takes about an hour (at a brisk stroll), through a pretty estuarine habitat of hedgerow flowers, rustling stands of bamboo and salt-tolerant shrubs. Black-winged stilts and other estuarine birds are a common sight, while the return leg of the path runs along the muddy banks of the Mondego, where a few fishermen still eke out a living from their painted wooden boats.

ARRIVAL AND DEPARTURE

By bus The bus station is on Av Saraiva de Carvalho, a twenty-minute walk east of the town centre and beach.

Destinations Aveiro (3–4 daily; 1hr); Caldas da Rainha (3–4 daily; 2hr); Coimbra (hourly; 1hr–1hr 15min); Leiria (9 daily; 1hr); Lisbon (2–5 daily; 2hr 45min–3hr).

By car Parking can be tricky in August but there's plenty of space during the rest of the year, either in the huge free car park near the clock tower (good for campervans) or anywhere along the long promenade, heading northwards.

By train The train station is next to the bus station on Largo da Estação.

Destinations Caldas da Rainha (3 daily; 2hr); Coimbra (hourly; 1hr–1hr 10min); and Leiria (2–4 daily; 1hr).

By taxi There's a rank outside the train station or call Radio Taxis ☎ 233 420 880.

GETTING AROUND

By bus Buses to Buarcos run from outside the bus and train stations (Mon–Fri every 30min, Sat & Sun hourly), also stopping in town at Rua da Liberdade. Regular buses to Praia do Cabadelo (Mon–Fri every 40min, Sat hourly, Sun every 2hr) leave from near the Jardim Municipal.

INFORMATION AND ACTIVITIES

Information Figueira da Foz turismo (daily 9.30am–1pm & 2.30–6pm; ☎ 233 422 610, ⓦ figueiraturismo.com) is on Avenida 25 de Abril, in the parade of cafés near the clock tower. There's another in Buarcos at the museum, just back from the seafront at Rua Governador Soares Nogueira 32 (Mon–Fri 9am–12.45pm & 2–4.45pm; ☎ 233 433 019).

Waterpark Aquapark, Av Dom João II 70, Cabo Mondego, Buarcos (mid-June–mid-Sept daily 10.30am–7pm; €8; ☎ 233 402 720, ⓦ teimoso.com), is a fun water-park with slides, chutes, a kids' play area and restaurant.

Football The local club, Naval (ⓦ naval1demaio.net) plays at the small Estádio Municipal, Apertado 2052, and has spent a few seasons bobbing between the top and second divisions.

Surfing Escola de Surf da Figueira at Praia do Cabadelo (☎ 233 412 413, ⓦ surfingfigueira.com) offers lessons and also rents out surf gear.

Swimming pool Piscina de Mar, Av 25 de Abril (June–Sept 10am–8pm; €7; ☎ 961 791 921), is a popular outdoor saltwater swimming pool, with a terrace and bar.

ACCOMMODATION

Aliança Rua Miguel Bombarda 12 ☎ 233 422 197, ⓦ hotelalianca.net. One block from the seafront, this has light, well-presented rooms (double-glazed windows, cable TV and wi-fi), some with balconies where you can sneak a view of the sea. There's a pleasant bar and restaurant downstairs. **€80**

Aviz Rua Dr Lopes Guimarães 16 ☎ 233 422 635, ⓦ site .pensaoresidencialaviz.com. This well-cared-for place with a friendly owner is on a quiet side-street, not far from the seafront, and you can park outside. Rooms are on the small and chintzy side, but are good quality with polished wooden floors, carved furniture, double-glazing and cable TV. **€60**

Costa de Prata Largo Coronel Galhardo 1 ☎ 233 426 620, ⓦ costadeprata.com. Recently renovated, this hotel is right on the seafront with some neat Art Nouveau touches: director's lamps and muted decor in the communal areas, a top-floor breakfast room and front rooms which boast fab sea views – avoid the back rooms which lack a view and have yet to be modernized. **€75**

★ **Paintshop Hostel & Bar** Rua Clemencia 9 ☎ 233 436 633, ⓦ paintshophostel.com. In the old part of town, this is a great English-run hostel with high-ceilinged dorms sleeping up to six, and three comfortable double rooms with shared bathroom on the top floor, all in a deceptively large townhouse. There's a communal kitchen/lounge with pool table, patio area and bar for sports TV and film nights. The very friendly owners can arrange surf lessons, bike hire and theme nights (bar crawls, pizza and barbecues). Free wi-fi and parking. Closed end Oct to March. Dorm beds **€20**; doubles **€50**

Sãozinha Ladeira do Monte 43 ☎ 233 425 243, ⓦ hospedariasaozinha.com. A family-run place that offers quiet, spotlessly clean en-suite rooms with tiled floors, rugs and dark-wood furniture: some have streetside balconies. It's a cool oasis, with parking outside, a 15min walk from the beach (it's signposted off Praça 8 de Maio). No breakfast available, but there's a café-*pastelaria* in the square. **€50**

Wellington Rua Dr Calado 23–27 ☎ 233 426 767, ⓦ lupahoteis.com. A reasonable, modern and central hotel, the three-star *Wellington*, three blocks from the beach, has tasteful rooms with en-suite bathrooms, cable TV and wi-fi, as well as its own bar. **€85**

EATING

Caçarola I Rua Cândido dos Reis 65 ☎ 233 424 861. Shellfish bar and restaurant with daily specials of crab, lobster, clams and the like – or if you're feeling brave, cow's hoof. There's a streetside deck for alfresco dining, and it's open late. Mains start at around €10–12. Daily 10am–2am.

3

3

Gelataria San Remo Largo D.M. Barraca 26, Buarcos ☎ 233 425 309. Something of a Buarcos institution, this is renowned for its fabulous crêpes, waffles and Italian ice cream, which come in an array of exotic flavours from around €1.50 a scoop; or you can just call in for a drink. It's in a lovely high-ceilinged former townhouse with a fine outdoor terrace facing the beach. Daily 8am–2am; Oct–March closes at midnight.

★ **Lisfoz** Rua Dr Francisco António Dinis 57 ☎ 233 429 203. This good-value *churrasqueira* serves up the best sardines in town (with the awards to prove it) but also has a decent menu of chicken, grilled squid and other grills from €5–10. Daily noon–3pm & 7–midnight.

Núcleo Sportinguista Rua Praia da Fonte 14–17 ☎ 233 434 882. You pay a little more if you're not a member of the Sporting Lisboa supporters club, but it's still a real bargain for the set meals (€8) in this buzzy

glass building. The menu features fish (salmon, octopus rice and the like) or meat (grilled chicken, pork etc) as well as a soup starter. Go for the mixed fish (around €7.50) and they'll keep refilling your plate, too. Daily 12.15–3pm & 7.15–10pm.

O Ferreiro Rua Capitão Guerra 4, Buarcos ☎ 233 421 403. This simple restaurant, just back from the Buarcos roundabout, is very reasonably priced (meat and fish dishes €9–12) with some less-usual options, such as vegetarian dishes and beef stroganoff. Daily noon–11pm.

★ **Plataforma** Avenida Infante D. Pedro, Praia de Buarcos ☎ 233 422 055. Right on the beach at the Buarcos end, by the car park, this is great for fish and shellfish with a sea view. It's not cheap – around €25 a head – but the fish is straight from the boat, and the daily specials are chalked on a board, from barnacles to lobster. Daily 11am–11pm.

DRINKING AND NIGHTLIFE

BARS AND CLUBS

Cristal Rua Académico Zagalo 28. This smart little bar is popular after dark for its lively streetside terrace – inside, DJs play music late into the night. Tues–Thurs 8pm–2am, Fri & Sat 8pm–4am.

NB Club Rua Cândido dos Reis ☎ 916 455 943, ⓦ noitebiba.pt. Inside the original casino building and opposite the new one, this is Figueira's top dance venue, with two dancefloors usually playing House or disco, though it doesn't warm up until well after midnight. Sat 11pm–6am; open other nights for specific events.

Oásis Avenida do Brasil, Praia da Claridade ☎ 233 413 236. You can't miss this bar-restaurant right on the beach: just look for the area of palm trees that gives it its name. Food is pricey here, but a sunset drink on the terrace is a treat. Tues–Sat 10.30am–10pm, Sun 10.30am–4pm.

Perfumaria Pub Rua Dr Calado 37 ☎ 233 426 442. A laidback, wood-panelled, arty bar on two levels connected

by a spiral staircase, with a pool table and a good (if pricey) cocktail list. Daily 5pm–4am.

★ **Zeitgeist Café** Rua Francisco António Dinis 82–84 ☎ 233 429 759. This modern café-bar serves a decent selection of cocktails and there's a DJ set and live music most Wednesdays (from midnight). Daily 5pm–4am.

ART AND ENTERTAINMENT

Casino Figueira Rua Dr Calado 1 ⓦ casinofigueira .com. One of the north's glamorous nights out, though not that exclusive. There's a fancy bar, all the usual games and slot machines, as well as frequent concerts and shows. Daily 3pm–3am.

Centro de Artes e Espectáculos Rua Abade Pedro ☎ 233 407 200, ⓦ cae.pt. Concerts, art-house movies, events and exhibitions are all staged at this modern cultural centre near the municipal museum.

DIRECTORY

Hospital Across the river: Hospital Distrital da Figueira da Foz, Gala, São Pedro ☎ 233 402 000, ⓦ hdfigueira.min -saude.pt.

Laundry Lavanderia Tinturaria Figueirense, Rua Cândido

dos Reis 15 ☎ 233 422 382.

Police PSP, Rua de Mortágua ☎ 233 407 560.

Post office Passeio Infante Dom Henrique 41–42 (Mon– Fri 9am–6pm).

Montemor-o-Velho

Thirty-two kilometres west of Coimbra, the keep and crenellated silhouette of the castle at **MONTEMOR-O-VELHO** brood over the flood plain of the Mondego. After it was taken back from the Moors at the end of the eleventh century, Montemor became a favoured royal residence – it was here in 1355 that Dom Afonso IV met with his council to decide on the fate of Inês de Castro, and here, thirty years later, that João of Avis received the homage of the townspeople on his way to Coimbra to be acclaimed Dom João I. Despite this royal attention, the town never really prospered, and there's not a lot to modern-day Montemor-O-Velho, though come on the second and fourth Wednesday of the month and you can experience the sprawling morning **market** which spills across the plain in the lee of the castle.

Castelo de Montemor-o-Velho

Rua Condessa de Valenças • Tues–Sun: June–Sept 10am–7pm; Oct–May 10am–5pm • Free • ☎ 239 687 316

Originally built in the thirteenth century, but with sixteenth-century additions, the **Castelo de Montemor-o-Velho** has little to see inside, save a Manueline church with a beautiful wooden ceiling, said to have been designed by Diogo de Boitaca of Belém fame. However, the views from the walkways are stunning, the lawns are a good place to let children run free and there's a nice terrace-café.

ARRIVAL AND DEPARTURE

MONTEMOR–O–VELHO

By bus Roughly hourly weekday Moisés buses (fewer at weekends) stop at Montemor-o-Velho en route between Figueira da Foz (30min) and Coimbra (1hr; ⓦ moises-transportes.pt).

By train The nearest train station is five kilometres southwest of town at Alfarelos, with regular services from Coimbra (every 30min; 35min) and Figueira da Foz line (every 30min; 35min). A taxi between the station and Montemor-o-Velho costs around €6.

EATING

A Grelha Avenida Fernão Mendes Pinto 3148 ☎ 239 689 372. Below the castle on the main street, this is the best place for lunch or an evening meal. The speciality is *charruscão da quinta*, a giant mixed grill, although the fresh fish is also good – try the sardines. Mains around €8. Sun–Fri 11am–11pm.

Beira Alta and Beira Baixa

SORTELHA

Beira Alta and Beira Baixa

The two historic mountain provinces of Beira Alta (Upper) and Beira Baixa (Lower) feature some of the most spectacular landscapes in the country, from upland plains of enormous boulders to towering mountain peaks. This harsh but beautiful landscape was home to the mighty warrior Viriatus, who used its remote wildness to his advantage when repelling the Romans. Later, as Portugal strived for nationhood, many of the towns near the disputed border with Spain acquired mighty castles, still in existence today.

The ancient town of **Viseu** is the capital of Beira Alta province and the only place of any real size in the region. The fast east–west A25 links Viseu to the mountain-top town of **Guarda** – with Spain another 40km to the east – while to the north, between the highway and the Douro River, are the high-sited castle-towns of the **planalto** (or tableland). Some, like medieval, walled **Trancoso**, or the star-shaped fortress town of **Almeida**, are worth a day of anyone's time.

South of the main highway rises the **Serra da Estrela** mountain range, whose landscape is protected under the auspices of the **Parque Natural da Serra da Estrela**. Mountain villages, tumbling rivers and glacial valleys are linked by an extensive series of hiking trails, though there's also road access to the major settlements, notably the enjoyable small town of **Manteigas**. The park's southeastern boundary is flanked by the university town of **Covilhã**, handy for the winter ski fields and the ascent of Portugal's highest mountain, Torre.

South and east of Covilhã lies the sombre plain of the lower province, **Beira Baixa**, whose parched landscape has its own mysterious beauty, dotted with cork, carob and olive trees. **Castelo Branco** in the south is the provincial capital, but most tourist attention is centred on the ancient hilltop villages rising dramatically from the surrounding plains, notably **Sortelha** and **Monsanto**. There's historic interest, too, in pretty **Belmonte**, halfway between Covilhã and Guarda, and in the extensive Roman remains at isolated **Idana-a-Velha**. Meanwhile, in the border hills and reservoirs of the **Serra da Malcata**, there are hiking, biking and wildlife-spotting opportunities.

Viseu

On a plateau between the coast and the mountains, VISEU was named "Viso" by the Romans because of its great views, and it was from an embankment just outside town that Viriatus, the head of a local independence movement, waged war against its Roman occupiers. According to most polls, modern Viseu has the best quality of city life in Portugal, and it doesn't take long to find out why. Its **old town**, clustered round a sturdy cathedral, is wonderfully unspoilt, while a burgeoning modern town is made up of wide avenues, leafy parks, a university and diverse array of shops, including the eye-popping **Palácio do Gelo** shopping centre. The town is also close to some of Portugal's best vineyards: fruity local Dão wines can be found in all of the restaurants.

NATURAL SWIMMING POOL, SERRA DA ESTRELA

Highlights

❶ Museu de Grão Vasco, Viseu Explore the works of one of Portugal's greatest artists in Viseu's fine museum. **See p.221**

❷ Trancoso This beautifully preserved, walled town is the best overnight stop in the Beira Alta tableland. **See p.228**

❸ Fortified walls of Almeida The extraordinary fortifications here are built in the form of a twelve-pointed star. **See p.232**

❹ Hiking in the Parque Natural da Serra da Estrela The mountain town of Manteigas is the best base for *serra* walks, including the half-day circuit to the Poço do Inferno waterfall. **See p.237**

❺ Belmonte An unsung treasure of a town, from the picturesque castle to its restored Jewish quarter. **See p.245**

❻ Village stay, Sortelha Stay the night in one of the restored houses in this walled village. **See p.247**

❼ Monsanto Houses hewn out of granite cling to a boulder-strewn hillside below a formidable castle. **See p.249**

❽ Idanha-a-Velha A mysterious ancient village set amid the burned plains of Beira Baixa. **See p.251**

HIGHLIGHTS ARE MARKED ON THE MAP ON P.220

The main annual event is the agricultural fair-cum-festival of the **Feira de São Mateus** which runs from mid-August until its climax on September 21 (Dia do São Mateus).

The old town

The lower town centres on the large square outside the town hall, known as the **Rossio**, from where you can climb up to the granite **Porta do Soar**, the fortified gateway to the jumble of alleys of the old town immediately behind the cathedral. Near the Rossio, up a tiled staircase on Rua Almeida Moreira, the attractive **Museu Almeida Moreira** has an eclectic display of art, furniture and porcelain in the former home of local collector Francisco Almeida Moreira (daily 10am–12.30pm & 2–5.30pm; free; ☎ 232 423 769).

BEIRA ALTA & BEIRA BAIXA

0   25
kilometres

N

HIGHLIGHTS

1 Museu Grão Vasco, Viseu
2 Trancoso
3 Fortified walls of Almeida
4 Hiking in the Parque Natural da Serra da Estrela
5 Belmonte
6 Village stay, Sortelha
7 Monsanto
8 Idanha-a-Velha

SPAIN

SPAIN

Otherwise, **Rua Direita** offers a second approach to the old town, along a winding medieval street that mixes boutiques and gift shops with key-cutters, florists, grocers and undertakers, many of the buildings displaying sixteenth-century Manueline windows and coats of arms. At the northern end of Rua Direita – just beyond the theatre, on the main avenue – stands the other surviving town gate, the **Porta dos Cavaleiros**. Beyond here, on the outskirts of town, lies the **Parque do Fontelo**, a municipal park laid out across the woods and gardens of the old bishop's palace.

The Sé

Praça da Sé · **Cathedral & cloisters** Daily 8am–noon & 2–7pm · Free · **Sacred Art Museum** Tues–Fri 9–noon & 2–5pm, Sat 2–5pm · €2.50

The wide cathedral square, Praça da Sé, is lined with noble stone buildings, including the striking twin-towered **Sé**, a Romanesque-Gothic cathedral built in the thirteenth century, but substantially added to over the years. The interior is truly striking, with a ribbed stone ceiling typical of Manueline architecture, while the neighbouring cloisters have some very attractive *azulejos*. Above the cloisters, the Sacred Art Museum houses the cathedral's rather uninsipiring religious art and sculpture collection, though it also has great views over the town and square.

Museu de Grão Vasco

Adro da Sé · Tues 2–6pm, Wed–Sun 10am–6pm · €4, free on Sun until 2pm · ☎ 232 422 049, ⓦ ipmuseus.pt

Inside the former Bishop's palace next to the cathedral, the **Museu de Grão Vasco** displays religious paintings and artefacts, including some beautiful Oriental porcelain and textiles. Its main appeal, however, is the paintings by local boy Vasco Fernandes, better known as "The Great Vasco" (Grão Vasco) and widely acknowledged as one of Portugal's best painters (see box below). His earliest work on display here is the fourteen panels tracing the *Life of Christ* (1501–06), which was commissioned for the altarpiece of Viseu cathedral – note the vivid *Adoration of the Magi* which topically presents Balthasar as a Brazilian-inspired Indian with feathered headdress (Brazil had been "discovered" by the Portuguese in 1500). His most famous work is *St Peter on His Throne* (1530–35) – the painting has been mounted freestanding so that you can see how the original frame and canvas were assembled.

4

ARRIVAL AND INFORMATION | VISEU

By bus The bus station is down Avenida Dr António José de Almeida, a five-minute walk from the Rossio.

Destinations Castelo Branco (2–5 daily; 2hr 30min–3hr); Coimbra (approx hourly; 1hr 15min–1hr 25min); Covilhã (approx hourly; 1hr 40min–2hr); Guarda (3–8 daily; 1hr 15min); Lisbon (hourly; 3hr 30min); Luso-Buçaco (5–7 daily; 1hr 45min); Mangualde (2–3 daily; 20min); and Porto (hourly; 1hr 45min).

By car There's metered parking all over the centre (free after 8pm, 2pm on Sat, and all Sun), though there's a four-hour limit – it's better to use the open-air car park on Rua do Hospital, by the *pousada*, where there's no time limit and you pay when you leave.

Information The turismo (mid-June to mid-Sept Mon–Fri 9am–8pm, Sat & Sun 9am–1pm & 2.30–6pm; rest of the year Mon–Fri 9am–6pm, Sat & Sun 9.30am–12.30pm

GRÃO VASCO AND GASPAR VAZ

Little is known about Vasco Fernandes, universally known as **Grão Vasco**; it can only be said that he was born in or near the city of Viseu, probably in 1475, and that he died in 1542 or 1543. There was no major artist living in Viseu at the time to mentor the young Vasco Fernandes, so it's assumed that he trained in Lisbon or even abroad. Even more problematic for art historians is that virtually all the works associated with him – up to 100 by some counts – have had to be identified by comparisons with the only two that he definitely signed, and with his known work on the surviving altar panels for Lamego and Viseu cathedrals. In many cases, his attributed works are collaborations, particularly with his Viseu contemporary **Gaspar Vaz** (1490–1569).

▲ Aveiro, Lamego, Chaves & Vila Real

VISEU

■ **ACCOMMODATION**
Avenida	6
Casa de Sé	2
Palácio dos Melos	3
Pousada de Juventude	1
Pousada de Viseu	7
Quinta d'Arroteia	5
Rossio Parque	4

Monument to Viriato

Casa da Ribeira

Rio Pavia

Weekly Market

LARGO CAST ANHEIRO DOS AMORES

R. DOS LOUREIROS

AVENIDA EMIDIO NAVARRO

AV. DOS CAPITEIS

AVENIDA EMIDIO NAVARRO

CALÇADA DE VIRIATO

RUA DOM JOSE DA CRUZ MOREIRA PINTO

AVENIDA DR. ANTONIO JOSÉ DE ALMEIDA

Porta Dos Cavaleiros

Teatro Viriato

LARGO MOUZINHO ALBUQUERQUE

Bus Station

RUA SERPA PINTO

RUA SILVA GAIO

CALÇADA DA VIGIA

Igreja da Misericórdia

PRAÇA DA SÉ

RUA SOAR DE CIMA

L. PINTOR GATA

Porta do Soar

RUA ALMEIDA MOREIRA

Museu Almeida Moreira

Museu Grão Vasco

R. DAS AMEIAS

Sé

RUA DIREITA

RUA DO GONÇALINHO

PRAÇA DOM DUARTE

RUA AUGUSTO HILARIO

RUA DR. LUÍS FERREIRA

RUA DOM DUARTE

RUA DIREITA

RUA ARVÔRE

AVENIDA SILVA PEREIRA

RUA DE JOÃO MENDES

Jardim das Mães

R. DO CARMO

LARGO DA SANT A CRISTINA

Câmara Municipal

PRAÇA DA REPÚBLICA (ROSSIO)

RUA FORMOSA

★ Taxi rank

AVENIDA ALBERTO SAMPAIO

RUA DA PAZ

R. VITORIA

LARGO GENERAL HUMBERTO DELGADO

RUA A. LOBO

RUA 5 DE OUTUBRO

R. CANDIDO REIS

Igreja dos Terceiros de São Francisco

RUA MIGUEL BOMBARDA

Igreja do Carmo

AVENIDA 25 DE ABRIL

RUA GASP AR BARREIROS

RUA DOM ATONIO ALVES MARTINS

Police Station

Parque Aquilino Ribeiro

RUA A. HERCULANO

AV. CANDIDO GUISMARÃO

RUA DO HOSPITAL

P

RUA J. BARROS

■ **BARS AND CLUBS**
Água Benta	2
Bar do Gelo	5
Hangar	1
Irish Bar	3
NB Club	4

● **RESTAURANTS**
Cacimbo	4
Casa dos Queijos	1
O Cortiço	2
O Hilário	3

0		100
	metres	

◄ Vouzela

► Parque do Fontelo & Campsite

► S. Mangualde, Guarda & Spain

4

& 1.30–5.30pm; ☎ 232 420 950, ⓦ turismodocentro.pt) in Casa do Adro on Adro da Sé has information about the whole region, including a booklet detailing the local archeological sites.

ACCOMMODATION

Avenida Av Alberto Sampaio 1 ☎ 232 423 432, ⓦ hotel avenida.com.pt. The location is excellent, and it exudes a stately air, with antiques and attractive photos in the communal areas. The smallish rooms and cramped bathrooms don't quite match up though, and there's street noise at the front. **€55**

★ **Casa de Sé** Rua Augusta Cruz 12 ☎ 232 468 032, ⓦ casadase.net. This small luxury hotel doubles as an antiques shop: the period furniture and fittings that decorate the communal areas and rooms are all for sale (from €30 to over €300). The rooms are varied, but all are plush with eighteenth-century flourishes – *azulejo*-lined bathrooms, period lamps, antique chairs and paintings. There's also a downstairs bar and tea room. **€90**

Palácio dos Melos Rua Chão do Mestre 4 ☎ 232 439 290, ⓦ hotelpalaciodosmelos.pt. Right by the Porta do Soar gate, this offers boutique, city-centre accommodation. Superior rooms in the main building retain a period feel, some with balconies; there's a more contemporary style in the annexe and in the classy restaurant. There's also parking – follow signs for Centro Histórico and then Porta do Soar. **€75**

Pousada de Juventude Rua Aristides Sousa Mendes, Portal do Fontelo ☎ 232 413 001, ⓦ microsites .juventude.gov.pt/portal/en. Viseu's backpacker choice is a plain, modern hostel by the main city park, a ten-minute walk northeast of Rossio, with five en-suite rooms and mini-dorms with either four or five beds. Dorm beds **€12**; rooms **€27**

★ **Pousada de Viseu** Rua do Hospital ☎ 232 457 320, ⓦ pousadas.pt. The country's largest *pousada* is a super-stylish conversion of a historic hospital, which opened in 1842 – photographs throughout the building show the work in progress. Spacious cherrywood rooms with granite bays – top-floor ones have terraces – overlook Viseu, while lounge-seats occupy the soaring glass-topped cloister-courtyard. It's a very calm space, with an outdoor pool, titchy indoor pool plus gym, spa (in the former hospital chapel), restaurant and parking. **€120**

Quinta d'Arroteia Póvoa de Sobrinhos, 3km east of town, N16 (Mangualde road) ☎ 232 478 450, ⓦ quinta darroteia.com. Exposed granite walls, a full-sized snooker table, an open fire in winter and a large pool in summer – perfect for a relaxing few days away from it all. No credit cards. **€70**

★ **Rossio Parque** Rua Solar de Cima 55 ☎ 232 422 085, ⓦ pensaorossioparque.com. A real treat if you can land one of the better rooms since they're large and airy, some with a view of the Rossio (though the cheaper rooms are smaller and more cell-like). Breakfast is also good, served in the restaurant downstairs, a popular dinner destination (mains around €10). **€35**

EATING, DRINKING AND NIGHTLIFE

For the cheapest eating, look along Rua Direita where several old-fashioned *tascas* and *casas de pasto* turn out full meals at lunch for around €5. The presence of students means there's a lively nightlife scene, with most of Viseu's late-night **bars** found in the old town near the Sé and Misericórdia churches.

RESTAURANTS

★ **Cacimbo** Rua Alexandre Herculano 95 ☎ 232 422 894, ⓦ cacimbo.pt. This contemporary diner is tops for an utterly reliable meal, with a long menu of fish including an excellent and very nutritious *pescada com todo* (steamed hake with potatoes and egg). Mains are mostly €8–10. Daily 9am–11pm.

Casa dos Queijos Travessa Escadinha da Sé 9 ☎ 232 422 643. In the heart of the old town, the "House of Cheese" is a quirky tavern full of smelly mountain cheeses and – up a narrow, creaky staircase – a traditional restaurant (lunch only) serving grilled meat and fish. Mains around €9. No credit cards. Mon–Sat 8am–8pm.

★ **O Cortiço** Rua Augusto Hilário 45 ☎ 232 423 853. This snug little restaurant boasts walls filled with messages of praise from heartily satisfied customers. The food's strictly traditional and a cut above most in town, and though dishes (*feijoada*, duck rice, roast goat and octopus) range from €13–16, many of them feed two. Daily 11am–11pm.

O Hilário Rua Augusto Hilário 35 ☎ 232 436 587. A friendly place just down from the Sé serving tasty *pataniscos* (cod cakes) and steaks for around €7–9. No credit cards. Mon–Sat 9.30am–11pm.

BARS AND CLUBS

Água Benta Largo da Misericórdia ☎ 232 469 531. Fashionable lounge bar where young professionals go to soak up the mellow atmosphere, with the occasional guest DJ playing the latest sounds – there's a great outdoor terrace. Daily noon–2am.

★ **Bar do Gelo** Palácio do Gelo, Quinta da Alagoa ☎ 232 483 931, ⓦ www.bardegeloviseu.com. Viseu's coolest bar, despite being on the ground floor of a shopping centre. Why? Because the bar itself, the chairs and sculptures are entirely made from permanently cooled ice

4

imported from Canada: it costs €10 to enter, which gives you 30 minutes inside and includes the hire of coat and gloves to keep you warm at -9°C while you down one of their excellent cocktails, from an ice glass. Daily 2pm–midnight.

Hangar Estrada do Aeródromo ☎ 936 014 763. For the determined clubber, there's a cool converted aircraft hangar outside the city near the aerodrome (on the Lamego road) where house is played well into the morning. July & Aug Wed & Sat only.

Irish Bar Largo Pintor Gata 7–8 ☎ 232 436 135. This Irish-themed bar draws a mixed crowd and sits on a charming square that catches the afternoon sun, so ideal for an early evening drink. Also has occasional live music. Mon–Sat 8.30am–midnight.

NB Club Rua Conselheiro Afonso de Melo 35 ⓦ noitebiba.pt. The standard choice for Viseu's students, playing a decent mixture of mainstream pop, house and r'n'b (check the website for club nights). Tues–Sat midnight–6am.

SHOPPING

Casa da Ribeira Largo Nossa Sra Conçeição ☎ 232 429 761. The Casa da Ribeira is home to a foundation that aims to maintain traditional arts and crafts, and there's usually someone on hand to show you the working loom and potters' wheel. There's plenty of traditional work to purchase, from the typical black Tondela earthenware to Viseu stained glass and decorative ironwork. There's also studio space where contemporary sculptors, basketweavers and wood restorers work. Tues–Sat 9am–12.30pm & 2–5.30pm.

Mercado The two floors of the domed Mercado Municipal (Mon–Fri 6.30am–7pm, Sat 6.30am–2pm), just west of Rossio (entrance on Av Dr António José de Almeida), are great for fresh food. A bigger weekly market (every

Tuesday), on the ring road by Largo Castanheiro dos Amores, is where Viseu buys its cheap clothes, pirated DVDs and chickens.

Palácio do Gelo Quinta da Alagoa ☎ 232 483 900, ⓦ www.palaciodogelo.pt. Most Portuguese cities boast giant shopping centres these days, but this one is truly impressive, with a basement water feature that blasts a jet of water the full height of its seven floors. As well as the usual panoply of local and international shops (H&M, Benetton, Mango, FNAC), there are also six cinema screens, an ice rink, bowling alley, restaurants and the famous *Bar do Gelo* ice bar (see p.223). It's around 2km from the centre: walk past the *pousada* and keep going. Most shops daily 10am–11pm.

DIRECTORY

Hospital Hospital Distrital de Viseu, Av Rei Dom Duarte ☎ 232 420 500, ⓦ hstviseu.min-saude.pt.

Pharmacy Farmácia Confiança, Rua Formosa 10 ☎ 232 480 340.

Police Rua Dom António Alves Martins ☎ 232 480 380.

Post office Largo General Humberto Delgado (Mon–Fri 9am–7pm).

Taxis There's a rank in Largo da Santa Catarina ☎ 232 478 931.

Mangualde and around

MANGUALDE, 15km east of Viseu along the A25, is a well-to-do town which traditionally flourished thanks to its position on the trading routes between the mountains and the coast. As a result, a tree-lined avenue leads into a centre of noble mansions, pick of which is the tiled baronial eighteenth-century Palácio dos Condes de Anadia (Largo Condes de Anadia; ☎ 232 622 366; Mon–Fri 2–6pm; €5), packed with period furniture and beautiful *azulejos*. Try and visit the town on a Thursday, when the weekly **market** enlivens the central streets.

Live Beach

Av Nossa Senhora do Castelo • June to mid-Sept daily 9am–7pm • €5.50, or €3.50 after 4.30pm • ☎ 282 622 048, ⓦ livebeach.pt

A side road just outside Mangualde is the unlikely setting for **Live Beach**, which locals proudly proclaim is Europe's first artificial beach, complete with 22,000 square metres of sand, salt water and all the paraphernalia associated with a real beach. In reality, it's really just a large swimming pool faced by a flat bank of sand, but on a hot summer's day you'll certainly appreciate the space and chance to soak up the rays, while the bars and restaurant are good value. After 7pm the venue is also used for frequent party nights and concerts; check the website for details.

Termas de Alcafache

Spa Mid-April to mid-Nov • ⓦ termasdealcafache.pt

A couple of kilometres northwest of Mangualde, the **Termas de Alcafache** sit by a Roman-era bridge which crosses the Rio Dão over a rock cleft. It's a charming little spot, with bathing in the gentle river, grassy picnic areas, a signposted riverside walk, and a couple of cafés that put out seats near the bridge. You can also take various treatments in the sulphurous waters at the spa building (see website for prices).

ARRIVAL AND INFORMATION

By bus There are 2–3 daily buses to Mangualde from Viseu (20min) and Guarda (50min).

By train The train station is 2km south of the town centre, on Rua da Estacão with 3 daily services to Guarda (55min) and Coimbra (1hr 10min).

Information Mangualde turismo, Largo Dr Couto (Mon–Fri 9am–5pm, Sat 10am–noon & 2–4pm, Sun 10.30am–noon

MANGUALDE AND AROUND

& 2–3.30pm; ☎ 232 613 980, ⓦ cmmangualde.pt), is adjacent to the Câmara Municipal, and has printed driving and hiking routes available, taking in places such as the Neolithic Anta da Cunha Baixa (signposted "Dolmen" from town, down the railway station road), a dramatic 4000-year-old funerary monument sited in a bucolic vineyard.

ACCOMODATION AND EATING

Casa de Darei Darei ☎ 232 613 200, ⓦ casadedarei.pt. A few kilometres out of Mangualde on the Penalva do Castelo road (north of the A25), in the midst of Dão valley vineyards, *Casa de Darei* is a working winery with both B&B rooms and self-catering apartments, plus a private river beach and hiking and biking trails. **€160**

Moinhos do Dão c/o Café Pinheiro, Rua Principal 27, Tibaldinho ☎ 232 610 586, ⓦ moinhosdodao.nl. Around 10km west of Mangualde (it's signed from the Fagilde exit on the A25) down a 1.5km track (fine for cars, take it slowly), you'll find this supremely relaxed ecofriendly holiday retreat on the Rio Dão. The owners have fashioned cheerily rustic rooms and studios from the old mill

buildings, and there are also wooden chalets. You might have to share a bathroom or fetch your own drinking water, and lighting is almost all by candle, but it's great fun for kids; while veggie-friendly meals are served communally most nights under the spreading fig tree. **€275–325** per week

O Valério Rua dos Combatentes da Guerra 48, Mangualde ☎ 232 611 955. This rustic restaurant (meals from €15) serves portions that are legendary: never mind a *meia-dose* (half-portion), it's the only place in Portugal we've found offering a quarter-portion of most dishes. Fab for pork, duck rice, eels and much more. Mon–Sat noon–3pm & 7.30–10pm.

Guarda

GUARDA, 70km east of Viseu, is Portugal's highest city, at an altitude of over 1000m. A somewhat dour town of solid granite, its name is apt, as the original fortifications helped to guard the residents – and the mountain hinterland – from Spanish invaders. There's not much left of the fortifications, but the old town retains an air of dignified grandeur, especially in the streets around the cathedral. Locals will tell you their city is *forte, farta, fiel e formosa* (strong, wealthy, loyal and beautiful), though come on an overcast winter's day and you may prefer to use *fria e feia* (cold and ugly). Either way, it makes a lively enough base from which to explore the surrounding area.

The Sé and around

Praça Luís de Camões • **Sé** Tues–Sun 10am–1.30pm & 3–6.30pm • Free

The heart of the historic centre is dominated by the **Sé**, a cathedral whose construction took around 150 years to complete (1390–1540). Not surprisingly it embraces various architectural styles, from its fortress-like Gothic exterior – including grotesque gargoyles – to later Manueline flourishes inside, including enormous twisted pillars and an intricate network of stone vaulting supporting the ceiling.

Around the cathedral you can see what's left of Guarda's original medieval fortifications. To the southeast lies the tall **Torre dos Ferreiros** (Blacksmiths' Tower, closed to the public), while the medieval jumble of streets between the old city gates – the **Porta da Erva** and **Porta d'El-Rei** – make up the old Jewish quarter and are the city's most ancient and interesting. You can climb the steps of the **Porta d'El-Rei** for some distant *serra* views.

Torre de Menagem

Daily: April–Sept 10am–1pm & 2–6pm; Oct–March 9am–1pm & 2–5pm • Free • ☎ 217 224 372

To the southwest of the Sé, the former keep, the **Torre de Menagem** is, at 1056 metres, the highest point in the city: there are fantastic views from the top, though it's a scramble up through a hatch in the roof to get there. Inside the keep you can watch a moderately engaging 20-minute 3D film tracing the history of the fortifications and town. Note that at busy times, you may have to wait, as only twenty people can visit the fairly small spaces at a time.

Museu da Guarda

Rua Alves Roçadas 30 • Tues–Sun 10am–12.30pm & 2–5.30pm • €2, free on Sun 10am–12.30pm • ☎ 271 213 460, ⓦ museudaguarda .imc-ip.pt

The city's history, art and culture is explored in the **Museu da Guarda**, housed in the seventeenth-century former seminary and Bishop's palace. There are some interesting Roman and prehistoric objects, sculptures, paintings and historic furniture, though you'd probably only want to visit on a wet day.

ARRIVAL AND DEPARTURE   GUARDA

By bus The bus terminal is on Rua Dom Nuno Álvares Pereira, below the market – it's a fifteen-minute (uphill) walk to the cathedral square.

Destinations Almeida (Mon–Fri 1 daily; 1hr 10min); Belmonte (3 daily; 25–45mins); Braga (2–7 daily; 4hr); Castelo Branco (3–5 daily; 1hr 40min); Coimbra (2–4 daily; 2hr 5min); Covilhã (3–7 daily; 45min); Figueira de Castelo Rodrigo (Mon–Sat 1 daily; 1hr); Lisbon (3–7 daily; 3hr 30min); Manteigas (Mon–Fri 2 daily; 1hr 20min); Sabugal (Mon–Fri every 2hr, Sat 1 daily; 45min); Seia (Fri & Sun 1 daily; 1hr 10min); Trancoso (1 daily on Mon, 2 daily on Fri; 1hr 30min); Vila Nova de Foz Côa (Mon–Fri 1 daily; 1hr 30min–2hr 15 min); and Viseu (3–8 daily; 1hr 15min).

By car There's metered parking (two-hour maximum) all over the town centre, though these spaces are free after 1pm on Saturday and all day Sunday. Alternatively, there's free parking at any time in the square outside the market or along Avenida dos Bombeiros Voluntários Egitanienses.

By train Guarda's train station is 5km northeast and downhill from the town centre, out towards the A25 – there's a regular bus service up to the bus station, and taxis outside.

Destinations Coimbra (6–7 daily; 2hr 30min–3hr); Lisbon (7 daily; 4hr 10min–5hr 25min); Mangualde (3 daily; 55min); and Porto (7 daily; 3hr 50 min–4hr 35min).

INFORMATION AND ACTIVITIES

Information Turismo, Praça Luís de Camões 21 (daily: April–Sept 10am–1pm & 2–6pm; Oct–March 9am–1pm & 2–5pm; ☎ 271 205 530, ⓦ www.mun-guarda.pt).

Kayaking Quebra Águas, Rua da Bela Vista 31 (☎ 963 058 375, ⓦ quebraaguas.pt), offer kayaking tours and other adventure sports in the surrounding district.

ACCOMMODATION

Filipe Rua Vasco da Gama 9 ☎ 271 223 658, ⓦ residencia-filipe.com. Van Gogh prints and marble in the public areas give way to more traditional rooms with parquet floors and heavy wood furniture, not to mention some rather garishly tiled bathrooms. Rooms 103, 104 and 108 have the best views of the church. €40

Pousada de Juventude Av Alexandre Herculano ☎ 271 224 482, ⓦ microsites.juventude.gov.pt/portal /en. At the youth hostel, a ten-minute walk out of the centre, there are ten small four-bed dorms, as well as four double en-suite rooms available. It's next door to a youth centre with free internet access. Dorm beds €13; doubles €28

★ **Santos** Rua Tenente Valadim 14 ☎ 271 205 400, ⓦ residencialsantos.com. Stylishly built around – and through – part of the original medieval city walls, this hotel has a glass lift that rises past suspended internal terraces and exposed stonework to rooms that frame views of the cathedral or countryside within granite sills. Beds are comfortable, and a nice buffet breakfast is included. Street parking almost outside (provided you can find your way there). €45

★ **Solar de Alarcão** Rua Dom Miguel de Alarcão 25–27 ☎ 271 214 392. Magnificent granite manor house

dating back to the seventeenth century. The atmospheric rooms come with huge antique mirrors, chandeliers, carved wooden ceilings and vintage shutters, while secure parking is available in the courtyard. Advance reservations essential. No credit cards. €65

Vanguarda Av Monsenhor Mendes do Carmo ☎ 271 208 390, ⓦ naturaimbhotels.com. The rooms in Guarda's most contemporary hotel feature gleaming bathrooms and sweeping views. It's on the edge of town (15min walk), though drivers will pass it on the way up from the A25 – you can't miss the steel wave-style roof. €50

CAMPSITE

Senses Camping Quinta do Rio, Faia ☎ 910 488 800, ⓦ sensescamping.com. A 15-minute drive (or €15 taxi ride), 8km northwest of Guarda, this stylish "glamping" site is run by a former DJ and sculptor. The rural riverside site has ready-erected bell tents (for 2–4 people, from €35 a night) and luxury "safari" tents (perfect for families, from €45), as well as wooden cabins sleeping two (from €40) and plenty of tranquil pitches. There's an on-site pool, bar and restaurant serving home-grown organic veg, while activities on offer include yoga, massage, arts workshops and horseriding. Pitch €9

4

EATING

Most of the town's **restaurants** are to be found between the Sé and the Igreja de São Vicente, with half a dozen alone squeezed into narrow Rua Francisco dos Passos. There really isn't too much variety on offer, although regional specialities – *chouriçada* (spiced sausage), *morcela* (black pudding), *cabrito* (kid), *javali* (wild boar) and trout from Manteigas – are all widely available.

★ **A Floresta** Rua Franciso dos Passos 40 ☎ 271 212 314. Rustic decor, friendly owners and an atmospheric old-town eating experience. The three-course *ementa turística* is a bargain at under €10, though there's also a long *à la carte* menu with most dishes priced between €6 and €8. Daily noon–4pm & 7–11pm; Oct–April closed Mon.

Aliança Rua Vasco da Gama 8 ☎ 271 222 235. Packed through the week, serving local dishes for local people – so, lots of pork and not much finesse. A good stop for lunch though, with mains around €8.50. Daily noon–2.30pm & 7–9pm.

A Mexicana Av Monsenhor Mendes do Carmo 7 ☎ 271 211 512. One of Guarda's best, and despite the name, the creatively prepared and presented food is Portuguese with a modern twist: fish with shrimp sauce, clam soup and the like for around €20. Mon, Tues & Thurs–Sun noon–11pm.

Belo Horizonte Largo de São Vicente 2 ☎ 271 211 454. A Guarda institution for over sixty years. A kindly old chef and matronly waitresses dish up meals from a menu strong on regional specialities (*chouriçada*, grilled goat, hare stew) that cost between €10 and €13. Tues–Sat 10am–midnight, Sun 10am–4pm.

DIRECTORY

Hospital Hospital Distrital, Av Rainha Dona Amélia ☎ 271 200 200.

Pharmacy Farmácia Central, Largo Dr João Almeida ☎ 271 211 972.

Police Largo Frei Pedro da Guarda ☎ 271 222 022.

Post office Largo João de Deus 22–24 ☎ 271 200 030 (Mon–Fri 8.30am–6pm).

Taxis There's a rank on Rua Alves Roçadas ☎ 271 221 863.

4

The Beira Alta planalto

Beyond Guarda and the mountains lies the Beira Alta tableland, or *planalto*, with its ancient, scattered villages separated by mile after mile of boulder-strewn scrub. It's a land of harsh winters, where even potatoes were hard to grow – in bygone days, roast or dried chestnuts were used as a substitute, plucked from the large trees that signal the entrance to many of the villages. Still, there's a history here that's central to Portugal's identity, starting with the border castles that typify the eastern *planalto*, in particular the stunning star-shaped fortress of **Almeida**. Other castles and fortified settlements of particular interest are those at **Castelo Rodrigo**, to the north of Almeida, **Castelo Bom** and **Castelo Mendo** to the south, and **Penedono** and **Marialva** to the west. There's a bygone wealth in the region, too, that sprang from the merchant trade of medieval Jewish settlements like **Trancoso**, which is easily the most attractive small town in the region. With a car, you could see the whole region in a couple of days, with the best overnight stops at Trancoso, Almeida or the upmarket holiday village accommodation at Marialva.

Trancoso

TRANCOSO is still largely contained within an attractive circuit of medieval walls. It's an uncommonly atmospheric little town, full of cobbled alleyways, well-kept gardens, shady squares and restored churches, all of which represent a tangible civic pride. It was here that Dom Dinis married the 12-year-old Isabel of Aragon in 1282, and later gave her the entire town as a gift; the wedding was solemnized in the small Capela de São Bartolomeu, not far from the town's surviving main gate, the Portas d'el Rei, which is surmounted by the Trancoso coat of arms.

4

Castelo

June–Sept daily 9.30am–12.30pm & 2–6pm; Oct–May Tues–Fri 9am–12.30pm & 2–5.30pm, Sat 9.30am–12.30pm & 2–5pm, Sun 9.30am–12.30pm & 2–4.30pm • Free

Like most *planalto* towns, Trancoso grew up around its **castelo** – and like any town with a castle, trouble was generally to be expected from one quarter or another. Even once the Moors had been finally vanquished, there were still centuries during which armies came and went across the tablelands, using Trancoso as a base or a defensive position. It's surprising so much of the walls still stand – never mind that they remain in such good condition – while its well-restored towers can be seen from afar as you drive towards town.

Casa do Gato Preto

Largo Luís Albuquerque • No public access

Medieval Trancoso had a large Jewish community, which lived in relative harmony (as in the rest of Portugal) until the late fifteenth century when Dom Manuel I ordered their expulsion. The former rabbi's house in Trancoso is known as the **Casa do Gato Preto** (House of the Black Cat), its facade featuring a prominent Lion of Judah. Other buildings in the old town also display features that hark back to a prosperous Jewish community quietly going about its business until religion and politics stepped in. The oldest houses, for example, have separate doorways, one for business and one used by the family, while others are marked with carved crosses, ordered by the Inquisition (active in Portugal from the 1530s onwards) to show that the inhabitants were "New Christian" converts.

ARRIVAL AND INFORMATION   TRANCOSO

By bus Buses stop near the main gate and the turismo. There's a direct service from Guarda on Monday morning, and two on Friday afternoon (1hr 30min), or you can take the hourly bus from Guarda to Celorico da Beira, from where there are two daily buses on to Trancoso. There's also a daily service (Mon–Fri) from Lamego (1hr 30min), and Viseu (1hr 10min), and express services to and from Bragança (3hr) and Lisbon (up to 5hr).

BANDARRA, THE COBBLER-PROPHET

The statue in Trancoso's Praça do Municipio might at first seem puzzling – a gentleman with a cobbler's last and shoe, and a rolled parchment in hand. It is the supposed likeness of the town's most famous son, **Gonçalo Bandarra**, a humble sixteenth-century shoemaker given to versifying – and, more to the point, coming up with prophecies that predicted the end of the world and the return of a hero-like king to save Portugal. The Inquisition took a dim view of this sort of thing and Bandarra was punished, and his verses banned, but the prophecies took on a life of their own with the later destruction of the cream of Portuguese nobility at the battle of Alcácer-Quibir in Morocco (1578). The young crusader-king Dom Sebastião – killed in battle – was held by many to be the hero-king who would one day return to free Portugal from the Spanish yoke, and Bandarra was posthumously elevated to the status of a Nostradamus figure. He was eventually honoured with a tomb in the town's Igreja de São Pedro.

By car Trancoso is 44km north of Guarda, just off the N102: parking isn't usually a problem, though things are much busier on market day, Friday.

Information The turismo is at Portas d'el Rei (June–Sept daily 9.30am–12.30pm & 2–6pm; Oct–May Mon–Fri 9am–12.30pm & 2–5.30pm, Sat 9.30am–12.30pm & 2–5pm, Sun 9.30am–12.30pm & 2–4.30pm; ☎271 811 147, ⓦ cm-trancoso.pt).

ACCOMMODATION

Convento Nossa Senhora do Carmo Freixinho, N226, 31km northwest of Trancoso ☎254 594 080, ⓦ hotel docarmo.com. For charming rural accommodation, drive the half-hour northwest to the village of Freixinho, just beyond Sernancelhe. The hotel is a splendidly restored sixteenth-century convent with simple rustic rooms and a dining room situated in the former chapel. **€70**

★ **Dom Dinis** Av da República 10 ☎271 811 525, ⓦ domdinis.net. Unpromisingly sited above the post office (follow signs for "Correios" to find it), this picks up markedly inside where rooms have laminate floors, good bathrooms, central heating and wall-mounted fans. Not much of a view, it's true, but it puts on a great spread for breakfast (an extra €4.50 per person) – fresh orange juice, *presunto*, cake and home-made pumpkin jam. Private parking. **€35**

Turismo de Trancoso Rua Prof Irene Avillez ☎271 829 200, ⓦ hotel-trancoso.com. The swish four-star on the edge of town (10min walk) seems out of place in homely Trancoso, and when guests are thin on the ground you'll rattle around. Rooms are good, though, and rates are best on weekdays and in winter. **€70**

Vale a Pena Largo Senhora da Calçada ☎271 811 219. Genial enough, with sweeping plains views from the back, and garage parking, but the en-suite rooms are old-fashioned and a bit musty. Although there's a sign on the side nearest the town walls, next to the tyres place (Auto Pneus), the entrance is around the back. No credit cards. **€35**

EATING AND DRINKING

★ **Àrea Benta** Rua dos Cavaleiros 30A ☎271 817 180, ⓦ areabenta.pt. The town's best choice, offering handsomely prepared meals – say, grilled squid with coriander vinaigrette, *cabrito* with chestnuts, or black-pepper steak – in an arty setting. (There's also a stylish cocktail bar a couple of doors down, called *Àgua Benta*, where you can have a dance at the weekend.) Most main courses cost around €8–10. Tues–Sat 12.30–3pm & 7.30–10pm, Sun 12.30–3pm.

O Brasão Rua Adriano Moutinho 3 ☎271 811 767. A simple, traditionally tiled place, where you know what to expect the minute you walk through the door – steaks, grills, chops and sausages, with nothing costing much more than €8 or €9. Mon–Fri noon–2.30pm & 7–10pm, Sun noon–2.30pm.

O Castiço Rua de São João ☎919 188 129. Stone-walled tavern with a comedy-rustic interior (don't trip over a pumpkin). The tap beer's a dark Boemia, while *petiscos* are of the cod-cake, sausage, octopus and boiled-egg variety. Daily 10am–midnight.

O Museu Largo de Santa Maria de Guimarães ☎271 811 810. The dishes of the day in this homely place are good value at around €6; otherwise it's €9–12 for grilled meat and fresh fish, with advance orders required for the speciality fondues and raclettes. Tues–Sun noon–3pm & 7–10pm.

Penedono and around

Isolated **PENEDONO** has a simply wonderful castle, the lichen-encrusted **Castelo Roqueiro**, visible from afar as you drive closer. The "rock castle" emerges from its granite base, and from the top there are far-reaching views, although the Rapunzel-style turrets and sparsely railed walkways are not for the faint-hearted.

Antas

Six kilometres south of Penedono (Trancoso road) lies the small village of **ANTAS** – an *anta* is a megalithic tomb, and a modern re-creation of one sits in the traffic roundabout on the main road. Follow the sign from here, through the village, east for 3.5km up a country road, and then park by the roadside sign for "Necrópole Megalítica da Lameia da Cima". It's a 1.5-kilometre walk from here up a dusty track to two megalithic **burial chambers**, 5000 years old, formed by overlapping stones. The cap stones are missing, but it's a scene of some mystery, with sweeping views down across the distant plain. If you're not travelling to the Alentejo, where more dramatic examples await, it's worth the hour's walk there and back.

Marialva

The tiny village of **MARIALVA** is dominated by its castle: here, within a complete circuit of walls dating from 1200, lies a deserted village where town hall, prison, watchtowers and houses stand in ruins, overgrown with olive trees and overrun by geckos. Depopulated for obscure reasons, the only buildings restored in modern times are the sixteenth-century **Igreja Matriz**, the stone keep and a lone bell-tower, with a geometrically cobbled square and *pelourinho* below. A timetable of hourly visits is posted (daily 10am–6pm; €1.50), but in practice you can ask at the turismo, and they'll let you in to wander through the roofless buildings, haphazard streets and doorways leading nowhere.

ARRIVAL AND INFORMATION   MARIALVA

By car Marialva is 23km north of Trancoso, just off the N102, a quick drive on a good road; there's also a winding, 28-kilometre back-road route from Penedono via Mêda.

Information The concrete-box turismo (June–Sept daily 10am–1.30pm & 3.30–7.30pm; Oct–May daily 9.30am–12.30pm & 2–6pm; ☏ 279 859 288, ⓦ cm-meda.pt) is below the castle gates.

ACCOMMODATION AND EATING

Casas do Côro Largo do Côro ☏ 917 552 020, ⓦ casasdocoro.pt. A mini-village-within-the-village of restored granite houses, terraces and gardens offering relaxed overnight accommodation. Minimalist chic vies successfully with four-poster beds and stone walls, while the outdoor pool is set amid manicured lawns and olive trees. Rooms and independent houses with kitchenette (sleeping from four) are available; breakfast is included, while a four-course dinner (€45) is served in the restaurant. Doubles €135; houses €175

Almeida and around

The most impressive of all the fortified border towns is **ALMEIDA**, within a mere cannon-shot of Spain. It's a handsomely preserved eighteenth-century stronghold, laid out in the shape of a twelve-pointed star and well worth a visit – particularly during the twice-monthly **feiras** (on the eighth day and last Saturday), and the annual bash on 1 September. The village within is charming, while a three-kilometre walk around the walls – now overgrown with grass, and grazed by horses – shows you the true extent of the fortifications, though you can only really appreciate their shape by looking at the aerial-shot postcards sold in the gift shops. If your interest is piqued, two more frontier fortresses – **Castelo Bom** and **Castelo Mendo**, around 20km south of Almeida – are both also easily seen in a quick trip from town by car or en route to the A25, which they straddle.

Almeida played a key role in the **Peninsular War**. Besieged here in 1810 by the Napoleonic army, the garrison held out for seventeen days until, on July 26, a barrel of gunpowder ignited and began a devastating fire. That should have been it for the town, and the decimated survivors gave themselves up, but they were reprieved when the Duke of Wellington later arrived with full army in tow – the French army disappeared into the night and Almeida was saved.

The town defences

Almeida's walls enclose a warren of cobbled lanes and whitewashed houses, punctuated by airy squares – inside the walled town, you'll also find the village post office, a bank with ATM, a grocery shop and a few cafés. The main entrance is still through the original two consecutive defensive tunnel-gates of the **Portas de São Francisco**, complete with a wide, dry moat between inner and outer walls. Immediately inside the gates, to the left, are the long infantry barracks, while a right turn, past the gardens and along the walls, leads to the **Casamatas** (opposite the fire station), an underground storage area with a capacity for five thousand men and their supplies.

You'll easily find your way up to what's left of the **castle**, blown up in 1810, the foundations now exposed under a modern walkway. Behind here, in one of the star-points, is the **picadeiro**, the restored cavalry barracks and horse-training area, whose stables offer short riding lessons and horse-and-buggy rides around town.

Castelo Bom

Tiny **Castelo Bom** preserves walled fortifications above an ancient village just 7km west of the Spanish border at Vilar Formoso. The Duke of Wellington's forces secured the whole area during 1812 and 1813 while advancing into Spain, with Wellington himself headquartered at a house in a nearby village – hence the brown tourist sign with the incongruous English place-name "Wellington".

Castelo Mendo

Four kilometres west of Castelo Bom, the preserved medieval village of **Castelo Mendo** is a gem. Two headless Celtic granite pigs guard the main gateway, through which cobbled streets twist up to a grassy knoll topped by a roofless church and the sketchy remains of the castle keep. It's a glorious spot, sitting on the lip of a sheltered bowl of land, with views across the undulating countryside.

ARRIVAL AND INFORMATION
ALMEIDA

By bus Buses stop in the square outside the main gate, with services on weekdays only from Guarda (1 daily arriving at 4.30pm; 1hr 10min), and Sabugal/Castelo Branco (3 daily; 1hr 30min–2hr).
By car Almeida is 45km northeast of Guarda; drivers can

park in the square outside the main gate.
Information The turismo is at Portas de São Francisco, just inside the inner gate (Mon–Fri 9am–12.30pm & 2–5.30pm, Sat, Sun & hols 10am–12.30pm & 2–5.30pm; ☎ 271 570 020, ⓦ cm-almeida.pt).

ACCOMMODATION AND EATING

Accommodation within the walls is not too badly priced, given the location and atmosphere. There are cheaper rooms outside the walls, by the GALP station, just down from the main gate, though the main road can be noisy; ask for a room at the back. If you don't eat in the *Fortaleza*, you'll probably end up down here anyway as both cheaper hotels have good-value **restaurants**.

A Muralha Bairro de São Pedro, opposite the GALP station ☎ 271 574 357, ⓦ amuralha.pt. The decent en-suite rooms have French windows opening on to balconies, while downstairs there's an unpretentious restaurant that serves a reputable steak (main dishes €7–10). **€40**
★ **Casa Pátio da Figueira** Rua Direita 48 ☎ 271 571 133 or ☎ 963 367 237. Four refined rooms nestled in a charming townhouse around the corner from the *Fortaleza*. It's very pretty inside, with exposed stone walls and tiled floors, and there are lovely gardens and a secluded

swimming pool. No credit cards. **€80**
Fortaleza de Almeida Rua das Muralhas ☎ 271 574 283, ⓦ hotelparadordealmeida.com. Formerly the *pousada*, this was built strictly for the views, across the rooftops to Spain. Inside it's a comfortable 1980s' rustic pastiche – agricultural equipment on the walls and 21 rooms with four-posters and enclosed latticework balconies. A good restaurant (mains around €18) serves regional cuisine, and shares the views with a shaded terrace. There's parking outside, follow the signs. **€85**

4

Granitus Largo 25 de Abril ☎271 574 834. A down-to-earth place, just outside the main gate, with a stand-up local bar where the bus drivers and policemen congregate. Inexpensive meals are served in the dining room, and there are a few café tables outside. You'll eat a good dinner for €16, lunch for less. Daily 10am–11pm.

Morgado Bairro de São Pedro, adjacent to the GALP station ☎271 574 412. At this slightly frayed guesthouse, the prevailing colours are brown (bathroom tiles and furniture) and yellow (bedspreads). That said, it has a restaurant with a welcoming ambience, *A Tertúlia* (closed Tues; mains €6–10), with fresh fish on the menu most days. **€40**

Castelo Rodrigo and around

The obvious route north of Almeida is up the N332 towards the Douro. After 20km – and 3km before the town of Figueira de Castelo Rodrigo – look for the signs to **CASTELO RODRIGO**, a fortified medieval settlement cresting an isolated hill. In the last few years, its huddled houses and cobbled alleys have been fully restored. Inevitably, there are tour buses, a couple of gift shops and cafés, and a slightly unreal, too-tidy air, but it's a great place to spend a couple of hours, with terrific views from all sides.

Castelo Rodrigo

The village is surrounded by a new road, punctuated by three surviving thirteenth-century gates – it's best to park outside if you have a car. Near the southeastern **Porta do Nascente** – facing the town of Figueira below – an inscription above the cemetery warns: "Consider with attention this place of terror, the end of this duplicitous world's vanities", a possible allusion to the castle's long and often violent history. Suitably chastened, enter the village, where the gatehouse now contains the *Sabores do Castelo* shop and bar, selling cheese, honey, smoked meats, local wines and liqueurs. The **castle** itself (daily: Oct–May 9am–6pm; June–Sept 9am–8pm; pay the €1 fee at the adjacent turismo) is built on a rocky outcrop, and remains impressive despite having been torched and sacked in the seventeenth century.

Figueira de Castelo Rodrigo

You'll inevitably pass through the bigger town of **Figueira de Castelo Rodrigo**, below the village, and it's an attractive enough place with a broad central square with fountains and a large church topped by a stork's nest. It provides a minor route to Barca d'Alva (the last settlement on the Douro River), a wonderfully scenic 20km to the north, or it's 35km from Figueira to Vila Nova de Foz Côa and its rock carvings.

Serra de Marofa

To or from Castelo Rodrigo, you might as well divert up to the **Serra de Marofa** viewpoint – signposted at the Pinhel junction on the Almeida road – an antennae-festooned summit, with a Rio-like Christ in Benediction looking out over Castelo Rodrigo, with Spain beyond.

ARRIVAL AND INFORMATION
CASTELO RODRIGO AND AROUND

By car Without your own car, Castelo Rodrigo is an unlikely visit. There is a daily bus (not Sunday) from Guarda, but only to Figueira (ie not the restored village) and then on to Foz Côa.
Information Castelo Rodrigo turismo is next door to the

castle (daily: Oct–May 9am–6pm; June–Sept 9am–8pm; ☎271 311 277, ⌨cm-fcr.pt). Figueira de Castelo Rodrigo turismo is on Largo Mateus de Castro (Mon–Fri 9am–12.30pm & 2–6pm; ☎271 311 365).

ACCOMMODATION

★ **Casa da Cisterna** Rua da Cadeia 7, Castelo Rodrigo ☎917 618 122, ⌨casadacisterna.com. Up at the castle you'll find this stylish, designer conversion of a village house, next to the old water cistern. Accommodation is

split between the main house, garden and annexe, and prices vary according to room (up to €120), but all are lovely, whether stone-walled mezzanine suite or rustic-chic romantic bolthole. **€85**

Falcão de Mendonça Rua Álvaro Castelões 20, Figueira de Castelo Rodrigo ☎ 271 319 200. Just off the town square, near the turismo, lurks a refurbished 1820 mansion that offers the best lodgings in town. There's a small covered swimming pool, courtyard bar and a silver-service atmosphere at the hotel's moderately priced restaurant, a formality ruined by the "Greatest Hits" radio piped in the background. €90

Transmontano Av 25 de Abril 66, Figueira de Castelo Rodrigo, at the top end of the square ☎ 271 313 263. The cheap choice in town with scuffed en-suite rooms on three floors, lackadaisical service and an inexpensive restaurant. €40

The Serra da Estrela

The highest mountains in Portugal, the peaks of the **Serra da Estrela** rise dramatically to the southwest of Guarda. The range is basically a high alpine plateau cut by valleys, from within which emanate two of the country's greatest rivers, the Mondego and the Zêzere – the only rivers to begin and end in Portugal rather than crossing the border from Spain. The mountains – snowcapped in winter – soon impose themselves upon any approach, while the lower flanks on either side of the range reveal a patchwork of small villages that retain much charm. Some Portuguese come to the *serra* to **ski** in winter; many more clog the narrow roads in summer looking for picnic space. A network of **hiking trails** covers the peaks and valleys, though relatively few people take to the paths to explore the region.

Around 1000 square kilometres of the mountain range is protected as the **Parque Natural da Serra da Estrela**, which stretches for around 55km from north to south and around 25km east–west at its widest point. From the west, access is from the N17, through the small service towns of **Seia** or **Gouveia** and then on over the high mountain roads, deep into the park; the smaller western-flank villages of **Linhares**, **Folgosinho** and **Loriga** offer a prettier introduction to the mountain landscape. The valley town and spa of **Manteigas**, pretty much in the centre of the park, is the single best base for hiking and touring, while the ski industry – such as it is – centres on the road between **Torre**, at 1993m, the country's highest peak, and **Covilhã**, south of Manteigas. Covilhã lies just outside the park proper, and is the only town of any size in the region.

4

GETTING AROUND   THE SERRA DA ESTRELA

Covilhã and Guarda can be reached by **train** or **bus**, and there are bus services to Seia and Gouveia, but none across the park itself or to any of the more interesting villages, except Manteigas. **Drivers** could see all the sights in a couple of days – a good route starts from Seia, climbs to the heights of Torre, cuts down the glacial valley road to Manteigas, then switchbacks west again to Gouveia and north to the pretty villages of Folgosinho and Linhares.

Linhares

The most historic village on the western flank of the *serra* is **LINHARES**, 6km off the N17 (20km southwest of Celorico da Beira and the A25) and 810m up, high on a slope overlooking the Mondego valley. It's a highly picturesque jumble of old stone houses linked by steps and cobbled alleys, offering fabulous views across the plains below.

MOUNTAIN LIFE

Over the last few decades life in the mountains has changed markedly. Farmers have moved from **stone mountain houses** to more modern dwellings on the valley floor while many of the former intensively cultivated Zêzere valley terraces have been abandoned in favour of spreading **pine plantation**. Meanwhile local village production is often now directed towards tourists – the local *queijo da serra*, an unctuous **mountain cheese**, and blankets from the wool of the grazing upland sheep, as well as rye bread, fruit preserves and **honey** from the fertile valleys are all widely available.

Near the parish church a path branches off towards Figueiró da Serra to the west (part of the T2 hiking trail), following a section of an old, paved **Roman road** – it's a lovely route, though the next stop, Folgosinho (see opposite), is around three hours away.

Castelo

Mon–Fri 10am–1pm & 2–6pm • Free

Built on an enormous outcrop of granite at the top of the village, the twin towers of the **castelo** date from 1169 when Linhares was a strategic military outpost. One of the towers had a clock added in the seventeenth century – you can go inside the tower and see its granite weights, while there are tremendous views to soak up from the castle walls.

ACCOMMODATION AND EATING   LINHARES

Cova da Loba Largo da Igreja, Linhares ☎ 271 776 119, ⓦ covadaloba.com. Opposite the church, this is a surprisingly modern and fashionable restaurant with a range of well-presented meat and fish dishes from around €13–15;

HIKING IN THE PARQUE NATURAL

In theory, various **hiking trails** cut across the Parque Natural da Serra da Estrela, though it's much harder to walk in the *serras* than it should be. The **park information offices** tend not to have English-speaking staff, and it's rare for the personnel to have any first-hand experience of the trails – often, you'll simply be pointed to dated or unreliable hiking guides and maps. Moreover, the **waymarking** (red-and-yellow paint marks) in the park is unreliable: maintenance doesn't appear to be a priority and signposting at village trailheads is woeful or non-existent. Well-prepared walkers will need to be self-sufficient if you want to complete the longer trails, which can be found on the park website ⓦ rt-serradaestrela.pt. The best time to walk is from May to October. For the day-hiker, who just wants a taste of the mountains, try the easy circular route from Manteigas to the Poço do Inferno waterfall (see box, p.240). Alternatively, you could tackle a short stretch of the lower-level T2 – Linhares to Gouveia, via Folgoshinho, is a good full day's walk, with facilities in each place – though you'll need to take a taxi back to your starting point.

---

the trout is always good and there's usually a vegetarian option. Mon, Tues & Fri–Sun 11.30am–midnight.

Quinta do Adamastor Figueiró da Serra, 7km southwest on the road to Folgosinho ⓣ 271 770 010, ⓦ quintadoadamastor.com. With lovely gardens, an impressive outdoor pool and restaurant (closed Tues dinner & Wed), this is a wonderful rural escape in a nineteenth-century stone mansion with ornate fittings.

Cosy rooms with scrubbed wood floors come with a/c, DVD players and minibars. **€90**

Taberna do Alcaide Linhares ⓣ 271 776 578, ⓦ tabernadoalcaide.serradaestrela.com. This country tavern serves local cheese, *serra* lamb and the like at around €9 for a main course, though it only opens at weekends. It also has three pretty if simple rooms, two en suite. Restaurant Sat & Sun 9am–midnight. **€40**

Folgosinho

FOLGOSINHO, 14km southwest of Linhares along a bumpy country lane (head back towards Carrapichana and turn left before the N17), is 100m higher than Linhares, with a mountain tang to the air, and is topped by not so much a castle as a perky, turreted clock tower clinging to the crags. There's a tree-shaded village square and a central kernel of granite houses, a few of which tout local produce and woolly jumpers (though it's shepherds' cloaks that are the more traditional habit). It's 11km by road to Gouveia from Folgosinho, or around three hours' walking on the T2 trail, whose paint marks you can pick up in the village.

EATING

O Albertino Largo do Adro de Viriato 8 ⓣ 238 745 266, ⓦ oalbertino-folgosinho.com. An earthy restaurant with a very meaty menu (suckling pig, wild boar, goat and veal all around €15), with every dish accompanied by *arroz de cabidela* (rice cooked with blood). Tues–Sat noon–4pm & 7.30–11.30pm, Sun noon–7pm.

O Mocas Rua do Outão 8 ⓣ 238 748 999. Cheery *Mocas* has a downstairs café and upstairs restaurant, with an inexpensive menu of half a dozen daily dishes (around €8) including the speciality sauasage, *morcela*. The unusual name of the restaurant, which means "stubs", is explained (in English) on the plaque outside, but it might have been better if they had kept it to themselves, since it's a reference to a particularly nasty kitchen accident that befell the present owner's grandfather. Mon & Wed–Sun 11am–11pm.

Gouveia

GOUVEIA is a small provincial town of well-kept gardens and terrace-cafés, with a striking blue-tiled Baroque **Igreja de São Pedro** – everything of interest is within five minutes' walk of the church. Although there are few onward buses into the mountains, it makes a good and lively base from which to explore the Serra villages if you have a car. There's also a bustling Thursday **market**.

Museu de Abel Manta

Ria Direita 45 • Tues–Sat 9.30am–12.30pm & 2–6pm, Sun 10am–noon & 2–5pm • Free • ☎ 238 493 648

Set inside seven small rooms of an interesting old seventeenth-century former winery, the **Museu de Abel Manta** houses a wide selection of contemporary Portuguese art donated by Gouveia-born artist and architect Abel Manta (1888–1982). None of the works are particularly memorable, except for the art by the man himself. Abel Manta lived and worked in Lisbon, Paris and Funchal, and his evocative paintings beautifully capture some of the towns and characters he encountered.

ARRIVAL AND INFORMATION   GOUVEIA

By bus Buses pull up in the centre of town, with regular services to Coimbra (3–4 daily; 2hr), Lisbon (3–4 daily; 4hr 30min) and Seia (Mon–Fri 3 daily; 30min).

Information The modern turismo is in the Jardim da Ribeira (Mon–Sat 9.30am–12.30pm & 2–6pm, Sun 10am–12.30pm & 2–5pm; ☎ 238 083 930, ⓦ cm-gouveia.pt), a small park below the market building.

ACCOMMODATION AND EATING

Casas da Mata da Cerca Cerca ☎ 238 492 315, ⓦ casasdamatadacerca.com. On the northeastern outskirts of Gouveia – but secluded enough to feel like you're in the middle of nowhere – this consists of rooms in two lovely houses surrounded by acres of mature woodland. €75

Monteneve Av Bombeiros Voluntários 12 ☎ 238 490 370, ⓦ montenevehotel.com. Inside two restored houses, this hotel is the best choice in town with chic en-suite rooms above a café. The entrance is a little hard to find even though it's on the main through-road. €50

O Júlio Rua do Loureiro 11A ☎ 238 498 016. This is the most reliable place to eat in town – strictly traditional, offering dishes like wild boar with onions, rabbit stew, or local kid and game from around €9. Mon & Wed–Sun noon–3pm & 7–9.30pm.

★ **Quinta das Cegonhas** Nabainhos, 6km east of Gouveia, Folgosinho road ☎ 238 745 886, ⓦ cegonhas .com. There are two rooms and two apartments to rent at this Dutch-owned seventeenth-century manor house, which revels in its country location and sweeping views. Also a shady campsite (open all year), swimming pool, bar and restaurant (meals served daily in summer, or by request). Doubles €60; apartments €65

Seia and around

The largest town on the western side of the *serra*, **SEIA**, 16km southwest of Gouveia, is well located as a base for mountain trips – though only if you have your car, as there's no onward public transport. The town centre is small indeed, and not particularly historic, but where Seia scores is its proximity to smaller, higher villages, such as **Sabugueiro**, and for the direct road route up to Torre peak, 30km to the southeast (see p.242).

Museu do Pão

Tues–Fri & Sun 10am–6pm, Sat 10am–10pm • €5 • ☎ 238 310 760, ⓦ museudopao.pt

The quaint **Museu do Pão**, a steep 1km above the town centre (on the Sabugueiro road), features rustic reconstructions of bread-making equipment and a traditional mill – if nothing else, you could emerge knowing the word for bread in 125 languages. The terrace café has excellent views and there's also a decent restaurant (Tues–Sun 12.30–3.30pm) and traditional *mercearia* (grocers) where you can buy home-made bread.

Sabugueiro

SABUGUEIRO, 10km east of Seia, is said to be Portugal's highest village (1050m), a cachet that has led to some rampant overdevelopment, certainly along the main road, which is now nothing more than a drive-through shopping experience. Mountain cheese, ham, rye bread, honey, leather coats, woolly slippers and fluffy toy mountain-dogs are piled high in the rash of souvenir shops – real mountain-dog pups (*cães*) are sold as a sideline, yelping piteously in tiny roadside cages. The surviving old village is at the bottom of the hill, near the Rio Alva. The slate-roofed stone cottages are in varying states of repair, although many have been restored and can be rented for a night's stay, but you'd do far better to visit on a day-trip from Seia or press on to Manteigas, 25km to the east.

ARRIVAL AND INFORMATION   SEIA AND AROUND

By bus The bus station is on the ring-road at the bottom of town, a few hundred metres from the centre. Destinations Coimbra (3–6 daily; 1hr 45min); Covilhã (Mon & Sun 1 daily; 1hr 40 min); Gouveia (Mon–Fri 3 daily; 30min); Guarda (Fri & Sun 1 daily; 1hr 10min); and Lisbon (3 daily; 3 hr 30min–4hr).

Information The turismo is opposite the market on Rua Pintor Lucas Marrão (Mon–Sat 9am–12.30pm & 2–5.30pm, Sun 9am–1pm; ☎ 238 317 762, ⓦ cm-seia.pt).

ACCOMMODATION AND EATING

Camelo Av 1 de Maio 16, Seia ☎ 238 310 100, ⓦ eurosol.pt. Agreeable, central three-star hotel with tartan-trimmed rooms, manicured grounds with a swimming pool, bar and well-regarded regional restaurant (closed Sun dinner & Mon). Follow the road through town (São Romão direction) to find it. **€50**

★ **Casas da Ribeira** Pôvoa Velha, 5km east of Seia, signposted off the Sabugueiro road ☎ 238 311 221, ⓦ casasdaribeira.com. Ten stone houses in an ancient village, ranging from studios to three-bed cottages, all equipped with kitchens, central heating and wood-burning stoves and fireplaces. A breakfast of fresh bread, ham, cheese and preserves is delivered to your door in the morning. Minimum two-night stay; no credit cards. Studios **€65**

Estalagem de Seia Av Dr Afonso Costa, Seia ☎ 238 315 866. Eighteenth-century townhouse with a granite staircase and a pleasant garden pool. Features and furnishings are a bit long in the tooth, and the relatively low price reflects this. It's just off the roundabout by the post office. No credit cards. **€60**

Restaurante Regional da Serra Av dos Combatentes da Grande Guerra 12–14, Seia ☎ 238 312 717. Just off the bottom of Praça da República, this place serves river trout, *cabrito*, sausages and so on. It's especially busy at lunch, and mains average around €7–10. Daily noon–11pm.

Loriga

The minor N231 road south of Seia (signposted initially to São Romão) winds for 18km to **LORIGA**, sitting at 770m above agricultural terraces that slope steeply down to the Loriga River. The fast-flowing water once powered woollen mills, and still irrigates the fields, while the settlement itself dates back at least to Roman times – there are traces of the Roman road signposted near Loriga and at Valezim just to the north.

INFORMATION AND ACCOMMODATION   LORIGA

Information Loriga turismo is on the EN231 into the village (Tues–Sat 9am–12.30pm & 2–5.30pm, Sun 9am–1pm; ☎ 238 951 175, ⓦ cm-seia.pt).

Casa do Meio da Vila Travessa do Figueiredo 6 ☎ 238 953 401, ⓦ casadomeiodavila.com. You can stay in a restored rustic stone village house here for a two-night minimum stay (three in high season); the website also features other larger houses that sleep up to ten. **€60**

O Vicente Rua Gago Coutinho 2 ☎ 238 953 127, ⓦ ovicente.com. Out on the N231, this welcoming place doubles as a crafts shop and restaurant with decent upstairs rooms (three nights minimum in high season). **€55**

Manteigas

If there's one town in the *serra* with a true mountain air it's **MANTEIGAS**, 700m up, whose whitewashed houses run along the contour above the Rio Zêzere. The approach from any direction is dramatic: from Sabugueiro and the west the road winds down in convoluted switchbacks; from Belmonte and the east the river scenery is at its most bucolic; while from the south there is the breathtaking descent down the glacial valley of the Rio Zêzere. The latter route brings you into town past the therapeutic spa of **Caldas de Manteigas** and to the fertile valley bottom of the Zêzere, with Manteigas itself spreading across the steep slope opposite.

There's no public transport further into the park from town, but with a car you can use Manteigas as a base to visit Torre, the glacial valley and ski fields, and the nearby villages. The town is on two of the official **walking trails**, but local routes are on the tough side since – south and west at least – you have to climb steep and far to get anywhere. There's one easy circular walk to the Poço do Inferno (see box below), though most other routes are point-to-point, requiring a taxi ride out or back, which can be easily arranged.

Skiparque

Largo Relva da Reboleira Sameiro • Daily 10am–5pm • ☎ 275 980 090, ⓦ skiparque.pt

The **Skiparque** is an artificial winter-sports slope and adventure park 8km east of Manteigas down the N232 Belmonte road. It's open all year round for dry-slope skiing and snowboarding, plus everything else from mountain-biking to hang-gliding. Half-day activities and ski lessons start at around €30, or you can go on four-hour guided walks for €6 a person (min four people). It pays to call ahead since it's either heaving (winter & weekends) or deserted, but there's a river beach, campsite (see p.242), restaurant and bar here in any case.

ARRIVAL AND INFORMATION   MANTEIGAS

By bus Bus services to Manteigas are limited to weekdays (though not public holidays) and liable to change. Manteigas turismo can confirm times, but currently there are services to/from Guarda (Mon–Fri 1 daily; 1hr 20min), Covilhã (Mon–Fri 1 daily; 1hr 30min) and Belmonte (Mon–

Fri 1 daily; 45min).
Information The English-speaking turismo (Tues–Sat 9.30am–12.30pm & 2–5.30pm; ☎ 275 981 129, ⓦ cm -manteigas.pt) is below GALP petrol station, opposite a small park and café.

ACCOMMODATION AND EATING

★ **Albergaria Berne** Quinta de Santo António ☎ 275 981 351, ⓦ albergaria-berne.planetaclix.pt. A friendly family takes good care of you in this simple, pine-furnished inn where rooms have their own baths. There's a swimming pool and a moderately priced restaurant (closed Sun dinner & Mon) where you'll eat heartily. It's down at the bottom of the town, by the river – a very steep fifteen minutes on

foot, or follow the signs coming in on the Caldas–Torre road. Closed two weeks Sept. €60
Casa das Obras Rua Teles de Vasconcelos ☎ 275 981 155, ⓦ casadasobras.pt. Follow the blue signs in town to find this restored eighteenth-century mansion, enlarged from an even older sixteenth-century house. Some rooms are a little dark, but the faded dining-room murals, games

---

A CIRCULAR WALK FROM MANTEIGAS TO THE POÇO DE INFERNO

The best circular walk **from Manteigas** is to the **Poço de Inferno waterfall** and back, which takes around four hours. Most of the paint-mark trail signs are missing or faded, but it's a straightforward route with some gorgeous views. The walk starts in the Zêzere valley bottom, from the small bridge and picnic area reached down the steep road behind the turismo.

Cross the bridge, turn left (signposted "Leandres") and walk for 500m along the road, past the recycling plant, before turning right onto a clear forestry track. Keep straight on, ever upwards through the woods – the first yellow paint sign is on a tree on the right-hand side (6min) and there isn't another until you reach a ruined white house in a clearing (45min) marked with the words "Matas Nacionais".

Five minutes after the house is the only turn off the main path – to the left (with paint marks before and after the turn). In another fifteen minutes the path ends at a bend in a tarmac road. Walk uphill (there's a yellow paint mark almost immediately) and it's twenty minutes further up the road to the Poço do Inferno, "Hell's Well", where the Leandres River pours down the narrow gorge into clear pools overlooked by viewing platforms.

To return, follow the minor road around past the falls, heading back towards Manteigas. This road actually runs steadily down to Caldas de Manteigas, though this would be a long (8km) and unnecessary return to Manteigas itself. Instead, after an hour, at a large water tank by the right-hand side of the road (there's also a white house, just before a small bridge) turn right down an ancient track – walled in parts – which drops in zigzags through the trees. Ultimately, there are several divergent paths, but as long as you keep going downhill you'll end up in the group of houses by the *Albergaria Berne* (another 30min) – from where it's a steep fifteen-minute climb into Manteigas proper.

room, uneven floorboards and cellar-like bar are delightful, and there's an enchanting garden with fruit trees and a secluded swimming pool. No credit cards. **€68**

Pousada de São Lourenço Pehnas Douradas, 12km west of Manteigas ☎ 275 980 050, ⓦ pousadas.pt. Reached by a series of switchbacks (follow signs from town) this marvellous *pousada* is best enjoyed in winter when log fires are roaring in the wood-panelled bar and the tartan curtains are drawn against howling mountain winds. That said, there are superlative views at any time of the year, and the panoramic restaurant is always worth a trip. **€120**

Serradalto Rua 1 de Maio ☎ 275 981 151. Spotless rooms with wooden ceilings and wonderful views. The guests' terrace is one of the best spots in Manteigas for a sunset beer, while full-length windows in the restaurant look out to the valley below – steak cooked on a hot stone at your table is the speciality. Restaurant closed Tues. No credit cards. **€45**

★ **Soadro do Zêzere** Estrada Nacional 232, Valhelhas, 17km east of Manteigas ☎ 275 487 114, ⓦ soadro.com. The inn is a sympathetic restoration of an old village house, with plenty of exposed stone and burnished wood and half a dozen unflashy but good-value rooms. There's a well-regarded restaurant on the premises too (closed on Tues). **€50**

CAMPSITE

Relva da Reboleira Largo Relva da Reboleira, Sameiro, at Skiparque ☎ 275 980 090, ⓦ skiparque.net.

The most convenient campsite is this year-round place near its own river beach, with a café and good facilities. It also handles bookings for stays at the fairly basic, but spectacularly located park site at Covão da Ametade, at the top of a glacial valley. Pitch **€5**

RESTAURANTS

★ **Dom Pastor** Rua Sá da Bandeira ☎ 275 982 920. Tucked away in an idyllic little lane by the river, *Dom Pastor* offers a creative take on traditional cuisine. It's a calm, contemporary space, constructed using local materials, and you can expect dishes such as fillet of perch with shrimp sauce or *bacalhau* with a corn-bread crust (mains €10–12). No credit cards. Mon & Tues–Sun 9am–midnight.

LusoPizza Rua Teles de Vasconcelos 15–17 ☎ 275 982 928. The pizza at this tiny restaurant/takeaway (just behind the park office) is the genuine article, and with prices at around €8–9 it's a good deal, with outdoor tables. No credit cards. Daily 11am–3pm & 7–midnight.

★ **Vallecula** Praça Dr José de Castro, Valhelhas, 17km east of Manteigas ☎ 275 487 123. Worth a special trip for superior dining in an old stone house on the village square. The emphasis is on local produce, with lamb, pork, rabbit, beef or game preceded by a starter of soft cheese with herbs, for example. Prices are fair (mains around €13), the owner affable and the regional wine list impressive. No credit cards. Tues–Sun noon–11pm.

Torre and around

The trans-mountain N339 between Seia and Covilhã climbs right across the bleak, scoured landscape of Portugal's highest mountains. The peak is known as **Torre** (1993m) after the stone *torre* (tower) added on the orders of Dom João VI in 1817 to raise the height to a more impressive 2000m. There's something typically Portuguese about that gesture, as there is about the summit shopping centre, with shops all selling smelly cheese and woolly slippers. Impressive in winter, when the ski lifts and surrounding slopes are bustling with skiers, at other times the natural beauty and grandeur at the top of Portugal's highest mountain is disfigured by the coach parking, radar domes and concrete buildings that house a café and restaurant.

It goes without saying that the route there is the best thing about Torre, and there's no better approach than the 15km from Manteigas up the dramatic glacial **Zêzere valley**. The valley road joins the N339 at the Nave de Santo António plateau, where you turn right for Torre (7km). En route to the peak you pass the vast statue of **Nossa Senhora da Boa Estrela**, carved into a niche in the rock, to which there's a massive procession from Covilhã on the second Sunday in August.

Penhas da Saúde

Around 10 km below Torre (towards Covilhã) lies the ski resort of **Penhas da Saúde** (1900m). The ski season runs from November to April (€25 a day, the same again for ski hire; ⓦ skiserradaestrela.com), but outside this time, it's a rather desolate-looking place with few facilities save a sprinkling of accommodation and some cafés. You can stretch your legs at the reservoir above, or stop on the way further down to Covilhã at a couple of signposted strolls, like that to **Pedra do Urso** (Bear Rock).

Covilhã

Just outside the eastern park boundary, and 44km south of Guarda, the prosperous town of **COVILHÃ** lies immediately below the highest peaks. It's busiest on winter weekends, when it's used as a base for trips to the ski slopes, but it has a life independent of the mountains, which makes it an agreeable place to visit at any time. Virtually every thoroughfare looks out across the plain below or up to the mountain crags – the café in the pretty town gardens has the best view, serenaded by practice sessions in the music conservatory opposite.

Praça do Município

Covilhã's favourite son is **Pêro de Covilhã**, who set out in 1487 to search for Prester John (legendary Christian priest and king) in what is now Ethiopia. He never found Prester John and never returned to Portugal, though Vasco da Gama found his report about India useful when he made his own celebrated voyage there in 1498. In front of the town hall on **Praça do Município** there's a huge, polished granite slab depicting Pêro de Covilhã's voyages and a decidedly queasy-looking statue of the man himself.

Museo de Lanifícios

Rua Marquês d'Ávila e Bolama • Tues–Sun 9.30am–noon & 2.30–6pm • €2, under-16s free • ⓦ museu.ubi.pt

A market town since the Middle Ages, Covilhã developed a textile industry in the seventeenth century using wool from the local sheep, which also provide the milk for the renowned *queijo da serra*. Later, the woollen industry harnessed water-power from the mountain streams; factories today, down on the plain below town, are powered by hydroelectricity. You can view the enormous vats used in the traditional wool-dyeing processes in the **Museo de Lanifícios**, located in the former Real Fábrica de Panos (Royal Textile Factory), a short walk downhill from the centre.

ARRIVAL AND DEPARTURE   COVILHÃ

BY CAR

Parking in the town centre is metered (4hr maximum; free after 8pm and on Sun). For longer stays, use the large, free parking area below the fire station (*Bombeiros*) – from the public gardens, head up past the *Covilhã Parque* hotel and *Telepizza*, turn sharp left at the garage (Pneus) and there's a blue parking sign immediately on the left.

BY BUS AND TRAIN

Both **train and bus stations** are 2km below the town, but a bus runs up the hill from here every ten minutes and

drops you at the **local bus terminal** outside the PSP (police station), where there's a bus information kiosk.

Bus Destinations Belmonte (3 daily; 30min); Castelo Branco (1–5 daily; 1hr); Guarda (3–7 daily; 45min); Lisbon (4–9 daily; 3hr 35min–6hr); Manteigas (Mon–Fri 1 daily; 1hr 30min); Penhas da Saúde (July–Sept only: 1 daily; 2 daily during Aug; 35min); Seia (Mon–Fri & Sun 1 daily; 2hr); Viseu (2–6 daily; 2hr).

Train Destinations Castelo Branco (6 daily; 1hr–1hr 20min); Lisbon (5 daily; 4hr 15min–5hr 15min).

ACCOMMODATION

There's a limited choice of **accommodation** in the old centre, while several business-oriented three- and four-star places are found below town (not really walking distance), down the road out to the main highway. Note that prices are cheapest everywhere in summer. At **Penhas da Saúde** (N339, 11km from Covilhã) there are a couple more hotels and the local youth hostel.

★ **Covilhã Jardim** Rua São Salvador 40 ☎ 275 322 140, ⓦ residencialcovilhajardim.com. Sited right by the public gardens, this has fifteen smart en-suite rooms, some with French windows and little balconies. The central location and genial family management make the prices something of a steal, there's pay parking right outside, and Covilhã's nicest café-bar and terrace on the ground floor. **€40**

Covilhã Parque Av Frei Heitor Pinto ☎ 275 329 320, ⓦ covilhaparquehotel.com.pt. Ten floors high and thus the best views in town, at least from the front rooms. It's two-star, and not quite as swish as the reception area suggests, with slightly worn decor and bathrooms on the basic side. But discounted summer rates are excellent, and there's direct access from the fire-station parking area. Its sister *Hotel Turismo* is a flashier three-star, with a pool and spa, but it's a long way below town. **€40**

Hotel dos Carqueijais Penhas road, N339, 5km northwest of Covilhã ☎ 275 319 120, ⓦ turistrela.pt.

For serious views, head out of town towards the mountains, to this four-star ski-oriented inn, with panoramic bar and restaurant, plus summer outdoor pool. Expect prices to be a lot higher at weekends in winter. **€60**

Pousada de Juventude Penhas da Saúde, 11km northwest of Covilhã ☎ 275 335 375, ⓦ microsites .juventude.gov.pt/portal/en. The huge 163-bed youth hostel is at 1500m, so the superb views are a given, and it also has a self-catering kitchen and bar, and some private en-suite rooms. Dorm beds **€12**, rooms **€45**

Solneve Rua Visconde da Coriscada 126 ☎ 275 323 001, ⓦ solneve.pt. The traditional three-star hotel overlooking the main traffic circle and square has been upgraded – the smart, business-like rooms are now either standard or superior (they come with a hot tub-bath and cost €10 or so more), and there's also a pool, spa and parking. The cavernous downstairs restaurant is pretty unbeatable value, with main dishes around €8 and including dishes like lasagne and stroganoff. **€40**

EATING AND DRINKING

Montiel Praça do Município 33–37 ☎ 275 322 086. Café and *pastelaria* downstairs, slightly genteel restaurant upstairs, filled to bursting with families for Sunday lunch. The menu concentrates on regional

specialities, trout to *cabrito*, and although some dishes are pricey the *pratos do dia* cost around €7 for a *meia dose* or €12 for a portion big enough for two. Daily 9am–10.30pm.

Ze do Sporting Rua Comendador Mendes Veiga 19
☎ 275 334 127. Locals plump for the steaks and grills
(including fish and seafood) at this renowned *churrasqueira*
– prices start at €8, though it's more like €15 for a decent
steak. It's down a backstreet behind the *Solneve*. Tues–Sat
noon–3pm & 7–10pm, Sun noon–3pm.

Beira Baixa

The area east of Covilhã and the A23 motorway forms the upper boundary of the
Beira Baixa, a landscape of undulating, heather-clad hills that extends to the Spanish
border. The sun-bleached fields, grazing livestock and extensive olive groves provide
a distinct contrast to the *serra* scenery, with visits concentrating on a series of
fortified towns and fascinating villages. With a car you can see the whole region in
a couple of days, and the best overnight stops are either at the underrated town of
Belmonte or in one of the atmospheric houses of medieval **Sortelha**. On the other
hand, travel by public transport is particularly difficult and slow. Only Belmonte
and **Sabugal** can be reached easily by bus, though if you're determined you'll also
get to Sortelha, while the provincial capital of **Castelo Branco** (on the Lisbon–
Covilhã train route) has services to **Monsanto** and **Idanha-a-Nova**. But isolated
destinations, such as **Idanha-a-Velha** and the **Serra da Malcata** nature reserve,
are impossible to see by public transport.

Belmonte

The delightful small town of **BELMONTE** springs one of the best surprises in the Beiras,
a charming place of sun-dappled squares, stone houses dripping with window boxes
and lazy dogs basking on the cobbles. There are curiosities at every turn, such as the
unusual pillory in the shape of an olive press, or the fire-blackened tree stumps outside
the castle, which are the site of Christmas Eve carols and gambols. Meanwhile, in the
Zêzere river valley, which Belmonte overlooks, vast peach and cherry orchards splash
a blaze of colour each spring.

Castelo and Igreja de Santiago
Largo de Santiago • April to mid-Sept Tues–Sun 9am–12.30pm & 2–6pm; mid-Sept to March Tues–Sun 9.30am–1pm & 2–5.30pm •
Castelo free; Igreja €1

For the Portuguese Belmonte is best known as the birthplace of **Pedro Álvares Cabral**
(1467–1520), the "discoverer" of Brazil, who was born in the tidily restored **castelo**
overlooking town. Cabral's father received the castle from Dom Afonso V, and adapted

---

PARKS, PATHS AND PROJECTS IN BEIRA BAIXA

The lower (*baixa*) Beira region is a surprisingly good place for hiking and outdoor activities;
better, in many ways, than the higher Serra da Estrela. It's the result of a diverse set of
interconnecting development projects, the main result of which is a growing series of reliable,
waymarked footpaths and readily available information. Castelo Branco sits at the centre of
the so-called **Naturtejo Geopark** (⊕ naturtejo.com), part of a wider pan-European project,
while a large section of Tejo River hinterland is contained within the **Parque Natural do
Tejo Internacional** – "internacional" because it's mirrored on the Spanish side of the river too.
There are good local walk circuits in many towns and villages, particularly between Monsanto,
the Spanish border and Idanha-a-Nova, and also around the so-called **Aldeias do Xisto**
(schist villages; ⊕ aldeiasdoxisto.pt), west of Castelo Branco; we've highlighted the best in this
Beira Baixa section, and you can pick up route leaflets and information in any local turismo.
There's even a long-distance hiking trail, the **GR12-E7** (total 80km), that connects Termas de
Monfortinho on the Spanish border with Idanha-a-Nova (some of the shorter walks connect
with this; details on the local council website ⊕ cm-idanhanova.pt).

it as the family residence, though it later fell into disrepair. The **Igreja de Santiago**, just outside the castle walls, contains the Cabral family pantheon (though not the tomb of Pedro Álvares, which is in Santarém), while one of two tiny stone chapels on a hillock opposite is inscribed with the Cabral family coat of arms – two goats within a shield. The Cabral trail also extends to the main through-road named in his honour, where there's a statue of the explorer clutching a large cross.

Judaria

Museu Judaico Rua da Portela 4 • April to mid-Sept Tues–Sun 9am–12.30pm & 2–6pm; mid-Sept to March Tues–Sun 9.30am–1pm & 2–5.30pm • €2.50

Belmonte's restored **Judaria (Jewish quarter)** is tucked below the southern wall of the castle. Belmonte once maintained one of Portugal's largest Jewish communities and records show that there was a synagogue here as early as 1297, but this fell into ruins after the Inquisition, when many Jews fled the country or were forced to convert to being "New Christians". The modern Sinagoga built in the Jewish quarter is now open for visits, while behind Largo do Pelourinho, in the old town, the **Museu Judaico** explores the history of Portuguese Judaism.

The town museums

All museums Rua Pedro Álvares Cabral • April to mid-Sept Tues–Sun 9am–12.30pm & 2–6pm; mid-Sept to March Tues–Sun 9.30am–1pm & 2–5.30pm • Admission to all museums, including Museu Judaico and Santiago church, €7.50 • ☎ 275 088 698

All the other town **museums** are located along the main Rua Pedro Álvares Cabral – start with the interpretation centre, **À Descoberta do Novo Mundo**, installed in the former Cabral palace, across from the town hall, which covers the New World discoveries of Cabral and others. Opposite lies the **Ecomuseu do Zêzere**, housed in a barn-like granite building, formerly a granary owned by the Cabral family. This provides the natural and geological background on the Zêzere River, while for an investigation of the local olive oil industry, follow the signs around the corner to the **Museu do Azeite**, housed in the former municipal olive-oil press.

Torre Centum Cellas

There's an extraordinary sight a couple of kilometres north of Belmonte, just off the N18 – drive 600m along the road from the Belmonte junction towards Guarda and then 400m up a side road to the right. The **Torre Centum Cellas** presents a very odd picture – rather like a child's brick building – with the further curiosity that no one quite knows what it was. The stone tower measures around 10m by 8m and stands three storeys high, and there are no fewer than forty intact window and door frames. Possibly it formed part of a Roman villa, and survived due to later use as a watchtower.

ARRIVAL AND INFORMATION   BELMONTE

By bus Buses drop you at the end of Rua Pedro Álvares Cabral, a 500-metre walk from the centre; long-distance express buses (to Lisbon and elsewhere) stop at Gingal junction on the N18, 2km below town.

Destinations Covilhã (3 daily; 30min); Guarda (3 daily; 25–45min); Manteigas (1 daily; 45min); and Sabugal (1 daily; 1hr 30min).

By car Belmonte is just 26km south of Guarda and 20km northeast of Covilhã, and it's also a handy stop en route to the Serra da Estrela, with Manteigas just 27km to the west. It's easy to park for free on the road into town, or up by the castle.

Information The turismo is on Praça da República (Tues–Sun 9.30am–12.30pm & 2.30–5.30pm; ☎ 275 911 488, ⓦ cm-belmonte.pt).

ACCOMMODATION AND EATING

Casa do Castelo Largo de Santiago ☎ 275 181 675, ⓦ casadocastelo.net. Located right outside the castle, offering good rooms at a decent price, a terrace café with sweeping views and a granite-walled restaurant serving upmarket regional food (mains €11–14, though the *prato do dia* for lunch is better value at €8). **€60**

Pousada Convento de Belmonte Serra da Esperança, 1km from town, follow the signs ☎ 275 910 300,

Ⓦpousadas.pt. The rather elegant rooms in this restored convent combine natural textures, light and space. There's a plunge-pool and terrace, and an excellent restaurant, where you'll eat smarter versions of traditional dishes for around €40 a head. €85

Sortelha

Twenty kilometres east of Belmonte, **SORTELHA** rises dramatically amid an unearthly, undulating highland plateau strewn with giant glacial boulders. It's an ancient place that, for most of its existence, has gone about its business quietly, though the wonderful rock-built fortress suggests some frontier excitement in times past. Today it presents itself as a museum piece – with some beautifully restored lodgings available – since the number of permanent residents in the old town barely struggles into double figures. From the modern quarters on the Sabugal road it's a five-minute walk uphill (follow "Castelo" signposts) to the fascinating walled old town – or you can drive up and park outside the main gate. A tight web of cobbled lanes wends between squat stone houses with red-tiled roofs, while rough carved steps in the castle keep offer a grandstand view over the valley below and the rock-speckled hillsides beyond.

ARRIVAL AND DEPARTURE   SORTELHA

By bus You can reach Sortelha by bus, but only from nearby Sabugal, 13km to the east, and only with any regularity during school term time (Sept–June, every weekday afternoon at 5.25pm); there's also a 1.30pm bus on Tuesdays and Thursdays. You'll have to stay the night, as the school-day return service isn't until the next morning. Otherwise, a taxi from Sabugal costs around €20.

ACCOMMODATION AND EATING

Sortelha has some enticing rustic **accommodation**, but advance reservations are recommended (and note that there are no credit card or banking facilities in Sortelha). As well as the **café and restaurant** in the old town there are a couple of places to eat on the main road below, one of which, *Restaurant O Celta* (closed Tues), also has a small *mini-mercado* attached.

Bar do Forno Esplanada ☎271 388 034. Friendly café with a stone-flagged terrace, right beneath the castle walls. There are sausage and cheese *petiscos* and other snacks, or they will rustle you up a steak and chips for under €10. Daily 10am–9pm; closed two weeks Sept.

Casa da Lagariça ☎271 388 116, Ⓦcasalagarica.com. An old stone village house, fashioned from a former grape store. Overnight accommodation is in two doubles or a twin room, sharing two bathrooms, a fully equipped kitchen and lounge. Prices go up to €80 in peak summer and winter season, but it's more reasonable at other times. They also have the smaller and similarly priced *Casa da Calçada* in the village, which has two double rooms available. €55

Dom Sancho I ☎271 388 267. The only proper restaurant in the old town, just inside the main gate, with a rustic stone-walled interior. Sample meat grills and game from a strictly traditional menu (mains €12–18), or you can just have a drink in the downstairs bar. Tues–Sat noon–2.30pm & 7–10pm, Sun noon–3pm.

Sabugal

SABUGAL is a pleasant place with a riverside setting on the Côa and a small old-town area of winding streets and noble mansions. The hill is topped by a neatly restored castle, but the setting isn't a patch on that at Sortelha. Most visitors will just drive on by, though Sabugal does make a good base for visiting the Serra da Malcata reserve (see p.248), as accommodation and restaurants are far better here than at the other town near the reserve, Penamacor, 35km to the south.

ARRIVAL AND INFORMATION   SABUGAL

By bus The bus station is at the bottom of town, by the market.
Destinations Belmonte (1 daily; 1hr 30min); Castelo Branco (Sun–Fri 1 daily; 2hr); Guarda (Mon–Fri every 2hr, Sat 1 daily; 45min); Penamacor (Sun–Fri 1–2 daily; 1hr); Sortelha (Sept–June Mon–Fri 1 daily plus 2 weekly on Tues & Thurs; 30min).
Information The turismo is in Castelo do Sabugal (April–Sept Tues–Fri 9.30am–1pm & 2–6.30pm, Sat & Sun

10am–1pm & 2–7pm; Oct–March Tues–Fri 9.30am–1pm & 2–5.30pm, Sat & Sun 10am–1pm & 2.30–5.30pm;

📞271 751 046, 🌐cm-sabugal.pt) – if you want to look around inside the castle walls it costs €1.

ACCOMMODATION AND EATING

★ **Robalo** Largo do Cinema 4 📞271 753 566. By far the best place to eat in town, and frankly worth a major detour in its own right. It serves trout from the Rio Côa, its own smoked sausage and fantastic lamb, steaks or *bacalhau*, all grilled over huge fireplaces burning holm oak; everything is served with organic salad and a garlic-and-pepper sauce that should have UN weapons' inspectors on alert; you can eat amazingly well for around €25. The owners offer simple rooms over the road in the *Hospedaria*

Robalo, which also has its own rustic tavern. Restaurant Mon–Sat noon–3pm & 7.30–11pm; also open on Sun in Aug noon–3pm & 7.30–11pm. Doubles €45

Sol Rio Av Infante Dom Henrique 58 📞271 753 197. This place situated down by the river bridge on the way into town has decent budget rooms with castle or river views, and a modest restaurant with mains around €11–15. Restaurant Mon–Thurs, Sat & Sun noon–3pm & 7–10pm. Doubles €35

Reserva Natural da Serra da Malcata

Between Sabugal and Penamacor, and reaching east from two local reservoirs to the Spanish border, spreads the **Reserva Natural da Serra da Malcata** (🌐icnf.pt). It's one of the least-visited Portuguese nature reserves – access isn't easy, and you really need to bike or hike to get much out of it – but it rewards the effort. If you're very lucky, you might get a glimpse of a wild boar among the trees, or catch sight of the magnificent golden eagle or black vulture. What you won't see – despite the emblem on all the promotional material – is the **Iberian lynx**, which is under serious threat of extinction. The last lynx was caught in the park in 1992, and there's been no sign of one now for many years – fewer than 200 are believed to exist in the wild, all now in Spain.

The reserve covers 16,000 hectares of heather-clad hills and oak woodland, with the reserve headquarters in Penamacor (see opposite). They can usually rustle up an English-speaking member of staff, and the office also sells a map and separate walking booklet in English. Note that not all the **hiking trails** are currently signposted, as neglect, forest fires and vandalism have taken their toll – but you can always follow our directions instead.

Barragem da Ribeira da Meimoa

To combine a scenic drive and walk, take the Penamacor road south of Sabugal and turn off after around 4km for the village of **Malcata**, near the Barragem do Sabugal. Just before you reach the village, turn off on a new minor road (not shown on most

---

A HIKE IN THE MALCATA RESERVE

An easy hike, the **Espírito Santo** trail (4.6km; 1hr 30min), through typical Malcata heather and oak-wood scenery, starts near the village of Quadrazais. We hesitate to say you can't get lost, but it would be difficult.

Drive 15km down the minor but good 538 road from Sabugal. At Quadrazais, take the Vale de Espinho road and 500m down this road take the right turn down a good dirt track (signposted "Reserva Natural, Rio Côa") for 300m to the River Côa. Drive over the bridge to the parking and picnic area and then walk up to the trail information board. Don't turn left for the chapel, but head straight up the track by the side of the wire fence and when you reach a T-junction after 750m, turn right. The track skirts the flank of a hill, through pine nurseries, and after 1.25km meets another T-junction at a ruined building, where you turn left (a wooden "PR1" marker shows the turn). Continue for another 1km, through shady oak, reaching a left turn on a rise with wind turbine views (again, there's a wooden "PR1" marker). Turn left here and it's then 1.6km around the other flank of the hill, dropping down to the chapel and river, where you started.

It's nice to combine this walk with lunch at the appealing *Trutal Côa* restaurant (open all year, lunch and dinner; closed Wed; 📞271 606 227), located at the trout farm, just a few kilometres away – it's sited 2km before the village of Vale de Espinho.

maps, signposted to Meimão) to wind right through a dramatic line of wind turbines before dropping into the rustic village of **Meimão**. From here, follow signs for "Barragem", which lead you above the edge of the reservoir and right to the dam wall of the **Barragem da Ribeira da Meimoa** (20km total drive from Sabugal).

You can cross the wall and park and then try to follow the eight-kilometre (2hr) trail, which is shown on the information board here, but suffers from a lack of signs. At the very least, you can walk out along the waterside track for a couple of kilometres and enjoy the views. The nearest facilities are further down the Penamacor road, at **Meimoa** (not to be confused with Meimão), 13km from Penamacor, which has a couple of simple restaurants.

Penamacor

Just outside the reserve, **PENAMACOR** has another medieval castle, not as impressive as those in Sabugal and Sortelha but still offering great views over the Serra da Malcata towards Spain. It's reached by a short but punishing climb up from the newer part of town, and the restored walls enclose a dilapidated village that's just beginning to get a face-lift. Back down the hill, the public gardens have more sweeping views over the southern plains of the Beira Baixa – there's an outdoor café here.

ARRIVAL AND INFORMATION

By car Penamacor is 34km southwest of Sabugal, which is a quick 35-minute drive. You'll need a car to get to the reserve, as there is no public transport. Once there, you're best off walking or cycling round the reserve itself.

RESERVA NATURAL DA SERRA DA MALCATA

Information The Reserva Natural da Serra da Malcata HQ is in Penamacor, at Rua António Ribeiro Sanches 60 (Mon–Fri 9am–12.30pm & 2–5.30pm; ☎ 277 394 467) – to find it, follow the main street uphill from the gardens and around to the left towards the church.

Monsanto and around

Ancient **MONSANTO** jealously guards its title of the "most Portuguese" village in the country, an award originally bestowed in 1948. Sited high on a hill above the plain, its houses huddle between giant granite outcrops, their walls moulded around enormous grey boulders – in the case of the **Casa de Uma Só Telha** ("the house with only one tile"), the entire roof is formed from a single rock. A few houses lie abandoned, but on the whole Monsanto seems to be doing well from Spanish day-trippers and from tourists still searching for the "real" Portugal. Gift shops aside, facilities are limited to a couple of cafés and a small *mercearia* (grocer's), but there's enough to do if you decided to stay the night and it certainly is an experience.

A fine driving **circuit east and south of Monsanto** leads to some fascinating border outposts, each with a well-marked walking trail. You can do it easily in a day, with time for a walk or two, before returning to Monsanto via Idanha-a-Velha (90km total trip).

A walk around Monsanto

A leaflet available from Monsanto turismo dutifully details every church, chapel, cross, decayed mansion and restored fountain in the village. The main cobbled path heads up to the **castelo** (always open; free), 700m up and offering remarkable views across the parched plains to the distant mountains. An enjoyable walk leads you around the castle and rock outcrops in a couple of hours, also dropping down to **São Pedro de Vir-à-Corça** chapel, in a grotto of cork trees below the crags. You'll pick up the walk-posts all over town, and there's an information board outside the turismo.

Penha Garcia

Heading down the N239, it's a ten-kilometre drive east from Monsanto to the similarly crag-bound village of **Penha Garcia**. A splendid trail (3km; 1hr) climbs up to the skeletal castle and then down into a rather magical gorge below a dam wall, where fossils of the furrows of giant trilobites have been found (some are on display in the village antiquary). There's a swimming area cut into the gorge terraces, with the trail leading back to the village via a fascinating series of old mills and watercourses. Have a drink in the *Frágua* (closed Mon), a bar built into the former forge (the archaic bellows are still *in situ*), while at weekends some of the local women fire up the village's communal bread oven and make bread to sell to visitors.

Salvaterra do Extremo

From Penha Garcia, the road sweeps on another 12km towards the Spanish border and the eminently missable collection of spa hotels and pensions that make up **Termas de Monfortinho**. However, turn south here at the roundabout (for Zebreira and Castelo Branco) and it's 15km down the N240 for the turn-off to sleepy **Salvaterra do Extremo**, which sits a little way inland from the Rio Erges (Erjas in Spanish), a tributary of the Tejo, which delineates the border. A signposted trail (10km; 3–4hr) takes in the old village, river and surrounding olive groves, but even if you're not up for this, at least walk the first one-kilometre section down an ancient stone pathway to the river viewpoint and bird hide, where eagles and vultures soar on the thermals.

Segura

A back road from Salvaterra do Extremo leads directly to **Segura** to the south (signposted as 6km, more like 9km), a small church-topped village also right on the Rio Erges and border. A waymarked ten-kilometre trail (3–4hr) takes you through more fine scenery, and includes the remains of the area's old lead mines.

Alcántara and the Spanish border

From Segura, it's around 35km to Idanha-a-Velha, via Zebreira, or 60km to Castelo Branco, but you might find a dash across the border irresistible. Just 20km southwest, across the Roman bridge at the border and down a fast road, is the small Spanish town of **Alcántara**. This sits high above the Rio Tajo (the Tejo in Portuguese) and is crossed by a magnificent bridge, also Roman. In the part-abandoned old town, crumbling mansions and churches have been colonized by storks whose unearthly machine-gun chatter accompanies any stroll through the quiet streets.

ARRIVAL AND INFORMATION   MONSANTO

By bus Buses from Castelo Branco (1–2 daily) stop at the parking area immediately outside the old village; the return service is at the early hour of 7.15am (though at 2.30pm on Sunday).

By car Monsanto is 48km northeast of Castelo Branco, and 25km south of Penamacor. There's a newer settlement right at the bottom of the hill and, further up, a small parking area outside the old village – don't be tempted to drive any further in.

By taxi For more distant local walks, you might need the services of Señor Adelinho, whose taxi (☎ 966 773 658) sits in the parking area – he lives above the *O Jovem* café opposite and is used to ferrying foreigners around (he speaks German, but no English).

Information The turismo is on Rua Marquês da Graciosa (June–Sept daily 10am–1pm & 2–6pm; Oct–May daily 9.30am–1pm & 2–5.30pm; ☎ 277 314 642). Walk up from the parking area to the church and turn right along the main street for the turismo and – eventually – the castle.

ACCOMMODATION AND EATING

Casa do Chafariz ☎ 914 253 793, ✉ casadochafariz1 @sapo.pt. A short way along the main street (signposted), this is a refurbishment of an old Monsanto house, with rooms built into the rock outcrops. Breakfast is available for a small extra charge. **€50**

Estalagem de Monsanto Rua de Capela 3 ☎ 277 314 481, ⊛ monsanto.homestead.com. The small village inn has undergone a couple of transformations in recent years, but it's currently offering ten en-suite rooms – nothing fancy, but perfectly good for the night – and a decently priced restaurant and bar (set menu €10, otherwise dishes €5–15). **€70**

Petiscos & Granitos ☎ 277 314 029. Eating out is fairly restricted in Monsanto – there are more gift shops than restaurants – but the restaurant-tavern on the way up to the castle is good for an atmospheric meal among the boulders. It's a bit on the pricey side (meals around €20), but the views are great. Daily 10am–midnight; closed Wed in winter.

Idanha-a-Velha

The isolated village of **IDANHA-A-VELHA** is 15km south of Monsanto by road, though closer by footpath. It might seem a forgotten backwater now, but it was a large Roman city in the first century BC and was later an important Visigothic settlement – one legend proudly records that the famous Visigothic king Wamba (reigned 672–680 AD) was born here (though at least two places in Spain claim him as well). During the fifteenth century, more local folklore has it that the inhabitants were driven from the village by a plague of rats, after which time the village fell into terminal decline. People do still live in Idana-a-Velha today – grazing sheep on the plains and tending allotments down by the river – but it often seems almost deserted. Indeed, the village looks much as it must have done when the rats moved in, and perhaps not very different from when the Romans left, either.

Around the village

Set amid burned plains and olive groves, the old village is still partly girded by a massive **Roman wall**. Down by the languid river the **Roman bridge** is still in use, while roses and vines are trained up the weathered walls of the houses, many built from plundered Roman stone. A stork's nest tops the ancient **basilica** – signposted as the Sé – while outside here stand the ruins of the **bishop's palace** and an even earlier Roman house. Perhaps the most fascinating restoration is of the old oil press or **Lagar de Varas**, with an ingenious pressing system utilizing two huge tree trunks, with roots intact. The basilica and the olive-oil-press building should be open during turismo office hours, but if not, just ask.

ARRIVAL, INFORMATION AND EATING · IDANA-A-VELHA

On foot There's no public transport to the village, although there is a great footpath from Monsanto (7km; 2hr). Walk down to the São Pedro de Vir-à-Corça chapel from Monsanto (red and yellow marks) and, behind the chapel, pick up the red and white markers that run down ancient tracks, through cork and olive groves, to Idanha-a-Velha. You wouldn't want to walk back uphill, though, so arrange a taxi in Monsanto first.

Information The turismo is on Rua da Sé, behind the Lagar (April–Sept daily 10am–1pm & 2–6pm; Oct–March daily 9.30am–1pm & 2–5.30pm; ☎277 914 280, ⓦcm-idanhanova.pt, ⓦidanha-a-velha.webnode.pt).
Eating and drinking There is a café in the village by the *pelourinho* but the nearest restaurants and accommodation are in Idanha-a-Nova, 20km to the southwest.

Idanha-a-Nova

The local municipal centre of **IDANHA-A-NOVA** is "nova" only in comparison with ancient Idanha-a-Velha. High above the nearby dam and Rio Ponsul, it presents a likeable, little-visited *zona antiga* of noble mansions and imposing churches. Not all has been tidily restored, and it's much the better for it, though the local council is making strenuous efforts to promote the town and its surroundings.

With history repeating itself in a rather neat way, there's a new town (*zona nova*) set even higher above the old – Idanha-a-Nova-Nova, if you like – where the planners have put the bus station, cultural centre, library and residential suburbs.

ARRIVAL AND DEPARTURE · IDANHA-A-NOVA

By car Idanha-a-Nova is 40km northeast of Castelo Branco and a quick 20km drive from the old village of Idanha-a-Velha, to the northeast. There are buses from Castelo Branco, though it's extremely unlikely that Idanha-a-Nova falls into any must-see itinerary – it does, however, make a handy base (or coffee stop en route) for seeing Idanha-a-Velha.

ACCOMMODATION AND EATING

Estrela da Idanha Av Joaquim Morão ☎277 200 500, ⓦestreladaidanha.pt. Up in the new town, this very agreeable three-star hotel sits right on top of the hill. There's a covered outdoor pool, and smart, spacious rooms with balconies and big views, and if you'd rather not eat in the restaurant it's just a twenty-minute walk down into town. **€60**

4

★ **Helana** Rua José Silvestre Ribeiro 35 ☎ 277 201 095, ✆ helana.com. There are one or two defiantly elderly cafés in town as well as this ubiquitously signposted stalwart, which serves a mix of pizzas, pasta and regional Portuguese dishes, including river-fish soup and sautéed wild mushrooms. You can eat for €15–20. Mon & Thurs–Sun noon–2.30pm & 7.30–10.30pm.

Pousada de Juventude Praça da República 32 ☎ 277 208 051, ✆ microsites.juventude.gov.pt/portal /en. There's not a lot of budget accommodation around in these parts, so it might pay to detour to Idanha for hostel dorms and rooms in a grand, restored mansion in the centre of town. Dorm beds €12; doubles €30

Castelo Branco and around

As capital of the Beira Baixa, **CASTELO BRANCO** has an air of prosperity compared to many of the nearby villages. Various frontier wars have robbed the town of much of its age-old history, save the sixteenth-century former town hall, a few handsome mansions, and some castle ruins at the top of town, where a garden *miradouro* offers sweeping views. Otherwise, it's a pleasant enough, predominantly modern town of sweeping boulevards, squares and parks, with a broad, leafy central avenue that's been opened up for pedestrians – there's also a daily **market** at the **Mercado Municipal**, down Av 1º de Maio, near the turismo. That said, you don't have to head very far out of town for some peace, quiet and natural beauty, with a string of stunning viewpoints and ancient villages within easy reach.

Jardim do Paço Episcopal

Rua Bartolomeu da Costa • Daily: Oct–April 9am–5pm; May–Sept 9am–7pm • €2

Flanking one side of the remaining old town is the **Jardim do Paço Episcopal**, the eighteenth-century garden of the old bishop's palace, whose twin showpiece staircases sport elaborate historic statues – on one, figures of the Apostles; on the other, the successive kings of Portugal, including three that, curiously, are much smaller than the others. The reason? They are the figures of the Spanish Habsburg rulers, Felipe I, II and III, whose sixty-year reign in Portugal is still cause for resentment.

Museu Tavares Proença Júnior

Largo Dr José Dias Lopes • Oct–April Tues–Sun 10am–12.30pm & 2–5.30pm; May–Sept Tues–Sun 10am–12.30pm & 2–7pm • €2, free on Sun morning • ☎ 272 347 880

The former bishop's palace now houses the **Museu Tavares Proença Júnior**, whose pride and joy is its large display of embroidered bedspreads, known as *colchas*. These lavish status symbols were originally produced in India and China where wealthy Portuguese commissioned them from local artisans. The craftspeople duly incorporated motifs from their own myths and culture – typically animals, flowers and mythical figures – which subsequently influenced Portuguese manufacturers in Castelo Branco.

Vila Velha de Rodão

27km southwest of Castelo Branco, down the A23 motorway

A quick drive out of town takes you to **Vila Velha de Rodão** on the Rio Tejo. Don't go into the village but keep on the Portalegre road until you reach the bridge and a brown sign pointing across the railway tracks for "Portas do Rodão"; at the top of the hill, turn at the "Ermida" sign. From the balcony in front of the restored Castelo de Rodão keep there are stupendous views of the serpentine Tejo River and the sheer walls of the **Portas do Rodão** (Rodão Gates) – the jaw-droppingly beautiful gorge that confronts rail passengers on the Lisbon–Castelo Branco line.

Foz do Cobrão and the schist villages

Follow the sign outside Vila Velha de Rodão for Alvaiade (7km) and, once there, follow a brown tourist sign to Foz do Cobrão, for another few kilometres

Foz do Cobrão is one of the region's typical schist villages, spectacularly sited in arid hills close to the **Portas de Vale Mourão** gorge – there's a viewpoint on the road in, just before the village. The schist villages (known as *aldeias de xisto*) are all seeing sustainable tourist investment of one kind or another, and the fruits in Foz do Cobrão are a river beach (*praia fluvial*) and a circular eleven-kilometre (4hr) hiking trail that takes in the gorge and, depending on your luck, the storks, eagles, vultures and otters that inhabit the valley. Park outside the *Restaurante Vale Mourão* at the top of the village, where there's a walk information board.

ARRIVAL AND INFORMATION

By bus From the bus station, turn right and it's a short walk up to the main Alameda da Liberdade.

Destinations Covilhã (1–5 daily; 1hr); Guarda (3–5 daily; 1hr 40min); Lisbon (7 daily; 2hr 30min); Monsanto (Mon–Fri 2 daily, Sun 1; 1hr 30min); Penamacor (Sun–Fri 1–2 daily; 1hr 20min); Sabugal (Sun–Fri 1 daily; 2hr); Viseu (2–5 daily; 2hr 30min–3 hr).

By car Grab a parking space where you can along the two avenues (Avenida 1° de Maio and Avenida de Nuno Álvares) approaching the Alameda da Liberdade, which

CASTELO BRANCO

is the main thoroughfare through town. Or try Largo de São João near the Paço Episcopal gardens.

By train The train station is 500m from the main Alameda da Liberdade, down Avenida de Nuno Álvares, with regular services to Covilhã (6 daily; 1hr–1hr 20min) and Lisbon (5 daily; 3hr 10min–3hr 45min).

Information The turismo is on Av de Nuno Álvares 30 (Mon–Fri 9.30am–7.30pm, Sat & Sun 9.30am–1pm & 2.30–6pm; ☎ 272 330 339, ⊛ cm-castelobranco.pt).

ACCOMMODATION AND EATING

Império Rua dos Prazeres 20 ☎ 272 341 720, ⊛ imperio dorei.pt. Behind the post office, in a quiet street close to the cathedral – follow Alameda da Liberdade around towards the gardens and museum. A friendly place with air-conditioned rooms and gleaming bathrooms; downstairs rooms are gloomier but cool in summer. No credit cards. €35

★ **O Jardim** Rua da Figueira 29–31 ☎ 272 342 850. Cosy restaurant with a big local reputation. Lunch is a bargain, but the *à la carte* prices are hardly off-putting, with grills from around €8 and house specials for €9–12, including great steaks – and many come specially for the prawn curry. It's signposted up an alley between Alameda da Liberdade and Largo da Sé, opposite Famácia Ferrer, just before the post office. Thurs–Tues noon–3pm & 7–10pm.

Praça Velha Largo Luís de Camões 17 ☎ 272 328 640, ⊛ pracavelha.com. This fashionable old-town restaurant presents a fairly traditional menu, but with a few contemporary twists – octopus *carpaccio*, for example, followed by a *feijoada* made with hare or *tournedos* with sheep's cheese. Prices are on the high side (mains from €13, though cheaper at lunch. Tues–Sat 12.30–3pm & 8–10.30pm, Sun 12.30–3pm.

Rainha Dona Amélia Rua Santiago 15 ☎ 272 348 800, ⊛ bestwesternrainhadamelia.com. Smart, spacious rooms in warm tones make this the best mid-range choice. The three-star hotel itself is a bit traditional (restaurant no one uses, souvenirs no one buys), but there's a buffet breakfast and garage parking. It's off the bottom of Av 1° de Maio. €55

Tryp Colina do Castelo Rua da Piscina ☎ 272 349 280, ⊛ solmelia.com. The fanciest place in town has a lofty location by the castle, rooms with soft-focus interiors and breathtaking views from the balconies and bar. There's also parking, a health club with sauna, Turkish baths and squash courts. Website room-only deals start at around €40. €55

4

Porto and the Rio Douro

PORTO RIVERFRONT

5

Porto and the Rio Douro

Lisbon might be the country's capital, but Portugal's second city, Porto, is very definitely not second best. Dramatically situated at the mouth of the Rio Douro, it's a massively atmospheric place that's well worth a couple of days of your time – more if you plan to make a serious assault on the famous port wine lodges of Vila Nova de Gaia, located just across the river. For a convenient trip to the seaside, the pretty town of Vila do Conde, 45 minutes to the north, offers a taste of what's to come as you head up the coast towards the Minho. East of Porto, meanwhile, the N15 or much faster A4 motorway runs inland to the *vinho verde*-producing towns of Penafiel and Amarante, the latter perhaps the single most attractive town in the region, set on the lazy Rio Tâmega.

Inevitably, however, it's the **Rio Douro** ("River of Gold") that defines the region, winding for over 200km from the Spanish border to the sea, with port wine lodges and tiny villages dotted above intricately terraced hillsides. It was once a wild and unpredictable river, though after the port-producing area was first demarcated in the eighteenth century, engineering works soon tamed the worst of the rapids and opened up the Douro for trade. The railway reached the Spanish border by the end of the nineteenth century, while the building of hydroelectric dams and locks along the river's length in the 1970s and 1980s turned the Douro into a series of navigable ribbon lakes.

It's possible to cruise all the way from Porto to Barca d'Alva on the Spanish border, while the drive along the Douro also makes for an unforgettable journey. But take the train at least part of the way if you can, since the main **Douro train line** is no slouch for scenery – particularly once you've reached the rough halfway point, marked by the port wine town and cruise centre of **Peso da Régua**. Just to the south of Régua, a slight detour takes in the delightful Baroque pilgrimage town of **Lamego** and the fascinating churches and historic buildings of its little-explored surroundings. Beyond Régua, the main stop is the idyllically set wine-town of **Pinhão**, and the train line continues to hug the river as far as its terminus at **Pocinho**, though the Douro itself still has a way to go, winding on to the border at **Barca d'Alva**. However, following the uppermost reaches of the Douro is impossible by road beyond Pinhão, with the N222 finally veering south of the river to reach the extraordinary collection of paleolithic rock engravings near **Vila Nova de Foz Côa**.

Porto

While *Portus Cale* (the Romans' "sheltered port") has a long history, modern **PORTO** largely eschews its distant past and presents itself to visitors as a busy commercial city rather than a prettified tourist destination. If that puts you off, it shouldn't, because commerce is written into Porto's DNA, from the great trading river at the heart of the city to the Baroque churches and Neoclassical buildings funded by merchants who made good. If it's never quite what you'd call gentrified – especially in the old riverside back-alleys – modern Porto does at least look better now than it has done for decades. Since 2001, when it was declared European City of Culture, many of the streets and squares have been reconstructed and historic buildings restored, particularly in the riverside *bairro* of **Ribeira** – now a UNESCO World Heritage Site – where the waterfront cafés and restaurants are an obvious attraction.

Highlights

❶ Fundação Serralves, Porto Don't miss the designer-style contemporary art gallery, surrounded by the city's most enjoyable park. **See p.269**

❷ Touring the port wine lodges, Vila Nova de Gaia Wine tastings and tours galore are offered by the country's leading port wine producers. **See p.270**

❸ Rio Douro river cruise Pass under the city bridges, or let the vineyards drift by, on a trip along the "River of Gold". **See p.273**

❹ Amarante A dreamy riverside town that's an upmarket weekend getaway. **See p.284**

❺ Lunch on the Douro Enjoy an alfresco riverside lunch at the stylish DOC restaurant near Peso da Régua. **See p.290**

❻ Manor-house stay, Lamego This pretty town is known for its *quintas* and *solares* – manor houses that offer restful nights in peaceful surroundings. **See p.294**

❼ Pinhão Road, rail and river hug the Rio Douro as far as this beautifully sited port-producing town with stunning local accommodation choices. **See p.295**

❽ Rock art at Foz Côa Some of the world's oldest works of art, dating back over 20,000 years. **See p.297**

HIGHLIGHTS ARE MARKED ON THE MAP ON PP.258–259

5

Once you've scooted around the commercial centre and seen the cathedral, the only two essential cultural attractions are the applied-art collections of the **Museu Nacional Soares dos Reis** and the world-class **Fundação Serralves** museum of contemporary art. Otherwise, tourism in Porto generally consists of lounging at a dockside café, enjoying a cruise on the Douro, swigging port across the river in **Vila Nova de Gaia** or taking the antique tram out to the local beach at **Foz do Douro**, at the mouth of the Rio Douro.

Avenida dos Aliados

Not quite all roads lead to the **Avenida dos Aliados** (just "Aliados" to locals), but most do. At the foot of the broad avenue – in the area known as Praça da Liberdade – are a couple of pavement cafés and an equestrian statue of Dom Pedro IV; at the head stands the statue of celebrated local boy Almeida Garrett (1799–1854), poet, novelist, dramatist and Liberal politician. Behind the statue at the top of the avenue is Porto's city hall, the **Câmara Municipal**, while off the bottom the **Estação de São Bento** might be a mere train station but it's one of the city's grandest buildings – the entrance hall contains 20,000 magnificent *azulejos* depicting two great themes, namely the history of transport and the history of Portugal.

Mercado do Bolhão

Rua Formosa • Mon–Fri 7am–5pm, Sat 7am–1pm

Heartbeat of the busy commercial area centred on Rua Formosa is the double-decker, wrought-iron **Mercado do Bolhão**. The structure might be a bit the worse for wear, as the years have taken their toll, but it's still the principal place in the city centre to buy meat, fish, fruit, veg and handicrafts. It's particularly good for bread (sold from little cabins in the middle), flowers and dried mountain herbs and teas, while one stall sells nothing but enormous mounds of garlic.

PORTO AND THE DOURO

HIGHLIGHTS

1 Fundação Serralves, Porto
2 Touring the port-wine lodges, Vila Nova de Gaia
3 Rio Douro river cruise
4 Amarante
5 Lunch on the Douro
6 Manor house stay, Lamego
7 Pinhão
8 Rock art at Foz Côa

5

Torre dos Clérigos

Rua São Filipe Nery • **Tower** April–Oct daily 9.30am–1pm & 2.30–7pm; Nov–March daily 10am–noon & 2–5pm • €2, binoculars €3 • **Church** Daily 8.45am–12.30pm & 3.30–7pm • Free

Best vantage point in the city centre is from the top of the Baroque **Torre dos Clérigos**, which towers 75m above the streets. The slender finger was the tallest building in Portugal when completed in 1763 and, having puffed up the two hundred-odd stairs, you can enjoy the sweeping views (you can rent binoculars at the ticket desk). Before you leave, step through the door into the associated church, the **Igreja dos Clérigos** – designed, like the tower, by busy Porto architect Nicolau

Nasoni, who, after half a lifetime spent in his adopted city, was buried in the church at his own request.

Around the Jardim da Cordoaria

The main university building in Porto flanks one side of the **Jardim da Cordoaria**, whose gigantic plane trees shelter impromptu card and chess schools. There are more monumental buildings to all sides, and a grouping of pavement cafés flanking Praça de Parada Leitão – you can catch the tram out towards Foz do Douro from here too.

5

PORTO'S ARCHITECTURE

Porto's churches in particular provide one of the country's richest concentrations of **Baroque** architecture. The style was brought to Portugal by Italian painter and architect **Nicolau Nasoni** (1691–1773), who arrived in Porto at the age of 34, and remained here all his life. The church and tower of Clérigos is his greatest work, though his masterful touch can also be seen in the cathedral and adjacent bishop's palace, and at the churches of Misericórdia, Carmo, Santo Ildefonso and São Francisco. All are remarkable for their decorative exuberance, reflecting the wealth derived from Portugal's colonies.

In the second half of the eighteenth century, out went the luxuriant complexity of Baroque and in came the studied lines of the **Neoclassical** period. Neoclassicism also incorporated hints of Gothic and Baroque art, but most of all, Islamic, which reached its apotheosis in the Salão Árabe of the Palácio da Bolsa. By the turn of the twentieth century Porto's Neoclassicism had acquired a distinctly French Renaissance touch, thanks largely to the architect **José Marquês da Silva** (1869–1947), who studied in Paris. His most notable works were São Bento railway station, the exuberant Teatro Nacional São João, and the distinctly less elegant monument to the Peninsular War that dominates the Rotunda da Boavista.

Not until the 1950s did Porto see the emergence of a style of architecture that it could call its own, with the beginning of the so-called **Porto School**, centred on the city's School of Fine Arts. This proved fertile ground for many of Porto's contemporary architects, including Eduardo Souto Moura (Casa das Artes, and the conversion of the Alfândega), Alcino Soutinho (the conversion of the Casa-Museu Guerra Junqueiro, and Amarante's Museu Amadeo Sousa Cardoso), and – most famously – **Álvaro Siza Vieira**, whose masterpiece in Porto is the contemporary art museum at the Fundação Serralves (1999). Earlier works of his can be seen in Leça da Palmeira, north of the city, such as the Piscina de Mar swimming pool (1966) and Casa de Chá da Boa Nova (1963), both hidden in the rocks by the shore – the Casa de Chá was a renowned café-restaurant for years but has currently been sadly abandoned to the elements and vandals.

A word should also be said about the city's famous **bridges** – there are five more besides the landmark Ponte Dom Luís I (see p.266), notably the Ponte do Infante, whose central 280-metre reinforced-concrete arch is the world's longest, and further east upriver, Gustave Eiffel's iron railway bridge, Ponte Dona Maria Pia. Best way to see them all is to take a river cruise (see p.273).

Centro Português de Fotografia

Campo Mártires da Pátria, Cordoaria • Tues–Fri 10am–12.30pm & 3–6pm, Sat, Sun & hols 3–7pm • Free • ☎ 220 046 300, ⓦ cpf.pt

The imposing Neoclassical building to the south of the Jardim da Cordoaria – distinguished by 103, mostly barred, windows – was the city's eighteenth-century prison, the Cadeia da Relação, which remained in use until 1974. It's now the headquarters of the **Centro Português de Fotografia**, which has restored the building's cells, chambers, workshops and internal courtyards as rather extraordinary exhibition spaces. Temporary shows cover anything from vintage Portuguese photography to contemporary urban work from Brazil and elsewhere, while up on the top floor is a collection of antique cameras and photographic equipment – from the "stereographoscope" of 1885 to all manner of classic Kodaks and Yashicas.

Igreja do Carmo

Rua do Carmo • Mon & Wed 8am–noon & 1–6pm, Tues & Thurs 9am–6pm, Fri 9am–5.30pm, Sat 9am–4pm, Sun 9am–1.30pm • Free

Beyond the north side of Cordoaria, across from the university, the eighteenth-century **Igreja do Carmo** has two instantly recognizable traits – its deliriously over-the-top exterior *azulejos* and the four saints atop the facade, seemingly poised to jump. Inside, the elegant gilt carvings are among the finest examples of Portuguese Rococo. The older and rather more sober **Igreja das Carmelitas** lies almost adjacent, but not quite, as a law stipulated that no two churches were to share the same wall (in this case perhaps to hinder amorous liaisons between the nuns of Carmelitas and the monks of Carmo).

As a result, what is probably the **narrowest house in Portugal** – barely 1m wide, and with its own letterbox – was built between them and, though now empty, remained inhabited until the 1980s.

Museu Nacional Soares dos Reis

Rua Dom Manuel II 44 • Tues 2–6pm, Wed–Sun 10am–6pm • €5, free on Sun & hols 10am–2pm • ☎ 223 393 770, ⓦ mnsr.imc-ip.pt

A five-minute walk from the Cordoaria, behind the hospital, stands the **Museu Nacional Soares dos Reis**. Serralves aside, it's the best museum in Porto and in fact was Portugal's first designated art museum, founded in 1833 to preserve works confiscated from dissolved monasteries and convents. The present building, into which the collection moved in the 1940s, was once a royal residence that served as the French headquarters in the Peninsular War.

The museum takes its name from sculptor António Soares dos Reis (1847–89), whose best-known work is here – *O Desterrado* (The Exile) – along with an extensive display of Portuguese art from the sixteenth to twentieth centuries. But it's the **applied and decorative art** that's perhaps most engaging – the museum contains excellent collections of gold jewellery, religious silverwork, Portuguese glassware, earthenware and textiles, delicate Chinese ceramics, noble French furniture, and painted screens and laquered cabinets from the Far East. Special exhibitions concentrate on particular periods, artists or themes, and you could spend hours here just browsing; there's also a garden and a good café, serving a daily lunch.

Jardim do Palácio de Cristal

Rua Dom Manuel II • Daily: April–Sept 8am–9pm; Oct–March 8am–7pm • Free

Follow Rua Dom Manuel II past the Soares dos Reis museum and you reach the **Jardim do Palácio de Cristal**, whose centrepiece pavilion – a kind of concrete tea-cosy – replaced a far more elegant 1860s iron-and-glass "Crystal Palace". The pavilion hosts varied concerts and events, and there's a popular open-air self-service café by the lake, but it's the surrounding **gardens** that are the real draw – with an avenue of lime trees and lovely river views from high vantage points on the south side. The municipal library is sited near the main entrance, while other buildings and galleries put on exhibitions, workshops, summer concerts and children's activities.

Sé and around

Terreiro da Sé • **Cathedral** April–June & Oct daily 9am–12.30pm & 2.30–7pm; July–Sept Mon–Sat 9am–7pm, Sun 9am–12.30pm & 2.30–7pm; Nov–March daily 9am–12.30pm & 2.30–6pm • Free • **Cloisters** April–June & Oct Mon–Sat 9am–12.15pm & 2.30–6pm, Sun & hols 2.30–6pm; July–Sept Mon–Sat 9am–6.30pm, Sun & hols 2.30–6.30pm; Nov–March Mon–Sat 9am–12.15pm & 2.30–5.15pm, Sun & hols 2.30–5.30pm • Cloisters, Sala Capitular and Tesouro €3

Porto's cathedral, the **Sé**, commands the eastern heights above the river, and there's a case for making this your first stop in the city, because the view from the terrace – of the old-town streets tumbling down towards the Douro – puts everything into perspective. On the north tower (the one with the bell), look for the very worn bas-relief depicting a fourteenth-century ship – a reminder of Portugal's (and Porto's) maritime past. Despite its great age – construction began in the twelfth century – there's no real sense of majesty inside the cathedral, with altar and chapels making little impact in the darkness. The **cloisters**, however, are a different matter, their arched walls filled with magnificent Baroque *azulejos*. Architect Nasoni added a grand, granite staircase, which climbs from the cloisters to the restored **Sala Capitular** (Chapter Room), with more *azulejos*, painted ceiling panels and views from the shuttered windows. In the **Tesouro** (Treasury), meanwhile, is the usual boggling array of silver and gold – beautifully lit for once.

5

CENTRAL PORTO

Antas & Bonfirm ▲   Antas & Bonfirm ▲

● **CAFÉS AND RESTAURANTS**

Antunes	1
Café Majestic	6
Café Progresso	5
Casa de Ló	3
Confeitaria do Bolhão	4
Dom Tonho	10
DOP	7
Filha da Mãe Preta	9
O Gancho	2
Rota do Chá	9
Verso em Pedra	8

■ **BARS AND CLUBS**

Boys 'R US	5
Clube Literário do Porto	7
Contagiarte	1
Está-se Bem	8
Maus Hábitos	4
O Meu Mercedes	9
Piolho d'Ouro	2
Tendinha dos Clérigos	3
Vinologia	6

Cedofeita, Rotunda da Boavista, Prelada Campsite, Centro Comercial Brasília, Boavista Stadium & Serralves ▲

Palálio de Cristal & Solar do Vinho do Porto ▲

▲ Alameda das Fontainhas (Fleamarket)

Massarelos & Foz do Douro ▲

Rio Douro

▼ Vila Nova de Gaia

Garagem Atlântico
Batalha Cinema
RUA S. ILDEFONSO
RUA EN REPAREDES
AV. RIO DE FREITAS
RUA A. HERCULANO
PRAÇA DA BATALHA
Teatro Nacional São João
RUA DO SOL
R. DE S. LUIS
RUA AUGUSTO ROSA
RUA CIMO DA VILA
R. PORTA SOL
Police
RUA DO DUQUE DE LOULÉ
PASSEIO DAS FONTAINHAS
RUA DO CATIVO
R. SARAIVA DE CARVALHO
R. ARNALDO GAMA
RUA MIRADOURO
Funicular dos Guindais
AVENIDA G. EIFFEL
Ponte Dom Luís I
City Wall
RUA 31
RUA DA MADEIRA
EST. S. BENTO
RUA DO LOUREIRO
RUA CHÃ
AV. DE VIMARA PERES
Casa-Museu Guerra Junqueiro
PRAÇA ALMEIDA GARRETT
Estação de São Bento
São Bento
AV. D. AFONSO HENRIQUES
R. S. SEBASTIÃO
CANDOMA
R. DE HUGO
Sé
Paço Episcopal
Tunnel
RUA DAS CANASTREIROS
R. DA ALFÂNDEGA
STCP
RUA TRINDADE COELHO
RUA DAS FLORES
RUA MOUZINHO DA SILVEIRA
Torre Medieval
R. P. VENTOSA
BAINHARIA
Igreja dos Grilos
RUA DOS MERCADORES
BARREDO
RIBEIRA
CAIS DA RIBEIRA
R. DO CIMA DO MURO
RUA DOS CLÉRIGOS
Igreja & Torre dos Clérigos
CARMELITAS
R. S. FILIPE NERY
R. DOS CALDEIREIROS
RUA DE TRÁS
RUA DO FERRAZ
Igreja Misericórdia
LARGO S. DOMINGOS
Palácio das Artes
Mercado Ferreira Borges
RUA DE SÃO JOÃO NOVO
Casa do Infante
PRAÇA DA RIBEIRA
P
PRAÇA DE LISBOA
R. S. BENTO DA VITÓRIA
TRAV. FERRAZ
RUA DA VITÓRIA
R. DR. SOUSA VITERBO
Police
PRAÇA DO INFANTE D. HENRIQUE
RUA INFANTE D. HENRIQUE
LARGO DO TERREIRO
RUA S. NICOLAU
CAIS DA ESTIVA
RUA DR. FERREIRA
MARTIRES
Jardim da Cordoaria
CAMPO MÁRTIRES DA PÁTRIA
Centro Português de Fotografia
Mosteiro de São Bento da Vitória
RUA S. MIGUEL
RUA DAS TAIPAS
Teatro de Marionetas
RUA DA BOLSA
RUA DE BELOMONTE
Palácio da Bolsa
Igreja de S. Francisco
RUA FERREIRA BORGES
RUA (COMÉRCIO DO PORTO)
Medieval Tower
R. DO QUITERIRINHO
R. REBOLEIRA
Renex
Palácio da Justiça
RUA DA RESTAURAÇÃO
RUA DR. B. DE CASTRO
Palácio de S. João Novo
RUA DAS VIRTUDES
LARGO DE S. JOÃO NOVO
R. S. JOÃO NOVO
Ig. de S. João Novo
MURO DOS BACALHOEIROS
RUA AFONSO ALBUQUERQUE
FR. ROC. SOARES
R. GONZAGA
R. ARMÉNIA
RUA NOVA DE ALFÂNDEGA
P
C. DAS VIRTUOUS
R. S. PEDRO MIRAGAIA
RUA MIRAGAIA
Ig. de S. Pedro de Miragaia
R. MTE. JUDEUS
R. DA BANDEIRINHA
Museu das Alfândegas

200
0
metres

5

On the south side of the Sé stretches the grandiose facade of the **Paço Episcopal** (not open to the public), the medieval archbishop's palace that was also rebuilt by the designer of much of eighteenth-century Porto, Nicolau Nasoni.

Casa-Museu Guerra Junqueiro

Rua de Dom Hugo 32 • Tues–Sun 10am–12.30pm & 2–5.30pm • €2 • ☎ 222 003 689

Behind the cathedral, the **Casa-Museu Guerra Junqueiro** is where the poet and writer Abílio Manuel Guerra Junqueiro (1850–1923) used to live and write his famous works, which reflected the revolutionary turmoil of the Republican era. He spent a lifetime collecting Iberian and Islamic art, and ceramics, glassware, glazed earthenware, jewellery and textiles are exhibited here in rooms recapturing the atmosphere of the era. The museum also hosts an active calendar of events, including fado performances and poetry readings.

Ribeira

Porto's waterfront – known as the **Ribeira** – has changed dramatically in recent years, from a rough dockside cargo zone to one of the city's major tourist attractions. The arcaded quayside, the **Cais da Ribeira**, is one long run of restaurants and cafés looking across the river to the port wine lodges on the other side. However, come down in the morning – before the parasols and blackboard menus have been put out – and the Ribeira still ticks along in local fashion. Between the postcards and touristy ceramics you'll find dusty grocery stores and a warehouse or two, piled high with bags of potatoes. Meanwhile, behind the arcades and heading up towards the cathedral is a warren of stepped alleys that thumb their noses at the riverside gentrification.

Ponte Dom Luís I

Porto's iconic double-decker bridge, **Ponte Dom Luís I**, provides one of the city's favourite photo opportunities. You can walk across either level to the port wine lodges, bars and restaurants of Vila Nova de Gaia – there's traffic on the bottom level, the metro across the top – and the upper level crossing especially (a nerve-jangling 60m above the water) is worth doing at least once. There are steps from the Ribeira up to the lower-level walkway, which lead past a café built on top of the surviving stone piers of an earlier bridge – a great location for a coffee with an unrivalled bridge and river view.

Casa do Infante

Rua da Alfândega 10 • Tues–Sun 10am–1pm & 2–5.30pm • Museum €2, exhibitions often free • ☎ 222 060 400

Just back from the central riverside stands the **Casa do Infante**, believed to be the house where Prince Henry the Navigator was born in 1394. Once the Crown's customs house, and later part of the Royal Mint, the solid mansion now contains the city archives as well as a museum displaying finds from excavations that revealed the remains of a large Roman palace. The prince himself gets a rather grandiose monument just up the road in the square also bearing his name.

Igreja de São Francisco

Rua do Infante Dom Henrique • Daily: Nov–Feb 9am–6pm; March–June & Oct 9am–7pm; July–Sept 9am–8pm • €3.50 • ☎ 222 062 100

The city's only truly Gothic church, the fourteenth-century **Igreja de São Francisco** (now deconsecrated), is even more remarkable for what lies within. Not only did it get a fabulously opulent Rococo makeover in the eighteenth century – the gilded interior has to be seen to be believed – but it also retains its catacombs, containing thousands of scrubbed human bones. It's an eerie sight for modern sensibilities, but reflects an earlier willingness to confront – and indeed embrace – mortality.

FROM TOP FUNDAÇÃO SERRALVES, PORTO (P.269); TORRE DOS CLÉRIGOS, PORTO (P.260) >

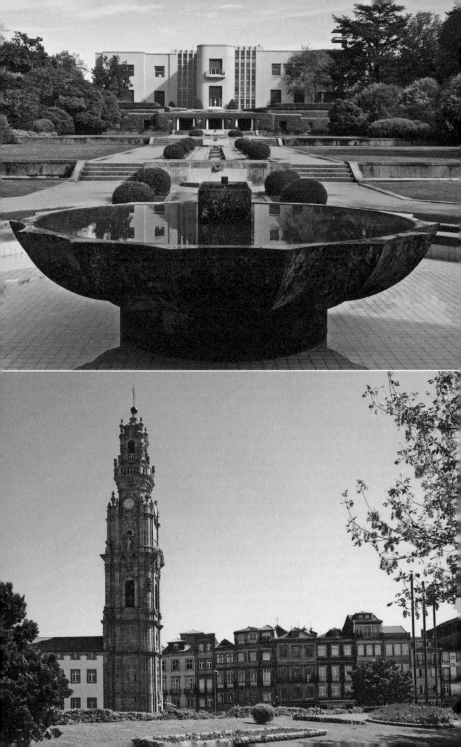

5

Palácio da Bolsa

Rua Ferreira Borges, at Praça do Infante Dom Henrique • Guided tours daily: April–Oct 9am–6.30pm; Nov–March 9am–12.30pm & 2–5.30pm • €7 • ☎ 223 399 000, ⓦ palaciodabolsa.pt

For an indication of the wealth pouring into Porto in earlier days, join a tour of the stock exchange – the **Palácio da Bolsa** – whose interior halls display an almost obscene richness. You don't need to buy a ticket to see the dramatic iron-, glass-and-tile **Patio das Nações** courtyard, a veritable cloister of commerce, whose side rooms contain a craft-and-jewellery store, wine bar and shop, and *O Comercial* restaurant – a rather grand space that is open to the public for a good-value lunch. But to delve any deeper into the building, to encounter over-the-top salons like the extraordinary **Salão Árabe** – inspired by the Alhambra in Granada – you'll have to bear with the rather pricey and fact-heavy guided visits.

Along the river

It's around 2km from the Ribeira along the riverfront pavement and quayside to the Ponte da Arrábida (heading west towards Foz do Douro). This is a good half-hour's walk, enough for most people to get a flavour of the Douro; there are several attractions en route, and you can then jump on the tram or bus #500 back to the city centre or on to Foz and the beach.

Museu das Alfândegas

Rua Nova de Alfândega • Tues–Fri 10am–6pm, Sat, Sun & hols 3–7pm • €3 • ☎ 223 403 000, ⓦ amtc.pt

The Neoclassical Alfândega, or customs house, was constructed on the riverbank between 1860 and 1880. It's a vast building, originally designed to store the cargo of up to forty ships, but now in service as the **Museu das Alfândegas**, which recounts the history of Porto, its trades and industries. The building also houses the Museum of Transport and Communications – the "car through time and space" exhibition entertainingly relates the development of the motor car.

Museu do Vinho do Porto

Rua de Monchique 45–52 • Tues–Sat 10am–12.30pm & 2–5.30pm, Sun 2–5.30pm • €2, free on Sat & Sun • ☎ 222 076 300

Housed in a handsome eighteenth-century former wine warehouse, the **Museu do Vinho do Porto** details the city's take on the history of the port wine trade. In many ways, this is the history of Porto itself and the museum tackles the subject with vim – displays and exhibits chart the development of the port wine business, linking the trade with the fortunes of the major port-wine families and showing how the city grew to become synonymous with wine in just a matter of decades.

Museu do Carro Eléctrico

Alameda Basílio Teles 51 • Mid-June to mid-Sept Mon 2–6pm, Tues–Fri 10am–7pm, Sat, Sun & hols 1.30–7pm; mid-Sept to mid-June Mon 2–6pm, Tues–Fri 9.30am–6pm, Sat, Sun & hols 2–7pm • €4 • ☎ 226 158 185, ⓦ museudocarroelectrico.pt

All Porto's trams make a fitting halt on the riverside outside the **Museu do Carro Eléctrico**. In the echoing spaces of a former power station, you can admire Iberia's oldest streetcar (1872) alongside many other gleaming vintage specimens.

Rotunda da Boavista

The northwestern edge of the city centre – 2km from downtown Aliados – is marked by the large park-cum-roundabout called Praça Mouzinho de Albuquerque but popularly known as the **Rotunda da Boavista**. The mighty obelisk in the centre commemorates the defeat of the French in the Peninsular War (1808–14), with a Portuguese lion squatting on top of a vanquished French eagle.

Casa da Música

Av da Boavista 604 • Guided tours daily at 11am in Portuguese and 4pm in English and Portuguese • €4 • ☎ 220 120 210, ⓦ casadamusica.com • Ⓜ Casa da Música

Rem Koolhaas' **Casa da Música** – a vast white wedge on a bare esplanade – looks as if the Mother Ship has landed, an impression reinforced by the steel staircase leading up into the black maw of the entrance. It was a coup for Porto, a flagship part of its urban regeneration programme, and opened to great fanfare in 2005. Attending a concert or event is clearly the best way to see the building, but there are daily, hour-long guided visits if you want to know more about its dramatic design and construction.

Igreja de São Martinho de Cedofeita

Largo do Priorado, off Rua Aníbal Cunha • Mon–Sat 8–10pm & 5–7pm

Located a few blocks off the Rotunda is the very simple **Igreja de São Martinho de Cedofeita**, which some claim has its origins as far back as the sixth century AD – making it the oldest church in Iberia. However, the existing Romanesque building is a thirteenth-century remodelling of a church whose existence can only be dated with certainty to 1118. Whatever its origins, Cedofeita is unique in being Portugal's only Romanesque church to have kept its original dome, supported by bulky exterior buttresses.

Fundação Serralves

Rua Dom João de Castro 210 • **Museum** April–Sept Tues–Fri 10am–5pm, Sat, Sun & hols 10am–8pm; Oct–March Tues–Fri 10am–5pm, Sat, Sun & hols 10am–7pm • **Park** April–Sept Tues–Fri 10am–7pm, Sat, Sun & hols 10am–8pm, plus July–Sept also open Mon 10am–7pm; Oct–March Tues–Sun 10am–7pm • Museum & park €7; park only €3; both free Sun 10am–1pm • ☎ 226 156 500, ⓦ serralves.pt • Ⓜ Casa da Música, or bus #502 from Bolhão or bus #203 from Rotunda da Boavista

If there's a must-see cultural attraction in Porto it's the contemporary art museum and park run by the **Fundação Serralves**, 4km west of the centre. The **Museu de Arte Contemporânea** is the work of Porto architect Álvaro Siza Vieira, and is a minimalist triumph of white facades and terraces strikingly set in an overwhelmingly green park. There's no permanent collection, but instead several changing exhibitions a year draw on the works of Portuguese and international artists, mainly from the 1960s to the present day. Other exhibitions are held in the separate, pink Art Deco **Casa de Serralves** in the grounds.

You can get an idea of the main building from the outside, and from the terrace café, more formal restaurant and museum shop (all free to enter), which means if the exhibitions aren't to your taste, you miss nothing by just visiting the **park**. Indeed, many people prefer this to the museum itself and it's easy to spend a lazy afternoon here, winding along swept gravel paths and clipped lawns before descending wooded tracks to the herb gardens and farmland beyond, grazed by goats and cattle. There are art installations dotted around and a tea house (open weekends only in winter) in a glade with a vine colonnade. July and August see a sequence of "Jazz no Parque" (Jazz in the Park) **concerts** held in the gardens.

Foz do Douro

5km west of the city centre • Bus #500 from São Bento, bus #203 from the Serralves museum and park, to central Foz, or #502 from Bolhão to Castelo do Queijo • Tram #1 (from Ribeira), or #18 (Igreja do Carmo) down to the terminus at Massarelos and change there to tram #1

Foz do Douro, formerly a fishermen's quarter but a distinctly more upmarket beach suburb these days, is on several bus routes, but it's a nice idea to take the tram at least one way – these drop you by the riverside gardens in Foz. The confluence of river and ocean is dominated by the squat **Castelo de São João**, beyond which stretch several kilometres of coves and beaches, backed by the cafés and bars of Avenida do Brasil,

5

which becomes the hub of Porto's summer nightlife. At the northern end stands the **Castelo do Queijo** (Cheese Castle), so-named because it was built upon boulders that apparently looked like cheese. From here, Avenida da Boavista (and bus #502) runs straight back into the city.

Vila Nova de Gaia

Quickest way to Gaia from Porto's upper town is to take the Funicular dos Guindais (see p.273) down from near Praça da Batalha and walk across the bridge; alternatively, buses #900, #901 and #906 run from São Bento station across the bridge and along the Gaia riverfront • For the upper station of the Teleférico de Gaia, take metro Line D from Ⓜ Aliados/São Bento to Ⓜ Jardim do Morro

Cross to the south side of the Rio Douro, over the Ponte Dom Luís I, and you leave the city of Porto for the separate town of **Vila Nova de Gaia** (or just Gaia), though the distinction is irrelevant to visitors. The riverfront here – facing Porto's Ribeira – also has a long line of cafés, bars and restaurants; cruise boats dock along the esplanade, while the wooden craft with sails are known as *barcos rabelos*, the traditional boats once used to transport wine casks downriver from the Douro port estates. The views are, if anything, better from Gaia than from the Porto side, looking back across to a largely eighteenth-century cityscape, with few modern buildings intruding in the panoramic sweep from Palácio de Cristal gardens to cathedral towers.

The port wine lodges

Gaia, of course, is completely synonymous with the **port wine** trade (see p.296) – you can't miss the dozens of company lodges and warehouses (known as *caves*), some in business for more than three centuries, that splash their brand names across every rooftop, facade and advertising hoarding. They almost all offer **tastings and tours**, conducted in English, with a view to enticing you to buy. Tours of the smaller, lesser-known companies tend to be more personal than those of larger producers, but they are all pretty informative and you'll soon know the difference between a tawny and a ruby, and which vintages are best.

Teleférico de Gaia

Lower station at Cais de Gaia, upper station at Ⓜ Jardim do Morro • Daily: Mid-April to mid-Oct 10am–8pm; mid-Oct to mid-April 10am–6pm • €5 one way, €8 return; children half-price • ☎ 223 723 709, ⓦ gaiacablecar.com

The new way to explore Gaia – and the best way to get some dramatic aerial shots of Porto and the river – is to take a ride on the **Teleférico de Gaia**, or cable car. It connects the upper station, near the top level of the Ponte Dom Luís I, with the far end of the Gaia riverside, in a five-minute, 600-metre journey that sees you suspended right above the rooftops of the historic port wine lodges.

VILA NOVA DE GAIA

5

Map labels:
PORTO
R. NOVA DA ALFÂNDEGA
R. INF. D. HENRIQUE
CAIS DA RIBEIRA
CAIS DE ESTIVA
Ponte Dom Luís I
UPPER LEVEL
LOWER LEVEL
Upper Station
Mosteiro da Serra do Pilar
Rio Douro
Boat Trips
Câlém
AV. DIOGO LEITE
AV. DA REPÚBLICA
Sandeman
Jardim Do Morro
Lower Station
LG. CRUZ
AV. RAMOS PINTO
Ramos Pinto
Ferreira
Graham's
Kopke
Croft
RUA LUIS DE CAMÕES
RUA DIOGO
General Torres
R. COSTA SANTOS
RUA SERRA PINTO
RUA BARÃO FORRESTER
Taylor, Fladgate & Yeatman
Cockburn
Burmester
Rozès
Câmera Municipal
Câmara De Gaia
Barros
Osborne
RUA CONSELHEIRO VELOSA DA CRUZ
R. BARÃO DO CORVO
Port Wine Company

● RESTAURANTS
Barão de Fladgate   2
Casa Adão   1

■ ACCOMMODATION
The Yeatman   1

Aurada
Real Companhia Velha

ARRIVAL AND DEPARTURE

BY PLANE
Porto airport (☎ 229 432 400, ⊕ ana.pt) is 13km north of the city in Maia. Metro Line E (daily 6am–1am, every 20–30min; one-way travel ticket €1.45) runs you directly into the centre in around half an hour – to Casa da Música (for Boavista hotels), Trindade, Aliados or Bolhão (for city-centre hotels), or São Bento or Campanhã (for onward train services). Taxis from the airport into the centre cost €20–25 – make sure you get one from the authorized rank outside the terminal.

BY BUS
Buses to Porto arrive at various stops and garages all over the city, though most are fairly central. Eurolines (international services) and several others use Campo 24 de Agosto, 1km east of the centre (⊕ Campo 24 de Agosto); Garagem Atlântico, Rua Alexandre Herculano, near Praça da Batalha, is a hub for several companies including the national operator Rede Expressos (⊕ rede-expressos.pt); Rodonorte (Estremadura, Ribatejo, Minho, Trás-os-Montes; ⊕ rodonorte.pt) and Santos (Beiras, Trás-os-Montes, Lisbon; ⊕ santosviagensturismo.pt) stop on Rua Ateneu Comercial, near Bolhão market; Minho services tend to stop near Praça da República, north of the centre (near Trindade metro); while Renex (Estremadura, Ribatejo, Lisbon, Algarve and Minho; ⊕ renex.pt) stop at Campo dos Mártires da Pátria 37, next to Palácio da Justiça.

PORTO

Destinations Amarante (up to 10 daily; 1hr); Barcelos (7 daily; 1hr 45min); Braga (every 1hr 30min; 1hr 15min); Bragança (6 daily; 3hr 30min); Chaves (5–10 daily; 2hr); Coimbra (8–10 daily; 1hr 30min); Guimarães (6–12 daily; 1hr); Lamego/Peso da Régua (3–5 daily; 3hr); Lisbon (hourly; 3hr–3hr 30min); Viana do Castelo (hourly; 1hr 15min); Vila Real (6–9 daily; 1hr 30min–2hr).

BY CAR
Driving into Porto is to be avoided, if possible – the city centre is congested and the one-way system confusing. You don't need a car to see the city, so the best advice is to park where you can and use public transport. Major suburban metro stations have parking – particularly at the football stadium, Estádio do Dragão – or use one of the signposted city-centre car parks or garages; following signs for "Centro" or "Aliados" will send you into the maelstrom. Garage parking is expensive – around €1 an hour between 8am and 8pm, slightly cheaper overnight – but you'll have little choice if your hotel doesn't have parking, as on-street metered parking is limited to two hours (though it's free after 8pm and at weekends).

BY TRAIN
Estação de Campanhã International, intercity and ALFA Pendular trains arrive at the Estação de Campanhã, 2km east of the city centre. With a ticket to Porto you can simply

5

change here onto any local train for São Bento station (see below), a five-minute ride away. Campanhã is also on the metro, or it's a €5 taxi ride into the centre.

Destinations Barcelos (14 daily; 1hr–1hr 20min); Coimbra (hourly; 1hr 15min–1hr 50min); Espinho (every 10–30min; 15–30min); Lisbon (hourly; 3hr 20min–4hr); Régua (13 daily; 1hr 45min–2hr 20min); Viana do Castelo (every 1–2hr; 1hr 30min–2hr).

Estação de São Bento is the city-centre station for suburban and regional services. There's a metro station here and taxis outside, though note that São Bento can be a bit of a zoo, with hawkers and touts much in evidence. You can buy tickets for any train at São Bento (even for Campanhã departures).

Destinations Aveiro (every 10–30min; 40–55min); Barcelos (14 daily; 1hr–1hr 20min); Braga (every 30min–1hr; 1hr); Guimarães (hourly; 1hr 5min); Régua (13 daily; 1hr 45min–2hr 20min); Viana do Castelo (every 1–2hr; 1hr 30min–2hr).

Train information There are information offices at both stations, or call ☎ 808 208 208 or consult the CP website, ⓦ cp.pt.

GETTING AROUND

You'll be able to walk – or perhaps more accurately, climb – between all the city-centre attractions, but you'll have to use public transport to get out to the Serralves art museum, the coast and the airport. There's an extensive bus network, and a swift metro system, while a funicular and a couple of old tram lines still remain in service. The local transport authority, **STCP** (☎ 808 200 166, ⓦ stcp.pt), has a useful website (English version available), and information offices (Mon–Fri 8am–7.30pm, Sat 9am–12.30pm) in Campanhã train station and Casa da Música and Trindade metro stations.

TICKETS AND PASSES

Andante card To use public transport you need a rechargeable Andante card (€0.50; ⓦ inhandante.com), available from ticket machines and from other marked Andante shops and kiosks (*Lojas Andante*). You credit the card with one, two or ten trips – the whole region is divided into concentric colour-coded zones, though everywhere you're going to want to go in Porto all falls within the same central zone. The current price for a single trip in the central zone is €1.15 – you can change transport for free within the hour. It sounds complicated, but in practice it isn't, and there are instructions in English at every station.

Andante Tour pass If you're doing a lot of travelling, buy an Andante Tour pass (24hr, €7, or 72hr, €15), which is valid on all metros, buses and trains (and is available on arrival at the airport).

Porto Card The turismos sell the Porto Card (€10.50 one day; €17.50 two days; €21.50 three days), which gives unlimited bus, metro and funicular travel plus discounts or free entry at many museums and monuments, tours, wine cellars, bars, restaurants and shops. There's also a stream-lined one-day version (no transport included) for €5.

BY BUS

Major city bus stops include Praça Almeida Garrett opposite São Bento station, Praça da Liberdade at the bottom of Avenida dos Aliados, Jardim da Cordoaria, and the inter-change at Casa da Música metro station.

BY METRO

The metro system (ⓦ metrodoporto.pt) runs on six lines, A to F, underground in the city centre and then overground to the airport and to suburban destinations. Hours of

---

OUR FIVE FAVOURITE PORT WINE LODGE TOURS

Around thirty port wine lodges in Vila Nova de Gaia are open for tours – our pick of the best is below. Most of the lodges are open daily between May and October; some close at weekends in winter, or are only open then by appointment. Some charge an entrance fee, though it's usually just a couple of euros and the amount is deducted from anything you buy.

Cálem ⓦ calem.pt. One of the best visitor centres, especially informative about the wine's history and the port-wine production process.

Graham's ⓦ grahams-port.com. A lodge originally founded by a Scottish family, and with a splendid tasting terrace overlooking the river.

Ramos Pinto ⓦ ramospinto.pt. The famous advertising posters of this Portuguese company did much to popularize port in the 1900s – there's a really good museum housed in the 1930s' period offices.

Sandeman ⓦ sandeman.eu. The black-hat-and-cape cut-out provides the most recognizable of company logos and the lengthy tour includes an explanatory film and a good museum.

Taylor, Fladgate & Yeatman ⓦ taylor.pt. Founded in 1692, and still an independent family firm, Taylor's has panoramic views from its salon, terrace and restaurant.

5

operation are daily from 6am to 1am (departures every 10–30min), and you need an Andante card (see p.272) to use the system. Other than for the ride in from the airport, or for the trip up the coast to Matosinhos or Vila do Conde, the metro isn't particularly useful for sightseeing, though there are handy city-centre stops at Trindade, Aliados, Bolhão and São Bento, and you can also use it to go to the Casa da Música at the Rotunda da Boavista and FC Porto's stadium, Estádio do Dragão. A spectacular ride to experience is Line D (from Trindade, Aliados or São Bento), which crosses the river to Vila Nova de Gaia along the top tier of Ponte Dom Luís I.

BY TRAM

Porto's trams (*eléctricos*) run 5km from the Ribeira along the river to Foz do Douro (25min), with a branch from the Igreja do Carmo at Cordoaria in the city centre (using this, change halfway at Massarelos, by the tram museum). The service operates daily (9.15am–7pm; departures every 15–30min), and you use your Andante card or other pass, or pay a flat €2.50 fare.

BY FUNICULAR

The quickest way from the city centre down to Ponte Dom Luís I (for Vila Nova de Gaia) and Ribeira is via the Funicular dos Guindais (every 10min: June–Sept Sun–Wed 8am–10pm; Thurs–Sat 8am–midnight; Oct–May Sun–Thurs 8am–8pm, Fri & Sat 8am–midnight; €1.80 each way, or use Andante card); the upper entrance is below Praça da Batalha, down

Rua Augusto Rosa; the lower is right by the bottom tier of the bridge. After a ninety-metre crawl through a tunnel, the carriage drops rather thrillingly down a steep one-in-three gradient beside the medieval city wall.

BY TAXI

A typical taxi ride across town costs €6–7, and most squares and major stations have taxi ranks (or call Radio Táxis ☎ 225 073 900).

TOURS AND CRUISES

River cruises Porto's stock-in-trade is the river cruise along the Douro. Services are daily and frequent in the summer, much reduced between November and February. The cheapest is the fifty-minute bridges cruise (€10), though there are also evening and dinner cruises, and full-day or weekend cruises, with prices ranging from €55 to €200. The longer cruises all operate via the port wine town of Peso da Régua, halfway along the Douro, where – depending on your choice – you're shuttled around a port wine lodge or take a trip on a steam train.

Tours There are also open-top bus tours (from €12), walking tours (from €12), bike tours (from €25), and all manner of other ways of seeing the city, from Segway to helicopter. **Reservations** Porto Tours, Torre Medieval, Calçada Dom Pedro Pitões 15, close to the Sé (daily 10am–7pm; ☎ 222 000 073 or ☎ 222 000 045, ⊛ portotours.com), can book all kinds of tours, including river cruises; trips can also be booked at the city turismos and São Bento train station.

INFORMATION

TURISMOS

As well as the year-round turismos listed below, where you can pick up a useful map and information, there are two summer-season information points, one in Campanhã train station and the other on the Ribeira waterfront.

Turismo Central, Rua Clube dos Fenianos 25, top of Av dos Aliados (daily: June–Oct 9am–8pm; Nov–May 9am–7pm; ☎ 223 393 472).

Turismo Sé, Casa da Câmara, Terreiro da Sé, opposite the cathedral (daily: June–Oct 9am–8pm; Nov–May 9am–7pm; ☎ 223 393 472).

Turismo Vila Nova de Gaia, Av Diogo Leite 242, next to Sandeman (Mon–Sat 10am–1pm & 2–6pm; ☎ 223 703 735, ⊛ cm-gaia.pt), is geared almost exclusively to

pointing you towards the port wine lodges.

Loja de Turismo, Praça Dom João I 43, one block east of Aliados (April–Oct Mon–Fri 9am–7.30pm, Sat, Sun & hols 9.30am–3.30pm; Nov–March Mon–Fri 9am–7pm, Sat, Sun & hols 9.30am–3.30pm; ☎ 927 411 817), is useful for general enquiries about northern Portugal.

WEBSITE AND BLOG

The city council's website, ⊛ portoturismo.pt (also in English), provides the same sort of information as the turismos, while there's more information about Porto and the north of Portugal on ⊛ visitportoandnorth.travel. For a different view of the city, check out ⊛ oportocool .wordpress.com, a blog of the city's fashionable hotspots.

ACCOMMODATION

Porto has a wide range of accommodation and rooms start at €25, though many of the older guesthouses are dog-eared, noisy or dodgy, or all three – budget on €40 for something tolerable and en suite. Nearly all the cheapest accommodation is in the city centre, rather than in the medieval streets nearer the river – there are concentrations along Rua de Cedofeita, Rua do Alamada, around Avenida dos Aliados, and near Praça da Batalha. There's a fair bit of boutique accommodation in and around the city centre, while the upmarket suburbs of Boavista and Serralves, west of the centre, contain most of the city's four- and five-star hotels, though the suburban location is a drawback for sightseers. Only a few hotels have their own parking, but some have negotiated cut-price deals with nearby car parks.

5

CITY CENTRE

★ **Duas Nações** Praça Guilherme Gomes Fernandes 59 ☎ 222 081 616, ⊗ duasnacoes.com.pt; map pp.264–265. A real budget gem, whose updated rooms have satellite TV, fan and central heating, and are double-glazed against the street noise. It's popular with backpackers, as some bunk-style rooms sleep four and prices come in as low as €12.50 per person. Best to book ahead if you want a private bathroom. Breakfast not included, but there's a café just outside. No credit cards. €30

★ **Eurostars das Artes** Rua do Rosário 160–164 ☎ 222 071 250, ⊗ eurostarsdasartes.com; map pp.264–265. Boutique style in a four-star hotel, occupying an impressively restored townhouse in a residential and shopping district near Soares dos Reis museum. Special offers go as low as €65, which is a good deal for a place with a garden and roof-deck, and rooms that come with hardwood floors, six-foot-wide beds and classy marble bathrooms. €100

★ **Grande Hotel de Paris** Rua da Fábrica 27–29 ☎ 222 073 140, ⊗ hotelparis.pt; map pp.264–265. Consistently recommended by readers, the *Grande Hotel* is actually more of a guesthouse in price and feel. The building retains many original fittings, with period furniture and high ceilings, while nice touches proliferate – thick bathroom towels, a small garden, and a good breakfast served in a splendid drawing room. Rear rooms have balconies and old-town views. €60

Grande Hotel do Porto Rua de Santa Catarina 197 ☎ 222 076 690, ⊗ grandehotelporto.com; map pp.264–265. Porto's oldest hotel (three stars) is steeped in nineteenth-century mercantile style, with lots of polished marble and crystal chandeliers, and an echoing gilt-tinged restaurant where breakfast is served. It's also in a very handy location, on the main pedestrianized shopping street. Rooms are on the dowdy side, but prices are pretty good, and even better during special promotions. Limited parking available. €85

Infante Sagres Praça Dona Filipa de Lencastre 62 ☎ 223 398 500, ⊗ hotelinfantesagres.pt; map pp.264–265. A boutique makeover has transformed Porto's central five-star into a glamorous, contemporary design hotel. The antique Persian carpets, crystal chandeliers, Chinese porcelain and stained-glass windows are all still there, but now you can also expect funky Portuguese custom-made furniture and chic cosmopolitan style. There's an open-air patio, good restaurant and Asian-style spa, plus parking nearby. €140

Pão de Açúcar Rua do Almada 262 ☎ 222 002 425, ⊗ residencialpaodeacucar.com; map pp.264–265. The building's a rather fab 1930s survivor, and while the rooms could all do with a style injection you do get shiny parquet floors and a fair amount of space. No question, though, that the best rooms (€85) are the half-dozen at the top that open out onto a private terrace overlooking the town hall. €65

Peninsular Rua Sá da Bandeira 21 ☎ 222 003 012, ⊗ hotel-peninsular.net; map pp.264–265. Comfortable family-run place with a range of rooms, all en-suite. Provided you steer clear of the very cheapest ones (windowless broom cupboards) you should also get an upgraded bathroom, a bit more space or a front view. €50

Porto Novo Rua Alexandre Herculano 185 ☎ 222 055 739, ⊗ residencialportonovo.com; map pp.264–265. Some guesthouses along this street are grotty, short-time places, but this is a reliable budget choice for clean if old-fashioned en-suite rooms. Insist on the top floor where the rooms have magnificent river views from their terraces. No credit cards. €35

★ **Rivoli Cinema Hostel** Rua Dr Magalhães Lemos 83 ☎ 220 174 634 or ☎ 968 958 637, ⊗ rivolicinemahostel .com; map pp.264–265. Co-owned by a bunch of art-grad, film-crazy friends, the classy *Rivoli* fills a bright and airy townhouse with film-themed four-bed dorms and double rooms, all sharing toilets and showers. It's by no means backpacker-only, but it is funky and communal – one big breakfast table, an outdoor roof terrace, kitchen and lounge – and they also organize things like poker nights and evening drinks. It's easily missed; go through the red door facing the Rivoli Teatro Municipal. Prices are a couple of euros per person higher at weekends. Dorm beds €19; doubles €44

RIBEIRA

Astoria Rua Arnaldo Gama 56 ☎ 222 008 175; map pp.264–265. An antique beauty, at the top of a hill overlooking the Douro. Creaky rooms have wooden double-doors, old dial-telephones and balcony views. Not all have private bathrooms (and those that do are often a slightly awkward fit, or lie across the hall) but there's a good breakfast served in a quaint dining room, and friendly service. No credit cards. €35

Carris Porto Ribeira Rua do Infante Dom Henrique 1 ☎ 808 203 615, ⊗ hotelcarrisportoribeira.com; map pp.264–265. Just a few steps up the hill from the Ribeira waterside, this newish four-star makes a decent base. It's been carved out of five old buildings, creating a dramatic lobby space of soaring stone arches and cutaway floors, with a stylish tapas bar off to one side. Handsome rooms feature hardwood floors, earth-toned fabrics and stylish bathrooms, while breakfast is several levels down in a restaurant that sits under huge granite arches and pillars. €90

★ **Douro** Rua Fonte Taurina 99 ☎ 222 015 135, ⊗ guesthousedouro.com; map pp.264–265. Super-cool waterfront B&B with windows right on to the Douro – a chic choice for a weekend getaway. Not all rooms have the river views (others look over the medieval street outside), but there's a sharp sense of style throughout and you couldn't be closer to the action. Parking nearby. €140

⭐ **Pestana Porto** Praça da Ribeira 1 ☎ 223 402 300, ⓦ pestana.com; map pp.264–265. Enjoying the Ribeira's best location, atop the medieval wall next to the river, this cluster of old buildings has been transformed into a boutique-style four-star hotel. Most rooms face the Douro, and corner rooms also overlook the bridge. A contemporary bar and restaurant occupies a raised terrace above the river, where a few outdoor tables are lit by candles on the walls. **€145**

VILA NOVA DE GAIA

⭐ **The Yeatman** Rua do Choupelo ☎ 220 123 100, ⓦ the-yeatman-hotel.com; map p.271. The most glamorous choice in town, this spectacular hotel is the business venture of one of Porto's most famous port-wine families. It sits amid historic port wine lodges but is thoroughly boutique in character, with dramatic views of Porto from room balconies and the Michelin-starred restaurant alike. You get not one but two infinity pools, one indoors, and connected to the fancy spa, and one outdoors, both with amazing panoramas. It wouldn't be a wine hotel without a wine cellar, and guests get a private tour with the sommelier of what's considered to be one of the best collections of Portuguese wine in the world. Rates vary considerably (from €139 depending on season, suites up to €800), and are room-only. **€185**

NORTH OF THE CENTRE

América Rua de Santa Catarina 1018 ☎ 223 392 930, ⓦ hotel-america.net; a 15min walk from the centre or bus #701/#702/#703 from Mercado do Bolhão; map pp.260–261. Well-regarded mid-range choice with bright and relatively spacious rooms. There's also private underground parking, a bar and what the hotel calls a "winter garden" and we call a conservatory with plants. **€65**

⭐ **Castelo de Santa Catarina** Rua de Santa Catarina 1347 ☎ 225 095 599, ⓦ castelosantacatarina.com.pt; a 15min walk from the centre or bus #701/#702/#703 from Mercado do Bolhão; map pp.260–261. This turreted folly of the most romantic kind makes a superb in-the-city retreat. The rooms aren't grand or expensive, but are furnished in period style and are perfectly comfortable, while breakfast is eaten in the lush *azulejo*-tiled gardens. There's parking too. **€70**

EAST OF THE CENTRE

⭐ **Pousada de Porto** Campanhã, N108 ☎ 210 407 600, ⓦ pousadas.pt; map pp.260–261. Porto finally has its own luxury *pousada*, a couple of kilometres east and upriver of Ribeira. The magnificently restored Baroque Palácio do Freixa dates from 1742, and enjoys a majestic riverside location. The main building sticks with period style and houses restaurant, bar and public rooms, while contemporary guest quarters – superbly appointed and many with classic Douro river views – are set in an adjacent former flour factory. Facilities are top-notch, from outdoor infinity pool with river view to indoor pool and spa, and the elegant restaurant and bar mean you don't have to make the slightly inconvenient trip into town and back if you don't wish to. **€150**

WEST OF THE CENTRE

Boa-Vista Esplanada do Castelo 58, Foz do Douro ☎ 225 320 020, ⓦ hotelboavista.com; bus #500 from São Bento; map pp.260–261. Ocean and river views are the thing at this traditional villa, set over the road from the fort at Foz do Douro – it's worth paying the extra €10 or so (and booking in advance) to be able to see the water. It's only a three-star, and rooms are comfortable if unexceptional, but there's a fine rooftop pool and sun terrace, plus bar, restaurant and parking. **€85**

Pousada de Juventude Rua Paulo da Gama 551, Pasteleira, 4km west of the centre ☎ 226 177 257, ⓦ microsites.juventude.gov.pt/portal/en; bus #504 from Ⓜ Casa da Música, or #207 from São Bento; map pp.260–261. It's a bit of a way out, and not ideal for night owls, but Porto's main hostel has wonderful views of the Douro as it drains into the Atlantic. Dorms are four-bed max, and there are 24 en-suite doubles, another 10 without bathrooms, and one self-contained apartment that sleeps four. It's essential to book ahead in summer. Dorm beds **€16**; doubles **€42**; apartment **€75**

Sheraton Hotel & Spa Rua de Tenente Valadim 146, Boavista ☎ 220 404 000, ⓦ sheratonporto.com; Ⓜ Casa da Música and taxi; map pp.260–261. The *Sheraton* has the five-star designer market wrapped up – a flash place of marble, steel and glass with elegant rooms featuring deep colours, hardwood furniture and massive beds; a "club" level offers a superior set of services. There's a fancy terrace-restaurant and juice bar, plus impressive spa facilities and parking. **€150**

EATING AND DRINKING

Both sides of the Douro have become the default places to spend the evening. Along Porto's **Cais da Ribeira** a dozen largely touristy fish restaurants are installed under the arches, with more simple places hidden along the backstreets. Over the bridge in **Vila Nova de Gaia** there's a mix of traditional fish places and international restaurants and bars. For cheaper meals look in the **city centre**, either around the university (facing the Jardim da Cordoaria) and near the Clérigos church (on streets such as Rua dos Caldeireiros) or up Rua do Bonjardim, or near Praça da Batalha. In the main market, the Mercado do Bolhão, you can also eat a very cheap lunch at a couple of little cafés amid the flower stalls. For the best local fish restaurants, you need to take the metro out to **Matosinhos**, a half-hour ride from the centre.

5

YOU'VE BEEN WARNED – PORTO'S DINNER SPECIALS

Porto's menus go big on grilled fish, seafood and *bacalhau*, but the most authentic local speciality is *tripas* (tripe) – the story goes that the inhabitants selflessly gave away all their meat for Infante Dom Henrique's expeditions to North Africa, leaving themselves only the tripe, and it's been on the menu ever since, cooked *à moda do Porto* (stewed with *chouriço* and white beans). Courtesy of returning emigrants, meanwhile, is the *francesinha* ("little French thing") – a mighty doorstep of steak, sausage and ham between toasted bread, covered with melted cheese and a peppery tomato-and-beer sauce. Don't plan on doing anything much after chowing down on either of these Porto belt-tighteners.

CITY CENTRE

★ **Antunes** Rua do Bonjardim 525 ☎ 222 052 406; map pp.264–265. Rustic restaurant that famously uses only wood-fired ovens to prepare the daily house specials – notably melt-in-the-mouth roast pork, served with gravy and sticky roast potatoes. Add a dessert and a carafe of house *rosado*, and you'll eat for €15. Mon–Sat noon–3pm & 7–10pm; closed 4 weeks in Aug/Sept.

Café Majestic Rua de Santa Catarina 112 ☎ 222 003 887, ⓦ cafemajestic.com; map pp.264–265. Best known of the city's *belle époque* cafés, with perfectly preserved decor (celestial cherubs, bevelled mirrors, carved chairs and wood panelling) and braided waiters flitting about to the strains of *The Blue Danube*. Come for coffee or afternoon tea – or maybe have a Caesar salad, club sandwich or *francesinha* for lunch (snacks from €6, mains €13–20). Mon–Sat 9.30am–midnight.

Café Progresso Rua Actor João Guedes 5, off Praça Carlos Alberto ☎ 222 322 647, ⓦ cafeprogresso.net; map pp.264–265. The best-known university café in town, founded as long ago as 1899, is less tweedy academic debate club these days and more of a contemporary, arty hangout, with occasional live music and events. Food tends towards croissants, snacks and sandwiches, though there's lunch and Sunday brunch (around €12) too. Mon–Thurs 7am–midnight, Fri & Sat 7am–2am, Sun 10am–5pm.

★ **Casa de Ló** Trav de Cedofeita 20A ☎ 220 119 738; map pp.264–265. A cracking café-bar set in the antique premises of a former bakery, purveyors of Porto's finest *pão-de-ló* (sponge cake) and *marmelada* (quince jelly), still available, lovingly wrapped in monogrammed paper. By day, it's a trendy little teahouse; by night, a relaxed bar, with weekend DJs starting around 11pm – and the best bit is the enclosed patio out back, with simple seats beneath ivy-clad walls. Mon–Sat 2pm–2am.

Confeitaria do Bolhão Rua Formosa 339 ☎ 223 395 220, ⓦ confeitariadobolhao.com; map pp.264–265. Open early for the traders, this traditional café and bakery opposite the market is a Porto classic – bread straight from the oven, speciality cakes and freshly squeezed juices. The shopper's lunch is good value (*bifinhos* to *bacalhau*, plus a daily buffet, dishes €5.50–8.50), and there's an associated

grocery up the street of the same vintage. Mon–Sat 6am–8pm.

★ **DOP** Palácio das Artes, Largo São Domingos 18 ☎ 222 014 313, ⓦ ruipaula.com; map pp.264–265. Well-known chef Rui Paula has returned to his native Porto to wow punters with more of the creative Portuguese cuisine that made his name. The sleek downtown premises are "a place to taste and be bold" – so expect a twist on tradition, like suckling pig in a cider sauce, or *caldeirada* with *gnocchi*. There are menus at €70 and €80, with wine pairings another €30 – and while you should just be able to rock up for lunch, dinner reservations are advised. Mon 7.30–11pm, Tues–Sat 12.30–3.30pm & 7.30–11pm.

Rota do Chá Rua Miguel Bombarda 457 ☎ 220 136 726, ⓦ rotadocha.pt; map pp.264–265. Push on through the rarified tea shop, stocked with tins and caddies of exotic brews, and you'll find a hideway café with a magical Eastern tea-garden with shaded seats and arbours. It's a great place for a lazy afternoon with a book, a big pot of fancy leaves and a cookie or two, or there are daily lunches (€7.50) and Friday- and Saturday-evening dinners (€13.50). Mon–Thurs 11am–8pm, Fri 11am–midnight, Sat noon–midnight, Sun 1–8pm.

RIBEIRA

★ **Dom Tonho** Cais da Ribeira 13–15 ☎ 222 004 307, ⓦ dtonho.com; map pp.264–265. Easy-going contemporary bar and restaurant, where anyone who's anyone comes when in town – weekend reservations advised. It looks flash (combining chrome, pine and glass with the original granite walls) but isn't stuffy, and the menu does fancy things with traditional dishes – such as deep-frying green beans in a tempura batter, serving sea bass in a salt crust or poaching *bacalhau* in extra-virgin olive oil (mains €15–30). There's also a bar-and-grill offshoot over the river on the Gaia esplanade, near the bridge, with right-by-the-water dining. Daily 12.30–3pm & 7.30–11.15pm; bar open until midnight, Fri & Sat until 2am.

Filha da Mãe Preta Cais da Ribeira 40 ☎ 222 055 515, ⓦ filhadamaepreta.com; map pp.264–265. Built into the arches, the *azulejo*-decorated upper floor provides a river view, or you can sit outside amid the souvenir stalls and strolling minstrels. It's resolutely local fare

– *arroz de marisco*, grilled fish, stuffed squid, not to mention the famous local *tripas* – but it is well regarded and not too pricey (dishes €8–15). Mon–Sat noon–3pm & 7–10.30pm.

0 Gancho Largo do Terreiro 11–12 ☏ 222 054 919; map pp.264–265. A bit of a bargain for a river view, with tables on a sunny square. A cheery family runs the place, scurrying out with meat and fish grills mostly in the €6–10 range. You can sit inside too, but really this is all about lunch in the sun with a Douro panorama. Mon–Sat noon–3pm & 7–11pm.

⭐ **Verso em Pedra** Rua Armenia 12, Miragaia ☏ 222 058 009, ⓦ versoempedra.com; map pp.264–265. The undisputed *francesinha* queen serves the coronary-on-a-plate a dozen ways (there are even veggie and seafood versions), from €9–14. There's also a straightforward menu of meat and fish grills, pastas and salads (mostly €8–10), served in the cafeteria-style interior or out on the street terrace in summer. Daily 11am–2am.

MASSARELOS

⭐ **Capa Negra** Rua do Campo Alegre 191 ☏ 226 078 380, ⓦ capanegra.com; map pp.260–261. A great diner-style grill house, packed at weekends, high days and holidays, and serving food until late. They champion their *francesinhas* but the steaks are just as good, or there's an extensive menu from shellfish to omelettes (most mains €10 to €20). If you like the good-time, filled-with-locals atmosphere, two other equally notable places just down the street, the *Gambamar* (no. 110) and *Galiza* (no. 55), offer a similar night out. Jump in a cab from the centre, it won't cost much to get here. Mon–Sat noon–2am, Sun noon–midnight.

MATOSINHOS

⭐ **Salta o Muro** Rua Heróis de França 386 ☏ 229 380 870; ⓜ Brito Capelo; map pp.260–261. The "Jump the Wall" is an engaging if cramped family-run *tasca* on a dockside Matosinhos street full of fish restaurants. Others might look more enticing, but stick with it – a handwritten menu offers the catch of the day, plus some home-style specials (*arroz de polvo*, baked sardines), and you'll get three courses, house wine and coffee for under €20. Or order a bottle from the wall racks and make the waiter use his cunning wine-claw/grab. Tues–Sat noon–3pm & 7–10pm; closed Aug.

VILA NOVA DE GAIA

Barão de Fladgate Taylor's, Rua do Choupelo 250 ☏ 223 772 951; map p.271. It's a punishing uphill hike (unless you take a taxi), but you're rewarded by the finest river and bridge views from the terrace of Taylor's port wine lodge restaurant. A fleet of smart waiters is on hand, but it's not really formal – lovely for an alfresco lunch – and not outrageously expensive either (mains around €15). Many dishes have a slug of port in the recipe, while others (like soya burger with wild rice, or pasta and New Zealand mussels) make a change from the prevailing traditional Portuguese cuisine. Mon–Sat 12.30–3pm & 7.30–10.30pm, Sun 12.30–3pm.

⭐ **Casa Adão** Av Ramos Pinto 252 ☏ 223 750 492; map p.271. Simple family-run riverfront restaurant with low prices (€6–14) for meat and fish grills, from steak and pork to salmon and seabass, as well as bigger platters for two or more (€20–30) of mixed grilled fish and the like. They're used to tourists, but it's the locals who pack in here at lunch (there might be a wait for a table), and with house wine at €5 a litre there's not much work done in nearby offices in the afternoon. Daily noon–3.30pm & 7–11pm.

NIGHTLIFE AND ENTERTAINMENT

Porto's ever-changing **bar scene** is spread over three distinct areas: down and around Ribeira, across the river in Gaia, and – unsurprisingly – around the university (near Praça Parada Leitão and on "Bar Street", Rua Galeria de Paris). There are more venues in beachside Foz do Douro, but most of the city's best clubs are fairly central (though the hard house and techno clubs tend to be further out, in Ramalde). Most bars don't open until 10pm and stay open until 2am, later at weekends (often until 4am). **Clubs** open (or really only get going) at midnight, and most don't close until 4 or 5am or later, with a standard €5–15 admission fee, more for special events and guest DJs – the entrance ticket usually gets you a free drink.

FESTA DE SÃO JOÃO

Porto lets its hair down – and we mean unravelling its flowing locks, Rapunzel-style – during the exuberant celebration that is the **Festa de São João**, St John's Eve (the night of June 23–24), in honour of John the Baptist, patron saint of the city. Be warned – for one night only it is considered fair game to bash total strangers over the head with squeaky plastic hammers, while Chinese lanterns drift off into the night sky. There are free concerts throughout the night and a massive firework display at midnight over the river at Praça da Ribeira. The bacchanalian party forms only part of the wider city festival, the **Festas da Cidade**, that runs throughout June and celebrates the start of the summer with concerts, dances, vintage car rallies, regattas, sardine grills and other wholesome entertainments – like the competitive *cascata* displays (dolls depicting Santo António, São João and São Pedro, complete with miniature houses, trains and cars).

5

CITY CENTRE

Boys 'R US Rua Dr Barbosa de Castro 63 ☎ 917 549 988; map pp.264–265. The number-one gay club in town – lashings of fashionable tunes and late-night drag acts for discerning punters of all ages. Wed & Fri–Sun 11pm–4am.

★ **Contagiarte** Rua Álvares Cabral 372 ☎ 222 000 682, ⊕ contagiarte.pt; map pp.264–265. Popular with an arty crew, this retro-chic two-storey club in a converted townhouse has different styles of music (changing each night) – reggae to world, folk to funk – with live acts and special events all part of the scene. Add a lovely outdoor terrace and you've got a top night out. Wed–Sat 10pm–4am.

★ **Maus Hábitos** Rua Passos Manuel 178-4º ☎ 222 087 268, ⊕ maushabitos.com; map pp.264–265. At the top of an innocuous staircase is "Bad Habits", a late-night, in-crowd venue for alternative music (jazz, funk, indie and world) and contemporary arts. It's not as exclusively hip as you might expect, and out-of-towners are more than welcome – coming for the daily veggie lunch is a good way for a first look around, and then you can check out what's coming up and what's on in the gallery. Restaurant Mon–Fri 12.30–3pm; gallery Wed–Sun 10pm–2am; bar Wed, Thurs & Sun 10pm–2am, Fri & Sat 10pm–4am.

Piolho d'Ouro Praça Parada Leitão 45 ☎ 222 003 749, ⊕ cafepiolho.com; map pp.264–265. The best-known of the student bars facing the university, the "Golden Louse" has a long tradition behind it – graduation plaques line the walls, and it used to be quite the revolutionary hangout. It's open virtually around the clock for cheapskate students nursing budget beers and basic bites to eat – and the sunny terrace is a good spot for sightseers – while there's a line of inexpensive *tascas* around the corner. Mon–Sat 7am–4am.

Tendinha dos Clérigos Rua Conde Vizela 80 ☎ 222 011 438, ⊕ tendinhadosclerigos.com; map pp.264–265. One for rockers – a cave-like bar and club with pool table and dancefloor, that's also a regular venue for up-and-coming bands. Tues–Sat 1–6am.

RIBEIRA

★ **Clube Literário do Porto** Rua Nova da Alfândega 22 ☎ 222 089 228, ⊕ clubeliterariodoportofla.wordpress .com; map pp.264–265. Above the bookshop and below the art exhibition, the literary club's piano bar is an elegant place to sit and chat with a view of the Douro. On Fri & Sat there are concerts and recitals, often involving their mini-grand. Daily 2.30pm–1am.

Está-se Bem Rua da Fonte Taurina 70–72 ☎ 222 002 249; map pp.264–265. A nice little *tasca* where a pre-club crowd hangs out, probably because drinks are cheap and there's no cover charge. Mon–Sat 6pm–4am.

O meu Mercedes é maior que o teu Rua da Lada 30 ☎ 222 082 151, ⊕ omeumercedes.com; map pp.264–265. The stalwart of the Ribeira scene not only wins the Porto bar name prize ("My Mercedes is bigger than yours") but is a wonderfully atmospheric joint to boot, a bit like an old stone-walled wine cellar with regular gigs. Wed–Sat 10pm–4am.

★ **Vinologia** Rua de São João 46 ☎ 936 057 340, ⊕ vinologia.eu.com; map pp.264–265. French-owned wine-bar-cum-tasting-shop that's a cosy place to get acquainted with Porto's top tipples. The enthusiastic English-speaking staff really know their stuff, and can recommend all sorts of ports from mainly small producers – from €1.50 a glass or tasting sessions from €6–15. Mon–Sat 2pm–midnight, Sun 6–10pm.

BOAVISTA

Labirintho Rua Nossa Senhora de Fátima 334 ☎ 226 007 023, ⊕ labirintho.com; ⓜ Casa da Música; map pp.260–261. Just a couple of minutes off the Rotunda, this is a great bar in a converted house, with a shaded back garden, gallery space and occasional live music. Mon–Sat 10pm–4am.

FOZ DO DOURO

Indústria Centro Comercial do Foz, Av do Brasil 835–843 ☎ 220 962 935, ⊕ industria-club.com; bus #500; map pp.260–261. A sophisticated dance club that gets packed in summer – it's not at the cutting edge of Porto's club scene, but it's still an impressively good night that sees Portugal's best DJs play to a cosmopolitan crowd. Thurs–Sat midnight–6am.

ARTS AND CULTURE

The **Casa da Música** concert hall has a wide musical remit, as well as being home of the **Orquestra Nacional do Porto**, one of the country's leading symphony orchestras. Otherwise, concerts of all kinds are held at a variety of venues, while in summer there's usually a series of **outdoor concerts** in the Jardim do Palácio de Cristal and at Serralves. Local **theatre** is almost always in Portuguese, though there's a strong tradition of contemporary dance and other visual and experimental genres. **Tickets** for most shows (usually in the range €10–40) can be bought in advance from the FNAC books and music store (see "Shopping", p.280), which also promotes gigs, events and talks. Porto's daily newspaper, the *Jornal de Notícias* (⊕ jnoticias.pt), is also a useful source of information.

Casa da Música Av da Boavista 604 ☎ 220 120 220, ⊕ casadamusica.com; ⓜ Casa da Música; map pp.260–261. Porto's major concert hall is a striking building with an international reputation, not just for

PORTO'S CALENDAR OF FESTIVALS

You can check exact festival and event dates on Porto's tourism website ⓦ portoturismo.pt. The following rundown mixes the annual highlights with some under-the-radar choices.

February/March Fantasporto (ⓦ fantasporto.com), the respected international fantasy, sci-fi and thriller film festival, has been a fixture in the city since 1980 and runs over ten days.

March–April Festival Intercéltico do Porto – Celtic sounds from Portugal, Galicia, Brittany, Wales, Ireland and Scotland.

May Fazer a Festa (ⓦ teatroartimagem.org) – international theatre festival held in a "theatre village" in the gardens of the Palácio de Cristal.

June As well as popular saints' days for São João (June 23–24) and São Pedro (June 29), June also marks the start of the respected PortoCartoon World Festival (until Sept), one of the biggest festivals of caricature in the world.

July The annual GLBT Porto Pride march and celebration takes place on the first or second week. The International Folklore Festival is held during the last week. The annual Festa da Cerveja (Beer Fest) begins in Foz do Douro and runs through to August.

August São Bartolomeu (Sun after Aug 24) – a procession in Foz do Douro culminating in a cleansing bathe (*banho santo*) in the sea. On the last weekend there's the Noites Ritual, an exclusively Portuguese music festival at the Palácio de Cristal.

September The Porto Jazz Festival is held during the month, and the Concurso Internacional de Música (International Music Competition) begins. The Festival Internacional de Marionetas do Porto (FIMP; ⓦ fim.com.pt) is a ten-day festival of dance, circus, puppetry and theatre.

classical concerts and recitals but early and contemporary music, fado, world, jazz, folk and experimental. Most tickets are €5–20, though some events are free. Ticket office open Mon–Fri 10am–7pm, Sat & Sun 10am–6pm.

Coliseu do Porto Rua de Passos Manuel 137 ☎ 223 394 940, ⓦ coliseudoporto.pt; map pp.264–265. Main city-centre venue for international acts, from rock, indie and pop to ballet, classical and big-stage musicals. Ticket office open Mon–Sat 1–8.30pm (Aug Mon–Fri 3–7pm).

Teatro do Campo Alegre Rua das Estrelas 57 ☎ 226 063 017, ⓦ planetario-porto.pt; bus from Casa

da Música interchange; map pp.260–261. An innovative playhouse putting on a vibrant blend of music, theatre, cinema, animation and public lectures; there's also a late-opening bar. Ticket office open Mon 2–10.30pm, Tues–Fri 1–10.30pm, Sat & Sun 3–10.30pm.

Teatro Nacional São João Praça da Batalha ☎ 223 401 900, ⓦ tnsj.pt; map pp.264–265. The city's major theatre and opera venue, for Portuguese and international productions – it's a gorgeously over-the-top building, inspired by Charles Garnier's Paris Opera. The programme is pretty varied and you can see a show for as little as €7.50. Ticket office open Tues–Sat 2–7pm, Sun 2–5pm.

SHOPPING

One of the city's abiding pleasures is its surviving **traditional shops**, often in beautiful Art Nouveau or Art Deco premises, in which you'll find anything from dusty bottles of vintage port to filigree gold jewellery. Even right in the city centre, people still do much of their day-to-day shopping at small, independent shops – in the line of shops below the Clérigos tower, for example, you could, if you so wished, buy an apple, a pair of shoes, a pig's tongue or a bucket. The main **market**, Mercado do Bolhão, still sees brisk business too, though most of the other neighbourhood markets have been eclipsed by the city's modern **shopping centres** – the biggest is NorteShopping, in the northwest at Senhora da Hora (on the metro). Porto's two main **shopping streets** are Rua de Cedofeita and the more upmarket Rua de Santa Catarina – these are where you'll find high-street fashion chains, designer boutiques, jewellers and shoe shops. Rua de Santa Catarina also has its own mall, Via Caterina, halfway up, as well as a few stalls selling beads, cheap jewellery and accessories, and some secondhand and "vintage" shops towards the top end. Rua de Miguel Bombarda (off Rua de Cedofeita) is at the heart of Porto's **"gallery and arts" district** and is the place for designers, delis, and urban arts and crafts.

ARTS, CRAFTS AND DESIGN

★ **Arcos de Miragaia** Rua de Miragaia 39–45 ☎ 918 294 551; map pp.264–265. Jorge Andrade's ceramics workshop under the arches is a great place to look for unique ("from my imagination") painted vases, contemporary *azulejo*

tiles, and creatively made platters and paperweights. Mon–Sat 10am–12.30pm & 2–7pm.

Lobo Taste Palácio das Artes, Largo São Domingos 20 ☎ 222 017 102; map pp.264–265. The personal project of interior designer Paulo Lobo, who presents his – and other

5

MARKETS, JUNK AND VINTAGE STUFF

If the **Mercado do Bolhão** (daily except Sun) whets your appetite, you might want to scour some of Porto's other markets, starting with the long-established Saturday-morning flea market, the **Feira de Vandôma** (Passeio das Fontaínhas). There's a more specialist market for **coins and collectables** (Sun morning, Praça Dom João I), while the **Feira dos Pasasarinhos** (Sun morning, Campo Mártires da Pátria, in front of the Cadeia da Relação) features birds, cages, and birds in cages. The **secondhand** scene is centred on the top (ie, grungier) end of Rua Santa Caterina, at shops such as Segunda Mão (Rua Santa Caterina 505), where you can buy anything from dodgy old Portuguese vinyl singles to retro household goods and vintage clothes.

designers' – reimaginings of traditional Portuguese arts and crafts. This means a rather gorgeous shop full of felt hats and flat caps in funky colours, plus contemporary ceramics, clay figures, designer basketware and fancy olive-oil gift sets, with many of the pieces in limited-edition series, signed by the artists. Mon–Fri 10am–7pm, Sat & Sun 4–8pm.

BOOKS AND MUSIC

Chaminé da Mota Rua das Flores 28 ☎222 005 380; map pp.264–265. Perhaps the most characteristic antiquarian bookshop (*alfarrabista*) in town, complete with rare tomes, antique decorations and giant music boxes that play punched metal discs. Mon–Fri 9am–12.30pm & 2.30–7pm, Sat 9am–1pm.

FNAC Rua de Santa Catarina 73; also at NorteShopping; ⓦfnac.pt; map pp.264–265. The city's biggest selection of CDs, DVDs, books, games and gizmos. Mon–Sat 10am–10pm, Sun 10am–8pm.

★ **Lello & Irmão** Rua das Carmelitas 144 ☎222 002

037; map pp.264–265. Porto's famous galleried Art Nouveau bookshop (1906), with its staircase just begging for a grand entrance, is a delight beyond words. There's a small café on the first floor. Mon–Fri 10am–7.30pm, Sat 10am–7pm.

FOOD AND DRINK

A Pérola do Bolhão Rua Formosa 279 ☎222 004 009; map pp.264–265. A great little grocery, founded in 1917, loved as much for its Art Nouveau facade as for its cluttered stock of *bacalhau*, port wine, cheese, cured sausages and smoked hams. Mon–Sat 9.30am–1pm & 2–7.30pm.

Loja de Vinhos do Douro e do Porto Rua Ferreira Borges 27 ☎222 071 669, ⓦwww.ivdp.pt; map pp.264–265. At the Porto and Douro Wine Institute's handily located shop and showroom you'll be able to taste a few wines and then buy from the well-stocked shelves. It's also a good place to ask about port wine tours or even arrange visits to the institute's labs and tasting chambers. Mon–Fri 11am–7pm.

DIRECTORY

Car rental Most international companies have both downtown and airport offices; it's far easier to pick up your car the day you leave Porto. Local companies include Auto-Jardim (ⓦauto-jardim.com) and Guerin (ⓦguerin.pt).

Football FC Porto, European champions in 2004 and winners of the Europa League in 2011, play at the landmark Estádio do Dragão in Antas, off Av Fernão Magalhães (ⓦfcporto.pt; ⓦEstádio do Dragão). Match tickets cost €15–60 depending on the opposition and seat location, or there are year-round stadium tours (July & Aug daily, otherwise Thurs–Sun only; €10; see website for schedules). The city's second team, Boavista FC, play at Estádio do Bessa, Rua 1 de Janeiro, off Av da Boavista (ⓦboavistafc.pt), west of the centre.

Hospital Centro Hospitalar do Porto, Largo Prof Abel Salazar, near the university ☎222 077 500, ⓦwww.chporto.pt. In an emergency, call ☎112.

Left luggage Coin-operated lockers at Campanhã and São Bento train stations.

Libraries Biblioteca Municipal Almeida Garrett, Palácio de Cristal, Rua de Entre Quintas 328 (Mon 2–6pm, Tues–Sat 10am–6pm; ☎226 081 000); or Biblioteca Municipal do Porto, Rua Dom João VI (Mon & Sat 10am–6pm, Tues–Fri 9am–7.30pm, except July & Aug Mon–Fri 10am–6pm; ☎225 193 480). There's an English-language library (Mon–Fri 2–7.30pm) and other services at the British Council, Rua do Breiner 155 (☎210 456 210, ⓦbritish council.org/Portugal).

Pharmacies Late-night and 24hr pharmacies (*farmácias de serviço*) operate on a rota basis; details posted in the windows and given in the daily *Jornal de Notícias*.

Police For English-speaking assistance go to the Esquadra de Turismo (Tourism Police Department), a branch of the PSP, Rua Clube dos Fenianos 11, next to the main turismo (daily 8am–2am; ☎222 081 833).

Post office Main post office, Praça General Humberto Delgado, by the town hall (Mon–Fri 8am–9pm, Sat 9am–6pm); also an office at Rua Ferreira Borges 73, near the Bolsa (Mon–Fri 9am–12.30pm & 2–6pm).

Vila do Conde

5

VILA DO CONDE, 27km north of Porto, has become quite a significant resort over recent years, but despite the increase in visitor numbers still retains much of its historic charm. In part, it's because the villas and apartments overlooking the beach are set away from the rest of town; the medieval centre, 1km inland on the north bank of the Rio Ave, still has its traditional fishing port and quiet, traffic-free streets, while the more modern town is a handsome place of boulevards, gardens and cafés. It has a fair reputation for festivals too, from food and crafts to film, and if you want more than just a beach then it's easily the best day out from Porto, especially as you can zip up and down quickly on the metro. The more developed sands of Póvoa do Varzim are just a few minutes beyond, at the end of the line.

Convento de Santa Clara

Largo Dom Afonso Sanches • No public access

The grand eighteenth-century **Convento de Santa Clara** is the town's major landmark. It sits high above the old bridge and, while it's not open to the public, it is worth climbing up to the *miradouro* for sweeping views of town and river. Running directly into the north side of the convent is a well-preserved, early eighteenth-century **aqueduct** which once carried water over a reputed 999 arches from Terroso, 5km north of town – the metro line to Póvoa do Varzim now cuts right through part of the remaining course. The other thing to note about Santa Clara is its long tradition of pastry-making – the so-called *doces conventuais* (convent cakes) are now available in cafés all over town, sickly-sweet affairs generally involving industrial quantities of sugar and eggs.

Around the Igreja Matriz

Anchoring the cobbled alleys and whitewashed buildings of the surviving old town is the beautiful Manueline **Igreja Matriz**. The neighbouring streets are largely pedestrianized, making it a nice area for a stroll, while every Friday the weekly **market** takes place, where you'll find everything from farm produce to traditional children's toys.

Museu de Rendas de Bilros

Rua de São Bento 70 • Tues–Sun 10am–noon & 2–6pm • €2 • ☎ 252 248 470

Vila do Conde is still known for its traditional lacework and embroidery (*rendas de bilros*), and there is an active lacework school in the interesting **Museu de Rendas de Bilros**, housed in one of the town's old manor houses. *Rendilheiras* (lace-makers) show off their skills most days, surrounded by lovely examples of lacework and historic lace-making tools and equipment. The museum is also a good place to buy lace, and you'll see more for sale in the market and in shops around town.

VILA DO CONDE FESTIVALS

A good time to visit Vila do Conde is for the nine-day **Feira de Gastronomia** (food fair; third week in Aug, ⓦ gastronomia.vconde.org), and there's also a renowned **Feira Nacional de Artesanato** (crafts fair; last week July to first week Aug; ⓦ fna.vconde.org). People also come from far and wide for **Curtas** (ⓦ curtas.pt), the European short-film festival held here for a week every July.

5

VILA DO CONDE

ACCOMMODATION
Forte de São João ... 2
Quinta das Alfaias ... 3
Manco d'Areia ... 1

RESTAURANTS AND CAFÉS
Adega Gavina ... 2
Ramon ... 1

Porto

Póvoa do Varzim

(M) (Vila do Conde)

N13 (Póvoa do Varzim), Viana do Castelo & Motorways

Centro de
Ciência Viva

Santa
Clara (M)

Rio Ave

N

Aqueduct

Casa de José Régio

Convento de
Santa Clara

RUA DAS DONAS

RUA DE SANTO AMARO

Market

RUA DE OUTUBRO

AVENIDA JOSÉ RÉGIO

Igreja
Matriz

RUA NS. DE FÁTIMA

RUA DA IGREJA

RUA 25 DE ABRIL

PRAÇA
JOSÉ
RÉGIO

PRAÇA DA
REPÚBLICA

Câmara
Municipal

Auditório
Municipal

CAIS DAS
LAVANDEIRAS

R. MISERICÓRDIA

LARGO DR
CUNHA
REIS

RUA S. BENTO

R. ANDRADE

Biblioteca
Municipal

AVENIDA DR. SOUSA PEREIRA

AVENIDA DR. JOÃO CANAVARRO

Museu de Rendas de Bilros

RUA DR. ELIAS DE AGUIAR

RUA CAIS DA ALFÂNDEGA

Museu da Construção Naval

Capela do Socorro

Rio Ave

N13 (Porto) &

AVENIDA DR. ARTUR CUNHA ARAÚJO

PRAÇA
CAMÕES

ALAMEDA DOS
DESCOBRIMENTOS

AVENIDA JÚLIO GRAÇA

AV. MARQUÊS DE SÁ DA BANDEIRA

RUA BENTO DE FREITAS

AVENIDA SACADURA CABRAL

AVENIDA DO FERROL

RUA ESTÊVÃO

RUA GASPAR MANUEL

Swimming
Pool

AVENIDA DO BRASIL

AVENIDA MANUEL BARROS

Forte de São
João Baptista

Praia Azul

Praia do Forno

ATLANTIC
OCEAN

0   200
metres

Museu da Construção Naval

Rua do Cais da Alfândega • Tues–Sun 10am–6pm • Free • ☎ 252 240 740

Down on the river, walking west takes you through the old **fishing quarter**. Vila do Conde's shipbuilding industry is among the oldest in Europe, and fishing boats reminiscent of fifteenth-century caravels are still constructed here, in the shipyards on the other side of the river. You can trace this heritage (and see replica vessels) in the excellent **Museu da Construção Naval**, housed in the impressive former royal customs house, the Alfândega Régia (1487). Further along the riverside you can't miss the conspicuously Moorish white dome of the **Capela do Socorro**, which bears witness to the conversion of Moorish craftsmen during the Inquisition.

The beach

The **beach** is a good fifteen-minute walk west of the town centre, and boasts long stretches of coarse sand that have been steadily developed right up the coast as far as Póvoa do Varzim. There are rock pools and a few cafés, while to the south the sands come to an end at the mouth of the Rio Ave, marked by the stumpy seventeenth-century **Forte de São João Baptista** (now a hotel), beyond which is a convenient little beach café with an excellent sea view.

ARRIVAL AND INFORMATION

VILA DO CONDE

By metro Metro Line B runs from Porto (Estádio do Dragão) every 20 minutes and takes around an hour – you need a Z6 Andante card to travel this far (total, with card, €5.80 return). There are two stations: get off at Santa Clara, 300m east of the convent, though quicker express services (50min) call at Vila do Conde station, still only five minutes' walk from the centre.

Information Turismo, Rua 25 de Abril 103 (June to mid-Sept Mon–Fri 9am–7pm, Sat & Sun 9.30am–1pm & 2.30–6pm; mid-Sept to May Mon–Fri 9am–6pm, Sat & Sun 9.30am–1pm & 2.30–6pm; ☎ 252 248 473, Ⓦ www .cm-viladoconde.pt).

ACCOMMODATION

Forte de São João Av do Brasil ☎ 252 240 600, Ⓦ forte .com.pt. The town's seventeenth-century pentagonal fortress now has a contemporary, minimalist style – inside, at least – and the rooms and public areas make the most of the ocean and river views. There's also a wine bar and chic restaurant (reservations advised). €85
O Manco d'Areia Praça da República 84 ☎ 252 631 748. The *azulejo*-lined stone staircase leads to a good, mid-range guesthouse with cosy, well-kept rooms. Don't expect up-to-the-minute decor and facilities, but the location is excellent. €50

★ **Quinta das Alfaias** Rua da Trás 220, Fajozes, 10km southeast of town ☎ 252 662 146 or ☎ 919 900 509, Ⓦ quintadasalfaias.com. A wonderfully elegant country house set in extensive gardens and orchards, with a large swimming pool and tennis court. It has four en-suite rooms with garden views, plus one suite (€90–105) and a couple of apartments (€110–200) – decor throughout is understated, with plenty of bare granite, and the style is traditional country-house. €80

EATING AND DRINKING

★ **Adega Gavina** Cais das Lavandeiras 56 ☎ 252 115 870. A small, unpretentious *adega* that overlooks the river and serves freshly caught fish – mackerel, squid and bream – grilled on the barbecue, and washed down with a jug of fruity house wine. A full meal is around €12. Tues–Sat noon–3pm & 7–10.30pm, Sun noon–3pm.

Ramon Rua 5 de Outubro 176 ☎ 252 631 334. The more upmarket place for fish, particularly shellfish – there's outdoor seating in the alley, a good-value set lunch and (providing it's not lobster) mains start at around €13. Mon & Wed–Sun noon–3pm & 7–11pm; closed 3 weeks in Sept.

Penafiel and around

While port wine defines the central and far eastern reaches of the Douro, closer to Porto it's actually *vinho verde* that holds sway, particularly around **PENAFIEL**, 35km east of Porto. The wine's origins lie with the Benedictine monks, who first grew vines on

5

precipitous valley terraces, while the Benedictine legacy also extends to a handful of glorious Romanesque churches secreted amid the rolling hills hereabouts. However, despite the promise, Penafiel itself comes as something of a disappointment. The few old streets of granite mansions behind a handsome Renaissance Igreja da Misericórdia are barely reason enough to stop – certainly not if you're reliant on public transport (and the train station is 3km from the centre in any case). Drivers, however, have the option of a pleasant half-day's tour, with wine tasting and church visits breaking up the onward journey along the Douro.

Quinta da Aveleda

Rua da Aveleda • **Tours** Mon–Fri at 10am, 11am, 2pm, 3pm & 4pm • €4.50; reservations required • **Shop** Mon–Sat 9am–noon & 1–5.30pm • ☎ 255 718 200, ⓦ aveleda.pt • Coming from Porto, leave the A4 at the "Penafiel Sul/Entre-os-Rios" exit

The charming, ivy-festooned **Quinta da Aveleda** is source of the local *vinho verde*. The guided tours include a visit to the bottling hall, and a wine and cheese tasting (and there's more on sale in the rather nice shop), but it's really the gorgeously unkempt, wooded gardens and their follies that make the visit.

Paço de Sousa

10km south of Penafiel, signposted off the N106

The Romanesque abbey church at **Paço de Sousa** – a pre-eminent Benedictine foundation – is the burial place of Penafiel's local boy made good, **Egas Moniz**, advisor to Dom Afonso Henriques, the first king of Portugal. On a mission to negotiate with the King of León, Moniz displayed the ultimate loyalty by offering himself as a sacrifice – an impressive gesture refused by the king, who rewarded Moniz with his liberty. The panels on Moniz' tomb tell his story, while outside the church is a shaded dell beside the Rio Sousa, just right for a picnic. There are a couple of cafés in the village below.

Boelho

12km southeast of Paço de Sousa, signposted off the N106 to Entre-os-Rios

Tucked up a minor country road, the church of São Gens at **Boelhe** is said to be the smallest Romanesque church in the country, and gains much of its appeal from its impressive position on a hill overlooking the Tâmega valley. From here, the N106 continues south to Entre-os-Rios, where you then have the choice of following the Rio Douro east along either bank (see p.288) towards Lamego and Peso da Régua.

Amarante

A quick drive from Porto takes you to the beautiful riverside town of **AMARANTE**, which hugs both sides of the Rio Tâmega, a handsome tributary of the Douro. Much of the town's history revolves around the thirteenth-century hermit Gonçalo, later made a saint, and most of the attractions bear his name or have some link to him. Although Amarante's sights are few, save a photogenic bridge, and a riverside main street of granite houses whose wooden balconies project over the Tâmega, it's popular with weekenders from Porto and foreign visitors. There's a definite air of prosperity about and it's certainly a fine place to spend the night, with a wide choice of accommodation, much of it still reasonably priced. Wednesdays and Saturdays – **market days** – are the most lively, though the action is all over by 3pm.

5

ACCOMMODATION
Casa de Calçada	3
Estoril	1
Navarras	4
Pousada de São Gonçalo	5
Zé de Calcada	2

CAFÉS AND RESTAURANTS
Confeitara da Ponte	2
Largo do Paço	4
Triunfante	1
Zé de Calcada	3

Igreja de São Gonçalo

Praça da República • Daily 8am–7pm • Free

Cross the old stone bridge over the Tâmega and you're confronted by the landmark **Igreja de São Gonçalo**, built on the spot where Gonçalo's hermitage once stood, although the holy site almost certainly dates back to pagan times. The saint's annual festival – now known as the Festas do Junho, celebrated over the first weekend in June – also goes in for a fair amount of pre-Christian jiggery-pokery, not least the traditional exchange of phallic cakes by unmarried couples. Moreover, in the church, a touch of the well-worn saint's tomb allegedly brings forward the happy wedding day for hitherto thwarted lovers.

Museu Amadeo de Souza-Cardoso

Alameda Teixeira de Pascoaes • June–Sept Tues–Sun 10am–12.30pm & 2–6pm; Oct–May Tues–Sun 9.30am–12.30pm & 2–5.30pm • €1 • ☎ 255 420 272, ⚑ www.amarante.pt/museu

The remodelled Renaissance cloisters around the side of São Gonçalo church contain the **Museu Amadeo de Souza-Cardoso**, largely based around the Cubist and avant-garde works of Amadeo de Souza-Cardoso (1887–1918). Born and brought up in Amarante, he spent his formative years as an artist in Paris but died young in the influenza pandemic of 1918. He's still relatively little known outside Portugal but the absorbing collection is well worth a look. There are also works by other Portuguese artists, as well as temporary exhibitions and a monthly cinema club.

Igreja de São Domingos

A steep granite stairway climbs from the main square, past the **Igreja de São Domingos**, whose bell-tower marks the hours. Take a quick look inside the intimate chapel – by

CYCLING ALONG THE TÂMEGA

In days gone by, the approach to Amarante was truly scenic, on the old Tâmega branch train line, with rattling wooden carriages snaking along a single-track route up the valley. Although long discontinued, part of the track now has a new lease of life as the **Ecopista da Linha do Tâmega**, a "green route" that's been opened from the old station at Amarante to that of Chapa, a shade over 9km to the northeast. In time, it's planned to extend the hiking and biking track as far as Celorico de Basto (22km from Amarante) and Arco de Baúlhe (40km), but even now, the shortish stretch to Chapa makes for a lovely day out, along the river valley, through pine and eucalyptus, over the occasional bridge and past abandoned buildings.

the door is an extraordinary carved wooden tablet showing Christ suspended upside down on the Cross, hoisted by three men operating a rope and pulley.

ARRIVAL AND INFORMATION   AMARANTE

By bus The bus station is on Av Primeiro de Maio, a five-minute walk south of the river, with regular services to and from Porto (up to 10 daily; 1hr), Vila Real (every 1hr 30min; 1hr 40min), Braga (5–7 daily; 1hr 20min) and Guimarães (5–8 daily; 50min).

By car Driving from Porto (60km) takes less than an hour via the A4 – traffic runs one-way only in town, around the two bridges. Parking is free along the river beside the

market, along the road under the new bridge, and in a parking lot beyond the hotel *Navarras*; everywhere else you'll need to feed the parking meters (2hr maximum).

Information Turismo, Alameda Teixeira de Pascoaes (daily: July–Sept 9am–7pm; Oct–June 9am–12.30pm & 2–5.30pm; ☎ 255 420 246, ⊛ amarante.pt/turismo), to the side of the main church next to the museum.

ACCOMMODATION

Casa da Calçada Largo do Paço 6 ☎ 255 410 830, ⊛ casadacalcada.com. A restored palace just above the bridge, stuffed with objets d'art and set in magnificent gardens. The thirty boutique-style rooms and suites vary in size, decor and outlook, while there's also a swimming pool and tennis court in the grounds. The Michelin-starred restaurant, *Largo do Paço* (see p.298), is what brings many here in the first place. **€130**

Estoril Rua 31 de Janeiro 49 ☎ 255 431 291, ⊖ mnestoril @hotmail.com. A star pick for budget travellers – pleasant, high-ceilinged en-suite rooms and, for a few euros more, a riverside balcony overlooking the bridge. Breakfast isn't included, but the cheery attached restaurant is a firm favourite for inexpensive riverside terrace dining – no need to go anywhere else if you're staying. **€35**

Navarras Rua António Carneiro ☎ 255 431 036, ⊛ hotel navarras.com. This central three-star choice has seen better days but rooms are shipshape and business-like, there's a

proper bath in the bathroom, and you can eat breakfast on the terrace (though the main-road traffic intrudes). Private parking is another boon. **€70**

★ **Pousada de São Gonçalo** Serra do Marão, Ansiães, 20km east of Amarante, IP4 (Vila Real direction) ☎ 255 460 030, ⊛ pousadas.pt. En route to the mountains, but still handy for Amarante, this little country-house chocolate-box of a *pousada* boasts big views and quiet rooms that guarantee a good night's sleep. There are only 15 rooms in the main house, and 10 more in a cottage annexe, while a sleek spa, terrace and glass-fronted pool offer a touch of contemporary style. The panoramic restaurant is good for traditional dishes (mains around €20). **€120**

★ **Zé da Calcada** Rua 31 de Janeiro 83 ☎ 255 426 814, ⊛ zedacalcada.com. Rooms are split over two houses on either side of the street, so try to get a room facing the river, rather than the road. The restaurant is the real draw (see p.298). **€50**

EATING AND DRINKING

Many of the places to stay have restaurants attached, though locals tend to eat in the cheaper places found near Largo Conselheiro António Cândido or up in the new town. The local hooch is Gatão, a fruity *vinho verde*. As the money has moved in, so the nightlife scene has moved up a notch or two, with a few late-opening esplanade bars found on the south side of the river near either bridge.

Confeitara da Ponte Rua 31 de Janeiro ☎ 255 432 034 ⊛ confeitariadaponte.com. The best place for tea and cakes is right by the bridge, with an ivy-festooned riverside terrace. The nuns of the (now ruined) Santa Clara convent

once made the town's famous *doces* (sweets), and you can sample them here, with home-made *bolos de São Gonçalo* (the saint's cakes), *pão de ló* (sponge cake) and others ready to be boxed up and taken away. Daily 8.30am–8pm.

5

★ **Largo do Paço** Largo do Paço 6 ☎ 255 410 830, ⓦ casadacalcada.com. In one of only two restaurants in the north of Portugal with a Michelin star, chef Vitor Matos does sublime things with local produce in a series of exquisitely presented tasting menus (from €55, lunch from €25). Everything changes with the seasons, but expect a creative twist on traditional dishes, which in autumn and winter might mean things like rabbit stuffed with pistachios and served with a mustard-and-herb crust or roast pigeon with sautéed cherries. Daily 12.30–3pm & 7.30–10.30pm.

Triunfante Rua Teixera de Vasconcelos ☎ 255 437 978.

A cheery granite-walled *adega*, where there's not much that costs over €5 – rabbit stew, *alheira*, steak, pork and *bacalhau* are generally on the menu. No credit cards. Mon–Sat 8am–10pm, Sun 8am–3pm.

Zé da Calcada Rua 31 de Janeiro 83 ☎ 255 426 814, ⓦ zedacalcada.com. Nicest of the riverside choices has a water-view terrace and good regional food (dishes €9–12), from a house *bacalhau* to *posta á Maronesa* (hefty steaks from the nearby Serra do Marão). They have also pioneered a weekday buffet lunch, where €8 gets you a choice of hot and cold dishes. Daily noon–3.30pm & 7–10.30pm.

Along the Douro

The **Douro river route** is one of *the* great European journeys, a careering 200-kilometre ride or stately cruise from Porto to the Spanish border. The full river journey there and back is in a class of its own, and pricey, all-inclusive cruises can take as long as a week, though short tours from Porto (see p.273) or Peso da Régua (see p.290) give you a flavour of the river. In many ways the train is best, though you'll have a lot more scope in a car to visit wineries, stay in rural *quintas* en route and hang around at the majestic dams to watch the boats come through the locks. Be warned that the roads are very winding and often fairly precipitous, though they are all in good condition. It can also take much longer than you think to get from A to B, so give yourself plenty of time.

North bank: along the N108

You can drive all the way from Porto, following the **N108**, though the first 40km or so is nothing special. Things pick up at **Entre-os-Rios** ("between the rivers"), 12km south of Penafiel, which is the point at which the Douro and Tâmega rivers meet. Stick to the N108 along the north bank and the road is set a fair way inland of the river for much of the route, though you'll get some stunning views at times before finally descending to Peso da Régua, 80km and a good couple of hours later.

THE LINHA DO DOURO – PORTUGAL'S BEST TRAIN RIDE

A true engineering marvel when it opened in 1887, the **Linha do Douro** (Douro Line) still thrills passengers today. In its heyday it crossed the border to Spain (for a through service to Salamanca and Madrid) and sprouted some stunning valley branch lines, but even though the branch lines are no more, it's still some ride – 160km of river-hugging track from Porto to Pocinho, via more than 20 tunnels, 30 bridges and 34 stations.

There are regular daily departures from Porto (São Bento and Campanhã) and you change on to the smaller Douro Line trains at Peso da Régua (just "Régua" on timetables). **Régua** also marks the point at which the Douro Line turns from a good route into a great one, sticking closely to the river from then on, clinging to the precipitous rocks as the river – and track – passes through the Douro gorge. Some of the stations are no more than a shelter on a platform, used by the local wine *quintas*, though there are useful stops at **Pinhão** (a pretty port-producing town), **Tua** (a cruise halt with a good restaurant) and finally **Pocinho** (for Vila Nova de Foz Côa and its rock art).

Currently five trains a day run from Porto to Pocinho at the end of the line (around 3hr 30min; €13 each way), so you can make the return trip in a day if you take a morning train; there are also summer weekend steam-train services between Régua and Tua. For **timetables**, see ⓦ cp.pt or call ☎ 808 208 208 (local-rate call in Portugal) or ☎ 707 201 280.

South bank: along the N222

Cross the bridge at Entre-os-Rios to the south bank of the Douro, and you're in for a treat of a drive along the increasingly picturesque **N222**. It's undoubtedly one of those "best in Portugal" routes, with the most compelling section the 40km or so between **Cinfães** and Peso da Régua, where the road hugs the terraced hills high above the glinting river. There's the occasional panoramic café, and iron gates at intervals announcing venerable *quintas* tucked into the hillside folds, while at the sleepy spa town of **Caldas de Aregos**, where the Douro has been dammed, there's a quayside marina and an outdoor café. The settlements beyond nearly all boast a Romanesque church, the most significant being **Santa Maria de Carquere**, a twisting 5km above the small town of Resende. Part of a convent dating back as early as 1099, this is now set amid family vineyards, with extensive views across the rolling hills beyond. The N222 eventually descends to Peso da Régua (though you can also cut south over the hills on the N226 to reach Lamego) and then embarks on its straightest but most river-hugging section, the relatively quick 25km to Pinhão.

Peso da Régua

PESO DA RÉGUA (usually just Régua) was declared the first capital of the demarcated port-producing region back in the eighteenth century. While it's Pinhão, further east, that's the more interesting place these days, Régua is still a popular stop – not least because it's the hub of the Douro river-cruise trade, with the boats disgorging hundreds of passengers for lunch, train trips and wine-lodge visits. Although it's not a particularly pretty place, and is dominated by a vertiginous motorway bridge, for most of the year there's an agreeable hubbub along the waterside promenade, where ornamental *barcos rabelos* lie anchored on the wide river. What's more, wine-trade patronage has resulted in some excellent local restaurants and enticing *quinta* accommodation in the vicinity.

Museu do Douro

Museum Rua Marquês de Pombal • Tues–Sun 10am–noon & 3–6pm • **Exhibition** 43 Rua da Ferreirinha • Tues–Sun 10am–1pm & 2.30–6pm • €6, ticket valid for both museum and exhibition • ☎ 254 310 190, ⓦ museudodouro.pt

Flagship building on Régua's riverfront avenue is the **Museu do Douro**, which tells you everything you ever wanted to know about the history of the river and its people, as well as the port wine story. It's actually laid across two sites, with a permanent display about the life and culture of the so-called Terra do Vinho on show at the exhibition area on Rua da Ferreirinha (the main inland street), and changing temporary exhibitions at the museum, whether it's photographs of old Douro bridges or shows by regional artists. There's also a restaurant at the museum site and, naturally enough, a wine bar with an esplanade-garden that's open during the summer months.

ARRIVAL AND INFORMATION

By train The train station is on Largo da Estação at the southeastern end of town (towards the bridges), reached along the waterfront avenue.

Destinations Pinhão (5 daily; 26min); Pocinho (5 daily; 1hr 25min); Porto (13 daily; 1hr 45min–2hr 20min); and Tua (5 daily; 42min).

By bus Buses stop outside the train station.

Destinations Guarda (daily; 2hr 30min); Lamego (every 2hr; 30min); Vila Real (every 2hr; 40min); and Viseu (2–6 daily; 1hr 10min).

Information The turismo is at Rua da Ferreirinha (daily 9am–12.30pm & 2–5.30pm, Nov–March closed weekends; ☎ 254 312 846, ⓦ cm-pesoregua.pt) – a 5min walk to the left of the quayside (Porto direction), near the large car park, at the end of the town's main street.

5

TOURS AND CRUISES

Tours Steam train services to Pinhão and Tua (complete with antique wooden carriages, food, wine and music) usually depart on Saturday afternoons between June and October, as well as Sunday mornings in September (€45 return, under-12s €25, reservations at ⓦ cp.pt, or at main train stations).

Cruises Between March and November, a huge variety of river cruises with various companies departs from, or passes through, Régua. Kiosks by the quayside sell tickets, or you can consult Porto Tours in Porto (ⓦ portotours.com) or Régua Turismo for full schedules. Short, hour-long cruises cost around €10, while longer tours run up to Pinhão and back (around €70, including lunch on board),

or combine a cruise with a trip on a steam train and a wine lodge visit (around €120).

Vineyard visits The many port wine *quintas* – or vineyard estates – around Peso da Régua offer vineyard tours and tastings. The turismo has plenty of information, as does the Rota do Vinho do Porto information centre, at Régua train station (Mon–Fri 9.30am–12.30pm & 2–6pm; ☎ 254 324 774, ⓦ rvp.pt), which produces a map of wine-related sites along the Douro (also available online). Douro Verde (ⓦ douroverde.com) also runs a tourist road-train service from Régua quayside (€7.50) that whisks you up to a viewpoint and throws in a brief lodge visit and tasting.

ACCOMMODATION

Accommodation in Régua itself is distinctly underwhelming, typified by the two high-rise eyesores close to the train station, but there are some fantastic riverside *quintas*, manor houses and wine-hotels within 10km of town. The former Solar da Rede *pousada* at Mesão Frio is currently closed, though may reopen under new ownership in the future.

★ **Quinta de Marrocos** Valdigem, 2km east, N222 Pinhão road ☎ 254 313 012, ⓦ quintademarrocos.com. Delightful family-owned *quinta* on the Douro's south bank where the grapes are still trodden by foot. There's swimming in the river from the estate grounds, B&B in rustic guest accommodation (and meals available for €25), while special weekend stays (€300 for 2 people) let you experience wine production here at first hand. They also offer cellar visits and tastings (€4–10, depending on type of visit). **€70**

★ **Quinta do Vallado** Vilharinho dos Freires, 6km

northeast, Corgo River road ☎ 254 318 081, ⓦ quinta dovallado.com. This historic *quinta* overlooks the Rio Corgo, a tributary, rather than the Douro itself. Owned for a couple of centuries by the famous port-wine Ferreira family, the striking house offers winery tours and tastings (well worth doing in any case), plus a selection of beautiful designer guest-rooms – five in the old manor house, and eight more in a sleek, modernist, slate-built extension set on a stunning panoramic terrace. There's also a lovely pool, plus bikes, fishing trips and boat tours available. **€130**

EATING AND DRINKING

★ **Castas e Pratos** Rua José Vasquez Osório ☎ 254 323 290, ⓦ castasepratos.com. Fanciest dining option in town is this impressive designer refurb of an old warehouse at the train station, offering restaurant, wine bar, lounge and wine shop, all rolled into one. You can snack in the wine bar on Portuguese and Spanish tapas, while the restaurant (dishes €10–25) goes in for artfully presented contemporary creative Portuguese cuisine. Wine bar daily 10.30am–11pm; restaurant daily 12.30–3pm & 7.30–10.30pm.

★ **DOC** Folgosa, 10km east, N222, Pinhão road ☎ 254 858 123, ⓦ restaurantedoc.com. There's no finer place on the Douro for an alfresco meal than this hip riverside restaurant with rolling vineyard views from its oh-so-cool

dining room and deck – it's only a 10min drive from Régua. Run by chef Rui Paulo of Porto's *DOP* (see p.276), the restaurant serves up sensational contemporary Portuguese food – think tuna carpaccio, *alheira* (sausage) samosa, and sea bass on wild rice, with starters at €6–10, mains around €20 and plenty of Douro wines by the glass. Daily 12.30–3.30pm & 7.30–11pm; esplanade bar 11am until late for drinks.

Gato Preto Av João Franco ☎ 254 313 367, ⓦ restaurantegatopreto.webnode.pt. The "Black Cat" is a reliable spot on the Régua quayside for an inexpensive meal, popular with locals, both bank manager and builder. Lunch around €8, dinner slightly more. Daily noon–3pm & 7–10.30pm.

Lamego and around

Although technically in the Beira Alta region, the charming town of **LAMEGO**, 11km south of Régua, is easily accessible from the Douro, with which it shares a passion for wine – in this case, Raposeira, Portugal's answer to champagne. It's overlooked by the fine Baroque shrine of Nossa Senhora dos Remédios – another of those decorative Portuguese stone stairways to the skies – which plays host to an annual pilgrimage from late August to early September. There are scores of noble manor-houses in the handsome town centre, and a series of extraordinary churches, monasteries and fortified buildings in the surrounding verdant valleys, a legacy of the twelfth-century Reconquista, when Lamego was among the first towns to be retaken from the Moors.

Much of Lamego's early wealth derived from its position astride a valuable trade route from the Beiras to the Douro, but the town's real importance stems from its history: in 1143, Lamego hosted Portugal's first parliament, when a group of clergy and noblemen assembled to recognize Afonso Henriques as the nation's first king. As such, Lamego lays claim to being the birthplace of both country and crown – a fact hotly disputed by Afonso Henriques' birthplace, Guimarães.

Sé

Largo da Sé • Daily 8am–1pm & 3–7pm • Free

Playing second fiddle to the sanctuary, Lamego's cathedral, the **Sé**, anchors the foot of town, a hybrid structure reflecting several bouts of rebuilding since it was first constructed in the twelfth century. The sculpted Gothic front is still impressive, though it's the rose-planted sixteenth-century cloister, with its pleasing arches and patterned *calçada* floor, that steals the show.

Museu de Lamego

Largo de Camões • Tues–Sun 10am–12.30pm & 2–5pm • €2, free on Sun 10am–12.30pm • ☎ 254 600 230

Facing the cathedral, and occupying the grand eighteenth-century Episcopal Palace, is the **Museu de Lamego**, whose star exhibit – officially classified as a "national treasure" – is a series of five panels (part of a larger polyptych) attributed to the great Portuguese painter Grão Vasco. They show various scenes, from *Creação dos Animais* (Creation of the Animals) to *Anunciação* (Annunciation) and were completed in Lamego between 1506 and 1511. The museum is also known for its collection of huge sixteenth-century Flemish tapestries.

Around the Castelo

Castelo Always open • **Torre de Menagem** Mid-June to Sept Tues–Sun 10am–noon & 3–6pm • Free

To reach the upper town, overseen by the castle, follow the small, steep Rua da Olaria from beside the turismo, passing an array of antiquated shops, grocers and *casas de pasto* selling regional bread, cheese, hams and smoked sausages. A right turn at the top takes you to the castle's southern gate, the **Porta do Sol**, while straight ahead along Rua de Almacave is the **Igreja de Almacave**, a simple Romanesque church with even earlier origins as a mosque. At the top of Rua de Almacave an alley on the right heads up along the town's massive thirteenth-century walls to the castle's north gate, the **Porta da Vila**, straddled by a sorry-looking wooden oratory constructed in the 1700s. This gives access to the **Castelo** itself, and its twelfth-century keep, the **Torre de Menagem** – if the tower's open, it's worth clambering up the rickety stairs onto the roof for the views.

Capela da Nossa Senhora do Socorro

Rua do Castelo, just past the Torre de Menagem

Within the castle walls, the small **Capela da Nossa Senhora do Socorro** was built – according to the inscription – on the site of Lamego's first cathedral, founded by the Suevian Idácio, who crowned himself Bishop of Lamego in 435. Further down the narrow street is a small circular *praça*, to the right of which, behind the wall, lies a thirteenth-century subterranean **cisterna** (water cistern). This is closed to visitors, but the enclosing wall itself is remarkable in that virtually every stone contains a different stonemason's mark.

Santuário de Nossa Senhora dos Remédios

Monte de Santo Estevão • **Staircase** Always open • **Chapel** Daily: May–Sept 7.30am–8pm; Oct–April 7.30am–6pm • Free

All eyes – and all steps – lead to the celebrated shrine and chapel of **Nossa Senhora dos Remédios** which embraces the city from the summit of a glorious Baroque staircase that starts at the end of Lamego's wide avenue of shady chestnut trees. It's no fewer than 611 steps to the top – climbed on your knees if you're particularly devout – with pauses on the way up at small chapels, decorated fountains and religious statues. You can return down the shaded forested tracks of the **Parque dos Remédios** on either side of the steps; early in the morning the air is filled with cuckoo calls and warbling birdsong.

The **Festas de Nossa Senhora dos Remédios** (nicknamed the Romaria de Portugal) kicks off on the last Thursday of August, and continues until September 8, with the main pilgrimage and procession on the last day, featuring white-frocked children, and bulls pulling the carriage that transports the image of Our Lady. Of course, it's also an excuse to party and, in addition to the religious ceremonies, there are also floral displays, fairground rides, folk music, dances and concerts all over town.

Capela de São Pedro de Balsemão

Balsemão, 3km northeast of Lamego • Tues 2–6pm, Wed–Sun 10am–12.30pm & 2–6pm; closed on the third weekend of every month • Free

The ancient **Capela de São Pedro de Balsemão** sits in a small square of granite cobbles in the tranquil hamlet of Balsemão. It's a pleasant, signposted, three-kilometre walk from Lamego, that starts at the Capela do Desterro, then heads through the old part of town and over the bridge. Believed to have been founded as early as the seventh century, the present chapel's foundations were laid in the tenth century during the Reconquista. Inside the dark, granite interior is the fourteenth-century sarcophagus of the Bishop of Porto, Dom Afonso Pires, who was born in Balsemão. Look out for the unusual statue of Nossa Senhora do Ó – the Ó refers to the shape of her pregnant belly, though others ascribe it to the exclamation uttered when seeing it: *Ó! Nossa Senhora, Mãe de Deus…*

Ucanha

15km southeast of Lamego • Take N226 (Moimenta da Beira road) for 12km, and look for the signposted left-turn just past Tarouca

For a trip into Lamego's medieval past, take a drive out to the old village of **UCANHA**, where a mighty fortified stone tollgate and ancient bridge (signposted "Torre Fortificada") straddle the lazy river. These sorts of buildings were once a common display of local power and influence – you paid a fee to the manor house to be able to cross the river – and the toll-house makes for an incongruous sight today in what's a real backwater. Like most other riverside villages, Ucanha also used to maintain a series of open-air washing pools, where the village women gathered to do their laundry and chat. These are no longer in use, but the whole scene is pretty as a picture, with a little bar at either end of the cobbled bridge, and a riverside path that runs up through the woods to a local river beach.

Mosteiro de Salzedas

Salzedas, 18km southeast of Lamego (N226) • June–Sept Tues–Sun 10am–12.30pm & 2–7pm; Oct–May Tues–Sun 9am–12.30pm & 2–5pm • Free • ☎ 254 677 458, ⓦ mosteirosalzedas.com

At **SALZEDAS**, 3km beyond Ucanha, the mildewed main facade of an Augustinian – later Cistercian – monastery overlooks the small village square. It dates from 1168, and was once enormously grand in scale and wealth, though it's been at the mercy of scavengers and the elements since the dissolution of the monasteries in 1834. Inside, a team of volunteers helps to clean and maintain the building, while outside are some abandoned courtyards and cloisters. You're usually free to wander in for a look around, though if you want a guided tour (and the chance of an English-speaker) you need to contact the monastery in advance. There are a couple of cafés in the village square.

THE ENTRUDO DOS COMPADRES AT LAZARIM

The unremarkable village of Lazarim (off the N2 Lamego–Castro Daire road) plays host to one of the oddest rituals to survive in Portugal. The **Entrudo dos Compadres** is a boisterous carnival that has taken place every Shrove Tuesday since the Middle Ages, with cavorting revellers taking to the streets wearing beautifully carved wooden masks, symbolic of the event's licentiousness. From a balcony, two colourful dolls loaded with fireworks are presented to the crowd – the *compadre*, carried by two young women, and *comadre*, toted by two young men. The couples proceed to recite insulting rhymes centring on sexual behaviour, after which the fireworks are lit and the dolls disintegrate in an explosive fury of smoke and flame, marking the end of the old year and the beginning of the new.

5

São João de Tarouca

17km southeast of Lamego, off the N226 (Moimenta da Beira road) • **Church** Tues 2–6pm, Wed–Sun 10am–12.30pm & 2–6pm • Free • The church is signposted to the right, past Mondim da Beira, 1.5km after the Ucanha junction on the N226, and it's another 3.5km from the turn

Evidence of the central role that Lamego played in the Reconquista, the fight back against the Moors, comes at the village of **SÃO JOÃO DE TAROUCA**, whose monastery of 1124 is thought to be the earliest on the Iberian peninsula to be founded by the Cistercian order – locals claim that Afonso Henrique himself, first king of Portugal, laid the founding stone. Whatever its erstwhile eminence, the monastery was thoroughly trashed after the 1834 dissolution, leaving a vast ruined shell of roofless monastic buildings, scattered tombstones and a lone bell-tower. The scale of the ruins is impressive, but only the adjacent Romanesque **church** – consecrated in 1169 – stands in anything like its original form. Inside, there's a fine carved choir and a Baroque organ (1766) whose central figure marks time with his arm during Mass, while *azulejos* in the transepts depict the life of St Bernard, including one of him standing in a wine barrel (a pre-Christian symbol of abundance).

Entry to the church is free, though if the guide accompanies you, pointing things out, you should tip him. There's a café nearby, and five minutes' walk downhill is a lovely Roman bridge over the Rio Varosa – a pleasant spot for a picnic.

ARRIVAL AND DEPARTURE

LAMEGO AND AROUND

By bus Lamego's bus station is right in the centre, a stone's throw from the main sights.

Destinations Braga (daily; 2hr 50min); Lisbon (2–4 daily; 5hr); Penafiel (3–5 daily; 1hr 40min); Peso da Régua (every 2hr; 30min); Porto (3–5 daily; 3hr); Trancoso (1–2 daily; 2–3hr); and Viseu (3–5 daily; 1hr).

By car The main avenue in town splits into two distinct halves (with separate names) either side of a central roundabout marked by a war-memorial statue of a soldier.

There's metered parking along the bottom half of the avenue (nearest the cathedral) and free parking along the top half (including on the large Largo da Feira market place, though not here on market day, Thursday).

By train The nearest train station is at Peso da Régua, 11km to the north: buses to Lamego leave from outside the station every couple of hours (30min), or take a taxi (around €20).

INFORMATION AND TOURS

Information The turismo is at the bottom of Av Visconde Guedes Teixeira (April–Sept Mon–Fri 9.30am–7pm, Sat & Sun 10am–1pm & 2.30–6pm; Oct–March daily 9.30am–12.30pm & 2–6pm; ☎ 254 612 005, ⓦ cm-lamego.pt).
Tours The two main local wine producers are the Caves da

Raposeira (ⓦ cavesdaraposeira.com), 1km from town, and the Caves da Murganheira (ⓦ murganheira.com), further out, on the road between Ucanha and Salzedas. For information about visits to local wineries, contact the turismo, since tours and tastings are not always possible.

ACCOMMODATION

LAMEGO

São Paulo Av 5 de Outubro 22 ☎254 613 114. Charm is in short supply in this tiled 1970s residential building above a parade of shops, but the plain rooms are big and those at the back look up to the old town and the Igreja de Almacave. Parking for guests. No credit cards. €35

Solar do Espírito Santo Rua Alexandre Herculano, entrance also on Av Dr Alfredo de Sousa ☎ 254 655 060. Comfortable if smallish en-suite rooms in the "Holy Ghost" guesthouse come with cool parquet floors and a/c. Those at the front with balconies have avenue and shrine views, though you also get some traffic noise. Private parking is a bonus, and there's a *pastelaria* below, from which come your breakfast rolls and croissants. €50

Solar dos Pachecos Av Visconde Guedes Teixeira ☎ 254 600 300. The smartest town-centre choice is this renovated, granite-walled *solar*. The rooms are light and airy, with baths or showers, and many have avenue views. Prices drop markedly out of summer. €75

AROUND LAMEGO

★ **Casa de Santo António de Britiande** Britiande, 5km southeast of Lamego, N226 ☎254 699 326, ⓦ casasantoantoniobritiande.com. In a handy location for touring the nearby Romanesque churches (bikes are available), this is a lordly, antique-filled manor house with its own *azulejo*-lined chapel and *pelourinho*, plus lovely orchards, gardens and a pool. There are four charming rooms in the house, and two separate garden apartments, with fireside or alfresco meals available by arrangement, as well as wine tastings and other local activities. €120

Casa dos Viscondes da Várzea Várzea de Abrunhais, 10km southeast, signposted off the N226 at Britiande ☎254 690 020, ⓦhotelruralviscondesvarzea.com. A palatial nineteenth-century *quinta* with shady verandas overlooking 180 acres of gardens, orchards and farmland. It's elegantly decorated throughout, with attractive wooden

furniture and traditionally tiled bathrooms. Meals, taken in a romantic *azulejo*-lined dining room, are a treat, and there's a pool. €150

Quinta do Terreiro Lalim, 7km south of Lamego, off N226 ☎254 697 040, ⓦquintadoterreiro.com. Another of the region's baronial eighteenth-century mansions, where you can stay in one of ten atmospheric granite-walled rooms, some with fireplaces. There's also a swimming pool, tennis court and cosy cellar-bar. €80

EATING AND DRINKING

For simple places serving inexpensive **regional food** head up Rua da Olaria, or at the back of the cathedral along Rua Trás de Sé ("Back-of-the-cathedral street") and Rua Direita. Local specialities include *fumeiros* (smoked meats), particularly *presunto* (ham) and *salpicão* sausages. The town's **food market** (closed Sat afternoon & Sun) is on Avenida 5 de Outubro, and there's a much bigger outdoor **weekly market** on Thursdays (at Largo da Feira), a colourful combination of local farm produce, trailers with grilled chicken, and clothes and shoes. The esplanade **bars and cafés** in the middle of the avenue are the hub for summertime evening drinkers and ice-cream addicts.

O Novo Largo da Sé 9 ☎254 613 166. The big draw here is dining at an outdoor table in front of the beautifully sculpted cathedral facade, though luckily the food is pretty good too. Lamego *presunto* is served with fried eggs, or stuffed into grilled trout, while the *bacalhau a casa* is baked with onions – dishes cost €8–14. Daily 10am–10pm; Nov–March closed Sat.

Trás da Sé Rua Trás da Sé 12 ☎254 614 075. The paint-daubed walls are lined with notepaper messages of congratulation, and the local food and wine is reliably good and fairly cheap – most dishes cost €7–10. There's a short menu, with a handwritten list of daily specials, including

the ubiquitous grilled trout stuffed with *presunto*. Daily noon–2.30pm & 7–10pm.

★ **Vindouro** Trav da Rua dos Fornos 19 ☎254 401 698, ⓦrestaurantevindouro.com. For a bit of Lamego glam, try this contemporary town-centre restaurant that cooks fancy regional dishes inspired by traditional Douro recipes in its wood-fired ovens. This means things like rack of lamb on ratatouille, *cabrito assado*, or risotto with wild duck and sun-dried tomatoes, with prices around €10–25. It's serious about its wines too, with most of the restaurant's Douro offerings also available to buy. Tues–Fri noon–2.30pm & 7.30–10pm, Sat noon–3pm & 7.30–10.30pm, Sun noon–3pm.

Pinhão and around

East of Peso da Régua, the minor N222 hugs the south side of the Rio Douro, with the train on the north side, until reaching the small port-wine town of **PINHÃO**, 25km to the east. It's a wonderful route and there's a real sense of arrival at Pinhão, where the river broadens and the terraced hills close in. Cruise boats tie up along a broad riverside esplanade, where a couple of bars look out over a fjord-like vista and there's a welcome breeze in the evening air. If you've come by car, don't miss the short, winding seven-kilometre drive up to the *miradouro* at the small village of **Casal de Loivos** (Favaios–Alijó road) – some say there's no better view along the whole of the Douro.

Wine House Quinta Nova

Estação do Pinhão, Largo da Estação 14 • **Shop** Mid-April to mid-Oct daily 10am–7pm; mid-Oct to mid-April Mon–Sat 9.30am–12.30pm & 2–6.30pm • Tastings €5–16 • **Museum** Tours daily at 11am, 3pm & 5pm; mid-Oct to mid-April closed Sun • €2.50 • ☎254 730 030, ⓦquintanova.com

Trains to Pinhão pull in at the delightful old station in town, clad in *azulejos* depicting the wine harvest. Part of the station has been converted into a classy wine shop run by *Quinta Nova* (see p.297), with all sorts of tasting packages available, pairing their wines with cheese or even chocolate. There's also a **wine museum** in the old station-staff living quarters, tours of which include a glass of *vinho*.

5

THE PORT WINE STORY

If ever a drink was synonymous with a country it's port – the fortified wine from Portugal's Douro region. For three centuries wine has been shipped down the Douro River to Vila Nova de Gaia, whose famous wine lodges (Sandeman, Graham's, Cockburn, Taylor's) reflect the early British influence on its production. A cellar tour here (see p.270) forms an integral part of any visit to Porto, while you can also follow the wine trail right along the Douro by train, car or cruise boat. To find out more, the country's port wine institute, the Instituto dos Vinhos do Douro e do Porto (𝕎 www.ivdp.pt), has a useful English-language website, while the Rota do Vinho do Porto (𝕎 rvp.pt) details the region's wine estates, attractions and events.

DEVELOPING A TASTE – THE EARLY DAYS

The clear distinction between port wine (*vinho do porto*) and other Portuguese wines wasn't made until the beginning of the eighteenth century, when Britain prohibited the import of French wines during the War of the Spanish Succession. Portuguese wines quickly filled the void and, following the **Methuen Treaty** (1703), the wine trade became so profitable that adulterated inferior wines were soon being passed off as the genuine article. This led to the creation of a regulatory body in 1756, the **Companhia Geral da Agricultura das Vinhas do Alto Douro**, and, the following year, the declaration of the world's oldest **demarcated wine region** (where port wine could now only legitimately be produced). Yet it wasn't until the mid-nineteenth century that it began to resemble today's fortified wine, when the addition of brandy to stop fermentation became widespread, enabling the wines to be transported over even longer distances.

THE DOURO WINE ROUTE

The port wine grapes are grown in a 600,000-acre demarcated region along both banks of the **Rio Douro**, stretching from Mesão Frio (near Peso da Régua) to the Spanish border. Sheltered by the Marão and Montemuro ranges, around fifteen percent of the region is under vines, which benefit from cold winters and hot, dry summers. The characteristic terraces can be seen along the length of the Douro, and they form a particularly beautiful backdrop to the small town of **Pinhão**, which is now the main centre for quality ports. The grapes are harvested at the *quintas* (vineyard estates) from September to October and crushed. After a few days fermentation is arrested by the addition of brandy – exactly when this is done determines the wine's sweetness – with the wine subsequently stored in casks until the following March. The final stage in the wine route is the transportation downstream to the shippers' lodges, where the wine is blended and matures.

WHAT'S IN THE BOTTLE?

Port wine is either **Ruby** (ie deep red) in style, **Tawny** (made from a blend of differently aged wines) or **white** – the first two are generally drunk at the end of a meal, or with cheese or dessert, the last served chilled as an aperitif. The finest reds are known as **Vintages**, wines from a single year that are bottled two to three years after harvest and left to mature. A vintage is only declared in certain years (just fourteen times between 1901 and 1999, for example), and the wine is only ready to drink at least ten to fifteen years after bottling, when the flavours are at their most complex, the wine deep purple and full-bodied. **Late Bottled Vintage (LBV)** is not of vintage quality, but is still good enough to mature in bottles, to which it's transferred after four to six years in the cask. All other ports are blended and are kept in the cask for between two and seven or more years, with the colour developing into various shades of Tawny – they are ready to drink when bottled. Of these, a **Colheita** ("Harvest") is a Tawny port made from grapes from a specific year and aged at least seven years in the cask; other fine wines are **superior Tawnies** dated 10, 20, 30 or 40 years old (the average age of the wines in the blend), while **Reserve** ports (both Tawny and Ruby) are decent blended wines, the best being the Tawny Reserve ports which have to spend at least seven years in the cask.

ARRIVAL AND DEPARTURE

PINHÃO AND AROUND

By train There are two through-trains a day from Porto to Pinhão (2hr 10min), or you can change in Peso da Régua (5 daily; 26min). Onward services are to Tua (5 daily; 15min) – change at Tua for the bus to Mirandela in Trás-os-Montes – and to the end of the line at Pocinho (5 daily; 1hr).

By car Beyond Pinhão, you can only follow the river by train or boat as the roads (on either side of the Douro) head for the hills, either to the wine- and olive-growing town of Alijó (15km northeast) or the rock art at Vila Nova de Foz Côa, 60km southeast.

ACCOMMODATION AND EATING

PINHÃO

Douro ☎ 254 732 404, ⊛ hotel-douro.pt. The best of the two adjacent budget places opposite the station, with a vine-covered terrace and simple en-suite rooms with balconies that overlook the water. It's hard to say what's more disconcerting – the cruise ships or the weekend steam trains, both disgorging their passengers below your window. The downstairs restaurant charges more than it should (dishes €9–12), but offers a few fish choices alongside the standard meat menu, and the house wine is excellent. Restaurant daily noon–3pm & 7–10pm. **€60**

Ponte Romana Rua da Ponte ☎ 254 732 978. Across the small bridge over the Pinhão River, at the back of town (Sabrosa road), this is the best of the non-hotel restaurants, with a river view if you get a seat by the window. You'll eat cheaply if you have the dish of the day at lunch, or for around €20 à la carte. Tues–Sun noon–3pm & 7–10pm. **Vintage House** ☎ 254 730 230, ⊛ cshotelsandresorts .com. Sumptuously decorated former warehouse on the Pinhão riverfront, whose rooms all have a water-view balcony or terrace. Boutique touches proliferate (guests help themselves to oranges piled in wicker grape-gathering baskets), and there are lovely grounds, a pool and a serious wine shop. *Rabelo* restaurant (mains from €20) comes into its own on a sunny day when you dine outside on a vine-covered terrace from a classy, contemporary Portuguese menu – non-guests are welcome, but a reservation is a good idea in summer for an alfresco lunch. The hotel also organizes tours, tastings and *quinta* visits. Restaurant daily 12.30–3pm & 7.30–10.30pm. **€160**

AROUND PINHÃO

★ **Casa de Casal de Loivos** Casal de Loivos, 7km north of Pinhão, Favaios–Alijó road ☎ 254 732 149, ⊛ casadecasaldeloivos.com. This old Douro manor house has an intimate house-party feel, and while the small rooms are traditional in decor they all open onto a stunning terrace with a pool, outdoor breakfast area and amazing views. It's the property of a rather exclusive wine producer, whose wines you'll be able to try if you dine here (€25). You'll find the house in the middle of the hilltop village, not far from the spectacular *miradouro*. **€100**

★ **Pousada Barão Forrester** Alijó, 15km northeast of Pinhão ☎ 259 959 467, ⊛ pousadas.pt. This splendid place is Alijó's main draw, named after the English port pioneer Joseph Forrester, made a baron by the Portuguese king and who drowned in the Douro in 1862 (weighed down, it is said, by his money belt). It's a genteel country house, with charming rooms, a formal restaurant, and terraces overlooking palm trees and a pool. **€90**

Quinta de la Rosa 1.5km west of Pinhão, on the north bank of the river ☎ 254 732 254, ⊛ quintadelarosa .com. A working wine estate with five rooms split between the main house and annexe, as well as two gorgeous larger suites (prices up to €120) and a swimming pool. The *quinta*'s own-label wines and olive oil are terrific and you can try them with a pre-booked lunch or dinner (€30), including wine and port) on their lush vine-covered terrace, which has views to die for. **€85**

★ **Quinta Nova de Nossa Senhora do Carmo** Covas do Douro, 10km west of Pinhão, on the north bank of the river ☎ 254 730 430, ⊛ quintanova.com. Truly fabulous, relaxing wine hotel in an eighteenth-century manor house on one of the most beautiful of Douro estates. Views over the vineyards and orchards to the river are stupendous, not least from the infinity pool, while country-chic rooms mix antique carved beds, polished floors and woven rugs with sharply styled, granite bathrooms containing select toiletries. It's a lovely, secluded space, offering its own vineyard tours and cellar tastings, plus bike and hiking trails, while meals (€30) are served outside under a century-old vine canopy. It's a fifteen-minute drive from Pinhão, or they can pick you up from Ferrão station at the bottom of the hill. **€150**

Vila Nova de Foz Côa

Sitting high above the Côa valley, 60km southeast of Pinhão, the small town of **VILA NOVA DE FOZ CÔA** would attract no interest at all had it not been for the discovery in 1992 of the most extensive array of outdoor **paleolithic art** in Europe. The engravings are of a similar style to those found in caves elsewhere, but their uniqueness lies in the fact that they are carved outside on exposed rock faces in a river valley. With the oldest dated at around 23,000 years, their survival is remarkable, and they are now under protection as both National Monument and UNESCO World Heritage Site.

There are three rock-art sites to visit, though the restrictions on numbers and visiting hours mean you can't see more than two in any one day. Depending on how keen you are, this might mean an overnight stop in Foz Côa, though there is no earthly reason otherwise to stay. Although the blistering midsummer heat and winter cold makes it hard to believe, the town benefits from a Mediterranean microclimate, proof of which is provided by the locally produced almonds, fruit, cheese, wine and – especially – olive oil, among the country's finest. The **monthly market** is on the first Tuesday of the month next to the football field, and the blossoming of **almond trees** draws the crowds in late February and early March.

Parque Arqueológico do Vale do Côa (PAVC)

Museu do Côa Tues–Sun 10am–1.30pm & 2–5.30pm • €5 • **Site visits** Tues–Sun 9am–12.30pm & 2–5.30pm • €10 per site, or €12 including museum, nocturnal visit €17 • ☎ 279 768 260, ✉ visitas@pavc.igespar.pt, ⊕ arte-coa.pt

The archeological park contains thousands of engravings on several hundred rocks, a good number of which are clustered around the three major sites. The engravings are of horses, deer, goats and other animals, as well as later, Neolithic, images of people – many are quite hard to make out, as unlike cave art they are not painted but were scratched or chipped with stones. Depending on the site, visits take place either in the mornings or afternoons, though night visits are sometimes possible, out of the sun's glare, when you can see the engravings more easily. If you only have time to visit one site, Penascosa is considered the most interesting.

Visiting the sites

The **Museu do Côa** (3km east of town, signposted) is the obvious place to start, since it expands in detail upon the discovery and history of the site, and also acts as a booking centre for the park. **Visits to the rock-art sites** have to be booked in advance, which can be done in person or by phone or email – in summer, two or three days in advance is recommended. The fee includes a guide and 4WD transport from the appropriate visitor centre (see "The sites", below); each trip has a maximum of eight visitors, and children under 3 are not allowed.

Canada do Inferno

From the museum, tours head out to the first site to be identified, that of **Canada do Inferno** (usually morning visits; tour lasts 1hr 30min), which lies near the abandoned Côa dam. It contains a wide variety of engravings, from bison to horses, some very close to the current water line and many more underwater since the construction of the Pocinho dam upstream raised the level.

Ribeira de Piscos

Trips to **Ribeira de Piscos** (usually mornings; 2hr 30min) head out from Muxagata, 1km off the N102 to Guarda, which has a bar beside the visitor centre. The engravings are spread out along the eponymous *ribeira* down to its confluence with the Côa – a beautiful place, but there's a lot of walking involved. The highlights are a tender engraving of two horses "kissing", some fine engravings of auroch bison (now extinct) and an exceptionally rare, paleolithic engraving of a man.

Penascosa

The least strenuous visit is to **Penascosa** (usually afternoons, 1hr 30min, plus evenings, 3hr), as the jeeps park right next to it. The starting point is the visitor centre in Castelo Melhor, just off the N322 to Figueira de Castelo Rodrigo. Penascosa's highlights include an engraving of a fish (one of very few such depictions worldwide), and a rock containing over a dozen superimposed animals, the meaning of which archeologists are at a loss to understand. The village itself has a gorgeous ruined castle and a couple of café-restaurants.

Quinta da Ervamoira

There's also a private site at **Quinta da Ervamoira** (closed Mon; visits by appointment: ☎ 279 759 229), a secluded vineyard on the west bank of the Côa, accessed from

Muxagata. It's owned by the Ramos Pinto port wine company, whose granite estate house is now a museum housing finds from Roman and medieval times.

ARRIVAL AND INFORMATION

VILA NOVA DE FOZ CÔA

By bus In Foz Côa the bus station is on the road in from Pocinho, 200m from the main avenue.

Destinations Bragança (2 daily; 2hr); Guarda (Mon–Fri 1 daily; 1hr 30min); Miranda do Douro (4–5 daily; 2hr 10min); Trancoso (2 daily; 40min); and Viseu (2–3 daily; 2hr).

By car Foz Côa is an hour's drive from Pinhão, over the hills along the highly scenic N222.

By train The train from Régua (5 daily; 1hr 25min) or Pinhão (5 daily; 1hr) follows the Douro River as far as its

terminus at Pocinho, which is little more than a railway station, a hydroelectric dam and a couple of restaurants. Vila Nova de Foz Côa is 8km south of Pocinho, and if there's no connecting bus into town, you can take a taxi for around €8.

Information The turismo is in the Centro Cultural, Av Cidade Nova (daily 9am–12.30pm & 2–5.30pm; ☎ 279 760 329, ⓦ cm-fozcoa.pt), in the same complex as the library, theatre, cinema and municipal museum.

ACCOMMODATION AND EATING

A Marisqueira Rua de São Miguel 35, down the pedestrianized continuation of the main avenue ☎ 279 762 187. A reliable stop for lunch or dinner – there is seafood, as the name suggests, including *arroz de marisco*, but in the end it's just as much a meat-and-potatoes place as anywhere else (meals around €15, lunch for less). For snacks and bread, visit *A Terrinca* bakery/tea room next door. Mon–Sat noon–2.30pm & 7–11pm.

Casa Vermelha Av Gago Coutinho 3 ☎ 279 765 252, ⓦ casavermelha.com. The only high-end place in town, with seven rather quaint rooms, plus picture-perfect lawns and a swimming pool. It's on the main avenue and is very easy to find – did we mention that it's extremely red (*vermelha*)? **€90**

Pousada de Juventude 1.5km northwest of town off the Pocinho road ☎ 279 764 041, ⓦ microsites .juventude.gov.pt/portal/en. Not a great location if

you don't have transport, but redeemed by good facilities and windswept views. It's more like a budget motel, with private rooms as well as dorms (with and without en-suite toilet), and also four-person apartments with kitchenette. Closed Dec. Dorm beds **€14**; doubles **€34**; apartments **€66**

★ **Quinta do Chão d'Ordem** 5km south, just south of Muxagata, off the N102 ☎ 279 762 427, ⓦ chaodordem .com. Eight bedrooms available on a working farm estate, with a cosy lounge and bar, tennis court and pool, and wine cellar in a converted dovecote. It's an artistically minded place with tasteful decor, and much of the produce, from the wine to the home-cured sausages, comes from the farm. **€60**

Vale do Côa Av Cidade Nova, facing the turismo ☎ 279 760 010, ⓦ hotelvaledocoa.net. The best mid-range place in town has spacious rooms with polished wooden floors, most with balconies, plus spotless bathrooms with bathtubs. **€60**

Barca d'Alva

The last Portuguese village along the Douro, **BARCA D'ALVA** is less than 2km from the Spanish border. Overlooked by mountains on all sides, and on a placid bend in the Rio Douro, it's a curious spot – on one hand, a long-abandoned railway line and a row of elderly cottages; on the other, a sparkling quayside with huge pontoons to accommodate the large Douro cruisers which disgorge passengers for a quick souvenir hunt. A few cafés and other places soak up any passing trade, but in the end it's the drive here, from north or south, that really warrants the trip, through beautifully sculpted Douro terraces of olives and vines, with sweeping views across the hills and into the river gorge. As there's no road along the Douro River in its latter stages after Pocinho, you have to approach via Foz Côa and Figueira de Castelo Rodrigo (in Beira Alta) or Torre de Moncorvo and Freixo de Espada à Cinta (in Trás-os-Montes).

ACCOMMODATION AND EATING

Bago d'Ouro Largo das Faias 29 ☎ 271 355 014, ⓦ bagodourohotels.pt. The simple river-facing rooms would suffice for the night, though you'd need a pretty good reason to stay. A daytime visit is more likely, for a

browse around the upmarket deli and lunch in the restaurant (mains from €10), where river fish from the Douro end up in dishes like *migas de peixe* (bread-based fish stew) and *peixinhos fritos* (mixed fried fish). **€50**

The Minho

BOM JESUS DO MONTE

6

The Minho

It's around 100km from Porto to the mouth of the Rio Minho, a broad river of even broader historical and cultural significance for the Portuguese since it marks the border with neighbouring Spain. The river has lent its name to the entire northwestern province, the MINHO, which encompasses a range of picture-postcard landscapes and features that could almost be Portugal in microcosm – dreamy river scenes, high mountains, rolling vineyards, historic towns, dramatic Atlantic beaches, ancient religious foundations and mysterious archeological sites. Add a modern network of roads – it takes only an hour or so to get from the main towns to remote hiking villages – and a useful regional bus and train network, and the Minho instantly appeals, as a sort of Portugal-in-a-nutshell experience, easily accessible straight out of Porto airport.

For a start, the region features many emblematic Portuguese traditions, whether it's the vast weekly market at **Barcelos** – a cross between a medieval fair and the biggest farmers' market you've ever seen – or the annual summer *romaria*, or carnival, at **Viano do Castelo**. The Minho's two principal historic towns, both in the south, are also steeped in tradition – handsomely preserved, medieval **Guimarães**, Portugal's first capital, and neighbouring **Braga**, the country's buttoned-up ecclesiastical centre. The Minho coast, meanwhile, as little as half an hour's drive from Braga, is the typical Atlantic swathe of sweeping duned beaches and wild surf. It's known as the **Costa Verde** (Green Coast), and is pretty much one long unbroken stretch of sand as far as the Spanish border, punctuated by several small-scale resorts and one decent-sized historic maritime town in Viana do Castelo.

Central Minho is characterized by the region's other major river, the **Rio Lima**, which idles through a succession of pretty towns where there's little to do but soak up the scenery – ideally, while staying in one of the boutique manor houses or country homes for which this area is renowned. Further east, the gentle charms of the Lima valley eventually give way to the mountains of the **Parque Nacional da Peneda-Gerês**, Portugal's only national park, which stretches north as far as the Spanish border and east into the next-door province of Trás-os-Montes.

To the north, the Minho region ends – where the country ends – with the **Rio Minho**, across which lies Spain. A string of compact fortified towns flanks the river on the Portuguese side, and the Minho train line from Porto terminates in the best of the lot, the spectacular walled town of **Valença do Minho**, a major crossing point into Spain.

Guimarães

GUIMARÃES never misses an opportunity to remind you of its place in Portuguese history. Indeed, it was here that the country's first monarch, Dom Afonso Henriques, was born in 1110, and the city became the first capital and court of the fledgling

Old capital, new projects p.307	The Viana Romaria p.322
Stairway to Heaven, Part II p.315	Portugal's Wonder Woman p.331
Braga's festivals p.317	Memory loss in Ponte de Lima? p.334
The Barcelos Cock p.320	Ponte de Lima's festivals p.335

FEIRA DE BARCELOS

Highlights

❶ **Pousada de Santa Marinha da Costa, Guimarães** Enjoy the views over Guimarães from a delightful hotel fashioned from a medieval monastery. **See p.308**

❷ **Citânia de Briteiros** Step back to pre-Roman times in the evocative ruins of a magnificent Iron Age hilltown. **See p.309**

❸ **Touring the cathedral, Braga** Follow the guide as he unlocks the secrets of the country's religious capital. **See p.312**

❹ **Feira de Barcelos** The spectacular Thursday *feira* is one of Europe's biggest weekly markets. **See p.319**

❺ **Monte de Santa Luzia** Ride up the funicular for one of the best views in Portugal from this breezy hilltop sanctuary. **See p.324**

❻ **Valença do Minho** A walk around the ramparts shows you the best of this historic Rio Minho fortified town. **See p.328**

❼ **Ponte de Lima** Whether staying in a manor house or boutique hotel – you won't regret a night in dreamy Ponte de Lima. **See p.334**

❽ **Soajo, Parque Nacional da Peneda-Gerês** The restored village of Soajo offers a glimpse of local life in this remote part of the country. **See p.346**

HIGHLIGHTS ARE MARKED ON THE MAP ON P.304

kingdom of "Portucale". Although Guimarães subsequently lost its pre-eminent status to Coimbra (elevated to Portuguese capital in 1143), it has never relinquished its sense of self-importance, something that's evident from the omnipresent reminder that *Portugal nasceu aqui* (Portugal was born here), the town's motto. With a carefully preserved kernel of medieval monuments, cobbled streets, delightful squares and honey-coloured houses, the old centre retains both a grandeur and a tangible sense of history that's helped earn it UNESCO World Heritage status. But it's far from a museum piece – its contemporary attractions were showcased during its stint as 2012 European Capital of Culture, while the local university lends it a youthful exuberance and lively nightlife, at its best during the end of May student-week festivities.

Castelo de Guimarães

Tues–Sun 10am–6pm • Castle and chapel of São Miguel do Castelo free; Torre de Menagem €1.50 • ☎ 253 412 273, ⓦ pduques.imc-ip.pt

Occupying a strategically sited hill and partly built into huge granite outcrops, the city's severe **Castelo** was originally built in the tenth century to protect the people of

THE MINHO

SPAIN

HIGHLIGHTS
1 Pousada de Santa Marinha da Costa, Guimarães
2 Citânia de Briteiros
3 Touring the cathedral, Braga
4 Feira de Barcelos
5 Monte de Santa Luzia

6 Valença do Minho
7 Ponte de Lima
8 Soajo, Parque Nacional da Peneda-Gerês

0   20
kilometres

Guimarães from attack by Moors and Normans. After centuries of use it fell into disrepair – and was used as a debtor's prison in the nineteenth century – but the castle was rebuilt in the 1940s to reflect the era of its greatest prominence under Afonso Henriques, the first monarch to call himself "King of Portugal". It's claimed he was born in the central keep – the **Torre de Menagem** – which is surrounded by seven fortified towers, and if – as is likely – Afonso was baptized here too, then it would have been in the small, squat Romanesque chapel of **São Miguel do Castelo**, nestling among trees just outside the walls. You're free to look inside the chapel and explore within the castle walls, where you can climb up to the ramparts and battlements for fine views of the town. For even better views you can climb the keep itself – reached from inside the walls over a high wooden bridge, followed by 77 steps to the top of a narrow tower.

Paço dos Duques de Bragança

Rua Conde Dom Henriques • Tues–Sun 10am–6pm • €5, under-14s free, free on Sun 10am–2pm • 📞 253 412 273, 🌐 pduques.imc-ip.pt

Dominating the lower part of the castle grounds is the grand **Paço dos Duques de Bragança**, originally built in the fifteenth century and serving as the medieval palace of the all-powerful Bragançan duchy until it fell into decline at the end of the sixteenth century. Successive uses, abandonments and unflattering restorations have rather mucked up its late-medieval majesty, and today part of the interior is used as a museum, housing an extensive collection of paintings (including a room of colourful pieces by modern artist José de Guimarães), applied art and weaponry. The top floor, meanwhile, is reserved as an official residence for the Portuguese president on any visit to the north of Portugal.

Along Rua de Santa Maria

For Guimarães at its most typical – by which we mean prettified and downright picturesque – take a walk along the narrow **Rua de Santa Maria**, which leads down from the castle area into the heart of the old town. You'll pass the impressive Baroque facade of the **Convento de Santa Clara** – now the Câmara Municipal (town hall), with the Biblioteca (library) opposite – before emerging in sloping **Praça de São Tiago**, which is ringed by cafés and restaurants. This forms almost a double square with neighbouring Largo da Oliveira, reached by walking through an ancient stone arcade that runs beneath the old medieval council chambers.

Largo da Oliveira

Legend, history and religion collide in the old town's most attractive square, **Largo da Oliveira**, with its appealingly rustic name (Olive Tree Square), stone arcades and painted houses with wooden balconies. There are no olive trees, though – the name relates to the tale of the Visigothic king Wamba, who is said to have pushed an olive-wood spear into the ground here, and refused to take up his crown unless the spear blossomed. Of course, it did bloom, and the supposed site is marked by a worn stone cross beneath an unusual four-sided **Gothic canopy**. The legend was enough to inspire Dom João I, who rode out from Guimarães to do battle with Castile at the Battle of Aljubarrota in 1385. Hedging his bets – just in case olive-sprouting miracles weren't the portent he hoped – the Portuguese king also called on the Virgin Mary for help, vowing to endow a monastic church in her honour if the battle went well. The Castilian army was duly scattered to the winds and Dom João I repaid the favour to the Virgin with the construction of the **Colegiada de Nossa Senhora da Oliveira** (Church of Our Lady of the Olive Tree; daily 7.15am–noon & 3.30–7pm), whose magnificent sculpted doorway faces the stone canopy in the square. The monastic buildings associated with the church later passed to the Portuguese state, and it's these that now house the Museu de Alberto Sampaio.

6

GUIMARÃES

● CAFÉS AND RESTAURANTS

Art & Gula	4
Casa Costinhas	3
Cor de Tangerina	1
Mumadona	2

■ BARS

Casa Amarela	2
Coconuts	1

■ ACCOMMODATION

Casa de Sezim	2
Mestre d'Aviz	5
Paço de São Cipriano	3
Pousada de Juventude	7
Pousada de Santa Marinha da Costa	4
Toural	6
Trinas	1

Museu de Alberto Sampaio

Rua Alfredo Guimarães • Tues–Sun 10am–6pm, July & Aug 10am–midnight • €3, free on Sun & hols 10am–2pm • ☎ 235 423 910, ⓦ masampaio.imc-ip.pt

Entered around the side of the Nossa Senhora da Oliveira church, the **Museu de Alberto Sampaio** shows off the region's religious treasures, from gold- and silverware to sculptures and frescoes. It's a beautifully restored space, with the collection displayed in the cloister and surrounding rooms, with two items above all taking pride of place. First is the masterpiece of medieval Portuguese silverware known as the *Triptych of the Nativity*, generally claimed to be captured Castilian war booty from the Battle of

Aljubarrota, although it was more probably made from melting down the king's silver measuring weights. The other precious relic displayed is João I's battle-worn tunic, handed over by the monarch as a gift to the church that would later embody his victory.

Museu Martins Sarmento

Rua Paio Galvão • Tues–Fri 9.30am–noon & 2–5pm, Sat & Sun 10am–noon & 2–5pm • €3 • ☎ 253 415 969, ⓦ msarmento.org

The city's archeological collections are held in the **Museu Martins Sarmento**, named after the nineteenth-century archeologist Francisco Martins Sarmento, who was born in Guimarães and first excavated the Iron Age site of Citânia de Briteiros (see p.309). The museum backdrop is the former convent of São Domingos, whose Gothic cloister and other rooms display a tantalizing selection of finds covering the entire prehistory of northern Portugal. Many of the finds from the Briteiros site and other major digs in the region are on show here, with highlights ranging from the intricately decorated Vilela votive offering (a 2500-year-old bronze piece depicting a ceremonial procession) to Iron Age granite warrior statues.

Penha and the Teleférico de Guimarães

Teleférico de Guimarães Nov–March daily 10am–5.30pm; April, May & Oct daily 10am–6.30pm; June, July & Sept Mon–Fri 10am–7pm, Sat, Sun & hols 10am–8pm; Aug daily 10am–8pm; April–Oct closed last Mon of each month • €4.30 return, children €2.15 return • ⓦ turipenha.pt

The peak of **Penha** (617m) is crowned by a dull grey church but offers spectacular views over Guimarães. The surrounding woods are the locals' favourite spot for a Sunday picnic, reached on paths that skirt round – and sometimes under – enormous moss-covered boulders. To get there, you need to head down Rua Dr José Sampaio (which starts near the Museu Alberto Sampaio) to the cable car station – the **Teleférico de Guimarães** – which is just a five-minute walk from the edge of the old town. By car or on foot, keep on Rua Dr José Sampaio and follow the signs, past the *pousada*; the signposted hiking route cuts up the switchbacks and it's about 3km (or a stiff hour) from town.

ARRIVAL AND INFORMATION   GUIMARÃES

Guimarães is around 50km northeast of Porto, and around 25km southeast of Braga. It's only a small place, and pretty much everything of interest is located in the old centre, where you'll easily be able to walk from sight to sight.

OLD CAPITAL, NEW PROJECTS

Guimarães' 2012 stint as European Capital of Culture prompted a cultural and architectural makeover for the city, though as visitors stick resolutely to the confined streets of the historic old town, the new attractions tend to get short shrift – even though they are mostly located just a few minutes' walk away. The old market building on Avenida Conde Margaride, for example, has been reborn as the **Plataforma das Artes**, an arts and culture space devoted to exhibitions, installations, workshops and other creative projects. Across the way, the converted buildings of a former plastics factory host exhibitions and events at the **Casa da Memória** (Memory House), where the city's history, culture, heritage and industry is explored. Other former industrial buildings have similarly been given a new lease of life as arts and cultural centres, like the **Centro para os Assuntos da Arte e Arquitectura** (CAAA; ⓦ centroaaa.org) – owned by a local association of artists and architects – or, just out of town, **Fábrica Asa** (ⓦ fabricaasa.eu). The project known as **Campurbis**, meanwhile – a partnership between council and university – aims to reinvigorate the former leather and textile district of Couros, with old factories again being put to new use as a Living Science Centre and Design Institute, among others. Further art and culture can be found at the well-established Centro Cultural de Vila Flôr (see p.309).

By bus The bus station is a fifteen-minute walk southwest of the centre at the bottom of Avenida Conde Margaride. There are regular daily services to Braga (express buses take 25min, local buses up to an hour), Porto (1hr), Vila Real (1hr) and Lisbon (up to 5hr).

By car The historic centre is partly pedestrianized, although metered parking is available in the streets around the old town walls. Free parking can be had at the big Largo das Hortas car park (follow signs to the Teleférico); there are also usually spaces on the far side of the Castelo (though not on Fridays, when it hosts a market).

By train With hourly services between Porto Campanha and Guimarães (1hr 10min), the train station is ten minutes' walk south of the centre – bear left from the station and take the first right down Avenida Dom Afonso Henriques, which takes you to the leafy boulevard of Alameda São Damaso.

Information The main Turismo da Alameda is at Alameda São Damaso 83 (daily 10am–10pm; ☎300 402 012, ⓦguimaraesturismo.com); there's also a branch office at Praça de Santiago 37 (Mon–Fri 9.30am–6.30pm, Sat & Sun 10am–6pm; ☎253 421 221).

ACCOMMODATION

As well as atmospheric accommodation in the old town, and a just-out-of-town *pousada* with grandstand views, there are also some lovely manor houses in the surrounding countryside offering rather fine lodgings. The former *pousada* in central Guimarães, *Nossa Senhora da Oliveira*, sited right in the heart of the old town, closed in 2013, but is expected to reopen as a rebranded hotel in the future.

Casa de Sezim Nespereira, 4km south of Guimarães off the Santo Tirso road – turn right at Covas ☎253 523 000, ⓦsezim.pt. A delightful aristocratic country estate owned by the same *vinho verde*-producing family for over six centuries. Eight of the rooms in the main eighteenth-century *solar* (manor) are furnished with Murano chandeliers and objets d'art, with four-posters in many. There's also a swimming pool and tennis court, and you're welcome to wander the vineyards, while things like walking tours and horseriding trips can be arranged. €115

⭐ **Mestre d'Aviz** Rua Dom João I 40 ☎253 422 770, ⓦhotelmestredeavis.pt. The best-value budget place in Guimarães, with pleasant rooms in a lovely converted townhouse, just outside the old centre. The best rooms have balconies, though those in the attic are also atmospheric. It even has its own neat living room and bar. Breakfast is extra. €45

⭐ **Paço de São Cipriano** Tabuadelo, 6km south of Guimarães off the Santo Tirso road – turn left at Covas ☎253 565 337, ⓦpacoscipriano.com. The owners of this stunning fifteenth-century country house have traditionally received pilgrims en route to Santiago de Compostela in Spain, and the property comes complete with a chapel and medieval tower. It's a thoroughly lovely retreat, with its own magical gardens and wooded grounds, plus orchards and vineyards – there are seven elegant rooms and a swimming pool. Afternoon tea and dinner are optional extras, as are guided tours of the estate. €110

Pousada de Juventude Largo da Cidade 8 ☎253 421 380, ⓦmicrosites.juventude.gov.pt/portal/en. On a quiet side street, the town hostel partly occupies a renovated mansion, with another part housed in a new wing. It's got dorms but it's not just for backpackers since there are also private rooms and simple four-bed apartments, plus its own gardens and courtyard, café, shared kitchen and parking. Dorm beds €14, doubles €38, apartments €68

⭐ **Pousada de Santa Marinha da Costa** Lugar de Costa, 2km southeast of Guimarães ☎253 511 249, ⓦpousadas.pt. A 20min walk from town, the finest city choice is the elegant hillside *pousada* fashioned from a twelfth-century Augustinian monastery, which uses its vast granite spaces to impressive effect; for example in the soaring, arched dining room (once the monks' *adega*), the wide, baronial corridors and majestic tiled bar. Water tinkles from fonts, the cloisters are intact, while a romantic terrace offers sweeping city views – and there's a fine swimming pool and lovely hillside gardens as well. Rooms in the main building are in the atmospheric updated monks' cells, though there's more space and better views in the newer wing. €150

Toural Largo do Toural, entrance in Largo A.L. de Carvalho ☎253 517 184, ⓦhoteltoural.com. Elegant townhouse renovated into a modern four-star establishment next to the music academy – expect delightful sounds to waft through the window. The rooms are spacious and plush, and there's a pleasant bar overlooking a central courtyard: it also has parking. €85

Trinas Rua das Trinas 29 ☎253 517 358, ⓦresidencial trinas.com. In a fine townhouse in a great position right in the old town, this good-value guesthouse has eleven modest, en-suite double rooms, a bit on the old-fashioned side but comfortable enough. Rooms overlooking the street have the atmosphere – rear rooms are noisier, although are double-glazed. €40

EATING, DRINKING AND ENTERTAINMENT

Old-town Guimarães has plenty of cafés and restaurants, with the best-located being those with outdoor tables in Praça de São Tiago and Largo da Oliveira – though menu-toting waiters go in for the hard sell at times and the food isn't always up to scratch. Local specialities are on the earthy side – like *chispalhada de feijão* (beans, sausage and pig's trotters) and *papas de sarabulho* (a blood and bread stew) – while desserts include the local honey cakes known as *melindres*, and *toucinho do céu* ("heavenly bacon"), a super-sweet concoction of sugar, almonds, eggs and lemon. The city's main festival is the **Festas Gualterianas** (for São Gualter, or St Walter), which has taken place on the first weekend of August every year since 1452.

CAFÉS AND RESTAURANTS

Art & Gula Largo Cónego José M. Gomes 39 ☎ 253 518 118, ⓦ artegula.com. The building is an old stone beauty in the historic core, with a first-floor dining room overlooking the square and town hall, but we especially like the romantic patio garden at the back. The menu's on the traditional side, *bacalhau* to *porco preto*, but in a restaurant that calls itself "Art & Gluttony" everything is beautifully cooked and presented (dishes €10–13). Tues–Sun noon–3pm & 7–10pm.

Casa Costinhas Rua de Santa Maria 68 ☎ 253 516 248. Sweet little granite house with a tiled bar serving the traditional cakes and pastries known as *doces regionais e conventuais*. Confections like *toucinho do céu* (available here) all once originated in Portugal's convents (this little caff is just around the corner from the old Santa Clara convent), and it's a perfect place to give in to your sweet tooth. Mon–Fri 8am–7pm, Sat 8am–2pm.

★ **Cor de Tangerina** Largo Martins Sarmento 89 ☎ 253 542 009. Hold on to your hats – creative organic veggie food from a good-natured cooperative is unusual enough in northern Portugal, but there's a charming tree-shaded terrace as well in this handsome old townhouse just below the castle. For meals, think things like a vegetable and mushroom *açorda* or tofu and veg cannelloni, with mains around €11 and lunch a good deal at €7–9. Otherwise, there are drinks, tastings, foodie workshops and music nights. June–Sept Tues–Sat noon–midnight, Sun noon–7pm; Oct–May Tues–Fri noon–3.30pm & 7.30–10pm, Sat noon–11pm, Sun noon–6pm.

Mumadona Rua Serpa Pinto 260 ☎ 253 416 111, ⓦ restaurantemumadona.com.sapo.pt. Cheapest feed in town at lunch is the set meal that gets you soup, a choice of main dish, drink and coffee, but to be honest it's not much pricier choosing off the menu – generous half-portions start at €5 in this bustling family-run restaurant that sees a largely local clientele (especially for lunch) despite its near-castle location. Mon–Sat noon–3pm & 7–10pm.

BARS

★ **Casa Amarela** Rua do Donães 16–24 ☎ 913 355 111. The "Yellow House" is a funky townhouse just off the historic squares, mixing bar, restaurant and live music. Drinks, and weekend gigs and DJs are upstairs in a smallish contemporary bar that opens out on to a roof terrace; good food is served downstairs, from tapas-sized dishes of fried chicken, grilled prawns or daily home-made quiche to *bacalhau*, steak or veggie mains (tapas €4, mains €10–13). Sun–Tues 10am–midnight, Wed–Sat 10am–2am.

Coconuts Largo da Oliveira 1 ☎ 253 516 664. Of the half-dozen bars on this lovely square, this is the pick of the bunch – best views, right on to the ancient cross and church, and a studenty interior fashioned from an infilled granite arcade. Nice cakes and pastries too. Sun–Thurs 10am–midnight, Fri & Sat 10am–2am.

ART AND CULTURE

Centro Cultural de Vila Flôr Av Dom Afonso Henriques 701, on the way to the train station ☎ 253 424 700, ⓦ ccvf.pt. The local cultural centre occupies an eighteenth-century manor house, with a separate theatre wing, plus late-opening café-bar and restaurant. There's an exciting year-round programme, from cinema, live music and theatre to opera, dance and arts workshops – and the terraced gardens are lovely too.

Citânia de Briteiros

Ancient Portuguese archeological sites don't come more mysterious or dramatic than the **Citânia de Briteiros**, an Iron Age hilltown that lies roughly halfway between Guimarães and Braga. It's one of dozens in the Minho region, large and small, most dating back to around 500 BC, although some are considerably older still. Home to a people known as the "Bracari", the extensive site at Briteiros, straddling a boulder-strewn hill, probably made a last-ditch stand against the invading Romans and was eventually abandoned by around 100 AD. Its significance is enormous – the hillside ruins may appear obscure today, but Briteiros is one of the earliest sites on the Iberian peninsula that could reasonably be described as an urban settlement.

The site

Rua de São Romão, Briteiros • Daily: May–Sept 9am–6pm; Oct–April 9am–5pm • €3, ticket includes admission to Museu de Cultura Castreja • ☎ 253 478 952, Ⓦ msarmento.org

The *citânia* was first uncovered by Guimarães archeologist Francisco Martins Sarmento in 1874, who showed evidence of habitation here going back several thousand years, though what's visible today dates mainly from around 200 BC. This era of the so-called Cultura Castreja (Castro Culture) probably saw Briteiros at its peak, home to as many as two thousand people, living in circular huts in family compounds – Sarmento rebuilt two of the dwellings to give an indication of the settlement's feel and look. There's a fair amount of guesswork involved when it comes to interpreting the foundations of more than 150 separate huts, but there are obvious cooking and sleeping areas while the central stones, it's thought, would have provided support for poles holding up thatched roofs. A few of the foundations are more extensive, including a building with stone benches, which may have been a meeting house, as well as two bathhouses – these had their own water supply and separate steam- and cold-water rooms. It displays a surprising level of urban sophistication for the Iron Age – including a clear pattern of streets and defensive walls – and the entire site is a hugely evocative place for a stroll, along rough cobbles and past ancient cork oaks.

Museu da Cultura Castreja

Rua do Solar, Briteiros • Daily: May–Sept 9.30am–12.30pm & 2–6pm; Oct–April 9.30am–12.30pm & 2–5pm • €3, includes admission to Citânia de Briteiros • ☎ 253 478 952, Ⓦ msarmento.org

Many of the finds from the site are on show in Guimarães at the Museu Martins Sarmento (see p.307), but once you're out here it's worth also calling in at the **Museu da Cultura Castreja** in nearby Briteiros. It's set inside an old manor house (once the family home of archeologist Francisco Martins Sarmento, and his HQ during the digs conducted at the archeological site), and puts the Citânia de Briteiros into wider context within the world of the Cultura Castreja, which extended throughout northern Portugal and into northwestern Spain. In particular, the museum displays the large, precisely incised stone known as the Pedra Formosa ("beautiful stone"), discovered at Briteiros in the eighteenth century and an object of some fascination for early archeologists. Once assumed to be a sacrificial altar, it's now generally agreed to have formed part of the inner wall in one of Briteiros' ritual bathhouses.

ARRIVAL AND DEPARTURE	CITÂNIA DE BRITEIROS
By car The site is around 15km from both Guimarães and Braga, reached via the small town of Briteiros – here, signs direct you to the *citânia* on the hill above town. There is limited parking on the road before the site and by the entrance.	**By bus** A few buses run from Guimarães direct to Briteiros (2–3 daily), from where you can either walk the 2km up to the site, or catch a taxi from the main square.

Braga and around

BRAGA is Portugal's most important religious centre, with churches by the bucket-load. It's also one of the country's oldest and most fought-over towns, probably first founded by the Iron Age Bracari people (hence the name) before falling into Roman hands, after which its history was one of conquest and reconquest. By the time Portugal was established as an independent country in the eleventh century it was already an important bishopric, and it's remained at the heart of national religious life ever since. Spend some time here and you soon become aware of the weight of ecclesiastical power, embodied by an archbishop's palace built on a truly presidential scale and religious festivities that set the tone for the rest of the country. The city's outlying districts also boast a selection of religious buildings, shrines and sanctuaries, notably

Portugal's oldest Benedictine monastic foundation at **Tibães**, and **Bom Jesus**, one of the country's most extravagant Baroque creations.

For all that, it would be too easy to fall into the time-honoured cliché that Braga is a traditional, conservative place of stultifying religiosity. True, there might be 35 churches in town, but there's also a fast-growing commercial centre, a renowned university and an underlying cultural vibrancy that led to Braga being named 2012 "European Youth Capital". The refashioned **city centre** is a pleasing place of wide boulevards and traffic-free

BRAGA

6

streets and squares, and it's easy to spend a day or so idling around, drinking coffee in its handsome cafés, some of them century-old survivors from more uptight days.

The smartening-up of Braga has come at a price – the network of fast roads, underpasses and modern tower blocks around the ancient town has angered many residents who feel that the old centre of Braga (the phrase "as old as the cathedral of Braga" is the Portuguese equivalent of "as old as the hills") should have been better preserved. Various tunnelling projects uncovered, and promptly destroyed, a number of Roman houses, but the plus side is that most of the central traffic is funnelled underground.

Praça da República

The heart of Braga is **Praça da República**, an arcaded square at the head of the old town, with a wide avenue in front marked by a trio of fountains. At the back of the square is the former town keep, the fourteenth-century **Torre de Menagem**, while in the arcade itself two traditional coffee houses still do the honours – the *Vianna*, in particular, is a gently fading period-piece. Pedestrianized shopping streets shoot off in all directions from Praça da República, like **Avenida da Liberdade**, with its central carpet of flowers, though it's **Rua do Souto** that is Braga's principal street, heading down towards the cathedral. Only in Braga, is the tempting refrain, would you find boutiques and bars alongside a selection of shops where you can buy a silver chalice, a life-sized ceramic saint and a bag of votive candles.

Paço Episcopal

Largo do Paço; No general admission • **Biblioteca** Entrance on Praça do Municipal; Mon–Fri 9am–noon & 2–8pm • Free

For centuries, the most impressive building in Braga has been the old Archbishop's Palace, the **Paço Episcopal**, a strident statement of intent in the very centre of the city. It's actually "buildings" rather than "building", since it's been extended and reconfigured many times, from medieval castle to aristocratic mansion – most of what survives today (it was much larger still in earlier times) dates from the sixteenth to eighteenth centuries and embraces a variety of architectural styles from Gothic to Baroque. There are some charming gardens around the back too. The palace has had a variety of uses in modern times, and currently accommodates part of the university and both the municipal archives and **library** (Biblioteca), the latter retaining its ornately furnished reading room.

Sé

Rua Dom Paio Mendes, entrance on Rua Diogo de Sousa • Daily: May–Sept 8am–7pm; Oct–April 8am–6.30pm • Free • ☎ 253 263 317, ⓦ se-braga.pt

The twin-towered **Sé**, or cathedral – properly, the Catedral de Santa Maria de Braga – stands opposite the Archbishop's Palace. It's a rambling structure founded in 1070 on the site of a Moorish mosque after the Christian Reconquest, though only the original main door (at the top of Rua Dom Paio Mendes) survives in its sculpted, Romanesque form. Everything else is a hotchpotch of often-conflicting styles – Braga's cathedral is no one's real favourite – although Archbishop Dom Diogo de Sousa (1505–1532) did at least have the foresight to commission architect-of-the-day João de Castilho to work on various aspects of the interior and exterior. You can walk into the cathedral for free, but you'll have to buy tickets at the desk to see the most interesting parts.

Tesouro–Museu da Sé

June–Sept Tues–Sun 9am–12.30pm & 2–6.30pm; Oct–May Tues–Sun 9am–12.30pm & 2–5.30pm • €3

Hardly surprisingly, the most domineering cathedral in Portugal also has the richest treasury in the country, containing representative chalices, crosses, goblets, coffers, vestments, paintings and ceramics from across the centuries. It is, dare we say, a bit on the dull side, and the only light relief comes from the displayed shoes of the diminutive Archbishop Dom Rodrigo de Maura Teles (1704–1728), who stood a mighty 1m 20cm tall. He commissioned 22 monuments during his term of office, among them the fabulous shrine at Bom Jesus.

Coro Alto and Capela dos Reis

June–Sept Tues–Sun 9am–12.30pm & 2–6.30pm; Oct–May Tues–Sun 9am–12.30pm & 2–5.30pm • €2

A separate ticket gives you a guided tour of the main chapels and choir, led by an attendant with giant comedy keys, opening and closing vast ancient doors as you go. First up is the Baroque **Coro Alto**, with its majestic carved seats, gilded organ and imposing archbishop's throne – the latter surmounted by a grand eighteenth-century clock stopped at a symbolic 3pm (the supposed hour of Christ's death). Then it's on to the fourteenth-century **Capela dos Reis** (King's Chapel), which is where ecclesiastical and royal power finally collide in Braga. The chapel contains the diminutive tombs of Henry of Burgundy and his wife Teresa of León – not only were they the founders of Braga cathedral, but also the parents of Afonso Henriques, first king of Portugal. You'll also be invited to look into the sarcophagus containing the supposedly mummified body of Archbishop Lourenço, though it's tricky to discern much through the clouded glass. Two other chapels are also on the tour – a gilded Baroque monstrosity dedicated to the first archbishop of Braga, now the city's patron saint, and a more sober affair with faded eighteenth-century frescoes and a painted ceiling.

Palácio dos Biscaínhos

Rua dos Biscaínhos • Tues–Sun 10am–12.15pm & 2–5.30pm • €2, free on Sun 10am–noon • ☎ 253 204 650

To get an idea of how the wealthy lived in the seventeenth and eighteenth centuries, visit the splendid **Palácio dos Biscaínhos**, which was donated to the city in the 1960s on the death of its last aristocratic owner. The Counts of Bertiandos had lived here for over three centuries and the grandiose complex now houses a small museum of decorative arts, paintings and sculpture from the seventeenth to nineteenth centuries, which, together with exquisite tiles and wooden ceilings, demonstrates some of the best Portuguese interior decor of the time. There are pretty landscaped **gardens** behind, complete with a 200-year-old Virginian magnolia tree.

Museu Pio XII

Largo de Santiago 47 • Tues–Sat 9.30am–12.30pm & 2.30–6pm • €2 for each part, or €4 for both plus the Torre Medieval • ☎ 253 200 130, ⓦ museupioxii.com

On the southern side of town, in a former seminary, the curious **Museu Pio XII** is divided into two parts: one traces the career of Portuguese portrait-painter Henrique Medina (1901–1988), while the other rounds up a wide-ranging archeological and sacred art collection. In the **Torre Medieval**, opposite, a further section of the museum narrates Braga's history across five floors of a bell-tower – but really, what you come here for is the fine view of town from the top.

Estádio AXA

Monte Castro, 2km north of the city centre • **Tours** Sept–May Mon–Fri 10.30am & 3.30pm; June–Aug 10.30am, 2.30pm & 4pm • 90min tour €5; 30min tour €3 • Reservations essential ☎ 253 206 860, ⓦ scbraga.pt • Bus #5 (every 30–60min) from Av Central

Braga's spectacular municipal stadium, known as the **Estádio AXA** – designed by Eduardo Souta Moura for the Euro 2004 football championships, and home of Sporting Braga – has become something of a contemporary icon for the city. It's hard not to be impressed by the architect's vision, which wedged two colossal stands into the Monte Castro hillside, with the bare rock cliff of an old quarry forming one end of the

6

ground. Both long and short tours take in the stadium interior and club museum, though if you're a Portuguese footy fan it's the longer tour you want, which also includes a visit to the changing rooms, press room and VIP areas.

Mosteiro de Tibães

Mire de Tibães, 6km northwest of Braga • Tues–Sun 10am–1pm & 2–5.30pm; guided tours at 11am, 3pm & 4.30pm • €4, under-14s free, free Sun 10am–1pm • ☎ 253 622 670, ⊛ geira.pt/msmtibaes • Bus #50 (4 daily; 30min) runs directly to the monastery from Praça Conde de Agrolongo, though last return is early afternoon; additional services on bus #11 (marked "Padim da Graça") involve a steep 10min walk up to the monastery

The oldest Benedictine foundation in the land – predating even the establishment of the Portuguese nation in the eleventh century – stands a few kilometres from the centre of Braga, close to the village of Mire de Tibães. The **Mosteiro de São Martinho de Tibães** was probably first founded in the tenth century, though its heyday coincided with the flourishing of nearby Braga in the seventeenth century, when Tibães was a fabulously wealthy monastery – it was for a time one of the country's main schools for master stonemasons and artists, until its dissolution by the state in 1833.

From the grand cobbled entrance – heavily grooved from the wheels of untold hundreds of carts – the tours (usually in Portuguese) take you round the old stables, and through beautiful **cloisters** lined with eighteenth-century *azulejos* showing the life of St Benedict. It is interesting to compare the ornate grand hall, where bishops were elected, with the spartan monks' cells, though perhaps most impressive of all is the huge church, a mishmash of Baroque, Rococo and Neoclassical styles. You can walk around on your own at other times, when you'll also be able to explore the hundred-acre monastic **gardens**, dotted with chapels, hermits' hideaways and little lakes. There are also two marked trails, a 45-minute one round the cultivated lower slopes, or a 90-minute one that climbs into the surrounding woodlands.

Bom Jesus do Monte

Monte do Bom Jesus, 5km northeast of Braga • Take bus #2, currently at 10min and 40min past the hour, from Av da Liberdade, near the main post office, to the foot of the stairway at Bom Jesus • **Funicular** Every 30min, daily 8am–dusk • €1.20 each way • Ⓦ estanciadobomjesus.com

If the endless churches and religious buildings of Braga leave you cold, the monumental Baroque stairway and pilgrim church of **Bom Jesus do Monte**, sited on a wooded hill 5km to the east, is unlikely to do the same. In the Portuguese way, it's both pilgrimage and picnic site – you might bring lunch and enjoy the wonderful views from the terrace at the top, while other visitors determinedly shuffle up the 116-metre-long, ornamental zig-zag, granite staircase, and doing it on their knees if they are particularly devout. The site was commissioned by Archbishop Dom Rodrigo de Maura Teles in 1723, although the whole complex – staircase, fountains, chapels and church – took sixty years to complete. There's a precise symbolism at work, with fountains representing the Five Senses and the Three Virtues, for example, while the chapels are adorned with sculpted scenes from the Passion of Christ. Linking all, meanwhile, are the bright, white, interleaved staircase walls, climbing to the church at the very top whose altar is dedicated to the inevitable Crucifixion of "Good Jesus of the Mount".

The walk up is certainly an experience, but you can also zip straight to the top using the hydraulic-powered, twin-cabined **funicular**, which was inaugurated in 1882 and is still going strong. The surrounding area is a public park with plenty of family-friendly attractions – woods to walk in, plus formal gardens and hidden grottoes, not to mention boating lake and pony-trap rides. A handful of day-tripper restaurants cater for the weekend and holiday crowds, and there are even a few hotels and pensions too, most taking full advantage of the sweeping views from the Bom Jesus heights.

ARRIVAL AND DEPARTURE   BRAGA AND AROUND

Braga is around 60km northeast of Porto, and a quick 45min drive up the motorway. It's a fair-sized city, although the old town – an oval of streets radiating out from the Sé – is easy to see on foot.

By bus The bus station is five minutes' walk from the central Praça da República. Local suburban buses operate from a variety of stops, though many use Praça Conde de Agrolongo as a terminus.
Destinations Arcos de Valdevez (10 daily; 1hr 30min–2hr); Barcelos (every 30min–1hr; 50min); Bragança (2–6 daily; 4hr 15min–5hr); Caldas do Gerês (5–11 daily; 1hr 30min);

Campo do Gerês (2–7 daily; 1hr 30min); Guimarães (every 30min; 40min–1hr); Lisbon (12 daily; 4hr 30min); Monção (2–4 daily; 1hr 45min); Ponte da Barca (2–4 daily; 1hr 15min); Ponte de Lima (3–10 daily; 30min–1hr); Porto (every 30min; 1hr); Viana do Castelo (4–10 daily; 1hr 40min).
By car A swirl of ring roads and a confusing one-way system does its best to keep you out if you're trying to enter

---

STAIRWAY TO HEAVEN, PART II

Close to Bom Jesus – 1.5km by road from the bottom of the staircase or a 20-minute walk uphill beyond the pinewoods at the top – there's a second pilgrimage staircase and shrine with an entirely different feel. The massive, white-domed **Santuário do Sameiro** is impressive in its way, and again affords fantastic views across the city of Braga and beyond. But the nineteenth-century church is swallowed up by swathes of surrounding concrete and approached by a grimly monolithic monumental stairway. It's on a similar scale to Fátima – a powerful reminder of the might and authority of the Roman Catholic Church in Portugal – and the main annual festival, on the first Sunday in June, sees the arrival of scores of thousands of pilgrims. There's a second huge event on the last Sunday in August too.

Braga and keep you in when you're trying to leave. If you're using SatNav, you're going to be hearing a lot of "Recalculating…". There are plenty of central, signposted underground car parks, while the side streets around Praça Mouzinho de Albuquerque are your best hope for free parking.

By train The train station lies west of the centre, a fifteen- to twenty-minute walk from the old town, down Rua Andrade Corvo. Direct trains run daily from Braga to Porto São Bento and Campanhã stations (every 30–60min; 55min–1hr 10min); change at Nine (10–20min) for Viana do Castelo and Valença do Minho.

INFORMATION, TOURS AND ACTIVITIES

Information Braga Turismo, Av da Liberdade 1 (Mon–Fri 9am–1pm & 2–6.30pm, Sat & Sun 10am–1pm & 2–6pm; ☎ 253 262 550, ⌨ cm-braga.pt), sells the Braga Card (€5, valid for two days) which gives hefty discounts on most town attractions and bus tours, and a ten-percent discount on some accommodation.

National park office The HQ of the Parque Nacional da Peneda-Gerês, Av António Macedo, Quinta das Parretas suburb (Mon–Fri 9am–12.30pm & 2–5.30pm; ☎ 253 203 480, ⌨ adere-pg.pt), is a 20min walk from the centre, and

supplies invaluable maps and walking guides for Peneda-Gerês national park.

Bike rental Rent bikes from Go By Bike (1hr €4, 1 day €12; ☎ 917 741 803, ⌨ gobybike.eu/aluguer) at Rua de São Marcus 76, located by *Bragatruthotel*.

Bus tours The Yellowbus (⌨ yellowbustours.com) hop-on, hop-off bus tour departs hourly from Av Central, passing the Sé and train station, and heading out to Bom Jesus and back (June–Sept from 10am–noon & 3–6pm; €10, children €5, includes ride on Bom Jesus funicular; ticket valid 24hr).

ACCOMMODATION

Albergaria da Sé Rua Dom Gonçalo Pereira 39–51 ☎ 253 214 502, ⌨ albergaria-da-se.com.pt. If you're on a budget this is a good first place to try, in a great position on a pedestrianized street a stone's throw from the cathedral and close to plenty of places to eat. It's nothing fancy, but the prices are good and there's friendly service. **€50**

Braga Melia Av General Carrilho da Silva Pinto 8 ☎ 707 299 707, ⌨ meliabraga.com. The *Melia* brings a touch of New York style to the suburban ring-road outside the city – from soaring, urban-chic lobby, restaurant and bar to fab spa facilities, and indoor and outdoor pool. Glam rooms in sober earth tones look over the swirling roads and city lights below – whisk back the dividing sheen curtain and your room doubles in size, revealing a deep stand-alone bath and sharply styled bathroom. It's a five-minute taxi ride to central Braga, and you're just a short drive from Bom Jesus. **€97**

★ **Bragatruthotel** Rua de São Marcos 80 ☎ 253 277 187, ⌨ truthotel.com. New owners have taken an ageing guesthouse and given it a contemporary lift – it's still a good-value choice in a conveniently located, handsome old building, but some of the revamped rooms have been designed and decorated by local artists, while dining area and lobby are designated "art spaces" for changing exhibitions. They've kept right on top of what visitors want, from pillow menu and slippers to bike rental and other services, and there are suites (€80) and family rooms too (€90). They can also sort out nearby parking for you. **€60**

Casa dos Lagos Estrada do Bom Jesus, Bom Jesus 71–73 ☎ 253 676 738, ⌨ casadoslagosbomjesus.com. A charming old manor house up at Bom Jesus (on the road just below the top of the steps), with three spacious, traditionally furnished rooms in the main house (opening out onto a veranda), and some more modern apartments in a separate annexe. There's a kidney-shaped swimming

pool and terraced gardens, and the views are sensational from all quarters. **€90**

Pousada de Juventude Rua de Santa Margarida 6 ☎ 253 616 163, ⌨ microsites.juventude.gov.pt/portal /en. Braga's youth hostel has half a dozen eight- and ten-bed dorms, and the bargain prices mean they tend to fill quickly in summer. You'll also need to book ahead if you want one of the three private double rooms. There are lockers for valuables, a kitchen, and a common room with satellite TV and a pool table. Dorm beds **€12**, doubles **€30**

São Vicente Largo de Infias ☎ 253 209 500, ⌨ hotelsao vicente.com.pt. Once upon a time, when businessmen made their fortunes in Brazil, they came home to build mansions like this rather grand affair, complete with its own private chapel. It's now a bijou hotel – with tastefully furnished rooms, restaurant and bar, and small summer-only outdoor pool – and while it does overlook a busy roundabout (the first one in Braga if you're arriving from the north on the N101), it's only a 10min walk from the centre. **€70**

Senhora-a-Branca Largo da Senhora-a-Branca 58 ☎ 253 269 938, ⌨ albergariasrabranca.pt. A useful place for drivers who want to stay centrally. It's in a quiet location, facing a leafy square, and has garage parking. **€55**

★ **Truthostel** Av da Liberdade 738 ☎ 253 609 020, ⌨ truthostel.com. Under the same ownership as the *Bragatruthotel*, and a similar reboot of an old guesthouse, this is their cheery, more youthful budget haven with rooms to suit most pockets. They've splashed a lot of colour around communal areas, and provided a lounge, continental breakfast and lots of city help and information (there's someone on the desk 24/7). Beds are either in mixed dorms or private singles, as well as simple en-suite doubles and twins, and the best rooms overlook the flower-filled pedestrianized avenue below. Dorm beds **€18**, doubles **€50**

BRAGA'S FESTIVALS

During **Semana Santa** (Holy Week), Braga is the scene of major celebrations which reach a climax in the three days before Easter Sunday, when local priests bless each house with a crucifix and holy water, while torchlit processions of hooded penitents known as *farricocos* parade by, spinning large rattles. Devout pilgrims meanwhile will be climbing the staircase at Bom Jesus on their knees, and there's a second major pilgrimage here for Pentecost (the seventh Sunday after Easter). Still a religious festival, but rather less buttoned-up, is the shindig associated with the **Festas de São João** (June 23–24), which is preceded by a festival of *gigantones* (giant carnival figures; June 18–20).

6

EATING, DRINKING AND NIGHTLIFE

Braga is known for its old-style cafés, and also has an abundance of **restaurants,** though most of these too are thoroughly traditional in character and cuisine. Local specialities include *caldo de castanhas* (chestnut soup) and *charutos de chila* (cigar-shaped squash pastries), with *rabanadas* (fried slices of milk-soaked bread with a sweet cinnamon sauce) for dessert. There is a more contemporary **bar** and **club** scene though it's largely out of town, with most of the action on and around Rua Nova de Santa Cruz, below Bom Jesus, where students from the Universidade do Minho gather. For details of local **cultural events**, including shows at the Theatro Circo, pick up the monthly what's-on booklet *Braga Cultural* from the turismo.

CAFÉS, BARS AND RESTAURANTS

★ **A Ceia** Rua do Raio 331 ☎ 253 263 932. A great-value local diner with a rustic feel – you might have to wait for a table, or bag a space at the bar. Spit-roast chickens, *bacalhau* and steaks are served in enormous portions from €5–6 for a *meia-dose* – if you're looking for a traditional treat, Thursday is *cozido* day. Tues–Sun noon–3pm & 7–10pm.

★ **Café A Brasileira** Largo Barão de São Marinha ☎ 253 262 104, ⓦ cafe-abrasileira.com. Originally opened in 1907, serving coffee imported from Brazil, this lovely old café has had a refit or two over the years but still looks the part, with its gilt reliefs, glass-topped tables and monogrammed wooden seats. Smart staff whisk around with snacks, cakes and sandwiches (€2–5), and the outside seats are perfect for watching the world go by. Mon–Thurs 7.30am–midnight, Fri & Sat 7.30am–2am.

Café Vianna Praça da República ☎ 253 262 336. The Art Nouveau *Vianna* hasn't quite kept its looks – tiles, marble and mirrors are all a bit on the tired side – but there's no arguing with its prime perch by Braga's showpiece fountains. There's a big menu of grills, salads and sandwiches, and it's uniformly good value (dishes €5–10). Mon–Thurs 8am–midnight, Fri & Sat 8am–2am, Sun 10am–7pm.

De Bouro Rua Santo António das Travessas 30–32 ☎ 253 261 609. This former Cistercian monastic lodging house has been buffed up into a *haute cuisine* establishment serving traditional Minho specialities, from *bacalhau a Lagareiro* (salt-cod cooked in olive oil) to *arroz de pato* (rice with shredded duck, served with pine-nuts). Most dishes are around €10, and bigger servings costing €20–25 easily serve two. Mon–Sat 12.30–3pm & 7.30–10.45pm; closed Dec & Jan.

Felix Taberna Largo do Praça Velha 17 ☎ 253 617 701. There's a bit more imagination gone into the traditional dishes served here – it's not straight-down-the-line meat and potatoes – and it's a handsome spot for a bit to eat (mains €9–12). If you don't fancy anything on the menu, the revamped old square the restaurant sits on also has several other choices, including a tapas bar on one side and veggie restaurant on the other, so something should suit. Mon–Thurs 6pm–midnight, Fri & Sat 6pm–1am.

★ **Livraria Mavy** Rua Diogo de Sousa 129–133. The glorious old Cruz bookshop, vintage 1888, with its sculpted wooden ceiling, double-arched glass doors and all, has a new life as a rather hip café-bar. It's a coffee-and-cake place during the day (cheap lunches too) and more of a cocktail and drinks joint at night, with the beautiful interior doubling as a *galeria* for the work of local artists. Daily 9am–2am.

Taperia Palatu Rua Dom Afonso Henriques 35–37 ☎ 253 279 772. Cool café-bar that offers up a range of Spanish-influenced dishes (€8–12), from tapas and *revueltos* (fancy scrambled eggs) to steaks and sharing platters. In spring and summer, the small patio garden really comes into its own. Daily noon–2am.

ARTS AND CULTURE

Theatro Circo Av Liberdade 697 ☎ 253 203 800, ⓦ theatrocirco.com. The big town-centre theatre is the arts hub for the city, with a full programme, from film to contemporary theatre. There's also a really good theatre café, restaurant and club (entrance around the side at Rua Dr Gonçalo Sampaio 18; ⓦ theatrocircocafe.com), worth checking out in any case.

Barcelos

There's little on first view to suggest that the small town of **BARCELOS** is in any way special – it has a few historical sights, a small medieval centre and an attractive riverside location, and in the normal run of things you might be persuaded to give it half a day. But the truly enormous square in the centre, the Campo da Feira, provides pause for thought, and all becomes clear if you turn up on a Thursday, when you'll coincide with the **Feira de Barcelos**, a gigantic open-air market with few equals in Europe, let alone Portugal.

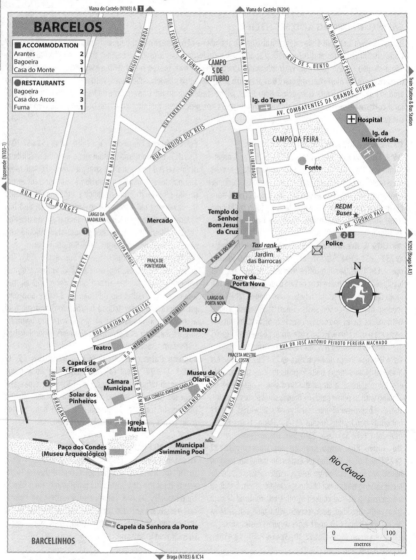

Campo da Feira

The vast **Campo da Feira** houses Barcelos' market every Thursday from dawn onwards – it's been held here since at least the early fifteenth century and, save a few modern refinements, there's still much that a medieval market-trader might recognize. Today the Feira may have its own Facebook page, but the close-set rows of modest smallholders offering up their surplus produce have surely changed little over the centuries. Beyond the fruit and veg, eggs, olives, herbs, cheeses, cured meats, breads and pastries there's the supporting framework of an entire rural economy on display here, from agricultural implements and animal yokes to chainsaws and wine-making gear – not to mention piles of cheap clothes, big pants, €10 jeans, counterfeit sportswear, lengths of cloth, brassy Portuguese pop CDs and rustic crafts. The local terracotta, white and yellow pottery – the *louças de Barcelos* – is a big deal, while Barcelos backs up its self-appointed role as "Capital do Artesanato" with a full array of other crafts, from earthenware figurines to traditional basketwork. The market is, in short, as valid a reason to visit Barcelos as you could want – if you can, stay the night before and make a real trip of it, then set your alarm clock for dawn and mingle with the stallholders as they set up for another timeless day at the *feira*.

Templo do Senhor Bom Jesus da Cruz

The gleaming white-painted Baroque church on the west side of the square is an obvious landmark. It's fronted by a rather nice formal garden of sculpted hedges and granite walls, while the cafés at the edge of the gardens have the best views in town. Just beware dusk, when birds gather in their hundreds for a chatter in the trees above, with inevitable consequences for anyone sitting or strolling beneath.

Torre de Porta Nova

Sitting prominently on the southwest side of the Campo da Feira, the solid stone fifteenth-century **Torre de Porta Nova** (currently closed for renovation) was once part of the city walls, and was used as a prison until 1932. Now the tower acts as a local handicrafts centre and shop, and is a good place to find out more about Barcelos arts and crafts.

Museu de Olaria

Rua Conégo Joaquim Gaiolas • Currently closed for renovation • ☎ 253 824 741, ⓦ museuolaria.org

Housed in the grand eighteenth-century Casa dos Mendanhas, the **Museu de Olaria** is the place to find out about the local ceramic wares. Started in 1963 as a private collection, it has since become a national display of some eight thousand pieces including fine ceramic figurines and urns – and anything bought in the shop will be of guaranteed provenance, which isn't always the case in the market.

Museu Arqueológico

Rua Dr Miguel Fonseca • Daily: May–Sept 9am–7pm; Oct–April 9am–5.30pm • Free

Above the town's medieval bridge stands what's left of the **Paço dos Condes**, once the Palace of the Counts of Barcelos, which was toppled by the Great Earthquake of 1755. Roofless and open to the elements, it's the backdrop to the **Museu Arqueológico**, which comprises a collection of gargoyles, sarcophagi, cornerstones and crosses, most notably the sixteenth-century carved crucifix that underpins the legend of the Galo de Barcelos (see p.320) – labelled "Padrão do Senhor do Galo", it's in the corner nearest the river, just in front of you as you enter. Note also the religious tombstone emblems of the various peoples to have lived in Barcelos through the ages: both Celtic and Catholic crosses, six-point Jewish Stars of David, and five-point Islamic pentagrams.

6

THE BARCELOS COCK

The legend goes that a Galician pilgrim, en route to Santiago de Compostela in Spain, was wrongly arrested for a crime in Barcelos and sentenced to hang. En route to the gallows, the pilgrim was escorted to the magistrate's house to make one final plea. The judge and his friends were sitting down to a roast dinner, at which the pilgrim proclaimed "As surely as I am innocent, that cock will crow if I am hanged". Up rose the bird from the table and the pilgrim was saved. This tale of the "Cock of Barcelos" – its scenes sculpted onto a cross in the town's archeological museum – has endured over the centuries to become a real Portuguese emblem, and you'll see the symbol all over the country, from the ubiquitous rooster-shaped ceramic figures to images reproduced on tea-towels and ornaments.

ARRIVAL AND DEPARTURE

BARCELOS

By bus The bus station is adjacent to the train station on the eastern edge of town – follow Avenida Alcaides de Faria straight ahead for fifteen minutes until it becomes Avenida Combatentes da Grande Guerra and you'll emerge on the Campo da Feira. Some buses to and from Porto, Braga and Viana do Castelo also stop opposite the *Hotel Bagoeira* on the Campo da Feira.

Destinations Braga (every 30min–1hr; 50min); Ponte de Lima (Mon–Fri 8 daily, Sat & Sun 1–2 daily; 55min); Porto (Mon–Sat 9–12 daily, Sun 1–2 daily; 1hr 45min); Viana do Castelo (2–8 daily; 50min).

By car Barcelos is 20km west of Braga – drivers should aim for the Campo da Feira, a giant car park for most of the week, though on Thursdays (market day) and Sundays parking is restricted and you should head for the streets below the Museu Arqueológico instead.

By train The train station is adjacent to the bus station (see above).

Destinations Porto (3–5 daily; 1hr); Valença do Minho (7 daily; 1hr 15min–1hr 50min); Viana do Castelo (11–12 daily; 30–40min).

INFORMATION

Barcelos Turismo Largo Dr José Novais 27 (mid-March to Sept Mon–Fri 9.30am–6pm, Sat 10am–1pm & 2–5pm, Sun 10am–1pm & 2–4pm; Oct to mid-March Mon–Fri 9.30am–5.30pm, Sat 10am–1pm & 2–5pm; ☎ 253 811 882, ⓦ cm-barcelos.pt), near the Torre de Porta Nova, just off the Campo.

ACCOMMODATION

★ **Arantes** Av da Liberdade 35-1º ☎ 253 811 326, ⓦ residencialarantes.webnode.pt. Choose the blue-tiled *Arantes* for a touch of old-fashioned charm, right on the main square. The best rooms have wrought-iron balconies with views over the Campo, and there's also a sunny breakfast room with its own balcony. Just avoid the cell-like rooms overlooking a central well. A *pastelaria* and *churrasqueira* of the same name occupy the ground floor. **€40**

Bagoeira Av Dr Sidónio Pais 495 ☎ 253 809 500, ⓦ bagoeira.com. In bygone days, the town's old market inn on the Campo offered really atmospheric lodgings. It's still pretty buzzy on market days, and the restaurant

(see below) is always worth a visit, but the inn itself has been overly modernized and sanitized, and there's not much character left – though you do get a top-floor bar and garage parking. **€55**

Casa do Monte Abade de Neiva, 3km west of Barcelos on the N103 (Viana do Castelo road) ☎ 253 811 519, ⓦ solaresdeportugal.pt. Delightful country manor house set in its own gardens and grounds, with three double and three twin rooms dressed with charmingly rustic furniture. Large gardens and a veranda give wonderful panoramic views and there's a swimming pool and tennis court. **€65**

EATING AND DRINKING

★ **Bagoeira** Av Dr Sidónio Pais 495 ☎ 253 813 088, ⓦ bagoeira.com. Showpiece restaurant on the square is the best place in town for regional cuisine, from *rojões* to *cabrito*, with the house specialities like *bacalhau na brasa* and *polvo na brasa*, grilled on huge ranges. Mains are around €6–12, in portions large enough to satisfy hungry market traders who've been up since before dawn. Daily noon–3pm & 7–10pm.

Casa dos Arcos Rua Duques de Bragança 185 ☎ 253

894 018. Down in the old town, near the river, the traditional old stone house is a local favourite for Sunday lunch. A long menu of regional specialities includes suckling pig and roast pork, while the house-special steak and *bacalhau* are always popular; mains around €10. Sun–Wed noon–3pm, Thurs–Sat noon–3pm & 7–10pm.

Furna Largo da Madalena 105 ☎ 253 811 117, ⓦ furnazinha.com. At times, the queues for the takeaway charcoal-grilled chicken stretch out of the door, which gives a fairly good idea of what to order. A half-bird, eaten in the restaurant, is yours for under €6, and there's also a big menu of other Portuguese grills and specialities, with most dishes costing €7–10. Tues–Sat 9am–10pm.

Viana do Castelo and around

For a first taste of the Minho coast, the historic maritime town of **VIANA DO CASTELO** is the principal port of call. Sited at the mouth of the Rio Lima, it has a landscaped waterfront, an appealing old town centre overlooked by the heights of Monte de Santa Luzia, and a great beach that lies just across the river. To call Viana

6

ACCOMMODATION

Casa do Ameal	2
Casa dos Costa Barros	5
Casa Melo Alvim	3
Jardim	6
Laranjeira	4
Navio Gil Eannes	7
Pousada do Monte de Santa Luzia	1

CAFÉS AND RESTAURANTS

Adega do Padrinho	5
Caravela	1
Casa d'Armas	6
Dolce Vianna	4
O Pescador	2
Os Três Potes	3

VIANA DO CASTELO

6

THE VIANA ROMARIA

The big event of the year is the pilgrimage-cum-carnival known as the **Romaria de Nossa Senhora d'Agonía** – dedicated to Our Lady of Sorrows. It lasts for several days over the nearest weekend to August 20, and is held in huge esteem by the locals who offer "um abraço dos Vianenses" (a big hug from the Vianense) to anyone who makes the effort to come.

Events kick off with a religious procession on the Friday, complete with carpets of flowers, while the Saturday sees a more carnival-like atmosphere with a no-holds-barred parade of decorated floats, local villagers in traditional costume and exuberant townsfolk. The blessing of the fishing boats on Monday morning is rather moving, when women in the fishing quarter, east of the centre, decorate their streets and bestow good wishes upon the fleet. And into the mix you can add *gigantones* (carnival giants) at every turn, plus bands, concerts and dances, and spectacular nightly firework displays.

---

a resort is probably a step too far – people certainly do come here in summer to laze on the sands, but the feel in the town at least is of a well-to-do place built on shipbuilding and trade, with elaborate period mansions and good-looking streets and squares to match. Tradition, too, still weighs strongly here, from the age-old Friday market held outside the former bastion walls to the annual *romaria* that ranks as one of the country's most impressive festivals.

Praça da República

Although badly worn, the Renaissance fountain in Viana's harmonious **Praça da República** sets the tone for a town whose earlier patrons spent well and wisely on their public buildings. One side of the square is taken up by the sixteenth-century, triple-galleried **Misericórdia** (almshouse), which forms part of the adjoining **Igreja de Misericórdia**, an impressive eighteenth-century structure lined with superb *azulejos* by master craftsman António de Oliveira Bernardes and his son Policarpo. Behind the fountain, the former **Casa da Câmara** stands foursquare above a medieval arcade – the stone reliefs either side of the coat of arms on the facade of this old city council chamber are of a globe and a caravel, twin symbols of erstwhile Portuguese imperial might. From May to September the square hosts a lively **Saturday-morning market**, while in the quiet streets and small squares to the south Viana's old town is at its most charming.

Museu do Traje

Praça da República • June–Sept Tues–Sun 10am–1pm & 3–7pm; Oct–May Tues–Sun 10am–1pm & 2–6pm • €2 includes entry to Museu de Artes Decorativas • ☎ 258 809 306

On the southwest edge of the square, the imposing yellow wedge – a former bank building – houses the **Museu do Traje**, or Costume Museum. It tells the story of the region's traditional clothes and costumes, from flax-planting to weaving, and displays a colourful array of wedding outfits, work gear and festival clothes, including the extraordinary *croça*, a rain cape made completely from straw.

Navio-Hospital Gil Eannes

Doca Comercial • Daily: April–Sept 9am–7pm; Oct–May 9am–5.30pm • €2 • ☎ 258 809 710, ⓦ fundacaogileannes.pt

Down on the waterfront, moored in the dock off Largo 5 de Outubro, the large white bulk of the **Gil Eannes** was Portugal's first hospital ship, built in Viana in the 1950s to support the cod-fishing boats and crew on the Newfoundland and Greenland seas. Later used as a cargo ship, and then finally scrapped in the 1990s, she returned to her home port after mouldering in Lisbon, and now serves as a

MONTE DE SANTA LUZIA, VIANA DO CASTELO (P.324) >

floating museum dedicated to the ship's history. Part of it is also used as a youth hostel (see p.326).

Museu de Artes Decorativas

Largo de São Domingos • June–Sept Tues–Sun 10am–1pm & 3–7pm; Oct–May Tues–Sun 10am–1pm & 2–6pm • €2, includes entry to Museu do Traje • ☎ 258 809 305

For a sense of the wealth that poured into and out of Viana during its mercantile heyday (from the seventeenth century onwards) it's necessary to walk five minutes east from the main avenue to the **Museu de Artes Decorativas**, which is housed in another of the town's lavish former residences, this time an eighteenth-century palace originally used by the archbishops of Braga. The beautifully maintained interior displays a large collection of ceramics, *azulejos*, furniture and art – often imported from Portugal's former colonies – while a modern extension hosts temporary exhibitions.

Castelo de Santiago da Barra

Guarding the river's mouth, at the western edge of town, is the **Castelo de Santiago da Barra**, commissioned by Philip II of Spain for the defence of the port. Outside the walls here, in the area known as Campo do Castelo, Viana's lively **feira** (market) takes place every Friday, from dawn onwards.

Monte de Santa Luzia

Santuário de Santa Luzia Daily: April–Sept 8am–7pm; Oct–March 8am–5pm • €1 • **Funicular de Santa Luzia** Nov–Feb Tues–Fri 10am–noon & 1–5pm, Sat & Sun 10am–5pm; March–May & Oct Mon–Fri 10am–noon & 1–5pm, Sat & Sun 9am–6pm; June–Sept daily 9am–8pm • €2 one way, €3 return • A taxi up to the sanctuary costs around €6

For a sensational view of the town, river and Atlantic coast you need to make your way up to the unmistakeable landmark basilica on top of **Monte de Santa Luzia**, which looms over Viana do Castelo. The funicular railway is a fun way to get there; otherwise it's a punishing thirty-minute walk up the steps which start just past the hospital – take note of the inscription at the bottom which translates as "My God help me get up". At the summit there's a café and restaurant, picnic tables among the trees, plus plenty of stalls selling "*artigos religiosos*". Other than its monumental presence, there's little interest in the **Santuário de Santa Luzia** itself, though the climb to the top of the dome (marked *Zimbório*) is emphatically worth it. A narrow winding staircase leads right through the building, past traffic lights laid on in summer to keep tourist hordes in check, and emerges on top of the dome itself. It's very steep and – at the top – pretty hair-raising when the wind picks up, but the magnificent views reward every effort.

Citânia de Santa Luzia

Monte de Santa Luzia • April–Sept Tues–Sun 9am–noon & 2–6pm; Oct–March Tues–Sun 10am–noon & 2–5pm • €2 • It's located right behind the *pousada*; follow the road up from the sanctuary

It's hardly surprising that such a magnificent – and easy to defend – site as the Santa Luzia hill was settled in very early times; indeed, excavations have revealed that Santa Luzia was continuously occupied from the Iron Age to the end of the Roman period. The remains of a "proto-urban" hilltown or **Citânia** – dating back to at least 500 BC – occupy the highest part of the hill, and the foundations of circular and oval-shaped dwellings, plus walls and paved streets, can be viewed from an extensive raised walkway. You can see very clearly that this was no out-of-the-way rustic backwater, but a town of shepherds, farmers, fishermen, tool-makers, weavers and potters, whose inhabitants went to extraordinary efforts over centuries to build and defend their settlement.

Praia do Cabedelo

Boats May–Sept approx hourly, 9am–dusk, but check with boatman for the last return • €1.10 each way • **Transcunha buses** Mon–Fri 6 daily, Sat & Sun 1–2 daily; 15min ride

Viana's nearest beach, the **Praia do Cabedelo**, is some distance from the historic town centre, south across the Rio Lima. Either take the ferry from the harbourside Praça da Liberdade, or a bus from the bus station, both of which drop you at the north end of the beach, where there's a cluster of café-restaurants and watersports outlets. The long, curving beach itself is terrific, if prone to the usual blustery conditions along this coast, with dunes and sand to spare even on the most popular of sunny days.

6

Vila Praia de Âncora

15km north of Viana do Castelo • Take the train from Viana station to Âncora-Praia, a 12–17min journey

North of Viana, the whole Minho coast is virtually one long beach. There are small holiday villages all the way up, though the flourishing resort of **Vila Praia de Âncora** is the only one near Viana with any kind of year-round life. It sits in the basin of the Rio Âncora, and has two forts guarding the bay: the Fortim de Cão, south of the estuary, and the better-preserved Forte de Lagarteira, to the north by a bustling fishing harbour. Legend has it that the river and town owe their name to a punishment doled out to the adulterous Queen Urraca of Navarre, drowned in the river by her jealous husband King Ramiro II of Asturias, Galicia and León with an anchor (*âncora*) around her neck. The beach, meanwhile, is a beauty, with an ocean-facing stretch of sand as well as a more sheltered area formed by a kink in the river estuary.

ARRIVAL AND DEPARTURE

VIANA DO CASTELO AND AROUND

By train Bus and train stations are integrated into a transport interchange (Estação Viana), combined with shopping complex and underground car park, located at the north end of Avenida dos Combatentes da Grande Guerra, which runs right through town and down to the river. Trains from Porto run inland via Barcelos, reaching the coast at Viana, then follow the coast north to Caminha. Destinations Barcelos (12 daily; 25–45min); Caminha (7–8 daily; 20–30min); Porto (3–5 daily; 1hr 45min); Valença do Minho (7–8 daily; 40min–1hr); Vila Praia de Âncora (8–10 daily; 12–17min).

By bus There are bus services all across the Minho from the bus station at the Estação Viana transport interchange (see above), but if you're heading up the coast to Caminha and

along the Minho to Valença it's usually better to go by train. Destinations Arcos de Valdevez (3–12 daily; 1hr 30min); Barcelos (2–8 daily; 50min); Braga (4–10 daily; 1hr 40min); Caminha (roughly hourly; 30min); Lisbon (2 daily; 5hr); Monção (1–5 daily; 1hr 20min); Ponte da Barca (6–8 daily; 1hr 30min); Ponte de Lima (Mon–Fri hourly, Sat & Sun 7 daily; 50min); Porto (3–14 daily; 1hr 35min); Valença do Minho (1–3 daily; 1hr 15min); Vila Praia de Âncora (2–16 daily; 20–30min).

By car Viana de Castelo is a quick, one-hour drive (80km) up the coast from Porto, with Ponte de Lima a 30min drive (26km) along the north side of the Rio Lima. Parking in town is easy in various places along the waterfront, and while you may have to pay, it won't be much.

INFORMATION AND ACTIVITIES

Information The Viana Welcome Centre, Praça da Liberdade (Sept–May Tues–Sun 10am–6pm; June–Aug daily 10am–7pm; ☎ 258 098 415, ⓦ vivexperiencia.pt). The main regional turismo is on Rua do Hospital Velho, at Praça da Erva (Mon–Sat 9.30am–12.30pm & 2–6pm; ☎ 258 822 620, ⓦ cm-viana-castelo.pt); it's housed in a lovely building dating from 1468 that was first used as a hospital for pilgrims travelling to Santiago de Compostela in Spain.

Bike rental and tours The Viana Welcome Centre rents out bikes (from €2.50 an hour or €11 a day) and can arrange bike tours (€22.50) and walking tours (€15).

Watersports Several local outfits rent surfing, kite-surfing and windsurfing gear, and can organize lessons and surf schools, including Viana Locals (☎ 258 325 168, ⓦ www .vianalocals.com) and the Surf Clube de Viana (☎ 258 826 208, ⓦ surfingviana.com).

ACCOMMODATION

★ **Casa do Ameal** Rua do Ameal 119, Meadela, 2km east off N202 (Ponte de Lima road) ☎ 936 070 630, ⓦ casadoameal.com. Handily placed for the town, and

a rare retreat, is this granite-walled, whitewashed noble mansion set in its own grounds. There's a pool with manicured lawn and sun-loungers, plus eight charming

6

apartments sleeping two or four (€140 for a four-bed room) featuring exposed stone walls and vintage furniture. **€90**

Casa dos Costa Barros Rua de São Pedro 28 ☎258 823 705, ⓦcasacostabarros.pt. One of the Manueline mansions in the old town offers good-value rooms for visitors, and while it's a pretty traditional setup – with fixtures and furnishings defiantly antique – you do get to sleep in one of Viana's characteristic sixteenth-century properties. **€70**

Casa Melo Alvim Av Conde da Carreira 28 ☎258 808 200, ⓦmeloalvimhouse.com. The town-centre choice for a gracious stay – a fabulously restored sixteenth-century mansion with elegant but understated rooms inspired by a period or a theme (Baroque to contemporary). Service is faultless, and there's a leafy garden and a good restaurant. Parking. **€130**

Jardim Largo 5 de Outubro 68 ☎258 828 915, ⓦresidencialjardim.pt. An old favourite, overlooking the main road and river at the bottom of town, the *Jardim* has straightforward rooms over five floors, enhanced by views of river, town or Monte de Santa Luzia, depending on which you choose. It's a bit noisy at the front, but pretty good value, especially considering the huge breakfasts. **€60**

Laranjeira Rua Cândido dos Reis 45–47 ☎258 822 261, ⓦwww.residencialaranjeira.com. Renovated townhouse with a bit of a budget boutiquey feel – some rooms are on the small side but the best ones have balconies facing Monte de Santa Luzia. There's garage parking too. **€80**

Navio Gil Eannes Doca Comercial ☎258 847 169, ⓦmicrosites.juventude.gov.pt/portal/en. Part of a former hospital ship moored at the docks, which has been turned into a youth hostel – so expect your dorm beds, and half-a-dozen private rooms, to be inside shipshape cabins. Facilities are pretty basic – there's only a common-room-cum-bar – but it makes for an unusual night's stay, and it is really cheap. Viana has a second hostel, too (details on the same website), which is a bigger, more modern affair a 15min walk from the centre. Dorm beds **€12**, cabins **€30**

★ **Pousada do Monte de Santa Luzia** Monte de Santa Luzia ☎258 800 370, ⓦpousadas.pt. The hilltop *pousada* is all about its fabulous views – beg for a room at the front (ideally 108, or the suite, 107, both with private terraces) to enjoy the best panoramas in Viana, right over the basilica and down to the river and coast. It's a handsome refurb of a 1918 hotel building, with rooms given a cheery, country-chic makeover, while public areas make the most of the view, whether from picture-window restaurant, arcaded terrace, grand lounge or stepped gardens. There's also an outside pool, backing on to the archeological remains and boasting more sweeping vistas from the sun-loungers. **€145**

EATING AND DRINKING

Viana's old town squares and wide avenues are made for dining alfresco, and there are plenty of places to soak up the atmosphere. For a historic backdrop aim for the cafés in lovely Praça da República, while in summer the riverfront comes into its own – there are restaurants and garden bars overlooking the docks and marina, and a few flash bars set alongside the renovated riverside prom.

Adega do Padrinho Rua Gago Coutinho 162–164 ☎258 826 954. There's a family feel and a down-to-earth folksy interior, though the belting traditional music might force you out on to the street-side tables. It's strictly local on the menu too, with a wide choice of meat and fish grills (€7–12), from pork to squid, all served in gigantic portions. Mon & Wed–Sun noon–3pm & 7–11pm.

Caravela Praça da República 62–68 ☎258 822 553. The outdoor tables on the square by the fountain are hard to resist, but have a peek at the interior too. Hollowed out behind the historic facade is a stylish *pastelaria* with mezzanine seating and counters groaning under the weight of delicious cakes and pastries. Daily 8am–7.30pm.

Casa d'Armas Largo 5 de Outubro 30 ☎258 824 999, ⓦcasadarmas.com. Mansion dining on the riverfront road – tapas and snacks on the terrace (€4–9) or a much fancier grill-house experience inside, with anything from lobster to *picanha* on offer (mains €16–22). Daily 12.30–3pm & 7.30–10.30pm, bar open until 2am.

Dolce Vianna Rua do Poço 44 ☎258 824 860. Tucked into a little hidden square (if you can find the regional turismo, you'll see the restaurant), the *Dolce Vianna* does pretty good wood-fired pizzas and almost-Italian pastas (€6–9); there's also a full Portuguese menu if this all seems dangerously exotic. Daily noon–3pm & 7.30–10.30pm.

★ **O Pescador** Largo São Domingos 35 ☎258 826 039, ⓦopescadorviana.com. The top fish place in town is a 5min walk away from the main avenue – come here for the grilled catch of the day (from €10) or share one of the many two-person specials (€21–30), from a *misto de peixe grelhado* (mixed grilled fish) to a monster *bacalhau* platter. Starters are along the lines of mussels, clams, grilled octopus or *escabeche* sardines. Mon–Sat noon–3pm & 7–10pm, Sun noon–3pm.

Os Três Potes Beco dos Fornos 7 ☎258 829 928. Undeniably touristy but also thoroughly charming – a sixteenth-century bakery, under a trailing vine, now the venue for live folk and fado music, bolstered by a pricey menu of Minho specialities, from *lampreia* to *cabrito* (dishes mostly €14–17). There are two entrances, both just off Praça da República – look for the cut-out figures in traditional dress. Mon, Tues & Thurs–Sun noon–3pm & 7–11pm.

Along the Rio Minho

At Caminha, 25km north of Viana do Castelo, road and rail turn decisively northeast and inland to run along the south bank of the **Rio Minho**. With Spain ever-present – just across the wide river – and crossings easily made, it's a fairly well-trodden tourist route, and the succession of historic frontier towns are used to Spanish day-trippers and visiting foreigners. You could just about see the lot in a day – from pretty **Caminha** to the country's northernmost town, **Melgaço**, 70km further east – but that would be to rush a region that's more suited to leisurely strolls, old-town rambles and summer afternoons spent at the nearest *praia fluvial* (river beach). With a night to spare, a stay in the fortress *pousada* of **Valença do Minho** is perhaps the best option, though admittedly this is the most touristy of the Minho towns. The **Linha do Minho** train line from Porto, via Viana do Castelo, runs to Caminha and Valença but no further, though there are plenty of local buses onwards to the old spa town of **Monção** and to Melgaço.

Caminha

At the broad sandy estuary of the Rio Minho, and straddling the Rio Coura, **CAMINHA** was a thriving port back in the seventeenth century, sending boats out across the empire. Those days are long gone – sleepy and provincial is closer to the mark now – but the thoroughly charming town is still worth a few hours' exploration, or even an overnight stop if you're in the mood for the beach or a quick ferry jaunt across to Spain. The main square, **Praça Conselheiro Silva Torres**, hints at past glories, with its majestic town hall, Renaissance clock-tower and sculpted fountain, though it's the magnificently decorated **Igreja Matriz** (follow the street under the arch beneath the clock tower) that reveals the wealth that once flowed through Caminha.

The nearest beach is just 2km southwest at **Foz de Minho** – an idyllic wooded peninsula where the Minho flows into the Atlantic. A wooden boardwalk hugs the water's edge, leading to a sheltered river beach, or head five minutes through the pines to a great Atlantic beach, with a little fortified islet just offshore and Spain visible opposite. There's another good ocean beach at **Moledo**, a further 2km southwest – both Foz and Moledo are signposted off the N13 (Viana road) as you head into town.

ARRIVAL AND INFORMATION   CAMINHA

By train The easiest way to reach Caminha is by train; the station is on Avenida Saraiva de Carvalho, a short walk from the centre. There are daily services to Viana do Castelo (7–8 daily; 20–30min; for connections to Porto) and to Valença do Minho (8–10 daily; 20–30min; for connections to Vigo in Spain).

By ferry Caminha has a ferry link to La Guardia in Spain, a pleasant ride across the river that leaves from beside the bridge over the Rio Coura – signposted "Ferry-boat", the dockside is a 3min walk from the central square. There are services throughout the year (July & Aug continuous service 8am–8pm; Sept–June Tues–Fri hourly 8am–noon & 2–6pm, Sat & Sun hourly 10am–noon & 2–6pm; foot passengers €1, cars €3).

Information Caminha Turismo, Praça Conselheiro Silva Torres (daily 9.30am–12.30pm & 2–6pm; ☎ 258 921 952, ⓦ caminhaturismo.pt), is located in the arcade by the clock tower.

ACCOMMODATION AND EATING

There are some good local accommodation choices in Caminha and, along with Valença, this is the best overnight choice along the river. Half a dozen cafés and restaurants put out tables around the central square; there's more of a bar scene down Rua Ricardo Joaquim de Sousa, which is the road through the arch from the clock tower, heading down towards the Igreja Matriz.

Casa de Esteiró Rua Benemérito Joaquim Rosas, 1km south of town, N13 ☎ 258 721 333, ⓦ casa esteiro.com. Originally an eighteenth-century hunting lodge, this charming house – crammed with family mementoes – is set in lovely gardens. There are two spacious suites in the house, plus three self-catering apartments (sleeping up to 4) in a separate house in the grounds. It's got a pool, and is only a few hundred metres' walk from the beach at Foz. Suites €100, apartments €120

Confeitaria Colmeia Praça Conselheiro Silva Torres 33 ☎258 722 456. The nicest café on the square sells a splendid array of local speciality pastries, including an almond-and-cream confection and a divine strawberry tart. There's also a little bar area where you can sample wines that are also for sale. Daily 9am–10pm.

Design & Wine Praça Conselheiro Silva Torres 8 ☎258 719 040, ⊛designwinehotel.com. Rio Minho visitors of old will scarcely credit some of the changes in these once somnolent towns, and Caminha's *Design & Wine* is typical of what monied tourism has wrought – a noble town mansion with a designer box full of river-facing rooms in over-the-top contemporary, street-art style. A sleek restaurant updates the Minho classics, offering Portuguese "tapas", *presunto* to clams, alongside mains (€15–18) like *cataplana*, locally sourced meats and risotto. **€90**

Galo d'Ouro Rua da Corredoura 15 ☎258 921 160, ✉residencialgalodouro@gmail.com. Easily visible just off the main square, this is friendly and full of character – for which read a bit old-fashioned, but cheap and serviceable. There's a fine *azulejo*-lined hallway, and stucco ceilings here and chunks of original stone wall there, though furnishings are more basic. No credit cards or breakfast, but the square's cafés are a step away. **€40**

Hotel Porta do Sol Av Marginal, 1.5km south of town, N13 ☎258 710 360, ⊛hotelportadosol.com. Caminha's biggest resort-style hotel is at the entrance to town, right on the river – you can cross the road and walk up the boardwalk to the beaches at Foz. It's a four-star place with nice enough rooms – they all have a balcony, though not necessarily a water view – plus panoramic restaurant, two pools (one for kids), sauna and spa, gym and tennis court. You can get here by train too – it's just 7min walk from Senhora d'Agonia station, the stop before Caminha. **€105**

Valença do Minho

The must-see historic sight along the Minho is the fortress of **VALENÇA DO MINHO** (or just Valença), whose walls and ramparts dominate the riverside and speak volumes about erstwhile neighbourly disagreements. The fortress has repelled innumerable Spanish and French invasions over the centuries, though the impeccably preserved old town has surrendered entirely to a modern-day army of wallet-waving visitors who file in through the narrow town gates and descend upon the gift shops. Even the regional tourist office describes Valença as a "shopping fortress". But most evenings you'll have old Valença to yourself, and can explore at your leisure – the only disadvantage being that many of the cafés and restaurants are either hauntingly empty for dinner or simply shut up shop once their captive audience has left for the day. There's a new town, south of the ramparts, home to all Valença's non-touristy businesses and services, while each Wednesday a huge weekly market is held on the wooded slopes around the old town to the east.

Around the walls and ramparts

The first defensive walls were built here in the thirteenth century, though the current layout – a dazzling system of double ramparts, with two separate old-town areas separated by a deep moat – is a classic piece of seventeenth-century military engineering. The entrance for traffic is through the **Portas da Coroada**, which leads into an outer town defended by half a dozen bulwarks. Another set of gates, the **Portas do Meio**, then leads across a stone bridge into the even older medieval town, again defended by an elongated star-shape of steep, angled walls, towers and turrets. Alternatively, you can enter directly into this older part of town via the pedestrian entrance of **Portas do Sol**.

The cobbled lanes and white-painted buildings **within the walls** have all been handsomely restored, though few visitors do much more than trawl up and down the couple of main streets, which are lined with boutiques and gift shops, pretty much all flogging the same vast selection of towels, sheets, pillow cases, nightwear, T-shirts and cheap souvenirs. Bewitching collection of traditional arts and handicrafts it is not – though if you need another Lionel Messi football shirt you're in luck.

If you're to come away from Valença with a more positive memory of its charms, you need to get off the street and up onto **the ramparts**, which can be accessed from virtually anywhere. From the precipitous walls, grassy mounds and winding footpaths, you can look down upon the buildings and the river far below, while exploring hidden

VALENÇA DO MINHO

▲ A3/IP1 (Porto, V.N. Cerveira & Viana) & Spain

▲ Tuy (Spain)

Rio Minho

★ Taxis

AV. ESPANHA

★ Roman Milestone

Museu Nucleológico

Town Hall

Portas do Sol

Portas do Melo

Portas da Coroada

AV. BOMBEIROS VOLUNTÁRIOS

LARGO SPORT CLUB VALENCIANO

AV. DE ESPANHA

Monção & Melgaço ▶

▼ Old Town & Pousada

▼ Bus & Train Station

Police

N

ACCOMMODATION	
Pousada de São Teotónio	1
Portas do Sol	2

● **CAFÉS AND RESTAURANTS**	
Churrasqueira Valenciana	2
Fortaleza	3
Pousada de São Teotónio	1

0 ———— 100
metres

6

tunnels, archaic towers and sentry-posts, and landscaped battlements complete with cannons. It becomes immediately apparent how difficult it would have been to vanquish Valença – the scale of the fortifications is immense – and you can spend a happy hour or two away from the shoppers, revelling in the fine views to all sides.

Núcleo Museológico

Rua Mouzinho de Albuquerque 67 • Tues–Fri 9.30am–12.30pm & 2–6pm, Sat 10am–noon & 2.30–5.30pm • Free

To find out about Valença's history, visit the small **Núcleo Museológico**. The labelling is all in Portuguese but the model of the original medieval town and the archeological finds, from Bronze Age swords to Roman vases, are pretty self-explanatory. On the way in you're confronted with a model of a siege engine of the type used to chuck big rocks across the river at Spain. Take a look, too, just behind the museum, where you'll find a **Roman milestone**, first erected in 43 AD and marking mile 42 from Braga to Tuy.

Tuy

The fortified town of **Tuy** in Spain lies just a couple of kilometres north of Valença, across an iron bridge designed by Eiffel. It's a tantalizing silhouette on the horizon, again complete with defensive walls and interesting old town, and if you've got time you may as well have a look around here too – it's an easy thirty-minute walk from Valença, or five minutes on the train, with services continuing on to Vigo.

ARRIVAL AND INFORMATION

VALENÇA DO MINHO

Everything of historic interest lies within the walls, and it only takes 15 minutes or so to walk from one end of old Valença to the other. Incidentally, street names are largely superfluous – there are only a few streets and alleys and you'll stumble upon everywhere sooner or later.

By car Valença is 28km northeast of Caminha, up the N13. There's plenty of parking by the outer castle walls, outside Portas do Sol (follow signs for "Fortaleza"), where you might need to pay €1 to one of the blokes directing you into a spare space. You can drive and park inside the walled town too – there's a large pay-and-display car park in front of the turismo – though you'll have to drive around the side of the walled town first and enter through the Portas da Coroada. Driving within the walls might seem a little freaky (some gates and alleys can be very narrow), but there's a rigid one-way system in force so you can't come to too much grief.

By bus The bus station is two blocks west of the train station on Avenida Sá Carneiro, five minutes' walk south of the walls (go up Rua Miguel Dantas to Largo da Trapichera). Destinations Lisbon (4 daily; 6hr 30min); Melgaço (8 daily;

40min); Monção (10 daily; 20min); Ponte de Lima (1 daily; 25min); Porto (2–7 daily; 3hr 30min); and Viana do Castelo via Caminha (1–3 daily; 1hr 15min).

By train From the train station, head up Av Miguel Dantas and you'll approach the old town from the Largo da Trapichera roundabout, at the bottom of the hill. Continue straight on up the tree-lined avenue and enter through the narrow Portas do Sol.

Destinations Barcelos (7–8 daily; 1hr 15min–2hr); Caminha (8–10 daily; 20–30min); Porto (4 daily, 2hr 15min); Viana do Castelo (7–8 daily; 40min–1hr); and Vigo, Spain (3 daily; 1hr 10min; connections to Santiago de Compostela and La Coruña).

Information The turismo (Mon–Sat 9.30am–12.30pm & 2.30–5.30pm; ☎ 251 823 329, ⓦ cm-valenca.pt) is in the old town, just inside the Portas da Coroada.

ACCOMMODATION

Accommodation in town is limited, though if you're heading for the *pousada* you're in for a treat. Otherwise, the choice is between a couple of uninspiring 1970s-style main-road hotels outside the walls (just up from the roundabout, on Av dos Bombeiros Voluntários, the Spain road).

Portas do Sol Rua Conselheiro Lopes da Silva 51, just inside Portas do Meio ☎ 251 837 134, ⓦ residencial portasdosol.com. The only other choice within the walls is an eight-roomed townhouse that's modestly priced for most of the year (rooms around €45), though rachets up

the cost in summer and other holiday periods. If you're going to stay, try and get one of the four rooms with river views. Breakfast not included. €70

★ **Pousada de São Teotónio** Baluarte do Socorro, inside the fortress ☎ 251 800 260, ⓦ pousadas.pt.

Set right by the northern ramparts, this *pousada* rejoices in sweeping views over the Minho from its lounge, sun-room and restaurant, while the outside terraces offer a panoramic place to sit and soak up the scenery. The best rooms also have terraces, as well as white walls and polished wooden floors, offset by vintage carved bed-heads, while public areas are big on terracotta tiles and chunky retro furniture. Enter town through Portas do Coroada and drive right through the old town, following the signs – you'll get there eventually. **€180**

EATING AND DRINKING

The few old-town cafés and restaurants are much of a pricey muchness – tapas and *bacalhau* to the fore, with a nod to their largely Spanish clientele – and, *pousada* excepted, it's hard to summon up any real enthusiasm for any of them. Two or three cafés in the cute Praça da República are best for an alfresco evening drink.

Churrasqueira Valenciana Rua Maestro Sousa Morais 8 ☎ 251826 547. Pretty much the cheapest place in the old town serves up a half grilled chicken and chips for €5, and other grills for not much more, and you can't say much fairer than that. It's theoretically open daily noon–3pm & 6–10pm, but sometimes closes in the evening.
Fortaleza Rua Apolinário da Fonseca 5 ☎ 251 823 146. Just outside the Portas do Meio, the house special here is *cabrito* (goat), although the chef also prepares a decent *arroz de marisco*; main courses cost €8–15. Dinner is best enjoyed at the outdoor tables so you can catch the last of the day's sun, setting over the ramparts. Daily noon–3pm & 7–10pm.

★ **Pousada de São Teotónio** Baluarte do Socorro, inside the fortress ☎ 251 800 260, ⓦ pousadas.pt. The *pousada* restaurant is the best in town, and given that prices in Valença are on the high side in any case, this should be your first choice. Dishes such as pan-fried saltcod with straw potatoes, or chicken with an *alheira* sausage stuffing (main courses €16–21), put a modern twist on the regional cuisine, and there's a good-value, if limited-choice, daily menu for €25. Daily noon–3pm & 7–10pm.

Monção

Like Valença, **MONÇÃO** too, was once fortified to the hilt, though its remaining walls are largely limited to a long stretch above the river, with an elevated promenade offering fine views across the Minho valley into Spain. Below are grassy banks, groves of trees and riverside pathways, with access down to the river through several surviving ancient gateways. It's a pleasant enough place to pause, centred on the spacious, mosaic-cobbled old town square, **Praça Deu-la-Deu**, with ramparts, *miradouro* and promenade at one end, seventeenth-century church at the other, and an attractive grid of narrow streets (reached down Rua 1 Dezembro) that curls around a simple Romanesque Igreja da Matriz. Spanish and Portuguese tourists tend to visit for the town's revived thermal-spa facilities; otherwise the town is liveliest on a Thursday, market day, or during the local festivals of Corpo de Deus (Corpus Christi, usually second week in June) and Virgem das Dores (Aug).

ARRIVAL AND INFORMATION   MONÇÃO

By bus The local bus station is on the western outskirts of town at Veiga Velha, but most services also stop near Campo da Feira.

Destinations Braga (2–4 daily; 1hr 45min); Melgaço (Mon–Fri 5 daily, Sat & Sun 1 daily; 40min); Porto (2–4 daily; 3hr); Valença (10 daily; 20min) and Viana do Castelo

PORTUGAL'S WONDER WOMAN

The main square in Monção has an uncommon name, Praça Deu-la-Deu, which celebrates the story of the town's much-heralded medieval saviour, a woman known as **Deu-la-Deu Martins** (the name means "God gave her"). In 1369, with the Spanish at the gates, the town under desperate siege and the mayor on the brink of capitulation, the mayor's wife commandeered Monção's paltry remaining flour stocks, whipped up some cakes and sent them over to the Spanish, offering "more if they needed them". The bold ruse worked, the Spanish forces thought better of attacking such an apparently well-supplied town, and Deu-la-Deu acquired everlasting fame, the honour of a tomb in the Igreja da Matriz, and a questionable modern statue at the head of the square on the *miradouro*.

(1–5 daily; 1hr 20min).

By car Monção is 16km east of Valença; the road to Spain crosses the bridge to Salvatierra, just outside town to the west. There's free parking in Campo da Feira (though not on market day, Thursday), by the bastion walls – for the town centre, walk straight ahead, under the old railway bridge, and at the end of the pedestrianized street turn left for the main square.

Information The turismo (Mon–Sat 9.30am–12.30pm & 2.30–6pm; ☎ 251 652 757, ⊛ cm-moncao.pt) is in a small handicrafts and cultural centre, the Casa do Curro, on Praça Deu-la-Deu.

ACCOMMODATION AND EATING

A night in Monção is hardly obligatory – and the nicest places are out of town in any case – but if you fancy it, there are budget rooms advertised in a couple of cafés on the square, and also in the streets around the Igreja da Matriz. Praça Deu-la-Deu is the best place for restaurants and cafés with outdoor tables, a couple of which lie near the *miradouro* with views over to Spain.

Cabral Rua 1 de Dezembro ☎ 251 651 775. Just off the main square (down the road to the side of *Restaurante Central*), this is a rustic place serving unpretentious regional cuisine, from *bacalhau a casa* (fried, with onions, tomatoes and potatoes) to local lamb (dishes €8–12) – there's always fresh fish too. An uneven stone wall forms one side of the dining room, just begging you to tuck your small change into the mortar alongside the collected escudos, cents and even the odd dollar bill and Chinese banknote. Mon–Thurs & Fri–Sun noon–2.30pm & 7–10pm.

Hotel Convento dos Capuchos Estrada de Melgaço ☎ 251 640 090, ⊛ conventodoscapuchos.com. The town's top hotel is a stylish conversion of an eighteenth-century convent just off the road to Melgaço. Contemporary rooms have been fashioned from the old cells, keeping the stonework and deep-set windows but adding a bit of designer flair; fancy restaurant, bar service in the cloister, outdoor pool and gardens complete the picture. **€150**

Solar de Serrade Mazedo, 3km south of Monção, off N101 to Arcos de Valdevez ☎ 251 654 008, ⊛ solardeserrade.pt. Aristocratic rooms, some with soaring ceilings, chandeliers and handcarved four-poster beds, in the seventeenth-century manor house of an excellent *vinho verde* wine estate. **€70**

Melgaço

MELGAÇO – the country's northernmost outpost – has a pretty, restored centre clustered round the towering keep of a medieval fortress. It's another Minho border town, perched high above the river, which merits a short coffee-break and a stroll around its cobbled streets and jasmine-draped cottages. Longer stays probably depend on how much of the local wine you plan to sample – the area around Melgaço produces the finest *vinho verde* in the country.

Castelo

Rua do Castelo • May–Sept Tues–Sun 10am–12.30pm & 2.30–7pm; Oct–April Tues–Sun 10am–12.30pm & 2–5pm • Outer walls free; keep €1

The tenth-century **Castelo** is a shadow of its former self but a small circuit of the walls offers a focal point for the old town. Outside the walls, a panoramic path provides sweeping vistas; inside you can buy a ticket to enter the keep, which contains a few archeological finds from the area, though it's the views from the roof that warrant the entry fee.

Solar do Alvarinho

Rua Direita • Daily 10am–12.30pm & 2.30–7pm; bar open later on Fri & Sat nights • ☎ 251 410 195

The local wine headquarters, **Solar do Alvarinho**, is housed in a fine granite mansion (its heraldic emblem dated 1687) on the old town's main street; there's a well-stocked tasting bar and wine shop here, as well as an exhibition area. Melgaço *vinhos verdes* are made from the Alvarinho grape, which produces a full-bodied wine with a much higher alcoholic content (around 12.5 percent) than other *vinhos verdes*, and consequently has the ability to age. The *solar* has details about the local *vinho verde quintas* (estates) which welcome visitors.

ARRIVAL AND DEPARTURE

By bus There are regular services to and from Monção (2–4 daily; 40min), and weekday buses to Lamas de Mouro in the national park (Mon–Fri 1 daily; 40min) and São Gregório on the Spanish border (Mon–Fri 3 daily; 30min), from where you can pick up connections to Orense.

By car Melgaço is 23km northeast of Monçao, and 11km

MELGAÇO

southwest of São Gregório on the Spanish border. It also provides easy access to the remote northern part of the Parque Nacional da Peneda-Gerês via the road to Lamas de Mouro. As you drive into town there's plenty of free parking around Largo Hermenegildo Solheiro and the fire station, from where brown signs point you to the castle, a two-minute walk away.

ACCOMMODATION AND EATING

Cantinho do Adro Rua Direita 30 ☎ 251 404 904. Sited just below the castle walls, in a pretty square by the church – you can get a decent meal here from a simple menu, with most dishes around €6–8. Daily noon–2.30pm & 7–10pm.
Quinta da Calçada 1km east of town, on the São

Gregorio ☎ 251 402 547, ⓦ quintadacalcada.com. The most charming local accommodation is this seventeenth-century rural manor house with three B&B rooms available; it also has a swimming pool, and gardens and grounds with lovely views. **€80**

The Lima valley

While it's the Minho that gives the region its name, it's the area's other river, the **Rio Lima**, which puts heart and soul into the Minho. Its delightful valley – dotted with ancient towns and Romanesque churches, and draped in morning mists – is a byword for beauty in Portugal, and forms an obvious route from Viana do Castelo, where the

PONTE DE LIMA

CAFÉS AND RESTAURANTS
Alameda	1
Casas das Cheias	3
O Brasão	2
O Mercado	4

ACCOMMODATION
Carmo's Boutique Hotel	5
Casa de Crasto	6
Casa de São Gonçal	1
Casa do Outeiro	2
Casa do Pinheiro	4
Moinho de Estorãos	7
Paço de Calheiros	8
Pousada de Juventude	9
São João	3

BAR
Os Telhadinhos	1

river meets the sea, eastwards to the Peneda-Gerês mountains. There are minor roads along north and south sides of the river, connecting a cluster of peaceful little settlements on the banks of the Lima and its tributaries, though the fast highway from Viana takes you quickly to the standout town of **Ponte de Lima**, with its famous market held right on the riverbanks. For slower travel around the region, the "Ecovia" bike-and-hike track runs along the riverside between Viana do Castelo, Ponte de Lima and Ponte de Barca.

Ponte de Lima

Largely sporting an air of sleepy indifference to the wider world, easy-going **PONTE DE LIMA** takes its name from the stone bridge that spans the wide Rio Lima at this point. It's an attractive town, set back from a handsome, landscaped riverside promenade – the scene is at its best every other Monday when Ponte de Lima's lively open-air market, the **Feira Quinzenal**, sprawls out across the riverside flatlands, where a sea of stalls sells anything from mobile phone accessories to trussed chickens. Ponte de Lima claims the first documented market charter in Portugal, dated 1125, which makes the bi-monthly market the oldest in the country (Feira Quinzenal dates are posted along the riverside and on the town council website). Otherwise, the pedestrianized old centre has no specific attractions beyond its restored stone mansions and tangle of back alleys, but it's one of those places that really repays a lazy day's stroll or a night or two's stopover. Local accommodation, in particular, is in keeping with the well-to-do air in town, with lots of historic manor houses and boutique properties providing a good excuse to stick around for a while.

The bridge and riverfront

There's been a fixed crossing over the river since at least Roman times (see box below). The current **bridge** was rebuilt in 1368 and once had seventeen arches – it's lost three over the centuries to riverbank improvements and raids during the Napoleonic assault in 1809. On occasions, the river encroaches upon the town – on the **Torre de São Paulo**, near the bridge, are marks showing the depth of historic floods, including the particularly severe one of 1987. Further down the riverfront is the old sixteenth-century keep and former prison, the **Torre da Cadeia Velha** (now housing the turismo), with the granite, arcaded **Mercado** building (market Mon–Fri 7am–7pm, Sat 7am–2pm), overlooking the riverside, just beyond here. If you keep going along the promenade and under the lime trees you'll see the fifteenth-century convent of **São Francisco e Santo António dos Capuchos**.

Parque do Arnada

Museu Rural Tues–Sun 2–6pm; free

Cross the bridge from town to find the manicured **Parque do Arnada** (or Parque Temático), whose formal gardens are divided into different styles including Roman and

---

MEMORY LOSS IN PONTE DE LIMA?

For the Romans in Portugal, the rising mists of the **Rio Lima** carried troubling echoes of the River Lethe, or the "River of Forgetfulness", one of the five mythical rivers of the Underworld. The Romans believed that if they crossed the river, or drank any of its water, their memories would be erased and they would never return home – which, according to local legend, is why the otherwise all-conquering Roman legion was brought up short here in the second century BC, its troops refusing to go any further. It took an enterprising general to splash across, and demonstrate that his memory remained intact, before the soldiers would follow. It's a nice tale, embraced by the modern town, which has a phalanx of Roman troop statues lined up on the town side of the river – being encouraged across the Lima by a mounted officer on the other side.

6

PONTE DE LIMA'S FESTIVALS

As if the huge bi-monthly market wasn't enough, Ponte de Lima offers several other major festivities throughout the year. The market itself goes into overdrive for four days over the second weekend in September with the **Feiras Novas**, or New Fairs, celebrated since 1826 – as much festival as market, with fireworks, fairground rides, folk music and *gigantones* (enormous carnival-like statues). There's a similarly traditional slant to June's **Feira do Cavalo** (Horse Fair), while on the day before Corpus Christi (usually early June) Ponte de Lima comes over positively pagan with its annual ritual of the **Vaca das Cordas** (literally, "Cow of the Ropes"), which involves an enraged and defiant bull being chased through town. This is one of many traditions with its origins in the ancient fertility cults brought to the Iberian peninsula by the Phoenicians – the bull is tied by its horns, led three times around the main church, and then jabbed with goads, after which the unfortunate animal charges through the town's streets before finishing up at the river. It is then led off to the abattoir, as the good people of Ponte de Lima prepare for the more sedate procession of **Corpo do Deus** the following day, which sees the streets covered with ornately patterned flowers. For more cultured pursuits, the annual two-week **Festival Percursos da Música** is held each July, a renowned arts festival presenting recitals, chamber music and opera as well as literature and philosophy events. The town's Teatro Diogo Bernardes is the main venue, hosting anything from dance to fado, with other performances also taking place in local manor houses and on the riverside itself.

Baroque; there's also a small hothouse. Go through the gardens to the small **Museu Rural**, which houses an interesting collection of archaic tools and farming implements. An annual **Festival de Jardins** (Garden Festival) is held along this side of the river every summer (May to Sept).

ARRIVAL AND DEPARTURE   PONTE DE LIMA

By bus The bus station is outside the old centre, on Rua Conde Bertiandos, fifteen minutes' walk from the river, though most arriving buses drop passengers closer in. Destinations Arcos de Valdevez (5–9 daily; 50min); Barcelos (2 daily; 55min); Braga (3–10 daily; 30min–1hr); Ponte de Barca (3–4 daily; 20–30min); Porto (4–7 daily; 2hr 20min); Valença do Minho (1 daily; 25min); and Viana do Castelo (Mon–Fri hourly, Sat & Sun 9 daily; 50min).

By car Ponte de Lima lies 26km east of Viana do Castelo, a half-hour drive on the A27. There's acres of free parking on the riverbank, except on *feira* days, when you'll have to find a space in town where you can.

INFORMATION AND ACTIVITIES

Information Loja de Turismo, Torre da Cadeia Velha (Mon–Sat 9am–12.30pm & 2–5pm; ☎ 258 942 335, ⓦ cm-pontedelima.pt), in the tower on the riverfront.
Bike rental Available from around the side of the market building (daily 9am–8pm; €2 an hr, €4 for 4hr, €6 for 8hr) – the Ecovia track (signposted from the old bridge) is ideal for cycling, with rides possible to the Lagoas de Bertiandos nature reserve (14km) and on to Ponte de Barca (18km).

ACCOMMODATION

Accommodation in Ponte de Lima itself is limited, though there is a staid three-star riverfront hotel next to the convent and a cheap guesthouse or two. What the town is famous for is its **rural tourism** properties – bed-and-breakfast and self-catering accommodation in a series of unique and atmospheric properties, from historic manor houses to boutique hideaways.

★ **Carmo's Boutique Hotel** Gemieira, 6km east on N203, Ponte de Barca road ☎ 258 938 743, ⓦ carmos boutiquehotel.com. Providing a real change of pace from the region's manor houses, the 15 rooms and 3 suites at *Carmo's* occupy a couple of postmodern blocks a few kilometres outside town – you'll drive right past if you're not careful. Inside, it's a chic, off-white delight of polished concrete surfaces, designer furniture and original art, with uniquely furnished rooms that romantics will love (think canopy beds, floaty fabrics, deep baths, robes and slippers, lotions and potions). There's an indoor plunge-pool and spa (treatments available) and outdoor summer pool on a grassy slope, with a classy dinner (€25) and drinks served in a book- and wine-filled lair that's less restaurant and more home-from-home lounge-bar (provided, that is, your home was designed by a flash architect). **€220**

6

Casa de Crasto São João da Ribeira, 1km east of town on N203, Ponte de Barca road ☎ 258 941 156, ⓦ solares deportugal.pt. A beautiful seventeenth-century property in verdant grounds, which, legend has it, was partly demolished by the owner in 1896 while looking for hidden treasure – the old kitchen and tower managed to evade his attention. Guest rooms are in the main house, and there's an apartment (sleeps 4, €140) for self-catering. **€80**

Casa de São Gonçalo Arcozelo, 1km west of Ponte de Lima ☎ 258 942 365, ⓦ solaresdeportugal.pt. Views of the town are outstanding from this nineteenth-century house, on the opposite side of the river and about 500m from the old bridge. Although rather elegant and furnished with antiques, it's very much a family home, and the charming garden is a lovely place for breakfast. There's just one double room and a two-person apartment (same price). **€65**

Casa do Outeiro Outeiro, Arcozelo, 2km northwest of Ponte de Lima ☎ 258 941 206, ⓦ solaresdeportugal.pt. Stately manor house that dates from the sixteenth century – its vast stone kitchen fireplace is original. The house is surrounded by a garden and woods, next to an old ivy-draped aqueduct, and guests have the run of the grounds and use of the swimming pool. **€80**

Casa do Pinheiro Rua Gen. Norton de Matos 50 ☎ 258 943 971, ⓔ turismo.casadopinheiro@gmail.com. A five-minute walk from the town centre, this old Minho mansion ("Pine Tree House") springs a pleasant surprise – lovely, high-ceilinged rooms, with the best on the first floor opening onto a lush garden complete with its own small swimming pool.

It's a good choice if you want rural-tourism-style accommodation without having to drive. **€75**

★ **Moinho de Estorãos** Estorãos, 7km northwest of Ponte de Lima ☎ 258 941 546, ⓦ solaresdeportugal.pt. Rustic charm aplenty in a converted seventeenth-century water mill in an idyllic location, next to a Romanesque bridge, with walking, fishing and swimming all at hand. Accommodation is in a self-catering apartment that sleeps two. Closed Nov to March. **€90**

★ **Paço de Calheiros** Calheiros, 7km northeast of Ponte de Lima ☎ 258 947 164, ⓦ pacodecalheiros.com. Country retreat of the Count of Calheiros, this magnificent seventeenth-century mansion is set in beautifully landscaped gardens with views over the Lima valley. The Count is in residence, happy to show off his family home – accommodation is in tastefully decorated bedrooms or self-catering apartments (same price), and guests get the run of the place, from swimming pool and tennis courts to shady gardens, orchards and vineyards. **€125**

Pousada de Juventude Rua Papa João Paulo II ☎ 258 943 797, ⓦ microsites.juventude.gov.pt/portal/en. Handy for the town centre, budget travellers could do worse than the decent modern hostel, which has both shared dorms and private rooms. Dorm beds **€12**, doubles **€32**

São João Rua do Rosário 6 ☎ 258 941 288. The only real low-cost option in town is near the bridge and riverfront, which means it can be noisy, though you've got a restaurant right below and cafés on the doorstep. Rooms are nice enough for the price – though the cheapest ones have shared facilities. No credit cards. **€35**

EATING AND DRINKING

Praça de Camões, by the old bridge, has a ring of outdoor cafés, while the narrow streets behind shelter some old (and not-so-old) *tasquinhas* where you can get stuck in to the local *vinho verde*. Regional specialities are earthy to the core – things like *sarrabulho* (rice cooked with blood), *rojões* (roast pork with blood sausage) and *bacalhau com broa* (salt cod baked with corn bread).

Alameda Alameda São João 40 ☎ 258 941 630. By the bridge on the town side of the river, this place has a big outdoor terrace and splendid views, and serves dishes in epic portions – a *meia-dose* at €9–10 should suffice. Tues–Sun noon–3pm & 7–10pm.

Casas das Cheias Passeo 25 de Abril 1, next to Torre de São Paulo ☎ 258 741 092. The "House of the Floods" gets it in the neck if the river rises, but in the meantime the affable owners rustle up bargain meals for local diners – big roasts, grills and stews, meat and fish, for €7.50 a *meia-dose*, €12 a *dose*, washed down with challenging *vinho verde* from a ceramic jug. It's only a titchy place, and a bit dingy inside, but there are sometimes a couple of tables laid outside, facing the river. Daily 10am–9pm.

★ **O Brasão** Rua Formosa 1 ☎ 258 941 890. A classy restaurant in an old stone mansion, just up the hill from the

river. The regional cuisine here gets a fancy twist or two, such as steak served with garlic and *vinho verde* sauce, and the weekend special is *rojões a Minhota* or Minho-style roast pork. Dishes cost €9–16. Mon, Tues & Thurs–Sun noon–3pm & 7–10.30pm.

O Mercado Mercado de Ponte de Lima, Rua António Magalhães ☎ 258 753 700. The market building has an upper level with three restaurants including the pick-of-the-bunch *Mercado* – there's terrace dining in summer and a full menu of regional dishes (€7–12) from *rojões* to *sarrabulho*, *bacalhau* to *polvo*. Daily noon–3pm & 7–10pm.

Os Telhadinhos Rua do Rosário 28. For a taste of what Lima used to be like, pop in to this stand-up *tasca* in a back street off the square, where red *vinho verde* is served to you in a little ceramic bowl. Snacks are of the pig's-ear-salad type. Daily 7am–midnight.

Ponte da Barca

Another old bridge over the Rio Lima is the centrepiece of the pretty, historic riverside town – **PONTE DA BARCA**, the "Barca" part of the name referring to the boat that once ferried pilgrims across the river, en route to Santiago de Compostela in northwestern Spain. Nowadays the Lima is spanned by a lovely sixteenth-century bridge, beside which is the shaded Jardim dos Poetas, dedicated to sixteenth-century brothers Diogo Bernardes and Agostinho da Cruz, monastic poets who were born in the town. Like the neighbouring Ponte de Lima, that's pretty much it, save for a fortnightly riverside **market** on Wednesdays (it alternates with Arcos de Valdevez), which draws hundreds of people from outlying hamlets. The only other time the small town becomes animated is for the annual **Feira de São Bartolomeu**, which takes place on August 19–24, with the big day on August 24; don't expect to get any sleep once the party starts.

Igreja de São Salvador

Bravães, 4km west of Ponte de Barca, N203

The many Romanesque churches of the Lima valley date from the medieval heyday of the pilgrimage route to Santiago de Compostela. They are often simple in the extreme, though enhanced by animated stone carvings, with the most renowned example being the **Igreja de São Salvador**, in a small hamlet just outside Ponte de Barca. If it's open (it often isn't) you'll be able to see its interior frescoes, but even if it's closed you can check out the vibrant quality of its sculpted doorways, featuring birds, oxen, sheep, people, and even monkeys. The church is right on the road from Ponte de Lima to Ponte de Barca – you can't miss it.

ARRIVAL AND DEPARTURE   PONTE DA BARCA

By bus Buses drop passengers near the bridge. Destinations Arcos de Valdevez (hourly; 15min); Braga (3–8 daily; 1hr); Lindoso (2 daily; 1hr); Soajo (2 daily; 45min); Ponte de Lima (3–4 daily; 20–30min); and Viana do Castelo (6–8 daily; 1hr 30min).
By car It's an 18km (20min) drive east from Ponte de Lima

to Ponte de Barca (N203); there's free parking in Campo do Curro, the large square to the side of the bridge. The town is handy for the Parque Nacional da Peneda-Gerês – about an hour (50km) on back roads to Caldas do Gerês or a straight 25km run east (N203) to Lindoso in the north of the park.

INFORMATION

Turismo Rua Dom Manuel I (May–Sept Tues–Sat 9.30am–12.30pm & 2–6pm; Oct–April Tues–Sat 9am–12.30pm & 2–5.30pm; ☎258 452 899, ⊛www.cmpb.pt) – from the bridge, walk 200m up the main Rua Conselheiro Rocha Peixoto and the office is down a street on the left.
National park office Adere Peneda-Gerês, Largo da

Misericórdia 10 (Mon–Fri 9am–12.30pm & 2.30–6pm; ☎258 452 450, ⊛adere-pg.pt), is a useful source of information about the nearby Parque Nacional da Peneda-Gerês; you can book village accommodation in the park here too. It's in a stone house just up the main street, in the sunken square on the left, before the turismo.

ACCOMMODATION AND EATING

★ **Casa Nobre do Correio-Mor** Rua Trás do Forno 1 ☎258 452 129, ⊛manorhouses.com. Pick your way around the name and address – "Noble House of the Head Postmaster" on "Back of the Oven Street", no less – and what you end up finding is a tastefully restored seventeenth-century manor house offering genteel accommodation. Ten rooms live up to their noble billing – pretty spacious and furnished with antiques – while there's also a pool, sauna, games room and lovely gardens. €90
O Moínho Campo de Cûrro ☎258 452 035. Dine on a nice raised terrace in an attractive stone building at the back of the square by the bridge. Local dishes (€9–15)

include things like large, juicy Minho steaks or roast pork served with *sarrabulho*. Mon & Wed–Sun noon–3pm & 7–10.30pm.
Pensão Restaurante Gomes Rua Conselheiro Rocha Peixoto 13 ☎258 452 288. Close to the bridge, on the main road, offering a standard grill menu (dishes €8–11) in a dull dining room. Upstairs, and under separate management, are a few old-fashioned rooms – these are undeniably cheap, and breakfast is served on a balcony overlooking river and bridge. No credit cards. €30
Quinta da Prova North bank of the river, just over the bridge ☎258 452 163, ⊛quintadaprova.com.

Spacious one- and two-bedroom cottages and apartments, all with kitchenette and living room – they are sited in different places on the estate, either overlooking the river from a delightful terrace or set back in the woods. No credit cards. Two people €70; four people €100

Arcos de Valdevez

A few kilometres north of Ponte de Barca, the Rio Vez, a tributary of the Lima, is overlooked by the hillside town of **ARCOS DE VALDEVEZ**. It's at its best – no real surprise – along the river, flanked by neat, wooded gardens and with a summer beach (*praia fluvial*) located a few hundred metres downstream from the old four-arched bridge. The old town, such as it is, stretches uphill behind the bridge, culminating in an unusual spiral Manueline pillory in the Praça Municipal. It's very much a traditional shopping town – a bucket, some wellies, a length of hosepipe and a kilo of peaches, no problem, designer clothes not so much. The peak of the town's activity takes place every other Wednesday, when the fortnightly Arcos market springs into action. Its major annual bash is the **Festa do Concelho**, held over the second week in August, featuring the usual giant figures, folkloric entertainments and blazing riverside pyrotechnics.

ARRIVAL AND DEPARTURE   ARCOS DE VALDEVEZ

By car Arcos is 5km north of Ponte da Barca, and makes a useful approach to the Parque Nacional da Peneda-Gerês – it's just 20km across the hills, on the winding N202 to Soajo.

By bus The bus station, 1km out of the centre near the river, has regular services to Braga (10 daily; 1hr 30min–2hr),

Monçao (4–6 daily; 45min), Ponte de Lima (5–9 daily; 50min) and Viana do Castelo (5–12 daily; 1hr 30min); arriving buses stop in the town centre on their way to the bus station. You can catch buses to Soajo (Mon–Fri 1–3 daily; 45min) and Lindoso (Mon–Fri 1–3 daily; 1hr) at the stops along the riverside Avenida Marginal.

INFORMATION

Turismo Rua Prof Dr Mário Júlio Almeida Costa, 200m north of the bridge (April–Sept Mon–Sat 9.30am–12.30pm & 2–6pm, Sun 10am–1pm & 2–5pm; Oct–March Mon–Sat 9am–12.30pm & 2–5.30pm; ☎ 258 520 530, ⊚cmav.pt).

National park office Parque Nacional, Rua Manuel Himalaia (Mon–Fri 9am–12.30pm & 2–5.30pm; ☎ 258 515 338) – turn uphill from the river at the fountain – has walk leaflets and a park map available.

ACCOMMODATION AND EATING

A Floresta Campo do Trasladário ☎ 258 515 163. Overlooking bridge and gardens, this is one of the few options in town for eating alfresco. Regional meats feature, as do fine garlicky beans, all served in generous portions – dishes from around €10. Daily noon–3pm & 7.30–11pm.

Casa dos Confrades Praça Municipal 10 ☎ 258 515 234. Right in the centre, flanking one side of the old square, this fine stone mansion has the most agreeable accommodation in town. Nice modern rooms face an

internal courtyard with its own pool and sweeping views over the hills. €70

★ **Quinta da Cortinhas** Paço, 1km south of town, Ponte da Barca road ☎ 258 931 750, ⊚solaresde portugal.pt. What was once a summer retreat now offers eight rooms in the lovely main house and another four in handsomely converted stables. Breakfast is served in an ornate tiled dining-room, and guests can also use the basement kitchens. A tennis court and pool in the small leafy grounds add to the appeal. €70

Parque Nacional da Peneda-Gerês

The magnificent **Parque Nacional da Peneda-Gerês** – Portugal's first and only national park – was established in 1971, and helps protect a natural world and a way of life that's all but disappeared from the rest of Portugal's mountain regions. In the lush valleys oak and laurel line the riverbanks, replaced by holly, birch, pine and juniper at higher elevations; a total of eighteen plant species – including the Serra do Gerês iris – are found nowhere else on earth. Shepherds and farmers inhabit remote granite-built

6

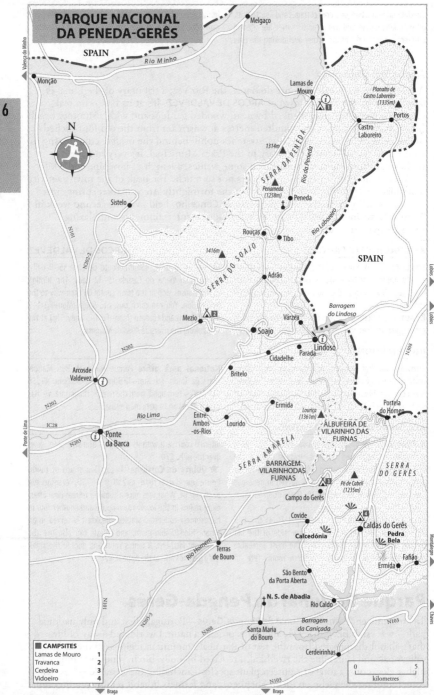

PARQUE NACIONAL DA PENEDA-GERÊS

SPAIN

Valença do Minho

Melgaço

Monção

Rio Minho

N

Lamas de Mouro

Planalto de Castro Laboreiro (1335m)

Portos

Castro Laboreiro

Sistelo

1314m

SERRA DA PENEDA

Rio da Peneda

Penameda (1258m)

Peneda

Rio Laboreiro

Rouças

Tibo

SPAIN

1416m

SERRA DO SOAJO

Adrão

Várzea

Barragem do Lindoso

Mezio

Soajo

Lindoso

Cidadelhe

Parada

Britelo

Arcosde Valdevez

Ermida

Louriça (1361m)

Portela do Homem

N202

N202

Rio Lima

Entre-Ambos-os-Rios

Lourido

ÁLBUFEIRA DE VILARINHO DAS FURNAS

IC28

N203

Ponte da Barca

SERRA AMARELA

SERRA DO GERÊS

Pé de Cabril (1235m)

BARRAGEM VILARINHO DAS FURNAS

Campo do Gerês

Covide

Caldas do Gerês

Pedra Bela

Calcedónia

N101

Rio Homem

Terras de Bouro

Ermida

Fafião

São Bento da Porta Aberta

N. S. de Abadia

Rio Caldo

N103

Santa Maria do Bouro

Barragem da Caniçada

Cerdeirinhas

N205-3

N308

N103

Braga

Braga

Lobios

Lobios

N308

Montalegre

Chaves

Ponte de Lima

CAMPSITES	
Lamas de Mouro	1
Travanca	2
Cerdeira	3
Vidoeiro	4

0 — 5 kilometres

villages, tending primitive domestic animals – *cachena* and *barrosa* cattle, *bravia* goats, *garrano* ponies and the powerful *Castro Laboreiro* sheepdog – that are long extinct elsewhere. In distant forested corners, remnants of the wildlife that once roamed all Europe still survive too, from wild boar to wolves.

If it sounds like a back-in-time backwater – well, parts certainly seem so, and there are high roads across boulder-strewn uplands where you'll rarely see another vehicle (and where goats very definitely have the right of way). But look closely at some of the beautifully kept villages, with their ancient customs and traditions apparently intact, and it's clear that tourism is playing its part in the park's preservation. Restored stone cottages and rustic houses are available for overnight guests in even the most remote of hamlets, while the unmade roads and dirt tracks of twenty years ago have acquired a layer of tarmac and a flurry of brown signs pointing out local attractions.

The park divides into several distinct regions, with the southern area easily seen from the spa town of **Caldas do Gerês**, while mountain-, forest- and water-based activities are centred on nearby settlements like **Rio Caldo** and **Campo do Gerês**. In the centre lie the traditional villages of **Soajo** and **Lindoso** – beautiful places to stay, if you fancy a quiet week hiking or touring – while the wild **Serra da Peneda**, in the north of the park, is one for real mountain aficionados. Here, you'll often have the steep forested valleys, and wind-blown *planaltos* dotted with weird rock formations, entirely to yourself. There's also a far eastern section of the park covered in the Trás-os-Montes chapter (see p.380).

ARRIVAL AND INFORMATION

By bus The roads into the park are pretty decent, but bus services are limited during the week and often non-existent at weekends. The main connections are from Melgaço (on the Rio Minho) to Lamas de Mouro in the north; from Arcos de Valdevez and Ponte da Barca (in the Lima valley) to Soajo and Lindoso in the centre; and from Braga to Caldas do Gerês in the south.

PARQUE NACIONAL DA PENEDA-GERÊS

Information The Parque Nacional da Peneda-Gerês (ⓦ adere-pg.pt) has park offices in the outlying towns of Braga, Ponte da Barca and Arcos de Valdevez. Within the park, the main office is in Caldas do Gerês, with smaller "gateway" offices (marked "Porta do PNPG") in Lindoso, Lamas de Mouro and elsewhere. All can provide maps, hiking guides and information.

ACCOMMODATION AND ACTIVITIES

Accommodation Apart from in Caldas do Gerês, accommodation is limited to a handful of hotels, rural guesthouses and village B&Bs, or camping at a few designated sites. But lots of traditional houses, particularly around Soajo and Lindoso, have been renovated and converted to simple self-catering use and are excellent value, starting at around €50 a night for 2 people, and up to €150 a night for something sleeping 6 to 8 people (there's usually a minimum two- to three-night stay). Bookings are largely through the park organization ADERE (ⓦ adere-pg.pt), either online or through any of their park offices. There are also properties available through Aldeias de

Portugal (ⓦ aldeiasdeportugal.pt) and other agencies.

Hiking Waymarked trails (*trilhos*) offer plenty of hiking opportunities, from short strolls to day-treks. There's a series of trail leaflets in English (available from park offices and local turismos), mostly for walks of around 10–16km that are fairly well marked with red and yellow pointers (though weather, wear-and-tear and landslides can affect waymarks and routes). The official park map doesn't show footpaths, so you'll need the "Série M888" 1:25,000 topographical maps produced by the Instituto Geográfico do Exército (ⓦ igeoe.pt), available online or in Portuguese bookshops.

Caldas do Gerês and around

Easy to reach from Braga, the old spa town of **CALDAS DO GERÊS** (sometimes known as Vila do Gerês) is the park's main resort. Despite a ring of pensions and hotels, it's still just about a village rather than town, spectacularly sited in a densely wooded valley and consisting of little more than a one-way system running either side of a babbling brook. Old folk still queue to taste the therapeutic waters that bubble out of a rock in the little spa building at the north end of the main street – though only those with a doctor's prescription are supposed to drink it. Contemporary pampering, meanwhile – hot tubs to volcanic rock massages – is on offer in the modern Águas do Gerês spa centre, also on the main street. Summer holidays and weekends aside, when day-trippers and spa tourists descend, it's a relaxed base from which to explore the surroundings – there are plenty of excellent local walks accessed from in or near town and you could easily spend two or three days tramping around the peaks, woodlands and waterfalls.

Parque das Termas

Entrance over the road from the arcaded gardens at the top of town • **Park** May–Oct daily 8am–6pm, Aug until 7pm; Nov–April Sat & Sun only depending on the weather • **Swimming pools** Mid-June to mid-Sept daily 10am–6pm, Aug until 7pm • Ⓦ aguasdogeres.com

Lazy summer afternoons are best spent at the **Parque das Termas**, a wonderful tree-shaded park either side of a gushing stream. You could easily while away half a day here, picnicking while sitting on granite slabs by the water, or stirring yourself for a spot of swimming, tennis or row-boat hire.

Pedra Bela

Drivers can take the road south of Caldas and turn left (signed "Ermida"), or north of Caldas and turn right (by the campsite) • On foot, the most direct approach is to take the cobbled ramp which heads steeply up opposite *Hotel Universal* on Caldas high street

For the best local views – a stunning panorama overlooking the Gerês range and Caniçada reservoir – make the trip up to the viewpoint of **Pedra Bela**, an hour's walk to the southeast of Caldas do Gerês. The tough climb is mostly on a dirt path which cuts off the road's corners. For a longer walk incorporating the viewpoint follow **trail PR3**, one of the region's best hikes. It starts from above the picnic site opposite the campsite/park-office turning, around 2km north of Caldas do Gerês on the Portela do Homen road. The ten-kilometre, half-day trail follows the *currals* or grazing pastures for cattle ranchers. Look for the red and yellow waymarks, which take you steeply uphill before levelling off to cross the mountain pastures, framed by weird granite outcrops.

Arado waterfalls and Ermida

From Pedra Bela, a delightful four-kilometre path heads southeast to the magnificent **Arado waterfalls**, a popular picnic spot, with refreshing pools for swimming. If you are driving, note the final approach road can be either treacherously muddy when wet or extremely bumpy when dry. The road then continues southeast to **Ermida**, a tiny farming community with an air of true isolation about it, though there are a few places renting out rooms and a couple of cafés: the total walk here from Caldas do Gerês is 11km (about three hours).

Trilho da Preguiça

One of the easiest and most rewarding of the local walking trails begins 4km north of Caldas do Gerês on the Portela do Homen road. The **Trilho da Preguiça route** (PR10) is clearly marked and the 4km walk will take most people around two and half hours. The first half, east of the road, heads steeply uphill through woods to a great viewpoint (1300m). You then descend and continue west of the road on a more gentle, picturesque path through a wooded valley, following a babbling brook with several small waterfalls and rock pools to cool off in.

Portela do Homen

13km north of Caldas do Gerês, N308

North of Caldas do Gerês, the narrow main road twists tortuously uphill into a series of deep, wooded valleys. A couple of kilometres before Portela do Homen, a small bridge crosses a stream with a superb natural bathing spot just north of the road, though note that in July and August parking is strictly forbidden along this stretch. **Portela do Homen** itself is a mountain pass with a deserted border post, its former customs buildings abandoned and surrounded by grazing cattle; drive right on through to enter Spain and the road to Ourense.

ARRIVAL AND INFORMATION

CALDAS DO GERÊS

By car It's 45km to Caldas from Braga, around an hour's drive. There's pay-and-display parking along the main street.

By bus Buses stop on the main street, Avenida Manuel Francisco da Costa, with regular services to Braga (5–11 daily; 1hr 30min) and Rio Caldo (6–12 daily; 25min).

Information The turismo is next to the handicrafts centre on the roundabout at the entrance to town (Mon–Wed & Fri–Sat 9.30am–12.30pm & 2.30–6pm; ☏ 253 391 133, ⓦ geres.pt).

National park office Centro de Educação Ambiente, Lugar do Vidoeiro (9am–12.30pm & 2–5.30pm: July & Aug daily; Sept–June Mon–Fri; ☏ 253 390 110), is 1.5km north of town on the Portela do Homen road, in an easily missed building by the entrance to the *Vidoeiro* campsite; it's the best place for walk advice and trail leaflets.

6

ACCOMMODATION

Gerês has plenty of accommodation, and prices tumble outside July and August (though many of the smaller places are only open from May to October). For budget rooms, try the string of guesthouses overlooking town on Rua do Arnaçó, which all have parking for guests; other good-value options are strung out along the road on the 8km down the valley to Rio Caldo.

Adelaide Rua do Arnaçó ☏ 253 390 020, ⓦ pensao adelaide.com.pt. Comfortable guesthouse in two separate buildings high up at the top end of the road; you'll want one of the rooms with a huge balcony for grandstand views. Guests can use a pool in town, and there's a lively restaurant if you can't face the trek down the hill at night. **€65**

Águas do Gerês Av Manuel Francisco da Costa 136 ☏ 253 390 190, ⓦ aguasdogeres.com. The town's principal spa hotel is an elegant place, restored several times over and featuring the most stylish rooms in Caldas. Fancy pool and spa facilities lie over the road, with all sorts of packages available if you want to indulge, while the associated Parque das Termas outdoor park and pools are just a short walk away. **€90**

Parque de Campismo do Vidoeiro Vidoeiro, 1.5km north of town, Portela do Homen road ☏ 253 391 289, ⓦ adere-pg.pt. Park-run campsite in shady, wooded grounds, just to the north of town by the river. Advance bookings advised in summer, which you can make in any national park office. Closed mid-Oct to mid-May. Pitch **€3.60**, plus **€4** per adult, plus **€3.75** per vehicle

Quinta Souto-Linho Av Manuel Francisco da Costa ☏ 253 392 000. A picture-book *turismo rural* property, more central than many, uphill just east of the high street. Grand rooms come with polished floors and fine views, and there's also an outdoor pool (open summer only). **€70**

★ **São Miguel do Gerês** Rua do Arnaçó 43 ☏ 253 391 360, ⓔ geral@pensaosaomiguel.com. Very friendly, small guesthouse with pristine rooms, each offering balconies with sweeping views over the wooded slopes. The bathrooms are showing their age but otherwise this is excellent value, with a generous breakfast to boot. **€50**

EATING AND DRINKING

A Lagôa Lugar do Vidoeiro, 1km north, halfway between town and the campsite ☏ 253 391 918. Uphill and out of town, by a cluster of cafés, this has a tranquil outside terrace by a babbling brook and a colossal dining area where you can tuck into well-prepared fish and grills – half-portions from €5 will do the trick for most. Daily noon–3pm & 7–11pm.

★ **Geresiana** Rua Augusta Sérgio Almeida Maia 1 ☏ 253 391 226. Stone walls and crisp white tablecloths set the tone for the best eatery in town, with a decent regional menu (dishes from €9–10). *Truta a Minhota* (trout stuffed with *presunto* ham) is always good, or there are grilled meats and a house *bacalhau* served with *grelos* (turnip tops). It's the salmon-pink building above the main street, opposite the spa. Mon, Tues & Thurs–Sun noon–3pm & 7–10.30pm.

Lurdes Capela Rua Dr Manuel Gomes de Almeida 77 ☏ 253 391 208. Pulls in the locals for two reasons – cheap €6 *combinado* dishes of steak and eggs, *alheira* and chips and the like, plus a more varied menu of local dishes (€8–11) from trout to *javali* (wild boar). It's at the bottom of the main street. Daily 11.30am–3pm & 6.30–10pm.

Rio Caldo and around

The village of **RIO CALDO**, 8km south of Caldas do Gerês, sprawls around the two bridges that cross the **Barragem da Caniçada**. Dramatically sited in a bowl surrounded by mountains, the large reservoir is a watersports centre – mainly for windsurfing and waterskiing – and the swimming is fine, too, though only in designated areas. For the best views of the water you need to get above Rio Caldo – either by staying at the *pousada* (N304, Braga road; see p.344) or heading the other way, 3km northwest to

São Bento da Porta Aberta (N304, Campo do Gerês road), whose austere sanctuary commands a terrace with a spectacular panorama. Pilgrims gather here at the beginning of July and again a month later (and on most Sundays throughout the year), at which times the traffic up here slows to a crawl.

Nossa Senhora da Abadia

13km west of Rio Caldo, off the N308 to Braga, turning off at Santa Maria do Bouro

One of the most revered places in Portugal, and accessible only by car, is the remote shrine of **Nossa Senhora da Abadia** – although not officially within the Peneda-Gerês national park, it's an easy drive here from Rio Caldo, though it can also be visited as a day-trip from Braga (30km southwest). Pilgrims come to pay homage to the twelfth-century wooden statue of the Virgin and Child and, while the church itself was largely rebuilt in the eighteenth century, outside are two earlier, elegant wings of monks' cells as well as a restaurant. It's pretty quiet for most of the year, though has a far livelier air during the main festival on August 15.

ACTIVITIES   RIO CALDO AND AROUND

Watersports Água Montanha in Rio Caldo (☎ 253 391 779, ⊛ aguamontanha.com) rents out canoes (from €6 per hr), pedaloes (€12 for 1hr) and motorboats (€35 for 1hr), as well as offering speedboat rides and family adventure packages, and can also arrange accommodation.

ACCOMMODATION AND EATING

Casa dos Santos ☎ 253 391 212, ⊛ casadossantos .com. For cheap rooms up at São Bento, try this homely place (just behind the *Mira Serra* restaurant). It's got simple rooms with smashing views, a patio garden full of lemon trees, and a rustic bar – and you can eat reasonably on the terrace at the neighbouring *Mira Serra*. The guesthouse also has some bunk-rooms (from €12 per person) and self-catering flats (from €45 per night), and can organize kayaking and quad-bike activities. €35

Pousada do Gerês Santa Maria do Bouro, 13km west of Rio Caldo ☎ 253 371 970, ⊛ pousadas.pt. This gorgeous conversion of a twelfth-century Cistercian monastery, set in the Gerês foothills, has been majestically restored and combines monastic simplicity with daring modern flare

– views from the rooms are magnificent, while cloisters, gardens, grounds, pool and grand restaurant all add up to a thoroughly spoiled stay. €150

★ **Pousada do Gerês-Caniçada** 5km south of Rio Caldo, N304, Braga road ☎ 253 649 150, ⊛ pousadas .pt. The old timber-and-granite hunting lodge has an enviable location, overlooking the reservoir from the southeast. It's a very attractive building, with a small-scale feel and lots of nooks and crannies to curl up in, and panoramic terraces to lounge on. There's also a swimming pool and a fine restaurant with more great views – river trout is a favoured dish here, alongside a decent menu of regional specialities, and you'll eat for around €40 a head. €125

Campo do Gerês

CAMPO DO GERÊS is little more than a cluster of houses huddled around a road junction, but it's surrounded by dense woodland and makes a pretty good base for local hikes and adventures. A typical day out on foot is the fine walk from the campsite (see opposite), following a forestry track east (signposted "Portela do Homen"). This eventually joins the road to Portela do Homen, from where it is a short walk to some superb natural bathing pools (7km/90min each way). Otherwise, there are all kinds of opportunities to rent mountain bikes, go riding or get out on the water at the local reservoir.

Museu Etnográfico de Vilarinho da Furna

1km south of Campo do Gerês • Tues–Sun 10am–12.30pm & 2–5pm • €2 • ☎ 253 351 888

Sited in quiet woodland not far from Campo, the **Museu Etnográfico de Vilarinho da Furna** is an emotive museum dedicated to the former village of Vilarinho da Furna, which was completely submerged by the building of a dam in 1972. There are farm implements, a re-created kitchen, and a series of black-and-white photos recording village life from days gone by. In the nearby dam itself, the **Barragem Vilarinho**

das Furnas, a dry summer sometimes reveals the ruins of the old village poking up above the waters.

Just outside the museum, you'll find **Roman column XXVII**, one of a series of carved granite posts lining the road from Santa Cruz, south of Terras de Bouro, to the border at Portela do Homen. This section, known locally as Geira, marks out miles XIV to XXXIV of the Roman Via Nova, a military road built in the first century AD. The route originally linked Braga with Astorga in Spain, a distance of 344km.

ARRIVAL AND ACTIVITIES   CAMPO DO GERÊS

By bus/car There are direct buses from Braga, via Rio Caldo, to Campo do Gerês (2–6 daily; 1hr 20min). In your own car, it takes under an hour (45km) from Braga along the N20/307, via Terras de Bouro.

Activities The *Parque de Cerdeira* campsite (see below) has mountain bikes for rent (€25 per day), and can also arrange activities like kayaking, horseriding, guided trekking and jeep safaris.

ACCOMMODATION AND EATING

There's a large choice of private rooms and self-catering apartments in and around Campo; just look for the signs. For campsite and hostel, in particular, it's best to book ahead, since this is a popular place to stay for outdoor enthusiasts – August is the really busy month, when prices rise across the board.

Albergaria Stop Rua de São João 915 ☎ 253 350 040, ⓦ albergariastop.com. Rather a nice lodge-style hotel; nothing fancy but the rooms have balconies overlooking an outdoor pool (mid-June to mid-Sept only). It's also got a tennis court and a few other public amenities, plus a decent restaurant open to nonguests (mains €8–12). Restaurant daily noon–2pm & 7.30–10pm. **€50**

★ **Parque de Cerdeira** Rua de Cerdeira 400 ☎ 253 351 005, ⓦ parquecerdeira.com. Set in verdant grounds just outside Campo, the local campsite is more of an outdoor leisure complex – not just tent pitches, heated washrooms and laundry service, but also bunkhouse accommodation with en-suite four-bed units and some very nice self-catering bungalows. Whichever accommodation you choose, you'll

have use of the open-air swimming pool, games areas, bar and restaurant, and minimarket. Pitch **€5**, plus **€5.50** per adult; bunkhouse **€17.50**; bungalows for 2 people **€70**, 4 people **€95**

Pousada de Juventude Rua da Pousada 1, Vilarinho das Furnas ☎ 253 351 339, ⓦ microsites.juventude .gov.pt/portal/en. The place where the dam construction workers once stayed is now the youth hostel, located a ten-minute walk from Campo do Gerês. It's a brightly presented, efficiently run base for outdoorsy types, with a fairly mixed bag as far as accommodation goes – not just dorms, but en-suite doubles and 4-bed bungalows with kitchenette. Dorm beds **€15**, doubles **€42**, bungalows **€90**

Lindoso

LINDOSO occupies a spectacular position, surrounded by mountains high above a glittering reservoir. Its prominent castle is a relic of more turbulent times – the village is very close to the Spanish border – though for once the castle isn't the most dramatic sight in the village. Here, instead, the honour goes to Lindoso's extraordinary collection of around fifty nineteenth-century granite **espigueiros** (grain stores), spread out on the slopes below the castle walls. Protecting the precious grain and the maize for the animal feed was a communal effort in this once-remote settlement, and the *espigueiros* are gathered together accordingly. They are raised off the ground on granite legs and have slots in the side-walls, which keeps the grain and maize away from vermin and allows dry air to circulate – and with each topped by a stone cross, the entire site resembles nothing less than a graveyard of elevated tombs.

Castelo

April–Sept Tues–Fri 10am–12.30pm & 2–6pm, Sat & Sun 10am–noon & 2.30–5pm; Oct–March, request access at the Porta do PNPG • €1.50

Rising above the village, Lindoso's ruined **Castelo** contains a museum chronicling the castle's military history and displays finds of local excavations. It's free if all you want to do is simply enjoy the guard's-eye view over the valley from the walls and battlements.

6

By car Lindoso is 25km east of Ponte da Barca (N203) and close to the Spanish border. If you're driving from Campo or Caldas do Gerês, the best route is to take the road via Portela do Homen into Spain, up to Lobios, entering Portugal again near Lindoso. There's free parking right beneath the castle walls.

By bus There are a couple of daily buses from Arcos de Valdevez and Ponte de Barca, but the timings usually mean that you would have to spend the night here.

Information Porta de PNPG, Lugar do Castelo (April–Sept daily 10am–7pm; Oct–March Tues–Sun 10am–12.30pm & 2–5pm; ☎ 258 578 141), just below the castle, opposite the church, is a modern information centre for the park.

ACCOMMODATION

Casa do Destro ☎ 258 577 534. In the shadow of the castle, with nine modern rooms and two spacious suites, all with good views, plus a pool on a large terrace. This is also an excellent place for a meal, its restaurant (mains €10–15; closed Wed) a surprisingly upmarket affair with a long list of starters and good, if pricey, steaks and *bacalhau* dishes. **€50**

Soajo

SOAJO is something of a puzzle. Set in a broad, fertile valley, amid a network of ancient cobbled tracks, cultivated fields and watermills, with higher grazing lands beyond, it's both a surviving centre of rustic tradition and designated centre for rural tourism. On the one hand, there are goat-herders, elderly black-clad widows and an ancient *pelourinho* in the time-worn central square; on the other, the stone houses are scrubbed suspiciously clean and linked by pristine paved alleys winding past carefully tended gardens filled with fruit trees and trellised vines. It's an idealized version of rusticity perhaps, but it does mean the village continues to thrive – and that staying in a beautifully renovated traditional house here or in neighbouring Lindoso is a joy (see p.341). It also means that there's a better-than-usual chance of something reasonable to eat with a couple of restaurants on the main road outside the village, and a café or two and a bakery inside the village. As in Lindoso, the main sight is a grouping of preserved *espigueiros* (grain houses), set apart from the houses on higher ground at the edge of the village. The best local walk is a four-kilometre return route via the neighbouring village of Adrão, along a cobbled lane with ruts worn into the stones over the centuries by ox carts.

By car Soajo is 20km east of Arcos de Valdevez (N202), a pleasant – and increasingly dramatic – half-hour drive over the hilltops. There's a sign off the main road for the *espigueiros*, where you can park. From Soajo, it's another 11km over the mountains on to Lindoso (N530), which you reach by crossing a reservoir.

By bus Services from Arcos de Valdevez (Mon–Fri 1–3 daily; 45min) drop you on the main road at the village entrance.

ACCOMMODATION AND EATING

★ **Casa do Adro** Largo da Eiro ☎ 258 576 327, ⓦ casadoadroturismorural.com. By the church in the square (follow the blue signposts), offering half-a-dozen rustic rooms in a beautiful eighteenth-century house. They make their own wine from the tumbling vines, and you eat breakfast in the old kitchen. There's a minimum three-night stay in July and August. **€50**

O Espigueiro de Soajo Av 25 de Abril, just up the Arcos road ☎ 258 576 136. Specializing in mountain goat, a chicken-and-rice stew and other rustic dishes, this restaurant – a couple of hundred metres up the main road – also has an outdoor terrace with valley views. Tues–Sat 11.30am–3.30pm & 7–10pm, Sun 11.30am–3.30pm.

Parque de Campismo de Travanca Bouças Donas, Cabana Maior ☎ 258 526 105. A summer-only campsite in a clearing in the trees, around 7km northwest of Soajo (on the Arcos road). Open July & Aug only. Pitches **€3.60**, plus **€4** per adult, plus **€3.75** per vehicle

Peneda

Far fewer tourists make the trek to the northern sections of the park, though the small mountain village of **PENEDA** is worth the effort. It's reached by a steep, twisting road and huddles under the towering granite summit of **Penameda** (1258m) – a rather stunning backdrop to the locally renowned **Sanctuário da Nossa Senhora da Peneda**, a miniature version of the pilgrimage church at Bom Jesus near Braga. The village itself is little more than a few religious artefact shops clustered around the main square, and often seems hauntingly empty, but for a couple of days a year at least (Sept 7 and 8) Peneda fills with pilgrims. The original focus of adoration was a curious stone which natural forces had sculpted into the form of a woman, who some said was pregnant. Come Christianity, the stone was adopted as the Virgin Mary and was duly incorporated into the late eighteenth-century church. There she remained until the 1930s, when somebody stole her; a gaudy plastic replacement now stands in her place.

6

ARRIVAL AND INFORMATION

PENEDA

By car Peneda is around 30km northeast of Arcos de Valdevez, signposted off the Soajo road. It's around the same distance south of Melgaço on the Rio Minho; coming this way, you'll enter the park at Lamas de Mouro, 8km north of Peneda.

Information The national park office, Porta do PNPG, Lamas de Mouro, Porto Ribeiro (April–Sept 10am–12.30pm & 2–7pm; Oct–March daily 10am–12.30pm & 2–5pm; ☎ 251 465 010, ⓦ adere-pg.pt).

ACCOMMODATION

Hotel da Peneda Lugar da Peneda ☎ 251 460 040, ⓦ hotel.peneda.net. Former pilgrim lodgings, now rebooted as a classy little three-star hotel, with its own bar and restaurant; it also lets out the attractive *turismo rural* property, the *Anjo da Guarda*, in the main square. **€90**

Parque Campismo Lamas de Mouro ☎ 251 466 041, ⓦ camping-lamas.com. The wooded campsite at Lamas has some bungalow shacks in the grounds, ideal for families, a natural pool nearby for swimming, and its own restaurant. Closed Oct–May. Pitches **€5**, bungalows **€60**

Trás-os-Montes

GIMONDE, IN THE PARQUE NATURAL DE MONTESINHO

Trás-os-Montes

The northeastern region of Trás-os-Montes (literally "Behind the Mountains") was once Portugal at its most remote. Cut off from the mainstream over the centuries – beyond the peaks of the Gerês, Marão and Alvão *serras* – this isolated region developed in its own individual way, characterized by strange traditions, harsh dialects and hard lives. Many fled to the cities in search of better things, and emigration was high; meanwhile others came to hide, such as the Jews who escaped here from the terrors of the Inquisition. Change came slowly, if at all, and Trás-os-Montes remained a land apart until as late as the 1980s and 90s, when fast new highways started to make inroads into the northern wilds. Investment in agriculture, industry and urban renewal has also done much to change perceptions of the region as backward and conservative, though those views still persist in much of the rest of Portugal.

You can get to the main towns quicker these days, but there are still places where you might feel like you are the first foreign visitor to arrive, and traditional village life continues as it has done for decades, if not centuries. This is especially true of the extreme north, hewn from dark granite, which has a challenging climate of long freezing winters and short boiling summers – hence its rather forbidding nickname of the *Terra Fria* (Cold Land). In contrast, the southern region – the *Terra Quente* (Hot Land) – covers the fertile hinterlands of the Douro, Corgo and Tua rivers, and presents a more pastoral landscape of olive groves, vineyards and orchards.

From the Douro and the south, the attractive town of **Vila Real** is the obvious starting point for a tour; it's also handy for access to the dramatic granite scenery of the **Parque Natural do Alvão**. Beyond Vila Real, fast highways run up to the border towns of **Chaves** and **Bragança**, which are the only other two places in the region of any significant size. Between them they hold the bulk of the historic and cultural interest, while each is also well placed for the great outdoors, with Chaves offering access (via Montalegre) to the eastern section of the **Parque Nacional da Peneda-Gerês** and Bragança being the jumping-off point for the magnificent **Parque Natural de Montesinho**. South and east of the Vila Real–Bragança highway, the landscapes are gentler for the most part but the journeys take longer, on winding routes through far less visited towns and villages. Some places, such as dramatically sited **Miranda do Douro**, above a dam on the Spanish border, the Roman bridge over the Rio Tua at **Mirandela**, or the small historic centre of **Torre de Moncorvo**, are worthy destinations in their own right. But often, it's simply the journey that counts, notably the tremendous backcountry route through the fringes of the **Parque Natural do Douro Internacional**, through unheralded towns such as **Mogadouro** and **Freixo de Espada à Cinta**.

BRAGANÇA

Highlights

❶ Castelo de Ansiães Discover Portugal's lost history in the abandoned medieval town and castle that once hosted the country's kings. **See p.360**

❷ São João das Arribas gorge Enjoy a day's walk from Miranda do Douro to a stupendous viewpoint over the dramatic gorge. **See p.364**

❸ Boat trip, Miranda do Douro A Douro cruise with a difference, this exciting boat trip plies the craggy gorge below ancient Miranda. **See p.365**

❹ Bragança An ancient citadel enclosing centuries of history and a revitalized town centre marks this once-remote regional capital. **See p.365**

❺ Parque Natural de Montesinho Hike in the hills before a night at the boutique "Lost Lobster". **See p.370**

❻ Chaves The Romans founded this lovely spa town with a picturesque riverside setting, and it's still a joy to behold. **See p.376**

❼ Piteus das Júnias Explore this wild northwest corner of the Parque Nacional da Peneda-Gerês. **See p.380**

HIGHLIGHTS ARE MARKED ON THE MAP ON P.352

Vila Real and around

VILA REAL sits on a high spur above the deep valley of the Rio Corgo, a tributary of the Douro. Founded and aptly named by Dom Dinis in 1289, "Royal Town" was once home to the largest concentration of nobility outside Lisbon, although today it has more of an industrial role, as well as being the home of the University of Trás-os-Montes. It's the nearest base for visiting the Parque Natural do Alvão (see p.355), while other local attractions include the ancient site at **Panóias** and the **Casa de Mateus** – the country house featured on the Mateus Rosé wine label. Despite its noble heritage, there's little of architectural interest in town save the odd surviving mansion, but it's a likeable place of broad avenues, sunny squares and old-town streets filled with a mix of day-to-day shops and craft stores – there's also a local produce **market** at the Mercado Municipal (Mon–Fri). Look out, in particular, for local straw work as well as the distinctive pewter-grey earthenware crockery (*olaria*) made in the nearby village of Bisalhães.

7

Museu da Vila Velha

Rua de Trás-os-Muros • Daily 9.30am–12.30pm & 2–6pm • €2, free on Sun • ☎ 259 303 320, ⓦ mvv.cm-vilareal.pt

The **Museu da Vila Velha** is the best place to find out about local history and to get a feel for the culture and traditions of the region. It's close to the foot of town, and you should definitely combine a museum visit with a walk to the end of the promontory on which Vila Real is built, for sweeping views from the nearby Capela de São Brás.

Casa de Mateus

Largo dos Condes, Mateus, 4km east of Vila Real • Daily: May, June & Sept 9am–7pm; July & Aug 9am–7.30pm; Oct, March & April 9am–6pm; Nov–Feb 9am–5pm • €10, gardens only €6.50, wine tastings €4 • ☎ 259 323 121, ⓦ casademateus.com • Bus from Rua Gonçalo Cristovão, outside Vila Real market (every 30min); fee charged for parking at the house

The **Casa de Mateus** (signposted "Palácio de Mateus") is probably the most familiar country house in Portugal, seen on the label of each bottle of Mateus Rosé, one of Portugal's major wine exports. The architect is unknown, though the building is often attributed to the Italian, Nicolau Nasoni (who built the landmark Clérigos church in Porto). It dates to around 1740 – the heyday of Portuguese Baroque – and although there are no special treasures, the house is an enjoyable evocation of its period, full of aristocratic portraits and antique furniture.

The main house ticket price includes a one-hour guided tour of the interior, including the chapel and special exhibition areas. You don't have to book in advance for the house tours, though as numbers are limited you may have to wait an hour for the next one. There are no such restrictions (or tours) for the delightful gardens (open same hours as the house), which are full of ponds, box hedges, statues and shaded avenues. There's also a shop, for local wines and produce, while wine tastings are offered in the *adega* (though not of Mateus Rosé, as you might expect – it's not actually made here).

Santuário de Panóias

Lugar do Assento, Vale de Nogueiras, 4km east of Mateus, 8km east of Vila Real • Tues 2–5pm, Wed–Sun 9am–12.30pm & 2–5pm • €2, free on Sun morning • The site is hard to reach by public transport, though by car it is well signposted beyond Mateus

The original settlement in the region was out at **Panóias**, whose fascinating sanctuary is all that remains of a once thriving town. At first sight it seems no more than a field of boulders, but this was the location of the temple of a particularly bloody sacrificial cult, later adopted by the Romans and dedicated to Serapis (a god of Greco-Egyptian origin, lord of life and death). There are three main sacrificial boulders, the uppermost and largest of which displays the remnants of a temple that once stood atop it; the tower above gives a

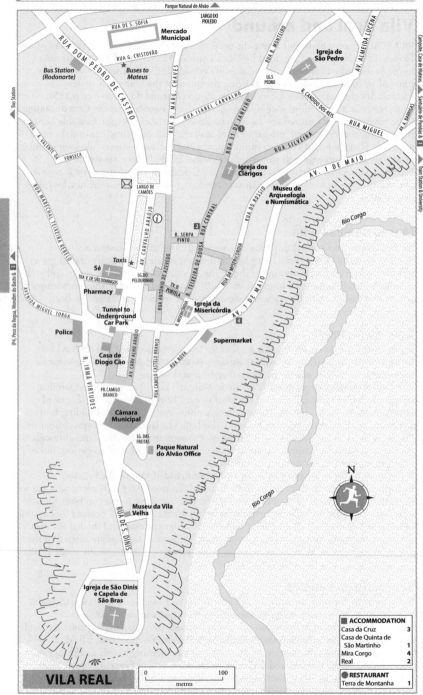

VILA REAL

0   100
metres

ACCOMMODATION
Casa da Cruz   3
Casa de Quinta de
  São Martinho   1
Mira Corgo   4
Real   2

RESTAURANT
Terra de Montanha   1

good overview. Much-eroded inscriptions on the boulders are in a strange mixture of Greek and Latin, as the Roman emperor at the time was from a Greek province.

ARRIVAL AND DEPARTURE

By bus The main bus station is just out of the old centre, on the corner of Avenida Cidade de Orense and Rua A. Valente de Fonseca, while Rodonorte (ⓦrodonorte.pt) services to Braga, Lisbon and Porto operate from Rua Dom Pedro de Castro by the *Hotel Miraneve*.

Destinations Braga (3–8 daily; 2hr 40min); Bragança (8–18 daily; 1hr 30min–2hr); Chaves (2 daily; 1hr 10min); Guimarães (1–5 daily; 1hr 30min); Lisbon (6–9 daily; 5hr);

VILA REAL AND AROUND

Mirandela (roughly hourly; 1hr); and Porto (6–12 daily; 1hr 30min).

By car Except for the one-way system around the central avenue, driving into town is fairly straightforward. There's a large underground car park at the southern end of the avenue, or try and find parking spots on Avenida 1º de Maio. For Casa de Mateus and Santuário de Panóias, take the N322 (Sabrosa road) out of town.

INFORMATION

Parque Natural do Alvão HQ Largo das Freitas, behind the Câmara Municipal (Mon–Fri 9am–12.30pm & 2–5.30pm; ☎ 259 302 830, ⓦicnf.pt).

Turismo Av Carvalho Araújo 94 (daily 9.30am–12.30pm & 2–6pm; ☎ 259 322 819, ⓦcm-vilareal.pt, ⓦrtsmarao.pt).

ACCOMMODATION AND EATING

Town-centre **accommodation** in Vila Real is pretty underwhelming and it's the *turismo rural* properties in the area that provide the nicer overnight stay. For the cheapest **restaurants** in town, look along Rua da Misericórdia and Rua Teixeira de Sousa; best **cafés**, meanwhile, are those on the pedestrianized avenue and square, near the Câmara Municipal. Incidentally, Vila Real might be in Trás-os-Montes, but it's also in the demarcated Douro wine region, so good **wines** are the norm in most restaurants.

Casa da Cruz Campeã, 12km west of Vila Real, N304, Mondim de Basto road ☎ 259 372 995 or ☎ 917 523 975, ⓦcasadacruz.com. Three rustic rooms and three apartments, all with lovely carved beds, in an eighteenth-century granite farmhouse, overlooking the Vale de Campeã. There's use of the kitchen, as well as a secluded swimming pool. €60

★ **Casa da Quinta de São Martinho** Mateus, 4km east of Vila Real, 300m from Casa de Mateus ☎ 259 323 986, ⓦquintasaomartinho.com. Country house swathed in ivy, with two B&B rooms in the main building and two self-contained apartments in the garden, complete with spiral staircase and exposed stone walls – the apartments will sleep a family of four. There's a swimming pool, and port wine tasting in the bar (the friendly proprietor being president of the Douro wine trail). €80

Mira Corgo Av 1º de Maio 78 ☎ 259 325 001, ⓦhotel miracorgo.com. This central four-star hotel is a pretty ugly

modern building, but secure a room overlooking the stepped terraces of the Rio Corgo and you won't be disappointed. There's an indoor swimming pool, and outdoor terraces for the views, as well as secure parking. €75

Real Rua Combatentes da Grande Guerra 5 ☎ 259 325 879, ⓦresidencialreal.com. First choice for budget travellers is this simple place above the *pastelaria* of the same name, where the well-kept, en-suite rooms have high white walls and polished wooden floors. A croissant, toast and pastry breakfast is included. €40

★ **Terra de Montanha** Rua 31 de Janeiro 28 ☎ 259 372 075. The tables are set inside huge, antique wine vats in this low-lit, rustic restaurant, and the friendly staff are enthusiastic about the traditional Portuguese menu. There's also a changing selection of hearty *pratos do dia* and a fine house red wine. Meals from around €20. Mon–Sat 12.30–2.30pm & 7.30–10.30pm, Sun 12.30–2.30pm.

Parque Natural do Alvão

The **Parque Natural do Alvão** is Portugal's smallest natural park, an area of 8000 mountainous hectares set between Vila Real and Mondim de Basto to the northwest. A mere handful of settlements (with a total population of fewer than 700) hugs the boulder-strewn terrain, with every centimetre of arable land between heroically terraced and tended, while other slopes are planted with pine whose scent carries in the air. Life, of course, has been hard and many of the villages are depopulated, but traditional agricultural methods (ox and plough, hand-scythed straw) cling on and some crafts (clog-making, weaving) have been revived. Drive-through visitors in a hurry don't always see the best of Alvão – at first sight, many of the settlements seem moribund or disfigured by ugly recent construction, while there are hardly any facilities within the park, rarely even a place to get a drink. But with just half a day to spare, you can easily do one of the two official waymarked walks, while another half-day gives you time to drive around a circuit of the most interesting villages and visit the one standout natural sight, the Fisgas de Ermelo waterfalls.

ARRIVAL AND INFORMATION
PARQUE NATURAL DO ALVÃO

Transport Access points to the park are Vila Real (5km southeast of the park boundary) or Mondim de Basto (15km from the main village of Ermelo, in the west). The N304 connects the two towns, and daily buses (not Sun) ply the route, and there are also regular weekday bus services from Vila Real to Agarez and to Lamas de Ôlo, both of which are on the marked walking routes. Alternatively, a taxi from Vila Real to Lamas do Ôlo, for example, shouldn't cost more than €25. However, to see the park properly,

certainly in a short time, you'll need a car. Be aware that signposting in the park leaves something to be desired and some villages are simply not signed at all.
Information There are park information offices in both Vila Real and Mondim de Basto, both hampered by the usual lack of anything you might call information, certainly in English. You could try the generally more helpful Vila Real turismo, or consult ⓦ icnf.pt.

ACCOMMODATION AND ACTIVITIES

Accommodation There's a distinct lack of accommodation (and no camping allowed) within the park, so the only real options are staying in Vila Real or Mondim de Basto. You might also consider the *Pousada de São Gonçalo* in the Serra do Marão (p.287), halfway between Vila Real and Amarante and close enough to the park for day-trips.

Hiking The good news is that, once you've found them, the two walking routes are well maintained, with proper red-yellow waymarks – you probably won't even need the photocopied route leaflets or park map that you might have managed to prise from the information offices.

Agarez and around

From Vila Real, it's only 5km to **AGAREZ** village, just above which starts the shorter of the two official walking routes; there's a walk information board on the left-hand side of the Lamas de Ôlo road, just out of Agarez. The **Galegos–Arnal circuit** (7km; 3hr) follows a lovely stone path, past an old watermill, before heading steeply up past the dung-spattered Galegos da Serra village to the Escola Ecológica study centre, 1000m high and with majestic views towards Vila Real. From here, the path winds down to the ancient farming hamlet of Arnal (whose chapel has an exterior chain-pull bell), and then you follow the minor road down the pretty Arnal river valley, past grazing cattle, back to Agarez.

Barragem do Alvão and Lamas de Ôlo

Drive further up the Lamas de Ôlo road and there's parking by the **Barragem do Alvão**, which is where the second park walking trail begins. The **Barragens–Barreiro–Lamas de Ôlo circuit** (13km; 4hr) is a magnificent high-plateau walk, starting between two dams (*barragens*) and circling around through the villages of Barreiro and Lamas de Ôlo (with the last 2km on the road from Lamas back up to the dams). You're walking at between 1100m and 1200m throughout, with amazing views all the way round, passing through vibrant blankets of purple and yellow heather and gorse, past frog-filled ponds, pine forests and precariously balanced boulders. **Lamas de Ôlo** itself is a partly abandoned mountain hamlet of granite houses and traditional *espigueiros* (grain stores). There's a basic café here – no sign, but it's near the bus stop – while the onward road between Lamas and Anta has more magnificent views, with Mondim de Basto and its conical mountain prominent in the distance.

Ermelo and around

There are several possible driving routes through the park from Vila Real to Mondim de Basto, but the loop through Pioledo and Cavernelhe towards Ermelo is thoroughly recommended, since you can detour to a spectacular rocky ledge overlooking the thundering waterfalls of **Fisgas de Ermelo**, in a craggy valley beyond. The parking and viewing area is some distance from the falls, though a tough hike gets you closer. Entering or leaving the park at the western side, you might as well take in **ERMELO** itself (1km off the N304), a sleepy hamlet that just about stirs itself to claim the title of "largest village in the park". The place has a few cafés, and nothing more in the way of services, but it's interesting to stop and look at the intricately plaited roofs of black slate that are typical of the village.

Mondim de Basto

The small, handsomely sited town of **MONDIM DE BASTO** lies on the northwestern side of the *parque natural*, an hour by road from Vila Real (N304) or slightly closer to Amarante, 30km back down the Rio Tâmega. There's little of historic interest, but Mondim is ringed by vineyards (they make *vinho verde* around here), and has a pretty floral garden in the centre and a municipal *parque florestal*, not to mention a useful range of accommodation nearby, and a couple of adventure-sports outfits that can arrange kayaking or rafting (around €75 a day). Lording it over the town is **Monte Farinha** (996m), which from a distance looks like a perfect child's drawing of a mountain; it's an eleven-kilometre winding drive up to the chapel at the top (follow signs to "N.S Graça" off the N312 Cerva road), and there's also a panoramic café. If you're really keen you can walk, on a well-signposted fourteen-kilometre (5hr) circuit from town, which cuts up through the road switchbacks.

ARRIVAL AND INFORMATION   MONDIM DE BASTO

By bus There are three buses a day from Vila Real (not Sun) to Mondim. To get to Amarante, you'll need to change at Fermil, 6km to the northwest, which also has connections to Guimarães and Braga. It's a short walk from the bus station to the public gardens.

Information The Parque Natural do Alvão information office is at Lugar do Barrio, 800m down the Celorico road by the Barrio primary school (Mon–Fri 9am–12.30pm & 2–5.30pm; ☎ 255 381 209). The turismo is on Praça do Município (Mon–Fri 9am–1pm & 2–5pm, Sat 10am–1pm & 2–5pm, Sun 10am–1pm; ☎ 255 389 370, ⓦ cm -mondimdebasto.pt).

ACCOMMODATION AND EATING

Accommodation in town is none too inspiring, particularly the two very cheapest places on the main avenue near the GALP petrol station. Manor houses out of town are the better choices. Mondim has several chips-with-everything restaurants, plus a supermarket, a grocer's shop, chemist and other services.

Casa do Campo Molares, 7km west of Mondim, just south of Fermil (Celorico de Basto road) ☎ 255 361 231, ⓦ casadocampo.pt. Extremely elegant manor-house accommodation, offering gorgeous B&B rooms with a touch of style, plus splendid gardens and a pool with mountain views. A couple of garden apartments have a bit more space (though they aren't self-catering), and there are also two large suites in the main house (€110). Give them some

---

THE TERRAS DE BASTO

Mondim de Basto is one of three towns with the same suffix: the others are Celorico de Basto, just to the southwest, and the larger Cabeceiras de Basto, 25km north (in the Minho). Together, the three Basto towns and their districts form the **Terras de Basto**, a region whose name comes from a number of life-sized Celtic warrior statues – beautifully incised with Celtic emblems on the torso and a shield on the belly – which were originally laid on warriors' graves. *Eu basto* ("I suffice") was their credo, expressing a willingness to face the enemy (Romans for the most part) single-handed.

notice and they can usually arrange dinner. **€90**

★ **Quinta do Fundo** Vilar de Viando, 2km south of Mondim (Vila Real road) ☎ 255 381 291, ⊛ quintado fundo.com. This relaxing first choice is set amid acres of *vinho verde* vines. It's full of family furniture and although the five rooms and two larger suites (€75) are a bit on the elderly side, it's a gorgeous spot with a pool, gardens and tennis court. Dinner (€30) is available on request. **€50**

Mirandela

It's around 65km from Vila Real to **MIRANDELA**, a neat provincial town on the Tua River that's been making an improbable name for itself in recent years as one of the world's jet-ski hotspots, hosting national and European championships. Otherwise, the town's most striking feature is its pedestrianized Roman bridge, stretching a good 200m across seventeen arches. There are pleasant riverside gardens and lawns, and – up the hill – a (very) small old town with a few surviving Baroque townhouses. There's also a proper, old-fashioned market building (walk up pedestrianized Rua da República; the market's best on Thursdays), while grocery stores and delis throughout town sell Mirandela's famed olive oil and olives (much of it *biológico*, or organically produced). The town is also known for its *alheira* sausages, draped across shop windows and served in every restaurant.

ARRIVAL AND INFORMATION   MIRANDELA

By bus Buses all stop on Rua Dom Afonso III, outside the old train station – to reach the town centre, turn right, then right again for the river and the Roman bridge, from where the road veers into the main Rua da República. Destinations Bragança (7–11 daily; 1hr); Chaves (Mon–Fri 3 daily; 2hr); Miranda (2 daily; 2hr–2hr 30min); Vila Flôr (4 daily; 40min); and Vila Real (14–22 daily; 1hr 10min).

Information Turismo, Rua Dom Afonso III, next to the old train station (June–Sept daily 10am–4pm; Oct–May Mon–Fri 9am–5.30pm, Sat & Sun 10am–4pm; ☎ 278 203 143, ⊛ cm-mirandela.pt).

ACCOMMODATION AND EATING

Dom Dinis Av Nossa Senhora do Amparo ☎ 278 260 100, ⊛ hoteldomdinis.com. A couple of places in town offer cheap rooms, but this large, riverside three-star hotel boasts the only views worth having (a front-facing room with balcony is a must), as well as an outdoor pool. The hotel's on the other side of the river from the old town, across the new bridge (which is adjacent to the old one). **€75**

★ **Flor de Sal** Parque Dr José Gama, across the bridge road from the Dom Dinis ☎ 278 203 063, ⊛ flordesal restaurante.com. A sleek, chic, contemporary Portuguese restaurant, with a riverside lounge-bar and deck that's just the place to while away an afternoon. The food's extremely good – fixed-price lunch from €15, otherwise from €40 a head – and it's a real surprise to find such a place in an out-of-the-way town like Mirandela. Restaurant daily 12.30–3.30pm & 7.30–11pm; bar daily 10am–2am.

Quinta Entre Rios Chelas, 3km northwest of town, N213 (follow the signs) ☎ 278 263 160, ⊛ quinta entrerios.pt.vu. The most agreeable overnight option where a dozen B&B rooms are located on an organic olive-oil estate, complete with pool and tennis court. **€75**

Vila Flôr and around

VILA FLÔR – the Town of Flowers – is 24km south of Mirandela and worth a quick stop if you're on your way into deep eastern Trás-os-Montes. It was given its name in the thirteenth century by Dom Dinis who, on his way to meet Isabel of Aragon, was clearly in a romantic frame of mind. Flowers are not so evident today, though handsome tree-lined squares and a striking twin-towered tiled church provide focus for a stroll. There's also a rather eccentric municipal museum, the **Museu Municipal de Berta Cabral** (not always open), and a few cafés in the old-town streets. Weekday buses call here on the run between Torre de Moncorvo and Mirandela, but you'd hardly want to stay the night in town – and in any case you need a car to see the more enticing surroundings, which primarily means the ruins of Ansiães, a twenty-minute drive southwest.

Castelo de Ansiães

The ruins are 5km south of the town of Carrazeda de Ansiães; you'll see the brown "Castelo" signs as you pass through the centre • Always open • Free • ⓦ castelodeansiaes.com

Twenty-one kilometres southwest of Vila Flôr – follow signs initially for Carrazeda de Ansiães – lie the intriguing ruins of an abandoned, medieval walled town. It's barely recognizable as such until you're almost upon it, winding up the 900m-high hillside to a craggy outcrop signposted simply as **Castelo de Ansiães**. You park by the outer gateway and make your way up a stone track, flanked by bramble-covered ruins, to a twelfth-century chapel with a carved Romanesque doorway. Beyond is the main gate and a complete circuit of partially ruined walls, which provides a breezy walk with beautiful views – otherwise, all that remains are fallen boulders and broken stones. It's hard to believe that five different kings, over a period of 500 years, made this their strategic base in the north – the last inhabitants of old Ansiães left in the mid-eighteenth century, when the nearby new town of Carrazeda de Ansiães was established.

7

Torre de Moncorvo

The 26-kilometre route southeast from Vila Flôr to **TORRE DE MONCORVO** is a tremendous drive, taking you into the steep mountains round the Douro valley. A network of narrow medieval shopping streets, granite-block walls and handsome mansions makes the small town a pleasant place to stop off for a few hours, with everything helpfully signposted, starting with the imposing sixteenth-century **Igreja Matriz** – the largest church in Trás-os-Montes, which took a century to build. A terrace here looks out over the distant hills, while following signs across the main square into the "*nucléo medieval*" takes you to the surviving town gate, the **Porta da Vila**. Aside from a couple of local museums, that, basically, is your lot, except for the annual burst of enthusiasm for the region's **almond trees**, the blossoming of which draws crowds of visitors in early spring. The sugared nuts are available in any number of local groceries and "*produto regionais*" shops, along with Moncorvo's famed cherries and lots of good Douro wines.

ARRIVAL AND DEPARTURE

TORRE DE MONCORVO

By bus The bus station is out on the main road, the N220. Destinations Freixo de Espada à Cinta (Mon–Fri 3 daily; 1hr); Miranda do Douro (2 daily; 1hr 45min); Mogodouro (2 daily; 1hr); Vila Nova de Foz Côa (3 daily; 35–40min); and Vila Real (1 daily; 2hr 5min).

By car Parking is mostly metered in town, though there's a free car park below the flyover on the way up into the old centre.

INFORMATION AND ACTIVITIES

Information The turismo is hidden away in the old centre (follow the signs) behind the Câmara Municipal, at Trav Campos Monteiro 21 (daily 9am–12.30pm & 2–5.30pm; ☏ 279 252 289, ⓦ cm-moncorvo.pt).

Tours CP, the Portuguese rail operator, runs almond blossom train-and-coach excursions here every spring (details on ⓦ cp.pt; click on "Outings"). Trains from Porto or Peso da Régua run to Pocinho, from where a tour bus follows a circuit through the hills, with stopoffs for views, walks and lunch, including a visit to Torre de Moncorvo (adults €35, bookings essential).

> ### AS FAR AS THE EYE CAN SEE
>
> The Trás-os-Montes **almond trees** are explained in the legend of a Moorish prince who married a northern-European princess. Though happy in summer, she grew sad and wistful in winter, and ached for the snow-clad hills of her homeland. The prince hurried to the Algarve, from where he brought back the almond trees, so that from then on, every February when the trees blossomed, the princess beheld white as far as the eye could see.

ACCOMMODATION

Campos Monteiro Rua Visconde de Vila Maior 55 ☎ 279 254 055. A quirky, creaky period-piece of a townhouse with reasonable budget rooms and its own parking around the back. It's fairly easy to find, signposted up the street off the main square. **€50**.

Casa de Santa Cruz Rua Cimo do Lugar, Felgar, 13km east of Torre de Moncorvo, off the N220 (Freixo de Espada road) ☎ 279 928 060, ⓦ casadesantacruz.com. Make the drive out to the quiet village of Felgar for a night in an imaginatively restored eighteenth-century manor house, located in a corner of the village square. It has its own pool,

and meals are available (€20) if you reserve ahead. **€85**

★ **Quinta das Aveleiras** Rua das Aveleiras, just out of Torre de Moncorvo on the Pocinho road ☎ 279 252 285, ⓦ quintadasaveleiras.pt. Relax in the surroundings of a lovely wine and olive estate, where classy self-catering accommodation is offered by the night in four restored buildings, sleeping two to six people (up to €220 a night). Pick of the bunch is the amazing circular *pombal* (pigeon house), which makes a unique and romantic bolt-hole for two – breakfast is provided in each property. And there's a pool, tennis court and bikes available. **€90**

EATING AND DRINKING

O Artur Carviçais, 16km east of Torre de Moncorvo, N220 (Freixo de Espada road) ☎ 279 098 000. Persevere with the drive for this in-the-know spot – and expect good-value meals served in a cheery roadhouse of red-checked tablecloths and stripped pine (mains from around €8). There are also some simple rooms above the restaurant, but dowdy Carviçais

is no place to spend the night. Tues–Sun noon–10.30pm.

O Lagar Rua do Hospital Velho 16, down the side of the Igreja Matriz ☎ 279 252 828. The best regional food in town – you'll eat well in an old, granite-walled olive-oil warehouse, and pay €20 if you stick to the excellent fruity table-wine. Mon–Sat noon–2.30pm & 7–10pm, Sun noon–2.30pm.

Freixo de Espada à Cinta

The southernmost town in Trás-os-Montes is **FREIXO DE ESPADA À CINTA**, around 40km southeast of Torre de Moncorvo. The mouthful of a name translates as "ash-tree of the sword of the belt" and supposedly refers to Dom Dinis hacking at a nearby tree as he announced the founding of the town. Hidden in the folds of the undulating Douro mountains, the town was once considered so remote that prisoners who had been granted an amnesty were allowed to settle here in obscurity. It doesn't feel quite so isolated any more, with a new town straddling one side of the main through-road (N221), and a small, surviving old town on the other, dominated by a surprisingly grand **Igreja Matriz** with a *retábulo* of paintings attributed to Viseu artist Grão Vasco. There's also a mighty keep, which affords great views from its bell tower, while beneath lies the town's spectacularly sited cemetery. Follow the signs ("*praia fluvial*") 4km east out of town, down a series of hairpin bends on the banks of the Rio Douro, and you'll end up at the local river beach and swimming spot.

ARRIVAL AND INFORMATION   FREIXO DE ESPADA À CINTA

By bus There are daily but infrequent weekday buses from Miranda do Douro, Torre de Moncorvo and Mogadouro, so you risk spending a lot longer here than Freixo really warrants (say an hour and a cup of coffee).

By car The drive here is marvellous, particularly the approach north from Barca d'Alva on the N221 (20km),

part of the Parque Natural do Douro Internacional, which follows a beautiful stretch of the Douro River, with viewpoints at strategic intervals.

Information Parque Natural do Douro Internacional regional office, Largo do Outeiro, in the modern town centre (Mon–Fri 9am–12.30pm & 2–5.30pm; ☎ 279 658 130).

ACCOMMODATION AND EATING

Cinta d'Ouro Av Guerra Junqueiro (the main through-road), opposite the market and municipal auditorium ☎ 279 652 550, ⓦ cintadouro.com. A rather fine restaurant above a bar and shop selling wines and *produtos regionais*. There's good *bacalhau* among other dishes, all at around the €9–10 mark, and cheap rooms too if you need them. Restaurant daily noon–2.30pm & 7–10.30pm. **€40**

Quinta do Salgueiro 3km north of Freixo on the Mogadouro road (N221) ☎ 279 652 007, ⓦ quintado salgueiro.com. A wine and olive estate with traditionally furnished B&B rooms and suites (up to €100). There's a rather nice pool in landscaped gardens, and some big views across the local hills and vineyards. **€80**

Parque Natural do Douro Internacional

The **Parque Natural do Douro Internacional** covers a long, thin 120-kilometre stretch of the Rio Douro as it flows along the border between Portugal and Spain. On the Portuguese side, the park runs from Miranda do Douro in the north, past Mogadouro and Freixo de Espada à Cinta to Barca d'Alva, the latter the point at which the Rio Douro officially enters Portuguese territory; there's also a southern section that encompasses a stretch of the Rio Águeda, further south in Beira Alta (near Figueira de Castelo Rodrigo). The park is extremely dramatic in parts, known for its sheer canyon walls and Mediterranean microclimate, and this combination of mild winters and its isolation from large human populations has led to the preservation of a rich variety of **animal species**, including a few surviving wolves and wild cats, as well as boar, otters, bats and amphibians. It is also home to over 170 **bird species**, including rare peregrine falcons, golden eagles, black storks and, in summer, Europe's largest concentration of Egyptian vultures.

The main problem for visitors is getting any sense of the park as a whole, since it's so elongated and necessarily remote from anywhere you're likely to be spending much time; you'll see the periodic brown park signs as you drive between Beira Alta and Bragança, but it's not immediately clear what there is to see or do. To make some sense of it, it's best to visit a park office and buy the official map. Armed with this, you can at least drive to the various spectacular viewing areas, to gaze down from the canyon-like cliffs into the Douro far below – that of **Penedo Dourão** is between Barca d'Alva and Freixo; there's another superb vantage-point at **Lagoaça**, 25km from Mogadouro; while close to Miranda do Douro is the magnificent **São João das Arribas** (see p.364). There's also a brown-signposted "Rota dos Castros" **driving route**, along minor roads linking a series of ancient fortified border posts.

INFORMATION AND ACTIVITIES

Information There are park information offices, in the small towns of Mogadouro, Miranda do Douro, Freixo de Espada à Cinta and Figueira de Castelo Rodrigo, but don't expect English to be spoken. For official information (in Portuguese), check ⓦ icnf.pt.

Hiking A number of waymarked hiking circuits thread through the park, but the route marks are not always properly maintained, and it can be difficult to get hold of the route leaflets, even in the park offices. Undoubtedly the best walk is the circular one from Miranda do Douro

(see p.364), which starts and finishes right in town.

Tours and activities Local adventure-tour operators, such as Torre de Moncorvo-based Sabor, Douro e Aventura (ⓦ sabordouro.com), offer activities including kakaying on the Douro (€30) and guided day-walks into the park (€20), though they are more geared to groups than individuals. In the end, your best bet might be a boat trip on the Douro itself – there are daily departures from Miranda do Douro (see p.365) through some of the most dramatic canyon scenery in the park.

Mogadouro

The old frontier fortress of **MOGADOURO** lies on the fringes of the Parque Natural do Douro Internacional. With the winding journey here from north or south half the attraction, it's hard to escape the impression of a town caught between past and present, ready to embrace tourism but not quite sure what it has to offer. Its main sight is the restored **keep** of a twelfth-century castle, set on a hill with extensive views over a patchwork of tilled fields, traditional pigeon houses and an imposing grain elevator – as well as the municipal swimming pool and stadium and a spreading line of suburban development.

ARRIVAL AND INFORMATION   MOGADOURO

By bus Buses stop in the main square, and services are usually frequent enough not to strand you in Mogadouro. Destinations Bragança (Mon–Fri 1–2 daily; 1hr 30min); Freixo de Espada à Cinta (Mon–Fri 3 daily; 1hr 15min);

Miranda do Douro (3 daily; 50min); Torre de Moncorvo (2 daily; 1hr); and Vila Real (Mon–Fri 3 daily, Sat & Sun 2 daily; 2hr 30min).
By car Mogadouro is 47km from Miranda do Douro and

58km from Torre de Moncorvo, both better overnight stops. In the centre of town is the wide, flower-bedded Largo Trindade Coelho, near which there's plenty of parking; the castle tower is visible from here, signposted straight up Rua Santa Marinha.

Information There's a turismo on the main square, Largo Trindade Coelho, which you don't need, and an information office for the Parque Natural do Douro Internacional, Rua Santa Marinha 4 (Mon–Fri 9am–12.30pm & 2–5.30pm; ☎ 279 340 030), which you might.

ACCOMMODATION AND EATING

Gabriela Sendim, 27km northeast of Mogadouro, N221 ☎ 273 739 180. Halfway to Miranda, there's the locally famed *Gabriela*, a traditional restaurant-with-rooms where a massive Mirandês steak (*posta*) is the order of the day (meals from around €15). Restaurant daily noon–3pm & 7–10pm. €50

Trindade Coelho Largo Trindade Coelho ☎ 279 340 010, ⓦ hoteltrindadecoelho.com. The functional, three-star hotel on the Largo really doesn't spring any surprises, but it would do for the night, The rooms and decor are in strict Portuguese country style, ie, unexciting and rather dated. €60

Miranda do Douro and around

7

Finally, at **MIRANDA DO DOURO**, you arrive at an eastern Trás-os-Montes town with a certain presence. In part, this is due to its location – across from Spain, and set above a magnificent gorge of the Rio Douro – but there's also history and tradition here in abundance. The border town was always at the forefront of fights with the Spanish, and was fortified to the gills in earlier times – until an apocalyptic explosion in 1762 destroyed its castle, killed hundreds and sent Miranda into a gentle decline. After the explosion, Miranda remained a neglected outpost for two centuries – sufficiently remote for a distinct language, **Mirandês**, to flourish. It is still spoken today and even taught in schools: local street and town signs are usually in both Portuguese and the Mirandês equivalent.

Modern Miranda might be small – with just a couple of thousand inhabitants – but it still retains the status of a city and boasts an outsized sixteenth-century cathedral and a charming old-town area from its glory days. What changed the character of Miranda completely, however, was the building in 1955 of the huge **Barragem de Miranda**, just below town. With the dam wall and border just a couple of kilometres away, there's a constant stream of Spanish tourists, who come to view the staggering gorge scenery, take a river trip and wander briefly around town. Stay the night, and you can also see a bit more of the Douro river gorge by driving out to the magnificent local viewing point – or even hiking there on one of the region's finest one-day walks.

Sé and around

The sixteenth-century cathedral, the **Sé**, overlooks Miranda's whitewashed townhouses and the Douro far below. In the eighteenth century, the see was transferred to Bragança and the adjacent Episcopal Palace allowed to fall into disrepair – today, the landscaped ruins form a handsome garden behind the cathedral, encircled by sections of the medieval walls. The **castle** remains, too, have been shored up and prettified, while the old streets and squares around are laid with clacking cobbles and lined with late-medieval facades. Below the castle on the other side of town, Miranda's other river, the tamer **Rio Fresno**, has also been dammed – it's now a landscaped park of whooshing fountains, winding paths and a waterside café.

Museu da Terra de Miranda

Praça Dom João III • June–Sept Tues 2–6pm, Wed–Sun 9.30am–12.30pm & 2–6pm; Oct–May Tues 2–5.30pm, Wed–Sun 9.30am–12.30pm & 2–5.30pm • €2 • ☎ 273 431 164

In the town-hall square near the cathedral, the **Museu da Terra de Miranda** is the repository of the region's stories and traditions, which sounds dull and worthy until

---

BAGPIPES AND STICK MEN

Trás-os-Montes is the heartland of the Portuguese **gaita-de-foles** (bagpipes), the main melody instrument of Trás-os-Montes traditional music. It's similar to the Scottish Highland war-pipe in shape but closest to the *gaitas* of Spanish Galicia and Asturias, all of which are drawn from the Moorish tradition (*ghaita* being the Moroccan word for a pipe). The old tradition of the pipes survives principally in Miranda do Douro, kept alive by Mirandês *gaiteiros* who play regularly for the **Pauliteiros**, local men in traditional outfits who prance around clattering wooden sticks together rhythmically (rather like an English morris dance). Like many such manifestations in the north (the stone pigs, the bonfire celebrations, the masked revels), it probably dates back to Celtic times. It's a performance which is more often seen at large nationwide festivals than in their home town, though the *Pauliteiros* make a special appearance every year during the Santa Bárbara *festa* (starts the Sunday following August 15). At this time you will also hear the local folk music, a tradition maintained at the town's *Casa da Música Mirandês* (music institute), by the ruined castle on Largo do Castelo.

7

you see the exhibits – from children's balloons made out of sheep's stomachs to fearsome-looking pagan masks worn by young men during local festivities. This is also the place to find out more about the town's stick dancers, known as the *Pauliteiros* (see above), whose performances enliven many a traditional festival.

Barragem de Miranda

Down the vertiginous hill below town lies the **Barragem de Miranda** hydroelectric dam and border – the road runs over the dam wall into Spain and on towards Zamora. It's one of the largest hydroelectric dams in the country and marks the point at which the Portuguese Rio Douro transforms itself into the Spanish Rio Duero. Boat trips through the gorge (see p.365) are an obvious attraction and they run year-round.

São João das Arribas gorge

The circular walk (20km; 6hr) from Miranda to the gorge at **São João das Arribas** is the best use of a spare day, though you can also drive there (partly on dirt roads, in good condition) for a picnic. The walk is waymarked with red and yellow paint stripes, and though many are faded they are still all (mostly) visible, making route-finding fairly straightforward. There is also a leaflet available in the park office showing the route; be prepared for barking dogs at farms all the way round.

The route starts by the turismo, where you follow the brown "Castros de Vale de Águia e de Aldeia Nova" sign – the road through the shops and buildings soon turns to a dirt track and the waymarks begin. At Castro de Vale de Águia (2.5km) are the first amazing views over a double bend in the river; at the rustic-in-the-extreme hamlet of Vale de Águia (4.5km) follow the "Aldeia Nova" sign along a tarmac road to Aldeia Nova (6.5km), where there's a bar (probably closed) and a sign for "São João das Arribas" and "Castro". Down this track, at the small chapel of **São João das Arribas** (8km), are simply extraordinary views of the Douro gorge, plus remains of the Iron Age, later Roman, *castro*. It's a great place for a picnic.

The no-risk return is to go back the way you came, though the actual waymarked route runs west through Pena Branca (12km) and then south to the Fresno River where you cross the low bridge (16km) and then head up past farms until you crest a hill and see Miranda (20km) ahead.

ARRIVAL AND DEPARTURE
MIRANDA DO DOURO

By bus Buses stop by the traffic circle, opposite the fire station.

Destinations Bragança (Mon–Fri 2 daily; 1hr 30min–2hr 15min); Freixo de Espada à Cinta (Mon–Fri 1 daily; 2hr);

Mirandela (2 daily; 2hr–2hr 30min); Mogadouro (3 daily; 50min); and Torre de Moncorvo (2 daily; 1hr 45min).

By car The town is split into old and new by a landscaped traffic circle, high above the river. There's lots of free parking all around here, and it's just a couple of hundred metres' walk up the avenue and through the walls into the old town.

INFORMATION AND ACTIVITIES

Information The turismo is on the main traffic circle (Mon–Sat 9am–12.30pm & 2–5.30pm; ☎ 273 430 025, ⓦ cm-mdouro.pt). The Parque Natural do Douro Internacional information office, on Rua do Convento (Mon–Fri 9am–12.30pm & 2–5.30pm; ☎ 273 431 457), is in the old town, at the back of the Episcopal Palace ruins (it's not immediately obvious, but is opposite the church that has been converted into the Biblioteca Municipal).

Boat trips From the quay (*cais*) at the dam, near the municipal swimming pool, Europarques (ⓦ europarques .com) runs boat trips on the Douro through the dramatic rock gorge (all year: Mon–Fri at 4pm, Sat & Sun and daily at Easter & in Aug 11am & 4pm; 1hr 30min cruise €16).

ACCOMMODATION

Miranda boasts a sizeable range of places to stay, all bar one clustered into two or three streets in the new part of town, just off the traffic circle. They are nothing particularly special, but anything down Rua do Mercado (the street closest to the top of the gorge) commands superb views.

★ **A Morgadinha** Rua do Mercado 57 ☎ 273 438 050. The best of the guesthouses on this street, with good-value, spick-and-span en-suite rooms – open your curtains in the morning to amazing dam views, and then gawp some more from the balcony over breakfast. €40

Parador Santa Catarina Largo da Pousada ☎ 273 431 005, ⓦ hotelparadorsantacatarina.pt. Right on the edge of the modern development outside the old town, with comfortable rooms offering dizzying views into the gorge – as do the bar and upmarket restaurant. €110

Santa Cruz Rua Abade Baçal 61 ☎ 273 431 374. The only place to stay in the old town, with an entrance on the square by the castle ruins. It's been done up over the years, and the rooms are modern if unexceptional, though some are definitely on the musty side. €50

EATING AND DRINKING

Locals maintain that Miranda is home to some of Portugal's most tender meat, in the form of *posta à Mirandesa*, basically a huge, thick, melt-in-the-mouth steak. You can sample it at just about every restaurant in town, although there's the usual local debate as to which place serves the best. The liveliest café-bar is the one in the Episcopal Palace gardens, open till the small hours in summer and with outdoor tables under the trees.

Capa d'Honras Trav do Castelo 1 ☎ 273 432 699. Old-town restaurant (just through the walls, on the right) that takes the flowing medieval capes traditionally worn during important events as its theme. As for the food, it's aimed at well-heeled tourists – meat grills and *posta* and no fewer than a dozen versions of *bacalhau*, with most dishes costing €10–12. Daily noon–3pm & 7–10.30pm.

★ **O Mirandês** Rua Dom Dinis 7 ☎ 273 431 418. This gets our vote for prime *posta à Mirandesa*, prepared by cooks beavering away in full view of the dining room, which looks out over the Fresno River. There's a straightforward menu of grills, meat and fish, and €20 gets you the works. Find it just off the traffic circle, below the old town avenue (the road is signposted "Universidade"). June–Sept daily noon–3pm & 7–10.30pm; Oct–May Mon–Sat noon–3pm & 7–10.30pm.

O Moinho Rua do Mercado 47 ☎ 273 431 116, ⓦ moinhomirandadodouro.com. All the Rua do Mercado restaurants are cavernous dining rooms with big windows onto the gorge, and with menus aimed squarely at Spanish day-trippers. This is no different, but it does also serve pizza and pasta and is remarkably good value, since you can easily eat for €10 or €12. Daily noon–3pm & 7–10pm.

Bragança

BRAGANÇA is the fascinating historic capital of Trás-os-Montes, settled since the very earliest times but acquiring a regional, and later national, importance from the twelfth century onwards. It's this medieval period that gave Bragança its distinctive hillside profile of a beautifully preserved old town and soaring castle keep, sitting inside a complete circuit of forbidding granite walls. Known as the Cidadela, or "citadel", it's the embodiment of the town's dynastic history under the sway of the dukes of Bragança – the extended family of Portuguese kings and emperors who ruled from 1640 (following independence from Spain) until the advent of the Republic in 1910.

It used to take an age to reach Bragança (and still does on the mountain road, the N103, from Chaves), but the fast IP4 highway from Vila Real easily puts the modern city on any northern Portuguese itinerary, while tourists from across the border in Spain are common. It's a pleasant place, despite the suburban eruption all around, and while the **citadel**, main **museum** and **riverside gardens** provide the most compelling reasons for a visit, the outlying Parque Natural de Montesinho is an additional draw. It's certainly worth staying a night or two, especially to experience early evening in the Cidadela, when the tourists have gone for the day and peace returns to the ancient streets.

Cidadela

The walled **Cidadela** is the obvious place to begin, and lies a fifteen-minute walk up the hill from the modern city centre. The hill above Bragança has been settled in one form or another since prehistoric times; the Romans probably had a small fortification here; and the current walled town and castle have stood since at least the twelfth century and formed the strategic base of the early Bragança dynasty.

Domus Municipalis

Walk up through the main gate of the Cidadela, and at the very top of the cobbled street stands the curious, pentagonal fifteenth-century council chamber known as the **Domus Municipalis**. Its meetings – for solving land disputes and the like – took place on the arcaded first floor; below was a cistern. Next to the Domus, the **Igreja de Santa Maria** features a fine painted ceiling, while opposite, the *Vila Café* (closed Mon) provides an outdoor terrace with courtyard views.

Torre de Menagem

Museu Militar Tues–Sun 9am–noon & 2–5pm • €1.50, free on Fri morning • ☎ 273 322 378

Dominating the walled citadel is the restored castle keep, the **Torre de Menagem**, which now houses a missable **Museu Militar**, although it's worth paying the entrance fee for the fine views from the top. At night, the whole fortification is floodlit and imposes itself even more dramatically upon the entire city. Round the other side of the keep, meanwhile, you'll find an ancient granite pig (see p.368) that forms part of a rather odd **pelourinho** (stone pillory).

Museu Ibérico da Máscara e do Traje

Rua Dom Fernando O Bravo 24–26 • June–Sept Tues–Sun 9am–1pm & 3–6pm; Oct–May Tues–Sun 9am–12.30pm & 2–5.30pm • €1 • ☎ 273 381 008, ⓦ museudamascara.cm-braganca.pt

There are more reminders of the pagan ways of the wild north in the **Museu Ibérico da Máscara e do Traje**, a few steps down the hill from the keep, which highlights the extraordinary ritual masks and ribboned costumes habitually seen in winter festivals on both sides of the border (kids get to crayon their own devil masks). This is a town, for example, where on Ash Wednesday (usually late February or early March) people dressed

---

BRAGANÇA'S FESTIVALS

Bragança's major festivals include the **Festa de Nossa Senhora das Graças** (Aug 12–22), featuring lots of cultural events and traditional music, and the **Romaria de São Bartolomeu** (Aug 24), an annual religious celebration involving solemn processions and rather wilder concerts and night-time festivities. The **Feira das Cantarinhas** (May 2 & 3) is a crafts fair dedicated to the clay water jug (*cantarinha*) which was once used to store the gifts given to a bride on her wedding day.

7

BRAGANÇA

N

Parque Natural de Montesinho HQ

São Francisco

Torre de Menagem (Museu Militar)

Santa Maria

CIDADELA

Domus Municipalis

São Bento

Museu Ibérico da Máscara e do Traje

Museu do Abade de Baçal

São Vicente

Misericórdia

Centro Arte Contemporânea

Sé

Cemetery

Praça Camões

Jardim António José Almeida

Cultural Centre

Rio Fervença

Bragança Shopping

Teatro Municipal

Bus Station

■ **ACCOMMODATION**
Arco da Velha   3
Pousada de Juventude   2
Pousada de São Bartolomeu   4
Senhora da Ribeira   1

● **RESTAURANTS AND BARS**
Lá em Casa   1
O Geadas   5
O Manel   4
Poças   3
Solar Bragançano   2

0   100
metres

PAGAN PIGS

Roughly sculpted **granite pigs** (known as *porcas* or *berrões*) are found all over northeastern Portugal and neighbouring Spain. Most date back a couple of thousand years, and their origins are obscure, though they are thought to have been Celtic fertility idols. The wild boar certainly holds sway in popular culture in these parts, so it's not hard to see where the inspiration lay in the earliest carvings. The most famous example of a *porca* is in the small town of **Murça**, off the IP4, halfway between Vila Real and Mirandela, where it sits on top of a granite plinth above a flowerbed in the town centre. Pig and town, incidentally, give their name to a ubiquitous Douro table wine, Porça de Murça (made by Real Companhia Velha), while the pig is in profile on Murça's *adega cooperativa* (wine co-op), the Caves de Murça. So there's no excuse not to drink the health of Portugal's pagan pigs.

---

as devils run around whipping penitents – the origins probably lie in an ancient fertility cult, when it was believed that Pan impregnated women simply by smacking them.

Museu do Abade de Baçal

Rua Abilio Beça 27 • Tues–Fri 10am–5pm, Sat & Sun 10am–6pm • €2, free on Sun morning • ☎ 273 331 595, ⓦ mabadebacal.com

The finest museum in town – and one of the best in the north – is the **Museu do Abade de Baçal**, housed in the handsome surroundings of an eighteenth-century former Bishop's Palace. The exhibits are beautifully presented, and range from Roman tombstones and imported lacquer boxes to aldermen's canes and weather vanes, while a series of 1930s watercolours by Alberto de Sousa depicts the northeast's unrivalled array of carved stone pillories – every village, however mean, has one, often centuries old.

Praça da Sé and around

Praça da Sé, around the cathedral, is essentially the centre of the modern town and while the cathedral itself is unexceptional, the surrounding area has been transformed almost beyond recognition in recent years. The old market was levelled to create the large square of **Praça do Camões** (part of the market facade was left *in situ*), with its shard of modern sculpture, and there's also a cultural centre and library (in a former convent), a contemporary art centre (with changing exhibitions) and landscaped town gardens.

A riverside walk

A walk down along the **Rio Fervença** is perhaps the best surprise – an ingenious network of paths, boardwalks and footbridges hug and crisscross the river as it rushes through a small gorge below town. You can follow this out under the castle walls, past olden-days reminders – chicken sheds, cabbage patches, tumbledown cottages (and one rather splendid gnome garden) – and in under ten minutes you're in open countryside.

ARRIVAL AND DEPARTURE   **BRAGANÇA**

By bus Local and long-distance buses operate out of what was once the train station, at the northern end of Avenida João da Cruz (note the benches, set on wheels on the old tracks). The various companies all post timetables at their office windows, including services across the border into Spain (Zamora and onwards).

Destinations Braga (2–6 daily; 4–5hr); Chaves (1–2 daily; 2hr 10min); Lisbon (6–11 daily; up to 7hr 30min); Miranda do Douro (Mon–Fri 1–4 daily; 1hr 30min–2hr 15min); Mirandela (7–11 daily; 1hr); Mogadouro (Mon–Fri 1–2

daily; 1hr 30min); Porto (7–20 daily; 3hr); Vila Nova de Foz Côa (1–3 daily; 1hr 45min); Vila Real (8–19 daily; 1hr 30min–2hr); and Vinhais (2–3 daily; 35min).

By car Bragança is 120km northeast of Vila Real, via Mirandela, on the fast IP4/A4, or a very winding 100km east of Chaves (N103). In Spain, the nearest big city is attractive Zamora, around 100km southeast. Driving into the city is easy; parking is a different matter, as the centre is almost all metered. For free, all-day parking, your best bet is up at the citadel.

INFORMATION

Turismo Av Cidade de Zamora (May–Sept Mon–Fri 10am–12.30pm & 2–6.30pm, Sat 9am–12.30pm & 2–5pm, Sun 9am–1pm; Oct–April Mon–Fri 9am–12.30pm & 2–5pm, Sat 10am–12.30pm; ☎ 273 381 273, ⊛ cm-braganca.pt).
Parque Natural de Montesinho HQ Rua Cónego Albano Falcão, Lote 5, Apartado 90 (Mon–Fri 9am–12.30pm & 2–5.30pm; ☎ 273 300 400, ⊛ incf.pt), located a few hundred metres down Av Cidade de Zamora, sign-posted off to the left – it's a very unassuming place, in a residential house.

ACCOMMODATION

There's a fair amount of cheap, if uninspiring, signposted central accommodation, or consider staying outside the city in one of the *turismo rural* options within the Parque Natural de Montesinho, most under half an hour's drive away. The nearest **campsite** to town, the *Parque Campismo do Inatel*, on the França road, isn't actually that good – there's better summer camping in the park at Rio de Onor (see p.374) or Cepo Verde (see p.375).

Arco da Velha Rua D. Fernao ☎ 966 787 208, ⊛ turismo braganca.com. A restored townhouse inside the *cidadela* – on your immediate right as you come through the main (west) gate – offering by-the-night self-catering accommo-dation with a homely, intimate feel. There are only a couple of rooms (sleeping up to five in total) and advance reserva-tions are essential. Parking available. **€90**

Pousada de Juventude Av 22 de Maio ☎ 273 329 231, ⊛ microsites.juventude.gov.pt/portal. Roughly 1km west of the centre, this modern hostel has a mix of accommo-dation, from smallish dorms to neat little private rooms (some suitable for families, €54) and a decent range of facili-ties, including laundry service and café-bar. Dorm beds **€13**, rooms **€32**

★ **Pousada de São Bartolomeu** Estrada do Turismo ☎ 273 331 493, ⊛ pousadas.pt. High up on the opposite side of the river, Bragança's best address is all about its castle and countryside views. Built in the late 1950s, it has a comfortable, country-house feel, rooms with wood-block floors and big balconies, plenty of exposed stone and a bar sporting a huge fireplace. There's a good regional restaurant (meals €40–50), and an inviting circular swim-ming pool. It's 1km by road from the centre – follow the signs – and you can walk down to river and town (steeply uphill on the way back) in around fifteen minutes. **€90**

Senhora da Ribeira Trav da Misericórdia ☎ 273 300 550. Follow the sign up the alley for a pleasant surprise. It doesn't look much, but inside are spotless rooms, nice and trim with matching decor, and decent bathrooms. And in the words of their brochure, "please visit Residencial Senhora da Ribeira, the best hotel in that king, at North East of the province of Trás-os-Montes. Thank You". **€45**

EATING, DRINKING AND ENTERTAINMENT

Bragança is a traditional town full of traditional restaurants; woe betide vegetarians. The municipal **market** is open daily (not Sun), although its distance from town means that central grocery stores are an easier option. Although it's a university town, there's not much in the way of **nightlife** save a couple of bars in the Cidadela and some others in an arcade five minutes' walk down Avenida Dr Francisco Sá Carneiro.

RESTAURANTS

Lá em Casa Rua Marquês de Pombal 7 ☎ 273 322 111. A convivial place, decked out in the kind of faux-rustic style so beloved of northern restaurateurs. It's the usual meat, fish and regional menu, with mains priced at €10–12. Daily noon–3pm & 7–10pm.

O Geadas Rua do Loreto ☎ 273 324 413, ⊛ geadas.net. Locals consider this the best choice for authentic regional food, from river trout to *cabrito*, with dishes ferried to your impeccably-set table by a fleet of uniformed waiters (meals around €30). It's a short way out of the centre (10min walk from the Sé, or downhill from the *pousada* and across the bridge). Mon–Sat noon–4pm & 7–11pm, Sun noon–4pm.

O Manel Rua Orobio de Castro 27, at Praça Camões ☎ 273 322 480. If you don't get your budget eats in the *Poças*, this is the other central favourite, good for no-nonsense grilled fish, steaks and pork in a telly-on upstairs dining room. Full meals from €15. Mon–Sat 12.30–3pm & 7.30–11pm.

★ **Poças** Rua Combatentes da Grande Guerra 200 ☎ 273 331 428. A reliable family-run place, in our Guide since the very first edition. It's usually popular enough to fill a couple of floors, and serves excellent-value meals (around €15, all in) – including garlicky clams, and grilled tuna – washed down with a great *vinho da casa*. There are budget rooms on the premises too. Daily noon–2.30pm & 7–10pm.

★ **Solar Bragançano** Praça da Sé 34 ☎ 274 323 875. Enjoyably old-fashioned *casa típica*, where you dine in chandelier-hung, oak-panelled rooms, or in the garden in summer. Mains start around €10, though for the regional dishes of which the restaurant is most proud – pheasant with chestnuts, say, or partridge cooked with grapes – it's more like €15 a serving. Tues–Sun noon–3pm & 7–10pm.

7

ARTS AND MUSIC

Teatro Municipal Praça Prof. Cavaleiro de Ferreira ☎ 273 302 744, ⓦ teatromunicipal.cm-braganca.pt.

Cultural anchor in town, with a good year-round music and theatre programme – there's also a cinema in the large adjacent shopping mall, Bragança Shopping.

DIRECTORY

Hospital Av Abade Baçal ☎ 273 310 800.

Pharmacy Farmácia Confiança, Av João da Cruz 76 ☎ 273 323 226.

Police PSP, Rua Dr Manuel Bento ☎ 273 303 400; GNR, Av General Humberto Delgado ☎ 273 331 864.

Post office Rua 5 de Outubro (Mon–Fri 8.30am–5.30pm, Sat 9am–12.30pm).

Taxis There's usually a fleet of taxis parked on Av João da Cruz, on the opposite side from the cafés, or call ☎ 273 322 138.

Parque Natural de Montesinho

There are still a few places in Portugal that truly feel like the middle of nowhere, and the **Parque Natural de Montesinho** is one of them. Located in the far northeast, hard up against the Spanish border, the heather-clad hills, verdant grass plains and dense oak forests look much as they have done for centuries. The park itself – lying north and west of Bragança – covers 751 square kilometres, and has a dwindling population of 8000 distributed between ninety-odd granite-built hamlets and villages, many of which have had so little mainstream contact that they retain their old Roman or Visigothic names. In many ways it's the same old story of rural abandonment, echoed by the similar desertion of many of the distinctive round pigeon houses (*pombal*, plural *pombais*), that are a feature of the region – the pigeons, it seems, like the people, prefer an easier existence in the cities rather than eking out a living in the countryside.

However, the park hasn't been entirely bypassed by modern life. Villages substantially unchanged since medieval times are connected by new roads and show the unmistakeable signs of *emigrante*-funded brick-and-concrete construction, while a long line of wind turbines snakes across the northern mountains. More positively, the local councils and park authorities are trying to promote tourism that's beneficial to the region. A flurry of brown signs points visitors towards *aldeias preservadas* (preserved villages), archeological and nature sites, picnic spots and local museums, and there's also a good network of hiking paths (see below).

WALKING IN THE PARQUE NATURAL DE MONTESINHO

There are currently a dozen waymarked **hiking trails** (*percursos pedestres*) in the natural park, mostly short (half-day, from around 8km), and well marked and maintained, though you should always expect changes and variations over time. There are free, glossy foldout brochures for each, available from the park information offices – they are in Portuguese but the route maps are useful. Boards at the starting points (usually in village centres) also show the routes; the waymarks are the usual red and yellow stripes and arrows. The walk at **Moimenta** provides a good introduction to the scenery, though if we had to pick just one route it would be that at **Montesinho**, which is a higher, more dramatic rock-and-reservoir circuit. The **Vilarinho** route is also interesting, winding through the *serra*'s characteristic heather hills and oak woods, though the route-marking is less than perfect on this – you have to be prepared to cross a river or two and not panic when you lose the waymarks at times. The park has also marked out a **two-day trail** (55km) that loops around Vilarinho and Montesinho (where you'd stay the night) – this uses red and white paint markers (which sometimes duplicate parts of other trails) but there's currently no walk brochure for this. Finally, if you were really keen to see more of the park on foot, consider staying at the *Lagosta Perdida* in Montesinho, which has prepared a series of self-guided hiking trails for guests that fan out from the village.

PARQUE NATURAL DE MONTESINHO

With just a day, and your own car, the western loop from **Vinhais** to **Moimenta** would show you some of the best scenery (and has one of the finest short walks). Contrasting villages such as **Gimonde** or fascinating **Rio de Onor** are also easily seen from Bragança, while if you plan on staying overnight in the park the no-contest winner is **Montesinho**, with its boutique guesthouse and excellent walking.

ARRIVAL AND INFORMATION   PARQUE NATURAL DE MONTESINHO

By car The two main access points for the park are Bragança and Vinhais, but public transport within the park is limited – you can only reach a very few villages by bus from Bragança, and the timetable does not allow for easy day-trips. Having your own transport opens up many more possibilities, especially in the far eastern and western sections of the park, home to countless little villages just waiting to be discovered.

Information There are park information offices in both Bragança and Vinhais, where you can pick up a free park map and walking brochures. The office in Vinhais is part of an excellent interpretation centre that's an essential visit in any case. There's official park information (in Portuguese) on ⓦicnf.pt.

ACCOMMODATION AND EATING

Accommodation is scarce, and cafés, shops and restaurants even more so – you may be better off heading another 20km or so up the França–Portelo road to the Spanish town of Puebla de Sanabria, where there are good hotels and restaurants and a better campsite than either on the Portuguese side.

Eastern park: Gimonde to Rio de Onor

There are local STUB buses from Bragança bus station to Gimonde and up to Rio de Onor via Varge. In neither case are you going to be able to make much of a day-trip, because of inconvenient departure times, but as there's good accommodation, a restaurant and a waymarked walk in Gimonde, and a summer campsite in Rio de Onor, an overnight stay might be the answer.

Gimonde and Varge

GIMONDE, 5km east of Bragança, is a collection of mostly traditional houses where the rivers Onor, Sabor and Igrejas all meet near a Romanesque bridge. Heading back towards Bragança there's a signposted turn for Rio de Onor, which leads you first through **VARGE**, where there are more ancient houses and a decent café-restaurant by the bridge. Beyond Varge is a bleak landscape of moorland, set against wild mountains that are snow-topped even in May.

Rio de Onor and around

Postcard-pretty **RIO DE ONOR**, on the Spanish border, is 25km north of Bragança, a half-hour drive though longer on the bus. Curiously, there are twin settlements here – one in Spain (called Riohonor de Castilla) and one in Portugal – but two stones marked with an "E" and "P" respectively, and a change from cobbles on the Portuguese side to tarmac on the Spanish, are all that have delineated the frontier for years. Until recently, the locals even mostly spoke a hybrid dialect known as *Rionorês*. The twin villages are sited in a lush valley on either side of the Rio Onor: schist-built houses with wooden balconies flank skinny alleyways, though some of the houses have been renovated, and there's a new bridge and parking area. Facilities are limited to an old **bar** in the Portuguese "half" of the village – complete with animal heads, antique keys and walking sticks – and a **shop** (signposted "Tienda"), down to the right on the Spanish side.

If you can get someone to point out the track you can walk over the hills on the old route to **Guadramil** (7km) and back, for a look at an even more decrepit village. There's also a new road, which provides a diverting circuit for drivers, back to Gimonde (30km), via Guadramil, Deilão and São Julião de Palácios.

⁎ TORRE DE MENAGEM, CHAVES (P.378) >

ACCOMMODATION AND EATING   EASTERN PARK

GIMONDE
Restaurante Típico Dom Roberto ☎ 273 302 510, ⓦ amontesinho.pt. Gimonde village has become something of a personal fiefdom of the family who run the restaurant by the bridge, with its cosy bar and rustic dining room (regional dishes from around €10, cheaper lunch available). Not only do they sell their own smoked sausages and other local produce, but they also have self-catering accommodation in half a dozen restored properties around the village, ranging from the old teacher's house to the manorial *Quinta das Covas*. An information office and

shop by the restaurant can show you the options; prices are room only (and €10 cheaper outside peak summer months), though breakfast is available. Restaurant open daily noon–11pm. €55

RIO DE ONOR
Parque de Campismo de Rio de Onor ☎ 273 927 036. There's a tree-shaded campsite – theoretically open April–Sept – at the entrance to the village on the Bragança side. Facilities are limited but it does have a café. Pitch €4, plus €4 per adult

Central park: França, Montesinho and around

The main touristed route in the park is the central spine north of Bragança, up to **França**, Portelo and then on to Puebla de Sanabria in Spain, with a side turning for **Montesinho**. The easy drive from Spain, and proximity to Bragança, mean the villages seem to have a little more about them than further east or west, and restored houses and riverside picnic areas are the result. STUB buses ply the route, and will get you to Montesinho if you want to stay the night.

França

Ten kilometres north of Bragança, unassuming **FRANÇA** is locally famous for its chestnuts and *chouriço*, while the village still has a number of tumbledown streets which remain rooted in the distant past. You can potter about by the **Rio Sabor** here quite happily, and a good track (left, off the main road, after the bridge) follows the course of the river for some way. There's a small café-bar in the village by the bridge, and horseriding and trekking with the Centro Hípico de França (ⓦ centrohipicofranca .com; €12 for a 30min trek).

Montesinho

Flanked by wind-whipped pine plantations and dramatic granite outcrops, the hardy village of **MONTESINHO** packs centuries of history into its manure-mottled streets. Chickens cluck behind wire in carefully tended allotments, while winter wood lies stacked up against solid slate-roofed houses, many of which have been handsomely restored. There's local honey on sale, and an artisan or two at work, but it's still hardly what you'd call touristy. It is the end of the line as far as the road is concerned (roughly 8km northwest of França), but the walking around here is magnificent, with a particularly good marked circular trail (8km; 3hr) running up to the mountain-ringed, turbine-flanked **Barragem da Serra Serrada**.

ACCOMMODATION AND EATING   MONTESINHO

There's plenty of rustically restored self-catering accommodation in the village (busy in July & Aug); you can also ask about rooms at the *Café Montesinho*, or at the other **café** in the *Casa do Povo* (parish rooms), by the water fountain, where they'll serve you a beer or a fearsomely murky shot of *licor Giesta*, which is home-made *aguardente* mixed with honey.

★ **Lagosta Perdida** ☎ 273 919 031, ⓦ lagosta perdida.com. Flagship accommodation is this boutique restoration of an old granite house in the middle of the village, run by a convivial Dutch–English couple. At the "Lost Lobster" chestnut-wood beams, polished floors and exposed stone set the tone for half-a-dozen agreeable guest rooms and enchanting public areas, including an

amazing central space with glass roof. There's ecofriendly solar- and olive-stone-fired power and a heated outdoor pool, while meals are also contemporary in style, using locally sourced ingredients. Dinner is €15 a head; room rates drop to €95 between Oct and April. They also offer horseriding at their riding centre in França (see above). €125

Western park

For the western park, access is easiest from the town of Vinhais, 31km west of Bragança. There's no useful public transport, so a car is essential, but you'll be able to see the best of the local scenery and dramatically sited villages in a single day, combining driving and some walking.

Moimenta

Leave Vinhais on the Spain (Espanha) road, through Rio de Fornos. It's 23km, a quick half an hour on a good road, through increasingly dramatic countryside, before arriving at tranquil **MOIMENTA**. There are new villas on the road above, but in the heart of the village Moimenta unfolds its charms slowly – filled with old stone cottages and rows of sagging wooden houses perched precariously atop granite pillars. The **circular walk** from here (8km; 2–3hr) – look for the route marker on the top road, by the green park information board – winds up to a viewpoint before taking in two bridges on the babbling Rio Tuela, the second a gorgeous medieval span with ancient stone-cobbled path leading all the way back up to the village. There's a very small shop in Moimenta, with an occasionally open tavern next door, and a café on the road above the village – you'll barely be able to get so much as a bag of crisps in any of them, though you might muster the fixings of a picnic in the shop. (Don't count on it: when asked where the nearest place to eat is, the villagers simply shrug and say "Spain".)

Dine

A new road runs from Moimenta over heather-and-gorse moorland towards Mofreita, with sweeping views north to Spain and the wind turbines on the distant snow-dusted mountains. When you reach the Mofreita road, turn right (for Vinhais) to find the enchanting village of **DINE**, constructed on descending cobbled streets that afford sweeping views of the valley. A cave excavation here unearthed bones, cooking implements, flints and arrowheads dating back to 4000 BC, and you might find someone in the small interpretation centre by the church who can show you around.

Vilarinho

On from Mofreita (Bragança direction), there are other signposted diversions – to the *aldeia preservada* (preserved village) of Zeive, for example – before you drop down into the more pastoral lands around the dung-spattered hamlet of **VILARINHO**. This has another good waymarked walk (8km; 3hr), as well as two basic village cafés, including the magnificently misnamed *Café Tropical*.

Gondesende

From Vilarinho, it's 16km back to Bragança, or you can cut south at Cova de Lua towards the Vinhais road again. You'll run through more pretty hamlets, such as **GONDESENDE**, which has a couple of *turismo rural* places offering rooms in self-catering houses, as well as the single biggest tourism complex in the region, the *Cepo Verde* campsite.

ACCOMMODATION AND EATING	GONDESENDE
Cepo Verde Lugar da Vinha do Santo, Gondesende, just up from the N103 Vinhais road ☎ 273 999 371, ⓦ montesinho.com. Rustic campsite and stone-and-wood	cabins set amid chestnuts and oak trees. There's an outdoor pool and restaurant too. Closed Oct–March. Pitch **€3.60**, plus **€4** per adult; cabins **€40**

Vinhais

The small town of **VINHAIS** is the western gateway to the Montesinho park, reached on the twisting white-knuckle ride along the N103 between Bragança (31km east) and Chaves (65km west). A tiny, walled old town hugs a prominent mound above a wide valley to the south, while a catwalk-style terrace off the main through-street offers amazing views down over manicured municipal lawns, ornamental waterways and immaculately tended fields. An information board across from the turismo on the main road marks the start of a nine-kilometre circular **walking trail** on farm tracks and paths, which runs via the **Parque Biológico de Vinhais** (see below), an eco-park just outside town, with nature trails, and animals from deer to donkeys. Vinhais is also known for its sausage – signs in town advertise it as the "Capital do Fumeiro" (Smoked Meat Capital) – and the various different types made in the region, including *chouriço*, *salpicão* and *alheira*, are all celebrated in an annual festival, the **Feira do Fumeiro** (second weekend in Feb; ⑩fumeiro.org).

Centro de Interpretação do Parque Natural
Casa da Vila • Tues–Sun 9am–12.30pm & 2–5.30pm • Free • ☎ 273 771 416

If you're heading for the Parque Natural de Montesinho, stop in at the **Centro de Interpretação**, an imaginatively conceived information centre in the Casa da Vila in the old town, with plenty of interesting audiovisual displays and useful pointers towards visiting the park's museums and archeological sites (*núcleos*).

7

INFORMATION, ACCOMMODATION AND EATING   VINHAIS

Information The turismo is on Rua Nova da Calçada, the main road through town (Mon–Fri 9am–1pm & 2–5pm, Sat & Sun 10am–1pm & 2–5pm; ☎ 273 770 309, ⑩ cm-vinhais.pt).

Casa de Mencha Rio de Fornos, 3km north of Vinhais ☎ 934 143 171, ⑩ casadamencha.com. A simple country house with a couple of cosy bedrooms, kitchen, a log fire and a balcony with views. To find it, drive out of Vinhais on the Spain/Montesinho park road. No meals available. €60

Parque Biológico de Vinhais Alto da Cidadelha, Vinhais ☎ 273 771 040, ⑩ parquebiologicodevinhais.com. The nearby eco-park has camping and cabin accommodation on site and an associated inn, the simple *Hospedaria do Parque*, 3km away in the village of Rio de Fornos. The bungalows sleep 4 to 8 people, and have a little kitchen; the inn is more for groups, but they have plenty of bed space and might be able to accommodate you. Pitch €3 plus €3 per adult; cabins €65; inn rooms €35

Restaurante Comercial Rua Nova da Calçada, on the main road, across from the turismo ☎ 273 772 169. Locals make a beeline for this place, which has dishes from around €6 and a special fondness for roast suckling pig. Daily noon–2.30pm & 7–10pm.

Chaves

One of the most attractive towns in Trás-os-Montes, riverside **CHAVES** lies 12km from the Spanish border, which tells you all you need to know about its erstwhile strategic importance – as do the connotations of its name, which means "keys". It's also a spa town of some repute, founded originally by the Romans in 78 AD, who built an impressive bridge here across the Rio Tâmega. After the Romans came a long line of squabbling forces, from Visigoths and Moors to the Spanish and French, which explains the surviving fortresses, towers and walls that ring the medieval old town. The history is obvious from the monuments, but the welcome surprise is the evident charm of Chaves, from its handsome squares and balconied old-townhouses to its intricately-planted flowerbeds and riverside gardens. The spa is an obvious money-spinner, and many do come to take the waters, but it's not the be-all and end-all. You could spend a happy couple of days here and never notice the spa, perhaps being more inclined to sample Chaves' other significant attractions – namely its smoked hams, sausages and red wine.

Ponte Trajano and the river

The wide curve of the Rio Tâmega is crossed by the sturdy first-century Roman bridge, the **Ponte Trajano** (after the Emperor Trajan), which is closed to traffic so you can easily

CHAVES

Montalegre   Spain & A25

Old Train Station
Bus Station

Hospital

AVENIDA NUNO ÁLVARES
AV. RIBEIRO DE CARVALHO
AVENIDA DO ESTÁDIO
AV. ANTÓNIO GRANJO
AV. IRMÃOS RUI E GARCIA LOPES
ESTRADA DE OUTEIRO SECO

N

Cinema

AV. FRANCISCO SÁ CARNEIRO
AV. XAVIER TEIXEIRA

Forte de São Francisco

AV. MIGUEL TORGA

Police Station

LARGO DO PICADEIRO

RUA DOS ALIADOS
RUA DRAGÕES
TERREIRO DE CAVALARIA

RUA DR. J. MARTINS

LARGO N.S. DA LAPA

Outeiro Machado

RUA BOMBEIROS VOLUNTÁRIOS

RUA TENENTE VALADIM

AVENIDA 5 DE OUTUBRO

R. JOAQUIM JOSÉ DELGADO
RUA 11 DEZEMBRO

RUA DE SANTO ANTÓNIO
LARGO GEN. BOMBEIROS
LARGO G. SILVEIRA
RUA CÂNDIDO DOS REIS
RUA DAS LANGRAS

Museu da Região Flaviense

Câmara Municipal

PR. DE CAMÕES

Igreja Matriz

Pharmacy

RESTAURANTS
Adega Faustino   1
Carvalho   2
Casa Costa   3

Museu Militar

RUA DIREITA

LARGO DO ARRABAIDE

ACCOMMODATION
Albergaria Jaime   3
Casa de Samaiões   6
Florinda   2
Forte de São Francisco 1
Kátia   4
Quinta de Santa Isabel 7
Termas   5

Braga & Vidago

Torre de Menagem

Misericórdia

RUA DAS CALDAS
RUA DA FAMÍLIA DE CAMÕES

AV. PEDRO ÁLVARES CABRAL

PRAÇA DO BRASIL

Termas de Chaves

Parque Termal

Rodonorte Buses

RUA DO SOL
RUA 25 DE ABRIL
CANTO DO TORROLADO

PONTE TRAJANO

Igreja de Madelena

LARGO DAS CALDAS

Piscina Municipal

Rio Tâmega

0   200
metres

6 , Vila Real, Porto & Valpaços   Vila Real & Porto   Bragança, Spain   & 7

stroll across and examine the Roman milestones erected in the middle. Both sides of the river have landscaped promenades, and a couple of newer footbridges allow you to walk a riverside circuit – and see, in the process, quite how small Chaves really is, with open countryside and mountains in full view beyond. The Madalena district, just across the Roman bridge, is almost like a separate village with its crumbling houses and handsome public gardens.

Termas de Chaves and Parque Termal

Largo das Caldas • ⓦ termasdechaves.com

The main gardens on the town side of the bridge, past the municipal swimming pool, are the site of the **Termas de Chaves** spa buildings and **Parque Termal**, in front of the landmark *Hotel Aquae Flaviae*. The various treatments offered here aren't really for casual visitors, but you can always join the elderly dames with their crocheted mug-holders to drink the sodium bicarbonate-laced waters at the little *nascente* (spring) in the circular, part-covered building in the square outside. The water emerges at a piping 73°C (the hottest spring water in Iberia) and is dispensed by a white-coated medic.

> ## PUTTING THE FIZZ BACK INTO THE SPAS
>
> It was the Romans who first developed the spas of northern Portugal, not only in Chaves (their name for the town was **Aquae Flaviae**) but also at several other nearby thermal stations. Even now, for example, **Carvalhelhos** spring water is a big deal in Portugal – it comes from a small town around 25km west of Chaves in the Barroso hills. But it's the historic spa of **Vidago**, 17km south of Chaves down the Rio Tâmega, that has the highest profile, centred on the opulent Art Nouveau *Vidago Palace Hotel* (⊛ vidagopalace.com), transformed into a five-star resort by top architect Álvaro Siza Vieira. A similar renovation has taken place at the old spa of **Pedras Salgadas** (another famous Portuguese mineral water), 20km south of Vidago, where there's new accommodation and revitalized spa facilities as well as more resort and leisure outlets.

Torre de Menagem and around

Museu Militar Torre de Menagem, Castelo de Chaves • June–Sept Mon–Fri 9am–12.30pm & 2–5.30pm, Sat & Sun 2–5.30pm; Oct–May daily 9am–12.30pm & 2–5.30pm • €1, includes entry to Museu da Região Flaviense

Up the hill from the river, the squat fourteenth-century keep, the **Torre de Menagem**, is all that's left of the castle (save the portions of surviving wall that crop up here and there in town). Inside is the **Museu Militar**, though if the terrace battlements are still closed to the public it's lost its major reason for a visit. The little floral gardens are a delight, though, and give a partial view of town, while there's a café kiosk outside as well.

The old town streets beyond the castle keep are highly attractive, such as atmospheric Rua Direita with its leaning houses and antique wooden balconies. Traditional shops are still much to the fore and it's not hard to find butchers, bakers and probably even candlestick makers if you looked hard enough. Loops of *alheira* sausage, smoked Chaves hams, traditional black pottery, and straw and wicker work are all widely available.

Museu da Região Flaviense

Praça de Camões • June–Sept Mon–Fri 9am–12.30pm & 2–5.30pm, Sat & Sun 2–5.30pm; Oct–May daily 9am–12.30pm & 2–5.30pm • €1, includes entry to Museu Militar • ☎ 276 340 500, ⊛ museudechaves.com

The main town museum, the **Museu da Região Flaviense**, is located in Praça de Camões, the town hall square, and is where many of the Roman-era artefacts are displayed, from coins and fragmented mosaics to engraved altars and milestones. (The remodelling of Largo do Arrabaide, just up from the bridge, has also unearthed the remains of the Roman thermal baths.)

Forte de São Francisco

The town's military past presents itself most forcefully in the dramatic, high-walled, seventeenth-century **Forte de São Francisco**, a short walk up from the town centre. It was originally a convent, but was fortified during the Peninsular Wars, and then eventually converted again, this time into a rather grand hotel. No one minds if you walk in through the main gate and take in the magnificent views from the ramparts, and there's also a tavern, bar and restaurant all open to the public.

ARRIVAL AND INFORMATION   CHAVES

By bus The bus station (Auto-Viação do Tâmega services; ⊛ avtamega.pt) is under ten minutes' walk north of the centre, behind the fort, by the old train station.
Destinations Braga (1–6 daily; 3hr); Bragança (1–2 daily; 2hr 10min); Coimbra (2–5 daily; 2hr 40min); Lisbon

(2 daily; 6hr 30min); Mirandela (Mon–Fri 3 daily; 2hr); Montalegre (Mon–Fri 4 daily, Sun 1 daily; 1hr 20min); Porto (7–12 daily; 3hr); Vila Real (hourly; 1hr 10min).
By car Chaves is around 65km northeast of Vila Real, and it's a quick drive on a good road. You can be in Spain in ten

minutes and in the city of Ourense (90km) under an hour later. There is ample parking in Chaves, often free (look for the word "gratis"), particularly in the streets around Forte de São Francisco and down by the riverside gardens.

Information The turismo is at the top of the Terreiro do Cavalaria gardens (Mon–Sat 9.30am–12.30pm & 2–5.30pm; ☎ 276 340 660, ✆ chaves.pt), near the fort.

ACCOMMODATION

Accommodation is plentiful, but spa business fills even the cheapest places in summer, so a reservation might be in order. Some town-centre budget places are a bit long-in-the-tooth; the best place to look for cheap rooms is down Rua do Sol, on the way to the river. A short drive out in the country might be a nicer bet if you don't mind not being in the centre.

IN TOWN

Albergaria Jaime Rua Joaquim José Delgado ☎ 276 301 050, ✆ albergariajaime.com.pt. This handsome, salmon-pink villa has been operating as a guesthouse since the late 1800s, although with rooms in a large rear extension it's now firmly in the hotel category. Rooms are reasonable without being remarkable, but it's a decent choice, with parking nearby, and the associated *Cyber Bar* terrace-esplanade below. **€60**

Florinda Rua dos Açougues ☎ 276 333 392. Blessedly cool rooms with polished wooden floors and trim bathrooms. It's a cosy old family house near the castle, whose front rooms have the town's characteristic wooden balconies. **€40**

★ **Forte de São Francisco** ☎ 276 333 700, ✆ forte saofrancisco.com. A chapel with tape-recorded Mass in the reception entry hall sets the tone for this atmospheric four-star hotel located in the fortress. The conversion is a sensitive blend of old and new, with pool, bar and replica traditional tavern, plus the house restaurant, the *Cozinha da Convento*, which offers a pricey take on updated regional cuisine. **€100**

★ **Kátia** Rua do Sol 28 ☎ 276 324 446. The pick of the bunch on this street of cheaper options has friendly

service and fine little rooms (some with balconies) above a good, inexpensive restaurant. You'd be hard pressed to find anything better in town for the money. **€35**

Termas Rua do Tabolado ☎ 276 333 280. A concrete hulk close to the river that's a classic case of better inside than out – you get nice big rooms with laminate floors and full bathrooms, heating and a/c and, though it can be noisy out front, it all seems pretty good value for money. Parking nearby. **€40**

OUT OF TOWN

Casa de Samaiões Samaiões, 5km south of Chaves ☎ 276 340 450, ✆ hotel-casasamaioes.com. A cross between an upmarket hotel and a *turismo rural*, this seventeenth-century *quinta* combines traditional four-poster beds with rather more contemporary furnishings. It's all set within lovely landscaped grounds complete with a charming pool with views. **€90**

Quinta de Santa Isabel Santo Estevão, 7km east of Chaves ☎ 276 333 210, ✆ quintadesantaisabel.com.pt. A traditional Trás-os-Montes country house with gardens and vineyards, 500m off the N103 to Bragança. Self-catering accommodation is in one of five rustic stone cottages which sleep two to four people. **€60**

EATING, DRINKING AND NIGHTLIFE

There are lots of **restaurants**, all pretty reasonable though few stand out from the crowd. Good Chaves *presunto* and local sausages are on every menu; at Christmas particularly it's traditional to eat octopus (*polvo*), brought up dried from the coast, then boiled with potatoes and greens. Two or three **cafés** by the Roman bridge are the best places for a sundowner, with a few late-night bars found on Largo das Caldas (by the riverside gardens) and down Travessa Cândido dos Reis.

★ **Adega Faustino** Trav Cândido dos Reis ☎ 276 322 142, ✆ adegafaustino.pt. A former wine cellar, with a cobbled floor and huge barrels lined up behind the bar. The wine is good, and it's great for *petiscos*, including things like bean salad and *presunto*, and grilled main dishes, with almost everything costing between €5 and €8. Mon–Sat noon–midnight.

Carvalho Largo das Caldas ☎ 276 321 727. Rated as the best in town for regional food, and consequently more expensive than most (mains €10–16), but certainly the place to try the definitive *arroz de fumeiro* (rice with

smoked meats) or *alheira* (sausage). There's always fish, too, and not just the ubiquitous *bacalhau* or *truta*. Tues–Sat noon–3pm & 7–11pm, Sun noon–3pm.

Casa Costa Rua do Tabolado ☎ 276 323 568. Primarily a grill place, with a daily handwritten menu of dishes from around €8–9. The speciality is *bacalhau à Costa* (oven-roast, with onions) or a gigantic Mirandês steak. There's also a vine-covered rear garden with bench-style tables, though it's not always open for dining. Daily 11am–3pm & 7pm–midnight.

7

Montalegre

The historic frontier town of **MONTALEGRE** is the entry point to the eastern stretches of the Peneda-Gerês national park – though you'd really need your own transport as there are no onward buses into the park. Even if you go no further, it's worth making the trip – 45km west of Chaves, and a ten-kilometre detour off the N103 – not least for the sudden looming of its dramatic medieval castle as you approach town, lording it over the surrounding plains. You can walk up to the surviving keep and ruined walls (always open; free), and then saunter through the few immaculately restored old-town streets below, and while this takes just twenty minutes, Montalegre is charming enough to stretch your visit to take in lunch. There are half a dozen restaurants in town, most near the dinky *pelourinho* square, just below the castle. All are big on the local Serra do Barroso produce, namely its huge steaks, smoked meats (*fumeiros*) and ham (*presunto*). There's even a whole festival dedicated to the products, the annual **Feira do Fumeiro e Presunto** (fourth week of January).

Around 8km south of town, a road leads to the huge **Barragem do Alto Rabagão**, around which you can pick up signs to swimming spots, old villages and walking trails.

Into the Parque Nacional da Peneda-Gerês

The easternmost parts of the **Parque Nacional da Peneda-Gerês** lie in Trás-os-Montes, cut off from the main section in the Minho region by the Barragem de Paradela and the towering Serra do Gerês mountain range. Drivers already in the main park can approach from the south on the stunning mountain route from **Cabril**, but from Trás-os-Montes it's much easier to drive via Montalegre, from where the park and its villages are well signposted. Montalegre has both park information office and turismo, where you should be able to pick up walking leaflets, but even without them you'll be able to find the trails, since for once they are properly signposted. The best walk is at **Pitões das Júnias**, which is itself the single best target in this section.

Pitões das Júnias

It's a terrific drive to **PITÕES DAS JÚNIAS**, 25km northwest of Montalegre, and set in one of the wildest corners of Portugal. The clustered brown-stone, red-tile buildings of the village are framed by the most extraordinary jagged peaks (*pitões*) of the Gerês mountains, and the surroundings simply beg you to get out of your car and walk. Happily, there's an enjoyable waymarked trail (4km; 1hr 30min) that descends a stone path into a hidden valley where a gloriously sited, twelfth-century monastery and plunging waterfall await. Follow the brown signs for "Mosteiro" and "Cascata" and then the paint marks, which take you first to the monastery, then along a stepped boardwalk to the waterfall viewing point before looping back to the village. Pitões may be isolated, but it expects visitors: there's a car park at the top of the village.

DEAD DRUNK

Montalegre is one of the Serra do Barroso settlements where you'll come across the so-called *Vinhos dos Mortos* – **Wines of the Dead**; try asking in local bars and restaurants. This is basically wine that matures in bottles buried underground, a practice that originated in 1809 when villagers, keen to protect their wine stocks from the invading French hordes, hid their bottles. When they dug them up again they were delighted to find that the contents tasted considerably better.

Tourém

Back at the turning off the Montalegre road, it's another 10km north to the traditional village of **TOURÉM**, across a wild plateau of heather and roaming cattle. This is another drive that needs no excuse, though Tourém itself is a gem, albeit one very liberally coated with dung. It sits in a neatly cultivated valley by a reservoir (where there's swimming), with a bridge connecting it with Spain on the other side. Another easy, marked trail (2.5km) heads through the village past a communal stone oven, before climbing to a viewpoint above Tourém.

Paredes do Rio to Paradela

The road from Montalegre runs southwest, passing **PAREDES DO RIO**, which sits high above the Rio Cávado in the valley below. Paredes itself is an ancient little place, notable for its *espigueiros* (grain stores).

Three kilometres further on, **OUTEIRO** is another charming cluster of old stone houses, this time overlooking the placid waters of the **Barragem de Paradela**, ringed by gnarled peaks. From here, you can head down over the dam and take the wild road towards Cabril for access to the main section of the park, or head south to **Venda Nova** and its own dam, 18km southeast on the main N103 (Chaves road).

Cabril

The fifteen-kilometre minor road over the top, south to **CABRIL**, climbs through wild mountain scenery of jutting granite outcrops before descending to the Rio Cabril and an old village surrounded on all sides by mountains. When the nearby Salamonde dam was created, parts of the village were submerged and the old bridge is still half under water. There's a nearby signposted campsite, and rooms available in a couple of simple local places, though it's only 8km on to Ermida in the Minho section of the park, with the main centre of Caldas do Gerês a similar distance beyond that.

ACCOMMODATION AND EATING

PITÕES DAS JÚNIAS

Casa do Preto ☎ 276 566 158, ⓦ casadopreto.com. An agreeable village restaurant and bar – the food is excellent, including produce from their own smokehouse. They also have decent guest rooms ("sober and engaging" they say, rather sweetly) in an adjacent building. **€50**

PAREDES DO RIO

Estalagem Rocha ☎ 276 566 147, ⓦ estalagemrocha .com.pt. It has neat little rooms, though no real reason to stay, and a rather more renowned rustic restaurant, cooking meat from its own farm (dishes around €10). **€40**

CABRIL

Ponte Novo ☎ 253 659 882. Overlooking the new bridge, this bar-restaurant has a riverside terrace for drinks, while inside you can eat a hearty stew or grilled trout (dishes €7–10). April–Sept daily noon–10pm; winter hours variable.

Alentejo

TEMPLO ROMANO, ÉVORA

Alentejo

The Alentejo covers a huge area, almost a third of the country, stretching south from the Rio Tejo to the northern mountain ranges of the Algarve – the name derives from the words *além do Tejo*, beyond the Tejo River. This is Portugal's garden, the bulk of the region given over to huge cork plantations, wheat fields and vineyards – and though much of it is flat, the region repays exploration, offering unexpected surprises, from ancient dolmens and superbly sited castles to Roman ruins and sweeping Atlantic beaches. Much of the population make a living from the huge agricultural estates known as *latifúndios*, which are handed down from generation to generation – many have been in existence since Roman times. The vast farms are generally wildlife friendly – the Alentejo is home to hundreds of species of bird, from black stork to great bustard, as well as wild boar.

For most visitors, the region's major draws are its towns, two of which have UNESCO World Heritage status: the spectacular fortified town of **Elvas**, and **Évora**, whose Roman temple, medieval walls and cathedral have put it firmly on the tourist circuit. Elsewhere in **Alto Alentejo** (Upper Alentejo), you'll find the dazzling hilltop villages of **Monsaraz** and **Marvão**, and the marble towns of **Estremoz** and **Vila Viçosa**, where the local marble quarries have given an opulent look to many of the buildings.

South of Évora, in the plains of **Baixo Alentejo** (Lower Alentejo), the attractions lie further apart and can be difficult to see without a car. However, there are some good overnight targets, including the main town of **Beja**, as well as nearby **Serpa**, **Moura** and **Mértola**, all enjoyable historic towns with a wealth of good accommodation. The coast, too, is an unexpected joy. Only a few small resorts – prime among them **Vila Nova de Milfontes** – attract summer crowds, but the beaches are superb and you can reach them all by public transport.

Évora

ÉVORA is one of Portugal's most historic and unspoilt cities: indeed its Roman temple, Moorish alleys, circuit of medieval walls, ensemble of sixteenth-century mansions and ochre-trimmed, whitewashed houses have resulted in it being awarded UNESCO World Heritage status. A vibrant university helps support a modern town that spreads beyond the old walls, though its current population of around 55,000 inhabitants is fewer than in medieval times, and its compact centre is easily explored within a day or two. Évora's agricultural roots are recalled on the second Tuesday of each month, with a huge **open-air market** held in the Rossio, south of the city walls, while the big annual

VILA NOVA DE MILFONTES

Highlights

❶ Templo Romano, Évora Enjoy a sunset drink near Évora's most impressive Roman remains. **See p.387**

❷ Cromeleque dos Almendres The Iberian peninsula's largest Neolithic stone circle, near Évora, is a hugely atmospheric site. **See p.393**

❸ Saturday market, Estremoz A classic Portuguese market, selling everything from earthenware to cheese, all locally made. See p.395

❹ Alter do Chão It's well worth the drive into the heart of the northern Alentejo plains to see the famous royal stud farm. **See p.397**

❺ Monsaraz Stay the night in one of the traditional houses in this fortified hilltop village. See p.410

❻ Mértola This quiet, historic riverside town exudes great charm. **See p.420**

❼ A Rota Vicentina Walk a section of this superb long-distance marked trail that wends its way down the west coast of the region. See p.425

❽ Vila Nova de Milfontes The Alentejo coast is quite distinct from that of the Algarve, with the estuary town of Vila Nova its finest resort. See p.426

HIGHLIGHTS ARE MARKED ON THE MAP ON P.386

event, the **Feira de São João**, takes over the city during the last ten days of June, with handicraft, gastronomic and musical festivals.

Praça do Giraldo is the city's central hub, with the main historic kernel just to the east. Within the surrounding city walls are several distinct old-town areas, with another concentration of sights in the streets between the main square and the public gardens. Meanwhile, to the north of the centre you can follow the course of the medieval **Aqueduto do Água Prata** (Silver Water Aqueduct), into whose ever-rising arches a row

ALENTEJO

HIGHLIGHTS

1. Templo Romano, Évora
2. Cromeleque dos Almendres
3. Saturday market, Estremoz
4. Alter do Chão
5. Monsaraz
6. Mértola
7. A Rota Vicentina
8. Vila Nova de Milfontes

of houses has been incorporated. Wherever you wander, nothing is more than a ten-minute walk from Praça do Giraldo.

Brief history

The original settlement was probably founded by the Celts, but it was the Romans who fortified the city in BC 57. Its position on trade routes allowed Évora to flourish and soon after, the Temple of Diana was erected. In 715, Tariq ibn-Ziyad began a 450-year period of Moorish rule which established the city's maze of narrow alleys. It was recaptured by the Christians in 1165, who began to construct the cathedral in 1186 (though it was not finished until the fourteenth century). The period from 1385–1580 saw the city prosper when the royal House of Avis established their court here, and it was during this period that most of Évora's finest buildings were built. In 1553, the Jesuits founded a highly-rated university, but this was closed down by the King's chief minister, Pombal, in 1759; he distrusted the Jesuits' influence. The Vauban-style defensive town walls were constructed in the seventeenth century under the French engineer Nicolas de Langres and remain little changed today. Once the Portuguese court moved nearer Lisbon, Évora drifted into relative obscurity for much of the nineteenth and twentieth centuries. However, the university was re-established in 1973 and in 1986, the town was awarded UNESCO World Heritage status as "the finest example of a city of the Golden Age of Portugal". It is now thriving again thanks to its lively student population and as a popular tourist destination.

Templo Romano (Temple of Diana)

8

The graceful **Templo Romano** stands at the very heart of the old city. It was built in the first or second century, supported by fourteen granite Corinthian columns, making it undoubtedly the most impressive Roman building in the country. Popularly known as the Temple of Diana (the Roman goddess of hunting), it was more probably dedicated to several Roman gods. The little square in front of the temple has an alluring kiosk-bar, while from the terrace you can look north across the rooftops – and see just how small contemporary Évora is, with the fields beginning only a few hundred metres away.

Igreja dos Lóios and Palácio dos Duques de Cadaval

Largo do Conde de Vila Flor • Tues–Sun 10am–12.30pm & 2–6pm • Church €3; church and palace €5 • ☎ 967 979 763

Directly opposite the Roman temple is the former conventual church, **Igreja dos Lóios**, dedicated to São João Evangelista, and belonging to the Duques de Cadaval, who still live in part of the adjacent ancestral palace. Inside the church – through the Gothic doorway – are some extraordinary floor-to-ceiling *azulejos*, created by one António Oliveira Bernardes early in the eighteenth century. They show scenes from the life of São Lourenço Justiniano, founder of the Lóios order. Hidden among the pews, two small trapdoors stand open to reveal both a Moorish cistern (the church and convent were built over an old castle) and a grisly ossuary containing the bones of the convent's monks. You can buy a combined ticket at the church if you also want to see the private art collection of the Cadaval dukes, housed in a few public rooms of the **Palácio dos Duques de Cadaval**, but it's probably one to skip.

The Sé

Largo Marquês de Marialva • Daily 9am–12.30pm & 2–4.50pm • Church €1.50; church and cloister €2.50; church, cloister and tower €3.50

The construction of Évora's impressive cathedral, the **Sé**, began just twenty years after Christians defeated the Moors in 1165 – hence its somewhat military-looking battlements and substantial towers. Its beautiful, if rather sombre, interior is lit up by

■ ACCOMMODATION		● CAFÉS		● RESTAURANTS		■ BARS AND CLUBS	
Albergaria do		Café Arcada	9	Adega Alentejana	6	Bota Alta	3
Calvario	3	Gelateria Zoka	5	¼ Para às 9	3	Molho Bico	1
Albergaria Solar		Quiosque Jardim	4	A Choupana	8	Páteo	2
de Monfalim	7	Diana	1	Botequim da Mouraria	5	Praxis Clube	4
Évora Inn Chiado		Pastelaria Conventual		O Fialho	2		
Design	8	Pão da Rala	11	Quarta-Feira	1		
Mar de Ar Aqueduto	2			Repas	10		
Monte da Serralheira	9						
Policarpo	3						
Pousada dos Lóios	4						
Quinta da Espada	6						
Riviera							

two huge Gothic rose windows. The more jaunty main chapel was an eighteenth-century Baroque addition attributed to João Frederico Ludovice (1673–1752), a German-born architect best known for his work on the Mosteiro Palácio de Mafra. The Gothic cloister is an attractive, tranquil space, though for most people the highlight is to climb up the tower onto the cathedral's cambered roof, which offers dazzling views over the town.

Museu de Catedral

Largo Marquês de Marialva • Tues–Sun 9am–11.30am & 2–4pm • €3.50

The **Museu de Catedral**, housed in the Cathedral chapter room, shows off the historic economic clout of the church. Its priceless treasures include a jewel-encrusted reliquary and a thirteenth-century ivory and wood statue of the Virgin, whose midriff opens out to display various Biblical scenes.

Museu de Évora

Largo Conde Vila Flor • Tues–Sun 9.30am–5.30pm • €4, free on Sun 10am–1pm • ☎ 266 702 604, Ⓦ museudevora.imc-ip.pt

The fascinating and well laid out **Museu de Évora**, housed in a beautiful former bishop's palace, is best known for its collection of fifteenth- and sixteenth-century Flemish paintings which were once displayed in the city's convents and churches. Highlight is a *retábulo* consisting of 19 pieces commissioned by the Bishop of Évora from Flanders in 1495, cementing the strong medieval trade links between the two countries. There are also still life by Portuguese painter Josefa da Óbidos (1630–1684) and archeological remains from Portugal's "Golden Age of Discoveries", including an ornate marble window-frame from a former Queen's palace (1506). In the basement, an archeological display includes finds from local burial mounds and Roman excavations, along with remains from Islamic houses.

Termas Romanas

Câmara Municipal • Mon–Fri 9am–5.30pm

One of the city's most significant Roman remains was uncovered in 1987 beneath the town hall, the **Câmara Municipal**, where during office hours you can walk in to view the **Termas Romanas** (Roman Baths), which date to the first century AD. Look down on it and you can see an arched brick doorway marking the entrance to an extraordinary sunken room which houses a circular steam bath 9m in diameter.

Antiga Universidade

Rua Cardeal Rei • Term time only Mon–Fri 9am–7pm, Sat 9am–1pm • Free • ☎ 266 740 800

In one of the liveliest corners of the city, you'll find the **Antiga Universidade**, whose beautiful courtyard is entered from Rua Cardeal Rei. Founded in 1559 by Cardinal Henrique, the future "Cardinal King", the university was closed down by the Jesuit-hating Marquês de Pombal during the eighteenth century, but reopened in the 1970s. You are free to wander in and view the brazilwood ceiling, *azulejos* and double cloister of marble columns.

Igreja de São Francisco and Capela dos Ossos

Igreja de São Francisco Praça 1 de Maio • Mon–Sat 9am–12.45pm & 2.30–5.10pm, Sun 10am–12.45pm & 2.30–5.10pm • Capela dos Ossos €2 • ☎ 266 704 521

The broad Praça 1 de Maio contains Évora's lively **Mercado Municipal** (closed Mon), where you can sample local produce – beneath the fish section is a wine cellar that offers tastings: it also hosts farmers' markets most weekends. On its eastern side, the **Igreja de São Francisco** is best known for its bizarre **Capela dos Ossos**, the "chapel of bones". During the fifteenth and sixteenth centuries, there were 42 monastic cemeteries in town which took up much-needed space. The Franciscans' solution was to move all the remains to one compact, consecrated site. This is the ghoulish result: a room lined with the bones and skulls of around five thousand former monks, inscribed with the reminder of our mortality: "*Nós ossos que aqui estamos pelos vossos esperamos*" ("Our bones that lie here are waiting for your bones").

Jardim Público and the Palácio de Dom Manuel

Just to the south of Praça 1 de Maio, the **Palácio de Dom Manuel**, with its reconstructed gallery – incorporating inventive horseshoe arches with strange serrated edges – lies within Évora's **Jardim Público** (Public Gardens). It was from the palace that Vasco da Gama is thought to have received the commission that changed the direction of the Portuguese empire, as the explorer established the sea route to India. From the garden walls, you can look out over the southern edge of the city, and see the **Ermida de São Brás** (Mon–Fri 8am–11am & 1–6pm; free; ☎266 708 362) just outside the city walls – this small church has been identified as an early work by Diogo de Boitaca, pioneer of the Manueline style.

ARRIVAL AND INFORMATION   ÉVORA

By bus The bus station (Terminal Rodoviária) is five minutes' walk from the western city walls along the Lisbon road; it's a ten-minute walk in total to Praça do Giraldo, or you can take one of the regular Trevo buses (see below).
Destinations Arraiolos (2–4 daily; 45min); Beja (7 daily; 1hr 15min); Elvas (3–4 daily; 1hr 30min); Estremoz (Mon–Fri 3 daily; 1hr 10min); Faro (3–4 daily; 4hr); Lisbon (hourly; 1hr 40min); Moura (1 daily; 1hr 25min); Portalegre (2–3 daily; 1hr 25min–1hr 45min); Reguengos de Monsaraz for Monsaraz (2–7 daily; 35min–1hr); Santarém (2 daily; 2hr); and Vila Viçosa (3 daily; 1hr).

By car Unless you are staying at a hotel with parking, drivers should park in one of the (mostly free) car parks around the walls, as the city centre has few parking places. There's always space on the massive Rossio (except on open-air market day). The Trevo bus (Mon–Fri 8am–8pm, Sat 8am–2pm; every 10min; €1 includes parking; ☜trevo.com.pt) acts as a park-and-ride service, circling all the car parks around the city walls and running into the historic centre.

By train Évora's train station is 1km southeast of the centre, with regular services from Beja (4 daily via Casa Branca; 2hr 15min) and Lisbon (4 daily; 1hr 55min). From the station, walk up through the Rossio and follow Rua da República straight ahead to reach Praça do Giraldo, the city's main square: it's a €6 taxi ride.

Information The turismo is at Praça do Giraldo 73 (daily: April–Oct 9am–7pm; Nov–March 9am–6pm; ☎266 777 071, ☜www2.cm-evora.pt/guiaturistico/) and posts useful bus and train timetables.

ACCOMMODATION

Accommodation prices in Évora are higher than in the rest of the Alentejo, but there's a more agreeable choice of places here than virtually anywhere else in the south, from simple rooms in family houses to ducal palaces. Outside the city, a large array of country houses also offer accommodation, most within a short drive. In summer you're advised to book in advance to guarantee a bed, though the turismo may be able to help.

★**Albergaria do Calvario** Travessa dos Lagares 3 ☎266 745 930, ☜albergariadocalvario.com. Stylishly converted inn partly set in a former sixteenth-century olive press that supplied olive oil to the adjacent convent. The plush rooms are arranged round an inner courtyard, and there's wi-fi and underground parking. The owners are keen foodies and provide an excellent organic breakfast, as well as tapas served in the bar. Mention Rough Guides when you book and you'll get a free room upgrade. **€110**

Albergaria Solar de Monfalim Largo da Misericórdia 1 ☎266 750 000, ☜monfalimtur.pt. The steps and sumptuous terrace leading to this restored summer ducal palace promise much, though the 25 rooms are a little less impressive. Pretty Alentejo furniture and furnishings decorate the communal areas, while breakfast is taken on the terrace, which has superb views. Parking (for a daily fee). **€60**

Évora Inn Chiado Design Rua da República 11 ☎266 744 500, ☜evorainn.com. It's easy to miss the entrance to this good-value guesthouse, which is on the top floor of a very central townhouse – its name comes from the contemporary furniture and art on the walls, some of which is for sale. The best rooms overlook the old town at the back, but all are individual and filled with funky furniture and fittings. There's also a communal lounge and kitchen. Breakfast €5 extra. **€58**

Mar de Ar Aqueduto Rua Cândido dos Reis 72 ☎266 740 700, ☜mardearhotels.com. This deluxe, ultra-modern five-star spa hotel is hidden behind a traditional facade. The rooms are huge, with glass-walled bathrooms, set round a fantastic garden with its own pool nestled against the city walls. A gym and restaurant complete its attractions. **€150**

Monte da Serralheira 3km south, beyond Bairro Almeirim ☎266 741 286, ☜monteserralheira.com. Dutch-owned farm with six good-value apartments (sleeping two or four people) each with terrace, sitting room, small kitchen and TV. It's very peaceful, there's a nice communal pool and table tennis, and you can rent a bike or ride a horse. Breakfast extra. **€65**

8

Policarpo Rua Freiria de Baixo 16 ☎ 266 702 424, ⓦ pensaopolicarpo.com. A former ducal summer palace with sixteenth-century *azulejos*, a granite staircase and fine views from many of its rooms. The staff are helpful and English-speaking and, if the rooms are fading a little (you pay €20 more for en-suite rooms), they still have charm; breakfast is eaten on the terrace. Parking. No credit cards. €40

Pousada dos Lóios Largo do Conde de Vila Flor ☎ 266 730 070, ⓦ pousadas.pt. One of the country's finest *pousadas*, housed in the former Convento dos Lóios and wrapped round superb inner courtyards, one with a pool. The rooms are lovely – many with traditional furniture, including some dramatic four-poster beds – and some in former monks' cells. You can also eat top-notch Alentejan specialities (mains €15–20; reservations required) in the sumptuous cloisters. €160

Quinta da Espada 4km north, Estrada da Arraiolos ☎ 266 734 549, ⓦ quintadaespada.pt. Five rustic-style rooms (some en suite) and two apartments (€200; three nights minimum let) in a nineteenth-century *quinta* set in pretty grounds, through which the Évora aqueduct runs. There's a sun terrace and pool, and dinner is available. €75

★ **Riviera** Rua 5 de Outubro 49 ☎ 266 737 210, ⓦ riviera-evora.com. A fine central option, with 21 individually styled rooms with stripped wooden floors, Alentejan rugs, pretty bedspreads and little marble bathrooms. Some rooms are more attractive (and bigger) than others, but all are good value. €55

EATING, DRINKING AND NIGHTLIFE

When the students aren't around, Évora goes to bed pretty early, but a few **bars** can provide a bit of late-night drinking – keep an eye out for flyers for club nights. **Concerts and cultural events** are advertised in the *Agenda Cultural* booklet, available from the turismo.

CAFÉS

Café Arcada Praça do Giraldo 7, at Rua João de Deus ☎ 266 741 777. The nicest perch in town, by the fountain at the top of the square, for perusing the comings and goings – also does good-value meals (around €15). Fri & Sat 8am–10.30pm, Sun–Thurs 8am–9.30pm.

Gelateria Zoka Rua Miguel Bombarda 14. This friendly café is famed for its lovely home-made ice cream – best enjoyed sitting at tables in the pretty square outside, if you can find one among the students. Daily 8am–2am.

Pastelaria Conventual Pão da Rala Rua do Cicioso 47 ☎ 266 707 778. This small, traditional café with *azulejos* on the walls has a counter filled with cakes and pastries whose recipes were originally concocted by nuns in local convents. Mostly egg- and almond-based and perfect for those with a sweet tooth, they have risqué names such as *beijinhas de freira* (nun's kisses). Daily 7.30am–8pm.

Quiosque Jardim Diana Largo do Conde de Vila Flor ☎ 266 707 642. The outdoor kiosk by the temple is the finest place in the city for a beer, as the fading sun dapples the cathedral and temple columns. Given its location, it's amazingly low priced. Daily 8am–8pm.

RESTAURANTS

¼ Para as 9 Rua Pedro Simões 9a ☎ 266 706 774. Lively local that serves the best fish in town – pricey mains from €12, but go for the huge *arroz de tamboril* or *marisco* and you can easily share the rice dishes between three people for €28 or so. Also superb starters such as cheese baked with oregano. Mon, Tues, Thurs–Sun noon–3pm & 7–10.30pm.

A Choupana Rua dos Mercadores 16–20 ☎ 266 704 427. Close enough to the main square to attract tourists aplenty, but good enough to appeal to locals, too, who tend to eat at the counter rather than in the adjacent tiled dining room. Grilled fish and meats such as *alheira* (chicken sausage) from €8–12. Daily noon–10pm.

Adega Alentejana Rua Gabriel Victor do Monte Pereira 21A ☎ 266 744 447. You'll find an authentic slice of the Alentejo at this rustic restaurant and bar, which is lined with agricultural implements, plates and giant barrels. Regional dishes feature the likes of *migas* and *açorda* (a garlic bread sauce cooked with meats), along with huge portions of grilled meats, all from €8. The daily specials are chalked on a board. Mon–Sat noon–3pm & 7–10.30pm.

★ **Botequim da Mouraria** Rua da Mouraria 16A ☎ 266 746 775. This tiny bar with counter seating serves excellent regional food, mainly tapas-style dishes (scrambled eggs and wild asparagus, roast peppers, wild mushrooms in garlic from €4–16) and a few market-fresh mains (say steak, or deep-fried squid with crispy potatoes from around €13). Mon–Fri 12.30–3pm & 7–10pm.

O Fialho Travessa das Mascarenhas 16 ☎ 266 703 079, ⓦ restaurantefialho.com. One of the city's top restaurants, specializing in traditional regional specialities such as partridge, hare and wild boar with apple sauce from around €14–18, and the wine list is excellent. Appetizers are particularly good (spinach with prawns, stuffed crab), as are the desserts. Tues–Sun noon–3pm & 7–10pm.

Quarta-Feira Rua do Inverno 16 ☎ 266 707 530. This simple but appealing Moorish Quarter tavern has a menu of mostly meaty Alentejan classics – *borrego, bife, lombinhos, rojões* – from €12.50. Tues–Sat 12.30–3pm & 7.30–10pm.

8

Repas Praça 1 de Maio 19 ☎266 708 540. The tables outside on the square, opposite São Francisco church, are the big draw – and you can just sit down for a drink (the locals order snails as an appetizer) – but it's also a cheap place to eat a steak and chips or all the other usual standards (from €8 or so). Mon, Tues & Thurs–Sun noon–10pm.

BARS AND CLUBS

Bota Alta Rua Serpa Pinto 93 ☎963 433 145. Small, intimate restaurant-bar with live fado sessions from 8pm; you're expected to pay a minimum of around €10 on food or drink, and you can eat decent mains from €12–15. Daily noon–3pm & 7pm–3am.

Molho Bico Rua de Aviz 91 ☎266 748 235. A pub-like music bar with tables out the front on an attractive square. There's live music most nights from 11pm, when things can get very lively. Daily 11.30am–3am.

Páteo Beco do Espinhoso, off Rua 5 de Outubro. Tucked at the end of a tiny alley, this lovely patio bar has tables and chairs under the shade of olive and lemon trees, a tranquil spot for a drink – it also does soups, snacks and wraps, and hosts occasional exhibitions. Daily 11.30–midnight (closes 8pm from Oct–April).

Praxis Clube Rua de Valdevinos 21A ☎266 708 177, ⓦpraxisclub.com. The town's only central club is the place to show your moves, especially in term time when the students are in town. There are two dancefloors, an esplanade and various chill-out areas. Wed–Sat midnight–6am.

DIRECTORY

Bike rental Évora Adventure Bike, Travessa do Barão 18 ☎266 702 326. Bikes from €15 a day.

Hospital Hospital do Espírito Santo, Largo Sr da Pobreza ☎266 740 100.

Police Police station (PSP) on Rua Francisco S Lusitano, near the Roman temple ☎266 702 022.

Post office Rua da Olivença (☎266 745 480; Mon–Fri 8.30am–6.30pm).

Taxis There's a rank in Praça do Giraldo.

Tours Knowledgeable local professor Libânio Merteira Reis (office in boutique at Rua 31 de Janeiro 15A ☎266 739 240, ⓦevora-mm.pt) runs customized tours round town and out to nearby megaliths, from €10 for half a day. You can also take guided 2–3-hour tours to the local megalithic sites with Ebora Megalithica (☎964 80 337, ⓦeboramegalithica.com) for around €25 per person.

Wine tours The helpful Rota dos Vinhos do Alentejo, Praça Joaquim António d'Aguiar 20–21 (☎266 746 498, ⓦvinhosdoalentejo.pt; Mon 2–7pm, Tues–Thurs 11am–7pm, Sat 10am–1pm), supplies a wine-route booklet detailing all the region's vineyards and arranges vineyard visits (book in advance).

ALENTEJAN WINES

The art of wine-making in the Alentejo was already well established when the Romans occupied the country's vineyards, but it is only relatively recently that **Alentejan wines** have become widely recognized as some of the best in Europe. Many of the region's vineyards were torn up in the eighteenth century to protect the newly demarcated port wines from the Douro region, while during the last century the Salazar regime encouraged farmers to replace their vines with wheat. It was only in the 1970s that wine co-operatives were re-established, and heavy investment in modern wine-making techniques saw the quality rise dramatically. What makes the wines stand out from elsewhere is that they are made from **local grape varieties** which thrive in the harsh soils: Touriga Nacional, Aragonez and Alicante Bouschet, Trincadeira and Periquita for the reds; and Antão Vaz, Arinto and Roupeiro for the whites. The region's cool winters, warm summers and perfect conditions for ripening grapes give the wines a full-bodied if youngish flavour. Many of the producers allow **visits** (usually around €6, which includes tastings), where you can find out about the wines, then sample them over dinner – several of the vineyards have restaurants as well as tasting rooms – while the larger ones, such as the *Herdade dos Grous* (see p.416), offer tours of their estate by jeep or even horseback. The best place to start is the headquarters of the Rota dos Vinhos do Alenjo (ⓦvinhosdoalentejo.pt) in Évora (see above), which can arrange tours to most of the nearby vineyards. Recommended estates to visit include Esporão (see p.410); *Quinta do Carmo* near Estremoz (ⓦbacalhoa.com), which is part-owned by the Lafite Rothschild group; and Adega Mayor (ⓦadegamayor.pt) in the Serra de São Mamede, whose landmark heaquarters is a stunning white edifice designed by Portugal's most famous architect, Álvaro Siza Viera.

Around Évora

Leave at least an afternoon or two to explore Évora's environs, which have some significant attractions. Some, like the castles at **Évoramonte**, warrant a quick stop en route elsewhere, though the famed carpet town of **Arraiolos**, just to the north, is a popular day- or overnight trip from the city. The administrative district of Évora also contains over a dozen megalithic sites – dolmens (funerary chambers), menhirs (standing stones) and stone circles – which have their origins in a culture that flourished here before spreading north as far as Brittany and Denmark. The stones of **Os Almendres**, in particular, provide one of the country's most extraordinary sights. With your own car, you can easily combine a visit to Os Almendres with the dramatic dolmen of **Zambujeiro**. While it's tempting to take the fast road to Beja and the south, there's an attractive detour to be made into deepest rural Alentejo, via the small historic towns of **Viana do Alentejo** and **Alvito** and the Roman ruins of **São Cucufate**. From Évora the first stop, Viana do Alentejo, is a simple twenty-minute drive down the ruler-straight N254. There's no reliable public transport along this route – you'll need a car.

Anta Grande do Zambujeiro

Brown archeological signposts at Valverde – 7km southwest of Évora, down the N380 (Alcáçovas road) – lead you through the university's agricultural faculty grounds to the **Anta Grande do Zambujeiro**, a huge burial chamber lying sheltered under a corrugated-iron roof. The last 1km of the approach is along a dirt track which is usually fine for cars if it hasn't been raining, but you can always leave your vehicle and walk if you're unsure.

Zambujeiro is the largest dolmen in the country, comprising eight standing stones which lean inwards to form a funeral chamber 8m high, with a six-metre diameter. The capstone is missing and the chamber itself is fenced off for safety reasons, but the twelve-metre-long approach corridor is still largely intact. The moving of such enormous stones must have challenged the ingenuity of the Neolithic builders, and there's still a real sense of mystery here, the only sound that of chirruping crickets in the ancient olive trees.

8

Os Almendres

The Iberian peninsula's largest and most impressive stone circle lies 13km west of Évora, just south of the small village of Guadalupe. To get there directly from Évora, take the N114 towards Montemor/Lisbon and follow the signs from Guadalupe. If you're approaching from the south, from Escoural and Valverde, you need to turn left in Guadalupe, at the *Café Barreiros*.

You are directed out along a dirt road (largely flat and in good condition, fine for cars), reaching the **Menir dos Almendres** after 2km. This is a single, three-metre-high standing stone set in a quiet olive plantation five minutes' walk from the road. Despite its obvious Neolithic origins, the local legend has it that it is the tomb of an enchanted Moorish princess, who appears once a year on the eve of São João and can be seen combing her hair.

Another 2.5km along the dirt road there's a parking area beside the extraordinary **Cromeleque dos Almendres**, where no less than 92 stones are aligned for 70m down a dusty hillside. Placed here in several phases, between six and seven thousand years ago, they are thought to have been erected in a horseshoe shape as some kind of astronomical observatory and site of fertility rituals. Even today, the power of the site is undeniable, the stones resembling frozen figures gazing across the surrounding cork plantation to a distant Évora.

Arraiolos

ARRAIOLOS, 21km north of Évora, is known for its superb **carpets** (*tapetes*), which have been handwoven here since the thirteenth century. Modelled on carpets from Persia, they have been much prized for centuries and adorn the interiors of any Portuguese manor or palace worth its salt. For carpet enthusiasts, Arraiolos is a dream – every second shop sells them, and you can spend €40 on a small square or €1500 or more on a fine example.

Carpets aside, it's a very pretty small town, with a ruined hilltop castle and brightly whitewashed houses trimmed in lavender. In the paved central square, Praça Lima e Brito, there's a sixteenth-century pillory and some ancient dye chambers, 500 years old, preserved beneath glass.

ARRIVAL, INFORMATION AND ACCOMMODATION ARRAIOLOS

By bus There are 2–4 buses daily between Arraiolos and Évora (45min).

Information The turismo (Mon–Fri 9am–12.30pm & 2–5.30pm, Sat 10am–12.30pm & 2–5.30pm; ☎ 266 490 254, ⓦ cm-arraiolos.pt) is at Praça do Município 27, in the town hall.

Pousada de Arraiolos Nossa Senhora da Assunção ☎ 266 419 340, ⓦ pousadas.pt. The lovely *Pousada Nossa Senhora da Assunção* is a serene hideaway, 1km or so out of town on the Pavia road. Set in beautiful grounds, it's built into a sixteenth-century former convent, though the rooms and pool are in a very contemporary style. **€170**

Viana do Alentejo

Castle Daily: April–Sept 10am–1pm & 3–7pm; Oct–March 9.30am–1pm & 2–5.30pm • Free • Buses from Alvito (Mon–Fri 1–3 daily; 20min) and Évora (Mon–Fri 3 daily; 35min).

VIANA DO ALENTEJO is a typically dozy southern-Alentejan town which nonetheless preserves a highly decorative **castle**, full of Mudéjar and Manueline features. The walls were built on a pentagonal plan by Dom Dinis in 1313, and the interior ensemble of buildings was expanded under Dom João II and Dom Manuel I in the late fifteenth century. From this latter period dates a sequence of elaborate battlements, with their witch's-hat towers and pinnacles, and the beautiful Igreja Matriz (parish church), which has a superbly carved door.

Alvito

ALVITO, 10km south of Viana do Alentejo, is a small town with great charm and an abundance of Manueline features. It's dominated by its **castle** built in 1494 and now a *pousada* (see below) – it's a curious Manueline–Mudéjar hybrid, a style seen also in the much smaller sixteenth-century **Ermida de São Sebastião**, on the edge of town, from where there are fine views across the cultivated plains below. In the few streets between the castle, the parish church and the town-hall clock tower, many of the houses have carved sixteenth-century windows and door frames, and if you seek out the town gardens, small market and typical *pelourinho* in the handsome main square, Praça da República, you've easily occupied an hour or two.

ARRIVAL AND INFORMATION ALVITO

By bus Buses run between Alvito and Évora (Mon–Fri 3 daily; 50min) and Viana do Alentejo (Mon–Fri 1–3 daily; 20min).

Information The turismo is at Rua dos Lobos 13 (Mon–

Fri 9am–12.30pm & 2–5.30pm, Sat 10am–12.30pm & 2–5.30pm; ☎ 284 480 808), and can point you in the direction of local rural guesthouses.

ACCOMMODATION

A Varanda Praça da República 9, Alvito ☎ 284 485 135, ⓦ avaranda-hospedaria.planetaclix.pt. Opposite the castle on Praça da República, this is a pleasant guesthouse, with spotless rooms and a baronial-style restaurant serving innovative mains such as *feijoada de gambas* from €15, and

if that's not enough, you can also enjoy a cocktail at its *Bar Lady Di*. Restaurant daily noon–3pm & 7.30–11pm. **€70**

Pousada de Alvito Castelo de Alvito, Alvito ☎ 284 480 700, ⓦ pousadas.pt. You'll certainly feel secure if you stay in the town *pousada*. The fifteenth-century castle was converted into a hotel in 1993, and now boasts very stylish rooms – some with fab views over town – a swimming pool in the garden and a quality if pricey restaurant serving local produce. **€120**

Évoramonte castle

Daily: June–Sept 10am–1pm & 2.30–6.30pm; Oct–May 10am–1pm & 2.30–5pm • €2 • Buses (Mon–Fri 3 daily) between Estremoz (20min) and Évora (50min) can drop you off on the main road, though it's a long uphill hike to the castle – realistically, you'll need a car

Twenty-nine kilometres northeast of Évora, along the N18 towards Estremoz, the castle at **ÉVORAMONTE** sits impressively atop a steep hillock high above the main road and modern village. While the castle stands on Roman fortifications, what you see today dates from 1306, with a Renaissance-style keep added in the sixteenth century. It was here in 1834 that the regent Miguel was finally defeated and the convention signed that put Pedro IV on the Portuguese throne. Legend has it that the signing took so long that there was only stale bread left to eat, causing the invention of the well-known Portuguese dish *açorda* (a soup of bread, coriander, garlic and olive oil). You can visit the three vaulted chambers inside the castle, though the terrace views are the main highlight.

The upper medieval village rings the castle mound and, with care, you can clamber around the walls and gate towers, and then wander down the cobbled main street to the small church and cemetery; head to the modern settlement on the main road for cafés and restaurants.

Estremoz

8

The appealing, walled market town of **ESTREMOZ** lies in the centre of a district rich in marble quarries – so much so that the material is used extensively in the most common-place surroundings, as you'll see when you wander its marble-clad streets and squares. It was once an important border settlement where Dom Dinis, an early monarch who set about fortifying Portugal's frontiers, chose to locate his hilltop palace. Meanwhile, down in the lower town, the vast main square known as the Rossio – properly, the Rossio Marquês de Pombal – has long been the site of one of Portugal's finest **markets**, held every Saturday. It starts and finishes early, so it pays to stay over in town on Friday night if you can. The Rossio also hosts Estremoz's annual **festival** (first weekend in Sept), as well as the huge five-day agricultural shindig in April known as the **Feira Internacional de Agricultura e Pecuária**, which mixes cattle shows, concerts and handicrafts.

Torre das Três Coroas

Pousada de Santa Rainha Isabel, Largo de Dom Dinis • Access via the *pousada*; ask at reception

The castle in Estremoz is now a *pousada*, set within the star-shaped ramparts of the upper town. However, you're allowed to climb the thirteenth-century **Torre das Três Coroas** (Tower of the Three Crowns), from where there's a splendid panoramic view across the plains to the castle of Évoramonte, 15km away. In front of the tower, there's a modern statue of Isabel, Dom Dinis's queen, who devoted her life to the poor, giving away food and money with unseemly enthusiasm for a monarch. The statue recalls a well-known episode, whereby her husband challenged her to reveal what was beneath her skirt: the bread she had hidden there had been was miraculously turned into roses.

Museu Municipal Professor Joaquim Vermelho

Largo de Dom Dinis • Tues–Sun 9am–12.30pm & 2–5.30pm • €2 • ☎ 268 339 219

Set in a nineteenth-century hospice opposite the Torre das Três Coroas, the **Museu Municipal** offers a fascinating insight into traditional Alentejan life and Estremoz handicrafts. A maze of rooms, including the building's former kitchen, displays rugged domestic utensils, hand-painted country furniture and intricately carved cork figures and tableaux. Best known of all, however, is the pottery of Estremoz, from dandy figurines and rural scenes to floral pots and jars inlaid with marble chips. There's a huge collection in the museum (as well as a ceramics *atelier* in the courtyard), with a story or tradition attached to each item – such as the role the pottery used to play in gypsy weddings. During the wedding procession, the bride would make a sudden dash for freedom across the marketplace, hotly pursued by the groom. With bride eventually captured, a fine Estremoz dish was thrown into the air and the couple pronounced man and wife at the moment that the dish fell to the ground in pieces.

ARRIVAL AND INFORMATION
ESTREMOZ

By bus Buses stop outside the old train station, from where it's a two-minute walk down to the Rossio.
Destinations Elvas (6 daily; 45min); Évora (Mon–Fri 3 daily; 1hr 10min); Lisbon (4–7 daily; 2hr 30min); and Portalegre (4–7 daily; 45min).
By car Estremoz is 46km northeast of Évora. There's plenty

of free parking in the Rossio (except on Saturday market day) and also outside the *pousada* in the upper town (follow signs for "Castelo").
Information The turismo is on the south side of the main Rossio (daily 10am–1pm & 2–6pm; ☎ 268 339 227, ⓦ www.cm-estremoz.pt).

ACCOMMODATION

★ **Alentejano** Rossio Marquês de Pombal 15 ☎ 268 337 300. A traditional place overlooking the Rossio, with

a dozen appealing rooms that come with flowery painted Alentejan furniture, brass beds and marble bathrooms.

There's a bar and café downstairs and a proper old country-style restaurant on the first floor, serving good regional food (daily 7am–midnight; mains €8–10). €50

★ **O Gadanha** Largo General Graça 56 ☎ 268 339 110, ⓦ residencialogadanha.com. The best bargain in town – an immaculately kept place, the large rooms come with a/c, tiled floors and decent bathrooms. Rooms 303 and 304 have terraces with castle views. It's good for families, too, as most rooms can easily accommodate an extra bed or divan. Breakfast not available. €35

Páteo dos Solares Rua Brito Capelo ☎ 268 338 400, ⓦ pateosolares.com. There's a very genteel ambience in this beautiful town mansion ("sober but rustic" they say, which is just about right). Rooms vary (some are classed "luxo" while suites have fireplaces and fancy massage baths), and there's a pool and gardens and an upmarket terrace restaurant (mains €15–22) that offers the nicest alfresco dining in town. Parking. €170

Pousada de Santa Rainha Isabel Largo de Dom Dinis ☎ 268 332 075, ⓦ pousadas.pt. The period-piece palace scores heavily on the charm front, with dramatic vaulted public areas, and guest rooms with carved wooden beds, heavy drapes and scintillating views. A pool and gardens are hidden within the battlemented walls, while the restaurant (mains around €20; open to nonguests) offers a slick variation on the usual Alentejan cuisine, with specials such as broad beans with *chouriço* or leg of pork with garlic and coriander. Parking. €170

EATING AND DRINKING

A Cadeia Quinhentista Rua Rainha Santa Isabel ☎ 268 323 400, ⓦ cadeiaquinhentista.com. Near the *pousada*, the old sixteenth-century jail is now a high-end café-bar and restaurant, serving Alentejan specialities such as *açorda* and grilled meats (around €14), as well as quality local wines. Café-bar daily 11am–midnight; restaurant daily 12.30–3pm & 7.30–10pm.

★ **Adega do Isaias** Rua do Almeida 21 ☎ 268 322 318. The finest old-style tavern in town, lined with giant wine jars. It serves most of its food straight from the huge outdoor chargrill – steak, lamb, pork, squid and more, from around €9. Mon–Sat noon–3pm & 7–10.30pm; closed 2 weeks in Aug.

A Ribatejana Largo General Graça 41A ☎ 268 323 656. Back-room *churrasqueira* that's great for spit-roast chicken, *leitão* (suckling pig) and grills at value-for-money prices (chicken from €5, other dishes €7–11). It's a bit rough and ready, but the food's tasty – and you may have to wait for a table at weekends if you leave it late. Mon & Wed–Sun noon–3pm & 7–10pm.

São Rosas Largo de Dom Dinis 11 ☎ 268 333 345. The classiest place in the upper town is a medieval-chic inn serving fancied-up regional cuisine (mains €12.50–20). There are lots of typical Alentejan dishes, such as *porco preto*, *borrego* and *migas*. Tues–Sun 12.45–3.30pm & 7.45–10.30pm.

8

Alter do Chão

North of Estremoz, the narrow but fast N245 thunders across the olive- and cork-lined plains to **ALTER DO CHÃO**, 48km away. It's a handsome town, with the rounded towers of its castle facing directly onto a shaded central square, though the chief reason for a visit – well worth the drive – is to see the royal stud farm.

Coudelaria Alter-Real

Tapada do Arneiro, signposted 3km north of town • 90min guided tours Tues–Sun at 11am & 3pm (English spoken) • €5 • ☎ 245 610 060, ⓦ alterreal.pt

The **Coudelaria Alter-Real** stud farm was founded by royalty in 1748 and Alter-Real Lusitano horses have been greatly sought after ever since – the Lisbon Riding School at Queluz and the Portuguese mounted police both use them. Guided visits show you the cosseted stallions in their vaulted stables, as well as the *picadeiro* (riding ring) and a collection of antique carriages. Some tours start with an impressive falcon-flying demonstration, and there's also a small museum and the possibility of arranging a riding lesson in the *picadeiro* (from €25). The annual stud show and sale is every April 24, a great day for a visit.

ACCOMMODATION AND EATING   ALTER DO CHÃO

Casa Arlindo Correia Alter Pedroso, 3km east of Alter do Chão ☎ 245 612 301, ⓦ pateoreal.com. For a real get-away-from-it-all retreat, stay at this rural guesthouse in the little hill village of Alter Pedroso. There are just four cosy rooms, and guests have the use of a kitchenette and living room – or head down to town for a meal in their associated restaurant, *Páteo Real* (see below). No credit cards. **€55**

Páteo Real Av Dr João Pestana 37 ☎ 245 612 301, ⓦ pateoreal.com. Easily the best place for lunch, just down from castle and square. It has a lovely vine-shaded terrace where you can enjoy a good meal of daily changing specialities, from roast lamb to *migas* with wild asparagus (dishes from around €7). Mon & Wed–Sun noon–11pm.

Crato

CRATO – 13km north of Alter do Chão – is an ancient agricultural town that has clearly seen better days and larger populations. A trio of imposing churches and the elegant **Varanda do Grão Prior** (an arcaded granite balcony) in the pretty main Praça do Município attest to the boom years of the sixteenth century. Indeed Crato's largely fifteenth-century castle was once among the mightiest in the Alentejo, but is currently being renovated after years of neglect. In the centre of town, you can't miss the dominant colour scheme – white with mustard-yellow trim – that adorns every single house, mansion to cottage.

From Crato, it's a 7km drive west along the N363 (towards Aldeia da Matato) to the **Anta do Tapadão**, which is reckoned to be the best-preserved dolmen in Portugal. The leaning stones are visible atop a small rise in the middle of grazing land away to the left; access is by foot along a farm track.

ARRIVAL AND DEPARTURE
CRATO

By bus There's one daily bus to Crato from Portalegre (20min), though the town is really only a coffee stop if you're driving – unless of course you fancy a night at the glam *pousada*.

ACCOMMODATION AND EATING

Pousada to Crato, Flor da Rosa Mosteiro da Flor da Rosa, 2km north of Crato ☎ 245 997 210, ⓦ pousadas .pt. This impressive Gothic monastery was founded in the fourteenth century but reopened in 1995 as a stylish hotel. The gardens are laid out in the insignia of the Order of Malta, in honour of the warlord Nuno Álvares Pereira, whose father founded the monastery. It's a magnificent building, marrying contemporary style with the convent buildings – there's a games room in the upper cloister and a lovely restaurant. **€180**

Portalegre

PORTALEGRE is the capital, market centre and transport hub of Alto Alentejo, a busy commercial town of around 20,000 people in the foothills of the Serra de São Mamede. Like most Alentejan towns, it has a whitewashed old quarter, but it's Portalegre's industrial history that looms large. Until the end of the seventeenth century, the town was a major textiles centre, though the 1703 Methuen Treaty largely put paid to the trade. However, reminders of a prosperous past still survive and lend the town a certain character. The largest tapestry factory – once housed in a Jesuit college in the lower town – has been beautifully restored as city council offices, while the great brick twin chimneys at the very top of town belong to the **Fábrica Robinson**, a cork factory originally established by an enterprising Yorkshireman (there are plans to turn this into a cultural centre).

All roads converge on the **Rossio**, the nineteenth-century square with a fountain that's at the heart of modern Portalegre. Beyond here the **town gardens** flank Avenida da Liberdade, the lower part featuring a renowned plane tree (*plátano*), planted in 1848, whose spreading branches are now so long they have to be supported by pillars.

Museu da Tapeçaria Guy Fino
Rua da Figueira 9 · Tues–Sun 9.30am–1pm & 2.30–6pm · €2.50 · ☎ 245 307 530

You can trace the history of local tapestry-making in the fascinating **Museu da Tapeçaria Guy Fino**, housed in a converted mansion. There are examples of old looms and a selection of the hundreds of different shades of wool that were once used in the manufacture of tapestries. Exhibitions change regularly, and there may be classical tapestry designs on show or displays of contemporary Portuguese art.

The old town

The old town is reached up steep cobbled streets lined with grand mercantile mansions, a legacy of the wealth from silk workshops and textile factories that once thrived here. **Rua 19 de Junho** – the main thoroughfare at the top of the old town – has some particularly fine examples. In nearby Rua do Carmo, you'll find the remains of Portalegre's thirteenth-century **Castelo** (Tues–Sun 9.30am–1pm & 2.30–6pm; free), whose old walls and remaining tower can be accessed via a series of modern wooden walkways, which offer fine views over the surroundings; there's also a small temporary-exhibition space.

ARRIVAL AND INFORMATION

By bus The bus station is on Rua Nuno Álvares Pereira, just west of the Rossio.

Destinations Beja (1–4 daily; 3hr 45min); Castelo de Vide (2 daily; 20min); Crato (1 daily; 20min); Estremoz (4–7 daily; 45min); Évora (2–3 daily; 1hr 25min–1hr 45min); and Lisbon (4–7 daily; 2hr 45min–3hr 45min).

By car There's lots of free parking by the gardens, near the Rossio.

PORTALEGRE

Information The turismo is at Rua Guilhermo Gomes Fernandes 22 (daily 9.30am–1pm & 2.30–6pm; ☎ 245 307 445, ⊚ cm-portalegre.pt). The Parque Natural da Serra de São Mamede HQ is at Rua General Jorge Conde de Ávilez 22 (Mon–Fri 9am–12.30pm & 2–5.30pm; ☎ 245 203 631, ⊚ icnb.pt), and has useful pamphlets with half-day waymarked walks in the *parque natural*, which spreads north and east of town.

ACCOMMODATION

⭐ **Convento da Provença** Monte Paleiros, 4km north of Portalegre, on the Marvão road ☎ 245 337 104, ⊚ provenca.pt. This restored convent is now a classy boutique *turismo rural*. Nine cool, tile-floor and oak-beam rooms look out over a pool and surrounding cork and olive groves, while the public areas have comfy sofas overseen by suits of armour. Breakfast can be taken on the terrace in the shadow of the ruined convent walls and arches. **€85**

⭐ **Mansão Alto Alentejo** Rua 19 de Junho 59 ☎ 245 202 290, ⊚ mansaoaltoalentejo.com.pt. The town's best choice up in the old town has traditional Alentejan decor (flowery painted headboards, country furniture) in twelve neat and decently sized en-suite, a/c rooms. **€45**

Nova Rua 31 de Janeiro 28–30 ☎ 245 331 212. Friendly place with 14 simple rooms, nicely turned out, with private bath and a decent breakfast served in the downstairs dining room. No credit cards. **€40**

EATING AND DRINKING

Casa Capote Rua 19 de Junho 56 ☎ 245 906 185. Swing-door tavern on one side, typical local restaurant on the other, where you can eat a starter, main and dessert for around €10. Daily noon–3pm & 7–9pm.

O Abrigo Rua de Elvas 74 ☎ 245 331 658. In the heart of the old town, this restaurant is a favourite with Portalegre families serving locally inspired Alentejan dishes, meat

and fish, from around €9. Mon & Wed–Sun noon–10pm.

⭐ **Santos** Largo Serpa Pinto 4 ☎ 245 203 066. You can eat on the outdoor deck in a pretty square, or in the rustic dining room. It's good for pork and fish (mains €6–10), while the mention of *sobremesas* brings out a mini photo album of amateur shots of puds on tables. Mon, Tues, Wed & Thurs noon–3pm & 7–11pm.

ENTERTAINMENT

Centro de Artes do Espetáculo Praça da República 39 ☎ 245 307 498, ⊚ caeportalegre.blogspot.com. The town's arts centre has a great programme of music, dance,

theatre and film, from world music gigs to symphony orchestras.

Castelo de Vide

Twenty kilometres north of Portalegre, the small town of **CASTELO DE VIDE** throws up one of the nicest surprises in the Alto Alentejo. A castle rises up above a fairy-tale townscape of bright white houses, while steep cobbled streets and placid squares are lined with well-watered pots of geraniums, tumbling house plants and two-metre-high sunflowers. Mineral springs pepper the local hills and the town is full of public fountains in gleaming *praças* and shaded gardens. It's one of those places that begs an aimless, meandering stroll, and it's very easy to find you've spent a couple of days here doing not very much at all quite happily.

With a car or a bike you can also spend an enjoyable day tracking down dolmens, menhirs and *antas*, which are the remains of an important **megalithic** culture that once flourished between the modern-day settlements of Castelo de Vide, the Barragem de

Póvoa and the village of Póvoa e Meadas, 10km to the north. The turismo has useful leaflets and more information.

Judiaria

The lower town stretches from the pretty public gardens to the main Igreja de Santa Maria, behind which are the cobbled lanes of the **Judiaria** – the old Jewish quarter – which was first established by Jews fleeing the Inquisition in Spain. It's a jumble of carefully kept cottages with distinctive granite door-frames, many with brilliant floral displays carpeting the steps. In one small square sits the **Fonte da Vila**, a Renaissance marble fountain dispensing Castelo de Vide's famed mineral water.

Sinagoga

Rua da Judiaria • Tues–Sun 9.30am–1pm & 2.30–6pm • Free • ☎ 245 901 361

Just off the precipitous Rua da Fonte lies the thirteenth-century **Sinagoga**, the oldest surviving synagogue in Portugal. From the outside it doesn't look very different to the houses from which it was originally adapted, but inside the tabernacle survives as part of a small museum detailing the life of Jews in the town.

Castelo

Daily: June–Sept 9.30am–6pm; Oct–May 9.30am–5pm • Free

At the top of the hill you reach the walls and gateway of the **Castelo**, whose foursquare keep squats within the wider fortifications of the original *burgo medieval* (medieval village). The views over the green and grey plains beyond are magnificent, while across town you can see the walls of the **Forte de São Roque**, Castelo de Vide's other defensive bulwark (always open; free) – there's nothing to see inside, though the nearby Praça Alta provides more sweeping views across the plain.

ARRIVAL AND INFORMATION

CASTELO DE VIDE

By bus Buses from Lisbon (2 daily; 4hr 10min) and Portalegre (2 daily; 20min) drop you at the central *pelourinho* by the town-hall clock tower, on Rua Bartolomeu Álvares da Santa.

By car There's ample free parking in clearly marked bays all around the main square and street.

Information The turismo is at Praça Dom Pedro V, just behind the town hall, through the arch (daily: June–Sept 9am–1pm & 3–6pm; Oct–May 9am–12.30pm & 2–5.30pm; ☎ 245 908 227, ⓦ cm-castelo-vide.pt).

ACCOMMODATION

★ **Casa Amarela** Praça Dom Pedro V 11 ☎ 245 905 878, ⓦ casaamarelath.pt. The most noble address in town, in keeping with the general ambience, is this lovely yellow mansion, its carved stone windows overlooking the main square. Beautiful rooms with plenty of space, marble bathrooms, antiques and polished wood. Parking outside. **€100**

Casa Machado Rua Luís de Camões 33 ☎ 245 901 515, ⓦ casamachado.com.pt. You'll find modern, spick-and-span rooms, sharing a patio and kitchen, at the western (bottom) edge of town, 300m from Porta São João. No credit cards. **€30**

Melanie Largo do Paço Novo 3 ☎ 245 901 632. Best value of the budget guesthouses at the western (town centre) end of the public gardens is provided by this friendly, English-speaking place with five nice, spacious rooms. No credit cards. **€35**

EATING AND DRINKING

Dom Pedro V Praça Dom Pedro V ☎ 245 901 236. The place for quality regional dishes, from the usual grills to country standards such as *arroz de lebre* (rice with hare) and *bacalhau com natas*. Mains cost €10–18, and you'll be hard pushed to resist trying one of the *doces conventuais*, the rich convent-recipe desserts that close any blow-out meal in these parts. Daily noon–10.30pm.

★ **Os Amigos** Rua Bartolomeu Álvares da Santa 43 ☎ 245 901 781. "The Friends" is just that, a cheery *churrasqueira* run by guys who dish up grilled platters (goat, pork, chicken and *bacalhau*) for €8–12 (most dishes feed two). It's great to eat out on the street, where the several cafés and bars over the road add to the general gaiety. Mon, Tues & Thurs–Sun noon–3pm & 7–10pm.

Marvão

By the time you've negotiated the winding road up to **MARVÃO** you're ready for sensational panoramas, and the remote border outpost doesn't disappoint. From the dramatically sited rocky outcrop high above the undulating *serra* there are unbeatable views, while within a complete circuit of seventeenth-century walls lies a higgledy-piggledy town of fewer than a thousand residents, inhabiting neat houses with granite windows and pitched red roofs. It's a fixture on the tourist trail of course, although many do no more than drive up for a quick look around, so spending the night here is an attractive proposition. There are few actual sights in the village save a couple of historical museums, and some displays, exhibitions and local handicrafts in the **Casa da Cultura** (daily 9am–12.30pm & 2–5.30pm; free), housed in the old town hall. But in the end, it's just as rewarding to simply climb up and down the switchback cobbled streets and sit awhile in the impeccably kept terrace gardens.

Castelo

Always open • Free

The town takes its name from Marvan, a Moorish ruler, and it was the Moors who built the town's first fortifications in around the eighth century. It passed into Christian hands in 1166, and the following century, Dom Dinis built the **Castelo** and walled town that stands today. You're free to walk into the castle and admire a huge *cisterna*, just inside the main entrance, still full of water, designed to supply the entire village, though most impressive of all are the views from the walls.

8

Cidade Romana de Ammaia

7km south of Marvão on the Portalegre road • Tues–Fri 9am–1pm & 2–5pm, Sat & Sun 10am–1pm & 2–5pm • €2.50 • Follow the signs for São Salvador de Aramenha from the Portagem junction

The **Cidade Romana de Ammaia** is located in a beautiful site in a wooded hollow, with Marvão high on its bluff in the distance. Sheep graze across the Roman remains, which include parts of the south gate, a bath complex, forum and temple, while a small museum occupies the kitchen and basement of an old Roman house.

ARRIVAL AND INFORMATION   MARVÃO

By bus Buses from Portalegre (Mon–Fri 1–2 daily; 40min) stop just outside the Portas de Rodão.

By car Marvão is 12km from Castelo de Vide and 17km from Portalegre. It's best to park at the village gate, the Portas de Rodão. You *can* drive further into the village, following signs for the turismo and castle, but it's narrow and unnerving.

Information The turismo is on Largo da Silverinha, on the way to the castle (June–Sept Mon–Fri 9am–7pm, Sat & Sun 10am–12.30pm and 2–7pm; Oct–May daily 9am–12.30pm & 2–5.30pm; ☎245 993 456, ⓦcm-marvao.pt).

ACCOMMODATION

Casa do Árvore Rua Doutor Matos Magalhães ☎245 993 854. A gleaming, traditional townhouse whose five genteel rooms have wooden floors, carved pine beds and great views from the living room and terrace. €55

★ **Casa Dom Dinis** Rua Dr António Matos Magalhães 8 ☎245 993 272, ⓦter-domdinis.com. On the corner across from the turismo, this house has charming rooms featuring striking murals and paintings, and there's a terrace with views (great for sunset-watching), though you can also pay extra for room 15, which has its own private terrace. Across the road is the *Castelo* café-bar, under the

same management, where you can sit outside under the spreading trees. €90

El-Rei Dom Manuel Largo de Olivença ☎245 909 150, ⓦturismarvao.pt. You'll find this spruce mid-range option in the first square through the gate, and there's parking right outside. It's worth paying €10 extra for the rooms that face out with expansive views, and some have little balconies or terraces. The in-house restaurant is a moderately priced place, too (mains around €12). €75

Pousada de Santa Maria Rua 24 de Janeiro 7 ☎245 993 201, ⓦpousadas.pt. The smartest place in the village is the small-scale *pousada*, converted from a couple of former village houses. Rooms are cute and cosy, and while

not all have views, those that do are blessed. The restaurant is the finest in Marvão (mains from €20). €120

EATING AND DRINKING

Casa do Povo Travessa do Chabouco ☎ 245 993 160. There's only a simple menu of basic grills and Portuguese dishes (€8–11) served here, but the killer attraction is the café terrace with big views to die for. Order a jug of *sangría* and settle in. Mon–Wed & Fri–Sun noon–10am.

Varanda do Alentejo Praça do Pelourinho 1 ☎ 245 993 272. Right in the middle of the village, by the *pelourinho*, and the best place outside the *pousada* to sample the regional cuisine. There's a good range of *petiscos* followed by dishes such as *migas* with *porco preto* or goat stew (mains €8–11). Daily 12.30–3pm & 7.30–10pm.

Elvas

The attractive hilltop town of **ELVAS** was once one of Portugal's mightiest frontier posts, strategically positioned just 15km from Spanish Badajoz, to the east across the Rio Guadiana. Its star-shaped walls and outlying forts are among the best-preserved military fortifications in Europe, a factor that subsequently helped gain the town UNESCO World Heritage status. Its military significance long past, and down to a population of around 25,000, it looks largely to tourism these days – Spanish day-trippers pop over to climb the steep cobbled streets and sit in the restored central square, while the vibrant **Monday market** (held on alternate weeks) is a big attraction, held just outside town behind the aqueduct. Otherwise, the town's main annual bash is its week-long **Festa de São Mateus**, starting on September 20 and including the largest procession in southern Portugal.

Brief history

Today's fortifications date largely from 1643–53 – that is, they were built during the Wars of Restoration with Spain (1641–68). Under the direction of a Dutch Jesuit, Padre Cosmander, an already impressive circuit of walls was supplemented by extensive moats and star-shaped ramparts. The result is considered to be the finest example of the Dutch school of fortifications anywhere in the world. In 1644, the garrison withstood a nine-day siege by Spanish troops, and in 1658, with its numbers reduced by an epidemic to a mere thousand, Elvas saw off a fifteen-thousand-strong Spanish army. During the Peninsular Wars in 1811, the fort provided the base from which Wellington successfully attacked Badajoz.

Praça da República and Largo de Santa Clara

The heart of town is the restored **Praça da República**, ringed by cafés and dominated by the mighty but ultimately underwhelming Igreja de Nossa Senhora da Assunção. A more interesting sight lies up the steep street behind the church in **Largo de Santa Clara**, a tiny, cobbled square built on a slope around a splendid sixteenth-century **pelourinho**. Criminals were chained from the four metal hooks near the top – the strung-up n'er-do-wells were unlikely to have appreciated the pillar's artistically twisted Manueline column.

Igreja de Nossa Senhora da Consolação

Largo da Santa Clara • Tues–Sun 9.30am–12.30pm & 2.30–7pm; Oct–April closes at 5.30pm • Free

The plain exterior of the small **Igreja de Nossa Senhora da Consolação** gives no clue as to the richness within. Inside you'll find a series of beautifully decorated columns rising up to a patterned cupola, while the walls are lined with ornate *azulejos*. The octagonal shape of the chapel probably pays homage to the Knights Templar: the sixteenth-century church replaced an older Knights Templar chapel that once stood nearby.

ELVAS

▲ Badajoz (N4)

ACCOMMODATION
António Mocisso 2
Quinta de Santo António 1
Quinta Vale de Marmelos 4
São João de Deus 3

● **RESTAURANTS AND CAFÉS**
Canal 7 1
O Lagar 3
O Machado 2

N

0   200
metres

◀ Forte da Graça

▶ Forte da Santa Luzia

Portas de São Vicente

Igreja de São Domingos

Igreja de São Pedro

Igreja dos Terceiros

Castelo

Cinema

Bus Station ★

RUA MOLTINHO DE ALBUQUERQUE

RUA DO PADRÃO

RUA DA BANDEIRA

RUA DO ESPIRITO SANTO

RUA S. PEDRO

RUA DE VILA BOIM

RUA BENT. COUTINHO

R. DE S. LOURENÇO

LARGO DE S. DOMINGOS

Library

RUA DOS CHILÕES

AV. DE S. DOMINGOS

Market

Pelourinho

Theatre

SAPATEIROS

RUA DA OLIVENÇA

PRAÇA DA REPUBLICA

ⓘ

RUA DA CARREIRA

RUA DE OLIVENÇA

RUA ALCAMIM

Portas de Olivença

Igreja de N.S. da Consolação

Igreja de N.S. da Assunção

Câmara Municipal

RUA DE CADEIA

RUA DA FEIRA

RUA CARRITO

R. FALCATO

R. ARGOS

RUA JOAO CASQUEIRO

RUA DO TABOLADO

AVENIDA GARCIA DE ORTA

P

P

P

P

P

P

LARGO DE SANTA CLARA

Police

RUA DE S. FRANCISCO

RUA DA MISERICORDIA

RUA PINTO

R. NOVA DA VIRGINIA

AV. DE ÉVORA

PR. 25 DE ABRIL

Military Prison

RUA 14 JANEIRO

Portas da Esquina

LARGO CISTERNA

Aqueduto da Amoreira

Jardim Municipal

AV. DE BADAJOZ

◀ **1** & Portalegre (N246)

◀ Estremoz (N4)

▶ Cidade Jardim

8

4

Castelo

Daily 9am–1pm & 2.30–5.30pm · €2 · ☎ 268 626 403

A pretty little quarter of whitewashed mansions and cottages surround Elvas' **Castelo**, to the north of the old town. A Roman fort was first built here, which was then developed by the Moors, though what you see today largely dates back to modifications made in the late fifteenth century. The admission fee lets you climb the battlements, with magnificent views over the surrounding plains (a view you can also enjoy from terraces outside the castle walls). Only from here do you start to appreciate the extent of the town's dramatic fortifications.

Aqueduto da Amoreira

The dramatic **Aqueduto da Amoreira**, at the entrance to town, was constructed between the late sixteenth and early seventeenth centuries. Its series of arches on five levels extend for seven kilometres and the chunky structure was a major factor in Elvas' invincibility – even under siege, the town had enough water to supply its citizens.

Forte de Santa Luzia

May–Sept Tues–Sun 10am–1pm & 3–7pm; Oct–April Tues–Sun 10am–1pm & 2–5pm · €3 · ☎ 268 628 357

Other buildings in the Elvas area that have UNESCO World Heritage status are the outlying forts, including the Forte da Graça (closed to the public), a couple of kilometres north, and the star-shaped **Forte de Santa Luzia**, 1.5km to the south on the Spain road. Built in 1687, the fort was used as a prison in Salazar's time, and is now a military museum, worth visiting for the chance to look across at the impressive ramparts of Elvas.

ARRIVAL AND INFORMATION

ELVAS

By bus The bus station is outside the walls on the Spain road: it's a longish walk in to the centre, so it's best to take a taxi for a few euros.

Destinations Estremoz (6 daily; 45min); Évora (3–4 daily; 1hr 30min); Lisbon (7 daily; 3hr 15min); and Vila Viçosa (2 daily; 35min).

By car Elvas is 40km east of Estremoz. There's parking by the entrances to the old town, though you can also follow the "Castelo" signs up through town – the narrow streets are a bit hair-raising at times, but there's a pay car park under Praça da República and lots of free parking by the castle.

Information The turismo is on Praça da República (Mon–Fri 9am–6pm, Sat & Sun 10am–12.30pm & 2–5.30pm; ☎ 268 622 236, ⓦ cm-elvas.pt).

ACCOMMODATION

António Mocisso Rua Aires Varela 15, off Rua de João d'Olivença ☎ 268 622 126, ⓦ residencial-antonio -mocisso.webnode.pt. Popular budget place in the jumble of streets (signposted) off the main square. The rooms are fairly compact, but you get a private bathroom, fridge, wi-fi and a/c at the lowest rates in town. Your room could be in one of several buildings nearby. No credit cards. Breakfast not included. €30

★ **Quinta de Santo António** Estrada de Barbacena, off the Portalegre road, 5km northwest of Elvas ☎ 268 636 460, ⓦ qsahotel.com. A very relaxed, informal rural estate with rambling wooded gardens, courtyards, fountains and an excellent large swimming pool. The handsome rooms have parquet floors, marble window seats and antique beds, and there are some two- and three-bedroom apartments too, plus a moderately priced restaurant. Child-friendly, there's a playground and various activities on offer including donkey rides on request. €70

★ **Quinta Vale de Marmelos** Estrada da Olivença, 3km south of Elvas ☎ 268 626 193, ⓦ quintavalede marmelos.co.uk. A charming rural *quinta* just outside Elvas with a self-catering cottage in the grounds, sleeping two, with its own roof terrace (€75). There's also a spacious room with a large balcony in the main house. You can use the communal pool and barbecue, with lovely gardens and fruit trees all around; meals on request. €83

São João de Deus Largo João de Deus 1 ☎ 268 639 220, ⓦ hotelsaojoaodeus.com. This beautifully restored four-star hotel right by the walls is the finest place in the town centre. Formerly a convent, it retains its grand sense of space and an interior of *azulejos* and warm colours. The rooms mix contemporary and traditional style, the restaurant occupies the old convent refectory, and there's a small terrace pool with city views. Parking. €70

EATING AND DRINKING

Elvas has a fairly good selection of **restaurants**, covering all price ranges. The best place to buy picnic supplies is the early-morning food **market** held Monday to Saturday at the bottom of Rua dos Chilões, by the walls. Elvas is not a late-night kind of place, but the **cafés** overlooking Praça da República can be relied upon for daytime drinks and stay open until around midnight.

Canal 7 Rua dos Sapateiros 16 ☎268 623 593. This backstreet grill house may lack sophistication, but is the best of the budget places – enormous helpings of chicken, suckling pig and the like for under €10. Daily noon–11pm.

O Lagar Rua Nova da Vendoria 7 ☎268 626 247. Good regional cuisine accompanied by a blessed blast of the air conditioning. Clams, cuttlefish, *bacalhau*, *açordas* and *cataplanas* sit alongside the usual grills, and the *porco*

alentejana is excellent. Most dishes cost €8.50–11.50. Mon–Wed & Fri–Sun noon–3pm & 7.30–10.30pm.

★ **O Machado** Rua de Cadeia ☎268 628 155. A favourite with lunching locals – and it has the advantage of shaded street-side tables. The chalkboard *pratos do dia* are always the best deal (otherwise mains cost €7–12), highlighting a changing selection of *bacalhau*, *porco* and other regional dishes. Daily noon–3pm & 7.30–11pm.

Vila Viçosa

The pretty town of **VILA VIÇOSA** is dominated entirely by its ducal palace – the last residence of the Portuguese monarchy – and by the coachloads of tourists who descend upon it for a quick visit before being whisked off again. Because of that, it's actually quite a pleasant place to spend the night, with an unhurried small-town atmosphere that survives the daily imposition of visitors. As at Estremoz, marble is the dominant building material: the road from Borba, 5km away, is lined on either side with enormous marble quarries, and in town everything, from the pavements to the humblest building, is made of the local stone.

Brief history

The dukes of Bragança established their seat here in the fifteenth century, originally in the castle and then, from the early sixteenth century, in the Paço Ducal. The family were always an influential part of Portugal's ruling elite, but it was only after Spain's Philip II took over the Portuguese throne in 1581, that the Bragança family became truly powerful. After sixty years of Spanish rule, Portuguese soldiers rebelled and occupied the palace at Lisbon. The Duke of Bragança was the obvious choice to take back the throne from the Spanish and he duly became Dom João IV of Portugal. From 1640 to the birth of the Republic in 1910, the dynasty continued to rule as monarchs. Although the Bragançan dukes and kings had lavish palaces all over the country, they often chose to stay in Vila Viçosa – indeed it was here that Dom Carlos slept the night before he was shot in a republican uprising in the capital in 1908. His son, Manuel II, also used the palace frequently before his eventual exile to Britain two years later. Afterwards, the family was banned from entering Portugal until 1950 so, it is alleged that when the current duke, Dom Duarte Pio – who still considers himself heir to the throne – was born (1945) it was in the Portuguese embassy in Berne, Switzerland, to ensure any possible future right of succession.

Paço Ducal

Terreiro do Paço • April–Sept Tues 2.30–5.30pm, Wed–Fri 10am–1pm & 2.30–5.30pm, Sat, Sun & hols 9.30am–1pm & 2.30–6pm; Oct–March Tues 2–5pm, Wed–Fri 10am–1pm & 2–5pm, Sat, Sun & hols 9.30am–1pm & 2–5pm • Tours €6; Armoury €3; Chinese porcelain collection €2.50; Coach museum €2 • ⓦ fcbraganca.pt

One whole side of the gleaming marble palace square is taken up by the **Paço Ducal**, which can only be seen on an obligatory one-hour guided tour. This is usually in Portuguese and none too revealing – and you might well pass up on the opportunity to visit the armoury, treasury, coach museum and Chinese porcelain collection (separate charges for all) that also form part of the complex. You are led dutifully through formal chambers and halls filled with regal furniture, glowering oil paintings and faded tapestries, and it's only in the more intimate private apartments that you get any real sense of the lives of the penultimate king, Dom Carlos, and his wife Marie-Amélia. There's a *Hello!* magazine fascination in gazing at the old family photographs and everyday objects on display which reveal their taste in fashion and food.

The old Bragança dukes were buried opposite the palace in the chapel of the **Mostéiro dos Agostinhos**, while the duchesses had their own mausoleum in the **Convento das Chagas**, just to the side of the palace – part of this is now the *pousada*. Before you leave the square, walk a little way up the road out of town (to Borba), where on the left the **Porta do Nós** is a Manueline stone gateway formed into the knot symbol of the Bragança family.

Castelo and around

Av dos Duques de Bragança • April–Sept Tues 2.30–5.30pm, Wed–Fri 10am–1pm & 2.30–5.30pm, Sat, Sun & hols 9.30am–1pm & 2.30–6pm; Oct–March Tues 2–5pm, Wed–Fri 10am–1pm & 2–5pm, Sat, Sun & hols 9.30am–1pm & 2–5pm • €3 • ⓦ cbraganca.pt

Avenida dos Duques de Bragança runs from the palace square past the thirteenth-century hilltop **Castelo**, built by Dom Dinis. It was the original home of the Bragança family before their larger, more lavish palace was built. You can take an hour-long guided tour of the interior, which now houses a moderately interesting museum dedicated to hunting and archeology, but you don't need to pay to climb the outer castle walls for views over town.

The original population of Vila Viçosa was based below the castle inside the walls of the old town. A few cobbled streets, white cottages and a sixteenth-century *pelourinho* are all that remain, along with the **Nossa Senhora de Conceição**, the pick of Vila Viçosa's 22 churches, filled with eighteenth-century *azulejos*.

ARRIVAL AND INFORMATION VILA VIÇOSA

By bus The bus station is opposite the municipal market at the foot of Largo Dom João IV – cross the square and it's a 200-metre walk up any of the streets ahead of you to the elongated main square, Praça da República.
Destinations Elvas (2 daily; 35min); Évora (3 daily; 1hr); Lisbon (3 daily; 2hr 40min–3hr).

By car Vila Viçosa is 35km southwest of Elvas, and 17km southeast of Estremoz. There's plenty of free parking in front of the palace or over in the town centre by the main squares.
Information The turismo is on Praça da República, in the town hall, near the upper (church) end (daily 9am–12.30pm & 2–5.30pm; ☎ 268 889 317, ⓦ cm-vilavicosa.pt).

ACCOMMODATION

Dom Carlos Praça da República 25 ☎ 268 980 318. Across the square from the turismo – so a great central position – this has decently sized rooms and is the most obvious budget choice. It's fine for a night, though the rooms are slightly overpriced. Breakfast not included. **€40**
★ **Pousada de Dom João IV** Terreiro do Paço ☎ 268 980 742, ⓦ pousadas.pt. Regal accommodation right by the palace in a converted sixteenth-century convent that retains its echoing halls, corridors, nuns' cells and cloister. Rooms are very elegant and the pool and gardens at the back are a hit with families. The restaurant (mains from

€20) is the glam dining spot in town, and there's nothing nicer than breakfast overlooking the orange trees in the peaceful cloister. Parking. **€150**
Solar dos Mascarenhas Rua Florbela Espança 125 ☎ 268 886 000, ⓦ solardosmascarenhas.com. Down the road between the palace and the main square, this converted mansion has stylish three-star accommodation, plus an outdoor terrace and decent pool. You can expect to pay an exta €20 or so per night at weekends. The restaurant (mains €15–18) offers a classier take on regional cuisine than most local places. **€70**

EATING

★ **0 Forno** Rua Cristovão de Brito Pereira 13 ☎ 268 999 797. A backstreet joint, just down from the square

(there are signs), that doesn't look like much but offers great budget dining (most dishes €6–12), and has a few

DON'T PICK THE FLOWERS

Every two years, the pretty little whitewashed town of **Redondo** (18km sout[...]
Viçosa) bursts into bloom during the extraordinary **Ruas Floridas**, a week-lo[...]
with a difference. In a revival of a nineteenth-century tradition, the cobbled[...]
are covered in flowers, shade canopies, human figures, exotic animals and l[...]
made entirely from coloured paper. Each street is responsible for choosing a[...]
might walk up to the castle through a steamy jungle complete with elephants and parrots a[...]
back down along a Brazilian beach; caricatures of the local women wash clothes in a paper
river, while wild boars root in paper acorns. At lunchtime, every single restaurant in Redondo is
crammed with local families and visitors; at night there are marching bands, dances, concerts
and bullfights. The event is biennial (odd years) and is usually held from the last day or two in
July through the first week in August (exact dates on the local town council website
Ⓦ cm-redondo.pt).

tables in the cobbled alley. It's mainly a grills place, but there are tasty *cozinha típica* specials such as *frango frito* (fried chicken), *favas* and *migas* that really hit the spot. Mon–Sat 12.30–3pm & 7.30–10.30pm.
Os Cucos Mata Municipal ☎ 268 980 806. At the top of the market square, in the town gardens, this popular place is particularly good for fish and there's a changing list of daily specials – you'll eat well for around €20. **Daily 12.30–3pm & 7.30–11pm; closed 2 weeks in Aug.**

Monsaraz and around

8

MONSARAZ – known locally as *Ninho das Águias* (Eagles' Nest) – is perched high above the border plains, a tiny village nestled into fortified walls close to the Spanish border. The views from the walls are magnificent: to the north and west, you survey a typically flat Alentejan plain of vineyards and olive groves, while to the south and east a watery expanse glitters far below the village, part of Europe's largest artificial reservoir behind the dam at Alqueva (see p.411). The village does its best to attract visitors with a series of little galleries, craft shops and restaurants, but it's really the **castle**, the higgledy-piggeldy streets and stunning views that keep people coming.

Four thousand years ago, the region around Monsaraz was an important centre of megalithic culture, and various **dolmens** (covered temples or tombs), **menhirs** (standing stones) and stone circles survive today. An hour and a half's driving circuit takes in most of these, and if you throw in lunch and a vineyard visit at nearby Reguengos that's a good day out.

Monsaraz

With a permanent population of only a few hundred, Monsaraz has just two main streets that run parallel to each other, Rua Direita and Rua de Santiago. The **Igreja Matriz** lies at the heart of the village, just off the main square that's home to a curious eighteenth-century **pillory**. The **Torre das Feiticeiras** (Witches' Tower) looms from the castle at the southern end of the village, part of a chain of impressive frontier fortresses, once ruled over by the Knights Templar and later the Order of Christ, who ensured the fortified town stayed in Christian hands long after it was taken from the Moors in 1167.

Cromeleque do Xerez

1.5km below the village; leave Monsaraz and follow the signs at the first roundabout for the Convento do Orada

The most impressive megalithic monument in the surroundings is the **Cromeleque do Xerez**, a square "circle" of 49 granite stones with a towering four-metre-high central

, which is thought to have been built to host fertility rites in Neolithic times. by the low walls near the convent and it's a two-hundred-metre walk to where e stones have been re-erected – they were moved here from their original site when the Alqueva dam was flooded.

São Pedro do Corval

It is an easy twenty-minute drive to **São Pedro do Corval**, off the Reguengos road, known for its ceramics workshops, many of which line the road. Some of these might tempt you to stop for a browse around – a few of the workshops and galleries also stock the hand-woven woollen scarves, rugs and blankets in which the region specializes.

Herdade do Esporão

Reguengos de Monsaraz, 15km west of Monsaraz • Tours at 11am, 3pm & 5pm • €6 • reservations on ☏ 66 509 280, ⓦ esporao.com • Wine bar daily 10am–6pm • Restaurant daily 12.30–3.30pm

Just south of the wine town of Reguengos, **Herdade do Esporão** is the oldest wine estate in the region, dating back to 1267 – though viniculture here has been bought bang up to date under Australian wine-maker David Baverstock. Visitors can tour the estate by Segway – or jeep if that doesn't appeal. As well as seeing the wine presses, cellars, bottling plant and vineyards, you can also visit the restaurant and bar to sample the estate's own olive oil as well as its wine.

ARRIVAL AND INFORMATION

By bus From Évora, you have to catch a bus to Reguengos de Monsaraz (2–7 daily; 35min–1hr) and change there for Monsaraz (Mon–Fri 3–5 daily; 35min). Buses stop right outside the town gates.

By car Drivers should use the various car parks outside the gates.

Information The turismo is on Rua Direita (daily 10am–1pm & 2–6pm; ☏ 266 557 136, ⓦ cm-reguengos -monsaraz.pt).

ACCOMMODATION

Several houses along Rua Direita and its continuation advertise **rooms**, sheltered behind thick walls in traditional Alentejan homes – cool in summer, warm in winter – many with stone floors, painted furniture, terraces and balconies. Prices are broadly similar (€70 a room including breakfast), cheaper outside peak summer season.

Casa Dona Antónia Rua Direita 15 ☏ 266 557 142, ⓦ casadantonia-monsaraz.com. A good first point of call, *Casa Dona Antónia* has a homely cottage interior and a lovely patio garden. The six double rooms and one suite are simple but cool and clean, and if you can stretch to an extra €10, you get a view thrown in. __€60__; suite __€90__

Estalagem de Monsaraz Largo de São Bartolomeu 5 ☏ 266 557 112, ⓦ estalagemdemonsaraz.com. Partly built into the walls, just outside the village, this superb inn is in a lovely old building. There are dazzling views from most rooms, as well as a lovely pool in a garden laden with lemon trees. __€80__

Monte Alerta Apartado 101, Telheiro ☏ 966 768 307, ⓦ montealerta.pt. A couple of kilometres from Monsaraz, *Monte Alerta* is a gorgeous rural retreat which has eight varied but pretty rooms, plus a pool, jacuzzi and fine gardens. __€85__

EATING

Casa do Forno Travessa Sabrosa ☏ 266 557 190. This welcoming place has a small terrace and a cosy interior serving Alentejan meat specialities such as *borrego no forno* (roast lamb), lamb chops and *migas* (most mains €9–11). Mon & Wed–Sun noon–3pm & 7–10pm.

★ **Xarez** Rua de Santiago 33 ☏ 266 557 052. The town's top choice is the stylish *Xarez*, just inside the main gate, which has a terrace with terrific views, an attractive stone interior and serves tasty tapas such as local cheeses, spicy sausages and hare tart. Main courses start at around €11, and usually include *bacalhau* and a fine steak cooked on a hot stone. Mon, Tues & Fri–Sun 11am–midnight, Wed 11am–5pm.

Moura

The pleasantly provincial town of **MOURA**, 50km south of Monsaraz, is a surprisingly opulent place full of grand mansions, pretty squares and pedestrianized shopping streets. It's also the closest town to the controversial Alqueva dam (see below). The Moors occupied the town from the eighth century until 1232 – an Arabic well still survives in the old town – and Moura is named after a Moorish maiden, Moura Saluquia, who ostensibly threw herself from the castle tower in despair when Christians murdered her betrothed and overran the town. But it was the discovery of naturally carbonated thermal springs in the late nineteenth century that prompted Moura's eventual prosperity. The spa water still dribbles from the Fonte das Três Bicas (Fountain of Three Spouts), but the spa no longer operates. Nevertheless, the adjacent **Jardim Doutor Santiago** gardens make a very pleasant place to stroll, with lots of shady trees.

Castelo

Daily 9.30am–12.30pm & 2.30pm–8pm • Free

West of the gardens rises the Manueline Igreja de São João Baptista, with the **Castelo** beyond, just past the large market building. Built by Dom Dinis over a Moorish citadel, it was largely destroyed by the Spanish Duke of Osuna in 1701, though one Moorish tower still survives, the **Torre de Menagem**. Inside is a motley collection of weapons, though most people head straight up to the top to enjoy the vista. The castle grounds, which have been attractively landscaped, also provide good views – a telescope is trained on the Alqueva dam wall, clearly visible 12km to the north – and form the background for various music and dance events, that take place throughout the summer (see the turismo website for details).

8

The Moorish quarter and the Núcleo Árabe

Núcleo Árabe Rua da Mouraria 11 • Tues–Sat 9.30am–12.30pm & 2.30–5.30pm • Free

Although Moura's Moorish occupation ended in 1232, a significant Moorish population remained in the part of town just to the south of the castle, off the elongated Praça Sacadura Cabral. Once a teeming hive of alleys, the former

---

THE BARRAGEM DE ALQUEVA

In February 2002 the floodgates opened on the controversial **Barragem de Alqueva** (Alqueva Dam), filled by the waters of the Rio Gaudiana and several tributaries. At 250 square kilometres (of which 69 square kilometres are in Spain), it's Europe's largest reservoir. Plans for the project started decades ago under the Salazar regime, with the aim of providing reliable irrigation in this arid region and jobs in the agricultural and tourism industries. There are many who still lament the destruction of over a million oak and cork trees in its construction and the resulting threats to the habitats of golden eagles and the even rarer Iberian lynx, plus the submerging of over 200 prehistoric sites. Meanwhile, the inhabitants of the former village of **Luz** on the east bank of the Guadiana, now submerged, were relocated to a facsimile village above the waterline which, despite similarities of appearance, has become something of a failed experiment; the younger villagers having left and the older ones are deeply dissatisfied.

The government points to the benefits of the dam, not least the hydroelectric plant, switched on in 2004, which provides enough electricity to supply the Évora and Beja districts combined. Smooth new roads also now radiate from the dam, which has become something of a tourist attraction in its own right, the deep waters lapping on one side, a sheer drop on the other. A little beyond the car park by the dam is a **Centro de Informação** (daily 10am–1pm & 2.30–5pm, to 6.30pm in July & Aug) which details how the dam was built and how it powers the area, as well as providing information on boat trips you can take on the waters themselves.

Moorish quarter is now a quiet residential neighbourhood, whose few narrow cobbled streets only spring to life once the heat of the day diminishes. Here you can still see the fourteenth-century "Poço Arabe" – the old Arab well – which forms the centrepiece of the **Núcleo Árabe**, a small museum that houses a collection of Arab artefacts.

Lagar de Varas do Fojo

Rua São João de Deus 20 • Tues–Sun 9.30am–12.30pm & 2.30–5.30pm • Free

Of Moura's few modest museums, the **Lagar de Varas**, just around the corner from the *Hotel de Moura*, is the most interesting. Housed in an old municipal olive-oil plant, which operated before machines took over in 1841, it is a beautifully cool, dark building featuring the restored wooden presses and vats plus a small exhibition about the production of olive oil.

ARRIVAL AND INFORMATION   MOURA

By bus Buses will either drop you centrally, at Praça Sacadura Cabral, by the castle, or at the bus station, outside the old train station, at the top end of Moura: from here, it's a 10–15min walk into the centre.
Destinations Beja (Mon–Fri 6 daily, Sat & Sun 2 daily; 90min); Évora (1 daily; 1hr 5min); Lisbon (1 daily; 3hr 10min); Serpa (Mon–Fri 6 daily, Sat & Sun 2 daily; 40min).
Information The turismo (Mon–Fri 9am–12.30pm & 2–5.30pm, Sat & Sun 10am–1pm & 2.30–5.30pm; ☎285 251 375, ⑩cm-moura.pt) is at Patio dos Rolins 13, which is opposite the gardens and spa, above the municipal swimming pool.

ACCOMMODATION AND EATING

A few pleasant **cafés** face the gardens and castle on Praça Sacadura Cabral, where you will also find the large fruit and vegetable market. In the narrow streets running back from here, there are plenty of **cafés and restaurants** serving inexpensive snacks and typically generous portions of Alentejan food. Rua Miguel Bombarda is the main pedestrianized shopping street.

Hotel de Moura Praça Gago Coutinho 1 ☎285 251 090, ⑩hoteldemoura.com. Moura's top hotel, signed to the south of town, is set in a former seventeenth-century convent which was turned into a hotel in 1900. Its facade is completely covered with *azulejos*, and inside there's a grand staircase, lavish rooms, patios, mirrored doors and a rambling garden with a swimming pool. **€70**
O Trilho Rua 5 de Outubro 5 ☎285 254 261. First choice for food is *O Trilho*, which serves moderately priced regional

dishes such as *açorda, bacalhau,* duck rice and *carne de porco à alentejana* (pork with clams and potatoes) from €9–13, as well as various dishes of the day. Tues–Sun noon–3pm & 7–10pm.
Santa Comba Praça Sacadura Cabral 34 ☎285 251 255, ⑩hotelsantacomba.com. The town's budget option is right by the castle: decent-sized rooms with air conditioning and cable TV, though front-facing rooms can be noisy. **€40**

Serpa

Thirty kilometres southwest of Moura, and the same again east of Beja, the small market town of **SERPA** offers the classic Alentejan attractions – a walled centre, a castle, and narrow, whitewashed streets of handsome bougainvillea-clad houses and lush gardens. The town has at various times been occupied by Celts, Romans and Moors, and its highest point is capped by the remnants of its **Castelo**. Beyond these few attractions, the delight of Serpa is in wandering its quiet, little-visited streets that spread for just a few hundred metres within the encircling walls. Centre of the settlement is the **Praça da República**, with its palm tree and cafés, while arched gates provide access to the more modern town beyond. To the south, the leafy **public gardens** provide shade in the hottest part of the day. The town's annual **feira** takes place on the closest weekend to Aug 24, and there are big celebrations each Easter in honour of Nossa Senhora de Gaudalupe.

Castelo

Tues–Sun 9am–12.30pm & 2–5.30pm • Free

Originally built by Dom Dinis in the fourteenth century, Serpa's attractive **Castelo** was partly blown up by the Spanish in the eighteenth-century War of Succession, though the keep survived and now houses a tiny archeological museum. You can also climb the surviving battlements for great views, and to track the course of Serpa's eleventh-century **aqueduct** (closed to the public), which retains an antique chain-pump at one end – this is best seen from just outside the town walls, on Rua dos Arcos. Near the castle entrance, the thirteenth-century **Igreja de Santa Maria** contains an altarpiece of intricate woodcarving, surrounded by seventeenth-century *azulejos*.

Museu Etnográfico

Largo do Corro • Tues–Sun 9am–12.30pm & 2–5.30pm • Free • ⓦ cm-serpa.pt

Flanking the eastern town walls, the small **Museu Etnográfico** (Ethnographic Museum) offers an interesting account of the changing economic activity of the town and the area as a whole. Its exhibits include a selection of ancient agricultural implements, olive presses and traditional local costumes.

ARRIVAL AND INFORMATION   SERPA

By bus The bus station is off Avenida de Paz in the modern southwest of town, ten minutes' walk from the old centre.

Destinations Beja (2–4 daily; 35min); Lisbon (1–3 daily; 3hr 45min); Moura (Mon–Fri 6 daily, Sat & Sun 2 daily; 40min).

8

ACCOMMODATION
Beatriz	2
Casa da Muralha	1
Casa de Serpa	3
Parque de Campismo	4

RESTAURANTS
A Adega	3
Adega Mólho-Bico	2
O Tapas	1

By car Cars can enter the walled town for access only, but you wouldn't want to risk the narrow streets in any case. There's plenty of parking all around the walls, with nothing more than five minutes' walk away.

Information The turismo is within the walls at Rua dos Cavalos 19 (April–Sept daily 10am–7pm; Oct–March daily 10am–6pm; ☎ 284 544 727, ⓦ cm-serpa.pt).

ACCOMMODATION

Beatriz Largo do Salvador 10 ☎ 284 544 423, ⓦ residencialbeatriz.com. This smart guesthouse near the church also has three apartments with kitchenettes (€60) – all rooms have private bath, wi-fi and a/c, and there's parking too. **€45**

★ **Casa da Muralha** Rua das Portas de Beja 43 ☎ 284 543 150, ⓦ casadamuralha.com. The only place to stay within the town walls, it's right by the aqueduct gate, with lovely rooms opening onto a tree-shaded courtyard garden. There are two rooms in the main house and two more in the garden, with painted Alentejan furniture, traditional cane ceilings and cool tile floors. Breakfast is a good spread of local produce. Discounts for longer stays. **€75**

Casa de Serpa Largo do Salvador 28 ☎ 284 549 238, ⓦ casadeserpa.com. A stylishly decorated, traditional house with a sunny patio and courtyard, offering half a dozen comfortable rooms, a warm welcome and free bike loan. No credit cards. **€65**

CAMPSITE

Parque de Campismo Eira de São Pedro ☎ 284 544 290, ⓦ cm-serpa.pt. Serpa's well-equipped municipal campsite is at the southwest corner of town, a bit closer in than the bus station, near the swimming pool complex (to which there's free access). Pitch **€6.50**

EATING AND DRINKING

A Adega Rua do Rossio 76 ☎ 284 543 433. A simple but usually bustling local that dishes up good and inexpensive grilled meats (mains under €8), and you can sit outside for a welcome breath of night air. Daily 10am–10pm.

Adega Mólho-Bico Rua Quente 1 ☎ 284 549 264. The weekend family favourite – a rustic grill house with stone floors and wooden benches, serving regional specialities

(pork, fish, steaks etc) from around €8–12. Mon, Tues & Thurs–Sun noon–11pm.

O Tapas Rua Quente 17 ☎ 284 544 063. As the name suggests, tapas is the speciality here – local sausage, cheese etc – though it also does fresh fish and grilled meats (around €10) and good local wines. Friendly staff, but service can be slow when it's busy. Mon–Wed & Fri–Sun noon–3pm & 7pm–10pm.

Beja and around

BEJA is the main town of the Baixa Alentejo (Lower Alentejo), though its population only numbers around 30,000. Its inland position means that it's frequently the hottest place in Portugal, something to bear in mind if you plan a visit during the summer months. Once past the modern suburbs, you'll find a laidback old quarter with a historic **convent** and an impressive **castle** dating from the thirteenth century. You can take in the sights in the compact historic centre in half a day, though it's not a bad night's stopover in any case, with plenty of good cafés and restaurants.

Commanding a strategic position in the centre of the plains, it has long been an important and prosperous city. Founded by Julius Caesar in 48 BC, it was named Pax Julia, in honour of the peace accord signed here between Rome and the Lusitanians, but later became Pax Augusta and then just Pax – this gradually became corrupted to Paca, Baca, Baju, and finally Beja. You can still experience the Roman influence to the north, at the atmospheric **Ruínas Romanas de São Cucufate**, where the history of three separate Roman villas is laid bare in a series of extensive excavations and reconstructions.

Museu Regional

Convento de Nossa Senhora da Conceição, Largo de Conceição • Tues–Sun 9.30am–12.30pm & 2–5.15pm • €2, free on Sun, also includes entry to Museu Visigótico • ☎ 284 323 351, ⓦ museuregionaldebeja.net

The highly impressive **Convento de Nossa Senhora da Conceição** was founded in the fifteenth century, with an array of Manueline arches and latticed embellishments that

BEJA

Ermida de Santo André

Train Station

RUA DA LAVOURA

Santo Amaro
(Museu
Visigótico)

Castelo
Sé
LARGO
DR. LIMA
FALEIRO
LARGO
DO
LIDADOR

Misericórdia

PR. DA
REPÚBLICA

Museu
Jorge
Vieira
LARGO DE
SANTA MARIA
Santa Maria
Salvador

LARGO
DOS DUQUES
DE BEJA
LG.
CONCEIÇÃO

Museu
Regional

Taxis
Tribunal
Jardim
Gago
Coutinho

Police
Station
Convento de
S. Francisco
Market

PRAÇA
DIOGO
FERNANDES

Library

Hospital

8

ACCOMMODATION

Bejense	2
Francis	5
Pousada de Juventude	6
Pousada de São Francisco	3
Rosa do Campo	1
Santa Bárbara	4

Bus
Station

N

Stadium

RESTAURANTS

A Pipa	1
Adega 25 Abril	2
Churrasqueira O Alemão	3
Luíz da Rocha	6
O Capitel	5
Pena	4

Parque de
Campismo

0   100
metres

Mertola & Castro Verde

enliven its low roofline. The convent was dissolved in 1834 and today houses the
excellent **Museu Regional**, with displays of rescued church art and Flemish paintings
gathered in the galleries around the convent cloister. It's the sumptuous tilework,
however, that first catches the eye – the walls of the cloisters and chapterhouse are tiled
from top to bottom with sixteenth- and seventeenth-century *azulejos*. There's also
a striking Rococo chapel, dripping with gold leaf. A stunning fifteenth-century
Mudéjar terracotta grille once linked the convent to the neighbouring palace – it was
through this delicate tracery that the convent's most famous resident, Sister Mariana
Alcoforado, first glimpsed her lover (see box, p.416).

Upstairs is a small archeological section, where Roman stonework and inscriptions
remind you of Beja's erstwhile importance. Much of the collection was found at the
extensive site of **Pisões**, 7km southwest of town (signposted from Aljustrel road; closed
Mon & Tues morning; free), where the walls of a Roman dam and the remains of rural
buildings of the first to fourth century AD can still be seen.

THE ERRANT NUN

During the seventeenth century, **Sister Mariana Alcoforado** lived in Beja's Convento de Nossa Senhora da Conceição, when her passionate affair with a French officer, Count Chamilly, became the talk of the town – and indeed, the whole country. The nun's scandalous missives to her lover, *Letters of a Portuguese Nun*, were published in Paris in 1669 and became the *Fifty Shades of Grey* of their day. Scholars have debated as to whether the nun actually wrote the original letters, but they were so popular that they inspired several imitations.

Museu Jorge Vieira–Casa das Artes

Rua do Touro 33 • Tues–Sat 10am–12.30pm & 2.30–6.30pm, Sun 2–6pm • Free • ☎ 284 311 920

A short walk up Rua do Touro from the Museu Regional brings you to the **Museu Jorge Vieira**. It's a quirky private showcase for the work of contemporary sculptor Jorge Vieira, whose surreal terracotta sculptures – part feminine, part grotesque – show a clear Cubist lineage from Picasso and Braque.

Igreja da Misericórdia

Praça da República • Mon–Fri 10am–5.30pm • ☎ 213 614 200

At the top of the Praça da República, you can't miss the sixteenth-century **Igreja da Misericórdia**, whose large arched porch once housed the town's meat market. Now it is home to a small handicrafts shop selling attractive cork products and ceramics produced by a local arts co-operative.

Castelo

Largo de Santo Amaro • April–Oct daily 10am–1pm & 2–6pm; Nov–March 9am–1pm & 2–5pm; Torre de Menagem closes 30min before castle • Free

Beja's impressive fourteenth-century **Castelo**, built by Dom Dinis, looms large beyond the town's unassuming cathedral. Its 40-metre-high Torre de Menagem boasts decorative battlements and dizzying views, making those from the walls below seem tame. The castle's internal courtyard now houses the town's turismo.

Igreja de Santo Amaro (Museu Visigótico)

Largo de Santo Amaro • Tues–Sun 9.30am–12.30pm & 2–5.15pm • €2, free on Sun, also includes entry to Museu Regional (see p.414) • ☎ 284 321 465

Beyond the castle walls, the small, whitewashed **Igreja de Santo Amaro** is one of the country's few extant buildings to date from pre-Moorish times, with motifs on its columns being dated back to the seventh century. Inside, the small **Museu Visigótico** displays an important collection of Visigothic archeological remains – look out for the amazing fifth-century iron sword, its handle inlaid with gold and amber.

Herdade dos Grous

Around 30km south of Beja just off the IP2 in the village of Albernoa • Daily 9am–6pm; wine tours from €5–25 depending on group size • ☎ 284 960 000, 🌐 herdade-dos-grous.com

Set in some of the Alentejo's most beautiful countryside, the **Herdade dos Grous** is one of the region's top wine estates, with 70 hectares of vineyards. They also make their own olive oil, breed cattle and champion show-jumpers, and can arrange fishing in the estate's private lake. Visitors can tour the winery, or explore the 730-hectare estate on foot, by tractor (€9), on horseback (€20), or even by hot-air balloon (€170; min four people). If you fancy a longer stay at this upmarket rural resort, there's a top-notch restaurant (daily 12.30–2.30pm; Fri–Sun also noon–2pm and 7.30–9.30pm), and smart accommodation (rooms from €125).

Ruinas Romanas de São Cucufate

Lugar de São Cucufate • May to mid-Sept Tues 2.30–6pm, Wed–Sun 10am–12.30pm & 2.30–6.30pm; mid-Sept to April Tues 2–5.30pm, Wed–Sun 10am–1pm & 2–5.30pm • €2.50 • ☎ 284 441 113, ⊛ www.cm-vidigueira.pt

Around 30km to the north of Beja and 1km beyond Vila de Frades, you'll pass the **Ruinas Romanas de São Cucufate**, a peaceful, rural spot, shrouded in landscaped grounds of rosemary, thyme and lavender. The first Roman villa was built here in the middle of the first century AD, but replaced by two successively grander constructions, with baths, grain stores, oil presses and servants' quarters. The third villa was abandoned in the fifth century and later reoccupied in medieval times as a monastery – the old wine cellar was eventually decorated with frescoes in the seventeenth century, after which the whole complex was abandoned once more. You can go inside a couple of the extremely rickety-looking ruins, used in spring by nesting birds.

ARRIVAL AND INFORMATION

By bus The bus station is five minutes' walk southeast of the old centre.

Destinations Évora (7 daily; 1hr 15min); Faro (3 daily; 2hr 50min); Lisbon (7–11 daily; 2hr 45min–3hr); Mértola (1–3 daily; 1hr 15min); Moura (1–6 daily; 1hr 15min); Portalegre (1–4 daily; 3hr 45min); and Serpa (2–4 daily; 35min).

By car Beja's old quarter is a circular tangle of streets, enclosed within a ring road that has largely replaced the town walls. Negotiate the one-way system and you can get fairly close to the historic centre by car, and there's signposted parking at various points (some of it metered, free at the weekends) – anywhere around the castle, gardens or bus station is convenient.

BEJA AND AROUND

By train Beja is on a branch off the Linha do Alentejo from Lisbon, which usually means changing trains at Casa Branca for trains to Lisbon (3–4 daily; 2hr 10min) or Évora (3–4 daily; 45min). The train station is five minutes northeast of the town centre.

By bike Bikes are available for free use around town – you'll see the racks – though you have to go through a form-filling procedure (take ID) at the turismo first.

Information The turismo is inside the Castelo (daily: April–Oct 10am–1pm & 2–6pm; Nov–March 9am–1pm & 2–5pm; ☎ 284 311 913, ⊛ rt-planiciedourada.pt), and can provide details of the town's various festivities throughout the year.

ACCOMMODATION

★ **Bejense** Rua Capitão J. Francisco de Sousa 57 ☎ 284 311 570, ⊛ hotelbejense.com. Beja's oldest hotel, first opened in 1889, has recently been given a boutique makeover, a lovely space filled with tiles, flowers and family photos. Contemporary-styled, high-ceilinged, a/c rooms have large bathrooms, satellite TV and free wi-fi. It's a welcoming place, with a bar; breakfast is served in a bright first-floor dining room. €45

Francis Praça Fernandes Lopes Graça, Lote 31 ☎ 284 315 500, ⊛ hotel-francis.com. A well-equipped if functional

three-star hotel with colour-coordinated rooms, many with big balconies. Best of all, there's a bar, gym plus parking, though front rooms can be noisy. €45

Pousada de Juventude Rua Prof Janeiro Acabado ☎ 284 325 239, ⊛ microsites.juventude.gov.pt/portal /en. The youth hostel is close to the bus station, with a good-sized common room, internet facilities and bike rental. The modern dorms are four- or six-bedded, and there are also six en-suite doubles. Dorm beds €14; doubles €32

> #### BEJA AIRPORT
> More than a few eyebrows were raised when a former military airbase opened as **Beja International Airport** in 2011. The logic was that, roughly equidistant from Faro and Lisbon, it would offer an alternative entry point to the south. But opening just as recession hit – and about as far from the coast as you can get in Portugal and a good 150km from the Algarve – it is perhaps no great surprise that the airport has hardly been a success, with very few airlines using it even in peak season. If you are one of the few passengers to arrive here, the airport (☎ 284 001 020, ⊛ ana.pt) is around 9km northwest of Beja – a shuttle bus (15min) serves Beja after most flights, or a taxi to town will cost €12–14.

8

CORKING STUFF

While travelling through the southern Alentejo, you'll pass mile upon mile of cork oak groves – so it may come as no surprise to learn that the district provides around fifty percent of the world's entire supply of **cork**. It has been an important Portuguese export since the late nineteenth century and a major crop for over seven hundred years.

Cork (*quercus suber*) consists of a layer of spongy cells called phellogen that appear under the bark during the first year of growth. The cells grow radially outwards to form a durable, impermeable material with excellent thermal properties – it's ideal to guard the tree against pests, fire and extremes of temperature, and also ideal as a material for humans to exploit. Importantly, the cork tree is also able to regenerate itself when a layer of cork is removed throughout the tree's life (usually over a hundred years) – and each regenerated layer is thicker than its predecessor. Using a curved axe, cork farmers are therefore able to strip away rectangular layers of cork every nine years, the time it takes for the cork layers to be 4–6cm thick – ideal for wine stoppers. The world's most productive cork tree, the 230-year-old **Whistler Tree**, in the northern Alentejo, has produced enough corks to stop up 100,000 bottles from a single harvest.

Cork trees cannot be harvested until they are at least 25 years old, and as a result, cork groves tend to be superb habitats for **wildlife**. Unfortunately this self-sustaining crop is under threat because of the growth in plastic and screw-top wine stoppers, forcing many farmers to rip up the cork groves for more viable crops, and destroying ancient habitats in the process.

★ **Pousada de São Francisco** Largo Dom Nuno Álvares Pereira ☎ 284 313 580, ⓦ pousadas.pt. Sumptuous *pousada* set round the cloisters and church of a former thirteenth-century convent – not surprisingly, the atmosphere is serene, with plush rooms modelled from former cells whose small windows keep out the heat. The excellent-quality restaurant and bar have outdoor tables in a palm-dotted garden with its own spacious pool and tennis courts. Parking. €120

Rosa do Campo Rua da Liberdade 12 ☎ 284 323 578, ⓦ rrc.pt.vu. Good for groups, with some large rooms of three beds or more, in a well-converted 1950s townhouse. It's a light, bright place, thanks to open planning and unusual roof lighting. No credit cards. €40

Santa Bárbara Rua de Mértola 56 ☎ 284 312 280, ⓦ hotelsantabarbara.pt. Good-value, a/c rooms with tiled floors and small en-suite showers/toilets. The best rooms overlook the pedestrianized street and have pocket-sized balconies. There's also a small bar. €45

CAMPSITE

Parque de Campismo Av Vasco da Gama ☎ 284 311 911. The municipal site is on the south side of town, past the stadium. It's fairly pleasant and shaded, and adjoins the local swimming pool. Pitch €4

EATING AND DRINKING

Adega 25 Abril Rua da Moeda 23 ☎ 284 325 960. There's an Alentejan farmer somewhere missing his tools, because they're all on the walls in this huge rustic *adega*. The menu is very meaty, though – try the mixed grill, a giant plate of meats for two at €14. Other mains from €7. Tues–Sat 12.30–3pm & 7–11pm, Sun 12.30–3pm.

★ **A Pipa** Rua da Moeda 8 ☎ 284 327 043. A barn-like restaurant with high ceilings hung with old yokes. Big, filling meaty mains from €8, though half-portions suffice for most. Good house wine too. Mon–Sat 12.30–3pm & 7–11pm.

Churrasqueira O Alemão Largo dos Duques de Beja 11 ☎ 284 311 490. The queues out the door at lunch are for the takeaway side of the operation – slip through into the simple tiled dining-room for unglamorous but inexpensive charcoal-grilled sausages, steaks and chicken from €6. Mon–Sat 10am–10pm.

Luíz da Rocha Rua do Capitão J. Francisco de Sousa 63 ☎ 284 323 179. In business for over a century, the café and tea room downstairs is one of Beja's big meet-and-greet destinations and is famed for its cakes, pies and pastries. Pop in for a *bica* and snack or an evening brandy, or head upstairs for inexpensive meals. Daily 9am–11pm; July–Sept closed Sun.

O Capitel Largo Eng. Duarte Pacheco ☎ 284 327 555. *O Capitel* has a sunny raised terrace facing an attractive square and the Tribunal building, a good spot for a drink or snack. At night, many move inside for the sports TV. Mon–Sat 7.30am–2am.

Pena Praça de Diogo Fernandes 19A ☎ 284 323 714. Come here if you fancy fish – there's more choice than on most local menus (lamprey, sardines, bream, squid) and the prices aren't too high (mains from €8–9). Mon–Sat 11am–10pm.

MERTOLA AND THE GUADIANA RIVER (P.420) >

Mértola

MÉRTOLA, 54km southeast of Beja, is as beautifully sited as any town in the south, set high on a spur above the confluence of the Guadiana and Oeiras rivers, guarded by the ruins of a Moorish frontier castle. It makes a fine place to stay the night, or longer, with a compact, somnolent old town full of attractions, and quiet rural surroundings that form part of the **Parque Natural Vale do Guadiana**. The region is home to the rare black stork and other endangered species, and the local hills, riverbanks and valleys have some excellent walks, especially round the old mining village of **São Domingos**.

Mértola's history goes back as far as Phoenician times, when it was an important river port, and it was later fortified and expanded by both Romans (as Myrtilis) and Moors (Martulah), before being taken by Dom Sancho II in 1238 as part of the Christian Reconquest. With the walled town occupying such a small area, successive conquerors and settlers simply built on what they found, which provides Mértola with its current fascination – the evidence of thousands of years of habitation visible in almost every building and street.

Museu de Mértola

Tues–Sun: July to mid-Sept 9.30am–12.30pm & 2–6pm; mid-Sept to June 9am–12.30pm & 2–5.30pm • €2 per museum, or €5 combined ticket for all museums plus Castelo & Alcácova do Castelo • ⓦ museus.cm-mertola.pt

Mértola has imaginatively created a series of ten mini-museums, allowing you to trace the town's art and history in a series of small, well-designed **exhibitions**. Most lie within the old walled town, signposted and easily found. The various exhibitions deal with a single facet of the town's history, such as the **Casa Romano**, showing the foundations of a Roman house discovered under the Câmara Municipal. In the **Museu Arte Islâmica** are gathered the inscribed funerary stones, glazed tableware and decorated urns discovered within the Moorish quarter, housed in a former granary, while the tiny **Museu de Arte Sacra** in the Misericórdia church concentrates on religious art, notably the three retables from the parish church depicting Sancho's ousting of the Moors. A co-operative set up to revive the traditional weaving industry showcases its methods in the **Oficina de Tecelagem**, next to the turismo. The most moving exhibit is five minutes' walk away in the modern part of town, where the **Basilica Paleocristã**, in Largo do Rossio do Carmo, preserves thirty funerary stones in a partial reconstruction of an early Christian temple. These inhabitants – "a man of social standing", or simply "son" or "daughter of" – were buried here, outside the city walls, over 1500 years ago.

Castelo and Alcácova do Castelo

Tues–Sun: July to mid-Sept 9.30am–12.30pm & 2–6pm; mid-Sept to June 9am–12.30pm & 2–5.30pm • €2 each, or €5 combined ticket for Castelo & Alcácova do Castelo plus all museums • ⓦ museus.cm-mertola.pt

From the **Castelo**, the layout of the walled old town and modern settlement beyond becomes clear. The arched main door and winding entrance lead into the central keep, which is Moorish in origin, though the rest of the castle dates from the thirteenth-century Christian Reconquest. The earlier Islamic inhabitants lived within the castle walls and, later, in the Moorish quarter, just outside, which now forms the **Alcácova do Castelo**, an excavated site with iron walkways over the ruins of the Moorish village as well as earlier Roman cisterns, a Christian baptistery and a later Christian cemetery.

Igreja Matriz

Wed–Sun 10am–1pm & 3–7pm • Free

The small parish church at the foot of the castle, the **Igreja Matriz**, is unusual for Portugal in that you can still clearly see its original incarnation as a Moorish mosque.

Built in the twelfth century, it became a church around a hundred years later but retains its Moorish arched doorway and a *mihrab* – a space behind the altar used for Muslim prayer.

Mina de São Domingos

North of town, across the bridge, the very attractive road to Serpa winds for 17km to **Mina de São Domingos**. The former pyrite and copper mines here were the largest in Iberia and until World War II were owned by a British company, whose reputation for harsh treatment of their workforce made them very unpopular hereabouts. The mines closed in 1965 and much of the scarred landscape has been imaginatively landscaped into woodlands around a large lake with an attractive river beach, a fine place for a stroll. You can also look round some of the old mining machinery and visit a miners' cottage, a titchy space of just 16 square metres.

ARRIVAL AND INFORMATION   MÉRTOLA

By bus Buses stop by the main Serpa/Beja traffic circle in the new town – follow the signs for "Mértola/Vila Real" for the five-minute walk down the road to Largo Vasco da Gama at the foot of the old town.

Destinations Alcoutim (Mon–Fri 1 daily; 50min); Beja (Mon–Fri 3 daily; 1hr 15min); and Lisbon (1 daily; 3hr 35min).

By car Don't even think of driving into the walled town

– park anywhere you like close to the walls or by the bus stops, though note there is a one-way system round the newer part of town.

Information The turismo (daily: July–mid-Sept 9.30am–12.30pm & 2–6pm; mid-Sept–June 9am–12.30pm & 2–5.30pm; ☎ 286 610 109, ⓦ cm-mertola.pt), is at Rua da Igreja 31, just inside the walls (signposted), hands out a useful map and has free internet access.

8

ACCOMMODATION

★ **Beira Rio** Rua Dr Afonso Costa 108 ☎ 286 611 190, ⓦ beirario.pt. The best rooms at this cheerful place (all modern and en-suite, most a/c) have balconies directly overlooking the peaceful river. A good buffet breakfast can be eaten on the terrace, and there's parking and free wi-fi in public areas. **€40**

Convento de São Francisco 1km out of town on the Alcoutim road ☎ 286 612 119, ⓦ conventomertola .com. This 400-year-old former convent is now a guest-house and artist's retreat. Stay in tasteful, rustic surroundings either in pretty studios with a terrace (two-night minimum stay), or a room in the convent itself with its own veranda and kitchen). They also let out a

bucolic "off grid" cottage (sleeps two; €250 a week) in the grounds, with views over the river and town. Breakfast on request. **€55**

Museu Rua Dr Afonso Costa 112 ☎ 286 612 003, ⓦ hotelmuseu.com. Tucked down by the river, this is the town's best modern option. The name comes from the fact that parts of a Moorish settlement and Roman store were revealed as it was being built – you can see an excavated Moorish building through a glass floor in reception. The best of the small but comfortable rooms face the river, and there's also a bar and attractive riverside terrace. **€60**

EATING AND DRINKING

Migas Mercado Municipal ☎ 927 302 372. By the entrance to the old town, below the old market, this modern café-restaurant has a terrace with fabulous views over the river. The speciality, not surprisingly, is *migas*, a heavy corn bread served with pork, but there are other meats and fish from around €8. Tues–Sun 10am–2pm & 5–11pm.

O Rapucho Av Aureliano Mira Fernandes ☎ 286 612 563. The best of a row of local places at the western end of the avenue, beyond the traffic circle in the modern town. This has fine fish, meat (including wild boar) and decent house wine. You can eat well here for around €15. Mon–Fri & Sun noon–3pm & 7–midnight.

ACTIVITIES

Boat trips/Kayaking/Bike hire Beira Rio Náutica, based at the *Beira Rio* guesthouse (Rua Dr Afonso Costa 108; ☎ 286 611 190, ⓦ beirario.pt) runs 1–2hr boat trips

up the river from €10 per person; they also rent out kayaks from €5 an hour and bikes from €6 a day.

Alcácer do Sal and Comporta

Coming from Lisbon and the west, **ALCÁCER DO SAL** is the first town of the Baixo Alentejo, 52km from Setúbal. It is one of Portugal's oldest ports, founded by the Phoenicians and made a regional capital under the Moors – whence its name (*al-Ksar*, "the town") derives. The other part of its name, *do Sal*, "of salt", reflects the dominance of the salt industry in these parts; the Sado estuary is still fringed with salt marshes.

Few stop longer than to stretch the legs – both Beja and the coast are less than an hour away – but it's an attractive enough place to spend some time, particularly along the waterfront promenade where there are various cafés and restaurants. A couple of roads back from the promenade, at its western end, lies a charming quarter of medieval houses where storks nest on any tall tower. Further uphill, above the town, stands the Moorish **castle**, now a luxury *pousada* (see below), from where you can look out over the Rio Sado and the distinctive green paddy fields which are still cultivated for rice.

Comporta

From Alcácer do Sal, the minor EN253 follows the banks of the Sado estuary to the nearest stretch of coast at **Comporta**, 26km west. It's a lovely drive and worth it, as the **beach** – signed just to the north of the village off the EN253-1 – is simply magnificent, a giant stretch of soft sands served by a couple of seasonal beach café-restaurants, though this may change if a planned tourist resort comes to fruition. You can continue up the EN253-1 onto the Tróia peninsula for the ferry back to Setúbal.

ACCOMMODATION AND INFORMATION   **ALCÁCER DO SAL**

Information The turismo is on Praça Pedro Nunes 1 (Mon–Sat 9am–5pm; ☎ 265 610 071, ⓦ cm-alcacerdosal.pt).

Pousada Dom Afonso II Castelo de Alcácer do Sal ☎ 265 613 070, ⓦ pousadas.pt. The former Moorish castle is now home to the fabulous *Pousada Dom Afonso II*, one of the classiest of the chain. The ancient shell of the castle makes a dramatic setting for the surprisingly contemporary rooms, and there's also a swimming pool and top-notch restaurant. **€145**

Santiago do Cacém and around

South of Alcácer, the only place that might tempt you to stop before the Alentejo coast is **SANTIAGO DO CACÉM**, an unassuming provincial town capped by a hilltop castle, with a decent regional museum and the fascinating Roman ruins of **Miróbriga** on its outskirts. It is close, too, to the impressive lagoon and beach at **Lagoa de Santo André**, and also marks the starting point of the 340km-long Rota Vicentina walking trail (see p.425).

Museu Municipal

Praça do Município • Tues–Fri 10am–noon & 2–5pm, Sat 2–6pm • Free • ☎ 269 827 375

In the centre of town, the bright white facade of the **Museu Municipal**, facing the municipal gardens off Avenida Álvares Pereira, was formerly a prison where "enemies" of the Salazar regime were locked up. You can see one of the re-created cells and experience how harsh and spartan life must have been for the prisoners. The building has been a museum since the 1970s, and it also displays coins and architectural finds from the area, as well as re-creations of traditional Alentejan bedrooms from the late nineteenth century.

Castelo

Mon–Fri 8.30am–dusk, Sat & Sun 8.30am–noon • Free

The modern town centres on its market, with what's left of the old town spreading up one of the hills to the **Castelo**, which was Moorish in origin but later rebuilt by the Knights Templar. The castle's defensive role became redundant by the nineteenth century, so the council decided it would make a handy place for the local cemetery for the neighbouring church. You can, however, still climb up to the battlements, a steep fifteen-minute walk up from town, for some fine views over town.

Ruinas Romanas de Miróbriga

Herdade dos Chãos Salgados • Tues–Sat 9am–12.30pm & 2–5.30pm; Sun 9am–noon & 2–5.30pm • €3, free Sun 9am–noon • ☎ 269 818 460, Ⓦ cm-santiagocacem.pt

The impressive **Ruinas Romanas de Miróbriga** are a short drive from town or around twenty minutes' walk – follow the Lisbon road (N120), and the ruins are signed right by a windmill on the hill. The site, which lies isolated amid Arcadian green hills, was probably inhabited during the Iron Age, but the Roman city here dates from the first century AD. For 200 years Miróbriga thrived on trade, a planned town set around its forum and temple, with recreational zones and residential areas – a "new town" of its era. By the fourth century AD it was in decline, and was then lost to history until the sixteenth century, and only first excavated in the nineteenth.

The ruins are extensive, scattered over the hills below the small interpretation centre. On top of the highest hill were three temples, one of which has been reconstructed. Below here was the commercial centre, complete with paved streets, houses and shops: one of the houses retains some second-century **wall paintings**, while the **bath complex** displays its underfloor heating. Alongside sits a beautifully preserved Roman **bridge** from the first century AD.

8

Lagoa de Santo André

Fifteen kilometres northwest of Santiago do Cacém, a sand beach separates the highly attractive lagoon of **Lagoa de Santo André** from the sea. The warm waters of the lagoon, only a couple of metres deep, are fringed by an extensive *reserva natural* of pinewoods and reeds, and development is consequently limited. There's a beach café and a couple of restaurants at the road's end, while beyond is the Atlantic, faced by kilometres of empty beach – though take care when swimming, as the undertow is notorious.

Badoca Safari Park

Herdade da Bodaca apartado 170 • Daily 9.30am–7pm • €16.50, children €14.50 • ☎ 269 708 850, Ⓦ badoca.com • It's 7km out of Santiago do Cacém, just off the IP8

Just inland from the Lagoa de Santo André, at Vila Nova de Santo André, the **Badoca Safari Park** is a great place for families. The main attraction is an hour-long tractor "safari" around a large enclosure where giraffe, zebra and deer roam free. There are also various shows and feeding sessions throughout the day.

ARRIVAL AND INFORMATION   SANTIAGO DO CACÉM AND AROUND

By bus The bus station in Santiago do Cacém is in Rua Moçambique in the centre of town, near the market. Destinations Lagoa de Santo André (Mon–Fri 3 daily; 30min); Lisbon (approx hourly; 2hr 15min); Porto Côvo (summer 5 daily, winter 1 daily; 1hr); Vila Nova de Milfontes (3–6 daily; 1hr 25min); Zambujeira do Mar (summer 4 daily, winter 1 daily; 2hr).

Information Santiago do Cacém's turismo is in Parque da Quinta do Chafariz, 100m from the bus station (Mon–Sat 9am–1pm & 2–5pm; ☎ 269 826 696, Ⓦ cm -santiagocacem.pt), and hands out a useful town map.

ACCOMMODATION

SANTIAGO DO CACÉM

Dom Nuno Av Álvares Pereira 7540 ☏ 269 823 325,
⊚ albdnuno.com. Accommodation is limited in Santiago
do Cacém, but if you do want to stay this is a reasonable,
central choice. The four-storey building is modern and
rooms are decently sized, if slightly in need of a revamp.
There's also a bar and small outside pool – a big bonus in

the summer. €90

LAGOA DE SANTO ANDRÉ

Al Tarik Lagoa de Santo André ☏ 269 708 600, ⊚ hotel
altarik.com. The apartment-style *Al Tarik* has self catering
rooms in a modern block, close to a minimarket and just
inland from the lagoon – it's well signed. €85

The southern Alentejo coast

Once south of the industrial town of **Sines** – avoidable unless you are on the trail of
Vasco da Gama, who was born here (see box below) – you'll encounter one of the least
developed coasts in Portugal, a wild, scrubby expanse of low hills and wave-pounded
cliffs. Low-key resorts cluster round the various cove beaches that you can find right
along the coast, including pretty **Porto Côvo**. Further south, **Vila Nova de Milfontes** is
the main – and by far the nicest – Alentejan resort, while **Almograve** and **Zambujeira
do Mar**, further south still, are both small seaside villages with stupendous beaches,
a short drive from the northern Algarve.

Porto Côvo

8

The former fishing village of **PORTO CÔVO** is a popular weekend retreat for Lisboetas, and
its tiny heart is now surrounded by modern holiday villas. The small centre consists of just
a few cobbled, whitewashed streets around the attractive central square, Largo Marquês de
Pombal. It's very crowded in August – when it turns into a sort of Lisbon-on-Sea – but for
most of the year the predominant sound is the whistle of the Atlantic breeze. To reach the
coast, head along the main pedestrianized **Rua da Vasco da Gama**, where you'll find most of
the village's dozen cafés and restaurants, plus a bank with ATM and various shops selling
beach gear and souvenirs. Bear left and steps lead down to a small fishing harbour where
you can take a **boat trip** (June–Sept only; €10) to the nearby **Ilha do Pessegueiro** (see
opposite). Bear right for the nearest cove **beach**, a lovely sandy wedge below cliffs – it's
generally sheltered even when the sea is rough elsewhere. Continue north along the coast
and it's a ten-minute walk to **Praia Grande**, the appropriately named "Big Beach",
especially so when the tide is low; it's got its own café-bar, so you could easily spend a day

VASCO DA GAMA

Vasco da Gama (1460–1524) was one of Portugal's greatest explorers – you'll find places named
after him all over the country as well as a town in India, a football team in Brazil and even a crater
on the Moon. He was born in **Sines**, the son of the town governor. In the 1490s he worked for
João II protecting trading stations along the **African coast**. His successes persuaded the next
king, Manuel I, to commission him to find a potentially lucrative **sea route to India**. He left Lisbon
in July 1497 with a fleet of four ships, reaching southern Africa in December – they named it
Natal ("Christmas" in Portuguese). By the following May they reached Calicut in southwest **India**,
and obtained trading terms there before departing in August 1498. The scale of their voyage can
be gauged by the fact that Vasco da Gama did not return to Portugal until September 1499, and
arrived with just two of his ships – half the crew had died. But Vasco da Gama was richly rewarded
by the king, his journey inspiring Camões to write *Os Lusiadas*, Portugal's most famous epic poem.
Vasco da Gama returned to India twice more, the final time in 1524 when he contracted **malaria**
and died in the town of Cochin. You can visit his birthplace in the otherwise missable industrial
town of Sines, where the Casa de Vasco da Gama in Sines' castle records his eventful life (Tues–Sun
10am–1pm & 2–5pm, July & Aug open til 6pm; free; ☏ 269 632 237, ⊚ sines.pt).

THE ROTA VICENTINA

The **Rota Vicentina** is a 340km long-distance footpath which runs from Santiago do Cacém in the Alentejo to Cabo de São Vicente in the Algarve. The northern, Alentejan half has two alternative routes: Porto Côvo is the beginning of 115km-long **Trilho dos Pescadores** (Fisherman's Trail), that follows coastal tracks long used by the local fishermen. Opened in 2012, it's relatively well marked with coloured arrows, and tracks the coast via Milfontes (a taxing first section, 20km), Almogrove (15km further), Zambujeira (another 22km) and into the Algarve at Odeceixe (18km on). It's tough going, much of it along towering cliffs, but no section is longer than 25km which means – in theory – you always have accommodation and a place to eat at the end of your day's walk. The inland alternative is the **Caminho Histórico** (Historic Way) which follows ancient pilgrimage routes from Santiago do Cacém, mostly inland, to Cabo de São Vicente. Be aware that, as with all Portuguese trails, way-marking can be sporadic and poorly maintained, so if you tackle the path, take a good map or GPS system – but it is worth the effort, as the route embraces some of the loveliest coastline in the country. Full details are on ⓦ rotavicentina.com.

---

here. Clifftop paths run north and south of town providing access to other coves and beaches. **Praia do Somouqueira** just to the north is named after the extraordinary rock formations and is popular at low tide when temporary beaches are created.

Ilha do Pessegueiro

The next beach south of Porto Côvo is at **Ilha do Pessegueiro** (Peach Tree Island), reached by car off the Porto Côvo–Vila Nova de Milfontes road. However, it's much nicer to walk, following the coastal path south from Porto Côvo. It's only a couple of kilometres and en route you'll pass the remains of a Bronze Age burial site.

The name actually applies to the mainland beach, another beautiful duned stretch of sand sitting below a small sixteenth-century fort. The island itself – with the matching ruins of another fort – is a few hundred metres offshore, clearly visible from Porto Côvo and reachable from there on local fishing **boats**, though not all are licensed to actually land on the island.

ARRIVAL AND INFORMATION

PORTO CÔVO

By bus Buses stop near Largo do Mercado, a short walk from the seafront.

Destinations Almograve (summer 5 daily, winter 1 daily; 45min); Lisbon (summer 7 daily, winter 1 daily; 2hr 30min–3hr); Santiago do Cacém (summer 5 daily, winter 1 daily; 1hr); Vila Nova de Milfontes (summer 7 daily, winter 1 daily; 25min); and Zambujeira (summer 5 daily, winter 1 daily; 1hr 10min).

Information The turismo (mid-June to Aug Mon–Sat 10am–noon & 1–5pm; Sept to mid-June Mon–Fri 9am–noon & 1–5pm; ☎ 269 959 124, ⓦ sines.pt) is on Largo do Mercado.

ACCOMMODATION

Boa Esperança Rua Conde Bandeira 4 ☎ 269 905 109. Two blocks north of Rua da Vasco da Gama, *Boa Esperança* has simple rooms in a wedge-shaped building on a small plot of land. No credit cards. **€70**

Porto Côvo Rua Vitalina da Silva 1–2 ☎ 269 959 140, ⓦ hotelportocovo.com. Popular with Portuguese families, this is Porto Côvo's top choice, by the campsite a few minutes' walk beyond the market building – it's a modern place with air-conditioned studios and one-bed apartments with kitchen wrapped around a small pool. **€88**

Zé Inácio Rua da Vasco da Gama 38 ☎ 269 959 136, ⓦ zeinacio.com. This is the best of several places offering rooms on the main street, a bright white building with large, comfortable rooms above a restaurant (so can be noisy) – the nicest rooms have sea views. **€75**

CAMPSITES

Ilha do Pessegueiro Camping Estrada da Ilha ☎ 269 905 178, ⓦ ilhadopessegueirocamping.com. The campsite, which also lets out bungalows, is a fair way inland on the road from Ilha do Pessegueiro to Vila Nova de Milfontes, but it is spacious with a minimarket and restaurant. Pitch **€7.50**

Parque de Campismo Porto Côvo Estrada Municipal 554 ☎ 269 905 136, ⓦ roteiro-campista.pt. On the Vila Nova road out of town and open all year, this has good facilities, including a children's playground, minimarket and pool (the latter only open in summer). Pitch **€8.50**

8

EATING AND DRINKING

A Ilha Praia da Ilha do Pessegueiro ☎ 269 905 113. This is a great little beach restaurant where you can choose fresh fish from the counter – it also serves interesting dishes such as fried eels. Mains around €10. Daily 8am–1am.

Doce Mar Rua da Vasco da Gama 35 ☎ 269 905 176. On the main street, *Doce Mar* is a good breakfast or lunch spot: it dishes up inexpensive snacks and a few main courses from around €7; with outdoor seating. Mon, Tues & Thurs–Sun 8am–midnight.

★ **Marquês** Largo Marquês de Pombal 11 ☎ 269 905 036. The *Marquês* is more like a classy Lisbon *cervejaria* than a local restaurant, with lovely tiles, stand-at-the-bar beers, oysters, fresh-from-the-tank lobsters, *feijoada* and other delights from around €12–15. Wed–Sun noon–10.30pm.

Miramar Rua Cândido da Silva 579 ☎ 269 905 449. The big draw here is the fantastic terrace overlooking the fishing harbour. The food's good, too, if a little pricey (mains €12–16), but there's usually plenty of fresh fish on the counter along with a few meat dishes. Daily 11am–11pm.

Vila Nova de Milfontes

VILA NOVA DE MILFONTES – 20km south of Porto Côvo – is the main and most attractive resort on the Alentejo coast, but though it gets very busy in high season, it's Portuguese families who predominate, injecting good humour and a relaxed atmosphere. The attractive whitewashed streets of the old town huddle around a striking, ivy-wreathed sixteenth-century castle facing the estuary of the Rio Mira. Built in 1599 to guard the town from North African pirates, the small castle was a hotel for many years, but is now closed to the public. The town's long, sandy river beach lies just a few minutes' walk to the west. Swimmers need to be aware of the strong river currents – the town beach has roped-off swimming areas that you should heed – and even more so at the beaches either side of town, where the breakers can be fierce. Make sure you swim close to the locals, however, and you shouldn't have anything to worry about. Even though the town beach is spacious, it gets busy in high season, when you might want to take the **ferry** (July & Aug daily 10am–7pm every 30min; €2 return) from the jetty at the foot of the castle across the estuary to **Furnas**, a long, sandy beach also accessible off the main coast road.

ARRIVAL AND INFORMATION   VILA NOVA DE MILFONTES

By bus Buses stop on Rua António Mantas, near the bank. Destinations Almograve (2–3 daily; 25min); Lisbon (3–8 daily; 3–4hr); Portimão (1 daily; 2hr 20min); Porto Côvo (summer 7 daily, winter 1 daily; 25min); Sagres (July–Sept 1 daily; 2hr); Santiago do Cacém (3–6 daily; 1hr 25min); and Zambujeira do Mar (summer 5 daily, winter 1 daily; 35min).

Land train A little land-train runs approximately every 30min from the campsite via the centre of town out to the end of the river beach (May–Sept 9.30am–1.30pm & 3–7.30pm, until midnight in Aug; €2.70; ☎ 917 911 309).

Information The turismo is on Rua António Mantas (daily 10am–1pm & 2–6pm; ☎ 283 996 599, ⓦ cm-odemira.pt).

ACTIVITIES

Boat trips In summer, various boat trips run from the town quay up the Rio Mira. Expect to pay around €6 for one-hour trips on traditional *Moliceiros* boats, or around €26 for half-day trips to the town of Odemira.

Canoeing and pony treks Half-day canoe hire is available at €15 a person from Ecotrails (ⓦ ecotrails.info), which also offers 90-minute pony treks from €35.

Horseriding You can go horseriding on the beaches around Pessegueiro (one hour from €20; day-treks from €60) with Herdade do Pessegueiro, Ilha do Pessegueiro (☎ 963 320 869, ⓦ herdadepessegueiro.typepad.com).

Surfing, kayaking and bike hire Surf Milfontes, Rua Custódio Brás Pacheco 38A (☎ 914 732 652, ⓦ surfmilfontes.com), offers surfboard rental and lessons (from around €35); it also rents out kayaks (€30 a day) and mountain bikes (€15 a day).

ACCOMMODATION

★ **Apartamentos Dunamar** Rua dos Médos 2, off Av Marginal ☎ 283 998 208, ⓦ dunamarmilfontes.com. In a prime location, high above the estuary, these smart a/c studio and one-bedroom apartments sleeping 4–6 people (with balconies and kitchenette) have great views and are just a few minutes' walk from the beach and town.

Parking; breakfast not included. **€85**

Cais Rua dos Carris 9 ☎ 283 996 268. This is the best budget choice in town, especially if you have one of the rooms with estuary views (€45), but even if your room doesn't have the best aspect – they are all fairly spacious with traditional furniture and modern bathrooms – there's

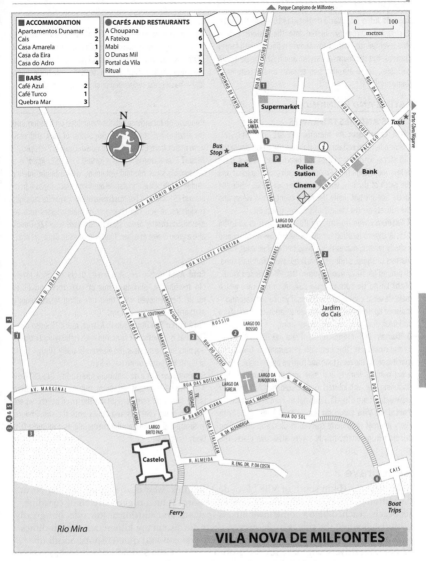

VILA NOVA DE MILFONTES

always the lovely vine-covered patio or first-floor terrace. No credit cards. **€40**

Casa Amarela Rua D. Luís de Castro e Almeida ☎283 996 632 or ☎934 204 610, ⓦcasaamarelamilfontes .com. The "yellow house" is the project of a gregarious backpacking owner, who has decorated stylish en-suite rooms (some with terrace) with art from his trips. Some rooms sleep up to four people (€20 a person) and there's a kitchen, lounge and free internet access. A separate mews-style block a couple of minutes away has more en-suite rooms arranged around

a large terraced area and kitchen. Laundry facilities available. Breakfast not included. No credit cards. **€60**

Casa da Eira Rua da Eira ☎283 997 001, ⓦaloja mentomilfontes.com. On the beach road, these small but modern rooms and self-catering apartments come with bright, contemporary decor, the best with balconies looking across a small garden towards the sea. Avoid the lower front rooms which face the road. The owners can also arrange various adventure activities including surfing, canoeing and cycling. **€60**

Casa do Adro Rua Diário de Notícias 10 ☎ 283 997 102, ⓦ casadoadro.com.pt. Tucked into the historic centre, this seventeenth-century townhouse is packed with family clutter – but the rooms are stylish and fresh, the best with balconies. There are also two terraces and a communal lounge. **€85**

EATING AND DRINKING

CAFÉS AND RESTAURANTS

★ **A Choupana** Av Marginal ☎ 283 996 643. This wooden bar and restaurant is right on the coast, down the cliff steps at the far end of the beach road: waves crash below you at high tide. An outdoor grill cooks up meat and the catch of the day, with mains from €12. But while the food's fine it's not really the main event – the views and the sunsets are the thing. Daily 8am–midnight.

A Fateixa Largo do Cais, off Rua dos Carris ☎ 283 996 415. A superb location on the riverbank below town and a shady terrace, makes this a good bet. It's fair value too – platters of squid, sardines, mackerel, swordfish and tuna, all around €8. Daily noon–10pm; Oct–May closed Wed.

Mabi Largo de Santa Maria 25A. A simple café which makes a great choice for breakfast, if you're self-catering – it dishes up delicious filled croissants, sandwiches, pastries and fresh orange juice. Daily 8am–8pm.

O Dunas Mil Marginal da Praia ☎ 283 996 420, ⓦ dunasmil.com. The best fish restaurant in town, five minutes along the coast road and high up on the right. There's a big outdoor terrace, and they specialize in *arroz* dishes (including one with lobster). Great mixed fried fish and tiger prawns, too, from €10–12. Daily noon–3pm & 7–10pm.

Portal da Vila Largo do Rossio ☎ 283 996 823. With every internal centimetre covered in tiles, and the ceiling dripping in greenery, this is a very attractive place. The

CAMPSITE

Parque Campismo de Milfontes ☎ 283 996 104, ⓦ campingmilfontes.com. This big campsite just north of town is set among shady trees and has excellent facilities, including slightly high-density teepees and bungalows. It also has a great swimming pool. Pitches from €30.

things to go include kebabs suspended on hangers and the sizzling hot-stone dishes (*da pedra*) of pork and veal, with mains from €10–14. Daily noon–3pm & 7–10pm.

Ritual Rua Barbosa Viana 4 ☎ 960 305 052. *Ritual* is a fashionable tapas bar and restaurant, with a bright interior studded with pillars and a small outdoor terrace. Tapas – from around €5 – includes *batatas bravas* or *alheira* (white sausage) croquettes, or you can choose from main courses such as mushroom risotto, pasta, steaks and salads (€9–12). There's also a good choice of wines. Mon & Wed–Sun 5pm–11pm.

BARS

Café Azul Rossio 20. A relaxed, classy bar in a lovely old townhouse, playing a mix of jazz, rock and blues music, best enjoyed with their refreshing frozen tequila margaritas. Daily 9pm–4am.

Café Turco Rua Dom João II. A large, mock-Moorish café-bar, that is a particular favourite with holidaying Lisboans – it puts on live music at the weekends. Daily 10pm–4am; in winter it's only open Sat & Sun.

Quebra Mar Praia da Franquia Apartado 51 ☎ 283 969 333. This has a decent restaurant, but the main draw here is the "tropical" terrace right on the river beach, where you can down cocktails and drinks until the small hours. In summer there are regular theme nights and guest DJs. Daily 9am–4am.

Almograve

ALMOGRAVE, 10km south of Vila Nova de Milfontes (west of the Odemira–Vila Nova de Milfontes road), is a diminutive, low-key resort sat on a rugged stretch of coastline. Its beach, reached below some low cliffs, is spacious and alluring at low tide, but greatly diminishes when the tide is in. However, there are also many kilometres of high dunes to north and south, riddled with tracks, where you can find quieter spots. South of Almograve, drivers can make for the promontory of **Cabo Sardão**, a dead-end road that culminates in a clifftop lighthouse, from near where there are magnificent panoramas of the rocky coastline.

ARRIVAL AND DEPARTURE
ALMOGRAVE

By bus Buses stop in the modern village, a block of houses and villas which sits back from the beach – a road and boardwalk run over the dunes to a huge car park above the sands.

Destinations Lisbon (1–4 daily; 3hr 50min); Porto Côvo (summer 5 daily, winter 1 daily; 45min); and Vila Nova de Milfontes (2–3 daily; 25min).

ACCOMMODATION AND EATING

Duna Praia Avenida da Praia ☎ 283 647 115, ⓦ dunapraia.webnode.pt. On the way to the beach you'll

pass the appealing *Duna Praia*, the best place to stay, with some rooms facing the dunes, and it also has its own pool

THE SOUNDS OF THE ALENTEJO

Every summer, you can enjoy two of Europe's top music fesitvals on the Alentejo coast. The otherwise missable town of Sines hosts Portugal's biggest festivals of world music every July. The **Festival Músicas do Mundo** (⊕fmm.com.pt) has taken place annually since 1999, with a main stage alongside the town castle and other events held at the beach or the Arts Centre. Folk, traditional sounds and jazz predominate and recent acts have included American jazz trio The Bad Plus, Mali singer Oumou Sangaré and Bilan from Cape Verde. Day-tickets are a modest €15 or so.

Just down the coast at Zambujeira do Mar is the **Festival Sudoeste** (⊕swtmn.com), usually held in mid-August. An annual event since 1997, the festival turns this sleepy coastal resort into a mecca for up to 30,000 music lovers. Three stages are set up for four days of concerts which, in recent years, have included sets by the likes of The Prodigy, Madness, Jessie J and the Ting Tings. One of the stages is dedicated to reggae. Camping is free on the site during the four days, or you can buy a day-ticket which is usually around €50.

and a decent restaurant. **€60**
Pousada de Juventude Rua do Chafariz ☎283 640 000, ⊕microsites.juventude.gov.pt/portal/en. This sleek,

modern youth hostel is ideally located close to the beach and has dorms for four, five or twelve people. Dorm beds **€15**; doubles **€45**

Zambujeira do Mar

The southernmost Alentejan resort is the small village of **ZAMBUJEIRA DO MAR**, 29km south of Vila Nova de Milfontes. The main street stops at the top of the cliff, where you can see the handsome beach below, whose rocky outcrops give some shade during the day. If the main beach is too crowded – and it gets smaller as the tide rises – there are good alternatives less than three kilometres' walk north or south, reached by clifftop paths. Zambujeira is small and laidback, attracting both locals and a backpacker crowd – it is particularly lively for the **Festival Sudoeste** (see box above). New villas have been tacked on to what was a tiny fishing village, and facilities are adequate: there's a small market, a bank, a few shops and half a dozen restaurants, all within a couple of hundred metres or so.

8

ARRIVAL AND INFORMATION

ZAMBUJEIRA DO MAR

By bus The bus stops at the top of the main approach road (which is closed to traffic from June–Sept); timetables are posted in the newsagent's window.
Destinations Aljezur (July–Sept 1 daily; 35min); Almograve (July–Sept 2 daily; 25min); Lisbon (2–4 daily; 4hr); Porto Côvo (summer 5 daily, winter 1 daily; 1hr 10min); Sagres (July–Sept 1 daily; 1hr 20min); Santiago do Cacém (summer 4 daily,

winter 1 daily; 2hr); and Vila Nova de Milfontes (summer 5 daily, winter 1 daily; 35min).
Information The turismo is on Rua da Escola (Tues–Sat 10am–1pm & 2–6pm; ☎283 961 144, ⊕cm-odemira.pt) and has details of private rooms: it can also check on space at the numerous rural-tourism properties in the surroundings.

ACCOMMODATION

Mar-e-Sol ☎283 961 171. The best of several places along the main street is the *Mar-e-Sol*, which has several spacious rooms that come with balconies above a restaurant. No credit cards. **€60**
Onda Azul Rua da Palmeira 1 ☎283 961 450. You'll find good-sized, modern rooms and quiet surroundings at the *Onda Azul* just east of the main street: it's above a decent restaurant. **€60**

CAMPSITE

Parque Campismo da Zambujeira ☎283 961 172, ⊕campingzambujeira.com.sapo.pt. The smart, local campsite is about 1km inland on the main approach road, and has a café-bar, swimming pools, games room and minimarket, as well as some apartments (€70) to rent. Pitch **€17**

EATING

Taberna Ti Vitório Rua Miramar ☎283 961 130. With outdoor benches just back from the clifftop, *Taberna Ti Vitório*

has a great reputation – it's been grilling fish and chicken for the locals for over fifty years. Daily noon–3pm & 7–10pm.

The Algarve

PRAIA DO AMADO

9

The Algarve

With many of the country's safest and loveliest beaches, and a year-round balmy climate, it is not surprising that the Algarve is Portugal's most popular region for holiday-makers. Inevitably, this also means stretches of the coast – in particular from Faro west to Albufeira – are heavily developed, though even here the beaches are first-rate, as are the facilities. Elsewhere in the Algarve, especially around Sagres and Tavira, the surroundings are more attractive, with laidback resorts and low-key development.

To the west of Vilamoura, you'll find the rocky outcrops and cove beaches for which the Algarve is best known, especially around the main resorts of **Albufeira, Armação de Pêra** and **Lagos**. The coast becomes progressively wilder as you head west, where attractive smaller resorts include the former fishing villages of **Salema** or **Burgau**, and the historic cape of **Sagres** – thought to be the site of Henry the Navigator's naval school. The string of villages along the rougher west coast, as far as **Odeceixe**, are quieter still, with limited facilities but fantastic wild beaches ideal for surfing.

The eastern coast between Faro and the Spanish border is very different. Most of it is protected within the **Reserva Natural da Ria Formosa**, a series of barrier islands fronted by extensive sandy beaches. That means taking a short boat trip to reach the sands, which has helped preserve the towns from large-scale development. The resorts here have a more Portuguese feel than those in the central stretch, and first-choice bases here would be **Faro** itself – capital of the entire region – **Olhão**, **Fuseta**, **Cabanas** or **Tavira**, all of which offer easy access to the sandbank islands.

Inland Algarve is still relatively undeveloped, especially around **Alcoutim** on the Spanish border. The Roman ruins of **Milreu** and the market town of **Loulé** are both worth an outing from Faro, while the old Moorish town of **Silves** is easily accessed from Portimão. Towards the west of the region, **Caldas de Monchique** is a quaint spa town in verdant woodland that makes up much of the picturesque **Serra de Monchique** mountain range.

GETTING AROUND AND INFORMATION   **THE ALGARVE**

By bus Buses link all the Algarve resorts and main inland villages. The principal regional bus companies are ⓦ eva-bus.com and ⓦ frotazul-algarve.pt, who sell three-day (€29) and seven-day (€36) passes. Several companies operate regular daily express buses between Lisbon and the Algarve (around 3hr 30min) including ⓦ rede-expressos.pt, ⓦ renex.pt and ⓦ eva-bus.com. EVA also runs a number of international buses from the Algarve, the most useful being the service from Lagos via the coast to Seville (3hr 50 min; €36 return).
Destinations Lisbon to: Albufeira (6–8 daily; 3hr 10min);

Alvor (6–8 daily; 4hr 10min); Armação de Pêra (6–8 daily; 3hr 20min); Faro (5–6 daily; 3hr 45min); Lagos (6–8 daily; 4hr 35min); Olhão (5–6 daily; 4hr); Portimão (6–8 daily; 3hr 40min); Tavira (5–6 daily; 4hr 15min); Vilamoura (6–8 daily; 3hr 50min); and Vila Real (5–6 daily; 4hr 45min).
By car Car hire is relatively inexpensive and will allow you to reach the more out-of-the-way inland villages and inaccessible cove beaches. The main east–west A22 highway from Lagos to the Spanish border offers fast and easy access to the region, linking with the A2 to Lisbon just northeast of Albufeira. Note, however, that it operates a

Highlights

❶ Olhão Its highly atmospheric old town has a superb market and it's the departure point for boat trips to some fabulous offshore-island beaches. **See p.441**

❷ Ilha de Tavira Take the ferry to this island with an enormous stretch of dune-backed beach – the best in the eastern Algarve. **See p.449**

❸ Rio Guadiana The river marking the border with Spain offers some of the region's least spoilt scenery, meandering north to the pretty village of Alcoutim. **See p.455**

❹ Boat trip, Lagos Explore the extraordinary rock formations and grottoes on a boat trip from the historic town of Lagos, from where Portugal's navigators once set sail. **See p.478**

❺ Surfing in Sagres The beaches around Europe's most southwesterly town are rated as some of the best in Europe – whatever your surfing skills. **See p.482**

❻ West-coast beaches A stunning variety of wave-battered sandy swathes grace the dramatic and largely undeveloped west coast between Sagres and Odeceixe. **See p.486**

HIGHLIGHTS ARE MARKED ON THE MAP ON PP.434–435

9

THE ALGARVE'S BEST BEACH RESTAURANTS

As you'd expect with so much coastline, the Algarve boasts some excellent beachside restaurants serving superb fresh fish as alluring as the sea views.

Beach Bar Burgau Burgau p.480
Boia Bar Salema p.480
Estrela do Mar Armação de Pêra p.465
Mar e Sol Praia da Rocha p.470

Raposo Sagres p.485
Rei das Praias Praia da Caneiros p.466
Restinga Alvor p.471
A Ruina Albufeira p.462

complex toll-charging system (see p.31).

By train The Algarve rail line (timetables on ☎ 808 208 208, ⓦ cp.pt) runs from Lagos in the west to Vila Real de Santo António on the Spanish border, calling at most major towns en route (you may have to change at Tunes, Faro or Tavira, depending on your destination). There are also fast daily connections between Faro and Lisbon. Details are given in the Guide.

Information A comprehensive calendar of cultural events can be found in *Agenda*, available free from tourist offices, cultural centres and larger hotels – the biggest affair is the Algarve International Music Festival (early summer), hosting major artists in various venues throughout the region. For general information, check the official tourist-board website, ⓦ visitalgarve.pt, or ⓦ algarvenet.com.

Faro and around

With its international airport, impressive shopping centre and ring of high-rise apartments, **FARO** has something of a big-city feel. However, the central area is a manageable size, boasting attractive mosaic-paved pedestrianized streets and marina-side gardens, while its university contributes to a lively nightlife, during term time at least. In summer, boats and buses run from the centre of town out to some excellent local beaches.

Originally a Roman settlement, the city was named by the Moors, under whom it was a thriving commercial port that supplied the regional capital at Silves. It then became Christian, under Afonso III in 1249, but was largely destroyed by the Great Earthquake of 1755 – so it comes as no surprise that modern Faro has so few historic buildings left. What interest it does retain is centred within and around the pretty **Cidade Velha** (Old Town), which lies behind a series of defensive walls overlooking the mudflats.

Cidade Velha

The only part of town to have survived the various violent historic upheavals is the **Cidade Velha**, or Vila-Adentro ("town within"), an oval of cobbled streets set within

HIGHLIGHTS
1 Olhão
2 Ilha de Tavira
3 Rio Guadiana
4 Boat trip, Lagos
5 Surfing in Sagres
6 West-coast beaches

9

FARO

◀ Olhão, Vila Real & Spain

RESTAURANTS	
Adega Dois Irmãos	2
Adega Nova	1
Aqui d'el Rey	7
Ginásio Clube Naval	6
República	3
Taberna Modesto	8

CAFÉS	
Café do Coreto	5
Gardy	4

ACCOMMODATION	
Adelaide	3
Aeromar	1
Eva	4
Faro	2
Sol Algarve	5
Tivoli Guest House	6

SHOPS	
Forum Algarve	1
Mercado	2
Rui Garrafeira	3

BARS AND CLUBS	
Âncora Bar	3
Bar Chessenta	4
Columbus Lounge Bar	4
Upa Upa	1

9

a run of sturdy walls. Bright-white houses are fronted by decorative balconies and tiling, a few now serving as antique shops, cafés or art galleries. The most central entrance is through the eighteenth-century town gate, the **Arco da Vila**, next to the turismo. From here, Rua do Município leads up to the broad Largo da Sé, which is lined with orange trees and flanked by the cathedral and a group of palaces, including the former bishop's palace.

Sé

Largo da Sé • Mon–Fri 10am–6pm (closes 5pm from Oct–May), Sat 10am–1pm • €3

Parts of Faro's squat **Sé** (cathedral) date back to 1251. The impressive structure became the Algarve's principal cathedral in 1577, but was sacked by the English under the Count of Essex in 1596 and then partially destroyed by the 1755 earthquake, so much of what you see today – a mixture of Gothic, Renaissance and Baroque styles – dates from the eighteenth century. Inside there's fine eighteenth-century *azulejo* tiling, though for most people the highlight is to climb the bell tower for superb views over the old town and the mudflats beyond.

Museu Municipal

Largo Dom Afonso III 14 • June–Sept Tues–Fri 10am–7pm, Sat & Sun 11.30am–6pm; Oct–May Tues–Fri 10am–6pm, Sat & Sun 10.30am–5pm • €2, free on Sun until 3.30pm • ☎ 289 897 400, ⊛ ipmuseus.pt

One of the oldest museums in Portugal, Faro's impressive **Museu Municipal** was founded as an archeological museum in 1894. Housed in a sixteenth-century convent with a beautiful cloister, its highlight is an almost intact mosaic showing the Roman god of water, Neptune, and the Four Seasons. Dating from the third century, it was originally excavated near the city's train station. Also on display are some fine Roman statues from Milreu (see p.438), exquisite Moorish lamps, vases and bowls, and a variety of Baroque and Renaissance paintings. The collection also includes Futurist works by Carlos Porfírio, one of the country's leading twentieth-century artists. In front of the building stands a forthright, crucifix-carrying statue of the conqueror Afonso himself, king between 1249 and 1279.

Around the marina

At the **marina**, attractive town gardens and outdoor cafés overlook the rows of sleek yachts, and at the end of the day much of Faro gathers to promenade here. At the northern end of the harbour is the small **Museu Marítimo** (Mon–Fri 2.30–4.30pm; free), a modest maritime museum with displays of model boats and local fishing techniques. Heading southwards from the marina along Rua Comandante Francisco Manuel, you can follow the railway line for an attractive walk along the seafront, with the town walls on one side and the mudflats on the other. A small arch through the old town walls offers another approach to the Cidade Velha, while from the jetty opposite here, ferries depart to the local sandspit beaches.

Núcleo Museológico

Rua Misericórdia 3 • Tues–Fri 9.30am–noon & 2–6pm • €1 • ☎ 289 805 992

Facing the marina-side gardens, the **Núcleo Museológico** is a small sacred-arts museum displaying religious artefacts recovered from the Misericórdia church that was destroyed in the 1755 earthquake. Its highlight is an unusual ivory statue of Christ from Indochina, the blood made from tiny rubies. You can also look around the Santa Casa da Misericórdia, the adjacent church; originally constructed in 1581, it was rebuilt after the earthquake in an Italian style.

9

Museu Regional

Praça de Liberdade 2 • Tues–Fri 10am–1.30 & 2.30–6pm • €2.50, free on Sun until 1.30pm • ☎ 289 878 238

Faro's likeable little **Museu Regional** is a refreshingly low-tech ensemble of items representing traditional Algarvian culture – perfect for an hour or so on a rainy day. There are agricultural implements, re-creations of house interiors, musical instruments and model fishing boats. Perhaps of most interest are the black-and-white photos that show what the town and local beaches looked like before the advent of tourism.

Igreja do Carmo and the Capela dos Ossos

Largo do Carmo • Mon–Fri 10am–1pm & 3–6pm, Sat 10am–1pm, Sun only for Mass at 9am; Oct–April Mon–Fri closes at 5pm • Church free; Capela dos Ossos €1

For ghoulish delights, it's worth seeking out the Baroque **Igreja do Carmo**, which enlivens an otherwise dull part of town. At the back of the church, you can buy a ticket to view the **Capela dos Ossos** (Chapel of Bones), set in an overgrown garden at the rear. The chapel is completely lined with the bones and skulls of monks disinterred from the cemetery next door and carefully arranged into neat patterns.

Igreja de São Pedro

Largo de São Pedro • Daily 8.30am–12.30pm & 3–6.45pm • Free

The **Igreja de São Pedro** is an attractive church originally built by the local fishermen in the late sixteenth century, though remodelled after the earthquake of 1755. Its finest decorative work is an altar (to the left of the main altar) whose central image is a gilded, wooden *Last Supper* in relief.

The beaches

Praia de Faro Buses #14 and #16 run from the marina gardens, or the stop opposite the bus station, calling at the airport en route, stopping just before the narrow bridge to the beach itself (every 45min, 7.15am–8pm; 30min) • **Ilha Culatra** From June to mid-Sept 5 ferries daily run from the jetty below Faro old town (first boat at 9.30am, last return at 7pm) • €5 return • ☎ 917 634 813

Faro's nearest beach, **Praia de Faro** – the only sandspit beach linked by a bridge – is a long sweep of beautiful sand with both a sea-facing and a more sheltered lagoon-facing side. Its proximity to both the airport and Faro means it's somewhat developed, with bars, restaurants and villas crammed onto a narrow strip – though out of season you'll probably have the sands to yourself. The beach is situated on the Ilha de Faro, southwest of town. In July, the area between the beach and the airport hosts the **Faro Bike Concentration** (🖥 www.motoclubefaro.pt), Europe's largest meeting of bikers, with plenty of live entertainment. Billy Idol and Portuguese star David Fonseca have appeared in recent years. In summer, ferries shuttle from Faro through narrow marshy channels to the town of **Farol** on the beautiful sandbar **Ilha da Culatra**, which has a fantastic sandy beach (see p.443).

Milreu

Estói • Tues–Sun: May–Sept 10.30am–1pm & 2–6.30pm; Oct–April 9.30am–1pm & 2–5pm • €2 • ☎ 289 997 823, 🖥 cultag.pt/milreu • Take the Estói bus from Faro bus station, which passes the site entrance

The Roman site at **Milreu** (pronounced *mil-rio*) is the Algarve's principal Roman excavation, just south of the attractive town of Estói, 11km north of Faro. The lavish villa that once stood here was inhabited from the first century AD and was constructed round a central peristyle – a gallery of columns surrounding a courtyard. You can also see the remains of one of the oldest Christian churches in the country, which was converted from a former Roman temple in around the sixth century. Southwest of the villa is an impressive bathing complex, with an underfloor heating system and striking

9

fish mosaics – there's also an *apodyterium*, or changing room, sporting arched niches for clothes. A small visitor centre shows what the villa would have looked like in its heyday.

ARRIVAL AND DEPARTURE   FARO

FARO AIRPORT

Flights land at Faro's international airport (🌐 ana.pt, flight information ☎ 289 800 800), 6km west of town, where there's a bank, ATMs, car rental companies and tourist office (daily 8am–11.30pm; ☎ 289 818 582). There are no direct public transport services to other resorts from the airport, which means heading first into central Faro.

By taxi A taxi from the airport into the centre of town (15min) should cost about €11–12, plus €2.50 for any luggage that goes in the boot; there's also a twenty-percent surcharge between 10pm and 6am, and at weekends.

By bus Local buses #14 and #16 also run from the airport to the centre (25min), costing €1.65 (departures roughly every 45min from 7am–8pm; buy tickets on board). Both stop outside the bus terminal in town (see below) and, further on, at the Jardim Manuel Bivar ("Jardim" on the timetables) by the harbour.

FARO TOWN

The compact town is simple to negotiate on foot, and all the hotels, restaurants and bars are extremely central. There is a town bus service, but you'll only need it to get to the beach and back to the airport.

By bus Faro's bus terminal (☎ 289 899 760) is on Avenida da República, just back from the marina. There's an English-speaking information office inside, though it is not always staffed. The RENEX bus terminal (for express buses to Lisbon, Porto and the Minho) is opposite.

Destinations Albufeira (approx hourly; 50min–1hr 15min); Castro Marim (5–9 daily; 1hr 35min); Estói (Mon–Fri 10–12 daily, Sat & Sun 9 daily; 20min); Fuseta (4 daily; 45min); Lisbon (5–6 daily; 3hr 45min); Loulé (every 30–50min; 40min); Monte Gordo (Mon–Fri 7–9 daily, Sat & Sun 4 daily; 1hr 40min); Olhão (Mon–Fri every 15–30min, Sat & Sun approx hourly; 20min); Quarteira (approx every 30min; 40min); Tavira (7–11 daily; 1hr); Vilamoura (approx every 30min; 50min); and Vila Real (6–9 daily; 1hr 40min).

By car Drivers will find plenty of metered parking around the harbour; free parking can be found in the streets around the train station or in the large Largo de São Francisco, just east of the old town.

By train The train station is on Largo da Estação, a few minutes' walk north of the marina.

Destinations Conceição (11 daily; 45min); Ferreiras for Albufeira (4 daily; 25min); Fuseta (15 daily; 35min); Lagos (9 daily; 1hr 50min); Lisbon (2–3 daily; 3hr 20min); Loulé (4 daily; 10min); Monte Gordo (11 daily; 1hr 5min); Olhão (15 daily; 12min); Portimão (9 daily; 1hr 30min); Porto (2 daily; 5hr 45min); Silves (9 daily; 1hr 15min); Tavira (15 daily; 40min); and Vila Real de Santo António (11 daily; 1hr 10min).

TOURS AND ACTIVITIES

Boat trips Various boat trips depart from Faro's jetty, below the old town walls, including the highly recommended two-and-a-half-hour trip to the Ilha Deserta (daily at 11am, 1pm & 3pm, weather permitting; €20; ☎ 917 811 856, 🌐 ilha-deserta.com), in the Parque Natural da Ria Formosa. The most southerly point of mainland Portugal, the island's official name is Ilha da Barreta, and there's little there, save one pricey café and a great beach.

Watersports and birdwatching Specializing in eco-tourism, Lands (☎ 289 817 466, 🌐 lands.pt) run kayaking and sailing-boat tours in the Ria Formosa, along with birdwatching, bike rental and walks around the region.

Land train A fun Comboio Turístico (land train; hourly 10am–dusk; €3.50) trundles from the marina to the Sé and through the modern town before skirting back to the marina via the market.

INFORMATION

Tourist office Faro's turismo, Rua da Misericórdia 8–12 (May–Sept daily 9.30am–7pm; Oct–April Tues–Fri 9.30am–5.30pm, Sat & Mon 9.30am–1pm & 2–5.30pm; ☎ 289 803 604, 🌐 cm-faro.pt) provides town maps and posts local and long-distance bus, boat and train timetables.

Regional tourist office Avenida 5 Outubro 18–20 (Mon–Fri 9am–12.30pm & 2–5.30pm; ☎ 289 800 400, 🌐 visitalgarve.pt) – a good source of information on the area as a whole.

ACCOMMODATION

Adelaide Rua Cruz das Mestras 9 ☎ 289 802 383, 🌐 adelaideresidencial.net. The friendly owner offers some of the best-value rooms in town, all with attached bathrooms and cable TV, and there's an airy breakfast-room-cum-snack-bar. Some rooms sleep three or four. **€55**

Aeromar Av Nascente 1, Praia de Faro ☎ 289 817 542, 🌐 aeromar.net. By the bridge to Faro's beach, this simple hotel has decent rooms above a restaurant with beach or (distant) airport views – you pay a little more for a terrace. A good option if you have an early flight. **€85**

9

Eva Av da República 1 ☎ 289 001 000, ⓦ tdhotels.com /eva/pt. The town's top hotel, offering bright rooms, the best with balconies looking across to the old town or the marina. There's a great rooftop pool and restaurant, and a courtesy bus to the local beach. Parking. **€175**

Faro Praça Dr Francisco Gomes 2 ☎ 289 830 830, ⓦ hotelfaro.pt. Modern four-star above (and accessed via) an office block. The rooms – largely geared to business travellers – are minimalist with minibar, cable TV and a/c; the best are on the top floors with views over town. The main attraction is the sunny roof terrace with its own restaurant and fine marina views. Free shuttle boat to Farol in summer. **€150**

Pousada Palácio de Estói Rua São José, Estói ☎ 289 990 150, ⓦ pousadas.pt. Around 11km north of Faro, this was the former nineteenth-century palace of the Viscount of Estói. Now it's a classic blend of old-style opulence – wood panelling, gilt mirrors and high ceilings – and contemporary flair, with a pool in the top part of the ornate former gardens, modern rooms, a plush bar and quality restaurant serving gourmet regional food. **€140**

Sol Algarve Rua Infante Dom Henrique 52 ☎ 289 895 700, ⓦ residencialalgarve.com. A popular two-star hotel, with bright rooms on several floors (there's a lift). Bathrooms are spotless, the rooms have a/c and cable TV and breakfast (included) is served in the downstairs dining room or on the little internal patio. Parking and wi-fi available. **€80**

Tivoli Guest House Praça Alexandre Herculano 6 ☎ 289 829 825, ⓦ pension-tivoli.net. Welcoming English-run place that has a mixed bag of airy, bright rooms with high ceilings and cable TV – the cheapest ones are on the ground floor with shared bath (€50) and there are also larger family rooms (€80). Some have showers and small balconies and you can use the communal kitchen and lovely roof terrace. No breakfast. **€55**

EATING, DRINKING AND NIGHTLIFE

The heart of the town is an attractive pedestrianized shopping area, where you can find innumerable **restaurants**, **cafés** and **bakeries** – the latter stocked with almond delicacies, the regional speciality. **Bars and clubs** are concentrated along the pedestrianized Rua Conselheiro Bivar and the parallel Rua do Prior. Things get going around midnight; soon afterwards, drinkers spill out onto the cobbled alleys to party.

CAFÉS

Café do Coreto Jardim Manuel Bivar ☎ 289 822 964. Glass kiosk café-bar with prime seating facing the marina. Serves everything from croissants to ice cream, cakes, beers and full meals (pizzas, crêpes etc from €10). Daily 8am–midnight.

★ **Gardy** Rua de Santo António 16 ☎ 289 824 062. Popular local *pastelaria* whose seats are always at a premium – excellent cakes, pastries and coffee, and good-value lunches. They also have a takeaway branch at Rua de Santo António 33, that sells the delicious local almond pastries. Mon–Sat 8.30am–8.30pm.

RESTAURANTS

Adega Dois Irmãos Largo Terreiro do Bispo 14 ☎ 289 823 337. Opened in 1925 by two brothers (*dois irmãos*) in a former welder's shop, this attractive tiled place is one of the oldest of the city's fish restaurants. The day's catch can be expensive (around €15), though the *pratos do dia* are usually better value. Despite the number of tourists passing through, service remains courteous and efficient, and there's a pleasant garden. Daily noon–4pm & 5.30–11pm.

Adega Nova Rua Francisco Barreto 24 ☎ 289 813 433. This old-fashioned *adega* seats diners on long, shared benches in a barn-like building. It's a buzzy place, serving big portions of good-value Portuguese food and jugs of local wine. Order *bife na pedra* and you can cook your own steak on a sizzling stone, brought to your table – you'll eat well for around €15. Daily noon–11pm.

★ **Aqui d'el Rey** Rua do Rapouso 6–8 ☎ 289 827 064. In a lovely old building close to the old town walls, this is a wonderful space that serves pricey but delicious, creative Portuguese cuisine (seafood spaghetti, monkfish rice) and also food from Portugal's former colony Angola. Expect chicken, rabbit or fish *moamba* (served with palm paste, garlic, okra and rice). Mains from €15. Daily 10.30am–11pm.

Ginásio Clube Naval Doca de Faro ☎ 289 823 869. The main draw here is a great terrace overlooking the tidal mudflats and the coast. The catch of the day includes fresh fish and seafood, often langoustine, clams and oysters and good-value rice dishes (around €9). Tues–Sun noon–3pm & 7–11pm.

República Avenida da República 40 ☎ 289 807 312. A small and intimate restaurant with arty decor: it serves up tasty local specialities including prawn kebabs, steaks and a fantastic *açorda de camarão* from €12. Mon–Sat 7–11pm.

Taberna Modesto Largo do Castelo 2 ☎ 916 577 044. This basic diner has alluring outdoor tables set out in the old town. There's a short, simple menu of fish or meat of the day at around €7–9. Daily noon–11pm; Oct–April closes at 6pm.

BARS AND CLUBS

Âncora Bar Rua 1 de Maio 11 ☎ 919 663 310. A pub-like bar with nautical decor – ropes, anchors, model boats and a ceiling of carved wood. It serves a good range of drinks and plays catchy sounds. Daily 6pm–4am.

9

Bar Chessenta 24 Rua do Prior ☎ 931 194 314. Small and smoky, but also Faro's main live-music bar which features everything from rock and pop to reggae and world music most weekends. Daily 1pm–4am.

★ **Columbus Lounge Bar** Jardim Manuel Bívar, corner with Rua João Dias ☎ 289 813 051. Fashionable bar with outdoor seats beneath the arcades of a former hospital, plus a cosy lounge area inside. It serves up fine *caipirinha* cocktails and hosts occasional live music. Tues–Sun 11am–1am.

Upa Upa Rua Conselheiro Bivar 51 ☎ 289 807 832. Laid-back and relatively early-opening music bar with a mixed clientele spilling onto outdoor tables on the widest stretch of this pedestrianized street. Daily 9pm–4am; Oct–April closed on Sun.

SHOPPING

Forum Algarve EN125 ☎ 289 889 300, ⓦ forumalgarve .net. You'll pass this giant shopping centre when heading into Faro from the airport – it's a brisk fifteen-minute walk from town up Rua Infante Dom Henrique. The attractive, Moorish-style pedestrianized complex has over 100 local and international shops, cafés, restaurants and a multiplex cinema. Daily 10am–midnight.

Mercado Largo Dr Francisco Sá Carneiro ☎ 289 897 250. Faro's bustling town market sits in a very grand building on three floors. There's a giant supermarket in the basement, while on the ground floor, stalls sell everything from dried figs and olives to fruits, cheeses, honey and fresh fish. There are also restaurants and souvenirs. Most shops Mon–Fri 8am–8pm, Sat 9am–1pm.

Rui Garrafeira 28 Praça Ferreira de Almeida ☎ 289 821 586. This deli-cum-off-licence sells a fantastic array of traditional sweets, cheeses, preserves and wines from the region. Mon–Sat 8.30am–8pm.

DIRECTORY

Football/Live music International games are some-times played at the 30,000-seat Algarve Stadium (☎ 289 893 200, ⓦ parquedascidades-eim.pt), the centre-piece of a cultural centre and sports park called Parque das Cidades, 6km north of Faro on the Loulé road. It also hosts various events including concerts – check the website for details.

Hospital Distrital de Faro, Rua Leão Penedo ☎ 289 891 100, ⓦ hdfaro.min-saude.pt. For emergencies call ☎ 112.

Police Rua da Policia de Segurança Pública 32 ☎ 289 822 022.

Post office Largo do Carmo (Mon–Fri 8.30am–6.30pm).

Taxis There's a rank in Praça Dr Francisco Gomes, by the town gardens; otherwise call ☎ 289 895 795.

Olhão and the islands

There are few actual sights in **OLHÃO**, 8km east of Faro, but with a vibrant market, attractive riverfront gardens and atmospheric backstreets, it's an appealing place to spend some time. It also makes a great base from which to visit the surrounding sandbank islands of **Armona** and **Culatra** or the **Quinta da Marim** environmental centre. The largely pedestrianized old town boasts some superb tile-fronted buildings, quirky shops and bars, while the flat roofs and narrow streets are striking and give a North African look to the place – perhaps not surprisingly, as Olhão had traditional trading links with Morocco. The town was granted its charter by exiled king João VI to thank the local fishermen who sailed a small boat, *O Caíque de Bom Sucesso*, across the Atlantic to Brazil in 1808 to give him the good news that Napoleon's troops had left Portugal. The amazing journey was completed with the most basic navigational aids, and a replica of the boat is now moored on the water behind the market: it occasionally runs boat trips along the coast – ask at the turismo for details.

Mercado

Avenida 5 de Outubro • Mon–Fri 7am–2pm, Sat 6.30am–3pm

The town's most obvious focus is the **mercado**, a bustling market held in two early twentieth-century redbrick buildings on the harbourside. Open from the crack of dawn, it sells meat, fruit and vegetables on one side, fish on the other, the latter full of tuna steaks the size of hubcaps and alarmingly large octopus and squid. Come on a Saturday morning and the market extends along the riverfront, a riot of chickens, flowers, fruit and local characters. In August, the gardens on either side host the

Festival do Marisco (Seafood Festival; ⓦfestivaldomarisco.com) with food stalls and nightly entertainment over five days.

Nossa Senhora do Rosário

Praça da Restauração • Tues–Sun 9.30am–noon & 3–6pm • Free

The old town's most prominent building is the seventeenth-century parish church of **Nossa Senhora do Rosário**, right in the middle of town. Outside, at the back of the church, an iron grille protects the chapel of **Nossa Senhora dos Aflitos**, where townswomen traditionally gathered to pray for their sailors when there was a storm at sea – if you look through the grille, you'll see the curious wax *ex voto* models of children and limbs left to bring good fortune.

Museu da Cidade

Praça da Restauração • Tues–Fri 10am–12.30pm & 2–5.30pm, Sat 10am–1pm • Free • ☏ 289 700 184

Behind the church of Nossa Senhora da Soledade you'll find the small but appealing **Museu da Cidade**, which has a small collection of archeological finds from the region,

> **FERRIES TO ARMONA AND CULATRA**
>
> Separate **ferries to** Armona and Culatra leave from the jetty at the eastern end of Olhão's municipal gardens, five minutes' walk from the market. The timetable (also on ⓦolhao.web.pt, or call ☎289 702 121) is posted at the ticket kiosk; if the kiosk isn't open, you can buy tickets on the ferries. The **Ilha da Armona** (15min) is accessible all year round, as are the villages of Culatra (35min) and Farol (45min) on the **Ilha da Culatra**. Note that in summer you can also get the boat to Farol from Faro.

from Bronze-Age pots to Islamic vases. Upstairs there are relics of Olhão's industrial heritage, with model fishing boats, oil presses and old black-and-white photos.

Ilha da Armona

Ferries June & Sept 10 departures daily; July & Aug first departure at 7.30am, then hourly from 9am–8pm; Oct–May 4 daily • €3 return

Ferries from Olhão drop their passengers at the southern end of **Ilha da Armona**, a narrow, nine-kilometre-long island flanked on the ocean side by idyllic, soft white sands. Ferries stop at the island's only settlement – little more than a cluster of holiday homes and seasonal cafés with a small shop – from where it's a fifteen-minute walk to the ocean. The section of beach nearest the ferry jetty can get busy in high season, but it doesn't take much effort to escape the crowds – just walk east. Continue east up the beach for two hours and you'll end up at Praia da Fuseta opposite Fuseta town (see p.445). There are no hotels on Armona, and camping on the beach is frowned upon, but there are some basic **bungalows** available to rent (see p.444).

Ilha da Culatra

Ferries June–mid-Sept 6 daily; July & Aug 7 daily; rest of year 4 daily • €3.10 return to Culatra, €3.70 to Farol

Ilha da Culatra is a six-kilometre-long strip of dunes dotted with narrow lagoons and faced by a wonderful sandy beach. The ferry stops first at **Culatra**, a working fishing village – you dock by a harbour bursting with fishing boats. When not at sea, fishermen gather to mend their nets, or hang out in the bars of the main town which has a permanent population of about a thousand. There are no cars – the main street is little more than a pavement – but it has its own school, church and assorted local fish restaurants. Walk south through the main street and across the boardwalks to reach the superb stretch of beach. **Farol**, the second ferry stop, is more geared to tourists, with fishermen's huts, seasonal restaurants and holiday homes gathered below a lighthouse, from where the beach stretches to the west: the further you walk, the quieter it becomes.

Quinta da Marim

Three kilometres east of Olhão, just off the N125 Olhão–Tavira road • Mon–Fri 8am–8pm, Sat & Sun 10am–8pm • €2.50 • ☎289 704 134 • Regular buses from Olhão and Fuseta drop you on the main road, from where it's a 5min walk

Quinta da Marim is an environmental educational centre and headquarters of the **Parque Natural da Ria Formosa**. It's a lovely quiet spot, set amid scrubby dunes and mudflats dotted with pines and gorse, well worth a half-day visit. You can follow a three-kilometre-long **nature trail** that leads from the car park past the visitor centre, along which you'll be able to view storks' nests, and the remains of Roman saltpans. Its highlight is one of the country's last remaining tidal mills; there's also a café at the visitor centre.

ARRIVAL AND INFORMATION   OLHÃO AND THE ISLANDS

By bus The bus terminal is on Rua General Humberto Delgado, five minutes' walk north of the centre.

Destinations Faro (Mon–Fri every 15–30min, Sat & Sun approx hourly; 20min); Tavira (9–10 daily; 40 min); and Vila Real de Santo António (10 daily; 1hr 20 min).

9

By train The train station is at the northern edge of town, off Avenida dos Combatentes da Grande Guerra. Destinations Faro (15 daily; 12min); Tavira (15 daily; 30min); and Vila Real de Santo António (11 daily; 1hr).

Information The turismo is on Largo Sebastião Martins Mestre (Mon–Fri 9.30am–1pm & 2–5.30pm; ☎ 289 713 936, ⓦ cm-olhao.pt).

ACCOMMODATION

Olhão does not have a great choice of **accommodation**, so it is best to book in advance in high season. If you are happy to cater for yourself, it's worth checking out ⓦ whiteterraces.com, which lets out some great traditional houses in the old town (minimum three-day lets) – many have roof terraces with sea views, and some have their own pool.

Bela Vista Rua Dr Teófilo Braga 65–67 ☎ 289 702 538. A long-standing favourite, with a range of simple, bright a/c rooms – some are completely tiled, though others lack windows – arranged around a flower-filled courtyard. No breakfast. €45

Bicuar Rua Vasco da Gama 5 ☎ 289 714 816, ⓦ pension -bicuar.com. Central, English-run guesthouse on a quiet pedestrianized street, with a variety of rooms, including family rooms and dorms sleeping four. All are well furnished with cable TV, most have private showers and balconies overlooking the old town, and guests can use a communal kitchen, wi-fi and book exchange. From the roof terrace there are great views. No breakfast. €50

Real Marina Avenida 5 de Outubro ☎ 289 091 300, ⓦ real-marina.com. The town's top hotel is an unattractive modern building that offers a range of luxurious facilities – most of the pristine rooms come with large

sea-facing balconies and flatscreen TVs. A glass lift shuttles from the ground floor, with its spa and restaurant, past the first-floor deck where there's a heated open-air pool. €85

CAMPSITES

Camping Olhão Pinheiros de Marim ☎ 289 700 300, ⓦ campings-camping.com. Around 3km east of town, next to Quinta da Marim, this upmarket site is set in substantial grounds and has its own pool (small fee charged), playground, tennis courts, minimarket, restaurant and bars. It's served by regular buses from Olhão. Pitch €6

Parque Orbitur Ilha da Armona Ilha da Armona ☎ 289 714 173, ⓦ orbitur.pt. *Orbitur* runs a series of simple beachside holiday bungalows sleeping up to six on the island of Armona. Reservations advised; one-week minimum stay in high season; closed Nov–March. €60

EATING AND DRINKING

CAFÉS AND RESTAURANTS

★ **A Bote** Av 5 de Outubro 122 ☎ 289 721 183. Near the fish market, this lively restaurant serves meat and fish dishes from an outdoor grill, accompanied by mounds of potatoes and salad, from €8. Mon–Sat 11am–4pm & 7–11pm.

Café Gelvi Rua Patrão Joaquim Casaca 24 ☎ 289 713 758. Best known for its ice creams, this bustling *pastelaria* and *geladaria* is in the corner of the fish market, with outdoor seats facing the water. Daily 8am–2am.

Indian Hut Rua Vasco da Gama 2 ☎ 289 703 082. The name changes frequently but this remains a reliable Indian restaurant in a fine old building, serving superb fish and prawn curries and a good range of veggie options from €8. Daily 11am–3pm & 6–midnight.

O Livramento Av 5 de Outubro 160 ☎ 289 706 763. One of the best of the fish restaurants on the harbour road,

dishing up superb *feijoada de mariscos* (seafood stew with beans), fish soups, *cataplanas* and daily specials, from around €9. Tues–Sun noon–3pm & 7–11pm.

BARS

Cais Club Mercado, Av 5 de Outubro ☎ 965 554 732. The liveliest of a row of bars behind the market, with outdoor tables facing the water – though most hit the inside bar and dance area as the night wears on. There's regular live music, usually folk or jazz. Daily 2pm–4am.

Casa Sete Estrelas Travessa Alexandre Herculano 6. If you fancy engaging with some of the local characters and fishermen, head to this rough-and-ready bar with football-themed decor. There's dirt-cheap wine from the barrel, animated banter and oodles of character. Tues–Sun noon–midnight.

ACTIVITIES

Football Olhão's football team, Olhanenses, has flown the flag for the region in the top Portuguese league in recent years, though its only league championship was in 1924. They host top league matches on alternate weekends from September to May at the small Estádio José Arcanjo (ⓦ scolhanense.com).

Guided walks and boat trips Natura (ⓦ natura -algarve.com, ☎ 918 056 674) offers a range of activities including guided walks and boat trips into the Ria Formosa lagoon, ranging from leisurely 2–3-hour birdwatching cruises which include a visit to an oyster farm (all year; €35), to adrenalin-rushing 2-hour powerboat rides to spot dolphins (June–Oct; €45).

Fuseta

Around 10km east of Olhão, and served by regular bus as well as the main Algarve rail
line, the fishing town of **FUSETA** (or Fuzeta) is one of the Algarve's least "discovered"
resorts, probably because of its shortage of accommodation. It is not the region's most
beautiful town, but it does retain some character as a working fishing port. Indeed its
daily routine revolves around the fishermen, whose colourful boats line up alongside
the river in town, though in summer Fuseta also attracts a lively community of
campers. The two communities usually mingle at the line of lively kiosk-cafés spreading
down from the ferry stop towards the river beach.

The town's backstreets straddle a low hill facing the lagoon, sheltered by the eastern
extremity of the Ilha da Armona. Many of the local fish find their way to the small
covered **market** on Largo 1° de Maio, on the road running parallel to the river. On
Saturdays the market expands into a flea market that lines the adjacent pedestrianized
Rua Tenente Barrosa. Continue up this road to reach the town's little palm-tree-lined
central square and Rua da Liberdade.

The waterfront of modern shops and apartments faces broad gardens that are largely
taken over by the campsite. Beyond this is the **estuary beach**, a fine stretch of white
sand that weaves up to a wooden lifeboat house, though more exhilarating and cleaner
waters are found over the lagoon on the Ilha da Armona (see p.443).

Praia da Fuseta

Ferries April–Sept daily approx every 15min from 9am–7pm, and often later; Oct–March 4 daily, last return at 6pm • €1.60 return

Regular **ferries** shuttle from the fishing quay at the back of the campsite across the
lagoon to **Praia da Fuseta** on the eastern end of the Ilha da Armona. The beach
immediately opposite the ferry stop gets fairly crowded in high summer, but you only
have to walk ten minutes or so either way from the holiday beach huts and seasonal
drinks kiosks to have beautiful, low dune-backed sands all to yourself. You can also
reach the sands by Aquataxis (☎962 539 810) for €5 one way per person.

ARRIVAL AND DEPARTURE
FUSETA

By bus Buses from Faro pull up at the waterfront near the
campsite (4 daily, 45min).
By train The train station is to the north of town, about
ten minutes' walk from the waterfront. It has regular
services to Faro (15 daily; 35min), Olhão (15 daily; 22min)
and Tavira (15 daily; 25 min).

ACCOMMODATION

Monte Alegre ☎289 794 222. Run by welcoming
Germans, around 2km northwest of Fuseta – signposted
Bias Sul – Monte Alegre consists of three well-equipped
apartments sleeping up to five, and a superb studio with its
own terrace. There's an outdoor swimming pool, stables for
horse rides and a pond full of resident frogs; all rooms have

---

TOP FIVE FAVOURITE COASTAL SPOTS
The Algarve is known for its wonderful beaches and dramatic coastline – here are our five
favourite places.
Ilha de Tavira Miles of soft, dune-backed sand without a hotel in sight. See p.448
Benagil This tiny village marks the start of a superb cliff-top path past an awesome sea cave.
See p.465
Praia da Figueira You'll have to walk to get here, but it's worth it to find this often-deserted
beach. See p.481
Praia da Bordeira A wild and wonderful stretch of sand in a remote corner of the Algarve.
See p.486
Praia de Odeceixe Follow the river valley to a superb bay with sheltered river swimming and
a wide sandy beach. See p.488

9

satellite TV and kitchenettes. Minimum one-week lets in high season. **€510** per week.
Parque de Campismo da Fuseta ❶289 793 459, ⓦjf-fuseta.pt. Beautifully positioned waterside campsite beneath the trees, with its own minimarket and bar. It gets pretty full in high summer, so it's best to book in advance. Pitch **€11**

EATING AND DRINKING

Fuseta Tapas Rua Tenete Barroso 59 ❶289 791 093. On the main pedestrianized square, this has a good range of *petiscos* (snacks) such as mushrooms with garlic and coriander, *chouriço* snails or *pasteis de bacalhau* (dried cod cakes) from €4, as well as the usual mains from €10. Tues–Sun 11am–3pm & 6–11pm.

Skandinavia Rua Tenente Barroso 11 ❶289 793 853. Near the market, the food here is not at all Scandinavian – it has friendly service and excellent seafood, grilled meat and fish from €7–9, with outdoor tables spilling onto the pedestrianized street. Mon & Wed–Sun noon–3pm & 6–11pm.

Tavira and around

Despite its inland position, **TAVIRA**, 30km east of Faro, is the most interesting and attractive of the eastern Algarve's towns. It straddles both sides of the broad Rio Gilão, the old town made up of white mansions with hipped roofs and wrought-iron balconies. Many visitors stay longer than planned – particularly after a visit to the superb island beach of the **Ilha de Tavira**, which lies within easy reach of the town by year-round ferry. There are also several quieter spots in the area, such as the holiday village of **Pedras d'el Rei** and nearby beach at **Barril** and, for some excellent seafood, the tiny fishing village of **Santa Luzia**.

Founded as long ago as 400 BC, Tavira was a powerful port trading with North Africa until the river began to silt up in the seventeenth century. It was also an important religious centre, with most of the town's 21 churches built in the fifteenth and sixteenth centuries. Following the Great Earthquake of 1755, Tavira was largely rebuilt with the graceful eighteenth-century townhouses and mansions that you see today. The old bridge was mostly built in 1667 on the foundations of a Roman structure; the other central bridge was put up by the army in 1989 as a temporary measure, but has held firm ever since. In the old-town streets on both sides of the river, numerous houses retain fine old doorways with traditional knockers in the shape of hands.

The riverfront

With its tranquil vistas and palm-lined gardens, the **riverfront** is the best part of Tavira for a wander. There are no sights as such north of the river, though the old streets hide many of the town's best restaurants. South of the river, the former town market building, **Mercado da Riberia**, houses a handful of small boutiques and waterfront cafés, with its central space hosting temporary exhibitions.

Beyond here, fishing boats and restaurants line up as far as the flyover. In summer, you can catch direct ferries to the Ilha de Tavira from here. Head under the bridge and you'll see the large new town **market** (Mon–Sat 8am–1.30pm), whose bustling interior is filled with an array of fruit and vegetables.

Núcleo Islâmico

Travessa da Fonte • May–Sept Tues–Sat 10am–12.30pm & 3–6.30pm; Oct–April 10am–12.30pm & 2–5.30pm • €2 • ❶281 320 568

Tavira is proud of its Islamic heritage and the interesting **Núcleo Islâmico**, spread over three floors, pays it homage. After an introductory video you visit the main exhibition area which displays pots, tiles and utensils from the time Tavira was under Moorish rule. Most impressive is a section of an earth-and-stone wall left *in situ*, though the

ACCOMMODATION
Imperial	3
Lagâos	1
Marés	4
Pedras del Rei	6
Pousada Convento da Graça	5
Vila Galé Albacora	2

BARS AND CLUBS
Almariado Bar	2
Bowling Bridge Bar	3
UBI	1

CAFÉS
Anazu	5
Pessoa's Café	6
Tavirense	7

RESTAURANTS
Abstrato	1
Aquasul	3
Barquinha	8
Bica	2
Capelo	10
O Simão	4
Quatro Águas	9

TAVIRA

museum's most valuable item is the Tavira Vase, dating from the eleventh century and lined with clay figures, probably made as part of a wedding dowry.

Igreja da Misericórdia

Rua da Galeria • Tues–Sat 9.30am–12.30pm & 2–6pm • Free

From the arcaded **Praça da República**, with its little modern amphitheatre by the river, it's a short climb up into the old town following Rua da Galeria. Ahead stands the **Igreja da Misericórdia** with a fine stone doorway carved by master mason André Pilarte (1551), depicting a series of mermaids, angels and saints. Inside

9

there's a striking *azulejo* interior showing scenes from the life of Christ, below a wooden vaulted ceiling.

Castelo

Mon–Fri 8am–5pm, Sat & Sun 10am–7pm • Free

A couple of hundred metres up from the main square are the ruins of the **Castelo**, which dates originally from the thirteenth century, though parts were rebuilt in the seventeenth century. Today you can clamber round the narrow walls (take care of steep drops) for great views over the town, or relax in the neatly tended gardens within the walls. Adjacent to the castle, the impressive church of **Santa Maria do Castelo** (open daily) is best known for being the final resting place of Paio Peres Correia, a warrior knight credited with helping to take back Tavira – and much of the Algarve – from Moorish rule in 1242.

Torre de Tavira

Calçada da Galeria 12 • Daily every 30min: June–Sept 10am–8pm; Oct–May 10am–5pm • €3.50 • ⓦ cdepa.pt

On the other side of the castle, you can take a lift to the top of the 100m-high **Torre de Tavira** for an unusual perspective of the town. A former water tower built in the 1930s, it now acts as an interesting Câmara Obscura – with images of the town projected onto a white disk, together with commentary in English.

Palácio Galeria

Calçada da Galeria • Tues–Sat: May–Sept 10am–12.30pm & 3–6.30pm; Oct–April 10am–12.30pm & 2–5.30pm • Exhibitions from €2

Just below the Torre de Tavira, the **Palácio Galeria** is a handsome palace with sixteen rooms and sixteen roofs. Partly dating from the sixteenth century, it's a fine building which is now used as a gallery for temporary exhibitions of local artists or on themes related to the history of the town.

Santa Luzia

A couple of kilometres west of Tavira, **SANTA LUZIA** is an earthy working fishing village which bills itself as the "King of the Octopus", with a number of seafood restaurants catering to day-trippers. Having strolled along the palm-lined waterfront and admired the octopus traps on the jetty, most people settle for a leisurely meal. In summer, local fishermen run two-hour trips into the lagoon for around €25 a head.

Barril

4km from Tavira • The miniature train runs daily 8am–dusk, except in bad weather, approx every 15–30min • €1 one way

From the bus stop and car park next to the *Pedras d'el Rei* holiday complex, you cross a short causeway to the terminal of a rather ancient-looking miniature train, which shuttles over to the beach at **Barril** on the Ilha de Tavira. Alternatively, you can walk alongside the tracks, past thousands of fiddler crabs on the mudflats beyond (10–15min). Once there, you'll find attractive former fishermen's houses that have been turned into a cluster of slightly pricey café-restaurants; there's also a small shop, showers and toilets. A long stretch of alluring sands lies a few minutes' walk right or left of the terminus – beyond the lines of anchors wedged into the dunes.

Ilha de Tavira

The **Ilha de Tavira** stretches southwest from Tavira almost as far as Fuseta, some 14km west, and the beach is enormous, backed by tufted dunes. The main path on the island

BOAT TRIPS TO ILHA DE TAVIRA

In summer you can catch ferries direct to Ilha de Tavira from the riverfront in **Tavira** (daily approx hourly: June & Sept 9am–6.30pm, last return at 7pm; July & Aug 8am–7.30pm, last return at 8pm; €2 return). There's also an all-year-round ferry that departs from the jetty at **Quatro Águas**, 2km east of Tavira – it's a thirty-minute walk, or you can take a bus from Tavira's bus terminal (see below). **Ferries** (daily: Oct–June 9am–5pm; July–Sept 8am–11pm; €1.40 return) take just five minutes to cross from Quatro Águas to the island. In high season they run every fifteen minutes or so; at other times they run approx hourly – always check with the ferryman what time the last boat returns. Alternatively, you can take a **water taxi** – Aquataxis (daily from 8am to dusk; ☏ 964 515 073) do the ride from Quatro Águas for €7 per person.

runs from the jetty through a small chalet settlement to the beach, where there are umbrellas and pedaloes for rent, and half a dozen bar-restaurants. In high summer this part of the beach is packed, though you only have to walk fifteen minutes or so to be clear of the crowds, and out of season you'll probably have the place entirely to yourself.

ARRIVAL AND INFORMATION   TAVIRA AND AROUND

By bus Tavira's bus terminal is by the river, from where it's a two-minute walk to the old bridge and Praça da República.

Destinations Cabanas (9–11 daily; 15min); Faro (7–11 daily; 1hr); Fuseta (9–11 daily; 25min); Lisbon (5–6 daily; 4hr 15min); Olhão (9–11 daily; 45min); Pedras d'el Rei (5–7 daily; 10min); Quatro Águas (4–5 daily; 5min); and Santa Luzia (every 40min; 15min).

By car Drivers will encounter a complicated one-way system in the central area; it's best to head for the metered car park under the flyover – follow signs to Quatro Águas.

By train The train station is 1km from the centre of town, straight up the Rua da Liberdade and at the end of Avenida Dr Mateus Teixeira de Azevedo.

Destinations Conceição (11 daily; 5min); Faro (15 daily; 40min); Fuseta (15 daily; 5min); Monte Gordo (11 daily; 25min); Olhão (15 daily; 28min); and Vila Real de Santo António (11 daily; 30min).

By road train A fun way to get your bearings is by taking the road train, which does a circuit from Praça da República out to Quatro Águas (daily approx hourly from 10am–dusk; €3.50 a circuit, or €5 for a day-pass).

By taxi Taxis line up opposite the cinema, or call ☏ 281 325 746.

Information The turismo is at Praça da República 5 (Oct–April Tues–Fri 9.30am–5.30pm, Sat & Sun 9.30am–1pm & 2–5.30pm; May–Sept daily 9.30am–1pm & 2–7pm; ☏ 281 322 511, ⓦ cm-tavira.pt).

ACCOMMODATION

TAVIRA

Imperial Rua José Pires Padinha 24 ☏ 281 098 135. Small, friendly guesthouse in a traditional townhouse above a decent restaurant. Opt for one of the rooms overlooking the gardens and river. Breakfast €5 extra. **€75**

Lagâos Rua Almirante Cândido dos Reis 24 ☏ 281 328 243. On the north side of the river, this place has simple but attractive rooms clustered round a pretty rooftop patio. It's above the top-notch budget restaurant *Bica* (see p.450). **€50**

★ **Marés** Rua José Pires Padinha 134–140 ☏ 281 325 815, ⓦ residencialmares.com. *Marés* has extremely pleasant rooms – the best have balconies facing the river – with tiled floors and *azulejos* in the bathrooms; there's also a roof terrace, sauna and free wi-fi. Family rooms are also available. **€92**

★ **Pousada Convento da Graça** Rua D. Paio Peres Correia ☏ 281 329 040, ⓦ pousadas.pt. Set in an immaculately converted sixteenth-century convent around beautiful cloisters and with its own church, this *pousada* is hard to

fault. Most of the plush rooms look down over the old town or a rural hillside, while the swimming pool sits inside Tavira's old town walls. During renovation work, the remains of a Moorish settlement were found and these can be viewed through a glass partition in the bar. There's also a highly rated restaurant that uses local ingredients. **€155**

ILHA DE TAVIRA

Camping de Tavira Ilha de Tavira ☏ 281 321 709, ⓦ campingtavira.com. If you fancy island living, this busy campsite is just a minute from the sands, off the path between the ferry terminal and the beach. Pitches are beneath the trees and it has a well-stocked minimarket and café. If you don't have your own tent, the campsite can rent out two-person tents from €33. Closed Oct–Easter. Pitches **€12**

QUATRO ÁGUAS

Vila Galé Albacora Quatro Águas ☏ 281 380 800, ⓦ vilagale.pt. Despite its address, this hotel is actually on

9

the opposite side of the estuary from Quatro Águas, 4km east of Tavira. It's a former tuna-fishing village that has been tastefully converted into a four-star hotel, with rooms in the old fishermen's houses either facing the river estuary or the enormous central courtyard (though some face the car park). The flower-filled courtyard also contains a large pool, games room, restaurant and bar; inside there's another pool and health club. The downside of its riverside position is a colony of voracious mosquitoes. Parking. **€160**

SANTA LUZIA

Pedras d'el Rei Santa Luzia ☎281 380 600, ⊚pedras delrei.com. The apartments and villas at this little resort just east of town are perfect for families, set in beautifully landscaped grounds. There's a central lawned area focused around an outdoor pool and overlooked by a café, bar and restaurant. Facilities include a playground, children's club, aviary and well-stocked shop, and residents get free passes for the train to the beach at Barril. **€105**

EATING AND DRINKING

TAVIRA

CAFÉS

Anazu Rua Jacques Pessoa 11–13 ☎281 381 935. A lovely, tiled riverfront café, which seems to catch the sun all day – a good place for breakfast, a light meal or a sunset drink. There's a games room/cybercafé attached. Daily 9am–midnight.

Pessoa's Café Rua Jacques Pessoa 22 ☎281 094 057. Cosy, arty café-bar with a few outdoor tables facing the river, serving a range of cakes, pastries and speciality teas. Mon–Fri 11am–11pm, Sat & Sun noon–11pm.

Tavirense Rua Marcelino Franco 19. For some of the best cakes and pastries in town, try this old-fashioned *pastelaria* opposite the cinema, where the locals go for breakfast and refuelling during the day. Daily 7am–2am.

RESTAURANTS

Abstrato Rua António Cabrita 34 ☎917 043 274. Small, fashionable restaurant which gives a modern twist to its fish and meat dishes (around €15), such as scallops, prawns in a curry sauce, or pork with apple and fennel. Mon & Wed–Sun 11am–3pm & 7–11pm.

Aquasul Rua Dr Augusto Silva Carvalho 13 ☎281 325 166. A hip and jazzy place on a quiet street, serving imaginative organic cuisine – goat's cheese with walnut salad, *picanha* (garlicky beef) and with a veggie dish of the day. Main courses are all around €13–15, though pizzas are less (from €7.50). May–Sept Mon–Sat 7–11pm; Oct–April Tues–Sat 7–11pm.

Barquinha Rua José Pires Padinha 142 ☎281 322 843. The best of some somewhat touristy places facing the river. Excellent *bacalhau à bras* and good fresh fish from €8. Mon, Tues & Thurs–Sun noon–3pm & 7–10pm.

Bica Rua Almirante Cândido dos Reis 22–24 ☎281 323 843. Always busy – book or get there early to guarantee a table – this unglamorous but excellent-value restaurant has tasty mains – grilled sardines, pork steaks and the like – for around €8. Daily noon–11pm.

O Simão Rua João Vaz Corte Real 10 ☎281 321 647. This is where the locals go to fill up on Portuguese steaks and grills from €6–9 – a bustling place which is even more appealing when it sets out its chairs on the riverside drag. Mon–Sat 9am–1am.

ILHA DE TAVIRA

Pavilhão da Ilha Ilha de Tavira ☎281 324 131. Between the ferry and the beach, this is the best place on the island for a full meal, with moderately priced fish and grills (from around €10) and a lively bar area. March–Oct daily noon–10pm.

QUATRO ÁGUAS

Quatro Águas Quatro Águas ☎281 325 329. Out by the ferry stop and overlooking the river, this highly rated seafood restaurant specializes in dishes such as *cataplana de marisco*, *bacalhau*, and excellent prawn and shrimp kebabs. Mains from around €12–15. Tues–Sun noon–3pm & 7–10pm.

SANTA LUZIA

Capelo Av Engenheiro Duarte Pacheco 40–42, Santa Luzia ☎281 381 670. Santa Luzia's best fish restaurant – slightly pricey but with a spacious *azulejo*-lined interior and a lovely outdoor terrace. Fresh fish, eels and clams from €13 upwards. Mon, Tues & Thurs–Sun noon–2am.

NIGHTLIFE AND ENTERTAINMENT

Almariado Bar Rua Borda de Água da Asseca 42, Tavira ☎964 282 303. The best of a row of bars along this stretch of the river. There are outside tables and a funky interior with comfy chairs and prints of film stars. Good sounds and a fun crowd. Tues–Sat 10am–2am.

Bowling Bridge Bar Estrada das Quatro Águas, Tavira ☎281 326 049. Wedged beneath the flyover by the river,

this sports bar attracts a young crowd thanks to its two bowling lanes and lively bar. Theme nights feature regularly, including Thursday for karaoke, live music on Fridays, and DJ sessions most Saturdays from midnight. Tues–Sun 3pm–2am.

UBI Rua Almirante Cândido dos Reis, Tavira ☎281 324 577. Follow Rua Almirante Cândido dos Reis to the

TAVIRA (P.446) >

9

outskirts of town, and you'll find Tavira's only club housed in a huge former factory. The locals warm up with a few pre-clubbing drinks in the *Bubi Bar* in the same building, open from 6pm. Club July–Sept Tues–Sun 11pm–4am; Oct–June Fri & Sat only.

ACTIVITIES

Bike rental Sport Nautica, Rua Jacques Pessoa 26 (☎914 741 368; Mon–Sat 9am–1pm & 3–7pm), rents out bikes from €6 a day.

Boat trips Sequa Tours (☎918 763 020, ⓦsequatours .com) runs hour-long boat trips round the lagoon for €12 a person, as well as 90-minute birdwatching tours from €20.

Cabanas

Six kilometres east of Tavira – past the golf course at Benamor – lies **CABANAS**, named after the fishermen's *cabanas* (huts) that formed the original settlement. Today a kernel of backstreets is still made up of pretty fishermen's houses along with a line of low-rise shops, cafés and bars facing a picturesque river estuary edged by a neat wooden walkway. Moored fishing boats testify to the village's former mainstay, though today the economy is largely driven by tourism thanks to the glorious sands on **Praia de Cabanas** over the estuary. Ferries shuttle passengers to the beach from a small jetty opposite *Restaurante O Monteiro* in the east of town (April–Oct 9am–dusk, every 15min; €1.50 return). Cross the dunes and you're faced with kilometres of golden sand, plus a couple of seasonal beach cafés.

ARRIVAL AND DEPARTURE   CABANAS

By bus 9–11 buses run daily from Tavira to Cabanas (15min), stopping at the west end of the waterfront.
By train The nearest station to Cabanas is 1km north at Conceição, on the Tavira-to-Vila Real train line – you'll have to walk into the centre from the station.
Destinations Conceição to: Faro (11 daily; 45min); Fuseta (15 daily; 10min); Olhão (15 daily; 30min); Tavira (15 daily; 5min); and Vila Real de Santo António (11 daily; 25min).

ACCOMMODATION

Casa Viana Largo Armação da Abóbora 5, Cabanas ☎281 325 730, ⓦcasa-viana.com. Near the jetty, this is the best budget option in town. The friendly guesthouse has large and spruce air-conditioned rooms in a modern building with a terrace on the seafront road. Free wi-fi. Closed late Dec. **€95**

★ **Forte de São João da Barra** Cabanas ☎281 370 495, ⓦfortesaojoaodabarra.com. This is probably the most sublime place to stay in the entire region, a stunningly converted seventeenth-century sea fort. Once you're inside the colossal castle gate, you enter a serene space with a big grassy courtyard and a swimming pool in one of the ramparts overlooking olive groves and the sea. The most atmospheric rooms, with cool stone interiors and period furniture, are in the old castle building, though there is an annexe with more modern fittings. **€150**

EATING AND DRINKING

★ **Noélia Jerónimo** Cabanas 8800 ☎281 370 649. At the eastern end of town in a modern building, with a terrace facing the water, this is the place to come for inventive home-made cuisine. Try the superb dory with coriander rice, or the octopus fritters. It also does fabulous salads, fresh tuna and a range of rice dishes for two, with mains around €10. Reservations advised in season. Mon, Tues & Thurs–Sun 10am–10pm.
Pedro Rua Capitão Batista Marçal 51, Cabanas ☎281 370 425. On the way to the jetty, this large, traditional building has an outdoor terrace and a long list of moderately priced fish (around €9–12), seafood and rice dishes. Daily 11am–11pm.

Cacela Velha

Perched on a low cliff facing the estuary, 10km east of Cabanas, the whitewashed village of **CACELA VELHA** is a reminder of how the Algarve must have looked half a century ago. Apart from a few café-restaurants, there are no tourist facilities, just a pretty church and the remains of an eighteenth-century fort – and even that houses a maritime police station and is closed to the public. Offering exhilarating views from its clifftop, Cacela is highly picturesque and, despite the Quinta da Ria/Quinta da Cima golf courses just to the west, it's rarely overrun by visitors. The only time the place gets busy is during the **Moorish Nights** in July – a four-day festival of Arabic food and Moorish-inspired events, including a souk.

The **beach** below the village is a delight. To get to it, follow signs to "Fábrica", just west of the village, around 1km downhill. Here a ferryman can take you over to the beach for €1.30 single (daily in summer but only during good weather the rest of the year).

ARRIVAL AND ACCOMMODATION   **CACELHA VELHA**

By bus There is no public transport to Cacela Velha, though you can ask to be let off the Tavira–Vila Real bus on the highway, just before Vila Nova de Cacela, 2km inland, from where it's a fifteen-minute walk down a side road to the village.

Cantinho da Ria Formosa Ribeira de Junco ☎ 281 951 837, ⓦ cantinhoriaformosa.com. Around 1.5km from Cacela Velha, near Fábrica and the golf course, the eight rooms in this blue-edged *rural hotel* have satellite TV and air conditioning, and views over the garden or fields. There are stables attached, and horse rides are on offer for around €20 an hour. **€80**

Vila Real de Santo António and around

VILA REAL DE SANTO ANTÓNIO (aka Vila Real) is a pleasant border town, the terminus for the trans-Algarve railway line. The ferry across the Guadiana from here to Ayamonte is still the most fun way to cross the border, but the construction of a modern road bridge just north of the town in the 1990s greatly affected the town's former role as the Algarve's main access point to Spain. Nevertheless, it's still an interesting place to spend a few hours, exploring a central grid of streets that radiates out from a handsome main square, **Praça Marquês de Pombal**, ringed by orange trees, low, white buildings and pleasant outdoor cafés. The square is named after the king's minister, who helped rebuild the original town after it was destroyed in a tsunami following the 1755 earthquake. Indeed the grid plan, built in 1774, is very similar to that of Lisbon's Baixa.

On the north side of the square, Rua Teófilo Braga, the pedestrianized main drag, leads inland from the riverfront Avenida da República to the **Centro Cultural António Aleixo** (Sept–June Mon–Fri 10am–1pm & 3–7pm; July & Aug Mon–Fri 4pm–midnight, Sat & Sun 8pm–midnight; free; ⓦcm-vrsa.pt), the town's former market building now used as an innovative space for temporary exhibits and the occasional film. The streets surrounding the cultural centre have a certain low-key charm, bristling with linen shops, electrical retailers and grocers, while the riverside **gardens** offer fine views across to the splash of white that is Ayamonte in Spain.

Ayamonte

Ferry Daily: July to mid-Sept every 30min from 8.30am, last return at 9pm Spanish time; mid-Sept to June hourly from 8.30am, last return at 7.30/8pm Spanish time • €1.70 each way

A fun day out is to take the **ferry** from Vila Real's harbour to the Spanish border town of **AYAMONTE**, with its tapas bars and palm-lined squares. It's a lovely twenty-minute ride across the Rio Guadiana, with the forts of Castro Marim visible to the west and the impressive bridge to the north. Remember that Spanish time is one hour ahead of Portuguese.

Monte Gordo

Vila Real's nearest beach lies 5km east of town at unglamorous **MONTE GORDO**, the last resort before the Spanish border. It's the most built-up of the eastern holiday

9

towns, with its own casino (⊛solverde.pt), and high-rise hotels overlooking the superb wide, clean sands, on which fishermen still tend to their nets after their stint at sea. In June expect to see a profusion of Harley-Davidson riders who descend for an annual bikers' meet.

Castro Marim

Castle Daily: May–Sept 10am–7pm; Oct–April 10am–5pm • Free

The little village of **CASTRO MARIM**, 5km north of Vila Real, is dominated by an impressive **castle**, built by Afonso III in the thirteenth century and once the headquarters of the Order of Christ (see p.494). The chapel within the castle was regularly visited by Henry the Navigator, though most of the building was destroyed by the 1755 earthquake. It's a good place for a wander, with fine views of the bridge to Spain from its walls; a small **museum** (daily 10am–1pm & 3.30–5pm; free) displays local archeological finds. The castle is also the centrepiece of the village's Medieval Days Festival over the last weekend in August, with re-creations of medieval life and plenty of entertainment, including access to the sixteenth-century **Fort of São Sebastião** on the opposite hill, which is otherwise usually closed.

The marshy area around Castro Marim forms the **Reserva Natural do Sapal**, where flamingos stop off to feed. One of the reserve's most unusual and elusive inhabitants is the ten-centimetre-long, swivel-eyed, opposing-toed, Mediterranean **chameleon** – a harmless, slow-moving lizard that's severely threatened elsewhere by habitat destruction.

ARRIVAL AND DEPARTURE

VILA REAL AND AROUND

By bus Buses to Vila Real either stop by the ferry terminal by the river or at a terminus just north of the train station. Destinations Alcoutim (Mon–Fri 1 daily; 1hr 15min); Castro Marim (Mon–Fri 12 daily, Sat & Sun 2 daily; 15min); Faro (6–9 daily; 1hr 40min); Manta Rota (Mon–Fri 4–6 daily, Sat 2 daily; 25min); Mértola (Mon–Fri 1 daily; 2hr); Monte Gordo (every 30min; 10min); Odeleite (Mon–Fri 1 daily; 30min); Olhão (10 daily; 1hr 20min); Seville (2 daily; 2hr 30min); and Tavira (9–10 daily; 40min).

By train Vila Real is the eastern terminal of the Algarve railway; the station is five minutes north of the riverfront. Destinations Faro (11 daily; 1hr 10min); Monte Gordo (11 daily; 5min); Olhão (15 daily; 55min); and Tavira (15 daily; 30min).

INFORMATION

Castro Marim turismo Praça 1 de Maio (Mon–Fri 9.30am–1pm & 2–5.30pm; ☎ 281 531 232), on the main street.
Monte Gordo turismo Av Infante Dom Henrique, east of the casino (Mon & Fri–Sun 9.30am–1pm & 2–5.30pm, Tues–Thurs 9.30am–7pm; ☎ 281 544 495, ⊛cm-vrsa.pt), with details of private rooms in town.

ACCOMMODATION

VILA REAL DE SANTO ANTÓNIO

Baixa Mar Rua Teófilo Braga, Vila Real 3 ☎ 281 543 511. This simple guesthouse has small, functional rooms – the best are at the front with great views over the river. No breakfast, but plenty of cafés nearby. **€45**

MONTE GORDO

Parque Municipal de Campismo Estrada Municipal, Monte Gordo 511 ☎ 281 510 970, ⊛cm-vrsa.pt. Monte Gordo's campsite is enormous, attractively set beneath pines near the beach on the Vila Real road. It gets very busy in season, but there's usually plenty of space the rest of the year. Pitch **€11**

Vasco da Gama Avenida Infante Dom Henrique, Monte Gordo ☎ 281 510 900, ⊛vascodagamahotel.com. This may be high-rise but inside it has a certain old-fashioned charm, and its position overlooking the beach can't be faulted. Facilities include tennis courts, pool, restaurant and playground. The best of the large en-suite rooms have sea views. **€150**

EATING

VILA REAL DE SANTO ANTÓNIO

Caves do Guadiana Avenida da República 80, Vila Real ☎ 281 544 498. The best place in town for a quality meal at moderate prices, with a pleasant vaulted interior. Mains include *caldeirada* (a type of fish stew) and tuna steaks, at around €9. Mon–Wed & Fri–Sun noon–2pm & 7–11pm.

Churrasqueira Arenilha Rua Cândido dos Reis 89, Vila Real ☎ 281 544 038. North of the market, this long-established restaurant with old black-and-white photos of the town on the walls serves up tasty grills from €10, as well as rice dishes such as *arroz de marisco* (€28 for two people). It also does good-value tapas from €3.50. Daily noon–3pm & 7–10pm.

MONTE GORDO

Jaime Praia de Monte Gordo, Monte Gordo ☎ 281 512 361. A little west up the beach from the casino, this simple beach shack draped with soccer scarves serves lunchtime snacks and is a great spot for a beer overlooking the fishing boats. Daily 9am–7pm; Oct–April closes at 6pm.

ACTIVITIES

Boat trips Rio Sul offers regular day-long boat trips from Vila Real up the Guadiana to the pretty riverside village of

Foz de Odeleite (☒ riosultravel.com); prices start at around €50 per person, which includes food and drinks.

Alcoutim

Some 40km north of Vila Real – and best approached by car along the road that hugs the Guadiana River – is the extremely attractive border village of **ALCOUTIM**. It has a long history as a river port, dominated in turn by Greeks, Romans and Arabs who all fortified the heights with various structures; the **castle** (daily 9am–7pm, closes 5.30pm from Oct–March; €2.50) dates from the fourteenth century and offers fine views over the river. The entrance fee includes access to a small archeological **museum** by the main gates, which traces the history of the castle, its active service in various battles and the remnants of earlier structures on the site. From the castle, cobbled backstreets lead down to the small main square, below which is the appealing riverfront. Currents are too strong for safe swimming, but you can take a boat across the river (around €1.50 single) to the Spanish village of **Sanlúcar**, a mirror image of Alcoutim, with its own ruined castle; or swim at the river beach (*praia fluvial*) in a small tributary off the Mértola road.

ARRIVAL AND INFORMATION

ALCOUTIM

By bus Thre are regular buses to Vila Real (Mon–Fri 1 daily; 1hr); Castro Marim (Mon–Fri 1 daily; 50min); and Mértola (Mon–Fri 1 daily; 50min).

Information A small turismo (May–Sept Tues–Thurs 9.30am–7pm, Mon & Fri–Sun 9.30am–1pm & 2–5.30pm;

Nov–April Tues–Thurs 9.30am–5.30pm, Mon & Fri–Sun 9.30am–1pm & 2–5.30pm; ☎ 281 546 179, ☒ cm -alcoutim.pt) is located on Rua 1 de Maio, just off the main Praça da República.

ACCOMMODATION

Estalagem do Guadiana Avenida de Espanha ☎ 281 540 120, ☒ www.grupofbarata.com. For upmarket lodgings, follow the signs to the *Estalagem do Guadiana*, a swish modern hotel with its own pool, tennis court and restaurant. The spacious rooms come with satellite TV and fine river views. Minimum stay of a week in August. **€85**

Pousada de Juventude Alcoutim ☎ 281 546 004, ☒ microsites.juventude.gov.pt/portal/en. The smart

fifty-bed youth hostel is around 1.5km north of the village; cross the bridge beyond Praça da República and follow the signs. As well as dorms and double rooms, it has apartments with a kitchenette (sleeping four), its own canteen and a swimming pool. There's disabled access, bikes for hire, and they can arrange kayaking on the river, too. Dorm beds **€14**; doubles **€45**; apartments **€90**

EATING AND DRINKING

O Soeiro Rua do Município 4 ☎ 281 546 241. The best-positioned place to grab a coffee, with outdoor tables facing the river; it also has an outside grill for great lunches and an upstairs restaurant serving local specialities (from €8) such as lamprey (an eel-like fish). Mon–Fri 10am–11pm.

Riverside Tavern Av Duarte Pacheco 3 ☎ 281 546 527. What little local nightlife there is can be found in this restaurant-bar, with a pool table, music TV and attractive outdoor terrace, where you can also eat fish and grills (from €11) or pizzas (from €7.50). Daily 10am–midnight.

9

Boat trips, kayaking and bike hire Fun River in Rua do Município, next to the quay (☎926 682 605, ⓦfun-river .com), runs short (€6 for 20min) and half-day (€50) boat trips, and rents out kayaks and bikes (both €15 for half a day).

The central Algarve resorts

The central Algarve from Faro to Lagos encompasses some of the region's best beaches – but also its most intense tourist development. Despite this, **Quinta do Lago**, **Vale do Lobo** and **Vilamoura** are low density and upmarket: purpose-built resorts with great facilities including marinas, top golf courses and tennis centres. These resorts don't have much traditional culture, though there's a little more of that at neighbouring **Quarteira**, a high-rise resort with a fine town beach and a renowned fish market.

Quinta do Lago and Vale do Lobo

Almancil is the turn-off point for the vast, luxury holiday resort of **QUINTA DO LAGO**, with its own golf courses and sports complex. Most day-visitors, however, head straight for the great beach, the **Praia do Ançāo**, reached over a wooden bridge from the car park at the end of the main Avenida André Jorge. The bridge heads across the western extremity of the Parque Natural da Ria Formosa; it also marks the start of two marked nature trails that lead either side of the inland waterways.

Facilities are similar at **VALE DO LOBO**, just to the west, where a great beach is backed by more serious-money hotels and swanky villas. The resort has a 24-hour reception as you enter the complex (☎289 353 000, ⓦvaledolobo.com), which can help with booking accommodation though nothing is very cheap. Nearby are golf courses, a riding school, and the **Vale do Lobo Tennis Academy** (☎289 357 850, ⓦpremier-sports.org), the most famous in the country. You can book lessons and coaching sessions here, though as even the world's top players come here to practise, courts get booked up well in advance.

Igreja de São Laurenço

Almancil • Tues–Sat 10am–1pm & 2.30–5pm, Mon 2.30–5pm • €2

Built in the early eighteenth century, the church of **São Laurenço** is famed for its superb tiled interior depicting the life and martyrdom of St Laurence, which is thought to have been painted in 1730 by influential artist Policarpo de Oliveira Bernardes. The church is around 12km northwest of Faro, near the Almancil turn-off from the N125, but is hard to reach without your own transport.

Quarteira

QUARTEIRA, 22km west of Faro, was one of the first fishing villages to be developed in the Algarve, and remains high-rise and downmarket. Stick to the palm-lined seafront promenade with its attractive stretch of beach – Praia de Quarteira – and it's a pleasant enough destination, which remains largely Portuguese in character. The main attraction is the bustling fish and vegetable **market** (Mon–Sat 8am–3pm; Sun vegetable market only 8am–2pm) by the working fishing harbour, to the west end of town, though there's also a good flea market each Wednesday, a couple of blocks east of the bus station.

Aquashow

Semino, EN396 • Daily June–Sept 10am–6pm • €22, children €15 • ⓦaquashowpark.com

At Semino, on the road between Quarteira and Loulé, **Aquashow** makes for a fun day out for families. There's a theme-park area with various rides including a rollercoaster through water, plus animal shows (sea lions, parrots and repiles) throughout the day. But the big attraction is the water-park zone which includes a panoply of slides, chutes and pools, including the terrifying vertical white falls and a descent down a helter skelter in the dark – all set in neatly landscaped grounds. Note that in high season the water park closes its gates when it hits 4000 people: aim to visit in June or September when it's quieter and there are fewer queues.

ARRIVAL AND INFORMATION   QUARTEIRA

By bus Quarteira's bus terminus is a couple of blocks back from the beach, on Avenida Dr Sá Carneiro, with regular services to and from Faro (approx every 30 min; 40min).

Information The turismo is right by the beach on Praça do Mar (May–Sept Mon & Fri–Sun 9.30am–1pm & 2–7pm, Tues–Thurs 9.30am–7pm; Oct–May closes at 5.30pm; ☎ 289 389 209).

GETTING AROUND

A **road train** trundles along the seafront, round town and back to the market every hour or so (May–Sept daily 10am–dusk; €2).

ACCOMMODATION

Aquashow Park Semino, EN396 ☎ 289 317 550, ⓦ aquashowpark.com. Right by the water park, this is a stylish modern four-star hotel whose plush rooms (which can interconnect for families) face the park or, better, the local woods and outside pool. The hotel has indoor and outdoor pools, a gym, spa and family activities, and guests have free access to the adjacent water park – check on the

website for some very good online deals. €150
Miramar Rua Gonçalo Velho 8 ☎ 289 315 225, ⓦ residencialmiramar.net. Near the market, this long-time favourite has a charming plant-lined internal terrace. The decent double rooms either look out over this, or have sea views. €70

EATING

Beira Mar Av Infante de Sagres 61–63 ☎ 289 314 748. Just past the turismo heading east on the seafront, this fab *pastelaria* serves an alluring range of cakes, pastries and inexpensive lunches, with seats facing the sea. Tues–Sun 8am–10pm.
Lendário Lote 2, Av Infante de Sagres 25E ☎ 289 308 067, ⓦ lendario.pt. For a touch of sophistication on the

pedestrianized seafront prom, this is a restaurant-cum-lounge-bar complete with piano, sports TV and a fine array of cocktails. Prices are surprisingly reasonable, and include *arroz de polvo* (€12), pasta (€8) and a filling *cataplana* (€35 for two). Mon noon–3pm, Wed–Sun noon–3pm & 7–10pm.

Vilamoura

Now virtually merged with Quarteira, **VILAMOURA** is a constantly expanding resort with a bewildering network of roads signposted to upmarket hotels and exclusive leisure facilities, including five renowned **golf courses**. It's perhaps *the* place in the Algarve to come and practise your swing, while another indication of the kind of clientele Vilamoura attracts is the ritzy **marina**, bristling with yachts and lined with pricey international cafés. Various stalls around the marina offer **boat trips** along the coast (€20 or so for a two-hour trip) and dolphin-watching (up to €50 for a full-day excursion).

Museu Cerro da Vila

Avenida Cerro da Vila • Tues–Sun: May–Oct 10am–1pm & 4–9pm; Nov–April 9.30am–12.30pm & 2–6pm • €2.50 • ☎ 289 312 153

The only historical sight in Vilamoura is just to the northwest of the marina, where the **Museu Cerra da Vila** archeological site displays the vestiges of a late Roman, Visigothic and Moorish colony. You can make out the foundations of a Roman mansion, baths and a fish-salting tank, together with well-preserved Roman mosaics laid out in a scrubby field.

By bus Regular buses between Vilamoura and Faro (approx every 30min; 50min) drop you next to the casino, one block from the impressive beach, the Praia da Marina.

Road train A road train runs from the marina and through the main town to Praia da Falesia (daily; hourly 10am–dusk; €3.50).

ACCOMMODATION AND EATING

O Tasquinho de Manel Escola de Vela, Vilamoura ☎289 315 756. Part of the sailing school, this simple place lacks the pretensions of the marina-side restaurants but has very moderately-priced fresh fish (around €9) and great views from the outdoor terrace. Tues–Sun noon–3pm & 7–11pm; Oct–April only open for lunch.

Sete Bloco 7, Marina de Vilamoura ☎289 313 243, Ⓦwww.setecafe.com. A fashionable chrome-and-steel café-bar part-owned by Portuguese soccer star Luís Figo,

and named after his shirt number (*sete* means seven). A good spot for a quiet drink by day, it gets lively after dark. Plasma TVs show the latest soccer action and guest DJs feature. Daily 9am–3am.

Tivoli Marina Apartado 65, Marina de Vilamoura ☎289 303 303, Ⓦtivolihotels.com. This enormous modern place is typical of the accommodation here – with every conceivable comfort, and giant rooms overlooking the marina or the beach. €130

Loulé

LOULÉ, 18km inland from Faro, has always been an important centre of commerce and is still best known for its markets. It has recently grown to a fair size, though its compact centre doesn't take long to look around. The most interesting streets, a grid of whitewashed cobbled lanes, lie between the remains of its Moorish castle (now a museum) and the thirteenth-century Gothic **Igreja Matriz**, with its palm-lined gardens in front.

Museu Municipal

Rua D. Paio Peres Correia 17 • Mon–Fri 9am–5.30pm, Sat 10am–2pm • €1.50 • ☎289 400 600

The remains of Loulé's castle enclose a mildly interesting **Museu Municipal**. Its main exhibit is an archeological collection that includes a range of Roman, Moorish and early Portuguese finds from Loulé and the surrounding area, as well as the foundations of a twelfth-century Moorish house, displayed under a glass floor. Head up the steps to the side of the museum to a kitchen, set out in traditional Algarvian style. You can also access the remains of the castle walls from here, for good views across town.

Mercado Municipal

Rua José Fernandes Guerreiro • Mon–Sat 7am–3pm

Loulé's most atmospheric attraction is its covered fruit and vegetable **market**, set in a late nineteenth-century red onion-domed building with Moorish-style windows, just southeast of the main Praça da República. Try and visit on a Saturday morning, when the market spreads into the surrounding streets – a medley of stalls selling everything from pungent cheese to cages of live chickens.

Saturday morning market

The main **Saturday morning market** (from around 9.30am) takes place around fifteen minutes' walk northwest of the centre – follow the signs to "IP1/Boliquieme". Stalls sell a motley collection of clothes, ceramics and agricultural produce on a patch of ground beautifully framed by a pair of dazzling white churches, including the curious, modern, beehive-shaped **Nossa Senhora da Piedade**. At Easter, the church is the starting point of a procession into town for Mãe Soberana, one of the Algarve's most important religious festivals.

ARRIVAL AND DEPARTURE

LOULÉ

By bus Buses from Albufeira (8–10 daily; 45min) and Faro (every 30–50min; 40min) pull in at the bus station on Rua Nossa Senhora de Fátima, a couple of minutes' walk north of the centre.

ACCOMMODATION AND EATING

Flôr da Praça Rua José Fernandes Guerreiro 44 ☎ 289 462 435. For good-value food, first choice is *Flôr da Praça*, opposite the main market, where fish and grills (from €8) are served in a bustling place with old photos and seashells on the walls. Mon–Sat 12.30–2.30pm & 7.30–11.30pm.

Loulé Jardim Praça Manuel de Arriaga 23 ☎ 289 413 094, ⓦ loulejardimhotel.com. A block south of Rua Nossa Senhora da Piedade, this welcoming three-star hotel boasts a bar, a small pool and smallish but comfortable rooms with cable TV. **€75**

Albufeira and around

ALBUFEIRA has long been one of the Algarve's most popular resorts – and it's easy to see why. The old centre is a highly picturesque medley of whitewashed houses atop low sandstone cliffs facing a fantastic town beach. But beyond, hundreds of modern buildings lie strung across the hillsides that spread east and west, around the town's marina. If you're looking for unspoiled Portugal, this isn't it. Nevertheless, Albufeira is undeniably fun, attracting a varied mix of holiday-makers.

Although the 1755 earthquake destroyed much of the town, there's still a Moorish feel to a few parts of central Albufeira – the original Arabic name of the town, *Al-Buhera*, means "Castle-on-the-Sea". There are some fine beaches either side of

9

the town, too. **Praia da Oura** and those further east towards **Praia da Falésia** are the more developed, while the cove beaches to the west, up to the swathe of sands at **Praia de Galé**, tend to be quieter. Inland, Albufeira is the nearest base for a couple of the Algarve's best family-orientated **theme parks**, while day-trips also run north into the hills to the pretty village of **Alte**.

Largo Engenheiro Duarte Pacheco and the beach

The focus of Albufeira is the somewhat tacky **Largo Engenheiro Duarte Pacheco**, a modern pedestrianized square with benches beneath palms and exotic trees. After dark, it's a magnet for families and promenaders, often serenaded by live performers and buskers. From the square, Rua 5 de Outubro leads – through a tunnel – down to the town **beach**, as good as any in the region, flanked by strange tooth-like rock formations.

Museu Arqueológico

Praça da República 1 • Tues–Sun: June to mid-Sept Wed–Fri 2–8pm, Sat & Sun 2–7pm & 8–10pm; mid-Sept to May Tues–Sun 9.30am–5.30pm • €1 • ☎ 289 599 508

Just above the tunnel to the beach, in the old town hall, the **Museu Arqueológico** presents a rather sparse but well laid out collection of artefacts gathered from the area from Neolithic times to the present. There are fragments of mosaics from a Roman villa, Visigothic rock tombs and jars, and even an Islamic silo excavated *in situ* beneath the museum.

The eastern beaches

Immediately east of Albufeira is a string of superb, cliff-backed cove beaches, all of which can be reached by local buses (8–12 daily) from the bus station. You can walk to the first beach, **Praia da Oura**, just 2km away, by heading down Albufeira's beach and up along a rocky bluff along a coastal path, and it can also be reached on the green bus route. This, though, has been extensively developed and you might want to push on by bus to **Olhos de Água** (green bus route) or neighbouring **Santa Eulalia** (on the green and blue bus routes) 7km further east – both former fishing villages with attractive beaches.

The western beaches

Most of the development further west of Albufeira is set back behind a further series of idyllic cove beaches. There are no direct buses to these resorts, though the Albufeira–Portimão service drops passengers on the main road, a steep two-kilometre walk away. Busy **São Rafael**, 3km west of Albufeira, and slightly quieter **Castelo**, 1km further on, sit above small beaches that only become crowded in peak season. A delightful clifftop path links the two resorts via the best cove found on this stretch, **Praia da Coelha**; it's reached down a sandy track, with no development apart from a seasonal beach café. Five kilometres west of Albufeira, you reach the extensive sands of **Praia de Galé**, where the beach spreads all the way to **Armação de Pêra**.

Quinta Miradouro

Álamos, Apartado 5008 • Mon–Fri 10am–1pm & 2–5pm • Shop free; tours €7.50, or €20–30 including transport from nearby resorts • ☎ 968 776 971, ⓦ winesvidanova.com

Just south of Algarve Shopping off the main EN125 (go past the car parks east of the shopping centre) lie the open fields of **Quinta Miradouro**, aka Cliff Richard's wine estate. This is actually one of three farms on a wine co-operative which produces strong Vida Nova wines – named after the "new life" the farms have breathed into exhausted vineyards. The co-operative has become something of a pilgrimage for Richard fans, who can be found posing for photos outside his nearby farm, Quinta do Moinho. Visits appeal equally to wine buffs, and include a talk about wine production, a look round the estate and the chance to sample recent blends, which you can purchase from the shop.

Zoo Marine

EN125, Guia • Easter–June, Sept & Oct daily 10am–6pm; July & Aug daily 10am–7.30pm • €24.50, under-10s €16.50 • ☎ 289 560 300, ⓦ zoomarine.com

Around 7km northwest of Albufeira, off the N125, **Zoo Marine** makes a great day out for families. Tickets allow entry to a variety of swimming pools, fairground rides, animal enclosures and an aquarium. Various shows take place throughout the day, including performing parrots and sea lions, and a spectacular dolphin show.

Krazy World

Lagoa de Viseu, Algoz • Easter–Sept daily 10am–6pm; Oct–Easter Fri–Sun 10am–6pm; some attractions closed in winter when prices are reduced • €10, under-13s €7 • ☎ 282 574 134, ⓦ krazyworld.com • Buses from Albufeira to São Bartolomeu de Messines stop near the entrance

Krazy World, around 13km north of Albufeira, is a sizeable zoo-cum-theme-park. Low-key and set in attractive farmland, the neatly landscaped park has crazy golf and traditional rides, a mini zoo-cum-petting-farm and a reptile zone complete with enormous pythons, crocodiles and a turtle city; there are some swimming pools to cool off in.

Alte

Around 30km northeast of Albufeira along the winding N124, **ALTE** makes a fine day-trip – though there is no direct public transport here so you'll need a car. Local tourist literature calls the village the prettiest in the Algarve and it is certainly attractive, consisting of a series of narrow, cobbled streets gathered on the hillside. It is a short walk up to the local springs, Fonte Pequena and Fonte Grande, where there's a small rocky pool, a stream and an old mill, now converted into a restaurant (see p.462) – it's a delightful spot, provided you don't coincide with the visiting tour groups.

ARRIVAL AND INFORMATION

ALBUFEIRA AND AROUND

By bus Albufeira's bus terminal is around 2km north of town. A red-route shuttle bus runs from the bus station to Avenida da Liberdade every 30 minutes (from 7am to midnight; Oct–May until 10pm; €1.40), which is a five-minute walk from the central square, Largo Engenheiro Duarte Pacheco.

Destinations Armacão de Pêra (Mon–Sat 12 daily, Sun 5 daily; 15–20min); Faro (approx hourly; 50min–1hr 15min); Guia (6 daily; 15min); Lagos (6–12 daily; 1hr 15min); Lisbon (6–8 daily; 3hr 10min); Loulé (8–10 daily; 45min); Olhos d'Água (every 30min; 10min); Paderne (5–8 daily; 20min); Portimão (Mon–Fri approx hourly, Sat & Sun 4 daily; 45min); and Silves (3–7 daily; 45min).

By train Albufeira's nearest train station is 6km north of

town at Ferreiras; a bus connects it with the bus terminal every 45 minutes or so (daily 7am–8pm), or a taxi costs about €12.

Destinations Ferreiras to: Lagos (9 daily; 1hr 10min); Faro (9 daily; 40min); Portimão (9 daily; 50min); and Silves (9 daily; 35min).

By car Central Albufeira is not an easy place to find a parking spot; it's best to follow signs to the out-of-town car parks.

Information The turismo (June–Sept Tues, Wed & Thurs 9.30am–7pm, Mon & Fri–Sun same hours but closed 1–2pm; Oct–May Mon–Fri 9.30am–1pm & 2–5.30pm; ☎ 289 585 279, ⓦ cm-albufeira.pt) is on Rua 5 de Outubro, by the tunnel to the beach.

GETTING AROUND

By bus If you're in Albufeira on a package holiday, you might well be staying in one of the resort-villages on either

side of town. The blue bus route is useful, running from the bus station via Areias de São João, Oura and Santa Eulalia

9

to Montechoro, a downmarket suburb to the northeast, known as "the strip". If you plan to use the buses a lot, consider a *bilhete turístico* day-pass for €4, or buy a *cartão recarregável* (rechargeable card; €3) on which you can load ten journeys for €8. Otherwise it is €1.40 a ride.

By road train A road train runs from the top of the improbable escalator at the eastern end of Praia dos Pescadores out to Montechoro (every 30min, 9am–10.30pm; 24hr in Aug; €2 a trip, or €3.50 for a day-pass).

ACCOMMODATION

★ **Dianamar** Rua Latino Coelho 36 ☎ 289 587 801, ⓦ dianamar.com. Top choice in town is this well-run Swedish-owned *guesthouse* in the nicest part of Albufeira, near the cliffs above the beach. En-suite rooms are pristine and breezy, and those at the top have great sea views, as does the communal roof terrace. Larger rooms can accommodate families. Price includes a fabulous breakfast, afternoon cake and a welcome bottle of wine. **€60**

Frentomar Rua Latino Coelho ☎ 289 512 005, ⓦ frentomar.com. Simple, clean rooms on a quiet side road. Get one with a sea view and you won't be disappointed, though these are usually snapped up quickly. Closed late Oct to May. No breakfast. **€60**

Sol e Mar Rua José Bernardino de Sousa ☎ 289 580 080, ⓦ www.grupofbarata.com. Though somewhat characterless, this four-star hotel is in a great position, with its entrance above the tunnel to the beach. It stretches down five floors to exit right on the beach, and the room balconies overlook the sands; there's live entertainment and a small covered swimming pool. Parking. **€110**

Vila Recife Rua Miguel Bombarda 12 ☎ 289 583 740,

ⓦ www.grupofbarata.com. This rambling hotel has its own garden and small pool. The communal areas are lined with *azulejos*, and while the en-suite rooms are on the small side they are comfortable, and the best have fine views. Closed Nov–April. **€75**

Vila São Vicente Largo Jacinto d'Ayet 4 ☎ 289 583 700, ⓦ hotelsaovicentealbufeira.com. A stylish hotel built in traditional style with tiled floors and whitewashed walls. It has its own small pool and a terrace facing the beach. You pay less for rooms facing the street, but it's worth the €20 extra for the sea views. All rooms are en suite with TVs and a/c. **€125**

CAMPSITE

Camping Albufeira Estrada de Ferreiras ☎ 289 587 629, ⓦ campingalbufeira.net. Around 2km to the north of town, off the N396, this is expensive but well appointed, complete with swimming pools, restaurants, bars, shops and tennis courts. There are regular red-bus route connections from the bus station; minimum one-week let in high season. Pitch **€17**

EATING

ALBUFEIRA

A Ruina Cais Herculano ☎ 289 512 094. Partly built into the old town walls, this superb old restaurant overlooks the beach – there are rooms and terraces at various levels. The lower, beachside area is the best place for those with kids, as they can play in the sand while you eat. The waiter will show you the latest fish catch, but check the price when ordering. Over €17 for most mains. Daily: April–Sept 12.30–3pm & 7–11pm; Oct–March noon–2.30pm & 6.30–10.30pm.

★ **A Tasquinha do Rossio** Rua Dr Santos Silva 58 ☎ 964 063 481. This is a fabulous little fish restaurant that's always popular. The speciality is *rodízio de peixe* – a mixed grill of the day's catch (€12.50) – or you can specify one fish for around €8. Tables spill out onto a quiet square. Tues–Sun noon–3pm & 6–10pm.

Casa da Fonte Rua João de Deus 7 ☎ 289 514 578. A popular spot set around a beautiful Moorish-style courtyard complete with *azulejos* and lemon trees – get there early if you want a courtyard table. There's a long menu, with mains from €11 – the fish kebabs are recommended. Daily noon–3pm & 6–11pm.

O Penedo Rua Latino Coelho 15 ☎ 289 587 429. With

tasteful contemporary decor and a terrific terrace overlooking the beach, this small, arty place serves Portuguese flavours with an unusual twist, such as seafood pasta and salmon with mint sauce (mains around €9). Daily 11am–3pm & 6.30–11pm; closed Jan.

O Zuca Travessa do Malpique 6 ☎ 289 588 768. Despite its proximity to the main square, this is the local's choice – a simple, family-run restaurant serving good-value and tasty meat and fish from €8. The tourist menu is recommended: around €13 for three courses and drinks. Daily noon–3pm & 6pm–midnight.

Royal Orchid Beco Bernardino de Sousa ☎ 289 502 505, ⓦ royalorchid-thaicuisine.com. Thai restaurant with sumptuous decor and tables laid out in a leafy courtyard. The long menu features noodle and rice dishes with fish, meat or seafood from €12–14 – there's also a range of vegetarian options. June–Sept Mon–Fri noon–2pm & 5pm–midnight, Sat & Sun 5pm–midnight; Oct–May daily 5pm–midnight.

ALTE

Fonte Pequeno Alte ☎ 289 478 509. A large rustic-style grill house with wooden benches laid out on a shady

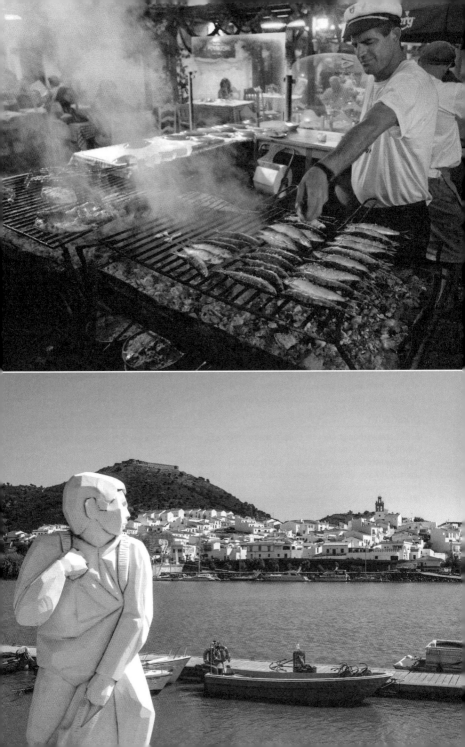

9

terrace, in the pretty village of Alte. It serves good regional dishes, such as bean and meat stew, or peas with poached

egg and sausage – a full meal will cost around €20. Tues–Sun noon–5.30pm; May–Sept also open 7–10.30pm.

DRINKING AND NIGHTLIFE

At night, the focus of Albufeira's lively bar scene is the pedestrianized **Rua Cândido dos Reis** where a good-time crowd parades past handicraft stalls and a menu of live soccer, or sits at bars which vie with each other to play the loudest music. Late-night clubs can mostly be found in the suburbs east of the centre, especially around Oura's Avenida Dr Francisco Sà Carneiro (aka The Strip).

Bizarro Bar Esplanada Dr Frutuosa Silva 30 ☎ 289 512 824. This attractive bar is high above the eastern end of the beach, with superb views over the sands from its front terrace. Mon–Sat 10am–10pm.
★ **Café Iguana** Rua Latino Coelho 59 ☎ 289 513 011. An attractive café-bar on the clifftop, whose terrace has fantastic views over the town and the beach. Serves baguettes and snacks as well as a range of drinks. Daily 8am–midnight.
Kiss Rua Vasco da Gama, Areias de São João ☎ 289 590 280, ⓦ kissclubalgarve.com. With five bars and two dancefloors, this glitzy place is regarded as the best club around. It often hosts international guest DJs (keep an eye out for flyers). It's 2km east of the old town; green and

blue bus routes pass nearby. May–Sept daily 1am–7am; Oct–April Fri & Sat 11pm–6am.
Matt's Bar Avenida Dr Francisco Sà Carneiro (The Strip), Oura ☎ 289 590 280, ⓦ mattsbar.net. Hip and fun bar/club with guest DJs, great music and alluring cocktails – its illustrious guests have included Ms Dynamite, Kenzie and Pixie Lott. May–Sept daily 8pm–4am; Oct–April Fri & Sat 8pm–4am.
O Farol Praia dos Pescadores, Albufeira ☎ 289 591 618. Once a fisherman's shack, this has been reborn as a modern beach bar/restaurant with a superbly positioned terrace touching the sands. A great spot for a sundowner, it also does good-value meat and fish dishes from €10. Daily 9am–11pm; Oct–April closes at 6pm.

ACTIVITIES

Boat trips Dreamwaves (☎ 962 003 885, ⓦ dreamwave algarve.com) runs daily boat trips to local caves, dolphin watching, and cruises on a mock pirate ship from €20–50. The trips leave from Albufeira's marina, a collection of

brightly coloured lego-like modern shops, bars and apartments clustered round in-your-face yachts and speedboats – it's downhill and 2km west of the town centre.

DIRECTORY

Banks and exchange ATMs are grouped around Largo Eng. Duarte Pacheco and along Av da Liberdade.
Health centre Urbanização dos Caliços, 2km north of the centre ☎ 289 598 400 (Mon–Fri 8am–8pm). The nearest hospital is in Faro or Portimão.
Markets A lively flea market takes place to the north of the centre at Urbanização dos Caliços, 2km north of the centre, on the first and third Tues of each month.

Pharmacy Farmácia Alves de Sousa, Av da Liberdade 103B ☎ 289 512 258.
Police Contact GNR at Av 25 de Abril 24 ☎ 289 583 310.
Post office In the new town on Rua Bartolomeu Dias 5–7 (Mon–Fri 9am–6pm).
Taxi There's a taxi rank on Av 25 de Abril. To order a cab call ☎ 289 583 230.

Armação de Pêra

ARMAÇÃO DE PÊRA, 15km west of Albufeira, fronts one of the largest beaches in the Algarve, which spreads east all the way to Galé. Beach aside, it is not the greatest looking of resorts; high-rise buildings and apartments straggle along the town's main through-road, tempered only by the pedestrianized promenade overlooking the central part of the sands. The remains of the town's fortified walls are at the eastern end of the resort, where a terrace in front of a little white chapel provides sweeping views. But the town beach is fine and if the main section is crowded, just head further east, beyond the cluster of traditional boats on the fishermen's beach towards Galé, where things are quieter. Aside from the **beaches**, the other local attraction is 4km up the main N125 at **Porches**, where the most famous of the Algarve's chunky and hand-painted pottery comes from – the main road is lined with shops that sell it.

The western beaches

9

The 10km or so of coast between Armação de Pêra and Centianes is largely flat and scrubby, with a series of delightful cove beaches that have mostly escaped any large-scale development, though you'll need a car to reach them. The closest to Armação de Pêra, 2km west, is **Praia da Senhora da Rocha**, boasting fine caves and strange rock formations below a pretty clifftop chapel. **Praia da Albondeira**, 5km west of Armação, marks the start of a superb coastal footpath that runs for 4km along clifftops all the way to Benagil (see below). A couple of kilometres west of Albondeira, the footpath passes **Praia da Marinha** below a craggy red-sandstone cliff, with the only trace of development being a seasonal beach restaurant and a tasteful villa complex a little up the hill.

After a further couple of kilometres, the path (and road) winds round to the next bay at **Benagil**, a tiny village consisting of a cluster of buildings with a couple of cafés above a narrow gully, its fine beach sitting beneath high cliffs. Fishing boats can take you out to an amazing sea cave, as large as a cathedral, with a hole in its roof. You can also walk to the top of it on the path that starts uphill by the restaurant *Algar* just above Benagil; take care of deep drops.

West of Benagil, the scenery changes again with coastal development crowding in around another appealing beach at **Praia de Centianes**, 3km away. From here, the road is lined with villas and apartments all the way to Carvoeiro.

ARRIVAL AND INFORMATION

ARMACÃO DE PÊRA

By bus Armacão de Pêra's bus terminal is at the eastern end of town.

Destinations Albufeira (Mon–Sat 12 daily, Sun 5 daily; 15–20min); Faro (5–7 daily; 1hr 20min); Lagos (6–8 daily; 1hr 15min); Lisbon (6–8 daily, 3hr 20min); Porches (6–8 daily; 10min); Portimão (6–8 daily; 30min); and Silves

(5–7 daily; 25min).

Information The turismo is on the seafront Avenida Beira Mar (May–Sept Mon–Fri 9.30am–7pm, Sat & Sun 9.30am–12.30pm & 2–7pm; Oct–April Mon–Fri 9.30am–1pm & 2–5.30pm; ☎ 282 312 145).

ACCOMMODATION

Holiday Inn Algarve Avenida Beira Mar 1 ☎ 282 320 260, ⓦ crimsonhotels.com/holidyinnalgarve. Right on the seafront, this plush, modern hotel has a pool and terrace overlooking the beach; there's also a restaurant, gym and live entertainment, but it's often block-booked by package companies. €125
Parque de Campismo Armação de Pêra ☎ 282 312 260, ⓦ roteiro-campista.pt. The shady campsite faces the unspoilt wetlands 1km out of the centre, back up the

N269-1 towards highway N125. It's well equipped, with its own pool, supermarket, restaurant and gardens; minimum three nights in high season. Pitch €16
Rosa Mar Rua Dom João II ☎ 282 312 377, ⓦ novo rosamar.com. If you don't mind high-rise living, these spacious apartments are good value. In a block back from the tourist office, they have heavy Portuguese decor, and some have sea-facing balconies. €60

EATING AND DRINKING

Estrela do Mar Largo 25 de Abril ☎ 282 313 775. The top budget choice is a simple shack right on the fishermen's beach offering bargain Portuguese staples from around €8; the grilled sardines are superb, as is the *bacalhau*. Tues–Sun 10am–midnight.

O Serol Rua Portas do Mar 2 ☎ 282 312 146. On the seafront near the fisherman's beach, this pleasantly old-fashioned seafood restaurant serves excellent fish *cataplanas* and a few grilled meat dishes from around €10. Mon, Tues & Thurs–Sun noon–3.30pm & 7–11pm.

Carvoeiro and around

A white-washed former fishing village nestled into sea cliffs, the small resort of **CARVOEIRO** must once have been very attractive, but now its small cove beach has to support the prostrate bodies of hundreds of tourists shipped in to what has become an overblown resort. The beach is pleasant enough though, with fishermen running boat trips from here to nearby caves for around €20. You can also visit the impressive rock

9

formations of **Algar Seco**, 1km east of town, where steps lead down low cliffs to a series of dramatic overhangs above blow holes and grottoes. They are accessible via the coast road, or by a road train that trundles out from Carvoeiro every forty minutes or so (April–Sept 10am–midnight; €3 round trip).

Praia da Caneiros and Praia Pintadinho

There are two superb cove beaches a few kilometres to the west of Carvoeiro, though you'll need your own transport to reach them. First up is **Praia da Caneiros**, with a rock stack jutting from the sea off its lovely beach and a superb beachside restaurant, *Rei das Praias* (see below). A couple of kilometres further on, **Praia Pintadinho** is almost as appealing, with a simpler café-restaurant.

Slide & Splash

Vale de Deus • Daily: April, May and mid-Sept to Oct 10am–5pm; June 10am–5.30pm; July & Aug 10am–6.30pm; early Sept 10am–6pm • €24.50, under-10s €18 • ⓦ slidesplash.com

For a change from the beach, the water chutes, slides, pools and aquatic fun at the **Slide & Splash** theme park make a great half-day outing, especially for older children; there are also cafés and a restaurant. It's a short drive from town, just outside Lagoa, signposted off the N125, or there's a dedicated bus that leaves Carvoeiro at 9.30am; check the website for details.

ARRIVAL AND INFORMATION

CARVOEIRO AND AROUND

By bus Buses stop near Carvoeiro beach, with regular services from Lagoa (every 40min; 15min) and Portimão (5–8 daily; 35min). Buses from Faro go via Lagoa (7–10 daily; 1hr 35min–2hr), where you'll have to change for the Carvoeira bus.

Information Carvoeiro turismo (June to mid-Sept daily 9.30am–7pm; Oct–April Mon & Fri–Sun 9.30am–1pm & 2–5.30pm, Tues–Thurs 9.30am–5.30pm; ☎ 282 357 728, ⓦ cm-lagoa.pt) is on Largo de Carvoeiro, just behind the beach, can help with private rooms.

ACCOMMODATION

Casa Rei das Praias Vale da Azinhaga ☎ 282 491 416, ⓦ reidaspraias.com. Just inland from the sands at Praia da Caneiros, this modernist villa is extremely stylish and includes indoor and outdoor pools, gym and spa. Plush, airy and spacious rooms come with terraces, free wi-fi and minibars. **€150**

O Castelo Rua da Casino 59–61, Carvoeiro ☎ 282 208 518, ⓦ ocastelo.net. This has modern rooms, the best with a superb view over the beach (€10 extra) – take the road that overlooks the beach uphill above the tourist office and it's a five-minute walk. Breakfast €6 extra. Minimum stay of one week in August and three days from Easter–mid Oct. **€50**

EATING AND DRINKING

A Fonte Escadinhas do Vai-Assar 10, Carvoeiro ☎ 282 356 707. Just west of the main street, *A Fonte* is one of the few restaurants with a local flavour, and there's an outdoor terrace, too. It serves good-value rice dishes and fresh fish from €10, as well as excellent *cataplana* (€26 for two). Daily noon–2.30pm & 6–10.30pm.

★ **Rei das Praias** Praia da Caneiros ☎ 282 461 006.

One of the Algarve's loveliest beach restaurants, set on stilts above the sands of this lovely cove. It's not cheap (mains from around €14), but the fresh fish and seafood is second to none – or you can just enjoy a cocktail, or a reasonably priced sandwich in the bar area. Restaurant daily noon–11pm; bar 9am–midnight.

Ferragudo

Facing the sprawl of Portimão across the Rio Arade estuary, **FERRAGUDO** is an attractive former fishing village centred on a strip of palm-fringed gardens that spread up to the cobbled main square, **Praça Rainha Dona Leonor**. A waterfront promenade lined with fish restaurants skirts the estuary, while the old town spreads uphill behind here, its warren of atmospheric cobbled backstreets gathered around the town church – from the church terrace there are great views. The town has an estuary beach, which gets progressively more appealing as it approaches the impressive **Castelo de São João do Arade**. The castle (closed to the public) faces its partner fort in Praia da Rocha across the river, both of which were built in the sixteenth century to defend Portimão against attack.

The nearest ocean beach lies a couple of kilometres south, where you'll find the broad sands of **Praia Grande** at the mouth of the Rio Arade, with a scattering of restaurant-bars.

ARRIVAL AND INFORMATION   FERRAGUDO

By bus Buses to and from Portimão (hourly 7.30am–7.30pm; 10min) stop on the main road by Praça Rainha Dona Leonor.
Information The travel agent Beroli, Rua 25 de Abril 40

(☎ 919 924 120, ⓦ algarve.tourismus.com; Mon–Fri 10am–noon & 3–5pm), is the best source of local information, and can arrange tours, boat trips and accommodation.

ACCOMMODATION AND EATING

A Ria Rua Infante Santo 27, Ferragudo ☎ 282 451 790. A small, friendly restaurant which lacks the outlook of some on this stretch, but serves good-value fish and grills (from €12) and a wide array of rice dishes, including a tasty *arroz de polvo* (octopus rice) – it's one of the first places you'll come to along the main harbour-front. Daily 10am–11pm.

Quinta da Horta Rua do Regato, Ferragudo ☎ 913 360 738, ⓦ quintadahorta.co.uk. If you aren't fussed about nudity, the best option is this "clothing optional" place just out of town – follow the concrete rivulet east for ten minutes and it is on the right. It sports a series of tasteful

cottages, as well as an apartment with kitchenette, set round a garden full of tropical plants with a small plunge pool, sauna and tennis court; the owners also offer meals and activities. **€82**

Taberna Casa Verde Rua 25 Abril 43, Ferragudo ☎ 926 329 943. On the main pedestrianized street, this atmospheric tavern serves a wonderful range of fresh *petiscos* (from €4) such as tuna with black beans, and prawns with garlic and *chouriço*. Good local wines, and if you're lucky, the owner's fishermen friends will start up a jamming session on their guitars. Mon–Sat 5pm–midnight, Sun noon–midnight.

Portimão

Sited on the broad estuary of the Rio Arade, **Portimão** has made its living from fishing since pre-Roman times but today is a sprawling modern port of around forty thousand people. Few of Portimão's buildings made it through the 1755 earthquake – the **Igreja da Nossa Senhora da Conceição** is a rare survivor, retaining a fourteenth-century Manueline door, though most of the church was rebuilt in the late seventeenth century. The surrounding streets are pleasant enough, filled with shops selling lace, shoes, jewellery, ceramics and wicker goods, while the main **shopping streets** are around the pedestrianized Rua Diogo Tomé and Rua da Portades de São José.

The most attractive part of town is the **riverfront**, where a series of squares – Largo do Dique, Praça Manuel Teixeira Gomes and Praça Visconde de Bivar – are filled with outdoor cafés by gushing fountains. Heading up the river and under the road bridge you'll find a series of open-air restaurants serving inexpensive grilled-sardine lunches. The narrow streets just back from the bridge – off **Largo da Barca** – are Portimão's oldest, with more than a hint of their fishing-quarter past.

ARRIVAL AND INFORMATION   PORTIMÃO

By train The train station is inconveniently located at the northern tip of town but a bus runs into the centre every 45 minutes (Mon–Fri only); a taxi costs about €6, or it's a fifteen-minute walk.
Destinations Faro (9 daily; 1hr 30min); Ferreiras for

Albufeira (9 daily; 50min); Ferragudo (9 daily; 5min); Loulé (9 daily; 1hr); Lagos (9 daily; 20min); and Silves (9 daily; 15min).
By bus Buses from all destinations pull up in the streets around Largo do Dique, close to the river.

9

PORTIMÃO

Destinations Albufeira (Mon–Fri approx hourly, Sat & Sun 4 daily; 45min); Alvor (6 daily, Sat & Sun 4 daily; 20min); Caldas de Monchique (Mon–Fri 9 daily, Sat & Sun 5 daily; 30min); Carvoeiro (5–8 daily; 35min); Faro (8 daily; 1hr 40min); Ferragudo (hourly; 10min); Lagos (hourly; 40min); Lisbon (6–8 daily; 3hr 40min); Monchique (Mon–Fri 9 daily, Sat & Sun 5 daily; 45min); Praia da Rocha (every 15–20min; 5min); and Silves (Mon–Fri 9 daily, Sat & Sun 7 daily; 40min).

Information The turismo (Mon–Fri 10am–7pm, Sat 10am–12.30pm & 2–7pm; ☎282 430 165, ⓦcm -portimao.pt) is on Largo 1 de Dezembro, inside the Teatro Municipal.

British consulate Apartado 609, Avenida Guanaré (Mon–Fri 9.30am–2.30pm; ☎283 954 082, ⓦbritish -consulate.net/Portimao.html).

ACCOMMODATION AND EATING

Dona Barca Largo da Barca ☎282 484 189. The town's most famous restaurant offers superb fish and regional dishes (around €9) served at outdoor tables in an attractive square. Specialities include *feijoada de buzinas* (shellfish with beans). Daily noon–3.30pm & 5.30–10.30pm.

Globo Rua 5 de Outubro 26 ☎282 405 030, ⓦhoteis algarvesol.pt. With Praia da Rocha down the road, there's not much cause to stay in Portimão, but if you do, this is the best option: boutiquey touches to the rooms and with its own gym, bar and great top-floor views. **€85**

U Venâncio Zona Ribeirinha Entre-Pontes 4 ☎963 456 901. The best of the row of smart but inexpensive fish restaurants north of the old bridge, on the riverfront. Go for the *rodízio* – all the fish you can eat for €12; other main courses from €8. Tues–Sun 10am–10pm.

ACTIVITIES AND SHOPPING

Boat trips All along the riverfront you'll be approached by people offering boat trips along the coast to see the local grottoes (2hr for around €20), while three-hour trips (around €35) also go up the Rio Arade to Silves (departure times depend on the tides). Santa Barnarda (☎282 422 791, ⓦsanta-bernarda.com) is a good option which offers half-day cave tours (€30) and all-day trips (around €60) on a *caravela* sailing ship.

Autódromo Internacional do Algarve Sítio do Escampadinho ☎282 405 600, ⓦautodromoalgarve .com. This modern race track, just north of the A22 motorway, hosts various motorbike and car racing championships – and also offers driving lessons and track rental, if you fancy getting behind the wheel yourself.

Aqua Shopping Rua de São Pedro 72 ☎282 413 536, ⓦaquaportimao.pt. This modern shopping centre, a kilometre northwest of the riverfront, features 117 stores including a hypermarket and a whole host of local and international shops, including Primark, H&M, Mango and Massimo Dutti. Most shops daily 9am–11pm.

Praia da Rocha

PRAIA DA ROCHA, 3km south of Portimão, has one of the Algarve's broadest beaches, a fantastic swathe of sand backed by low cliffs. The eastern end of the beach is overlooked by the walls of an old sea fort, the **Fortaleza da Santa Caterina**, which was built in 1691 to guard the mouth of the Rio Arade – the fort's terrace offers splendid views across the ocean in one direction, and over a modern marina and the estuary the other way. Sadly, the rest of Praia da Rocha is a splodge of ungainly high-rise hotels, bars and a casino that sit on the clifftop, with the beach reached down steep steps from the elevated main street, Avenida Tomás Cabreira. But at least most of the bars, restaurants and hotels boast fine views of the sands and sea – and it remains pretty lively whatever time of year you visit.

ARRIVAL AND INFORMATION   PRAIA DA ROCHA

By bus There's a bus from Portimão every 15–20 minutes (7am–11.30pm; 5min), stopping in front of the *Hotel Jupiter* on Estrada da Rocha.

By car Drivers should note that the main coast road is one-way west to east; it is best to park on the main drag in

from Portimão, Estrada da Rocha.

Information The turismo (May to mid-Sept daily 9.30am–7pm; mid-Sept to April Mon–Fri 9.30am–1pm & 2.30–5.30pm; ☎282 419 132) is on the pedestrianized section of the main Avenida Tomás Cabreira.

ACCOMMODATION

Bela Vista Av Tomás Cabreira ☎282 450 480, ⓦhotelbelavista.net. Recently renovated to incorporate a modern wing, restaurant, pool and spa, this is the most stylish place to stay on the seafront. The original building is a mock-Moorish mansion built in 1918 by the wealthy Magalhães family as a wedding gift. The rooms and communal areas are an exquisite mixture of carved wood,

stained glass, and yellow, white and blue *azulejos*. Parking. **€200**

Casa Três Palmeiras Apartado 84, Praia do Vau, 2km west of Praia da Rocha ☎282 401 275, ⓦcasatres palmeiras.com. In a sublime position on a clifftop above a little beach, this sleek villa is a superb example of 1960s chic. Glass-fronted rooms curve around a terrace with a

■ ACCOMMODATION		● RESTAURANTS		■ BARS AND CLUBS	
Bela Vista	2	Cervejaria Marisqueira		Bar Miradouro	2
Casa Três Palmeiras	1	Praia da Rocha	1	Katedral	1
Vila Lido	3	Mar e Sol	2	Moonlight Bar	3

9

pool, where breakfast is served in summer. Rooms and communal areas are spacious and tastefully furnished and there's free wi-fi. Parking. Closed Dec & Jan. €204

★ **Vila Lido** Av Tomás Cabreira ☎282 424 127, ⓦhotelvilalido.com. A beautiful, blue-shuttered, early twentieth-century villa, in its own small grounds facing the fort. The front rooms have superb views over the beach, and the best come with their own terrace. Very friendly owners, and a superb breakfast is served on the terrace. Closed mid-Nov to mid-March. €110

EATING AND DRINKING

Cervejaria Marisqueira Praia da Rocha Rua Bartolomeu Dias, Edifício Colunas, off Av Tomás Cabreira ☎282 416 541. With an outdoor patio and bustling interior, this attracts a largely Portuguese crowd for excellent, good-value daily specials, fresh fish and seafood (from €10). Mon–Sat noon–3pm & 6–11pm.

Mar e Sol Areal da Praia da Rocha ☎282 483 235. Best value of the row of beach restaurants, each under a carapace of steel girders. Good salads, fresh fish and grills (around €9) and a great place to catch the sunset. Daily 11.30am–11pm.

BARS AND CLUBS

Bar Miradouro Av Tomás Cabreira miradouro. Superbly positioned kiosk café-bar, next to a natural rocky viewpoint above the beach – outdoor tables catch the last of the day's sun. Good for snacks, smoothies and cocktails. Daily 10.30am–midnight.

Katedral Av Tomás Cabreira ☎282 417 900, ⓦkatedral -disco.com. Housed in a futuristic cube on the clifftop, this is the largest and highest-profile club in town, with an early opening bar downstairs. Daily midnight–4am; bar open from noon.

Moonlight Bar Av Tomás Cabreira Ed. Guiomar Lj.7 ☎282 417 918. The best of a row of attractive clifftop bars on this stretch, with bright decor, lively sounds, sports TV and a superb terrace facing the beach to while the night away. Daily 9am–4am.

Alvor

Set slightly inland on the Rio Alvor, the port of **ALVOR**, 6km west of Praia da Rocha, briefly achieved fame as the place where Dom João II died in 1495. Although much of the town was razed in the 1755 earthquake, it still boasts a sixteenth-century Igreja Matriz with Manueline doors and pillars carved into fishing ropes and plants. Despite the inevitable development, the old core around the church and the central Praça da República retains some character, while the harbour itself is a delight, lined with colourful fishing boats and aromatic fish restaurants. Two-hour **boat trips** to various places along the coast leave from here (around €25 a person).

From the harbour it is a short walk uphill to the ruins of Alvor's **castle**, which dates back to the thirteenth century but now houses a children's playground. From here, Rua Padre David Neto leads onto Rua Dr Frederico Romas Mendes, the main drag lined with bars and restaurants. This stretches down to the riverside **Largo da Ribeira**, marked by a modern statue of a fish, where you'll find half a dozen fish restaurants overlooking the picturesque Rio Alvor. Head right as you face the river and a path leads up the estuary for a tranquil walk; bear left and it is a ten-minute stroll past fishermen's huts and riverside cafés to the **Praia de Alvor**, an enormous beach backed by café-bars.

Quinta da Rocha

On the peninsula between the mouths of the rivers Alvor and Odiáxere, **Quinta da Rocha** is an extensive area of copses, salt marshes, sandy spits and estuarine mudflats, forming a wide range of habitats for different types of animals – including 22 species of wading bird. Birdwatching tours of the protected wetlands are run by a voluntary environmental group, A Rocha (ⓦarocha.org). To explore independently, take the turning off the main N125 opposite Mexilheira Grande and follow any of the tracks into the wetlands (there are no marked trails).

ARRIVAL AND INFORMATION

ALVOR

By bus Buses pull in on the eastern edge of the old town, with services from Lagos (6 daily, Sat & Sun 4 daily; 20min); Lisbon (6–8 daily; 4hr 10min); and Portimão (6 daily, Sat & Sun 4 daily; 20min).

Information The town's turismo is in the centre of town at Rua Dr Alfonso Costa 51 (daily May–Sept 9.30am–7pm; Oct–April Mon–Fri 9.30am–1pm & 2–5.30pm; **☎**282 457 540).

ACCOMMODATION AND EATING

Despite its resort status, Alvor has a surprising lack of central **accommodation**. Most of the hotels are away from the centre, with a cluster of high-rise options a good 2km east of the town facing the beach. **Bars and restaurants**, however, are plentiful, mostly clustered around the waterfront Largo da Ribeira and its approach roads.

Buganvilia Rua Padre Mendes 6 **☎**282 459 412. Just down the hill from the turismo, this modern guesthouse has spotless en-suite rooms. There's also a roof terrace and decent downstairs restaurant. One-week-minimum let in August. No breakfast. €60

Churrasqueira Mercado de Alvor Mercado de Alvor **☎**282 458 248. Up near the castle, by the market, this local grill house serves bargain chicken with or without *piri-piri* for under €7, along with other dishes. Tues–Sun 8.30am–midnight.

Restinga Praia de Alvor **☎**282 459 434. Down on the beach, 1km south of the town, this bar-restaurant sits on the cusp of a large dune and offers great views to go with its moderately priced fish and grills (mains around €12); there's another branch on the waterside in Alvor. Daily 9am–9pm.

Zé Margadinho Largo da Ribeira 9 **☎**282 459 144. Operating since 1890, this bustling place is opposite the old fish market, with outdoor tables facing the river and freshly grilled fish from around €9. Daily 10am–10pm.

Silves

Eighteen kilometres northeast of Portimão, **SILVES** is well worth at least a half-day's visit, with its superb castle, whose dramatic red ring of walls gradually reveal themselves as you approach. While under Moorish occupation, the town was the capital of the Algarve – indeed it was the Moors who named the region *al-Gharb* ("the west"), and built Silves into a well-fortified and sophisticated place. The town's golden age came to

9

an end, however, in 1189 with the arrival of **Sancho I** and his large, unruly army of Crusaders, who laid siege to thirty thousand Moorish inhabitants in the citadel for three months. When the Moors' water and food supplies finally ran low they agreed to open the citadel gates in return for Sancho guaranteeing the safety of its inhabitants. The Crusaders, however, ignored Sancho's pledge and killed some six thousand Moors as they gleefully took the fortress. Silves passed back into Moorish hands two years later, but by then the town had been irreparably weakened, and it finally fell to Christian forces for good in 1249.

Fortaleza

Daily: mid-July to mid-Sept 9am–7pm; mid-Sept to mid-July 9am–5.30pm; last entry 30min before closing • €2.50, or combined ticket with Museu Arqueológico €3.60

The Moorish **Fortaleza** is slightly less impressive inside than seen from a distance despite recent renovations of the fairly sparse remains within the walls. There is a Moorish-style garden, café and access to the wonderful vaulted thirteenth-century water cistern, the **Cisterna Grande**, which once served the town. Some 7m in height and supported by six columns, it can hold enough water to supply 1200 people for a year and in use by the modern town up until the 1980s. The cistern is said to be haunted by a Moorish maiden who can be seen sailing across the underground waters during a full moon. The castle walls offer impressive views over the town and surrounding hills.

Sé

Rua da Sé • Mon–Fri 9am–1pm & 2–6pm, Sat 9am–1pm • €1 • ☎ 282 442 472

Sited below the fortress, Silves's **Sé** (cathedral) was built between 1242 and 1577 on the site of the Grand Mosque. It's an impressive edifice that was the Algarve's most important church until the bishopric moved to Faro shortly after the 1755 earthquake. The tombs lining the cathedral walls are of bishops and Crusaders who died taking Silves back from the Moors. Opposite the Sé, take a quick look in the newer **Igreja da Misericórdia** (free), a sixteenth-century church with a fine Manueline doorway; it also hosts temporary exhibitions.

Museu Arqueológico

Rua das Portas de Loulé 14 • Daily: mid-July to mid-Sept 9am–7pm; mid-Sept to mid-July 9am–5.30pm; last entry 30min before closing • €2, or combined ticket with Fortaleza €3.60 • ☎ 282 444 832

Below the Sé is the town's **Museu Arqueológico**. It's engaging enough, despite a lack of English-language labelling, and romps through the history of Silves from the year dot to the sixteenth century with displays of local archeological finds. At the centre of the museum is an Arab water cistern, which boasts a 18-metre-deep well – you can also access some of the old town walls from here.

ARRIVAL AND INFORMATION   SILVES

By train The train station lies 2km out of town (a taxi will cost around €4), with regular services to Faro (9 daily; 1hr 15min) and Lagos (9 daily; 35min).

By bus Buses stop near the market on the riverfront at the foot of town, with regular services to Armação de Pêra (5–7 daily; 25min) and Portimão (Mon–Fri 9 daily, Sat &

Sun 7 daily; 40min).

Information The main turismo is in Praça do Município (Mon–Fri 9am–1pm & 2–5pm; ☎ 282 440 800, ⍵ cm-silves .pt), which doubles as an exhibition space tracing Silves's Moorish heritage. There is also an information post by the car park near the market building (same hours; ☎ 282 442 255).

ACCOMMODATION AND EATING

★ **Café Inglês** Rua do Castelo 11 ☎ 282 442 585. The town's social hub, up by the castle, is a fun and funky

restored townhouse which sells delicious home-made snacks as well as full meals, including pizzas, curries and pasta, from around €8; it has a roof terrace, outside seats, live music at weekends, poetry nights and the occasional art exhibition. Tues–Fri & Sun 10am–1pm, Sat 1pm–1am.

Colina dos Mouros Pocinho Santo ☎ 282 440 420, ⓦ colinahotels.com. The top choice in town is this modern hotel, across the river opposite the fortress, which has an outdoor pool, and rooms with superb views over the town. €80

Marisqueira Rui Rua Comendador Vilarinho 27 ☎ 282 442 682, ⓦ marisqueirarui.com. Despite its humble appearance, this is justifiably rated for its seafood, with fantastic fish soup and a very long menu including *massa de peixe* (fish stew with pasta); main courses start at €11. Mon & Wed–Sun noon–11pm.

The Serra de Monchique

The **Serra de Monchique** is a rolling mountain range separating the Algarve from the neighbouring Alentejo district. Its slopes are made up of deciduous oaks and chestnut woods and it's one of the few areas of Portugal that shows off dazzling autumn colours. Its highest peak – at nearly 900m – is **Fóia**, from where, on a clear day, the views stretch over the south coast of the Algarve and west across to Cabo de São Vicente. Sadly this area also bears the brunt of the summer fires that seem to rage annually, though the woodland is generally quick to recover.

Parque da Mina

Vale de Boi • Daily: April–Sept 10am–7pm; Oct–March 10am–5pm; closed Mon from Nov–Feb • €10, under-12s €6 • ☎ 962 079 408 • ⓦ parquedamina.pt

Some 15km from Portimão, the **Parque da Mina** is a small theme park on the site of a disused mineral mine. There are woodland walks, a mini-farm and an old distillery as well as the chance to visit the gallery of the former copper, quartz and iron mine, operational until the 1960s.

Caldas de Monchique

Set in a beautifully wooded ravine, **CALDAS DE MONCHIQUE** was a spa even in Roman times and was once popular with Portuguese royalty. It was sympathetically restored in 2000, transforming a somewhat ramshackle spa resort into a tourist village – and the results have been fairly successful. The cobbled, tree-shaded main square, fronted by the pseudo-Moorish windows of the former casino (now an exhibition hall), is surrounded by lovely nineteenth-century buildings and the wooded setting is a delight. At the foot of the village, the modern **thermal spa** (ⓦ www.monchiquetermas .com) offers specialist treatments – including water massage, jet-showers and a steam room – and you can stay here too, in various renovated buildings around the village (from €140; book though the spa website), which all have use of an outdoor pool and kids' club.

Monchique

MONCHIQUE, 6km from Caldas, is a sizeable hilltown best visited for its **market**, held on the second Monday of each month (by the helipad): check out the local smoked hams and distinctive wooden furniture – especially the distinctive x-shaped chairs. There's also a weekly Sunday market on the main square, Largo 5 de Outubro, though the town is liveliest during the Traditional Sausage Fair in March, when restaurants lay on special menus. The old town is dotted with beautifully crafted metal sculptures of local characters made by a contemporary Lisbon artist, which you can spot on the waymarked route to the ruined seventeenth-century monastery of **Nossa Senhora do Desterro**, signed uphill from the bus station. Only a rickety shell of this Franciscan church remains, but it's a lovely fifteen-minute walk up.

9

There's a beautiful, winding 8km drive from Monchique up to the Serra's highest peak at **Fóia**, though the summit itself – bristling with radio masts, and capped by an ungainly modern complex sheltering a café-restaurant and shop – can be an anticlimax, especially if clouds obscure the views. On a clear day, however, the vistas are superb.

ARRIVAL AND INFORMATION — SERRA DE MONCHIQUE

By bus Frequent buses run from Portimão to Monchique's bus station (Mon–Fri 9 daily, Sat & Sun 5 daily; 45min) on the main Largo 5 de Outubro. Most of these call into the centre of Caldas de Monchique (30min) en route, though some stop on the main road a minute's walk above the spa's main square.

Information Monchique's turismo (Mon–Fri 9.30am–1pm & 2–5.30pm; ☎282 911 189, ⓦ cm-monchique.pt) is on Largo de São Sebastião, 100m up the steep Fóia road.

ACCOMMODATION AND EATING

CALDAS DE MONCHIQUE
Albergaria do Lageado Caldas de Monchique ☎282 912 616, ⓦalbergariadolageado.com. This pleasantly old-fashioned inn has tiled floors, white walls and elderly bathrooms, but the rooms (not all a/c) are spacious and airy, there's a pool and decent restaurant. Closed Nov–March. €55

MONCHIQUE
Abrigo da Montanha Corte Pereiro, Monchique ☎282 912 131, ⓦabrigodamontanha.com. A couple of kilometres out on the Fóia road, this country inn is great if you want to stay in rural solitude, with a pool, great views

from most of the bare-wood-floored rooms, and its own restaurant. €75

A Charrete Rua do Dr Samora Gil 30–34 ☎282 912 142. A great, traditional restaurant specializing in award-winning "mountain food" – meat and fish cooked with beans, rice, goat and the like from around €12. Mon, Tues & Thurs–Sun 10am–1pm.

Estrela de Monchique Rua do Porto Fundo 46, Monchique ☎282 913 111. The best budget accommodation option in Monchique is at this simple but welcoming guesthouse, a stone's throw from the bus terminal, with decent double rooms. No breakfast. €35

Lagos

LAGOS is one of the Algarve's most attractive and historic towns, its centre enclosed in largely fourteenth-century walls at the mouth of the Ribeira de Bensafrim. For all its historical significance, Lagos's main attraction is its proximity to some of the region's best beaches. To the east is the long sweep of **Meia Praia**, while to the west – from **Praia de Dona Ana** to **Porto de Mós** – you'll find the series of coves, caves and rock stacks for which the Algarve is best known. Boat trips run along the coast all year round, while a popular side-trip is inland to **Lagos Zoo**.

Brief history

During the early 1400s, Prince Henry the Navigator lived for much of his time in Lagos while he was developing his sea school in nearby Sagres. Over the next century it was from Lagos that many of Portugal's great explorers set off for the New World, including local boy Gil Eanes, who in 1434 became the first European to round Cape Bojador (today's Western Sahara). In 1577, Lagos became the administrative capital of the Algarve and within a year, Portugal's Crusader king Dom Sebastião gathered his troops in the town before their disastrous failed Crusade to Morocco, when the king and most of his court were killed in the battle of Alcácer-Quibrir; in Praça Gil Eanes, an oddly undignified statue commemorates the monarch. Much of Lagos was destroyed in the 1755 earthquake and Faro took over as capital in 1776. As a result the town went into a long decline, until tourism revived its fortunes in the 1960s. Since then it has developed into a major resort – though it also remains a working fishing port and local market centre.

LAGOS

BARS AND CLUBS

Bon Vivante	2
Cervejaria Ferradura	1
Grand Café	4
Stevie Ray's	3

RESTAURANTS

A Forja	4
Adega da Marina	1
Casa do Zé	4
Mullens	1
Nahnahbah	5
Taberna de Lagos	3
The Garden	3

ACCOMMODATION

Casa da Moura	4
Lagosmar	6
Marazul	6
Marina Rio	5
Pousada de Juventude	2
Tivoli Lagos	3

0   100
metres

Meia Praia & N125/A22

Boat
Trips

Marina

Swing Bridge

Train Station & Meia Praia

Doca dos Pescadores

LARGO
ROSSIO DE
SAO JOÃO

Bus
Station

AV. DOS DESCOBRIMENTOS

RUA VICTOR DA COSTA SILVA

RUA LUCINDA SANTOS

R. DR. JOSÉ CABRITA

R. A. CAETANO

RUA DO CONVENTO DA SRA. DA GLORIA

RUA VASCO DE GAMA

RUA VASCO DE GAMA

RUA ANTÓNIO CRISÓGNO DOS SANTOS

Laundry

RUA NOVA DA ALDEIA

RUA DA BARREIRA

RUA JOSÉ VIERA

RUA DO CEMITÉRIO

TRAVESSA DO CEMITÉRIO

RUA DA CAPELINHA

Centro
Ciência Viva

Mercado

RUA DO CARACOL

R. DR. SILVA

R. JOSÉ PELLITT

R. DUBRINHA

RUA CONS JOAQUIM MACHADO

RUA DOS PELREIROS

Supermarket

RUA DR. JOSÉ ALMEIDA

RUA CAMACHINHOS

R. DOS FERREIROS

RUA DAS PORTAS DE PORTUGAL

RUA QUINTAIS

R. DO JOGO DA BOLA

TRAV. 1 DE MAIO

R. GIL EANES

R. GIL EANES

PR. LUISE DE CAMÕES

PR. GIL EANES

Town
Hall

Buses to
Meia Praia

RUA INFANTE DE SAGRES

R. DO CANAL

TV. DO PAÇO

RUA LARANJEIRA

A. B. VIANA

R. 1 DE MAIO

R. M. POMBAL

R. AFONSO ALMEIDA

R. LIMPNHO

RUA MARREIROS NETTO

Pharmacy

RUA DA BARROCA

R. DAS ALEGRIAS

R. DR. ATALAIA

RUA DE FERRADURA

RUA 1 DE MAIO

RUA DA EXTREMA

RUA DR. J. TELO

Mercado dos
Escravos

RUA 25 DE ABRIL

RUA CÂNDIDO DOS REIS

R. DA OLIVEIRA

RUA LUIS DE AZEVEDO

RUA SOTEIRA DA COSTA

R. DA SILVA LOPES

RUA MENDONÇA PESSANHA

Cinema

Jah-Shaka

R.S. DA GRAÇA

PRAÇA
INFANTE
D. HENRIQUE

Santa
Maria

AV. DOS DESCOBRIMENTOS

Ribeira de Bensafrim

RUA DE GIL VICENTE

RUA CARDEAL NETO

RUA LANCAROTE DE FREITAS

Centro
Cultural
de Lagos

TR. DO FORNO

R.S. GONÇALO

PR. DA
REPÚBLICA

Santo
António

LAGOS

Police

R. H. C. SILVA

Museu
Municipal
Dr José
Formosinho

RUA CASTELO DOS GOVERNADORES

Hospital

Forte Ponta
da Bandeira

Praia da
Batata

RUA DR. MENDONÇA

R. 5 DE OUTUBRO

TV. DAS ALMS

RUA DR. ALBERTO SILVEIRA

R. DO JARDIM

RUA GEN. ALBERTO SILVEIRA

JÚLIO DANTAS

BOMBARDA

R. MIGUEL

RUA DA PORTA DA VILA

LARGO
DAS
PORTES
DA VILA

RUA INFANTE DE SAGRES

R. D. ESCOLAS PRIMÁRIAS

ESTRADA DO BOER

Town Walls

Town Walls

Praias

N

9

Mercado dos Escravos

Praça do Infante • Mon–Sat 10am–12.30pm & 2–5.30pm • €1.50; combined ticket with Museu Municipal and Forte da Bandeira €5 • Ⓦ cm-lagos.pt

The most unsavoury aspect of Portugal's historical forays overseas can be seen at the **Mercado dos Escravos**, site of Europe's first slave market, opened in 1444. The current arcaded building was built as a guards' mess in 1691 and later acted as a customs office: it now serves as a small exhibition space detailing the awful reality of the slave trade. Displays include the written accounts of the first 230 slaves to be sold in Lagos, along with artefacts brought over by them. You can also see the skeleton of a slave that was found dumped on a rubbish tip at the edge of town.

Igreja de Santo António and the Museu Municipal

Rua General Alberto Silveira • Tues–Sun 10am–5.30pm • €3; combined ticket with Mercado dos Escravos and Forte da Bandeira €5 • ☎ 282 762 301, Ⓦ cm-lagos.pt

The **Igreja de Santo António**, largely rebuilt after the 1755 earthquake, has a wonderful, lavishly decorated interior – a riot of ornate carvings, gilding and decorative tiles. The church forms part of a visit to the adjacent **Museu Municipal Dr José Formosinho** – an eclectic collection, to say the least. Alongside barrowloads of Neolithic axe-heads, statuary and local religious art are jars containing misshapen animal foetuses, a display of models of Algarvian chimneys, and fossils, the 1504 town charter, and assorted swords and cannonballs.

Forte Ponta da Bandeira

Cais da Solaria, Avenida dos Descobrimentos • Tues–Sun 10am–6pm • €3; combined ticket with Mercado dos Escravos and Museu Municipal €5 • Ⓦ cm-lagos.pt

Stroll along the waterfront Avenida dos Descobrimentos to see the remains of Lagos's once impregnable walls and fortifications, which include the squat seventeenth-century **Forte Ponta da Bandeira**, guarding the entrance to the harbour. Despite its modest size, this was considered one of the most advanced forts of its age; inside there's a pretty chapel, exhibition space and fine views over the water.

The town beaches

A **road train** (May–Sept hourly 10am–11pm) runs from Lagos marina along Avenida dos Descobrimentos and out via the beaches of Praia de Dona Ana and Porto de Mós to the headland at Ponta da Piedade • €4

The small **Praia da Batata**, by the Forte Ponta da Bandeira, is the first of a series of lovely cove beaches. Head up the hill (towards Sagres) and it's about 15 minutes' walk to the next beach, tiny **Praia do Pinhão**. Five minutes further, across the cliffs, is **Praia de Dona Ana** – the classic Algarve cove, with a restaurant built into the cliffs. Out of season the beach is superb, though in summer the crowds can get overwhelming.

Beyond here, you can follow a path around the cliffs and coast to **Praia do Camilo** – sometimes a bit less crowded – and right to the **Ponta da Piedade**, a headland whose lighthouse is a popular spot to watch the sunset. This marks the final point of call for the road train from Lagos.

Porto de Mós

Beyond Ponta da Piedade, the coast sweeps west to the beach of **Porto de Mós**, another 45 minutes' walk on the coast path, a lovely, broad beach with its own restaurant. The path then continues on as far as Luz, another hour away; it's a splendid stretch, high above the ocean, until the obelisk above Luz comes into sight, from where you scramble down the hillside and into town.

Meia Praia

9

The coast east of Lagos is very different to the western coves, made up of a 4km-long swathe of beach, **Meia Praia**, backed by low dunes and beach restaurants. You can walk to the beach via the marina and fishing harbour in around twenty minutes, or there's a regular bus service from Avenida dos Descobrimentos, which travels the length of the beach.

Lagos Zoo

Barão de São João • Daily: April–Sept 10am–7pm; Oct–March 10am–5pm • €14, under-11s €10 • ⓦ zoolagos.com

Around 8km north of Lagos, just off the main N120, **Lagos Zoo** is an extensive area of semitropical parkland which houses flamingos, toucans, owls and parrots, small mammals such as wallabies and porcupines, and farm animals in a special children's enclosure. Highlight is the "monkey lake", where gibbons and smaller animals wander semi-free. There's also a shop, restaurant and playgrounds.

ARRIVAL AND INFORMATION
LAGOS

By bus The bus station is a block back from the main riverfront road, Avenida dos Descobrimentos.

Destinations Albufeira (6–12 daily; 1hr 15min); Aljezur (4–6 daily; 50min); Alvor (6 daily, Sat & Sun 4 daily; 15min); Armação de Pêra (10 daily; 50min); Burgau (7–9 daily, 4 daily on Sun; 20min); Faro (7 daily; 2hr); Lisbon (6–8 daily; 4hr 35min); Luz (8–11 daily, 4 daily on Sun; 15min); Portimão (hourly; 40min); Sagres (approx hourly; 1hr); and Salema (5–8 daily; 35min).

By car There is plenty of parking for drivers (metered on the town side of the marina).

By train Lagos is the western terminal of the Algarve railway line and its train station is across the river, a

fifteen-minute walk from the centre via a swing bridge in the marina; taxis are usually available if you can't face the walk.

Destinations Faro (9 daily; 1hr 50min); Ferragudo (9 daily; 25min); Ferreiras for Albufeira (9 daily; 1hr 10min); Loulé (9 daily; 1hr 20min); Meia Praia (9 daily; 5min); Portimão (9 daily; 20min); Silves (9 daily; 35min); Tunes (13 daily; 50min–1hr).

Information The turismo is in the Antigos Paços do Concelho, Praça Gil Eanes (mid-June to mid-Sept daily 9.30am–7pm; mid-Sept to mid-June Mon–Fri 9.30am–6pm, Sat & Sun 9.30am–1pm & 2–5.30pm; ☎ 282 763 031, ⓦ cm-lagos.pt).

ACCOMMODATION

★ **Casa da Moura** Rua Cardeal Neto 10 ☎ 967 177 590, ⓦ casadamoura.com. Tucked into a quiet street at the top end of the old town, this is a gem of a place – a 100-year-old townhouse given a boutique makeover. There's a Moorish-style patio garden with a small pool; stylish, large rooms; communal bookshelves and oodles of character. Breakfast is taken on an upstairs terrace with views over the old town walls. **€150**

Lagosmar Rua Dr Faria e Silva 13 ☎ 282 763 523, ⓦ lagosmar.com. This small family hotel is on a (usually) quiet street with its own bar; there's free wi-fi and the best of the smallish rooms have little balconies. **€90**

★ **Marazul** Rua 25 de Abril 13 ☎ 282 770 230, ⓦ hotelmarazul.eu. Beautifully decorated guesthouse in the heart of the old town, with bright rooms and communal areas tiled in *azulejos*. Bedrooms (most en-suite) vary in size, but all come with TVs and some have terraces with sea views. Closed Jan. **€60**

Marina Rio Av dos Descobrimentos 388 ☎ 282 780 830, ⓦ marinario.com. A friendly, modern four-star facing the

harbour (though the back rooms look over the bus station). The rooms are very comfy with balconies and good facilities, while the hotel also has a games room, small rooftop pool and a sundeck. Limited free parking or paid-for garage parking. **€111**

Pousada de Juventude Rua de Lançarote de Freitas 50 ☎ 282 761 970, ⓦ microsites.juventude.gov .pt/portal/en. A contemporary, well-designed youth hostel, with several dorms plus a few en-suite doubles (book in advance for these). There's a pleasant courtyard plus internet access, laundry facilities and currency exchange. Dorm beds **€18**; doubles **€40**

Tivoli Lagos Rua Nova da Aldeia ☎ 282 790 079, ⓦ tivolilagos.com. The most upmarket hotel in the town centre is built round a central garden area with its own pool. Not all the rooms are spacious, and some overlook a busy street, but the best have terraces with good views. There are two restaurants, a bar, indoor and outdoor pools, and a health club, plus a courtesy bus to its own beach club at Meia Praia. Parking. **€140**

9

EATING AND DRINKING

★ **Adega da Marina** Av dos Descobrimentos 35 ☎ 282 764 284. A great barn of a place with rows of tables serving very good value food, including huge portions of charcoal-grilled meat and fish; the house wines are great and there's occasional live music. Most mains under €10. Daily noon–2am.

A Forja Rua dos Ferreiros 17 ☎ 282 768 588. This is one of the best places in town for fresh fish, at good-value prices (from around €9) – the giant salmon steaks, for example, are superb. It also serves a few meat dishes, salads and tasty starters. Mon–Fri & Sun noon–11pm.

Casa do Zé Rua Portas de Portugal 65 ☎ 282 760 212. On the corner with the market, where filling fish dishes are served at good-value prices. It's very much a locals' choice at lunchtime, with the outdoor seating soaking up a brisk trade – daily specials cost around €7 and the tourist menu is around €10. Daily 6am–2am.

Mullens Rua Cândido dos Reis 86 ☎ 915 045 650. This atmospheric *adega* serves moderately priced international dishes (curries, pasta and good steaks for around €10); the drinks are inexpensive and there's regular live music. Daily 8pm–2am.

Nahnahbah Travessa do Forno 14 ☎ 966 207 702. Fun-time café-restaurant famed for its inexpensive tasty organic burgers (around €9) – including El Kilo, a self-explanatory heart attack in a bun for €35. Also serves salads, pasta and cocktails to a youthful crowd, many from the nearby hostels. Tues–Sun 6pm–11pm, usually closed Jan.

Taberna de Lagos Rua Dr Joaquim Telo 1 ☎ 919 426 240. Lovely, high-ceilinged 400-year-old mansion converted into a sophisticated bar-restaurant that attracts an arty crowd. Dishes include steaks, pasta and fish (from around €16), as well as less-pricey salads and snacks (from around €7). There's an upstairs room which hosts the occasional salsa session, while a DJ takes over late most weekends. Daily 12.30pm–1am.

The Garden Rua de Lançarote de Freitas 29 ☎ 913 187 142. As the name suggests, the big draw here is a large patio garden, with tables beneath shady trees. There's a bit of everything on the menu, from good cocktails, pasta and burgers (from €6) to Moroccan-influenced mains such as couscous, tagines and *kefta* (around €10). Daily 3pm–midnight.

BARS AND CLUBS

Bon Vivante Rua 25 Abril 105 ☎ 282 761 019. This late-night bar/club at the top of the main pedestrianized street has drinking on three floors and a superb roof terrace – a great spot to watch the sun go down. Daily 6pm–4am.

Cervejaria Ferradura Rua 1 de Maio 26A. An atmospheric *cervejaria* covered in soccer scarves and posters, where locals hole up on stools around a horseshoe-shaped bar and tuck into inexpensive shellfish *petiscos*. Mon–Sat 10am–2am.

Grand Café Rua Senhora da Graça 7 ☎ 282 762 622. In a fine high-ceilinged building decked in gold leaf and velvet, this is one of the town's coolest hangouts, with an outside terrace, guest DJs and a lively crowd. April–Sept daily 9pm–4am; Oct–March Fri & Sat 9pm–4am.

Stevie Ray's Rua Senhora da Graça 9 ☎ 282 760 673, ⓦ stevie-rays.com. Lagos's premier jazz, blues and latin club, with live music every Fri and Sat, plus music other nights in a relaxed and pleasant venue. Tues–Sat 9pm–4am.

ACTIVITIES

Balloon rides Barlavento Balloons (☎ 914 532 300, ⓦ barlaventoballoons.com.pt) offer hot-air-balloon rides across the region, usually departing from Aeródromo de Lagos, though exact routes depend on weather conditions.

★ **Bike tours** Innovative British-run outfit, The Mountain Bike Adventure (Porta da Vila Lote 2 ☎ 918 502 663, ⓦ themountainbikeadventure.com), offers various half- and full-day mountain coastal or mountain-bike tours (€30–55) as well as bike holidays.

Boat trips Avenida dos Descobrimentos is lined with stalls offering boat trips, and kayak tours to the amazing grottoes and sea caves along the surrounding coast, as well as dolphin "seafaris", with most departing from the marina.

It's worth shopping around for the best deal, but most cost around €15–20 per person for a 45-minute trip up to around €50 for half-day excursions.

Surf and bike rental Jah-Shaka (Rua Cândido dos Reis 112 ☎ 282 798 006, ⓦ jahshakasurf.com; daily 9am–8pm) sells and hires out surf gear and mountain bikes (surfboards and bikes from €20 a day) and can also arrange surf lessons and fishing trips..

Surfing and kitesurfing Extreme Algarve (☎ 918 674 079, ⓦ extremealgarve.com) offer surfing and kitesurfing lessons (from €55 a day), as well as surfing/kitesurfing holidays, based at its own central Lagos villa.

LISTINGS

Banks and exchange Banks and ATMs are grouped around Praça Gil Eanes.

Hospital Rua do Castelo dos Governadores, adjacent to the Santa Maria church ☎ 282 770 100, ⓦ chbalgarvio .min-saude.pt.

Laundry Lavandaria Míele, Av dos Descobrimentos 27 (Mon–Fri 9am–1pm & 3–7pm, Sat 9am–1pm).
Pharmacy Silva, Rua 25 Abril 9 ☎ 282 762 859.
Police Rua General Alberto Silveira ☎ 282 780 240.
Post office Rua Portas de Portugal, just off Av dos

Descobrimentos (Mon–Fri 9am–6pm).
Supermarket Intermarché, Av dos Descobrimentos 15 (daily 8am–8pm, until 10pm in July and August).
Taxis There are ranks in front of the post office or call ☎ 282 763 587.

The western Algarve

The coast west of Lagos, as far as Sagres, remains one of the least spoiled parts of the Algarve, largely thanks to the Parque Natural do Sudoeste Alentejano e Costa Vicentina which prohibits large-scale building on the coastline west of Burgau. As a result, the resorts – certainly west of **Luz** at **Burgau** and **Salema** – remain largely low-rise and low-key. Most of the coast is linked by a craggy coast path and you can easily walk between the villages: Salema to Luz, or Luz to Lagos, in particular, are beautiful routes.

GETTING AROUND   THE WESTERN ALGARVE

There are regular **buses** (5–8 daily) from Lagos calling at Luz (15min), Burgau (20min) and Salema (35min). Other local beaches, near Figueira and Raposeira, can't be reached by public transport, but they are much less visited as a consequence.

Luz

Five kilometres west of Lagos, the mass of white chalets and villas that makes up the resort of **LUZ** piles up behind a sweeping beach set below towering cliffs. There's not much of a centre to Luz, but there's an attractive palm-lined beachside promenade that leads from the sands to a *miradouro* beneath the village's old fort – now a restaurant – and the church. Halfway along the promenade lie the **Termas Romanas** (daily 9am–7pm; free), scant remains of a Roman house, fish-preserving tanks and a bathhouse. Walkers can take the **path to Lagos** which starts at the eastern end of the beach. At the Algarve Sports Club, follow the private road uphill and make the steep scramble up to the obelisk on the cliffs, from where a gentle path careers along the tops to Porto de Mós, Ponte das Piedade and Lagos: from Luz to Lagos takes around two hours.

ACCOMMODATION   LUZ

Most **accommodation** in Luz is in modern tourist complexes and villas that are usually block-booked in summer, though the hotel and campsite we list below often have vacancies. For self-catering, ⓦ starvilla.com has a good range of quality, decent-value self-catering options in and around Luz. Book early and you can get very good deals.

Belavista da Luz Praia da Luz ☎ 282 788 655, ⓦ belavistadaluz.com. Around 1km uphill on the road towards Sagres, this is Luz's only hotel proper, a smart four-star with tennis courts, a health club, restaurant and pool. All the rooms are spacious with balconies. **€155**

Camping Valverde Estrada da Praia da Luz ☎ 218 789 211, ⓦ orbitur.pt. Close to the EN125 highway and a good 3km from the beach, this is nevertheless well-equipped, with a restaurant, bar, pool, supermarket and kids' playground. Pitch **€35**

EATING AND DRINKING

Fortaleza da Luz Rua da Igreja 3 ☎ 282 789 926. Above the west end of the beach, you can dine in style in a seventeenth-century former sea fort with a lovely sea-facing terrace. Organic vegetables and home-made ice creams compliment a choice of Algarvian and international cuisine (mains from €10–14). There's live music on

Thursdays. Daily 11am –11pm.
Kiwi Pastelaria Avenida dos Pescadores 4 ☎ 282 789 646. The perfect beachside café, right on the promenade, serving inexpensive fresh croissants, juices, salads, sandwiches, ice creams and pizzas (from €7). Daily 9.30am–7pm.

9

Burgau

Once past the modern suburbs, **BURGAU**, 5km west of Luz, is a pretty little former fishing village of narrow cobbled lanes which tumble down a steep hillside to a fine sandy beach set below low cliffs. Fishing boats still line the lower roads, which double up as slipways, while narrow alleys weave around to a *miradouro* viewpoint. In July and August the village is somewhat mobbed, but at other times it retains a distinct character, with locals cooking fish on tiny grills outside their homes.

ACCOMMODATION AND EATING
BURGAU

A Barraca Largo dos Pescadores 2 ☎282 697 748. This clifftop restaurant (AKA The Hut) is a top spot for mid-priced meat dishes and seafood (around €10–12), including the speciality, *cataplana*. It's best in summer since, at other times, plastic sheets over the terrace put paid to the wind but also the views. Mon & Wed–Sun noon–3pm & 7–10pm; closed one month in winter.

Beach Bar Burgau Praia de Burgau ☎ 282 697 553. This high-profile beach restaurant has a splendid terrace on the beach – waves crash around it at high tide. It serves tasty fresh fish and grills (€11–15), or just pop in for a drink. Daily: bar 10am–midnight; restaurant noon–3pm & 7–10pm.

Casa Grande ☎282 697 416, ⓦcasagrandeportugal .com. At the top end of town on the road towards Luz, this is a lovely old English-run manor set in its own grounds. The rooms (of varying sizes) have soaring ceilings and families can be accommodated. There's also a good restaurant attached, the *Adega Casa Grande*, which serves tasty Portuguese cuisine and weekend wood-fired pizzas. **€80**

Praia do Burgau Rua da Fortaleza ☎962 505 429, ⓦhotelpraiadoburgautfmhotels.com. On a hillside at the east end of town, this is a friendly three-star place with small but decent rooms. The top-floor rooms with balconies have superb views and there's a small pool. **€70**

Salema

At the bottom of an attractive valley, Salema is no longer the thriving fishing village it once was, but its tight warren of fishermen's houses above the eastern end of a fine, sandy bay now form the hub of an attractive resort. Many of the old houses are now converted into inexpensive holiday lets: look for signs in the windows. A plume of modern development spreads steeply uphill, but at least the white villas are in keeping with the old town, and its beach only gets busy in high season.

ACCOMMODATION
SALEMA

A Maré Praia de Salema ☎282 695 165, ⓦalgarve .co.uk. On the hill above the main road into town, this good-value and attractively renovated house has a lovely sea-facing terrace and airy breakfast room. En-suite rooms are small but spotless. **€80**

Quinta dos Carriços Praia de Salema ☎282 695 201, ⓦquintadoscarricos.com. An excellent campsite with well-spaced pitches in beautifully landscaped grounds with

plenty of trees for shade. Good facilities include a minimarket, restaurant, bar and launderette – there's also a naturists' zone and bungalows sleeping 2–4 (from €75). Pitch **€22**

Salema Rua 28 de Janeiro ☎282 665 328, ⓦhotel salema.com. Plonked ungraciously by the cobbled square just back from the beach, this modern hotel block offers small but pleasant rooms with their own balconies and skewed sea views; there's also a bar. Closed Nov–March. **€94**

EATING AND DRINKING

Boia Bar Rua das Pescadores 101 ☎282 695 382, ⓦboiabar.com. Salema's top restaurant is a swish place facing the beach, with snappy service; *caldeirada* (fish stew) is the speciality (though you need to order it in advance), otherwise fresh fish (€9–13) is the thing to go for. Also does inexpensive sandwiches. Daily 10am–10pm.

Mira Mar Travessa do Mira Mar 6 ☎919 560 339. This simple beach restaurant has a sea-facing terrace and serves excellent fresh fish (from around €10), as well as tapas, veggie dishes and a fine *sangría*. May–Sept Mon–Fri & Sun 10am–10pm.

Praia da Figueira

The small village of Figueira on the N125, around 3km northwest of Salema, is the starting point for a rough track (signed "Forte da Figueira") to the isolated sands of

Praia da Figueira, that lie below the ruins of an old fort. It's one of the least-visited beaches along this stretch – possibly because it's a 20–30min walk to get there, though the path passes through lovely countryside on the way. There are no facilities so take your own food and drink.

Nossa Senhora de Guadalupe

Estrada Nacional 125, Raposeira • Tues–Sun 10.30am–1pm & 2–6.30pm • Free; exhibitions €2 • ☎ 282 620 140, ⓦ cultalg.pt

Between Figueira and Raposeira, a sign points off the main N125 to the chapel of **Nossa Senhora de Guadalupe**, reached down the old road which runs parallel to the highway. Built in the thirteenth century by the Knights Templar, and said to have been frequented by Henry the Navigator, the chapel stands in rural solitude, but it's a pleasant place to stroll around or have a picnic. A small, rather unimpressive exhibition space details the chapel's links with Henry the Navigator.

Praia do Zavial and Praia da Ingrina

The little-visited **Praia do Zavial** can be reached from the small village of Raposeira, which is on the main EN125. It has a great beach which is popular with surfers and also has a fine café-restaurant of the same name (☎282 639 282; Tues–Sun 10am–dusk). Another couple of kilometres around the bay, **Praia da Ingrina** is more sheltered and sandy, good for beachcombing amid the rock pools, though there's no public transport to either beach, so you'll need a car.

Sagres and around

Sagres is the southwesternmost habour in Europe. Spread over a flat, scrubby headland above a working fishing port, it is not a handsome town, but its dramatic position attracts a growing number of families, backpackers, divers and surfers,

■ BARS AND CLUBS		● RESTAURANTS		■ ACCOMMODATION	
Água Salgado	1	A Grelha	1	Mareta View	3
Dromedário	2	Mar á Vista	2	Martinhal Beach Resort	1
Rosa dos Ventos	3	Raposo	4	Memmo Baleeira	2
		Vila Velha	3	Pousada do Infante	4

9

drawn by warm waters, surf schools and the string of magnificent local beaches. **Modern Sagres** is little more than a main road – Rua Comandante Matoso – connecting the lively fishing harbour and Praia da Baleeira at one end with the main square at the other, all backed by a new town of white villas and apartments. The small square, **Praça da République**, is the main focus of town, an attractive cobbled space lined with squat palms. Its liveliest day is August 15 when celebrations and fireworks celebrate the local saint's day.

Brief history

Sagres and its rugged cape, Cabo de São Vicente, were once thought to mark the edge of the known world, which is why **Henry the Navigator** is believed to have set up his **school of navigation** here in the fifteenth century. It was here too that the caravel was developed – a revolutionary boat that could sail further than any European had been before. During Henry's lifetime, Portuguese navigators colonized the Azores and Madeira and began trading with ports along the west coast of Africa. After Henry's death in 1460, his school continued to train and equip sailors who went on to become the most famous of Portugal's great explorers: **Vasco da Gama** (1460–1524), who opened up the sea route to India; **Pedro Álvares Cabral** (1468–1520), who "discovered" Brazil; and **Ferdinand Magellan** (1519–1522), the first European to cross the Pacific. Once Lisbon became the main departure point for the Portuguese explorers, however, Sagres lost some of its importance and slipped back into obscurity. Its small sixteenth-century Fortaleza de Baleeira was damaged by Francis Drake in 1587 and further ruined in the 1755 earthquake; most of today's town was built after tourism revived its fortunes in the 1960s.

The beaches

Most people spend their days in Sagres on one of the excellent beaches, five of which are within walking distance of the town. Three are on the more sheltered coast east of the fortress, with the best, **Praia da Mareta**, just five minutes' walk southeast of the main square. Further on is the slightly scrubby harbour beach, **Praia da Baleeira**, but you're better off walking another five to ten minutes over the cliffs above the harbour to the longest beach, **Praia do Martinhal**, which is particularly good for families and backed by a purpose-built resort. West of the fortress, **Praia do Tonel** is a wilder location, popular with surfers. It's a longer walk to the beautiful **Praia de Belixe**, 2km down the road from Sagres to Cabo de São Vicente, which is overlooked by a small fortress (closed to the public). Wherever you swim, take care – there are some very strong undertows, especially on the west side of the fortress.

SAGRES SURFING

The west coast of the Algarve has gained a reputation as one of Europe's best **surfing** destinations, with Sagres as its surfing capital. Its position at the bottom corner of Portugal means that there are nearly always excellent surfing conditions, whatever the weather. The swell "wraps" round Cabo de São Vicente, producing relatively gentle waves in the bays between Sagres and Lagos, ideal for the less experienced. With swell sizes of up to 5m, the beaches north of Cabo de São Vicente face the full brunt of the Atlantic so are best for experienced surfers – legs of the World Surfing Championships are held at nearby Praia do Amado. Indeed, it can be decidedly dangerous and inexperienced surfers are best off going with a surf school – which can give one-off lessons or courses from around €55 a day – or a surf camp, which throws in accommodation and transport to the best beaches. Top surf camps in the region include ⓦfreeridesurfcamp.com, ⓦalgarvesurfschool.com, ⓦinternationalsurfschool.com and ⓦsurf-experience.com.

FROM TOP BOAT TRIP FROM LAGOS (P.478); PRAIA DE ODECEIXE (P.488) >

9

Porto da Baleeira

Porto da Baleeira is a working fishing harbour, around fifteen minutes' walk from the main square along Rua Comandante Matoso: it's an earthy place lined with boat-repair yards and fishing fleets – watching the day's catch come in is always an event. You can book various boat trips and **diving** courses from here – try Diverscape (☎965 559 073, ⓦwww.diverscape.com), which offers half-day dive trips from around €45 and various diving courses from around €240.

Fortaleza

Daily: May, June & Sept 9.30am–8pm; July & Aug 9.30am–8.30pm; Oct–April 9.30am–5.30pm • €3; free on Sun before 2pm • ☎282 620 140, ⓦcultalg.pt/sagres

Henry the Navigator's **Fortaleza** looms over the town, with Rua da Fortaleza running directly up the headland towards its massive bulk; it is better to walk this way than to follow the road signs which take you on a detour to a giant car park set well back from the fort. You enter the fort via a tunnel through the impressive walls – these are all that remain of the defences that once enclosed this dramatic headland jutting into the Atlantic; the rest were brought down by the 1755 earthquake. Opposite the tunnel entrance, you'll see a huge pebble **Rosa dos Ventos** (wind compass), which was used to measure the direction of the wind. No one is sure whether the compass dates back to Henry's time, though the much-restored chapel of **Nossa Senhora da Graça** alongside is certainly from the fifteenth century.

The only other buildings within the walls are a shop, café and exhibition space showing maps of Portugal and other nautical memorabilia – though their ugly concrete construction does little to enhance the beauty of the site. Still, it's pleasant to wander around the walls or out to **Ponta de Sagres**, a headland with a small lighthouse beacon offering superb views along the coast, past fishermen dangling lines suicidally off the immense cliffs.

Cabo de São Vicente

The dramatic, cliff-fringed **Cabo de São Vicente** – Cape St Vincent – is the most southwestern point of mainland Europe. The Romans called this Promontorium Sacrum and thought the sun plunged nightly into the sea here – it later became a Christian shrine when the relics of the martyred St Vincent were brought here in the eighth century (see box below). Today, tourist stalls selling trinkets line the approach road to a **lighthouse** – the most powerful in Europe – and a ruined sixteenth-century Capuchin convent, which survived the 1755 earthquake but not

---

ST VICENT

St Vicent was born in Zaragoza in Spain in the first century AD and became the town's deacon during the early days of Christianity in Iberia. He was later imprisoned in Valencia and sentenced to death in 304 AD during the days of Christian persecution. It is said that while he was being burned alive, the room filled with light and the voices of angels, and he was proclaimed a martyr and then a saint. In the eighth century, his remains – which had somehow survived the fire – were miraculously washed up in an unmanned boat piloted by ravens at what is now Cabo de São Vicente. Perhaps more credible is the theory that Christians took whatever was left of Vincent with them to flee invading Moors, arriving at the safe outpost of the Cape where they later built a chapel to house his remains. In 1173, Afonso Henriques, Portugal's first Christian monarch, had the saint's remains moved to Lisbon. Legend has it that the faithful ravens followed them to the capital, and guarded over him in the cloisters of Lisbon's Sé (cathedral), until the last raven died in 1978. Today São Vicente remains Lisbon's patron saint.

the dissolution of the monasteries in 1834: its remaining walls today shelter a small shop and café.

The sea off this wild set of cliffs shelters the highest concentration of marine life in Portugal, including rare birds such as Bonelli's eagle – there's a **birdwatching festival** here in autumn (wbirdwatchingsagres.com). If you can, it's worth visiting the cape at sunset, when the views are breathtaking.

ARRIVAL AND INFORMATION

SAGRES AND AROUND

By bus Buses from Lagos stop just by Praça da República and then continue on to the harbour, Porto da Baleeira. Destinations Cabo de São Vicente (Mon–Fri 2 daily; 10min); Lagos (approx hourly; 1hr); and Salema (Mon–Fri 4–8 daily, Sat & Sun 3–4 daily; 35min).

Information The turismo on the main Avenida Comandante Matoso (Tues–Sat 9am–12.30pm & 1.30–5.30pm; ☎282 624 873, wcm-viladobispo.pt) can give details of local bus timetables and events.

ACCOMMODATION

Mareta View Praça da República ☎282 620 040, wsagresholidays.com. Right on the main square, this bills itself as a "boutique hotel" and it certainly has a clean, modern feel with bright rooms, some facing the sea. There is also a fashionable bar, attractive garden and free wi-fi, as well as an Italian-style café downstairs. **€120**

★ **Martinhal Beach Resort** Quinta do Martinhal ☎282 240 200, wmartinhal.com. The upmarket, family-friendly *Martinhal Beach Resort* is almost a village in its own right, with a small supermarket, a fantastic spa, various pools, restaurants and playgrounds dotted around the grounds which slope down to Martinhal beach. The stylish villas are modern and very well designed for families, while the classy hotel is better for those travelling without kids. On-site facilities include a gym as well as access to a whole raft of sports and activities including tennis, padel tennis, kayaking, surfing and cycling. Of the

three restaurants, *O Terraço* offers excellent fine dining, while the more relaxed beachfront *As Dunas* specializes in fresh fish. **€280**

Memmo Baleeira Rua das Nau ☎282 624 212, wmemmobaleeira.com. This stylish four-star is in a prime location overlooking the fishing harbour, and has a restaurant and bar overlooking landscaped lawns and the pool. Rooms are bright, white and minimalist with flatscreen TV, and there's also a spa, bike hire and in-house surf school. Parking. **€145**

Pousada do Infante ☎282 620 240, wpousadas.pt. This is an attractive clifftop mansion with Moorish elements and splendid views of the fortress from its bar-terrace. Rooms are large and comfy with luxurious bathrooms. There are also tennis courts, a restaurant and pool in the grounds. Parking. **€125**

EATING AND DRINKING

RESTAURANTS

A Grelha Rua Comandante Matoso ☎282 624 193. A simple grill house run by old-timers, who are never hurried. Good-value meat– the chicken *piri-piri* is recommended – as well as *bacalhau* dishes and *cataplanas*. Mains from €9. Daily 8am–midnight.

Mar á Vista Sítio da Mareta ☎282 624 247. On a scrubby patch of ground just off the road to Praia da Mareta, this pleasant restaurant serves a long list of good-value fish, omelettes and salads (around €11 for mains), with good views from its outdoor tables. Mon–Wed & Fri–Sun 10am–10pm.

★ **Raposo** Praia da Mareta ☎282 624 168. Lovely wood-and-chrome beach bar-restaurant right on the sands. Food is good value if you steer clear of the pricey seafood and wines. Expect to pay around €20 a head. By day it's full of surfers enjoying a drink. Daily 10am–10pm.

Vila Velha Rua Patrão António Faustino ☎282 624 788. The Dutch owners of this traditional restaurant give

an international twist to Portuguese ingredients, such as spaghetti with mushrooms and Dutch cheese and pork with mango sauce, in a pretty white house. Mains from €13. Tues–Sun 6.30–10pm.

BARS

Água Salgado Rua Comandante Matoso 8650 ☎282 624 297. Bright, lively bar with cool music, free wi-fi, a TV and table football. Also does crêpes, pizzas and breakfasts. Daily 10am–2am.

Dromedário Rua Comandante Matoso ☎282 624 219. Fashionable little bar-bistro with Egyptian-inspired decor, serving a mean range of cocktails and juices. Occasional live jazz and karaoke. Daily 10am–3am; Oct–April closes Tues.

Rosa dos Ventos Praça da República ☎282 624 480. Atmospheric bar, which also does simple food, in an old townhouse on the main square – the wonderful large terrace at the back faces the Atlantic. Mon & Wed–Sun 10am–2am.

9

The west coast

The Algarve's **west coast** faces the full brunt of the Atlantic, whose crashing breakers and cooler waters have largely deterred the developers. Nevertheless, the rocky coastline is punctuated by fantastic broad beaches accessible from the small village of **Carrapateira**, or the prettier and livelier villages of **Aljezur** and **Odeceixe**. This is popular territory for surfers, campervanners and hardy nudists who appreciate the remote beaches, but be warned: the sea can be dangerous and swimmers should take great care. The designation in 1995 of the stretch of coast from Burgau to Cabo de São Vicente and up through the Alentejo as a nature reserve – the **Parque Natural do Sudoeste Alentejano e Costa Vicentina** – has afforded the rugged scenery a certain amount of protection, though it also means that accommodation is scarce and it certainly helps to have your own transport.

Carrapateira and its beaches

Some twenty kilometres to the north of Sagres (served by one weekday bus from Vila do Bispo and Aljezur) is the low-key village of **CARRAPATEIRA**. There's not much to the village itself, but most people are drawn by the nearby **Praia da Bordeira**, a spectacular beach backed by giant dunes, a tiny river and crashing surf. A couple of kilometres south of Carrapateira (signed off the main road), there's a further fantastic broad, sandy bay, **Praia do Amado**, with a couple of seasonal cafés. Backed by low hills, it's particularly popular with surfers, and there's a **surf school** here (☎962 846 771, ⓦalgarvesurfschool.com) which offers equipment rental and surf courses from €50.

Museu do Mar

Rua do Pescador 7 • Tues–Sat: June–Sept 11am–6pm; Oct–May 10am–5pm • €2.60 • ☎282 970 000

Carrapateira's only real site is the modern **Museu do Mar** at the north end of town up a steep side-road. The museum explores the village's relationship with the sea, with a modest assembly of traditional tools and crafts and some evocative photos; there are also great views across the coast from its café.

ACCOMMODATION AND EATING
CARRAPATEIRA AND ITS BEACHES

Dunas Rua da Padaria 9, Carrapateira ☎282 973 118. The best local place to stay is a very pretty building on the beach side of the village, which has a number of simple rooms overlooking a flower-filled courtyard; there are also six apartments sleeping two or four and free wi-fi. **€55**

Monte Velho Herdade deo Monte Velho ☎966 007 950, ⓦwonderfulland.com/montevelho. With your own transport, the best option, especially if you like solitude, is reached down a bumpy track 5km south on the road to Vila do Bispo (follow signs to Vilarinho/Herdade do Beiçudo stables). Set in wild countryside on a breezy hill,

all rooms (some of which sleep up to five) come in contemporary styles and have terraces. The owners can arrange horse-riding, mountain-bike hire, surf lessons and massages. **€120**

O Sítio do Rio Praia da Bordeira ☎282 973 119. Around 1km back from the beach towards Carrapateira, this is a great little restaurant which uses largely organic produce – fresh soup, simple grills and veggie dishes from €10, with an outdoor terrace. Mon & Wed–Sun noon–3pm & 7–10pm; closed mid-Nov to mid-Dec.

Aljezur and around

ALJEZUR (pronounced "alj-ezoor"), 16km north of Carrapeteira, is the liveliest town on this coast, though some way inland from any beaches. The main coast road passes through a prosaic, modern lower town where you find banks, the post office and a range of cafés and restaurants. The more interesting historic centre spreads uphill beyond the bridge over the Aljezur River, a network of narrow cobbled streets reaching up through whitewashed houses to the remains of an eleventh-century Moorish **castle**. It's a lovely walk up to the castle with sweeping views over the valley, via a cluster of museums – though only the Casa Museu Pintor José Cercas (see below) is really worth a visit.

Casa Museu Pintor José Cercas

Rua do Castelo 2 • Mon–Fri 10am–1pm & 2.30–5pm • €2, includes entry to all the town museums • Tickets must be bought from the main Museu Municipal, which details the town's history, on Largo 5 de Outubro

The **Casa Museu Pintor José Cercas** displays the works and collections of local artist José Cercas, who lived in the house until his death in 1992. His well-observed landscapes and religious scenes are complemented by the attractive house and pretty garden.

Praia da Arrifana and Monte Clérigo

From May to September, two buses daily run from Aljezur to Praia da Arifana and Monte Clérigo, though you'll need your own transport the rest of the year; at Arifana, drivers may need to park at the top of the cliff and walk to the beach as parking spaces are limited.

Some 10km southwest of Aljezur, **Praia da Arrifana** is a superb, sandy sweep set below high, crumbling black cliffs which shelter a tiny fishing harbour. The beach is excellent, and surf competitions are sometimes held here. Several simple café-restaurants lie along the road above the beach, all serving grilled fish at moderate prices.

At the top of the cliff – at the headland, **Ponte da Arrifana** – are the ruins of an old seventeenth-century fort, largely destroyed by the 1755 earthquake. From here, you can pick up a coastal walk north, via the remains of an Islamic community at Ponte da Atalaia, all the way to **Monte Clérigo**, a pretty little holiday village of pink- and white-faced beach houses facing a superb, family-oriented beach tucked into the foot of a valley. The fine 2hr walk forms part of the signed Trilho dos Pescadores (see p.425) – keep the sea on your left and you can hardly get lost. The views are excellent, down into the deep, green waters and along the fragmented coast. There are some superb deserted strands below – not easily accessible – while the clifftop path, 100m up, runs through the brush- and herb-carpeted dunes, filled with flowers in the spring.

ARRIVAL AND INFORMATION

ALJEZUR AND AROUND

By bus The bus stops on Aljezur's main street. Destinations Carrapateira (Mon–Fri 1 daily; 25min); Lagos (4 daily; 50min); Lisbon (2 daily; 5hr); Odeceixe (3–4 daily; 30min); Portimão (2 daily; 55min); and Santiago de Cacém (2 daily; 2hr 30min).

Information The turismo (Mon–Fri 9.30am–1pm & 2–5.30pm; ☎ 282 998 229, ⍟ cm-aljezur.pt), at Rua 25 de Abril 62, the main through-road, does its best to help with private rooms.

ACCOMMODATION

Accommodation options are somewhat limited around Aljezur. The town itself has just one hostel, though there are a few guesthouses in the suburb of Igreja Nova, 1km north of the centre. If you fancy self-catering, Carpe Vita (☎ 963 256 581, ⍟ carpe-vita.com) lets out a variety of tastefully renovated houses in Aljezur old town, sleeping from two (€95) to five (€115) people.

WALKS IN AND AROUND ALJEZUR

The active historical society in Aljezur has marked out an attractive 4km **Circuito Histórico** around the old town, with historical sights marked by plaques in English and Portuguese. Before the river silted up in the fifteenth century, Aljezur was a major port, and the route passes buildings such as the tollhouse, once used to check weights and goods as they arrived. The town also marks the crossover point of two major long-distance walking trails: the **Via Algarviana** (⍟ viaalgarviana.org), which runs for 300km from Alcoutim in the west to Cabo de São Vicente in the south; and the **Rota Vicentina** (see p.425), which runs for 340km from Santiago de Cacém in the Alentejo, sharing the southern route to Cabo de São Vicente with the Via Algarviana.

9

ALJEZUR

Amazigh Design Hostel Rua da Ladeira 5, Aljezur ☎ 282 997 502, ⓦ www.amazighostel.com. Near the market at the bottom of the old town, this funky modern hostel is in a classily renovated old building with lots of bleached wood and exposed brickwork. Geared up for local surfers (surf packages available), there's a pleasant communal lounge and kitchen, dorms sleeping 6–10 people, plus free wi-fi. Breakfast €3 extra. Dorm beds €15; doubles €50

Dom Sancho Largo 1 de Maio, Igreja Nova ☎ 282 998 119. This simple *hotel* with comfortable rooms overlooks a pedestrianized street with plenty of cafés on its doorstep, in the suburb of Igreja Nova, 1km from the tourist office, just off the Monchique road – the bus from Lagos loops through Igreja Nova on its way out of Aljezur. €40

ARRIFANA

Pousada de Juventude Urbanização Arrifamar, Lote 43–44, Praia da Arrifana ☎ 282 997 455, ⓦ microsites .juventude.gov.pt/portal/en. A smart, modern youth hostel around 1km from the beach as you approach from Aljezur, with its own canteen and fine sea views. Four-bed dorms €17; double rooms €47

CAMPSITE

Parque de Campismo do Serrão Herdade do Serrão ☎ 282 990 220, ⓦ parque-campismo-serrao.com. The local campsite, 7km northwest of Aljezur, and 4km from the lovely beach of Praia Amoreira, has its own pool, supermarket, restaurant and tennis courts among dense trees. Pitch €16

EATING AND DRINKING

Pont'a Pé Largo da Liberdade 12, Aljezur ☎ 282 998 104. Near the market at the foot of the old town, this buzzy restaurant (mains around €10) offers grills, salads and a fine *arroz de tamboril* inside a cosy diner or on an outdoor terrace. Live music most weekends competes with the sound of the resident frogs. Daily noon–3.30pm &

6.30–10.30pm.

Ruth O Ivo Rua 25 de Abril 14, Aljezur ☎ 282 998 534. A small restaurant that specializes in top-quality local dishes such as goose barnacles with sweet potatoes and fish with pasta (mains from €10). Mon–Fri & Sun noon–3.30pm & 6.30–10.30pm.

ACTIVITIES

Bike rental/tours Algarve Adventure (Vale da Telha J189 ☎ 282 098 126, ⓦ algarve-adventure.com) rents out bikes for €10 a day and offers guided bike tours from €35 per person.

Donkey treks Burras Artes (Vale da Amoreiras, Apartado 19

☎ 289 998 331, ⓦ burros-artes.blogspot.com) offers 90-minute (€10 per person), half-day (€20) and one-day (€32) donkey treks along the trails around Aljezur (minimum three people). The donkeys carry your luggage and children if required.

Odeceixe

The attractive village of **ODECEIXE** tumbles down a hillside opposite the broad valley of the Odeceixe River, below the winding, tree-lined main coast road. Sleepy out of season, its character changes in summer when it attracts a steady stream of surfers, campervanners and families, lured by a superb beach and a very laidback atmosphere. Everything centres on the single main street and a small square, **Largo 1 de Maio**, where you'll find some lively bars, plenty of cafés, a couple of minimarkets, post office, bank and craft shops.

Praia de Odeceixe

The beach, **Praia de Odeceixe**, is 4km west of the village, reached down a verdant river valley, the fields either side neatly cultivated with corn. A road-train trundles between village and beach during July and August (approx hourly 10am–5pm), but it's a lovely walk along the road as well, following the river to a broad, sandy bay framed by low cliffs. It is one of the most sheltered beaches along this stretch of coast, offering superb surfing and relatively safe swimming, especially when the tide is out. There's lots of parking above the bay, as well as a cluster of houses and cafés, some offering *quartos*.

ARRIVAL AND DEPARTURE ODECEIXE

There are 3–4 **buses** daily to Odeceixe village from Lagos (1hr 15min) via Aljezur (30min).

ACCOMMODATION

Casa Celeste Rua Nova 10 ☎282 947 150, ⓦcasa celeste.web.pt. You can stay right on the main street, in spacious, attractively decorated rooms in a traditional townhouse – avoid the lower rooms which are a bit too close to the street for comfort. **€60**

Residência do Parque Rua do Correio 15 ☎282 947 117. On the main street by the post office, this friendly backpackers' haunt has a mixed bag of en-suite rooms – the best are on the top floor with small balconies. There's also a hammock lounge downstairs and huge off-season reductions. **€35**

EATING AND DRINKING

Chaparro Rua do Correiro, Odeceixe ☎282 947 304. The top choice for eating and drinking, opposite *Residência do Parque* – they serve local treats such as *piri-piri* prawns and goose barnacles (mains from €9), and there's a blackboard menu for the catch-of-the-day as well. If it's warm, you can sit outside at wooden benches to eat. Daily noon–3pm & 7–10pm.

Dorita Praia da Odeceixe ☎965 283 914. In a superb spot just above the beach, this German-run café-restaurant does tasty and healthy grills as well as quiches and cakes – one of the owners is a trained nutritionist. If you fancy staying, there are lovely en-suite rooms (plus a tiny one with shared facilities), the best of which have sea-facing balconies (€65). Daily 10am–10pm.

O Retiro do Adelino Rua Nova 20, Odeceixe ☎282 947 352. An excellent-value local restaurant, with tables in a covered courtyard, serving dishes such as grilled octopus and squid from €9. Daily noon–11pm.

ACTIVITIES

Surfing The Odeceixe Surf School (☎282 994 191, ⓦodeceixesurfschool.com) offers three-hour lessons from €35 and rents out equipment from €10 an hour.

Contexts

History

There is evidence of human life in Portugal going back 30,000 years, to a time when ice covered much of Europe. Around 22,000 years ago, the first Paleolithic hunter-gatherers – concentrated in the sheltered river valleys of the upper Douro and Tejo – began to leave animal engravings on the rocky river flank, most famously around Vila Nova de Foz Côa. The purpose of the etchings remains a mystery, although their unerringly lifelike nature suggests that shamanic ritual may have been involved. Over the following millennia, as the ice receded, early man extended his range further into the part of the Iberian peninsula that later became Portugal.

The first man-made stone structures made their appearance 6000 to 7000 years ago, in the form of communal tombs or **antas** (dolmens), most of which follow a basic design of a circular stone-walled chamber, roofed with flat slabs and originally covered with soil and rubble. Associated with the *antas* is a fertility cult, whose most obvious remains are a series of vertically planted, stone **menhirs** (heavy cylindrical stones, some carved into unarguably phallic forms) – egg-shaped boulders bearing vaginal symbols are believed to be the female equivalents. The largest surviving dolmen in the country is the Anta Grande do Zambujeiro, near Évora, though there are scores of others sited across the Alentejo and Beira regions. There's also a series of Neolithic **stone circles** (most dramatically at Os Almendres, near Évora) whose exact purpose is still unclear, though they may have had religious or even time-keeping significance.

How long this "granite civilization" lasted is unclear, though by 2000 BC it was well integrated into a broader western-European megalithic culture, as testified by the development of symbolic rock art. Particularly fine examples of Neolithic art are the carved shale funerary plaques from Alentejo and Algarve, mostly in the form of stylized owls or other birds of prey, probably divinities; the plaques may also have been symbols of tribal power or affiliation.

Cultura Castreja

The end of the Neolithic era, around 1000 BC, saw the development of northern Portugal's **Cultura Castreja**, based around fortified hilltop towns – called **citânias** – and villages (*castros*). There were contacts with trading peoples from across the Mediterranean, including the Phoenicians, who settled along Portugal's Atlantic coastline (c.900 BC), and the Mycenaean Greeks. A curious testament to this cultural mingling is found at Panóias, close to Vila Real, where an engraved text next to a sacrificial altar bears a bilingual Latin and Greek inscription dedicated to the Greco-Egyptian deity of Serapis.

c20,000 BC	5000–2000 BC	700–600 BC
Paleolithic hunters jazz up their caves with animal engravings in the Upper Douro	Neolithic stone circles are erected, most notably near Évora	Celts bring their northern customs to hilltowns such as Citânia de Briteiros near Braga

With the arrival of **Celtic peoples** in Portugal (from 700 BC onwards), life in the *citânias* and *castros* became more sophisticated. The Citânia de Briteiros, near Braga, and Citânia de Sanfins de Ferreira, north of Porto, were both substantial settlements of farmers, artisans and traders who lived in houses on paved streets, defended by formidable walls. Remains and relics from settlements in neighbouring Trás-os-Montes reveal more about this well-established society. The famous granite statues of wild sows and boars – *berrões* or *porcas* – may once have been worshipped as part of a fertility cult (there are notable examples at Bragança and Murça). Meanwhile, from both Minho and Trás-os-Montes come the life-sized statues of Celtic warriors, whose popular name – *figuras de basto* – alludes to their bravery: *eu basto*, "I suffice" (in defending the people), was their motto.

Rise and fall of the Romans

The **Romans** arrived in the Iberian peninsula in 210 BC, spreading out from the Mediterranean coast and quickly colonizing the south. Inland, however, it was a different matter, with the various Celt-Iberian tribes determined to defend their homeland against the invaders. The **Lusitani** of central Portugal in particular are still remembered for their heroic resistance, starting in 193 BC and keeping the Romans busy for years, if not decades. Their leader was one Viriatus, who kept the Lusitani in charge of their own destiny until he was betrayed in 139 BC – the Roman army smashed through and quickly pacified the Portuguese interior as far north as the Minho. Even so, it's easy to believe that in the far north and east, in isolated hilltowns and mountainous areas, the influence of the Romans was never very strong.

By 60 BC the Romans had founded a capital – **Olisipo** (Lisbon) – and established satellite towns throughout the Alentejo, including Évora, Santarém and Beja. Later, the southern Roman provinces became known as Lusitania, with a separate province to the north that covered the Minho, ruled from its main settlement at Braga. There are Roman remains and excavations – major and minor – in all these areas, and while Portuguese Roman archeological sites are generally insignificant compared to those elsewhere in the Mediterranean, the excavations at **Conímbriga** (near Coimbra) do at least give a sense of scale of Roman settlement and occupation.

WHAT DID THE ROMANS EVER DO FOR US?

Well, there are the roads, obviously, and the aqueducts, and the crops, and the language. As elsewhere in Europe and beyond, the influence of **the Romans** in Portugal was far-reaching and long-lasting. They introduced the fundamentally Portuguese staples of olives, vines and cereals, planted on massive agricultural estates (*latifundia*) in the Alentejo that still exist today in their essential forms. Surviving bridges, aqueducts and Roman roads – extremely elegant and amazingly durable – mark out many now-obscure settlements as having once had a more illustrious past. And the very basis of the early Portuguese language derived from the Latin spoken throughout the Empire. Even centuries after the fall of Rome and the end of Empire, when Visigoths and, later, the Moors were the dominant forces in the Iberian peninsula, many people in many town and villages lived a life that still bore heavy Romanized characteristics, from agricultural methods to legal processes.

First century BC	193–139 BC	711 AD
The Romans occupy southern Portugal, planting vines and citrus fruits	Local warrior Viriatus becomes a scourge of the occupying Romans	The Moors decide Iberia looks a promising place to colonize

By the fourth century AD, as elsewhere in Europe, so-called "barbarian" **Germanic tribes** were nibbling away at the Roman sphere of influence in Portugal, while Christianity was already well established. With the fall of the Roman Empire, the Suevi and then the Visigoths took their opportunities – the latter prevailing after 585, when a unified **Visigothic kingdom** was established across most of the peninsula, ruling from their capital in Toledo, Spain.

The Moors and the Reconquista

The Visigothic kingdom endured until it met its first real political and social challenge – the crossing of the Straits from North Africa in 711 of the **Moors**, largely Berbers from Morocco. Long riven by internal conflict, the Visigothic kingdom collapsed and the Moors advanced, almost without opposition. In Portugal they reached as far as Coimbra and the centre of the country, but preferred the milder south, particularly the established towns and agricultural estates of the Tejo valley and the Alentejo. However, it's the southern coast of Portugal that is most associated with the Moors – the land they knew as **al-Gharb** (Algarve), or "the west", with their capital at the walled town of Silves.

It was a time of civility and no little prosperity. Although the land was held under Muslim law, freedom of worship was granted while the Moors introduced their own **agricultural improvements** – from better irrigation (imported from the harsher climate of North Africa) to the planting of citrus fruits, rice and cotton. Towns as far away from the Algarve as Lisbon, Santarém and Évora acquired a distinct Moorish character that's still evident today.

The unconquered lands between the Douro and the Minho, however, never saw Moorish influence, and it was here that the Christian Reconquest – known in Portugal as the **Reconquista** – first took root. As a region, or county, of the Spanish kingdom of León, by the ninth century this northern land of mountains, forests and rivers was known as "**Portucale**", and by the eleventh century it was big – and occasionally obstreperous – enough to be thought of as a separate country. The nominal "Counts" of Portucale began to flex their muscles and eventually, under Henry of Burgundy, declared their independence. The kingdoms of León and Galicia had other ideas about this fledgling nation, but under Henry's son, **Afonso Henriques**, Portucale moved decisively towards self-determination. Following the battle of São Mamede (1128) – where he defeated his own mother, loyal to the kingdom of León – Afonso declared himself to be prince (and later "king", in 1137) of Portugal and announced that his capital would be at Guimarães.

Reconquest from the Moors followed quickly in the central regions close to Afonso's new power base of **Coimbra**, which became capital in 1143. Santarém and Lisbon both fell in 1147, after mighty sieges, and Afonso's new kingdom spread south as far as the Alentejo. That was the easy part, however, and it took another hundred years or so before the Moorish stronghold of the Algarve was breached – Silves was brutally sacked in 1189 and, though control later ebbed and flowed between Moorish and Christian forces, the writing was on the wall.

When Faro fell in 1249, the borders of the kingdom of Portugal were set – and have remained almost unchanged ever since. The first **Cortes** (Parliament) was called in Coimbra in 1211, though the country's capital was ultimately transferred to **Lisbon** in 1260 by Afonso III.

1073	1137	1249	1279–1325
Afonso is crowned king of Portucale, a small area to the north of the Moorish Iberia	Afonso Henriques becomes the first king of Portugal proper	Portugal boots out the last Moors from the Algarve	The country's borders are demarcated by a series of forts

THE KNIGHTS TEMPLAR

Founded as a chivalric order in France in the early twelfth century, the **Knights Templar** played an important part in wresting back control of Moorish-controlled land in the nascent state of Portugal. From a castle in Soure in central Portugal – granted in specific exchange for their help against the Moors – the Knights were at the forefront of battles and sieges like that at Santarém, fighting alongside Afonso Henriques as he swept south. They were given authority over lands they had conquered, which made them a power to rival that of the established Church and the other nobles, and in 1160 they moved their headquarters to the strategic site of **Tomar**. Within a century their power and influence in Europe was such that Philip IV of France suppressed the Order (1307), which was later officially dissolved by the Pope in 1312. In Portugal, however, it was too well entrenched in political and religious life simply to disappear – and under Dom Dinis, it was re-established as the **Order of Christ**, which took over the lands and possessions of the Templars, though under royal jurisdiction. The Order continued to play a significant role in the development of Portugal, whose kings and princes became its Grand Masters, thus further enmeshing Church, State and politics to mutual benefit.

Consolidation of the nation

The long reign (1279–1325) of **Dom Dinis** – son of Afonso III – did much to set on a firm footing the Portuguese kingdom that had emerged from the *reconquista*. With Castile still nibbling at the borders, new castles were built and towns fortified to safeguard the eastern side of the country – the Treaty of Alcanizes (1297) with Castile eventually granted Dom Dinis the security he craved. Trade and agriculture were prime concerns too, with Dinis' far-reaching reforms earning him the soubriquet *O Lavrador* (the farmer), while an interest in the arts and culture expressed itself in the founding of Portugal's first university at Lisbon in 1290 (later relocated to Coimbra). Dinis also made Portuguese the official language of the country, founded the Portuguese navy, and promoted various other legal and social reforms – in many ways establishing an early national identity for the country that echoed down through the following centuries.

The reigns of Dinis' successors were less tranquil, and the **Burgundian dynasty** – which started with the founding father of the country, Afonso Henriques – ended with the death of the ninth Burgundian monarch, Fernando I, in 1383. Although two years of factional fighting and Castilian intrigue followed, Portugal emerged not only intact but strengthened. With the country's independence under threat yet again from Castile, as rival claimants to the throne squared up to each other, a solution arrived in the shape of João, illegitimate son of Dom Pedro I (the king before Fernando) and Grand Master of the noble House of Aviz.

At the decisive **Battle of Aljubarrota** (1385), fought in the heart of Estremadura, João triumphed against the odds, defeating (indeed, crushing) the powerful Castilian army – with, it's claimed, the help of the Virgin Mary. Divine intervention or not, João built the abbey at Batalha in honour of his victory and was crowned **João I**.

A newly confident Portugal had no further fear of Castilian meddling, and began to look elsewhere for support, trade and alliances. English soldiers had played a part at Aljubarrota, and an Anglo-Portuguese alliance was cemented with

1290	1385	1386	mid-1400s
One of the world's first universities is founded at Coimbra	English archers help Portugal to repel Spanish invaders	The Treaty of Windsor cements Portugal's friendship with England	Henry the Navigator encourages expeditions to the New World

the 1386 **Treaty of Windsor** – one of the oldest surviving international alliances in the world – and the subsequent marriage of João to Philippa of Lancaster, daughter of John of Gaunt, in 1387.

Emergence of the maritime empire

Given its geographic location, it was hardly surprising that Portugal looked west and south – across the oceans – from the earliest settled period of its nationhood. There had always been the Crusades to keep knights and nobles occupied, and Morocco and North Africa were also tantalizingly close – João I took **Ceuta** in 1415, which was the first real step towards anything approaching an imperial policy.

However, it was to be João's third son, Henry, who transformed Portugal's maritime fortunes – he's known, aptly, as **Prince Henry "The Navigator"** (1394–1460). Henry became fascinated by the prospects of African trade and exploration and, after being made governor of the Algarve (1419) and then Grand Master of the Order of Christ (1420), was eventually in a position to fund his pursuits. At Sagres, on the Algarve, Henry developed an ocean-going ship, the caravel, which would drive Portugal's later explorations, while cartographers and navigators were quizzed for their expertise.

By 1430 both **Madeira** and the **Azores** had been colonized, and by the 1440s the **west coast of Africa** had been reached – importantly, avoiding the Muslim-dominated land routes across the Sahara and thus opening up a new line of trade for Portugal. The **Cape Verde** islands were explored in 1456 and, two years after Henry's death, in 1462, Sierra Leone was reached. It took another quarter of a century to round the Cape of Good Hope – named (Cabo da Boa Esperança) by Portuguese mariner **Bartolomeu Dias** – which was the true catalyst for expansion.

In 1498, when **Vasco da Gama** used decades of Portuguese maritime know-how to sail on around Africa and reach India, the economic floodgates opened. Under Dom Manuel I, the Portuguese Crown was to reap the extraordinary rewards of its sailors' endeavours, becoming one of the world's richest countries in the process. With imperial Spain similarly active in the New World, the **Treaty of Tordesillas** (1494) effectively divided the globe between the two countries.

Manuel I and the Golden Age

Four hundred years after it had first carved itself out a niche in the Iberian peninsula, Portugal was a world power. By the beginning of the sixteenth century, the country's "**discoveries**" in Africa and the Orient – and their exploitation for trade – had made Portugal a super-power. There was a Portuguese presence in Brazil (after 1500), India (1505), the Persian Gulf (1515) and Macau (1557), with untold riches – from gold, silver, precious metals, spices and slaves – filling the royal coffers.

The main beneficiary of this trade-built windfall was **Manuel I** (1495–1521), the king known as *O Venturoso* – "The Fortunate" indeed. His reign is often referred to as a "Golden Age" and it's difficult to argue with that assessment when confronted with the greatest manifestations of this huge wealth – the magnificent buildings erected in his reign that bear the architectural description **Manueline** (a term first used, incidentally, in the nineteenth century). The swirling maritime motifs, the twisted ropes and

late 1400s	1494	1498	1495–1521
An elephant is paraded around Lisbon as an example of exotic wealth	Spain and Portugal agree to divide the New World's trade routes	Vasco da Gama opens up the Spice Route to India	Manuel donates his name to a flamboyant architectural style

JEWS AND THE INQUISITION IN PORTUGAL

Jews had long settled in Portugal, and in many ways the country seemed more tolerant of the faith than others in Europe. Even when Spain turned decisively against **the Jews** in 1492 – forcibly expelling them en masse – Portugal at first refused to join the clamour. When Manuel I became king in 1495, there was still much sympathy in royal circles for the plight of the Spanish Jews, many of whom relocated across the border. But realpolitik soon intervened and Manuel felt sufficient pressure to order his own expulsion of the Jews in 1496. Many left altogether – to the Netherlands, or to hide away in remote parts of the Portuguese kingdom where the royal writ scarcely reached. There are enclaves in Trás-os-Montes and the Mountain Beiras where Jewish communities survived under the radar for centuries. Others took the official way out by becoming forced converts, known as "New Christians", a process that took on a more public face after 1531 with the activities of the **Portuguese Inquisition** – never as fierce as in neighbouring Spain, but still with the capacity to harm and to change lives forever. Stone crosses carved on lintels over ancient doors in small towns across Portugal tell the story of families forced to deny their old faith and proclaim their new one.

columns, the elaborate vegetation and heraldic devices – whether at Batalha, Tomar, Belém or Setúbal, these symphonies in stone speak of a desire to make a confident statement about a newly endowed empire.

After Manuel came his eldest son **João III** (1521–57), and the Portuguese empire continued to thrive and expand, as well as making significant new trading contacts in China and Japan. It can barely have seemed possible that it would end, such was its extent, wealth and glory, and yet within twenty years of João's death, Spain was back in charge.

Under the Spanish yoke

The seeds of disaster had already been sown under Manuel I and continued with the reign of his son João III. Such a huge **empire** was hard to administer and local governors difficult to control. The Ottoman Empire had its own ideas about where spheres of influence should be established, Indian and North African ports became difficult to defend, and pirates continued a running battle against Portuguese ships. In addition, although the wealth was pouring in, it was also pouring out again – personally commissioned abbeys and palaces, designed and decorated by the day's leading architects and artists, didn't come cheap.

João's heir was his three-year-old grandson **Sebastião**, most of whose reign was spent under a regency. The boy was devout, came of age in 1568 and promptly set about pursuing new religious and imperial endeavours, unaware that the old ones were already crumbling. Morocco was his eventual target, ostensibly to safeguard Portuguese trading outposts on the India route, but Sebastião was also happy to dress up the invasion as a Crusade. He took an army of 17,000 from Lisbon to Cadiz and then to Morocco, where it was annihilated at the battle of **Alcácer-Quibir** (1578) – thousands were killed, including Sebastião himself, riding into battle.

Spain saw its chance and renewed its long dormant claim to Portugal. Sebastião's uncle, Philip II of Spain, scion of the House of Habsburg, saw off a multitude of pretenders in battle and marched into Lisbon to proclaim himself **Filipe I** of Portugal

1531	1581	1640	Late 1600s
The Inquisition ruthlessly expels or converts Jewish citizens	Political manoeuvrings see Philip II start a period of Spanish rule	Portuguese troops place a Portuguese Duke on the throne	The country fills its coffers with gold and diamonds from Brazil

– he was recognized as such by a meeting of the Cortes in Tomar in 1581. Sixty years of direct Spanish rule followed, largely under viceroys appointed by Filipe and his sons, Filipe II and III. Their intention was to rule Portugal as a separate kingdom, though part of a dynastic union, and the country kept its currency, laws and government.

It made no difference to the Portuguese, who were never going to take to Spanish rule. Filipe himself was judged to be an unrightful ruler, and faced loud whispers that the last young Portuguese king, Sebastião, had never died at all, while various pretenders and mysterious Arthurian-style "sleeping kings" emerged from the woodwork over the years. Heavy taxes further upset both the nobility and the population at large, while Spain's own political pretensions – sending an Armada against England, Portugal's long-time ally, for example – simply made Portugal's position worse.

The House of Bragança takes power

With Spain embroiled in the Thirty Years' War, and waging constant battles with France, matters came to a head in 1640 when Filipe III ordered Portuguese nobles to Spain to help put down an uprising in Catalunya. That was enough for many, who kicked Filipe's governor out of his palace in Lisbon and bestowed the throne upon the Duke of Bragança, from one of the most powerful families in the country. He became **João IV** (1640–56), first king from the Portuguese **House of Bragança**, the dynastic family that was to reign until the Republic was declared in 1910.

The newly independent Portuguese Crown made it very clear, very quickly, that Spanish concerns were now of secondary importance. João's oldest surviving daughter, **Catherine of Bragança**, was used as a blatant lure for reviving relations with England and – in the face of continuing Spanish opposition – she was married to Charles II of England in 1661. Continuing skirmishes with Spain – some political, others military – were finally ended by the 1668 **Treaty of Lisbon**, mediated by England, in which Spain recognized Portuguese sovereignty.

The House of Bragança was to preside over something of a second Golden Age for Portugal, kick-started by the fortuitous **discovery of gold and diamonds in Brazil**. The colony had been a source of revenue since the arrival of the Portuguese in 1500, with hardwoods, tobacco, cotton and sugar exported and traded, but the discovery of gold at the end of the seventeenth century – in the inland area that became known as Minas Gerais (General Mines) – changed the game.

The Portuguese Crown, impoverished by the long struggle with Spain, couldn't believe its good luck. It no longer needed to rely on the troublesome Cortes (Parliament) for funding and so simply stopped calling it, and the new-found riches meant that Portugal could buy textiles, manufactured and luxury goods, guns and pretty much anything else it needed from England and other European countries. The **Methuen Treaty** of 1703 formalized the trading relationship with England, expanding the market for Portuguese wine while allowing in English cloth tax-free.

The newly absolutist Crown enjoyed its greatest period of prosperity under the long-serving **João V** (1706–50), who did what all monarchs-with-money do – spent it, lavishly. Unequalled in Europe as a patron of the arts, João also built magnificent monuments to his own importance, chief of which was the extraordinary – some say obscene – palace-convent at Mafra, which has almost become a byword for lavish excess.

Early 1700s	1755	Late 1700s	Early 1800s
Poor decisions and lavish building programmes bankrupt the state	A huge earthquake flattens Lisbon	The Marquês de Pombal rebuilds the capital, modernizes the country and ejects the Jesuits	British forces help to repel Napoleon's invading army

Pombal and the 1755 earthquake

João was succeeded by his dilettante son, **José I** (1750–77), who had better things to do (mainly hunting, fishing and shooting) than rule a country. From the outset of his reign, power in the land instead was vested almost entirely in the hands of the monarch's Secretary of State, one Sebastião José de Carvalho e Melo, better known as the **Marquês de Pombal** (1699–1782).

Pombal's influence on Portuguese life was incalculable. Although not of royal birth he gave the country a single-minded, regal, autocratic direction, best seen in his reaction to the defining event of the age, the **Great Earthquake of 1755**, when the capital Lisbon was razed to the ground. His response ("Bury the dead, heal the living") was typically pragmatic, and Lisbon itself emerged from the rubble with a new, planned, ordered look that reflected the man himself.

Pombal's reforms chimed with the prevailing Age of Enlightenment, and Portugal's systems of trade, commerce, manufacturing, law and education were all overhauled. Pombal abolished slavery in Portugal, ended discrimination against "New Christian" converts and also took on the established Church – believing in particular that the Jesuits were acting as a break on further reform. Where there was opposition, it was dealt with ruthlessly, and when an assassination attempt on Dom José I in 1758 implicated the high-ranking Távora family, Pombal had them swiftly executed.

Such a personal hold on power relied on particular circumstances, and with the death of his royal "protector" José I, and the accession of the king's unsympathetic daughter, **Maria I** (1777–1816), Pombal's time was over. His reforms largely endured, however, while in "Pombaline" Lisbon – with its gridded plan, open squares and low-built earthquake-proof buildings – Europe was bequeathed one of its most gracious capital cities.

Napoleon – and the independence of Brazil

While the Portuguese monarchy had largely managed to keep the country out of foreign squabbles for over a century, it was **Napoleon** who dragged Portugal squarely into European affairs. In an attempt to wage economic war against the British he ordered the Portuguese to close their ports to their oldest allies and, when they proved understandably reluctant, Napoleon ordered in his generals, who in 1807 marched across Spain for Lisbon.

The royal family had already fled into exile in Brazil, and it was to be the British who led the fight for Portugal in the ensuing **Peninsular Wars**. British forces landed in Portugal in 1808, under their commander Arthur Wellesley, later Duke of Wellington, and – after victories and setbacks – finally wore the French down. Wellington's fortified "Lines of Torres Vedras" and the significant **Battle of Buçaco** (1810) gave the French army pause for thought, and when Napoleon turned his attention towards Russia he withdrew his army from Portugal in 1812, pursued by Wellington.

Even after the final defeat of Napoleon in 1815, Dom João VI and the Portuguese royal family remained in **Brazil**, with Portugal effectively a British military protectorate. Portugal was destitute – ravaged by war and the comings and goings of invading and protecting armies – and rumblings of domestic discontent grew louder, inspired by the advent of a liberal constitution in Spain, drawn up after the defeat of Napoleon. Brazil meanwhile had

1821	mid-1800s	late 1800s	1910
Safe from Napoleon, the Portuguese royal family return from Brazil	Instability in the court leads to virtual civil war	Lisbon's trams set forth as part of a public works programme	Portugal's last monarch flees to England at the birth of the Republic

been elevated from colony to kingdom in 1815 and was now an equal partner in a "United Kingdom of Portugal, Brazil and the Algarves" – subservient no longer.

In 1820, a liberal Cortes in Portugal formed a government, drew up a new constitution and, a year later, demanded the king's return from Brazil. João acceded but his attempts to maintain his United Kingdom split his family and came to naught. His queen, Dona Carlota, refused to accept the proposed limits on royal authority and was dispossessed of her title and position – becoming a figurehead of reactionary, absolutist opposition. João's son Pedro, meanwhile, was left in Brazil to rule as regent, but instead proclaimed **Brazilian independence** in 1822 (with that independence finally recognized by Portugal in 1825).

The death of the monarchy

The struggle between Liberals and Absolutists in Portugal, and between reform and repression, was set to define the rest of the century. After João VI's death in 1826, Pedro I of Brazil took the same route as his father before him and returned to Portugal as **Pedro IV**, but his reign – as of those of his daughter and grandsons – was mired in constitutional conflict that occasionally bordered on civil war. The monarchy – deprived of its cash-cow of Brazil, following that country's independence – was almost bankrupt, and the dynasty became fundamentally split between a Portuguese and a Brazilian line. The enduring influence of the Church stifled social progress, and old imperial interests in Africa were lost as Britain, Germany and Belgium carved up the continent between them; there were industrial disturbances and political unrest as **Republicanism** gained a foothold.

The endgame approached for the ruling family. **Dom Carlos I** (1889–1908) was assassinated as he travelled across Lisbon in 1908, killed by a shot from a Republican crowd. His oldest son also died in the attack, and the younger son, **Manuel II**, took up the throne. He was the last of the Braganças – and indeed the last of all – to be king of Portugal, forced into exile on October 5, 1910, by a **Republican revolution**. The royal yacht sailed from Ericeira to Gibraltar and on to Britain – all attempts to restore his throne failed and Manuel lived on in exile in London until his death in 1932.

The rule of Salazar

The first **Portuguese Republic**, although widely welcomed by parts of society (and rejected by others, notably the Church), never achieved its goals. Divisions among the Republicans, the cyclical attempts at violent overthrow of the new regime by monarchists, and the weakening of the country's economy kept the Republic in permanent turmoil. There were 45 changes of government in sixteen years, and several brief dictatorships and military uprisings.

Into such a volatile situation stepped **Dr António de Oliveira Salazar** (1889–1970), a pro-Church professor of economics at Coimbra University, who joined the regime in 1928 as Finance Minister. So effective was Salazar was quickly established as the leading light in the regime and appointed **Prime Minister** in 1932, while retaining close control over government spending and economic planning. A new constitution in 1933 gave him overarching, authoritarian powers under Portugal's **Second Republic** – powers that Salazar personally exercised until 1968.

early 1900s	1916–18	1928	1932–68
Political instability witnesses 45 changes in government in 16 years	Initially neutral, Portugal finally joins ally Britain in the war against Germany	Economics professor Dr António Salazar makes his mark as an impressive Finance Minister	Salazar rules Portugal as a virtual dictator

A FASCIST REGIME?

It's still a matter of hot debate as to whether **Salazar's regime** was fascist or simply deeply authoritarian and rightwing. The things it was opposed to certainly put it in the prevailing fascist camp – against communism, socialism or liberalism of any kind, with a repressive streak that was mirrored in both Germany and Italy. Political organizations were highly controlled, with his own party, the **National Union**, dogmatically supportive of the regime. Elections were rarely contested, rigid Catholicism became an integral part of the state education system, and censorship of the press was widespread. Salazar established a **secret police force** (the PVDE, later the PIDE) in 1933, modelled on the Gestapo, which kept tabs on leftwing political opponents and jailed many of them in detention camps on the Azores and the Cape Verde islands. During the Spanish Civil War, Salazar offered assistance to the Nationalists and turned over Republican refugees and sympathizers to Franco, knowing that they were certain to "disappear". Salazar's Portugal may not have been outwardly as brutal as Nazi Germany, or post-Civil War Spain under Franco, but there's little doubting the desensitizing effect his policies had on the country for decades.

Salazar's so-called **Estado Novo** or "New State" stabilized the economy but sowed the seeds of its prolonged downfall with its narrow, nationalistic outlook. There was no trickle-down effect as far as wealth was concerned, and Portugal remained woefully underdeveloped. The vast agricultural estates of the Alentejo saw no real improvement – scenes of rural work and life in the 1950s could have come straight out of a medieval engraving – and **emigration** was widespread. Large Portuguese populations in France, the US and elsewhere are a direct result of these impoverished years.

Portugal still had an empire, which ardent **colonialist** Salazar was determined to defend as part of "Greater Portugal", but the tide was turning in Africa and India. Goa was lost in 1961, while guerrilla activity increasingly spelled trouble for Portugal in Angola, Mozambique and Guinea-Bissau. The country began to find itself internationally isolated, economically stagnant and out of touch with the rising anticolonial sentiment in the world.

The end came in 1968 when Salazar suffered a brain hemorrhage and was replaced by his long-time colleague **Marcelo Caetano**. Salazar lived on until 1970 (apparently under the illusion that he was still Prime Minister), but the one-man state he had constructed was dismantled surprisingly quickly.

Revolution and democracy

Initially, after Salazar, there were limited government attempts to appease opposition at home, but it was unrest in the colonies that increasingly became the focus of dissent. The wars against the independence movements in Africa took a huge financial and personal toll, and an increasing number of younger soldiers and officers began to question Portugal's colonial isolationism. Many joined the revolutionary **Movimento das Forças Armadas** (Armed Forces Movement; **MFA**), while senior officers – up to the level of General António Ribeiro de Spínola – began openly to support democratic reform and military withdrawal from Africa. Thousands of other young men fled Portugal to avoid conscription.

1939–45	1950–65	1960s–1973	1974
"Neutral" Lisbon becomes a hotbed of wartime spies, including Ian Fleming	Salazar funds the construction of the Lisbon metro and a bridge over the Tagus	Portuguese troops increasingly sent abroad to contain uprisings in its colonies	The Carnation Revolution overthrows the old regime

On **April 25, 1974**, the Caetano government fell to a coup known as the *Revolução dos Cravos*, or **Carnation Revolution**. The signal was the playing of a song on the radio called *Grândola, Vila Morena'*, by a banned Portuguese political singer-songwriter; the carnations were the flowers handed to the revolutionary soldiers by the people who came out to celebrate a peaceful coup in which no shots were fired.

It was an exciting and liberating time for Portugal. Although there had been no general clamour for freedom at home before the coup, the days and weeks after April 25 saw a surge in popular political participation, with mass demonstrations and demands for change. A military junta sponsored by the MFA took charge, under the leadership of **General Spínola**, and prepared for eventual civilian government. It was not all plain sailing and the country saw increasing friction between communists and democrats, conservative peasants and liberal urban elite, north and south. The Church was still strong in the conservative north of the country, where ecclesiastical Braga saw itself as a bulwark against godless communism; in the Alentejo in the south, peasants enthusiastically grabbed the land and set up collective farms.

Portugal's first **free election** for half a century was held on the first anniversary of the Revolution, in April 1975, paving the way for a new constitution to replace that of Salazar's Estado Novo. After a so-called "hot summer" of political intrigue, there was one last twist as a communist-led counter-coup by elements of the MFA tried to seize power on November 25, 1975. The Carnation Revolution was safeguarded by the actions of General António dos Santos Ramalho Eanes, who put down the uprising, and new elections in April 1976 finally cemented **democratic government** in Portugal.

The Socialist Party won most seats and former exile **Mário Soares** became Portugal's first democratically elected Prime Minister, with the respected figure of General Eanes elected as President. Ultimately, right and left contested power for the next decade as Portugal came to terms with its new status, but Eanes and Soares provided a crucial consistency. Soares lost office between 1978 and 1983, but Eanes remained as President until 1986 – when he was replaced by none other than Soares, who had the distinction of becoming the first civilian President for sixty years.

END OF EMPIRE

The 1974 Revolution had a profound impact on **Portugal's former colonies**, which were not only granted **independence** virtually overnight – with no planning in place – but also lost large parts of their administration and labour force. The Portuguese troops went home, leaving a power vacuum, while hundreds of thousands of Portuguese citizens also relocated back to Portugal – the so-called *retornados*. Guinea-Bissau and Mozambique initially found independence beneficial (though damaging civil wars later followed), but Angola dissolved into full-scale civil war from the outset, which took decades to resolve. In East Timor, thousands were slain as Indonesia invaded in 1975 – they remained in brutal occupation until 1999. Only Cape Verde and Macau avoided bloodshed, though political maturity took time to evolve. In Portugal itself the colonial **retornados** posed yet more problems, as the mother country struggled to house and employ them. Their peaceful integration has been one of modern Portugal's greatest successes – though in the ongoing economic crisis the situation has been reversed, with many thousands of Portuguese people seeking better lives in the thriving economies of Angola and Mozambique.

late 1970s	1986	Early 1990s	1998
Thousands of refugees flood into Portugal from its former colonies	Political stability is ensured with entry into the European Community	European funds transform the country's infrastructure	Lisbon hosts the successful Expo 98, which spawns a new district and bridge over the Tagus; Portuguese author José Saramago wins the Nobel Prize for Literature

Portugal in Europe: the 1980s and 1990s

Portugal's entry into the **European Community** in 1986 brought with it the most important changes since the Revolution. With the help of a massive injection of funds, Portugal enjoyed unprecedented economic growth as roads, industry and communications received heavy investment. In 1992 Portugal assumed the presidency of the European Community, the year when all remaining trade and employment barriers were removed and the EC became the **European Union (EU)**.

The late 1990s saw a huge boost in Portuguese self-esteem. Lisbon's **Expo 98** was an enormous success, and the following year, **Portugal's last colony** – Macau – was handed back to Chinese rule, largely without the problems encountered by the UK with Hong Kong. Portugal also played a major role in the fate of former colony **East Timor**, which had endured a bloody 24-year rule by Indonesia following the 1974 Revolution. A UN-organized referendum in August 1999 saw an overwhelming vote in favour of independence. The Portuguese had been pushing for this for two decades – the feeling was of a long-standing obligation to a former colony that had finally been fulfilled.

Twenty-first-century Portugal

With EU funds flooding in, the first decade of the new millennium saw the country's infrastructure develop beyond recognition. Ambitious new roads and bridges were built; there was a new transport system in Porto and Lisbon's metro system was greatly expanded; and a series of fancy stadiums were built for the successful **2004 European Football Championships**.

Not surprisingly, Portugal was a flag-waver for the EU, and in December 2007 the draft constitution for the European Union – the so-called **Lisbon Treaty** – was signed in front of the Mosteiro dos Jerónimos in Belém. Portugal will forever be associated with the fundamental workings of the Union as a whole.

However, attitudes towards the EU have changed markedly since the global crash of 2008 and subsequent **European economic crisis**. Portugal plunged towards an inevitable request for an EU bailout, which ended Portugal's second Golden Age of lavish building as abruptly as the earthquake of 1755 had ended the first one. The new buzzword is austerity, managed by right-of-centre Prime Minister Pedro Passos Coelho, a previously little known former businessman and fado fan who was voted into power in June 2011. He quickly sold off state assets, including some of Portugal's power companies to China, and dramatically hiked tax rates, but despite these efforts the country is mired in recession. By 2013, unemployment stood at 18 percent, including 43 percent of those under the age of 25.

Despite massive **social change and economic restructuring**, the economy remains ill-equipped to compete successfully in the international arena. The bulk of Portugal's **industries** remain small or medium in scale, and have now to compete with Eastern European enterprises which have the advantage of lower labour costs and new EU funding. The country is also vulnerable to drought, especially in the south, affecting both **agriculture** – still a significant employer – and tourism. Unforeseen developments have even damaged traditional industries such as cork production: Portugal produces around half the world's cork, but the shift by wine-makers to plastic stoppers has threatened livelihoods.

1999	2004	2007
Portugal gives up its last colony, Macau	The Euro football championships are hosted in a series of state-of-the-art stadiums	Portugal joins the PIGS – that infamous band of countries (Portugal, Italy, Greece and Spain) whose failing economies threaten the future of the Eurozone

The future?

It's not all bad news. Successive governments have heavily promoted technology in work and education and there's been considerable investment in **communications technology**. Not only does Portugal have one of the world's highest densities of mobile phone use, it's also one of the few European countries with virtually universal high-speed internet coverage.

The country's dependence on imported energy has also been addressed by an ambitious **alternative energy programme**. An enormous solar farm near Moura in the Alentejo supplies the electricity needs of 30,000 homes, while northern Portugal boasts the world's biggest wind farm – the aim being for the country to produce over thirty percent of its primary energy from clean sources by 2020. **Tourism**, too, remains a reliable earner. Porto has joined Lisbon as a major city-break destination, and there is no sign that the popularity of the Algarve's beach resorts is dwindling.

2009	2010	2013
National superstar Cristiano Ronaldo becomes the world most expensive footballer when he is sold by Manchester United to Real Madrid for £80 million	Portuguese artist Paula Rego is made a British Dame	Garrett McNamara breaks the record for surfing the world's biggest wave – around thirty metres high – off the Nazaré coast

Fado – the people's soul

Portugal's most famous musical form, **fado** (or "fate"), opens a window onto the Portuguese soul. It's an urban music, a thing of night-time and bars, the origins of which are debatable but certainly involve influences from Portugal's overseas explorations. The essence of fado is *saudade* – an impossible-to-translate word that is nonetheless usually summed up as a "yearning" or "beautiful melancholy", and it's this that is expressed by the lyrical and sentimental expression of a solo singer, usually accompanied by the *guitarra* and *viola de fado*. The Portuguese are often mystified as to what a non-Portuguese-speaker could get from fado, since so much of its meaning lies buried in the poetic lyrics, but the beauty of soaring vocals over a silvery *guitarra* is certainly seductive.

Two working-class districts of Lisbon – **Mouraria** and **Alfama** – are considered the birthplace of fado, while the university city of Coimbra also has its own separate tradition. In both places – not to mention in towns and resorts across the country – you'll find clubs devoted to fado where you can experience something of the mystery that attaches itself to the art form. Many clubs are expensive, some are tourist-traps, some are both, and you may find the most memorable fado of all is performed by an unadvertised performer – when you're present at a special, real moment of fado you'll know it. **Fado clubs** are social places, with eating, drinking and informality, but during a song set in a good club the waiters don't serve, and the music is treated with due reverence.

Lisbon fado

The greatest name in fado – still – is **Amália Rodrigues**, who had an immeasurable impact upon the direction of fado through her recordings. Born in 1920 in the Alfama district of Lisbon, her death in October 1999 saw three days of official mourning announced in Portugal. Though over the course of her long singing career she ventured into other musical forms, her style and most celebrated recordings have become a central reference point for what people mean by fado.

It's not unusual for well-known Lisboan *fadistas* to run their own clubs. **Maria da Fé** owns the fado house *O Senhor Vinho*, where she and other notables perform. Seated at the long tables in the *Clube de Fado* in Alfama, you might well hear the owner **Mário Pacheco** himself, a fine guitarist and the last to play with Amália, accompanying another celebrated *fadista*, **Ana Sofia Varela**.

Coimbra fado

Coimbra fado has a very different style to that of Lisbon, reflecting that city's ancient university traditions. It's typically performed by students and Coimbra graduates, and is an exclusively male domain. As well as more formal songs that are less personally expressive than the Lisbon fado, there is also a strong aspect of *guitarra*-led instrumentals.

The most famous Coimbra *guitarra fadista* of the latter half of the twentieth century was **Carlos Paredes**, who combined enviable technical mastery with genuine feeling and expression, placing the fado guitar centre-stage alongside the singers it traditionally accompanied. Coimbra's instrumental fado continues to evolve in both traditional and new combinations: most of **Pedro Caldeira Cabral**'s compositions aren't fado as such, but they and his immense virtuosity on the *guitarra* can be seen as part of the legacy of Coimbra fado.

Nova canção and música popular

Coimbra fado also embarked on a new journey towards the modern Portuguese ballad, whose progenitor was the great **José Afonso**. He had a classic, soaring fado-style voice and his first recording, with Luís Góes in 1956, comprised fados from Coimbra together with his own more personal, contemporary songs. It's these, and his drawing upon regional traditional music and fado, that first formed the genre known during the last years of the Salazar dictatorship as **nova canção** ("new song"). Although censorship and the restriction of performing opportunities caused some songwriters to move and record abroad, Afonso remained in Portugal, masking his social and political messages with allegory, when necessary.

After the 1974 Revolution, an ever-growing number of singer-songwriters turned to contemporary matters in their music – social, cultural, political – and *nova canção* became known simply as **música popular**, both drawing on popular tradition while taking on board new influences from Latin America, Europe and North Africa. Afonso died in 1987, but his music is still very much a touchstone, while other singers and songwriters, such as **Amélia Muge**, continue to mix rural and fado traditions. You'll frequently hear songs by Afonso, Sergio Godinho and other *nova canção* leaders in the repertoire of fado singers.

Contemporary fado

Contemporary *fadistas* start with **Mariza**, now a veritable world-music superstar who frequently tours the globe. Also listen out for **Mísia**, **Cristina Branco**, **Kátia Guerreiro**, **Mafalda Arnauth** and male singers **Helder Moutinho** and **Camané**. At the same time, **Dona Rosa**, a blind former busker, is now receiving international acclaim after years of performing her very personal fado on the streets of Lisbon.

Many performers move in and out of fado, or mix aspects of it with other genres. For example, **Dulce Pontes** began in the world of rock-pop ballads, then for her second CD, *Lágrimas*, she performed fado and while she explores other genres it has remained a strong thread in her music. The music of long-standing Lisbon band **Madredeus** – a manicured blend of classical guitars and keyboards surrounding the songbird vocals of **Teresa Salgueiro** in songs largely by band leader Pedro Ayres Magalhães – while not fado as such is, nevertheless, replete with the reflective melancholy of *saudade*.

Playing fado – guitar and viola

The dominant instrument of fado is the **guitarra**, although its body isn't "guitar-shaped", but that of an Arabic lute, introduced over a thousand years ago by the Moors. Two designs evolved – the Lisbon *guitarra*, usually used for accompanying singers, and the larger and richer version more suited to Coimbra fado, with its strong *guitarra*-virtuoso strand. Both have six pairs of steel strings.

The *guitarra* is usually accompanied by a six-string guitar of the Spanish form, known in Portugal as a **viola**. Though the *viola de fado* is usually a normal Spanish guitar, there is a remarkable range of other specifically Portuguese violas. The version encountered most often, particularly in the north, is the *viola braguesa*, which has five pairs of strings and is usually played *rasgado* (a fast, intricate, rolling strum with an opening hand). A slightly smaller close relative, from the region of Amarante, is the *viola amarantina*, while other varieties include the ten- or twelve-stringed *viola campanica alentejana* and the *viola beiroa*.

Books

There are plenty of books available in English covering Portuguese history and society, and also lots of fiction in translation. It's always worth checking the latest output from UK publisher Carcanet Press (ⓦcarcanet.co.uk), which has a series entitled "Aspects of Portugal". Publishers are given below for books published only in Portugal.

ART, CULTURE AND BIOGRAPHY

Helder Carita and Homem Cardoso *Portuguese Gardens*. A huge, beautiful tome, lavishly illustrated with photographs and plans, with a scholarly text.

Miles Danby *The Fires of Excellence*. Magnificent and detailed study of the Oriental architecture of Spain and Portugal, illustrated with specially commissioned photographs.

Júlio Gil and Augusto Cabrita *The Finest Castles in Portugal*. A superb illustrated survey of Portuguese castles, let down a little by pedestrian text.

Matthew Hancock *Xenophobe's Guide to the Portuguese*. An irreverent and affectionate look by Rough Guide author, at what makes the Portuguese Portuguese. It contains cultural insights ranging from why the nation is so child

friendly to Portuguese driving habits, business etiquette and why coffee and salted cod are so revered.

Luís Lourenço and José Mourinho *Made in Portugal*. The authorized biography of Portugal's most successful football manager José Mourinho, tracing his career from translator with Bobby Robson at Sporting Lisbon to manager of European Champions Porto, and onwards to a multi-million-pound salary with Chelsea.

Anne de Stoop *Living in Portugal*. A glossy coffee-table tome filled with beautifully evocative photographs of Portugal's sights and architectural gems, from palaces and rural houses to *pastelarias* and restaurants.

FICTION

Monica Ali *Alentejo Blue*. Best known for *Brick Lane*, which looked at the difficulties Asian immigrants face in London, Monica Ali here turns her gaze to expat immigrants and would-be emigrants in a small, rural Alentejan village. Ali, who has a holiday home in the region, creates an atmospheric but ultimately inconsequential world where nothing much happens – evoking perfectly the Alentejo.

António Lobo Antunes *An Explanation of the Birds; The Natural Order of Things; Act of the Damned; The Return of the Caravels;* and *South of Nowhere*. Psychologically astute and with a helter-skelter prose style, Antunes is considered by many to be Portugal's finest contemporary writer after Saramago. *The Return of the Caravels*, a modern "take" on the Discoveries, is a good place to start.

Mario de Carvalho *A God Strolling in the Cool of the Evening*. Set in the third century AD, this fascinating novel traces the life of a Roman magistrate whose Lusitanian town is threatened by subversive Christians and the prospect of attack from the Moors. Summing up the circumstances that ultimately destroyed the Roman Empire, the book won the Pegasus Prize for Fiction in 1996.

★ **Lídia Jorge** *The Migrant Painter of Birds*. Born near Albufeira in 1946, Lídia Jorge is one of Portugal's most respected contemporary writers. This beautifully written novel describes a girl's memories as she grows up in a small village close to the Atlantic, and in doing so poignantly captures a changing rural community.

Ray Keenoy, David Treece and Paul Hyland *The Babel Guide to the Fiction of Portugal, Brazil and Africa*. A tantalizing introduction to Portuguese literature, with a collection of reviews of the major works of Lusophone fiction since 1945.

Eugénio Lisboa (ed) *The Anarchist Banker and Other Portuguese Stories; Professor Pfiglzz and His Strange Companion and Other Portuguese Stories; The Dedalus Book of Portuguese Fantasy*. These collections of twentieth-century short stories give more than a taste of the exuberance and talent currently proliferating in Portuguese literature. Stories by old favourites – Eça de Queirós, Pessoa, José Régio and Miguel Torga – are included, too.

Pascal Mercier *Night Train to Lisbon*. This slow-burner by a Swiss philosophy professor explores the adventures of an elderly teacher in Bern. Spontaneously giving up his job, he sets off on a train to learn more about an inspirational Portuguese writer. Piecing together the writer's life in pre- and post-revolutionary Lisbon, the teacher begins an insightful journey of self-discovery.

José Rodrigues Miguéis *Happy Easter*. A powerful and disturbing account of the distorted reality experienced by a schizophrenic, whose deprived childhood leads him to a self-destructive and tragic life in Lisbon; evocatively written and a gripping read.

★ **José Luís Peixoto** *The Piano Cemetery*. Loosely based on a real Portuguese marathon runner who died in the

1912 Stockholm Olympics, Peixoto's novel is a dazzling fragmented mosaic of episodes from the lives of carpenters who run a piano workshop in Lisbon. The workshop introduces romance, intrigue and betrayal into three generations of a family fated to repeat each other's mistakes, but who are ultimately bonded by a deep loyalty and love. Beautifully written, it's the sort of book that you want to reread the minute you've finished it.

★ **Fernando Pessoa** *Book of Disquiet; A Centenary Pessoa; The Education of the Stoic: The Only Manuscript of the Baron of Teive*. The country's best-known poet wrote *The Book of Disquiet* in prose; it's an unclassifiable text compiled from unordered fragments, part autobiography, part philosophical rambling. Regarded as a Modernist classic, the Penguin edition is the most complete English version. *A Centenary Pessoa* includes a selection of his prose and poetry, including his works under the pseudonym of Ricardo Reis. *The Education of the Stoic* was compiled in 1999 from the Pessoa archives in Lisbon. Written under the heteronym the "Baron of Teive", it is a bleak work exploring the impossibility of producing perfect art by an artist who bins all his output before destroying himself.

★ **Eça de Queirós** *The Sin of Father Amaro; The City and the Mountains; Cousin Bazilio; The Maias; The Illustrious House of Ramires; To the Capital; The Yellow Sofa; and Three Portraits*. One of Portugal's greatest writers, Eça de Queirós (or Queiroz; 1845–1900) introduced realism into Portuguese fiction with *The Sin of Father Amaro*, published in 1876. It was recently given contemporary treatment in a successful Mexican film, *The Crime of Father Amaro*. Over half a dozen of his novels have been translated into English; always highly readable, they

present a cynical but affectionate picture of Portuguese society in the second half of the nineteenth century. His *English Letters*, written during his long stint as consul in England, is also recommended.

José Régio *Flame Coloured Dress*. Like Eça de Queirós, Régio examines how society imposes restrictions on everyday life. *Flame Coloured Dress* is a series of vivid short stories, each one about the struggles of a woman but in very different circumstances, from a society woman to one suffering abject poverty.

Erich Maria Remarque *The Night in Lisbon*. Better known as author of *All Quiet on the Western Front*, German author Remarque writes with a similar detachment in this tale of a World War II refugee seeking an escape route from Europe. One night in Lisbon, he meets a stranger who has two tickets, and within hours their lives are inextricably linked in a harrowing and moving tale.

Mário de Sá-Carneiro *The Great Shadow* and *Lucio's Confessions*. *The Great Shadow* is a collection of short stories set against the backdrop of Lisbon in the early 1900s as the author describes his obsession with great art. Sá-Carneiro, who committed suicide at 26, writes with stunning intensity and originality about art, science, death, homosexual sex and insanity. Similar themes appear in *Lucio's Confessions*, in which a *ménage à trois* between artists ends in a death.

★ **José Saramago** *All the Names; Baltasar and Blimunda; Blindness; The History of the Siege of Lisbon; The Year of the Death of Ricardo Reis; The Gospel According to Jesus Christ; The Stone Raft; The Tale of the Unknown Island; Manual of Painting and Calligraphy; The Cave; The Double; Seeing; Death with Interruptions; Small Memories; The Trip*

EÇA DE QUEIRÓS

In a series of outstanding novels, the writer **Eça de Queirós** (1845–1900) turned his unflinching gaze on the shortcomings of his native land. While his earlier novels, such as *The Sin of Father Amaro* (1875) and *Cousin Bazilio* (1878), reveal a clear debt to French naturalism in their satirical intent, his mature writings offer a more measured critique of contemporary Portuguese society. Novels like *The Illustrious House of Ramires* (1900) work by gradually building up a picture of decadence and inertia, through an assemblage of acutely observed vignettes tinged with a sardonic but always affectionate humour.

Eça's cosmopolitan outlook was a result of both his background and of the fact that he was extremely well-travelled. Born out of wedlock, he was brought up by his paternal grandparents in the north of Portugal in an atmosphere of liberal political ideas. He studied law at Coimbra University, where he joined a group of young intellectuals (known as the "Generation of 1870") dedicated to the idea of reforming and modernizing the country. His adult years were spent as a career diplomat and for much of the 1870s and 1880s he was a consul in England, first in Newcastle upon Tyne, then in Bristol.

Oddly enough, it was at Newcastle that Eça wrote much of his masterpiece *The Maias* (1888), a complex portrayal of an aristocratic, land-owning family unable, or unwilling, to adapt to changing times. Focusing on three generations of male family members, Eça brilliantly conveys what he sees as a peculiarly Portuguese indolence and hedonism that invariably acts as a curb to good intentions – a condition that becomes a metaphor for the country's inwardness and lack of ambition.

of the Elephant; and Cain. Saramago (1922–2010) won the Nobel Prize for Literature in 1998 and is Portugal's most famous contemporary writer. His novels have come thick and fast and are mostly experimental, often dispensing with punctuation altogether; Blindness even avoided naming a single character and was recently made into a successful film, directed by Fernando Meirelles. Start with Ricardo Reis, whose theme is the return of Dr. Reis, after sixteen years in Brazil, to a Lisbon where the Salazar dictatorship is imminent and where Reis wanders the streets to be confronted by the ghost of the writer Fernando Pessoa. In Baltasar and Blimunda, Saramago mixes fact with myth in an entertaining novel set around the building of the Convent of Mafra and the construction of the world's first flying machine.

Antonio Tabucchi Declares Pereira; Requiem: A Hallucination; and Fernando Pessoa (with Maria José de Lancastre). Tabucchi is a highly regarded Italian author who lived in Portugal for many years and is a biographer of Pessoa. In Declares Pereira he has re-created the repressive atmosphere of Salazar's Lisbon, tracing the experiences of a newspaper editor who questions his own lifestyle under a regime he can no longer ignore. The book has recently been made into a film by Roberto Faenza. Requiem: A Hallucination is an imaginative and dream-like journey around Lisbon. The unifying theme is food and drink, and the book even contains a note on recipes at the end.

Miguel Torga The Creation of the World and Tales from the Mountain. Twice nominated for the Nobel Prize before his death in 1995, Torga lived and set his stories in the wild Trás-os-Montes region. His pseudonym "Torga" is a tough species of heather that thrives in this rural, unforgiving landscape, where the fiercely independent characters of his books battle to survive in a repressed society. Torga's harsh views of rural life in Tales from the Mountain led to the book being banned under the Salazar regime.

Gil Vicente Three Discovery Plays: Auto da Barca do Inferno, Exortação da Guerra, Auto da Índia. Three plays from the sixteenth-century scribe who some consider the Portuguese equivalent of Shakespeare, with the original archaic Portuguese versions alongside English translations, and copious notes.

Robert Wilson A Small Death in Lisbon. A policeman attempts to find the murderer of a girl found dumped near a beach on the train line to Cascais, opening up a can of worms stretching back to the last World War. The novel presents an evocative account of the seedier side of contemporary Lisbon, though its potted summary of the World War II is less convincing. A gripping page-turner from a British author who lives in Portugal.

Richard Zimler The Last Kabbalist of Lisbon. Kabbalah is a mystical art based on an esoteric interpretation of the Old Testament. American author Zimler, now a resident of Porto, writes an intense and compelling story of a Jewish kabbalist attempting to discover the mystery behind his uncle's murder during the massacre of New Christians in Lisbon in 1506. Based on historical fact, the story has been a bestseller in Portugal, Italy and Brazil.

FOOD AND WINE

Jean Anderson Food of Portugal. The best of the cookbooks by non-Portuguese writers; a wonderful tour of the gastronomic horizon with easy-to-follow recipes.

Rainer Horbelt and Sonja Spindler Algarve Country Cooking (Vista Ibérica, Portugal). A series of regional recipes based round local anecdotes and the four seasons; well translated from German and a charming insight into rural Algarve traditions.

★ **Tessa Kiros** Piri Piri Starfish. A range of great Portuguese recipes, but the big pull here is the photos that are so good you could eat them.

Richard Mayson The Wines and Vineyards of Portugal. A wide-ranging, award-winning account of all you need to know about Portuguese wines by a passionate expert in the field.

Charles Metcalfe and Kathryn McWhirter The Wine and Food Lover's Guide to Portugal. A true labour of love, and an encyclopedic guide to the country's finest wine, regional cuisines, gastro destinations, food shops, markets and more. It's an essential luggage-item for anyone interested in visiting Portugal's vineyards and is based on serious research – the wine-critic authors have tasted every wine mentioned in the book!

Ana Patuleia Ortins Portuguese Homestyle Cooking. All the classics: easy-to-follow regional recipes collected by a first-generation Portuguese-American, peppered with fun anecdotes, stories and photos.

GUIDES

Brian and Eileen Anderson Landscapes of Portugal (Sunflower Books, online only; ⓦ sunflowerbooks.co.uk). Regional books with maps and small photos detailing walks – covering the Algarve, Lisbon areas and northern Portugal; there are also car tours and some practical information.

Bethan Davies and Ben Cole Walking in Portugal. Dependable guide to trekking in the national parks of Gerês, Serra da Estrela, Montesinho and Serra de São Mamede.

Chris Nelson and Demi Taylor Surfing Europe. A glossy tome for the dedicated surfer, with tips on how to find and surf the best Atlantic waves from Orkney to Morocco. The Portugal section is detailed and comprehensive, backed up by some fine colour photographs.

Oleg Polunin and B.E. Smythies *Flowers of South-West Europe: A Field Guide*. The best available guide to Portuguese flora.

Laurence Rose *Where to Watch Birds in Spain and Portugal*. Comprehensive guide to some of Europe's finest and most environmentally sensitive wildlife sites, with practical information on how to get there and when to go. Interesting reading for amateurs as well as being invaluable for ardent ornithologists.

HISTORY AND POLITICS

Nigel Cliff *The Last Crusade*. A kind of Hilary Mantelesque treatment of the Age of Discoveries, focussing in particular on Vasco da Gama's mammoth voyage to India. Placing it firmly in the context of earlier crusades, Cliff neatly captures the historical misunderstandings between – and driving passions of – the great cultures of the East and West.

Peter Daughtrey *Atlantis and the Silver City*. British researcher Daughtrey argues the case that Silves, in the Algarve, was the fabled city of Atlantis, claiming it matches 60 of Plato's clues and that its demise probably was the result of a similar earthquake to the one that flattened Lisbon in 1755. A fascinating premise.

★ **Edward Paice** *Wrath of God*. Vivid, readable and evocative account of Lisbon before, during and after the Great Earthquake of 1755.

★ **José Hermano Saraiva** *Companion History of Portugal*. An accessible, generously illustrated and concise history of the country written especially for non-specialist foreigners by the author of the bestselling Portuguese original. Includes easy-reference glossaries of historical figures and places.

Ronald Watkins *Unknown Seas: How Vasco da Gama Opened the East*. The fascinating story of Vasco da Gama's voyage and triumphant return, which paved the way for the runaway expansion of the Portuguese empire. It's a well-told tale that rattles along.

Patrick Wilcken *Empire Adrift*. The Portuguese royal family fled from the French to Brazil in 1807 and established a court in exile there for 13 years. It was a move that was to change both Brazil and the path of the monarchy in Portugal, as this lively account of the fluctuating fortunes of João VI and his family shows.

POETRY

★ **Luís de Camões** *The Lusiads; Epic and Lyric; Selected Sonnets*. Portugal's great national epic, *The Lusiads* (*Os Lusíadas*) was written in 1572, taking Virgil's *Aeneid* as its inspiration. The Oxford Classics is a good verse translation by Landeg White. *Epic and Lyric* includes extracts from *The Lusiads* together with other shorter poems, while *Selected Sonnets* shows the development of his remarkable lyrical poetry both before and after his experiences in Africa and India.

Sofia de Mello Breyner *Breyner Log Book: Selected Poems*. Evocative selection of translated poems from one of the country's foremost writers, winner of the 1999 Prémio Camões.

Fernando Pessoa *Pessoa: Selected Poems*. Pessoa wrote his poetry under several different identities, which he called heteronyms. Those wanting a brief introduction to the range of his different "voices" are well served by Jonathan Griffin's elegant translations of four of them. *A Centenary Pessoa* is a superlative anthology of poems, prose, letters and photographs, and the most comprehensive selection of Pessoa's output yet published in English. *Fernando Pessoa*, available only in Portugal (Hazan, Portugal), is a revealing collection of documents and photographs of the author at work, with an introduction by Antonio Tabucchi.

Pedro Tamen *Honey and Poison: Selected Poems*. Lisbon law graduate Tamen is regarded as one of Portugal's leading contemporary poets; his poems of passion capture the distinctive sights and emotions of a country which has moved from dictatorship to democracy during his lifetime.

TRAVEL WRITING

William Beckford *Recollections of an Excursion to the Monasteries of Alcobaça and Batalha; Travels in Spain and Portugal (1778–88)*. There's rarely been a more entertaining traveller in Portugal than the wildly wealthy Beckford – eccentric seems a woefully inadequate description – and his journals and tales still delight.

Paul Hyland *Backwards Out of the Big World*. A fascinating and sympathetic account of a journey through Portugal by a man who knows the country's people, history and literature as few foreigners do.

★ **Marion Kaplan** *The Portuguese: the Land and its People*. A readable, all-embracing volume, covering everything from wine to the family, poetry and the land. A little dated perhaps, but still the best general introduction to the country.

Rose Macaulay *They Went to Portugal*. Old-school travel writing that takes a Brit's-eye view of visits to Portugal through the ages, from medieval times onwards. There was a follow-up volume, *They Went to Portugal, Too*.

Fernando Pessoa *Lisbon: What the Tourist Should See* (*O que o turista deve ver*) (Livros Horizonte, Portugal). Written in English and Portuguese (but only available in Portugal), Pessoa's 1925 guidebook describes a Lisbon that is largely recognizable today.

Portuguese

If you have some knowledge of Spanish you won't have much problem reading Portuguese. Understanding it when it's spoken, though, is another matter: pronunciation is entirely different and at first even the easiest words are hard to distinguish. But it's well worth the effort to master at least the rudiments – certainly the locals will be pleased you've made an effort and you'll be congratulated on even your most excruciating manglings of the language.

The **pronunciation and phrasebook guide** below will equip you with the basics, and there's also a full **menu reader**, so you shouldn't ever be stuck for choice in a restaurant. For more detail, purchase the *Rough Guide Portuguese Phrasebook*, set out dictionary-style for easy access.

Pronunciation

The chief difficulty with pronunciation is its lack of clarity – consonants tend to be slurred, while vowels are nasal and often contracted to the point of being ignored.

CONSONANTS

C is soft before E and I, hard otherwise unless it has a cedilla – açucar (sugar) is pronounced "assookar".

CH is somewhat softer than in English; chá (tea) sounds like "shah".

J is pronounced like the "s" in pleasure.

G as in English, except before E and I, when it's also like the "s" in pleasure.

LH sounds like "lyuh" (Batalha is pronounced "Batalyuh").

M as in English, except at the end of a word when it's more like a nasal "-ng" – com (with) is pronounced "kong" (without sounding the G).

Q is always pronounced as a "K".

S before a consonant or at the end of a word becomes "sh", otherwise it's as in English – Cascais is pronounced "Kashkaish", adeus (goodbye) is "a-day-ush".

X is also pronounced "sh" – caixa (cash desk) is pronounced "kaisha".

VOWELS

E at the end of a word is virtually silent unless it has an accent, so that verde (green) is pronounced "verd", while café is pronounced "ca-**feh**".

Ã and Õ The tilde renders the pronunciation much like the French -an and -on endings, only more nasal.

ÃO Sounds something like a strangled yelp of "Ow!"

cut off in midstream (as in pão, bread – são, saint – limão, lemon).

EI and OU Sound like the "ay" in day and the "oh" in dough respectively (though when other two vowels come together they continue to be enunciated separately).

Portuguese words and phrases

GREETINGS AND QUESTIONS

hello; good morning	olá; bom dia	what's this called in Portuguese?	como se diz isto em Português?
good afternoon/night	boa tarde/noite	can you write it down?	pode escrever isso?
goodbye, see you later	adeus, até logo	do you know…?	sabe…?
everything all right?	tudo bem?	could you…?	pode…?
it's all right/OK	está bem	it doesn't matter	não faz mal
I don't know	não sei	you're welcome	de nada
I don't understand	não compreendo		

do you speak English?	fala Inglês?	what's your name?	como se chama?
where are you from?	de onde é?	my name is…	chamo-me…
I am from…	sou de…	what time is it?	que horas são?

USEFUL WORDS AND SIGNS

yes; no	sim; não	campsite	um parque de
please	por favor/se faz favor		campismo
thank you	obrigado/a*	Is there a…near	Há um/a…aqui
sorry; excuse me	desculpe; com licença	here?	perto?
today; tomorrow;	hoje; amanhã; ontem	Do you have a room?	Tem um quarto?
midday, noon/midnight	meio-dia; meia-noite	I'd like a room for…	Queria um quarto para…
where; what	onde; que	one person/	uma pessoa/
when; why	quando; porquê	two people	duas pessoas
how; how much	como; quanto	with two beds/	com duas camas/
with; without	com; sem	a double bed	um casal
here; there	aqui; ali	with a private	com casa de
near; far	perto; longe	bathroom	banho privado
this; that	este/a; aquele/a	It's for one night/	É para uma noite/
now; later	agora; mais tarde	one week	uma semana
more; less	mais; menos	May I see it?	Posso ver?
big; little	grande; pequeno	How much is it?	Quanto custa?
open; closed	aberto; fechado	OK, I'll take it	Está bem, fico com ele
push; pull	empurre; puxe	I'd like to make a	Queria fazer uma
entrance; exit	entrada; saída	reservation	reserva
danger; dangerous	perigo; perigoso	I have a reservation	Tenho uma reserva

*Obrigado agrees with the sex of the person
speaking – a woman says obrigada, a man
obrigado.

TRANSPORT

Where is…	Onde é…
the bus station?	a estação de camionetas/ terminal rodoviária?
the bus stop for…?	a paragem de autocarro para…?
Is there a bus to…?	Há uma camioneta/ autocarro para…?
Where does the bus to…leave from?	Donde parte o autocarro para…?
Stop here please	Pare aqui por favor
Where is the railway station?	Onde é a estação de comboios?
Is this the train for…?	É este o comboio para…?
What time does it leave? (arrive at…?)	A que horas parte? (chega a…?)
I'd like a ticket to…	Queria um bilhete para…
one-way/return	ida/ida e volta

ACCOMMODATION

I'm looking for a…	Procuro…
pension/	uma pensão/
hotel/	um hotel/uma
youth hostel/	pousada da juventude/

DRIVING AND DIRECTIONS

Which is the road to…?	Qual é a estrada para…?
left, right	esquerda, direita
straight ahead	sempre em frente
air; tyre	ar; pneu
oil	óleo
petrol; diesel (unleaded)	gasolina; gasóleo (sem chumbo)
Fill it up please	Encha, se faz favor
diversion	desvio
roadworks	obras
no entry	passagem proibida
no parking	proibido estacionar/ estacionamento proibido
Can I park here?	Posso estacionar aqui?
motorway	autoestrada
tollbooth	portagem
petrol station	bomba de gasolina
driving licence; documents	carta de conduçao; documentos

SHOPPING

what's that?	O que é isso?
I want to buy…	Quero comprar…
how much is it?	Quanto é?
I'd like a bag	Queria um saco
slices/sliced	fatias/fatiado

fresh; can (tinned)	fresco; lata (em lata)	November	Novembro
litre	litro	December	Dezembro
market	mercado		
minimarket/grocery	minimercado/mercearia	**NUMBERS**	
supermarket	supermercado	one	um/uma
organic/organic	biológico/produtos	two	dois/duas
produce	biológicos	three	três
weight/to weigh	peso/pesar	four	quatro
kilo	quilo	five	cinco
unit	unidade	six	seis
bakery; butchers	padaria; talho	seven	sete
bank; exchange	banco; câmbio	eight	oito
bookshop; laundry	livraria; lavandaria	nine	nove
correios; selos	post office; stamps	ten	dez
(dois) selos	(two) stamps	eleven	onze
pharmacy/chemist	farmácia	twelve	doze
includes VAT	incluído IVA	thirteen	treze
		fourteen	catorze
DAYS OF THE WEEK		fifteen	quinze
Sunday	Domingo	sixteen	dezasseis
Monday	Segunda-feira	seventeen	dezassete
Tuesday	Terça-feira	eighteen	dezoito
Wednesday	Quarta-feira	nineteen	dezanove
Thursday	Quinta-feira	twenty	vinte
Friday	Sexta-feira	twenty-one	vinte e um
Saturday	Sábado	thirty	trinta
		forty	quarenta
MONTHS		fifty	cinquenta
January	Janeiro	sixty	sessenta
February	Fevereiro	seventy	setenta
March	Março	eighty	oitenta
April	Abril	ninety	noventa
May	Maio	100	cem
June	Junho	101	cento e um
July	Julho	200	duzentos
August	Agosto	500	quinhentos
September	Setembro	1000	mil
October	Outubro	2000	dois mil

MENU READER

BASICS

Açucár	Sugar	mexidos/quentes/	scrambled/soft-boiled/
Arroz	Rice	estrelados)	fried)
Azeite	Olive oil	Pão (trigo/centeio/	Bread (wheat/rye/
Azeitonas	Olives	caseiro/intégral)	rustic/wholemeal)
Broa	Cornbread	Pimenta (preta/branca)	Pepper (black/white)
Farinha	Flour	Queijo	Cheese
Manteiga	Butter	Sal	Salt
Massa	Pasta	Salada	Salad
Molho de tomate	Tomato/chilli sauce/	Vinagre	Vinegar
	piri-piri		
Omeleta	Omelette	**IN A RESTAURANT**	
Ovos (cozidos/	Eggs (hard-boiled/	Ementa (turística/do dia)	Menu (set menu)
escalfados/	poached/	Prato do dia	Dish of the day
		Carta dos vinhos	Wine list

Dose (uma dose/ meia dose)	Portion (full/half)
Pequeno almoço	Breakfast
Almoço	Lunch
Jantar	Dinner
Petiscos	Snacks, tapas
Entrada	Starter
Sobremesa	Dessert
Prato	Plate
Chávena	Cup
Copo	Glass
Garrafa	Bottle
Faca	Knife
Garfo	Fork
Colher	Spoon
Conta	Bill

COOKING TERMS

A vapor	Steamed
Assado/no espeto	Roasted/spit-roasted
Bem passado/mal passado	Well done/rare
Caril	Curry
Caseiro	Home-made
Cozido	Boiled/stewed
Empada	Pie
Ensopado	Soup or stew
Estrelado	Fried
Frio	Cold
Frito	Fried
Fumado	Smoked
Gratinado	Gratin
Grelhado/na grelha	Grilled
Guisado	Stewed
Mexido	Scrambled
Molho	Sauce
Na brasa	Chargrilled, braised
No churrasco	Chargrilled
No forno	Baked
Panado	Breadcrumbed and fried
Picante	Spicy/hot
Piri-piri	With chilli sauce
Quente	Hot
Recheado	Stuffed
Salgado	Salted
Salteado	Sautéed

FISH (*PEIXE*) AND SHELLFISH (*MARISCOS*)

Ameijoas	Clams
Anchovas	Anchovies
Atum	Tuna
Besugo	Bream
Camarões	Shrimp
Caranguejo	Crab
Carapau	Mackerel
Cherne	Sea bream
Chocos	Cuttlefish
Congro	Conger eel
Dourada	Bream
Enguia	Eel
(Peixe) Espada	Scabbard fish
Espadarte	Swordfish
Gambas	Prawns
Garoupa	Grouper
Lagosta	Lobster
Lampreia	Lamprey (similar to eel)
Linguado	Sole
Lulas	Squid
Mexilhões	Mussels
Ostras	Oysters
Pargo	Snapper
Perceves	Goose barnacles
Pescada	Hake
Polvo	Octopus
Robalo	Sea bass
Salmão	Salmon
Salmonete	Red mullet
Santolas	Spider crabs
Sapateiras	Common crabs
Sarda	Mackerel
Sardinhas	Sardines
Tamboril	Monkfish
Truta	Trout
Vieiras	Scallops

MEAT (*CARNE*), POULTRY (*AVES*) AND GAME (*CAÇA*)

Almôndegas	Meatballs
Bife	Steak
Borrego	Lamb
Bucho	Haggis
Cabrito	Kid goat
Carne picada	Mincemeat
Chouriço	Cured sausage
Coelho	Rabbit
Cordeiro	Lamb
Cordoniz	Quail
Costeleta	Chop/cutlet
Dobrada	Tripe
Enchidos	Smoked sausages
Entrecosto	Spare rib
Escalope	Escalope
Farinheira	Floury sausage
Febras	Thin pork steaks
Fiambre	Boiled/cured ham
Fígado	Liver
Frango	Chicken
Fumeiros	Smoked meats
Javali	Wild boar

Leitão	Suckling pig
Linguiça	Cured sausage
Lombo	Loin, fillet or tenderloin
Medalhão	Medallion
Moela	Gizzard
Morcela	Black pudding, blood sausage
Paio	Cured sausage
Pata/Pé	Hoof/foot
Pato	Duck
Perdiz	Partridge
Perna	Leg
Perú	Turkey
Picanha	Brazilian sliced rump steak
Pomba	Pigeon
Porco	Pork
Presunto	Smoked ham
Rim	Kidney
Salpicão/salsicha	Smoked sausage/sausage
Tripas	Tripe
Vitela	Veal

VEGETABLES (*LEGUMES* OR *HORTALIÇAS*) AND SALAD (*SALADA*)

Abacate	Avocado
Abóbora	Pumpkin
Agriões	Watercress
Alcachofra	Artichoke
Alface	Lettuce
Alho	Garlic
Alho Francês	Leek
Batatas (fritas/ cozidas/a murro)	Potatoes (French fries/ boiled/jacket)
Berlingela	Aubergine
Cebola	Onion
Cenoura	Carrot
Coentro	Coriander
Cogumelo	Mushroom
Couve	Cabbage
Couve-flor	Cauliflower
Ervilha	Pea
Espargos	Asparagus
Espinafre	Spinach
Fava	Broad bean
Feijão	Bean
Feijão-frade	Black-eyed bean
Feijão-verde/-vermelho	Green bean/kidney bean
Grão(-de-bico)	Chickpea
Nabo	Turnip
Pepino	Cucumber
Pimento	Sweet pepper
Salsa	Parsley
Tomate	Tomato

FRUIT (*FRUTA*)

Ameixas	Plums
Ananás/Abacaxi	Pineapple
Cerejas	Cherries
Damascos	Apricots
Figo	Fig
Framboesas	Raspberries
Frutas silvestres	Berries, forest fruits
Goiaba	Guava
Laranja	Orange
Limão	Lemon
Maçã	Apple
Manga	Mango
Maracujá	Passion fruit
Melancia	Water melon
Melão	Melon
Meloa	Cantaloupe or Carmargue melon
Morangos	Strawberries
Pêra	Pear
Pêssego	Peach
Romã	Pomegranate
Tangerina	Tangerine
Toranja	Grapefruit
Uvas	Grapes

DESSERTS (*SOBREMESAS*), SWEETS (*DOCES*) AND PASTRIES (*PASTÉIS*)

Arroz doce	Rice pudding
Bolo	Cake
Broa de mel	Soft cornflour and honey cake
Doces conventuais	Sweet egg-based "Convent desserts"
Gelado	Ice cream
Maçapão	Marzipan
Mel	Honey
Mil-folhas	Puff pastry (mille feuille)
Pastel de nata	Custard tart
Pudim, Pudim flan	Crème caramel
Queijadas	Cheese cakes
Suspiro	Meringue
Tarte	Tart
Torta de arroz/feijão/ cenoura/chila de amêndoa/ amendoim/noz/ nata/mel	Roll...with rice/beans/ carrot/pumpkin ...with almonds/ peanuts/walnuts or nuts/pumpkin/cream or custard/honey

PORTUGUESE SPECIALITIES

| Açorda (de marisco) | Bread-based stew (with shellfish, garlic and coriander) |

Alheira	A fried pork-free "sausage" from Trás-os-Montes, traditionally of minced chicken and bread – more like a rissole than a sausage	Caldo verde	Cabbage/potato broth (with or without *chouriço*)
		Canja de galinha	Chicken broth with rice and boiled egg yolks
		Cataplana	The name of the copper cooking vessel – most commonly used to cook shellfish, particularly clams (*ameijoas*), with smoked ham, pepper and onion
Ameijoas à Bulhão Pato	Clams sautéed with garlic and coriander (named after a 19th-century Portuguese poet)		
Arroz de… …cabidela/pato/ polvo	Rice… enriched with chicken blood/with shredded duck/with octopus	Chanfana	Goat/kid stew, braised in red wine, a Beiras dish
Arroz de mariscos	A thick, soupy seafood rice	Coelho à caçadora	"Hunter's rabbit", a stew with tomatoes and garlic
Bacalhau…	Dried salt cod, soaked and then cooked…	Cozido à portuguesa	Boiled casserole of pork, beef, blood sausage, offal, beans, cabbage and carrots, served with rice
com batatas e grão	with boiled potatoes and chickpeas		
à brás	fried, with egg, onions and potatoes	Empada de frango/atum	Chicken/tuna pie
na brasa	roasted with sliced potatoes	Ensopado de borrego	Lamb stew
à Gomes de Sá	sliced, baked with potatoes, served with boiled eggs and olives; speciality of Porto, named after a 19th-century cod merchant turned chef	Espetada mista	Mixed meat kebab; *espetadas* of squid/ shrimp are also common
		Feijoada	White bean stew: *à moda de Trás-os-Montes* (with root vegetables, cabbage, beef and *chouriço*); *à moda do Porto* (with *chouriço* and tripe)
à lagar (lagareiro)	roasted in lots of olive oil (a *lagar* is an olive-oil press), served with roast potatoes		
com natas	baked with cream	Filetes (de pescada)	"Fillets", nearly always battered or breadcrumbed fish fillets, served with tomato rice
com todos	"with everything", ie boiled potatoes, cabbage and eggs (a Christmas dish)		
		Francesinha	The "little French thing", a Porto speciality – a grilled steak, ham and sausage sandwich, smothered in melted cheese, doused in spicy beer-and-tomato sauce
Bifana	A grilled/fried pork-steak sandwich		
Bife de atum de cebolada	Tuna steak with stewed onions, cooked in an earthenware dish		
Bife à Portuguesa	Beef steak, topped with mustard sauce and a fried egg	Frango no churrasco	Barbecued chicken; sometimes with *piri-piri* (chilli) sauce
Cabrito assado no forno	Oven-baked kid goat	Frango na púcara	Chicken casserole made with wine, port and brandy (a *púcara* is the earthenware pot it's cooked in)
Caldeirada de peixe	Fish stew, with a base of onions, tomatoes and potatoes		
Caldo de castanhas	Chestnut soup		

Isca de bacalhau	Battered cod fishcake		vegetables (originally
Lanches	Sweet bread/brioche		from the Alentejo)
	stuffed with ham	Prego no pão/prato	Steak sandwich; with
Leitão assado	Roast suckling pig		a fried egg on top
Lulas recheadas	Stuffed squid (with	Rodizio	Brazilian buffet of
	meat and herbs)		sliced, barbecued
Massa(da) de...	Soupy pasta dish, usually		meats, served with
	with *peixe* (fish)		black beans, rice
Migas (à alentejana)	Fried maize-bread-		and salad
	based dish	Rojões (à Minho)	Cubed pork
	(with pork, garlic		(marinaded in wine,
	and spices)		cumin and garlic),
Papas de sarrabulho	Thick blood-and-		roasted with chunks
	bread-based		of blood sausage and
	stew with herbs		potato
	and spices	Sopa à alentejana	Garlic/bread soup with
Pastéis de carne	Puff pastries stuffed		poached egg on top
	with sausage meat	Sopa de tomate	Tomato soup, in the
Pastéis/bolinhos	Codfish-and-potato		Alentejo often made
de bacalhau	cakes		with quails' eggs or
Pescada com todos	Poached hake, with		beaten egg
	potatoes, boiled eggs	Tremoços	Pickled lupin seeds
	and greens	Tripas à moda do	Tripe stewed with
Porco à alentejana	Pork cooked with clams,	Porto	beans and vegetables
	served with fried	Truta com/recheado	Trout stuffed with
	potatoes and pickled	com presunto	smoked ham

Glossary

Adega Wine cellar, winery (also wine bar or restaurant)
Alameda Promenade
Albufeira Reservoir or lagoon
Aldeia Small village or hamlet
Alto/a Upper (area of a town)
Anta Prehistoric megalith tomb (also dolmen)
Armazém Warehouse
Artesanato Handicraft shop
Avenida Avenue
Azulejo Glazed, painted tile
Bairro Quarter, area (of a town); *alto* is upper, *baixo* lower
Baixo/a Lower (area of a town)
Barragem Dam
Biblioteca Library
Cais fluvial Quayside terminal
Caldas Mineral springs or spa complex
Câmara municipal Town hall
Campo Square, field or sports arena
Capela Chapel
Capela dos ossos Ossuary
Casa de povo Village/community hall
Castelo Castle
Castro Fortified hilltown
Centro comercial Shopping centre

Centro de saúde Health centre
Centro histórico Historic centre
Chafariz Public fountain
Cidade City
Citânia Prehistoric/Celtic hill settlement
Claustro Cloister
Convento Convent (or old church)
Coro Choir stalls (in church)
Correios Post office (abbreviated CTT)
Cruz, cruzeiro Cross
Dom, dona Sir, Madam (courtesy titles, usually applied to kings and queens)
Eléctrico Tramcar
Elevador Elevator or funicular railway
Ermida Chapel, not necessarily a hermitage
Espigueiro Grain shed on stilts
Esplanada Seafront promenade, terrace
Estação Station
Estrada Road
Farmácia Pharmacy
Feira Fair or market
Festa Festival or carnival
Fonte Fountain or spring
Forte, Fortaleza Fort
Freguesia Parish (*junta da freguesia* is the local council)

Grutas Caves

Igreja Church; *igreja matriz* is a parish church

Ilha Island

Infante/a Prince/princess

Jardim Garden

Lago Lake

Largo Square

Livraria Bookshop

Manueline Flamboyant style of Late Gothic architecture developed in the reign of Manuel I (1495–1521)

Menhir Prehistoric standing stone

Miradouro Belvedere or viewpoint

Moçárabe Moorish-Arabic (usually of architecture or a design)

Mosteiro Monastery (or old church)

Mudéjar Moorish-style architecture and decoration

Nossa senhora (N.S.) Our Lady – the Virgin Mary

Paço Palace or country house

Palácio Palace or country house; *palácio real*, royal palace

Parque Park

Parque nacional/natural National/Natural park

Pelourinho Pillory

Poço Well

Pombal Pigeon house

Ponte Bridge

Portagem Tollbooth on motorway

Praça Square

Praça de touros Bullring

Praia (fluvial) Beach (river beach)

Quinta Country estate, farm or villa

Retábulo Altarpiece

Ria Lagoon

Ribeiro Stream

Rio River

Romaria Pilgrimage or festival

Sala do capítulo Chapterhouse

Sé Cathedral

Serra Mountain or mountain range

Solar Manor house or mansion

Termas Thermal springs or spa complex

Torre de menagem Keep or tower (of a castle)

Tourada Bullfight

Vila Town

Small print and index

A ROUGH GUIDE TO ROUGH GUIDES

Published in 1982, the first Rough Guide – to Greece – was a student scheme that became a publishing phenomenon. Mark Ellingham, a recent graduate in English from Bristol University, had been travelling in Greece the previous summer and couldn't find the right guidebook. With a small group of friends he wrote his own guide, combining a highly contemporary, journalistic style with a thoroughly practical approach to travellers' needs.

The immediate success of the book spawned a series that rapidly covered dozens of destinations. And, in addition to impecunious backpackers, Rough Guides soon acquired a much broader readership that relished the guides' wit and inquisitiveness as much as their enthusiastic, critical approach and value-for-money ethos.

These days, Rough Guides include recommendations from budget to luxury and cover more than 200 destinations around the globe, as well as producing an ever-growing range of eBooks and apps.

Visit **roughguides.com** to see our latest publications.

Rough Guide credits

Editor: Amanda Tomlin
Senior editor: Andy Turner
Layout: Nikhil Agarwal
Cartography: Rajesh Mishra
Picture editor: Natascha Sturny
Proofreader: Diane Margolis
Managing editor: Monica Woods
Assistant editor: Dipika Dasgupta
Production: Charlotte Cade

Cover design: Wilf Matos, Nikhil Agarwal
Editorial assistant: Olivia Rawes
Senior pre-press designer: Dan May
Creative operations manager: Jason Mitchell
Publisher: Joanna Kirby
Operations coordinator: Helen Blount
Publishing director (Travel): Clare Currie
Commercial manager: Gino Magnotta
Managing director: John Duhigg

Publishing information

This fourteenth edition published Januaury 2014 by
Rough Guides Ltd,
80 Strand, London WC2R 0RL
11, Community Centre, Panchsheel Park,
New Delhi 110017, India
Distributed by the Penguin Group
Penguin Books Ltd,
80 Strand, London WC2R 0RL
Penguin Group (USA)
345 Hudson Street, NY 10014, USA
Penguin Group (Australia)
250 Camberwell Road, Camberwell,
Victoria 3124, Australia
Penguin Group (NZ)
67 Apollo Drive, Mairangi Bay, Auckland 1310,
New Zealand
Penguin Group (South Africa)
Block D, Rosebank Office Park, 181 Jan Smuts Avenue,
Parktown North, Gauteng, South Africa 2193
Rough Guides is represented in Canada by Tourmaline
Editions Inc. 662 King Street West, Suite 304, Toronto,
Ontario M5V 1M7
Printed in Malaysia by Vivar Printing Sdn. Bhd.

528pp includes index
A catalogue record for this book is available from the
British Library
ISBN: 978-1-40935-867-1

MIX
Paper from responsible sources
FSC www.fsc.org   FSC™ C018179

Help us update

We've gone to a lot of effort to ensure that the fourteenth edition of **The Rough Guide to Portugal** is accurate and up-to-date. However, things change – places get "discovered", opening hours are notoriously fickle, restaurants and rooms raise prices or lower standards. If you feel we've got it wrong or left something out, we'd like to know, and if you can remember the address, the price, the hours, the phone number, so much the better.

Please send your comments with the subject line "**Rough Guide Portugal Update**" to ✉ mail@uk .roughguides.com. We'll credit all contributions and send a copy of the next edition (or any other Rough Guide if you prefer) for the very best emails.

Find more travel information, connect with fellow travellers and plan your trip on ⓦ roughguides.com

Acknowledgements

Matthew Hancock Thanks to everyone who helped me research this book, including Sílvia Aires at ARPT Centro de Portugal, Vitor Carriço, Debbie and Steve at the Paintshop Hostel, Daniela Resenterra, Jenna Osborne/Turismo de Portugal, Gary Drewett, Nuno Pina/Pousadas, Monica Bessone, Nuno Alegre, Julia, Karla and Mette Hallas-Moller, Peter Brinkman, Luis Santos, Eva and Mats, Ana Rodrigues, Jonas Van Vossole, Luke and Paula Pimenta-Tilley, and especially Mandy, Alex and Olivia for their usual at-home support.

Readers' updates

Thanks to all the readers who have taken the time to write in with comments and suggestions (and apologies if we've inadvertently omitted or misspelt anyone's name):

Barbara Abelho; Tony Boas; Matthew Brady; Linda Briskin; Louis Campbell; Nell Carter; Dilum Coppens; Zoe Crick; John Death; Theresa Duda; Peter Fishbourne; Mari Fflur; Stan Fletcher; Antonio Gavinho; Ines Guise; Anja Laan; John Launder; Fernando Machado; Dorothy McCord; Mariana Mineiro; Paulo Nugas; Virpi Oliveira; Clive Paul; Philip Prowse; Suzanne Rennie; Nicolas Rouquette; Kevin Sharpe; Manuel Sousa; Ray Smith; Bill Thompson; Helen Thornton; Carol Tritton; Rhoda Van Vugt

ABOUT THE AUTHORS

Matthew Hancock fell in love with Portugal when he taught in Lisbon, then walked the 775-mile Portuguese/Spanish border. For this edition he researched and wrote the sections on Lisbon, Coimbra and the Beira Litoral, the southern Alentejo and the Algarve. Now a journalist and editor living in Dorset, he is also author of the *Pocket Rough Guide to Lisbon* and co-author of the *Rough Guide to Dorset, Hampshire and the Isle of Wight.*

Jules Brown first visited Portugal in 1985 and has contributed to the guide in one way or another ever since. For this edition he researched and wrote the sections on Estremadura and Ribatejo, Beira Alta and Beira Baixa, Porto and the Rio Douro, Trás-os-Montes and the northern Alentejo.

Index

Maps are marked in grey

Map symbols

The symbols below are used on maps throughout the book

✈	Airport	⅏	Waterfall	🏛	Stately home	▲	Peak
★	Bus/taxi	⋀⋀	Spring	✛	Chapel	⛰	Mountain range
Ⓜ	Metro station	≈	Swimming pool	⛪	Monastery		Rocks
🅿	Parking	⛴	Boat	✡	Synagogue		Cliff
ⓘ	Tourist office	⊥	Gardens	⛷	Skiing		Church
☏	Telephone	⌒	Cave	⛳	Golf course		Building
@	Internet café/access	⋔	Abbey	🍇	Vineyard		Market
✉	Post office	Ψ	Fortress	⊠–⊠	Gate		Stadium
✚	Hospital	■	Tower	● – ●	Cable car		Park
♦	Place of interest	⋁	Viewpoint	—	Wall		Beach
⊙	Statue/monument	⋂	Arch	- - -	Footpath	⊞	Cemetery
ⵊ	Lighthouse	⋀	Campsite	⌣	Bridge		
∴	Ruins	⌂	Mountain refuge/lodge				

Listings key

■ Accommodation
● Eating and drinking
■ Bars and clubs
● Shops